Ready for Sea

Ready for Sea

THE BICENTENNIAL HISTORY OF THE U.S. NAVY SUPPLY CORPS

RADM Frank J. Allston,
SC, USNR (Ret.)

FOREWORD BY

RADM R. M. Moore, SC, USN
CHIEF OF SUPPLY CORPS

Naval Institute Press
ANNAPOLIS, MARYLAND

Library of Congress Cataloging-in-Publication Data

Allston, Frank J., 1930-
Ready for sea : the bicentennial history of the U.S. Navy Supply Corps / Frank J. Allston : foreword by R.M. Moore.
p. cm.
Includes bibliographical references and index.
ISBN 1-55750-033-9 (alk. paper)
1. United States. Navy. Supply Corps—History. 2. United States. Navy—Supplies and stores—History. I. Title.
VC263.A795 1995
359.8′0973—dc20 95-13662
CIP

Printed in the United States of America on acid-free paper ∞

02 01 00 99 98 97 96 95 9 8 7 6 5 4 3 2

First printing

Book design and composition by
Wolf Song Design, Champaign, Illinois

To the wives, husbands, and children who have remained at home and preserved family integrity while naval agents, pursers, paymasters, Pay Corps officers, and Supply Corps officers have provided "Service to the Fleet" for two centuries.

Contents

Foreword

RADM R. M. Moore, SC, USN
CHIEF OF SUPPLY CORPS

The Supply Corps has had a proud heritage and unmatched record of service to the country and our Navy. In 1795 when the Continental Navy was in its infancy, our ancestors set this standard of excellence and devotion to duty. Today, the men and women of the Supply Corps team, military and civilian, officer and enlisted, around the world, at sea and ashore, continue this splendid tradition.

This chronicle is a celebration of that tradition and a celebration of you—the men and women of the Corps. As chief of Supply Corps, I am proud of our heritage and of your accomplishments. I hope you will read this history with a sense of reverence for the thousands of officers of the Corps who have made us what we are today.

On this our 200th anniversary, we look back on the contributions and sacrifices of those who have gone before and forward to the challenges of the future with a renewed dedication of "Service to the Fleet."

Preface

Naval literature has traditionally recorded epic sea battles and the role of protecting the commerce of nations. Little has been written about the efforts of those behind the scenes who have supplied fleets with the food, clothing, ammunition, and weapons to carry out their missions. Over the 200 years of Navy supply, the basic mission of providing needed materials to elements of the Fleet has remained unchanged, but naval combatants have grown tremendously in size and complexity. As the Navy advanced from sail to nuclear power, from muzzle-loading guns to missiles, and from hardtack to freshly cooked steaks, demands on the Navy supply system have increased accordingly.

This bicentennial history traces the United States Navy Supply Corps from its beginnings, with appointment of Tench Francis as the young nation's first purveyor of public supplies in 1795. Through a series of organizational and nomenclature changes, the Supply Corps today is the world's most competent, efficient group of naval businessmen and businesswomen.

From a brief introduction of a fledgling nation struggling to assert its place in the world and an upstart Navy modeled along the lines of Great Britain's Royal Navy, this work examines the evolution of the Corps. The concurrent evolution of the "corporate home" from the Bureau of Provisions and Clothing in 1842, through the Bureau of Supplies and Accounts in 1892, to the Naval Supply Systems Command in 1966, is covered. The Navy's businessmen originally were civilian naval agents and pursers until Congress authorized commissioning of pursers in 1812. Pursers were redesignated paymasters in 1860. A separate Pay Corps was established in 1871, and the chief of the Bureau of Provisions and Clothing was given the additional title of paymaster general. The Pay Corps was renamed the Supply Corps in 1919. The first women were commissioned as officers in World War II. A Navy Department reorganization replaced the bureau system with the systems command structure in 1966.

The primary reason I was asked to undertake this project, upon my retirement from the Naval Reserve in 1985, was my background and experience as a professional communicator. My first challenge was to determine how best to present the 200-year history of the Navy's businessmen and businesswomen in the most readable, interesting, and, above all, factual manner. I concluded that the story of the Supply Corps is the story of the people who have provided "Service to the Fleet" over two centuries.

The method I chose to tell this story was to select a manageable number of individuals from available published material about literally thousands of Supply Corps officers and their predecessors. Next came the decision to prepare free-standing "cradle to grave" vignettes and to present them chronologically within a continuum of Navy and Supply Corps history. My purpose in adopting this approach has been to emphasize the dedication, creativity, initiative, and professionalism of the Navy's businessmen and businesswomen.

All the chiefs of the Corps and vice admirals have been included in recognition of their policymaking responsibilities. The criteria applied in the selection of the balance of the vignettes include outstanding service, heroic actions, and unusual duties. These vignettes are then presented chronologically. Where more than one period of service qualified, the vignette is placed within the time frame of the earliest. As a result, some officers who rose to senior status are presented early in their careers as junior officers. Some experiences of captains and Flag officers are positioned and titled as paymasters or junior officers. This is vivid demonstration of the fact that Supply Corps leadership traits usually manifest themselves early in an individual's Navy career. This review of the Corps' history ends with Fiscal Year 1994 on 30 September 1994.

At least two serious attempts were made—in 1934–38 and again in the 1950s—to record the history of the Navy Supply Corps. Although no published book resulted from these efforts, much valuable information was compiled. However, with additional information gathered since then, such a mass of data was accumulated that I had to make continuing editorial judgments in selecting which material, in my opinion, best exemplified the Corps' motto, "Ready for Sea." In this context of limited time and space, many events and stories had to be condensed or eliminated. All of the material, including documents, books, messages, article reprints, oral autobiographies, and photographs assembled for this project have been placed in the Navy Supply Corps Museum at Athens, Georgia, except where return to the contributor was specified. This material is available for review.

This work, which has been in process during the administration of the four most recent chiefs of the Corps, has been sponsored by the Navy Supply Corps Association, the professional organization of Navy Supply Corps officers—Regular, Reserve, and retired. It is important to note that many Supply Corps officers have contributed to this effort, but that no government funds have been expended in the research, writing, printing, distribution, or marketing. This has been truly a labor of love.

The competent and motivated men and women of the Supply Corps have demonstrated over the past 200 years that they have been uniquely qualified to meet the Navy's logistical challenges of today and the future. The accomplishments of these dedicated Supply Corps officers have been made possible with the support of the thousands of highly trained, skilled, and dedicated enlisted personnel in supply ratings and civil servants employed within the Navy supply system.

The United States Navy Supply Corps is proud of the record it has compiled over its two centuries of service to the Navy and to the nation. As this is written, the Corps is facing many challenges, and the Corps of today is ready to meet them. The Supply Corps of the future may very well be quite different from the one that has evolved since 1795, but one fact remains clear: Whatever assignments the Navy gives its businessmen and businesswomen in the future, the Supply Corps will always be "Ready for Sea."

Acknowledgments

Preparing a literary work of this nature, covering a period of two centuries, requires the input of many people, and I have been blessed with the cooperation and assistance of some of the best. To attempt to name them all is to court disaster, so I shall single out a few.

First, I thank Rear Admiral Ted Walker who, as chief of Supply Corps in 1985, had the confidence in me to ask that I undertake this project. I have been fortunate to have the cooperation and support of his three successors: Rear Admirals Dan McKinnon, Jim Miller, and Bob Moore. While I have invested my time on a purely volunteer basis, the Navy Supply Corps Association has reimbursed me for travel, research, postage, and other out-of-pocket expenses. I emphasize that no appropriated funds were involved in this project. Special thanks go to Kaye Morris, NSCA administrative officer, for her prompt response to my many requests.

This task would have been impossible without the support of my family, especially my wife, Barbara, a former CIA analyst and historian, who is experienced in researching and abstracting published material. She has painstakingly reviewed several iterations of the manuscript, questioned my statements, and stoutly maintained that if she could not understand what I wrote, probably nobody else could. My two sons, James and John, both history buffs, have made loans of valuable source material from their personal libraries. Jim has also been my data processing consultant throughout the 10 years this project has been underway.

Two individuals with the Supply Corps family—Nan Dimond, former public affairs officer of the Naval Supply Systems Command, and Dan Roth, curator of the Navy Supply Corps Museum—have been especially helpful over the years. No request of mine was ever turned down by either of these special people. I also appreciate the support of Nan's successor, Liz Van Wye, and her associate, Laurie Tall, and Val Hogue, editor of the *Navy Supply Corps Newsletter,* who published my "Lore of the Corps" series of articles based on the material collected for this book. The first of these articles appeared in the January-February 1993 issue. I am also appreciative of the assistance of public affairs officers of three NAVSUP field activities: Jo Avalos, FISC Oakland; Mary Markovinovic, FISC San Diego; and Phil Sheridan, ASO.

Another special group of people at the Naval Historical Center at the Washington Navy Yard made important contributions: Dr. Dean C. Allard, director; Dr. William S. Dudley, senior historian; Bernard F. Cavalcante, head, Operational Archival Branch, and his associate, Araina Jacob; and two drilling Supply Corps Reservists, CAPTs Bill McClintock and Woody Tiernan, both trained historians.

In-depth research among 18th- and 19th-century records at the National Archives, Library of Congress, Naval Historical Center, Naval Academy Library, and other sources in the Washington-Annapolis area was competently undertaken by Dr. William Calderhead, retired Naval Academy history professor, assisted by Jeff Charlston. During the final year of the project, Lois Waber, an experienced secretary and my neighbor, competently handled researching, cataloging, and filing the immense amount of material that flowed into my home office. She also assisted with typing and data entry into my word-processing system.

VADM Ken Wheeler and RADM Bernie Bieri thoughtfully invited me to attend the 1993 reunion of the famous Navy Finance and Supply School class of 1939–40, where I was privileged to meet and interview some of the true heroes of the Supply Corps. When I started the project in 1985, I set out to interview all of the living former chiefs of the Corps, including Admirals Wheeler, Bieri, Murrey Royar, John Crumpacker, Hersh Goldberg, Wally Dowd, Gene Grinstead, and Andy Giordano. In all, I conducted more than 50 personal interviews and at least as many telephone interviews. These individuals were completely open and willing to put their experiences on the record.

In addition to the contributions of those living officers and other individuals profiled or credited in the text, dozens of present and former Supply Corps officers provided information for this project. I single out CAPT Nick Schmitt, CO, FISC Pearl Harbor; CAPT Ken Chase, OIC, Cheatham Annex, FISC Norfolk; and CDR Matthew Lechleitner, who supplied information on the evolution of the BuSandA Field Branch into the Defense Finance and Accounting Service Cleveland. Also, I am indebted to RADM Charlie Blick, who supplied a set of CAPT Earle Chesney's Eggburt cartoons; CAPT Tom Brown, who maintained and contributed copies of reports made by Supply Corps officers who experienced the 7 December 1941 attack on Pearl Harbor; and CAPT John Mulhern, who did yeoman work in Philadelphia in researching the life of Israel Whelen, Tench Francis's successor. LT Phil Stevens, in the NAVSUP Reserve Division, was extremely helpful in ferreting out needed information from BuPers and other Washington-area sources. When I first started on this project, three fellow Naval Reservists stepped up to join the effort. RADM Tom Hill provided essential guidance and assistance in the selection of computer hardware. CAPT Chris Isely set up a computer program to catalog the the significant flow of material voluntarily submitted to me. CAPT Bill Redman, Jr., was an early contributor by reviewing several books and directing my attention to useful passages. CAPT Bill Tonner provided a frequently used reference, a copy of the 1940 edition of the *Register of Commissioned and Warrant Officers of the United States Navy and Marine Corps*. LT Frederick P. Schmitt first brought to my attention CAPT Cecil Sherman Baker's 1939 collection of Supply Corps abstracts by contributing a copy, which has been extremely valuable to me throughout this endeavor.

I am also indebted to Dr. William N. Still, Jr., a former holder of the Secretary of the Navy Research Chair in Naval History, and director emeritus, Department of Maritime History and Nautical Archaeology, East Carolina University, and a former Navy storekeeper. He graciously invited me to spend the better part of a day going through his collection of World War I Navy messages and documents, copied those I needed, and responded promptly to many follow-up requests.

I also thank relatives of deceased Supply Corps officers for sharing personal insights: Alice Arnold and Marjory Fowler about their husbands; Nancy Williams Baker and Roy O. Stratton, Jr., on their fathers; and Rogers S. Bagnall about his grandfather, RADM J. J. Cheatham.

Several other individuals who made significant contributions to this project include Paul Stillwell, director, History Division, U.S. Naval Institute; Roger Bohn, a dedicated member of the Civil War Roundtable, who opened his extensive personal library to me; and RADM Phil Whitacre, a good friend whose encouragement and faith sustained me through frustrating times.

The Research Department staff of Nichols Library, Naperville, Illinois, was of enormous help in directing me to the proper sources in response to my frequent inquiries and never failed to located a desired publication through the interlibrary loan system.

Finally, but most important, I want to pay special tribute to Mary Giles and William C. Ackermann. Mary Giles provided professional editing of the manuscript and patiently explained why her suggested modifications were necesary to enhance the readability of the final product. CAPT Bill Ackermann, business manager of the University of Illinois Press, retired from the Supply Corps Reserve in 1994 and has been my constant, reliable consultant in publishing matters. Without his assistance, this work would have been exceedingly more difficult.

Ready for Sea

Introduction: The Formative Years

Personnel who provide supplies and services have been assigned to ships since the eleventh century. They have been called variously ship's clerk, purser, supercargo, paymaster, or supply officer. The contributions of these supply specialists have contributed significantly to the success of maritime nations over the years, but their accomplishments rarely have been recorded in official naval journals. The early providers of essential supplies and services to fleets were civilians, often relatives or friends of ships' captains. The supply function, as with many others in the U.S. Navy, has its roots in Britain's Royal Navy. American naval customs, traditions, and early shipboard and shore organizations reflect this British heritage.

Formal administration of the Royal Navy began in the thirteenth century and was expanded in 1546 when King Henry VIII appointed the first Navy Board. With only minor modifications, this administrative system remained in effect until 1832. The Royal Navy Board was responsible for building and repairing ships, managing navy dockyards, purchasing and distributing stores and provisions, and paying personnel. It consisted of a treasurer, a controller, a surveyor of victuals, and a clerk of acts, known collectively as the *four principal officers* of the Royal Navy. A surveyor of victuals submitted an annual estimates of stores needed for the following year and purchased and accounted for all stores and provisions. The Navy Board instituted a primitive system of checks to ensure administrative honesty that required the four principal officers to watch one another. According to Michael Lewis, the British naval historian, these checks created "a mutual suspicion society." This was probably warranted because courts martial records and auditors' reports indicate that the Royal Navy was riddled with nepotism, favoritism, and corruption.

Paymasters in the Royal Navy

Eighteenth-century Royal Navy regulations defined the status of its paymasters as tradesmen, paid at the rate of 12 pence a month. Ashore, naval storekeepers and pursers were stationed at each royal dockyard. Storekeepers received and inspected stores and timber for ship construction, examined invoices for all receipts, returned all unfit stores, maintained storage facilities, and issued stock.

Until 1775, when the 13 North American British colonies initiated their struggle for independence, the Royal Navy protected supply lines between the mother country and the British dependencies. Before the start of hostilities, the American colonies provided Great Britain with substantial amounts of raw materials, including such items for navy use as tar, pitch, and tall, white-pine timber, which was ideal for ships' masts. The British maintained several supply depots in the Colonies. A fleet of Royal Navy storeships transported food, ordnance, equipage, square rigging and fittings, and general supplies to the far-flung British Fleet.

The Navy and the Continental Congress

When the American Revolution began, the Continental Congress moved to create its own navy to perform the functions previously supplied by the Royal Navy. That decision was a courageous one because the new Continental Navy would face a British Navy many times its size.

On 13 December 1775, Congress appointed a Marine Committee with one representative from each of the original 13 colonies. In one of its first actions, the Marine Committee adopted the British system of agents in 13 major commercial centers in America and several foreign countries to provide material and supplies for the budding Continental Navy. Most of the men the board appointed were experienced in ocean commerce as continental agents. They supervised construction of Continental Navy warships in their respective ports and purchased everything needed to outfit the ships, ranging from anchors, cannons, and sails to blankets and provisions.

Congress established uniform standards for officers in 1776, but did not set uniform standards for seamen, who usually wore long, baggy trousers. Shipboard pursers ordered clothing, called *slops,* through naval agents for sale to crew members. The government did not set standard specifications for material to be used in the manufacture of clothing to be sold to crews, and quality control was virtually nonexistent. As a result, slops available to crewmen often disintegrated after first washing or soaking by sea water. Officers ordered their own tailor-made clothing.

The First American Navy Board

On 6 November 1776, Congress appointed the first American Navy Board at Philadelphia to relieve the burden of the Marine Committee. The board was charged with conducting the Navy's business for the Middle Atlantic states.

Congress appointed a second Navy Board at Boston for the eastern states on 10 July 1777. The Eastern Navy Board operated more independently than the Philadelphia Board because of the great distance from the seat of government. It functioned under a broad charter granted by John Hancock, president of the Marine Committee, who told the board that it was responsible for overseeing all naval and marine affairs of the United States of America within the four eastern states under the direction of the Marine Committee. The board was also charged with directing the building, manning, and fitting for sea all armed vessels of the United States and to provide all materials and stores necessary for that purpose.

American Navy Boards were the early equivalents of modern supply agencies and inventory control points. They were basically similar to the Royal Navy Board, except that their scope was on a regional basis rather than on a national basis. Each had a secretary, treasurer, and paymaster. As a result of difficulty in staffing the boards, individual members often served in more than one capacity. In addition to serving the logistical needs of the fleet and shore establishment, the Middle Atlantic Navy Board faced logistics problems of its own. It was forced to relocate when British troops captured or threatened significant portions of the East Coast, including cities where the board met.

The Continental Navy boards took over the functions of supply ashore and borrowed the naval agent concept from the British. However, the Americans lacked the sophistication of the Royal Navy's logistical system, which had been developed over many years. This was a major factor in the British navy's success against the Continental Navy during the early days of the Revolutionary War.

Although pursers were embarked in Continental Navy ships, they were little more than civilian navy agents afloat. They were, for the most part, political appointees, often with no previous experience and little or no training. Pursers did not achieve commissioned officer status until 1812.

A Navy Agent and John Paul Jones

Although navy agents stayed pretty much out of the limelight and were generally unheralded, some were not adverse to standing up to politicians and naval heroes when the latter put what they considered undue pressure on them. One of these was Colonel John Langdon, navy agent at Portsmouth and a former member of the Marine Committee of Congress, who was supervising the building of *Ranger* on orders of the committee.

Congress had given Captain John Paul Jones command of *Ranger*. Jones immediately charged that *Ranger* was oversparred and too light for the 20 guns specified. He tried to obtain a new set of spars from Langdon, who did not jump to comply with Jones's every wish. Langdon's first priority was to complete, launch, and fit out the frigate *Raleigh*. Jones insisted on the best equipment and many spare parts for his ship. He maintained that it was up to Langdon to provide them. Jones was particularly upset that Langdon provided *Ranger* with fewer than 30 gallons of rum for a crew of 150 despite the fact that there was an ample supply of rum in New England. Langdon also would not give Jones a boatswain's whistle. Apparently, he believed the captain should command the attention of his crew by strong voice, as Langdon had done when he was a ship's master at sea. Jones further complained over the quality of *Ranger*'s sails and charged that Langdon was of no assistance in recruiting a crew for his ship. Langdon was so exasperated by Jones's repeated demands that he told the flamboyant captain he knew as well as Jones "how to equip, govern or fight a ship of war."

The incensed Jones wrote to the secretary of the Marine Committee to report that Langdon had not provided the assistance he required of an agent. "He thinks himself my master," Jones complained, "and he, who was bred in a shop and hath been about a voyage or two at sea under a nurse, had once the assurance to tell me that he knew as well as myself how to fit out, govern and fight a ship of war!" Jones's claim that Langdon was not knowledgeable in maritime matters was inaccurate at best. Langdon had been master of four different merchantmen before becoming a shipowner.

The Board of Admiralty

Congress realized that the Marine Committee was extremely ineffective in administering the Navy, and on 28 October 1779, replaced it with a new entity, the Board of Admiralty. The board was to keep accounts; make proper entries; obtain regular and exact returns of all naval war stores, clothing, provisions, and all other articles; and report to Congress.

In one of its first actions, the Board of Admiralty demanded an accounting from the Navy boards and continental agents, but compliance with this order was not universal. As a result, the board decided to correct and verify accounts itself. Buried in administrative minutiae, the Board of Admiralty neglected the broader aspects of administering the Navy. Many Continental Navy agents resigned or were discharged for failure to render accounts, for general inattention to their jobs, and, in some cases, for outright dishonesty. By the summer of 1781, when the accounting system was in a state of collapse, members of the Board of Admiralty chose to resign. Wartime battle losses and a severe shortage of funds left the Navy with only three small, lightly armed frigates, resulting in a sharp reduction in the number of pursers on active duty.

The four organizations to which Congress delegated administration of the Navy—the Naval Committee, the Marine Committee, the Board of Admiralty, and the Agent of Marine—accomplished little of note. Most of the men assigned to these entities were farmers, lawyers, and businessmen who had little or no experience or knowledge of maritime affairs. The one notable exception was Robert Morris, the highly respected financier of the Revolution.

Robert Morris and the Navy

In February 1781 Congress established an Executive Department with a secretary of marine in charge, but no qualified individual would accept the post. In mid-1781, Congress temporarily assigned the duties of the Board of Admiralty and operational control of the fleet to Robert Morris, who was then superintendent of finance. Morris obviously had the confidence of Congress, which appointed him agent of marine in August 1781. In this position, the versatile Morris would administer the Navy, including the purchase of stores and provisions, and assume the formidable task of settling and paying the Navy's overdue accounts. Finally, the Navy had the services of an able and conscientious man who brought administrative leadership to his task.

Morris moved quickly to close most Navy offices, but he retained the Eastern Navy Board until two additional men-of-war—*Alliance* and *Deane*—could be fitted out for further cruises. When that task was completed, the Eastern Navy Board transferred all its remaining stores, records, and books to the superintendent of finance, a position Morris continued to hold.

Morris was determined to take charge of the Navy's finances and move forward by using the experienced accountants in his Office of Finance to settle Navy accounts. He also appointed new naval agents in several eastern ports, including experienced businessmen knowledgeable in maritime affairs, to assist in auditing and paying accounts.

A Permanent American Navy

The question of establishing a permanent American Navy became a matter of contentious debate in Congress and also provoked pointed discussions among Americans in every walk of life. In a report to the Continental Congress on 31 July 1783, Robert Morris strongly supported establishment of a navy. However, he pointed out that no money was available for construction of ships, docks, and naval arsenals, or for the support necessary for the United States to establish a permanent and credible presence at sea. Congress was preoccupied with broader national financial problems and had difficulty securing financing for the navy that Robert Morris proposed. He appointed Joseph Pennell to be commissioner for settling accounts of the Marine Department.

Pennell advised Congress in September 1783 that he would have difficulty in tracing the marine accounts through the different stages, obtaining the proper vouchers and settling old accounts. He feared that the office he had inherited was in greater confusion than he had suspected and that his predecessors had kept no book of accounts. He charged that records were insufficient for audit, with at least $150,000 missing from the books and $80,000 in unexplained receipts. Financial problems were not confined to the capital and to the Navy organization ashore, however; the fleet also had its share. In October 1783, John Paul Jones wrote to Robert Morris that the crew of the *Bonhomme Richard* had not been paid for four years.

The 13 new states were slow to recognize the interdependence of men, weapons, and material, supplemented by a strong industrial base and an effective logistical system. As long as its merchant fleet had no protection on the high seas, it would be difficult for America to have an effective presence in worldwide commerce. The Continental Congress agreed that the nation needed a real Navy with armed frigates and appointed a Naval Committee to determine the cost of converting and fitting out four warships. Robert Morris was instrumental in arranging funding for the construction of 13 new frigates.

A Marine Committee was authorized to build and supervise operation of the new ships. Continental agents in coastal cities in America and overseas supervised the building and provisioning of the frigates. The fledgling government also issued the first set of regulations for governing the establishment, organization, and operation of its Navy.

Professional Business Managers Afloat

Congress finally recognized the need for trained officers to manage the business affairs of ships of the line. The Continental Navy assigned seagoing American businessmen, called *pursers* or *supercargoes*. They met their ships' material needs and operated the first informal ship's stores for sale of clothing, candles, and other items for personal use of crew members.

Although early American pursers had a much better reputation than their English counterparts, who were considered cheats, trust in American pursers was limited. They were required to whistle continuously while conducting inventory to assure they were not consuming raisins intended for the crew's pudding. The profits that pursers could make on sales to the crew were restricted by law. Markups ranged from 10 to 50 percent, depending on the item. Profiting from sales to the crew was common practice in the early days of the American Navy because pursers were not naval officers. They remained civilians given warrants to sail in American Navy ships, primarily to handle finances and subsistence.

A group of seagoing bandits, operating out of the ports of Algiers, Oran, Tripoli, and Tunis along the Mediterranean coast, began to harass merchant ships. These renegades, known collectively as the Barbary pirates, made a livelihood out of boarding ships and imprisoning the crews until substantial tribute was paid. When the United States refused to pay tribute, U.S.-flagged ships were seized and sailors imprisoned. In 1787, the United States signed a treaty with Morocco without having to pay tribute. Concluding concurrent treaties with the other states proved impossible, however. Some Americans remained hostages in prisons along the Barbary Coast for years. (By 1794, the Barbary pirates had seized 13 American ships and more than 100 seaman held hostage. Despite heroic efforts by Stephen Decatur in rescuing American captives, the United States responded to pressure from captives' families and paid nearly $800,000 ransom.) Under these troubling circumstances, the United States could not justify the costs of American commerce in the Mediterranean, and all the American trade in the area ceased.

Abolition and Revival

Even though sea power had played a critical role in gaining independence, the Continental Congress, buffeted by financial woes, allowed its Navy to pass out of existence in 1785. When President George Washington took office in early 1789, a modest Navy was revived and assigned to the War Department. Almost immediately, new financial problems arose. Inflation was of such concern in 1791 that, on 31 May, the Board of Admiralty asked Congress for legislation requiring payment of wages and bounty expenses in specie.

Alleged negligence in Army procurement prompted Congress to enact legislation on 8 May 1792 to transfer responsibility for procurement of military supplies from the secretary of war to the secretary of the treasury. Procurement of all public supplies also became the responsibility of the secretary of the treasury.

Six New American Frigates

There was one positive outcome of this humiliating experience. Congress enacted the Naval Armament Act of 1794, which authorized construction of six new frigates—the first U.S. naval vessels to be built since the Revolutionary War. Thus the young nation again set about reestablishing a credible navy. The decision to invest in another navy highlighted the need for a professional officer corps. The 1794 legislation authorized the secretary of war through his subordinate, the secretary of the navy, to appoint a full complement of officers for the recently authorized frigates.

In April 1794, the secretary of the treasury delegated the procurement of military supplies to Tench Coxe, commissioner of revenue. Following appropriation of funds for the construction of the new ships in early June, Coxe began the process of procuring supplies and assigning responsibility for their construction by appointing agents in Portsmouth, Boston, New York, Philadelphia, Baltimore, and Norfolk.

Tench Francis and the New Ships

Coxe assigned the major responsibility for procuring supplies for the new shipbuilding project to Tench Francis, a well-placed Philadelphia businessman who served as a treasury agent involved in the purchase of military supplies. However, Coxe retained for himself heavy involvement in details of frigate construction.

The lively June 1794 correspondence exchanged between Coxe and Francis involved a series of transactions regarding material and services in conjunction with building the six new warships. Francis contracted with shipwrights and carpenters in the interior of Connecticut and Rhode Island to go to Georgia and cut the approximately 2,400 tons of live oak and shape the timber for the frigates. Coxe wanted the cut timber shipped out of Georgia before winter, but by late September it was still not ready. The carpenters from New England were unable to handle the task, so Francis replaced them with carpenters from Philadelphia at higher wages. In order to secure funds to pay the higher wages, he caused quite a stir when he requested $35,000 in cash without going through proper channels.

Despite the mercurial nature of political support for the Navy from the start of the Revolution, through the Confederation period, and into the Federal period, America's leadership understood the need for a strong presence at sea. The experience of the first 20 years of American naval history vividly demonstrated the need for development of a more professional organization if the young nation was to be a world-class sea power.

Notes

Sources for material used in this chapter and not cited earlier include:

Navy Supply Corps Newsletter, February 1970, September 1973.

Wellborn, Fred W. *The Growth of American Nationality, 1492–1865.* New York: Macmillan, 1951.

Additional sources for material:

Leiner, Frederick C. "The Norfolk War Scare," *Naval History,* Summer 1993. (On President Jefferson's plan to substitute gunboats manned by civilian sailors for a professional navy.)

McKee, Christopher. *A Gentlemanly and Honorable Profession: The Creation of the U.S. Naval Officer Corps, 1794–1815.* Annapolis: Naval Institute Press, 1991.

Miscellaneous Letters Received by the Secretary of the Navy, 1801–85. The original letters are on file at the National Archives in Washington and microfilm copies are on file at the Naval Historical Center.

Morison, Samuel Eliot. *John Paul Jones: A Sailor's Biography.* Boston: Little, Brown, 1959.

CHAPTER ONE

The Navy's First Professional Business Managers

1795–1814

Congress accepted the fact that the Navy had become a national institution and committed to establish it permanently with a professional officer corps, setting the stage for the development of an effective naval business arm. What was needed next was the selection and training of talented business managers, afloat and ashore. Selection criteria specified that early Navy business officers had to possess expertise in procuring material for building and outfitting ships; supplying them with sails, guns, and other necessary supplies; and feeding, clothing, paying, and arming officers and enlisted personnel. Past experience made it vital that candidates be capable of accounting properly for all transactions.

Tench Coxe, who had survived the tribulations of bearing responsibility for all military purchases, resigned the naval procurement function in late December 1794. Whether motivated by an excessive workload or frustration over repeated delays in obtaining materials for construction of the six new frigates, Coxe gave up a major part of his duties when he relinquished responsibility for military purchases.

Tench Francis, who had been serving as agent for military purchases at Philadelphia, assumed the Treasury Department duties performed on behalf of the War Department on 31 January, 1795. He was to head a new office in Treasury that would include responsibility for the Agency for Naval Armament. Tench Coxe also sent a letter to the secretary of war to submit a list of 17 projects involving the new frigates in which his Treasury office had been involved for nearly a year.

Secretary of the Treasury Alexander Hamilton, acutely aware of the long history of financial corruption in European governments, had campaigned for five years for a single government procurement agency. On 23 February 1795, Congress approved Hamilton's plan by enacting legislation requiring that "there shall be in the Department of the Treasury an officer to be denominated 'Purveyor of Public Supplies' whose duty it shall be to conduct the procuring and provisioning of all arms, military and naval stores, provisions, clothing, Indian goods, and generally all articles of supply requisite for the service of the United States."

To fill this newly authorized position, President Washington nominated Tench Francis, and the Senate approved Francis's appointment the following day. The selection put in place an official who could provide the centralized direction to government purchasing that Alexander Hamilton had envisioned. This move was designed to further Robert Morris's strongly held belief in competitive bidding for government contracts. In 1781, Francis had teamed with Matthias Slough to bid successfully for one of the first contracts awarded under the Morris system.

The scope of Francis's new assignment was broad, but his most immediate task was to expedite cutting and shipping of the timbers and delivery of other supplies for construction of the six new frigates. In recognition of this first centralized supply function, the U.S. Navy Supply Corps traces its birth to the appointment of Tench Francis.

LORE OF THE CORPS

Tench Francis, Jr.

Purveyor of Public Supplies, 1795–1800

Tench Francis, the man to whom the Supply Corps traces its beginning, became the first purveyor of public supplies in 1795. Francis entered into the office with an impressive background as a businessman, Treasury Department official specializing in military supplies, and colonel of reserves.

Although he was born in Talbot County, Maryland, in 1731, Francis is considered a Philadelphian, having moved there at the age of eight. He married Anne Shippen Willing, sister of Thomas Willing, a Philadelphia businessman and friend of Robert Morris. In 1754, Francis and his father opened a large mercantile firm. Two years later, he and his brother-in-law formed a partnership, Willing and Francis, which was in business for nearly 50 years. Francis enjoyed a successful career as a businessman and financier, acting for many years as agent for the proprietary interests of the Penn family.

At one time, Francis was suspected of harboring Tory sympathies, but was later exonerated. He became a staunch anti-Tory and donated 5,000 pounds sterling for support of the Revolutionary Army. In 1775, he joined the Third Battalion of Philadelphia Associators as a captain. Later that year he was appointed a colonel in the Pennsylvania Militia.

After the Revolution, under the Articles of Confederation, Francis assisted the Secretary of the Treasury Alexander Hamilton and Robert Morris in resolving financial matters. Hamilton sought Francis's advice on techniques for detecting the presence of base metals in counterfeit coins in bulk quantities of coinage when the new secretary was compiling his famous *Report on the Mint.* Tench Francis was active in a number of business and civic endeavors, served as first cashier of the Bank of North America from 1781 to 1792, and signed documents authorizing a loan of $50,000 to the new federal government. From 1792 to 1794, the firm of Willing and Francis was a major supplier to the War Department, selling more than $20,000 in supplies during the two-year period. The firm was also instrumental in procuring timber for construction of the first ships for the U.S. Navy.

In his new position as purveyor of public supplies, Francis presided over the centralized function of procuring and distributing government military supplies. In June 1795, Secretary of War Timothy Pickering complained about the delay in cutting live-oak timbers for the new frigates. He asserted that continuing the existing plan meant that "the business in every yard will be kept in a lingering condition, at a heavy expense, without completing anything." Francis and Tench Coxe eventually resolved that problem by bringing in new woodcutters.

Procuring and arranging shipment of items of tribute to be paid to rulers of Barbary powers occupied much of Francis's time. Meanwhile, he continued to manage the business affairs of Willing and Francis while serving concurrently as purveyor of public supplies. America was gradually being drawn into the war between Great Britain and France, but Willing and Francis continued to trade with the British. The firm lost a large shipment of rum when its merchant ship *Mount Vernon* was captured just outside Delaware Bay by the French privateer *Flying Fish.*

Tench Francis died on 1 May 1800, but the office of Purveyor of Public Supplies continued to function until it was abolished in 1812.

Sources

Naval Documents Related to the Quasi-War between the United States and

France, Naval Operations from January 1800 to November 1800. 2 vols. Washington: U.S. Government Printing Office, 1937.

Naval Documents Related to the United States Wars with the Barbary Powers, vol. 1: *Naval Operations, Including Diplomatic Background from 1785 through 1801.* Washington: U.S. Government Printing Office, 1939.

Navy Supply Corps Newsletter, February, May 1976, January–February 1985.

The New Frigates and Relations with France

Although construction progressed slowly, the six new frigates—*Constitution, President* and *United States* (44 guns each) and *Chesapeake, Congress* and *Constellation* (36 guns each)—were the finest ships of their class afloat when completed. The Navy's early contracting officers had done their jobs competently if not expeditiously.

On the diplomatic front, the United States signed additional treaties with the Barbary states in 1796 and 1797, lessening the threat to American commerce in the Mediterranean. Meanwhile, the French Revolution was underway and friction between United States and French naval forces had steadily eroded sympathy in the new American republic for the French government.

French demands for bribes to keep the peace, moreover, generated public support for the United States to strengthen its Army and Navy. Many members of Congress believed that it was important to remove the Navy from the jurisdiction of the War Department through formation of a separate Navy Department. American merchant vessels were given permission to defend themselves, and naval vessels and privateers were authorized to capture armed French vessels. The United States formally abrogated treaties with France. Although there was no formal declaration of war between the two nations, the Quasi War with France had begun.

Pursers as Commissioned Officers

The war with France was another milestone in the evolution of the U.S. Navy Supply Corps. For the first time, pursers served aboard ships of the line as officers. Between March 1794 and June 1798, the War Department received about 350 applications for officer appointments in the Navy. Pursers were authorized warrant officer status.

Congress removed the Navy from jurisdiction of the War Department on 30 May 1798, and a new Navy Department came into being as a separate entity. The new department continued to rely on navy agents for the purchase of all supplies and for the performance of duties of general disbursing agents. They received their commissions from the president, with the advice and consent of the Senate, for four years. The practice, with its beginnings in the Royal and Continental navies, of paying agents a stated percentage of the public monies they disbursed in foreign ports was continued by the new Navy Department. Congress did not abolish the position of navy agent until 1866.

Naval storekeepers were usually civilians employed at navy yards and receiving stations and at foreign naval depots established to support the Fleet. They were under the direction of the commanding officers of yards and stations. These storekeepers made requisitions on navy agents for the purchase of supplies, were in charge of all stores, and were accountable for the distribution of such stores to ships and to shore facilities.

In the new organization, the Navy gave commissioned pursers great responsibility as ships' business agents, more encompassing than that of paymasters who would succeed them in the nineteenth century. The early pursers maintained their ship's payrolls and paid the crew, issued provisions, conducted inventories, sold personal items to the crew, and purchased fresh food in foreign ports where there was no navy agent.

The Role of Pursers

From the beginning, pursers were a small group in the U.S. Navy. Only 123 men received appointments from March 1798 to July 1814. Of these, 52 began their careers during the Quasi War with France. A purser required large amounts of cash to carry out his enormous responsibilities. He requisitioned this money, with the approval of his captain, and thereafter was required to account for the total amount. According to U.S. Navy historian Christopher McKee:

> A successful purser needed to be accurate, systematic, and hardworking, and to possess a compulsive fondness for detail, for the paperwork burden of the job was staggering.
>
> To fulfill his payroll function, the purser was required to maintain six records—general muster book, register, payroll, slop account, provision book and monthly muster book. In addition to these primary records, the purser was required to keep dozens of other records.

A purser's life was anything but routine, and many a good man failed at the tasks required of him. Cruises were long and hard, and there was a great deal of turnover in the crew. These factors, coupled with a requirement to submit monthly reports to Philadelphia, added to the purser's burdens. His general muster book for a cruise could have as many as 1,000 entries as a result of personnel turnover.

Running the Company Store

Mirroring its Royal Navy heritage, the U.S. Navy required its sailors to purchase their own uniforms. When civilian pursers had been embarked in Navy ships, they sold uniforms to American seamen at high prices, charging what the traffic would bear. Warrant pursers were saddled with the legacy of their civilian predecessors, who were suspected of gouging the crew. Responding to complaints from the Fleet, Congress enacted legislation in 1799 to establish stores aboard ship, where pursers sold slops—shirts, trousers, outer and under jackets, shoes, stockings, flannel drawers, blankets, and mattresses. Sailors did not purchase slops for cash, but they were charged against their individual pay accounts, and pursers added a commission of 5 percent for each transaction. When cruises ended or when sailors otherwise left their ships, pursers balanced out the accounts.

Because pursers handled both the sale of slops and the pay accounts, the system created the potential for two perceived abuses. First, the purser could increase his cash flow by issuing more slops than the sailor might need and charge it to the sailor's account. Second, he might profit by charging an excessive amount. Sailors frequently accused pursers of both practices. The fact that actual cash did not change hands facilitated the pursers' potential for personal enrichment.These shipboard businessmen also sold articles of secondary necessity and luxuries, such as tea, coffee, sugar, and tobacco and charged commissions ranging up to 50 percent on these sales.

The mere fact that pursers' compensation was derived, in part, from the profit of sales caused friction with other officers. In addition, significant losses through theft and spoilage compounded the perception of pursers' incompetence. In fact, most pursers were honest. Pursers were often accused of being profiteers because they had income in addition to the same cash compensation allowed by law to sailing masters and chaplains for a year's active duty. The annual salary amounted to $581 through the Quasi War with France, $552 from 1801 through 1813, and $570 thereafter. Except for an occasional modest amount of prize money, sailing masters and chaplains were limited to pay and rations. As the men who ran the company store for a captive clientele, pursers' potential income was second only to that of ships' captains.

Pursers took great risks in sailing in U.S. Navy ships. When their host ships were engaged in combat, particularly when in pursuit of the enemy, pursers often were commanded to throw their inventory overboard in order to lighten ship. Without special relief from Congress, they bore such losses personally.

Developing guidelines for provisioning American ships was a major responsibility of Navy Secretary Benjamin Stoddert, who worked directly with navy agents. No detail seemed too small for the secretary's attention. In July 1798, he wrote to warn the agents against overloading ships with stores. The secretary was keenly interested in the acquisition, stocking, issuance, and accounting for slops.

The Office of Accountant of the Navy

Secretary Stoddert was responsible for the Navy's operations throughout the world, and he needed a separate office to account for the expenditure of public monies. Hence, on 16 June 1798, the Office of Accountant of the Navy was established in the Navy Department, not in the Treasury Department, as was the case with most other federal agencies. The War Department had been granted accounting independence earlier when it had jurisdiction over the Navy Department.

The first accountant of the Navy was William Winder, a planter from the Eastern Shore of Maryland, who was appointed in July 1798 but did not report to Philadelphia until September. Not only did Secretary Stoddert have difficulty in getting Winder on the job, but he also had difficulty keeping him at his desk. Winder finally resigned in January 1800, and Thomas Turner, the former mayor of Georgetown, was appointed to the position and served for the next 16 years.

Turner lost no time in casting the office in his own mold and setting a new standard of performance. In the 16 months he had actually occupied the position of accountant, Winder had processed and passed on to the Treasury Department accounts totaling only $546,000. In the first 15 months of his tenure, Turner settled $3.12 million in Navy accounts.

The Accountant of the Navy as Second-ranking Officer

The accountant of the Navy rapidly became the unofficial second-ranking officer of the Navy Department, with his own virtually independent fiefdom. The secretary and the accountant were the only two Navy officials whose appointment required Senate confirmation.

Accountability was a major issue, not only for pursers afloat, but also for anyone who handled the Navy's money and paid its bills. The early-nineteenth-century Navy placed large sums of money in the custody of navy agents ashore and pursers afloat. Lesser sums were entrusted to ship captains, squadron commanders, and even junior officers who entertained and recruited prospective sailors. The recipient of funds gave the government a receipt for the amount and assumed responsibility for it. He either had to prove that the money was spent for legitimate purposes or repay any discrepancy. Determining the legitimacy of the expenditures was the primary responsibility of the accountant of the Navy and his staff. As Christopher McKee describes the competence of the staff, "They fulfilled this charge with rigor, integrity and pickiness that make a twentieth-century Internal Revenue Service or General Accounting Office auditor seem downright permissive."

Turner, the typical orderly, systematic accountant, was appalled by the laxness of Navy pursers. "It is really wonderful that the officers in the Navy should be so extremely inattentive and commit so many blunders," he observed. "The system laid down for them is plain and simple and requires nothing but a little attention to enable them to exhibit all their returns correct." The system's basic principle, according to Turner, was that all vouchers submitted in proof of expenditures must be "fair, explicit, and unequivocal."

Pursers afloat often had difficulty complying precisely with these seemingly simple instructions because literally thousands of individual transactions required an equal number of pieces of paper. Fighting a war was not a clerical job and usually did not lend itself to precise record-keeping or meticulous accounting.

In the first decade of the Navy's existence as a separate entity from the War Department, the only recourse the federal government had to settle and collect debts owed by pursers was to institute suit in federal court. During that period, which included the undeclared war with France and the Barbary Coast hostilities, the problem of delinquent accounts of pursers lessened. The accounts of 17 pursers failed to explain only a total of $37,900.16, an average of $2,229.42. Of that amount, $20,296.55 in unaccounted funds was charged against pursers lost in *Pickering* and *Insurgente,* and $8,273.95 was charged against Purser John Lyon, whom McKee describes as "a compulsive gambler."

When Tench Francis died in May 1800, he was succeeded as purveyor of public supplies by Israel Whelen, another prominent Philadelphia businessman.

LORE OF THE CORPS

Israel Whelen

Purveyor of Public Supplies, 1800–1806

Israel Whelen, a banker, had a shipping business in Philadelphia and was active in state and national politics. He had applied for appointment as collector of the Port of Philadelphia before Tench Francis died. He apparently was in the right place at the right time, and President John Adams appointed him as Francis's successor rather than to the lesser post of port collector.

Born at Philadelphia in December 1752 into a family of Quakers, he married Mary Downing in May 1772. Whelen entered the Revolutionary Army under General George Washington in the summer of 1776. Israel Whelen devoted his personal service and fortune to the Revolutionary cause and rose to the rank of commissary general of the Army and financial agent of the government. His relationship with the Society of Friends was interrupted, not severed, and he returned to the faith when hostilities ceased.

Whelen conducted an extensive shipping business on High (later Market) Street in Philadelphia. He subsequently served in the Pennsylvania senate, where he was a member of a three-man committee appointed to secure congressional approval of the Jay Treaty with Great Britain. He was a member of the Electoral College in December 1796 that elected John Adams the second president of the United States.

Israel Whelen was the Philadelphia agent of the Phoenix Insurance Company of London and one of founding directors of the Bank of the United States when it was established in 1791. He was also president of the Board of Brokers and one of the corporators of the Lancaster Turnpike Commission, which he later served as president.

He suffered heavy financial losses when the government of Napoleon I seized seven cotton-laden ships he had consigned to French ports. Although the French allowed damages to the United States under the Louisiana Purchase agreement in 1804, the government did not reimburse individual losses.

When Whelen was nominated for collector of the Port of Philadelphia in May 1800, 151 prominent Philadelphians signed a letter of recommendation to President Adams. Before Adams could act on the nomination, Tench Francis died on 12 May. The president appointed Whelen to succeed Francis as purveyor of public supplies on 18 May.

Secretary of the Navy Benjamin Stoddert advised Navy officials on 28 May that the president had ordered offices of the Navy Department to be moved from Philadelphia and opened at Washington on 15 June 1800. Personnel of the offices of the Secretary and Accountant of the Navy were instructed to regulate their affairs accordingly. They were authorized a salary advance and "perhaps a little more, but this cannot at present be counted upon." Stoddert also authorized personnel to send to Washington such things as could be spared as soon as the owners pleased, but "Mr. Whelen, the purveyor, must be consulted in every instance."

During his tenure as purveyor, Whelen was responsible for arranging insurance for government cargoes and for accounting for goods to be delivered as tribute to rulers of the Barbary states. The account of the United States for the Barbary powers, which he maintained, amounted to $168,303.61 on 12 October 1801.

Israel Whelen died in October 1806 at the age of 54, and his remains interred in the Friends burial grounds at Philadelphia. A newspaper of the day paid him tribute:

> Few men have experienced greater vicissitudes of fortune, or supported them with equal moderation; as a senator, conciliating, active and intelligent; even his political opponents were unable to withhold from him the tribute of their esteem and affection. In private life his exalted integrity secured to him, under the most trying exigencies, the unlimited confidence of his numerous friends. In his domestic relations, every endearing quality waited to render his loss irreparable. Such a man will be long remembered and deeply lamented. Whilst we regret his loss, let us endeavor to imitate his virtues.

Sources

"A History of the Navy Supply Corps." *Navy Supply Corps Newsletter,* February 1970.

Naval Documents Related to the Quasi-War between the United States and France, Naval Operations from January 1800 to November 1800. 2 vols. Washington: U.S. Government Printing Officer, 1937.

Naval Documents Related to the United States Wars with the Barbary Powers, vol. 1: *Naval Operations, Including Diplomatic Background from 1785 through 1801.* Washington: U.S. Government Printing Office, 1939.

"Navy Supply Corps." *Navy Times,* 13 February 1955.

Scharf, J. Thomas, and Thomas Westcott. *History of Philadelphia,* vol. 3: *1609–1884.* Philadelphia: L. H. Everts, 1884.

The First U.S. Navy Yards and the Reduction of Forces

The first American navy yards were established in Washington and Portsmouth, New Hampshire, in 1800, and in Philadelphia, New York, Boston, and Norfolk in 1801. As Washington increasingly became the focal point of federal activities, the Navy Department moved from Philadelphia to the new capital city on the Potomac River.

In 1801, as it had done at the end of the Revolutionary War, Congress again took what was to become a frequent and regular action by drawing down American armed forces when the nation was not involved in a declared war. The president was authorized to sell all but 13 Navy vessels, of which only 6 were to be kept in commission. In addition, all commissioned officers and all pursers were discharged from service.

Drawing down American military forces proved to be an unwise move because the rulers of some Barbary Coast states were still requiring the United States to pay annual tribute. In early 1801, Tripoli declared war on the United States. Faced with a war he had not declared and did not want, President Thomas Jefferson, in May 1801 ordered Commodore Richard Dale to take a small squadron of ships to determine what effect a show of force might have. However, the American squadron, separated from America by 4,000 miles of water, was poorly supported by Congress.

The First Underway Replenishment at Sea

Support of U.S. Navy ventures far from friendly shores was always a major challenge. American Navy ships were not always welcome in foreign ports, but creative minds sought other means of providing the necessary material needs of deployed ships. The result was the first recorded replenishment at sea in 1804 when the ketch *Intrepid* resupplied Commodore Edward Preble's forces off Tripoli with provisions, clothing, and ammunition. This historic event enabled Preble to continue his blockade.

Having turned aside the threats posed by the Barbary States and France, the young nation appeared to be on the threshold of emerging from the shadow of former British rule. Realization that the United States was an island nation which, although rich in many resources, lacked many others essential to solidifying her independence led to increased awareness of the importance of worldwide trade. The United States adopted a policy of neutrality, and U.S. merchant ships began to fan out to all corners of the globe. However, the expanding power of aggressive European nations such as England, France, and Spain threatened America's independence as well as its neutrality.

In May 1803 war resumed between the British and French. Unable to recruit sufficient manpower for its large fleet, the Royal Navy turned to the impressment of American seamen. In this environment, Congress authorized $852,500 for construction of 188 gunboats for defense against British incursions.

At Peace, but Preparing for War

Technically in a peacetime status, but with war clouds on the horizon, Navy supply was largely a matter of supporting the Fleet and conducting routine procurement and accounting. Navy agents continued to provide these supporting functions at shore bases. Excerpts from letters addressed to the secretary of the Navy reveal the nature and scope of the agents' day-to-day activities.

In September 1807 Navy Secretary Robert Smith received a letter from the navy agent at Portland, Maine, reporting that workers building gunboats under Commodore Preble were in arrears in their pay. According to the Portland agent, "During the latter part of Commodore Preble's life, he was so extremely low that we could not hold any conversation with him respecting pay."

The purchase, storage, and quality control of saltpeter, an essential ingredient of gunpowder, was a major concern of George Harrison, navy agent at Philadelphia. Gunpowder and saltpeter were subjects of frequent correspondence between Secretary Smith and Harrison, who regularly reported on the status of his negotiations with powder manufacturers throughout the first decade of the century. Saltpeter delivered to the Philadelphia Navy Yard often contained a substantial amount of dirt and marine salt. This required remanufacture by purifying, kiln drying, and packing in tight casks to protect it from deterioration while in storage. It was not until May 1811 that George Harrison could report to Smith that an adequate supply of quality saltpeter was available at Philadelphia.

Over the years, offers of assistance were often made by merchants, government employees, and ordinary citizens; most sought reimbursement but others did not. The secretary was besieged with letters requesting contracts for the Navy. John Marrast of Norfolk wanted to supply candles, a Mr. Ricketts, of Alexandria desired to supply bread, and Joseph Warren Revere of Massachusetts wished to supply copper.

The secretary and his staff considered procurement of provisions and the diet of crews especially important. Sailors in the eighteenth and nineteenth centuries ate regularly, if not especially well, twice a day. They subsisted mainly on dried meat, hard biscuits, raisins, peas, pudding, and grog (watered-down rum) despite continuing efforts to improve their diets.

In May 1808 Navy Agent J. Blount informed Secretary Smith that he was convinced that split peas were not only better for immediate use but also kept much better on long voyages in the summertime. Blount sent a barrel of split peas to the Washington Navy Yard and proposed that an experiment be made by using them on board ships.

Congressional Involvement

Congress enacted legislation in March 1809 that dealt with a variety of accounting matters, including a provision that "every purser of the Navy give bond, with one or more sufficient sureties, in such sums as the President of the United States may direct, for the faithful discharge of the trust reposed in him." This requirement had previously existed for government officials entrusted with large sums of public money, and the new legislation extended it to Navy pursers and Army paymasters. The legislation limited compensation of navy agents to 1 percent of the public monies they distributed.

Early Congresses showed a proclivity to micromanage military budgets, and individual members sometimes waged personal vendettas against the U.S. military establishment. The actions of Congressman John Randolph of Virginia is a case in point. Randolph was opposed to standing military and naval establishments. His favorite target was the financial operations of the Navy, which he examined in great detail.

In May 1809 the House of Representatives appointed him to chair a committee "to investigate and report whether monies drawn from the Treasury since the 3rd of March 1801 have been faithfully applied to the objects for which they were appropriated and whether the same have been regularly accounted for." McKee describes the resulting Committee of Investigation as "primarily a fishing expedition" in search of evidence that Randolph and his allies hoped to use to embarrass President James Madison, Treasury Secretary Albert Gallatin, and former Secretary of the Navy Robert Smith. Randolph went to work with a vengeance and the committee spread a wide net. Navy yards were convenient and especially vulnerable targets because of the ample opportunity they offered for charges, real or alleged, of fraud, favoritism, and fiscal irresponsibility on the part of commanders. The easy availability of disgruntled current and former employees fueled Randolph's campaign against the Navy.

Randolph listed four areas of Navy supply and financial management he planned to investigate: (1) the nature and amount of extra allowances made to officers of the Navy beyond the compensation allowed by law; (2) the manner in which advances were made to pursers; (3) principles on which their accounts were settled; and (4) the nature of pursers' emoluments other than the pay allowed them by law. Obviously, the investigation of pursers was intended to put the spotlight on their profits from sales of slops.

Accountant of the Navy Turner listed in considerable detail the "extra allowances" made to officers in addition to pay. He showed that they were normal reimbursements for travel and living expenses while the officers were engaged in official duties. As a result of Turner's effective testimony, the committee moved on to more fertile grounds. It next questioned whether pursers were able—and, in fact, compelled—to account for the money advanced to them for official purposes. Then, the committee delved into pursers' profits on sales of slops.

In June, Paul Hamilton told Randolph, "In the settlement of their [pursers'] accounts they must exhibit a satisfactory voucher for every expenditure." Hamilton described how advances were made to pursers and how the advances were charged to them when included in an ultimate settlement of accounts. Dissatisfied with Hamilton's responses, Randolph introduced a resolution calling for a reduction of the Navy and military establishments.

Secretary Hamilton continued to be involved in detailed dealings with navy agents and suppliers. In November 1811 Representative Randolph appeared at the Navy Office to interrogate Secretary Hamilton and Chief Clerk Charles W. Goldsborough. His most serious discovery was that Purser Robert W. Goldsborough, the deceased brother of the chief clerk, had not possessed a valid bond.

Congress was impressed with the obvious competence of Thomas Turner, but Secretary Hamilton was not held in high regard. Under Randolph's intense prodding, the Navy's clerks prepared a series of reports to Congress. The report on profits from sales of slops appears to have mollified the committee. Less satisfactory was the report on pursers' total outstanding balances in excess of $30,000, of which nearly $13,000 was attributed to the account of the late Purser Goldsborough.

Even as the reports were flowing from the Navy's offices to Congress, the House investigation died out when war clouds gathered. Nothing might have come of the Senate probe had not Senator William Branch Giles of Virginia proposed a candidate for appointment to the highly lucrative post of purser of the Washington Navy Yard. When Giles learned that Lewis Deblois, a politically connected Washington businessman, had been appointed to the coveted post, he was furious.

Senator Giles set out to discredit Deblois's suitability as a purser, but Hamilton claimed the appointment was made without his consent. President Madison also said that he had nothing to do with it. Yet Delbois became purser of the Washington Yard, an office to which no one would admit appointing him.

On 30 March 1812 the Senate enacted legislation making the appointment of pursers subject to the advice and consent of the Senate. The legislation voided all existing purser appointments, requiring the incumbents to be nominated and confirmed anew as of 1 May 1812. Giles's action, apparently born of pique and politics, had taken its toll by raising so many questions about pursers' operations and profits that some congressional action was inevitable. In testimony before the Senate committee, Secretary Hamilton said that he needed only 13 pursers, but 38 were already on active duty.

The legislation forced Secretary Hamilton to decide which pursers to nominate for new commissions. It was not until 13 April that President Madison forwarded Hamilton's list of 26 men to the Senate for reappointment. Hamilton was called back to the Senate to defend the list, which included the name of Lewis Deblois. The senators, disturbed that the most recent settlements of purser accounts had been in 1808, wanted to know how Hamilton arrived at 26 required pursers. Hamilton was better prepared for this visit to the Senate than he had been on previous occasions and somehow managed to convince the senators to confirm all 26 nominees.

With attention focused on the threat of war, questions about pursers disappeared while other issues took center stage. As the mood of the country shifted steadily toward war during the latter months of 1811, President James Madison knew that his army and navy were substantially smaller than, and probably no match for, their potential British adversaries. Thus, he struggled to find an accommodation by which war could be averted.

A Movement toward War

In the period from 1810 to 1812 the Navy had two afloat units—the Northern Division based at New York and a Southern Division based at Norfolk. On 16 May 1812, ships of Commodore John Rodgers's Northern Division engaged the British sloop *Lille Belt,* also known as *Little Belt.* In the ensuing action, the British ship was severely damaged, with 9 sailors killed and 23 wounded. Action reports failed to clarify who had hailed first and who had fired first. When the British demanded reparations for damage to *Little Belt,* Secretary of State James Monroe refused. Americans living in the western territories believed that the British in Canada had stirred up Indian attacks. Congressmen from western and southern states, dubbed "war hawks," strongly advocated using force against Britain.

The Royal Navy's impressment of American seaman and disruption of U.S. ocean commerce continued, and American sentiment mounted against the English crown. Although united for the most part in anger at the English, Americans were divided over whether the country should go to war again. The British impressed an estimated 10,000 Americans between 1796 and 1811. The State Department complained vigorously but to no avail, and the practice continued although U.S. complaints resulted in return of about one-third of those seized.

In his State of the Union message in November 1811 President Madison announced his decision to continue pursuing peace while preparing for war. While strengthening both the Army and the Navy, the United States would advise the British and French of its willingness to ease trade restrictions.

The war hawks in Congress failed to muster sufficient votes to pass Madison's plan, which included building 12 74-gun ships of the line and 10 additional frigates. Congress did approve stockpiling timber and funds to repair and fit *Chesapeake, Constellation,* and *Adams* and also construction of a dry dock. As a result of the congressional action, the United States was moving toward war without the needed resources.

The Details of Supply

Congress enacted legislation to abolish the office of Purveyor of Public Supplies and assign its functions to each government agency, including the departments of War and Navy. Around the nation, apprehension over impending war was widespread, but at the Navy Department it was business as usual. A sampling of correspondence between the Secretary of the Navy Paul Hamilton and agents and pursers in the field provides an insight into the problems of supply, finance, organization, and administration.

In November 1811 Joseph Kerr, a contractor in Chillicothe, Ohio, advised Secretary Hamilton that sending provisions from New Orleans to Washington would be risky. Kerr revealed plans to drive cattle to the Washington Navy Yard to be slaughtered, and the meat to be packed there. Through the spring of 1812, prospective suppliers continued to solicit the secretary's approval of various tenders for goods and services. Richard Parrott purchased hemp at a low price the previous fall and had from $60,000 to $80,000 worth on hand. Paul Pritchard, the respected shipbuilder at Charleston, was completing a vessel that could serve as a brig or schooner. Stephen Girard, a well-known Philadelphia merchant, offered first quality beef, boasting, "There is not a single shank bone to the barrel."

The details of supply continued to occupy much of Secretary Hamilton's daily routine. Just two weeks before war broke out, he wrote to Purser Samuel Hambleton, who had been ordered to duty at New York to support gunboats there, that a contract had been made with Seth G. Macy of Hudson, New York, for a "considerable supply" of blue cloth for

Navy use. Hamilton also instructed Hambleton to requisition a necessary supply of slops from the navy agent for issue to gunboat crews at Newport, Rhode Island. For these issues, the Secretary authorized Hambleton to charge a commission of 12½ percent. He also advised Hambleton that the New York navy agent would advance him up to $2,000 to enable him to provide a supply of small stores. Hambleton was provided "a suitable room" at public expense to enable him to keep articles of clothing and also a room in which to keep his accounts. The secretary authorized a steward for each of the gunboats and one extra steward for the purser.

LORE OF THE CORPS

Purser Samuel Hambleton, USN

Period of Service: 1806–51

Purser Hambleton had the famous blue flag made that carried the often-quoted dying words of Captain James Lawrence, "Don't give up the ship." This was the banner under which Master Commandant Oliver Hazard Perry led his American forces into the Battle of Lake Erie.

Samuel Hambleton was born into a distinguished family of the Eastern Shore of Maryland at the Talbot County town of Martingham in 1777. He served for a short time as a merchant's clerk and eventually became one of his family's most outstanding members.

In 1806 he was appointed a purser in the fledgling U.S. Navy. His first duty was at New Orleans. He subsequently was transferred to New York City and, in 1812, to Newport, Rhode Island, where he and Perry became good friends. When Perry left to assume command of the Lake Erie Squadron, he took Hambleton along with him.

Hambleton was 36 when he served as purser aboard Perry's flagship, *Lawrence*. The young purser was severely wounded during the Lake Erie encounter when he was struck by a cannonball that dropped from the rigging while he was the guns. He survived the encounter.

Samuel Hambleton's younger brother, John, followed him into the Navy as a purser. Little is known of Samuel Hambleton's Navy duties after the war, although he remained on the active list until his death in 1851.

Source

From a Lighthouse Window. Saint Michaels, Md.: Chesapeake Bay Maritime Museum, 1989.

War with Great Britain

On 30 June 1812 Congress finally voted the long-anticipated declaration of war against Great Britain. Upon this action, Hamilton issued instructions to his officers: "You are with the force under your command entitled to every belligerent right to attack and capture, and to defend."

Material shortages were reported almost immediately. On 9 July Commodore Thomas Tingey wrote to the secretary from the Washington Navy Yard that the frequent requisitions from naval stations at Gosport, Virginia, Wilmington, North Carolina, and Charleston, South Carolina, were rapidly drawing down his ordnance stocks. Two days later, Tingey recommended that muskets, bayonets, pistols, and cutlasses be ordered from Philadelphia, where apparently a greater supply existed.

Despite spending considerable time fending off his adversaries in Congress, Hamilton devoted much of his time to keeping a tight rein on the Navy's funds. This meant continued direct communication with the merchant suppliers.

Predicting the arrival of British men-of-war off New York, the inventor Robert Fulton wanted to be prepared for such an event, and he reminded Secretary Hamilton that the Navy still owed him $2,500 on money appropriated for torpedo experiments. Fulton proposed that he construct 10 or 12 torpedoes with all operating apparatus. He also promised to make preparations for employing them against the British and assured the secretary that, if he did not use the funds in a manner satisfactory to Congress, he would refund the money.

As formal hostilities commenced, Hamilton's navy agents recommended actions they felt were in the interest of security. Constant Tabor, navy agent at Newport, wrote to the secretary on 5 July 1812 to express concern about British raids along the coast and the possibility that they might seize provisions. He asked permission to move the provisions at his discretion 15 or 20 miles up the river into a port that British ships could not enter.

Later in the month, Lieutenant Colonel Wharton, commandant of the Marine Corps, wrote to the secretary that he found it necessary because of the difficulty of transport by sea to order that 100 uniform coats be made in New York for the men stationed there. Because the Navy had no appropriated funds for the manufacture of Marine uniforms in New York, Wharton requested that Hamilton have Chief Clerk Goldsborough forward $1,800 for that purpose.

The original American strategy had been for Commodore Stephen

Decatur to form a cruising squadron and sail under Commodore Rodgers's flag but to keep his squadron separate from Rodgers's. However, Hamilton decided that the two squadrons should cruise off their respective stations of New York and Norfolk. He wanted them to stay close to the coast in order to protect American merchant ships returning to ports between Norfolk and New England. They could meet occasionally but were not to join forces unless they expected to meet a superior force.

While Rodgers's squadron was deployed in the Atlantic, many crewmen came down with scurvy. The illness, a constant threat to seamen, was the subject of a continuing research into methods to combat it. D. Lamarier of Philadelphia read a copy of Rodgers's report and contacted Hamilton with a description of plants that could be used to combat scurvy.

A New Age for Pursers

In order to meet wartime requirements, the Navy was forced to recall 18 pursers who had been laid off during the earlier drawdown period. Newly recruited pursers were relatively mature men who averaged 27 years of age, about 5 years older than the typical new lieutenant of the line. Pursers were also much better educated then line lieutenants; 12 were college graduates and 5 were attorneys. Early-nineteenth-century pursers knew how to work within the regulations but were amazingly creative when faced with situations not specifically covered and found new and different ways to accomplish their objectives.

Late in 1812 Secretary Hamilton proposed to add the duties of navy storekeeper to those of purser at shore stations. This proposal was not popular with storekeepers, and on 30 December Faris Craven, Navy storekeeper at Portsmouth, New Hampshire, wrote to the secretary and advised him that the position of storekeeper was necessary because of the quantities of goods at the Portsmouth Yard. Hamilton dropped the idea of eliminating storekeepers.

Pressure on pursers afloat and ashore mounted during the War of 1812 as they struggled to maintain the flow of supplies required to prosecute the war and maintain proper records of all transactions. Although the war put them under greater pressure, the higher volume of supplies meant increased income for pursers from commissions on materials sold to the increased number of ships and naval personnel.

Pursers' Duties in the War of 1812

During the War of 1812, ships' pursers performed a variety of duties that today are the responsibility of ships' supply officers. The nineteenth-century purser procured, stowed, dispensed, and accounted for food, clothing, and the pay of officers and men. The normal supply channel required pursers to procure the necessities through the navy agents of their respective stations. When acceptable local supplies were not available through normal channels, pursers could request permission of the secretary of the Navy to make purchases outside the system.

Purser Edwin T. Satterwhite, U.S. Brig *Vixen* at Charleston, advised the secretary on 11 September 1812 that winter clothing available there was of poor quality and exorbitantly priced. Gwin Harris, purser at St. Mary's Station, had advised Satterwhite that Winn and Butler of New York could supply the needed clothing "of a quality much superior to those of Charleston, and at prices below those heretofore paid." Satterwhite requested that the secretary provide instructions for the purchase.

Purser Craven Turner reported to the Navy secretary on the condition of the buildings and material when he arrived at his new duty station, the Portsmouth Navy Yard, in October 1812. Turner was impressed by Portsmouth and its New England setting, the harbor, the town, and its population, but he was appalled at the deteriorating timbers that had been assembled for construction of a 74-gun frigate authorized in 1799. He noted that preparatory work had been done, but construction had not been completed. The purser proposed that workers at Portsmouth could build the frigate in 90 working days. He also recommended Portsmouth as the logical site to stock materials for the repair of damaged ships, citing the "safe and commodious nature of the harbor."

Turner had noted that the yard's superintendent occupied one of two apartments in the dwelling house, with the other vacant and available. Obviously enthusiastic over the prospect of being purser of an expanded Portsmouth Navy Yard, Turner made an unusual proposal to Secretary Hamilton: "I will most cheerfully take due care of the Yard and property therein without any further compensation than the right of residence you were pleased to give me."

By November 1812 the British blockade had cut off the supply of Georgia timbers for repair of battle-damaged ships and for resumption of building frigates. Commodore Tingey, at the Washington Navy Yard, recommended speedy arrangements for furnishing the navy yard at Portsmouth with suitable materials for rebuilding a frigate.

The British Surrender a Prize U.S. Ship

In an age when warfare was conducted under vastly different rules of engagement than those of the present, it was still legal for American merchant ships to trade under British license. Navy officers opposed the practice vigorously and attempted to check it. In one amazing and amusing incident, Purser Henry Denison, prize master of the captured British licensed trader *Ariadne,* was ordered to put into the closest U.S. port. Before he could comply, he used his British license and what he called "a little finesse" to avoid identification as American by two Royal Navy warships. The British, assuming *Ariadne* and Denison were British, put aboard nine impressed American seamen to assist in working the ship. Purser Denison and the suddenly freed seamen made their way in *Ariadne* safely to Boston. He smugly reported the incident, and his role in it, to Secretary Hamilton by letter.

Although the Navy was achieving unexpectedly successful individual actions against the Royal Navy in the Atlantic, the British blockade of American ports had substantially reduced the volume of American commerce. As a result, the national treasury experienced a sharp decline in revenues from customs fees. Although both combatants had become dissatisfied with the progress of the war, the spectacular success of the young and outnumbered Navy, which was full of fight, raised national morale and encouraged President Madison and Congress to stay the course.

Navy Expansion and a New Secretary of the Navy

In late 1812, Congress debated the merits of increasing the size of the U.S. Navy to meet the threat posed by the much larger Royal Navy and its 74-gun ships of the line. Finally, on 23 December, Congress approved the first major naval construction legislation in 10 years. On 13 January 1813, President Madison signed the Act to Increase the Navy of the United States, which authorized the building of 10 frigates, 4 of 74 guns and 6 of 44 guns.

Madison was unhappy with administration of the Navy and especially with Secretary Paul Hamilton, who resigned in December 1812. Madison promptly appointed William Jones, a former sea captain who took over in January 1813 as Hamilton's successor. One of his first acts, apparently purely political, was to replace the venerable Chief Clerk Goldsborough.

For their part, the British were not happy with their forces committed to the American war. The Royal Navy asked for additional resources for the North American Station, but the Admiralty, faced with worldwide commitments, was at first reluctant to provide more ships. In January 1813, the Admiralty relented and sent reinforcements. The British government hoped this additional commitment, bringing the total ships in the reinforced North American Squadron to 98, would enable the Royal Navy to turn the tide to victory in the Atlantic. Slow progress on construction of the 74-gun frigates further complicated the situation for the American Navy, now faced with enhanced strength of the enemy. In fact, not one of the new ships was to be completed during the war.

Problems at St. Mary's

Meanwhile, the lack of funds and guidelines continued to plague the Navy's pursers. Purser Nathaniel W. Rothwell relieved Purser Gwin Harris at St. Mary's, Georgia, in late December 1812. A week after assuming his new post, Rothwell wrote to Jones to report that he was astonished to find it so difficult to procure funds, provisions, slops, and other items. He also reported that a substantial amount of money was due officers and seamen at St. Mary's.

He indicated that he had no barrels of provisions salted against spoilage in stock, fewer than 100 barrels available in Savannah, and that he was unable to purchase flour. He also informed the secretary that his commodore had directed him to request one year's salted provisions and "a few barrels of flour" because all the provisions would be exhausted by the time a supply of pork and beef could arrive. Not waiting for the secretary's response, Rothwell contracted to purchase 200 barrels each of pork and beef.

Rothwell also explained his plan to procure funds inasmuch as he could not negotiate a bill of $1,000 at the St. Mary's bank. He advised the secretary that he had tentatively accepted a proposal by the bank in Savannah that he pay a discount. He said he intended to implement this arrangement unless he received a remittance or contrary instructions from Jones. The purser revealed that he had a demand from the commanding officer of Marines for funds—a demand with which he would comply when he had funds.

Other officers envied and distrusted pursers because of the additional income they received from commissions on sale of supplies. Occasionally, this animosity resulted in attacks. An incident in Purser Rothwell's home at St. Mary's in late September 1813 illustrates the extent to which one officer went in voicing his opinion. In a letter to Secretary Jones, Commodore Campbell charged Sailing Master Winslow Foster with unauthorized entry into Rothwell's home in a drunken state, using improper language, and exhibiting conduct unbecoming an officer. Jones first ordered Foster's dismissal then reversed himself, but Foster was arrested on other charges less than a month later.

The Institutionalization of Contracting and Purchasing Procedures

Congressional interest in the administration of the Navy continued under the stewardship of Secretary Jones. In December 1812, Representative Langdon Cheves, chairman of the House Naval Affairs Committee, requested that Lieutenant Charles Morris provide information to expose the causes of mismanagement in the naval establishment and that he make suggestions on reform. Cheves also asked Morris pointedly about the existence of abuses, waste, and extravagance in building, repairing, equipping, and supplying naval forces.

Morris responded in January 1813. "The present mode of supplying the Navy through navy agents is one great source of abuse and extravagance," he reported. He said he believed that compensation of agents through commissions on purchases induced higher prices. Morris pointed out that he was not accusing the agents of doing so, but that the present regulations exposed the Navy to a costly temptation for abuse and personal gain.

As a remedy for this potential risk, Morris proposed that agents receive fixed salaries, advertise for sealed proposals, and be bound to accept "those most favorable to the Government." He also suggested that agents be required to take an oath that they had complied with all regulations. Morris particularly criticized the lack of a regular system for determining allowances for stores and furniture for each class of vessels. He claimed that this void allowed commanders to implement their own ideas on how to arrange their own ships.

Morris's recommendation was that, in addition to requiring sealed proposals, the Navy take steps to ensure full contract compliance and to make no advances to contractors without proper security to indemnify the Navy against their failure to perform. He proposed that the Navy regulate the armament, equipment, and allowances of the various stores for each class. Morris went on to point out that delays in refitting Navy ships not only increased expenses but also took the ships out of service too long. He also complained that too many artisans were employed in some of the yards, that ships' officers had too much discretion in the alteration of vessels, and that officers discharged from ships in the yards were not subject to sufficient accountability. The allocation of too many resources to the gunboat program initiated by Thomas Jefferson was another point of criticism. Morris told the secretary that the gunboat program should be carefully reexamined and suggested that a board of professionals be appointed to oversee the program.

In early February Secretary Jones proposed a reorganization of the

Navy Department to Congressman Burwell Bassett, who had succeeded Representative Cheves as chairman of the Committee of Naval Enquiry. Jones suggested to the Senate the formation of a Naval Purveyor Department, "with as many deputies as necessary," appointed by the president and confirmed by the Senate. Jones recommended that purveyor's deputies reside in "some of our central seaports where the state of the market and the information necessary to form contracts to advantage can be best known and effected with the best security." He proposed that the secretary's office retain the control and general direction of all important contracts the purveyor negotiated. Secretary Jones also asked for increased appropriations to employ two additional clerks, to appoint additional captains, and to fund construction of six of a new class of larger corvettes. To offset these costs, he suggested a reduction in the number of gunboats.

Apparently swayed by Jones's rationale, Congress approved another naval expansion act on 3 March 1813. Armed with this new authority, Jones issued instructions to the naval constructor at the Washington Navy Yard and to the navy agents, stressing the importance of inventorying and purchasing materials for ship construction as expeditiously as possible.

These were important steps in the evolution of Navy supply. Bassett, Cheves, Jones, and Morris all played important roles in reining in senior Navy officers and agents in the conduct of procurement. This modest first step in institutionalization of contracting and purchasing procedures had a long-term impact on progress along the road to a more professional Navy, especially Navy supply.

Jones and the Coastal Cities

The Naval Expansion Act was significant to continued success against the Royal Navy. Jones was convinced that the British would tighten their blockade, and he believed that smaller vessels could be built faster, would be better commerce raiders, and might be successful against the blockade. Meanwhile, he was frustrated by the wide dispersal of gunboats, which he described as "scattered in every creek and corner." He was concerned about waste and extravagance and so decided to reduce the number of active gunboats to 50 and apportion them among stations from New York to New Orleans. The remainder were to be laid up, ready for emergency service.

By April 1813 Jones had been in his post as Navy secretary for only three months, insufficient time to comprehend naval strategies and finances fully. Charlestonians were nervous about the potential threat the British fleet posed to their city and did not hesitate to let Washington know of their concern. Secretary Jones termed Captain John H. Dent's deployment of ships beyond coastal waters as irresponsible when their primary missions were largely defensive. He was also upset when Dent, the commanding naval officer at Charleston, appointed a navy agent at Beaufort, South Carolina.

Citizens of New York City also were frightened, and Jones's order to reduce the number of gunboats added to their nervousness. Secretary Jones was concerned with replenishing provisions and water for the flotilla defending New York from a position off Sandy Hook. In the event Captain John Lewis did not think it prudent to bring the force, which he personally commanded, back to New York for resupply, Jones instructed him to order the navy agent to use replenishment at sea by "employing a shallop occasionally to convey the supplies to the flotilla."

Supply Details and the Secretary

Jones quickly found himself immersed in dealing with problems—large and small—of naval agents, pursers, and suppliers. The secretary's correspondence reveals the type and scope of the issues of the time: procurement, storage, distribution, transportation, and financing.

One of the transportation problems involved providing light cannons for ships under construction on the eastern Great Lakes. The only reliable method of transporting the guns to the staging point at Pittsburgh was by wagon. Jones dealt with Isaac Robbins of Alexandria, Virginia, who arranged with 11 subcontractors to transport 12 cannons from Washington to Pittsburgh.

The threat to coastal towns meant that supplies ordered for delivery to ships and ports along the Atlantic seaboard often required diversion to inland locations. Because Baltimore was being threatened with bombardment from both land and sea in May 1814, R. Pindell, a contractor at Hagerstown, Maryland, proposed a plan to prevent loss of Navy yarn. He suggested delivering the yarn, for which he had contracted, to the navy agent at Pittsburgh or Lexington, Kentucky.

In June, John Jacob Astor advised the secretary from New York that experience had proved that "the best and safest mode of keeping bread was to be put it up in good rum puncheons." In his letter, Astor assured Jones that bread stored this way would keep for two or three years.

The Royal Navy blockade and other wartime economic realities took their toll on civilian contractors. Foot and Hinman Company of New York signed a contract to supply the Navy with 300 bolts of duck cloth. As of October 1813, the company had delivered 218 bolts but had become insolvent and asked to be released from delivering the balance.

In February 1813 Dennis Carroll, a former Briton residing in Washington and experienced in executing provisions contracts for the Royal Navy, contacted Secretary Jones regarding salted provisions for the Navy. Carroll later advised the secretary that he had shipped 100 barrels of Navy beef from Baltimore to Washington in December 1813 because ice would block the water in January and February and that "the British would no doubt return in the spring."

The Secretary and a Chesapeake Privateersman

In September 1813 Joshua Barney, well-known privateersman from Baltimore commanding a flotilla defending the Chesapeake Bay, informed Secretary Jones that his flotilla needed a purser on the flagship. Barney asked the secretary to appoint his son as purser.

Commodore Barney wrote to the secretary again in March 1814, noting that his flotilla was still without a purser. He told the secretary that he was providing one month's pay to each recruit. However, the navy agent at Baltimore required a purser's requisition and, without a purser, Barney could not supply one. In April, Barney advised Secretary Jones that shipment of provisions for New Orleans must be via circuitous routing on account of the British blockade. As a result, a flatboat had been loaded at Shippingsport, Pennsylvania, with 140 barrels of pickled beef, 74 barrels of pickled pork, and 100 25-pound casks of gunpowder. Later in the month, Barney warned Jones that it was impossible to put provisions, other than salt, on board the gunboats. He pointed out that the gunboats had no hold or place to put the bulky bread and he would not trust liquors or small stores to the riverboat crews.

By May, Barney had his purser—not his son but a Mr. Skinner. Barney reported that Skinner wanted to draw money from the navy agent at Baltimore to purchase extra articles for the crews of the ships in the flotilla. Skinner claimed that he could purchase the desired items 20 to 25 percent cheaper by using cash.

Supply Problems and the Adjudication of Disputes

The Office of the Secretary of the Navy was frequently called upon to adjudicate disputes, often petty, involving navy agents, pursers, and suppliers. Typical of these involved Dr. John Bullus, the agent at New York, and the purser of the frigate *John Adams.* The men clashed over the latter's purchase of carpeting in June 1814. The purser presented his bill for $136, but Bullus required him to wait until his ship returned from a cruise because he had not authorized the purchase. Jones's response is not known.

Other samples of the secretary's correspondence are illustrative: Jahaziel Sherman, agent at New York, wanted to know which Albany bank to use to obtain notes to pay the company from which Captain Macdonough took a ship; R. Meade, navy agent at Cadiz, Spain, strongly recommended Cadiz as a trading port when the War of 1812 ended; Reid and Hart were made temporary agents by Commodore Macdonough on Lake Champlain in 1813; William Welling, a New York contractor, contended that well-seasoned ash was superior to oak in making barrels to store provisions; and the Navy Accountant's Office notified the secretary that, although many official records were deliberately destroyed when the British sacked Washington, all of the papers in his office were saved.

Supplying raw materials for construction of the 74-gun ships of the line continued to be a major problem. A shortage of live-oak timbers so severely hampered progress at the Portsmouth Navy Yard that most of the carpenters were laid off and the less desirable white oak was substituted. In July, Captain Isaac Hull, commandant at Portsmouth, wrote to the secretary regarding the timber situation and sought permission to build a $2,000 shiphouse to cover building ways because of the extreme cold and heavy snows at Portsmouth. Stating that the money for the proposed shiphouse would be "well laid out," the secretary approved Hull's request in August.

While Hull was experiencing difficulties in obtaining the supplies he needed, the Royal Navy was having much better luck in procuring needed supplies from coastal New England towns. New Englanders, seething under the political and economic frustrations of what they termed "Mr. Madison's War," were willing to supply food, water, and wood to British vessels on the North American Station for a price.

The frustrations of the New England states led radicals to demand secession, but moderates wanted only to amend the Constitution. In October 1814, the New England states presented a report to Congress, an act that implied secession, but increasing hostilities initiated by the British destroyed any credence the threat may have had.

Supplying the Navy in the Northern Lakes Theater

Early in the war, it became obvious that naval control of the eastern Great Lakes and Lake Champlain was necessary to the success of British military operations. Supplying the small American fleet operating in these waters was an early test of American logistics planning. With no major centers of commerce on the American lakes littoral, all supplies necessarily had to come from Philadelphia or Pittsburgh, each several days away by overland routes. To expedite the flow of naval stores and purchases, Oliver Ormsby, a Pittsburgh merchant, was appointed navy agent in that city in February 1813.

Commodore Isaac Chauncey was appointed commander of American naval forces on Lake Erie and Lake Ontario in September 1812 and took charge of building a U.S. Navy squadron on Lake Ontario with purchased schooners and a corvette. Chauncey had difficulty recruiting sufficient sailors in the wilderness to man the ships in his squadron. Oliver Hazard Perry, an ambitious, intelligent 28-year-old officer with 14 years of Navy experience, came to Chauncey's rescue with an offer to serve under his command and bring 100 seamen from Rhode Island.

Appointment of navy agents and contractors was frequently a source of controversy for the secretary. A Mr. Walter, a government agent at Ontario, questioned the ability of Eli Luther, who was employed by Dr. Bullus, navy agent at New York, to transport naval stores and seamen to Lakes Ontario, Erie, and Champlain. During the winter of 1812-13, separate fleets were under construction on the three lakes. The procurement of men, materials, and supplies at Erie, Pennsylvania, and at Sackets Harbor and Plattsburgh, New York, was especially challenging. Although timber was plentiful along the wooded shores of the lakes, other materials had to be transported great distances over primitive roads and barely navigable rivers. Ship carpenters and other workmen, sailors, guns, and naval stores for the Lake Erie and Lake Ontario fleets came from New York City.

Augustus Porter was navy agent at Lake Ontario. During the winter of 1812–13, he had placed a quantity of naval stores with a private storekeeper at Buffalo and Manchester, Vermont, after being unable to place them under the care of an authorized naval agent or storekeeper. He was forced to report to the secretary that the stores left at Buffalo had been destroyed by a British attack and that he had only unauthorized private receipts to show for it.

Despite the logistical obstacles and the mixed results of early naval actions, the Americans gained control of Lake Erie when Perry's flotilla won a decisive battle on 10 September 1813. That control was to last through the balance of the war.

Opposing Forces in the Gulf of Mexico

On the southern coast along the Gulf of Mexico, opposing forces maintained a careful watch on one another. New Orleans was the major base for operations of the U.S. Navy in the Gulf. However, most of the material needed to build and outfit, repair and refit warships, including cannon shot, gunpowder, cordage, canvas, and ballast, was unavailable at New Orleans. Supplies were obtained from northern industrial centers, and exorbitant transportation expenses significantly inflated prices. Costs escalated dramatically in 1813, when a new shipyard was constructed and a severe hurricane required costly repairs to the station.

In February 1813 Secretary Jones warned John K. Smith, the navy agent at New Orleans, to curb spending. A month later, Jones ordered Captain John Shaw, commanding officer of the New Orleans Station, to reduce the number of gunboats and men under his command. The high costs incurred at New Orleans remained an issue throughout the remainder of the war, although the secretary made it quite clear that he did not hold Navy Agent Smith responsible. The extreme heat and humidity took a constant toll on the wooden ships, as well as on the men assigned to them.

The smaller vessels at New Orleans had no pursers assigned. Their needs were supplied by Purser Thomas Shields, who was based ashore and requisitioned supplies through the navy agent when necessary. Cruising ships, such as brigs or sloops, normally had their own pursers embarked.

Captain Shaw redesignated *Louisiana* as a cruising vessel rather than a stationary block ship. In December 1812, he proposed appointing the brother-in-law of a fellow naval officer as purser. Faced with losing significant commissions, Purser Shields protested to Brigadier General James Wilkinson, who immediately opposed Shaw's move. This dispute became the subject of voluminous correspondence between Shaw and Shields and soon brought Secretary Hamilton into the dispute. Available records do not indicate any action on the part of Hamilton, who would soon leave office. However, new Secretary Jones sided with Shields and ordered Shaw to dismiss *Louisiana*'s purser.

In June 1813 Shields, who remained Shaw's strong critic, refused to advance monies to men at the New Orleans Station even when Shaw ordered him to do so. Shields cited Navy Department regulations that forbade him from making the requested advances. For nearly a week, the two exchanged long, verbose, and sarcastic letters daily. The two disputants finally turned to the secretary for arbitration. Again, Jones backed the purser and instructed Accountant of the Navy Thomas Turner, "I wish to correct the errors of Captain Shaw who appears to fancy himself as supreme and to forget that there is any other authority."

Congress voted in February 1813 to annex West Florida, portions of which had been in dispute with neutral Spain, which claimed all of Florida. General Wilkinson was ordered in March to seize the disputed port of Mobile from the Spanish. When Wilkinson's troops went ashore from

New Orleans-based Navy ships on 10 April, Shaw's six gunboats blockaded the entrance to Mobile Bay. The siege was brief and bloodless, resulting in capitulation by the Spanish on 13 April. By mid-year U.S. Navy forces in the Gulf had dwindled to six gunboats and one ship to patrol and defend more than 300 miles of Gulf coast line. Secretary Jones declined to provide additional resources, reflecting the low priority the Navy assigned to New Orleans. Shaw was relieved in October by Master Commandant Daniel T. Patterson, who reached many of the same conclusions Shaw had about conditions at New Orleans. In 1814 Patterson advised Jones that he would meet with the purser of each station and send to the secretary a list of supplies and the quantities of each required.

Pacific Ventures

Captain David Porter had attempted in late 1812 to comply with Commodore William Bainbridge's orders to become part of a commerce-raiding cruise in the South Atlantic. Bainbridge failed to make a planned rendezvous with Porter on three occasions when he was delayed each time by actions against the British farther north. Exercising the discretionary portion of his sailing orders, Porter decided to realize his long-held desire to sail into the Pacific to claim new lands for the United States and to chart previously uncharted coasts. He set sail for the Pacific on 26 January 1813 in *Essex,* thus opening a new theater of operations for the U.S. Navy. There was no British opposition along the west coast of South America, where several provinces were rebelling against their Spanish rulers. Great Britain paid little attention to that area of the world until the presence of Porter's *Essex* was considered a threat to British whalers operating in the area.

The Navy's normal supply lines did not extend into the Pacific, requiring Porter's Pacific excursion to draw support solely from civilian sources in ports along the way. When *Essex* arrived at Valparaiso, Chile, she was welcomed by the rebels. Porter spent eight days in replenishing his food, water, and wood. During the next 10 months, he completed an impressive cruise in which he captured 11 British commercial vessels and a belligerent Peruvian privateer and freed a captured American whaling ship.

Gloomy War Prospects

At the start of 1814, prospects for an American victory over Great Britain were extremely gloomy. The British controlled the Atlantic Coast through a blockade that extended from New Orleans all the way to the Canadian border. The U.S. Treasury was practically empty, and the threat of secession by New England remained. When Napoleon abdicated on 13 April and brought an end to France's war with England, the British were free to send veteran troops to relieve hard-pressed Canada and take the land war to America on its home ground.

Before the British reinforcements arrived in Canada, American Generals Jacob Brown and Winfield Scott scored tactical victories in upstate New York, and Captain Thomas Macdonough's flotilla of 13 small ships achieved a stirring victory over a British flotilla on Lake Champlain, but the Royal Navy still controlled the entire Atlantic Coast. In early August, a large detachment of Wellington's regulars reinforced the British squadron in the Chesapeake. A force of more than 4,000 British troops occupied Washington and burned government buildings, but they left homes and stores unharmed.

With the U.S. Navy effectively bottled up, official facilities of the capital city in ruins, British regulars pouring into America, and American militiamen running away, the young country's future was in doubt. The British were stymied at Baltimore and withdrew after deciding that success would not be worth the cost.

A 10,000-man British expeditionary force moved on to assault New Orleans. There, waiting for them, was General Andrew Jackson. When the British attacked on 2 January 1815, Jackson's irregulars turned back three determined charges by the veteran British regulars, who lost 2,000 men. American casualties were 13. Although the combatants did not know it, the war was already over. A peace treaty had been signed at Ghent, Belgium, on Christmas Eve, 10 days earlier.

The United States was able to leverage startling victories on both land and the lakes into an acceptable treaty. The Treaty of Ghent did not give the United States anything for which the nation went to war, but it did end the fighting. It also did not require the United States to give up any of the sovereignty it had won at great cost in the Revolution.

The United States returned to peace with a strong national pride intact, and Americans were happy to be finally free of European entanglements. The performance of American officers and seamen had been a revelation to the British, who developed a healthy respect for their Yankee adversaries. During the war, commissioned pursers performed professionally, earning acceptance of their fellow officers.

Service to the Fleet Begins

Although few in number, pre-1815 pursers, with some exceptions, were a talented lot. On the average, they were about five years older than the typical new lieutenant and two years younger than the newly appointed master commandant or sailing master. The Navy's pursers, expected to be capable of assuming and discharging considerable responsibility, and handling and accounting for large sums of money, were also usually better educated than their line peers.

There is little in the records to determine the basis on which secretaries of the Navy chose the 123 pursers who served from 1794 through 1814. In *A Gentlemanly and Honorable Profession,* Christopher McKee points out that information on the backgrounds of those chosen is equally sparse. Where prior experience of pursers is recorded, eight had been merchant captains or supercargoes before being appointed; seven had been clerks in stores, merchant countinghouses, or banks; six had been in business; and five had been attorneys. Some candidates for appointment as pursers benefited from having relatives serving as Navy officers who influenced appointments for their kin.

During the War of 1812, pursers assumed many of the functions previously performed by agents, bringing the same degree of professionalism to shore activities that they had demonstrated afloat. With this demonstrated competence, along with reforms in contracting and financial accountability instituted by Congress and Secretary Jones, Navy supply made great strides during the war. The foundation had been laid for the eventual formation of an organization dedicated to "Service to the Fleet."

Having survived war against the greatest economic, political, and military power on earth and come out of the experience intact, the United States had become a recognized world power.

Sources

Sources for material used in this chapter and not cited earlier include:

Dudley, William S., ed. *The Naval War of 1812: A Documentary History.* Vols. 1 and 2. Washington, D.C.: Naval Historical Center, Department of the Navy, 1985, 1992.

Leiner, Frederick C. "The Norfolk War Scare." *Naval History,* Summer 1993. (On President Jefferson's plan to substitute gunboats manned by civilian sailors for a professional Navy.)

McKee, Christopher. *A Gentlemanly and Honorable Profession: The Creation of the U.S. Naval Officer Corps, 1794–1815.* Annapolis: Naval Institute Press, 1991.

Miller, Nathan. *The U.S. Navy: An Illustrated History.* Annapolis: Naval Institute Press, and New York: American Heritage Publishing, 1977.

Miscellaneous Letters Received by the Secretary of the Navy, 1801–85. The original letters are on file at the National Archives in Washington, and microfilm copies are on file at the Naval Historical Center.

Navy Supply Corps Newsletter, February 1970, September 1973.

Paullin, Charles O. *Paullin's History of Naval Administration, 1775–1911.* Annapolis: Naval Institute, 1968.

Wellborn, Fred W. *The Growth of American Nationality, 1492-1865.* New York: Macmillan, 1951.

CHAPTER TWO

Protecting and Expanding Trade and Commerce

1815–60

When the War of 1812 ended, the U.S. Navy had a major piece of unfinished business—dealing with the Barbary corsairs who had continued to harass American ships since 1807. Congress declared war on the pirates on 3 March 1815. The most powerful fleet ever assembled by the United States, with two squadrons commanded by Commodores Stephen Decatur and William Bainbridge, prepared for action.

On 20 May Decatur sailed with his squadron of eight warships for the Mediterranean. Bainbridge's nine-ship squadron arrived on the scene in midsummer. The two squadrons cruised independently but impressed the leaders of Algiers, Tunis, and Tripoli with their power. The pirate nations quickly agreed to sign on terms favorable to the United States. The treaties included most-favored-nation status, the end of payment of tribute, and freedom for all American prisoners without payment of ransom.

Deployment of 17 U.S. Navy ships across the Atlantic at one time extended the Navy's supply lines far beyond any previous logistical effort. Decatur, who believed that the Barbary states would violate the treaties when the American ships departed, convinced Secretary of State James Monroe to maintain a U.S. Navy force in the Mediterranean. When the two squadrons met at Gibraltar in mid-October 1815 for the return home, two frigates and several smaller ships were left behind to protect American commerce from a resumption of pirate attacks.

A New Era of Reform

The United States had achieved naval success in the War of 1812 despite the inefficiencies of the Navy Department, which was run by well-meaning but relatively inexperienced civilian secretaries. The wartime secretaries Paul Hamilton and William Jones had no background in naval strategy and tactics and spent most of their time in the job on manning and supplying the Fleet and protecting their political flanks. Their staffs had little or no professional expertise. The Navy's senior leaders knew how to work within the system that existed during the war, but the situation also led to intense rivalries as the leaders maneuvered to gain position. In 1814 a new era of reform and expansion of the U.S. Navy began with the appointment of Benjamin W. Crowninshield, a Salem, Massachusetts, businessman with significant experience at sea, as secretary of the Navy. While still in office, Jones had proposed a detailed plan for further reorganization of the Navy Department. Congress endorsed this plan, with modifications suggested by senior naval officers and Crowninshield. In February 1815, Congress created a Board of Navy Commissioners and named three experienced captains as members. The board, under the superintendence of the secretary of the Navy, was responsible for all logistical functions, including procuring naval stores, and supplies and for constructing, arming, equipping, and deploying warships.

The reorganization reflected the widely held opinion that, under both Hamilton and Jones, the Navy Department was grossly inefficient. If that were true, the historian J. C. A. Stagg asks, how was it that "a department so poorly run could perform so creditably in the War?" Perhaps, as Stagg suggests, it was because the Navy Department was unable to control the Navy's officers closely, giving fleet and shore commanders a great deal of latitude in determining their operations, which led to outstanding individual accomplishments.

As a result of strong criticism, the Office of the Accountant of the Navy was abolished in 1817 and its functions were reacquired by the Treasury Department. In 1822, however, Congress reconsidered that action and reestablished the office.

The Navy and Western Hemisphere Pirates

On 3 March 1819 Congress authorized President Monroe to commence action against pirates operating in the Atlantic and the Gulf of Mexico. Historians estimate that between 1815 and 1822 as many as 3,000 ships were attacked by pirates, with American-flag vessels the primary targets.

The press reported the incidents in lurid detail, and the American public was duly incensed. Monroe tried to solve the problem through diplomacy supported by the Navy's muscle, but when his diplomatic gestures failed, he assigned a more active role to the Navy. Although isolated pirate attacks on American-flag ships continued, the Navy reported in mid-1826 that frequent attacks on American commerce had been halted.

Pursers of the Yard

Secretary Crowninshield sent a circular to all agents on 27 November 1817, advising them that all accounts must be settled within one year and that the secretary of the treasury would establish quarterly reporting dates. In 1818, pursers were appointed to serve ashore at navy yards, taking over many of the functions previously performed by agents. However, pursers did not replace agents at other stateside locations or at foreign ports. For the first time, Navy regulations listed the duties and privileges of pursers, who had become commissioned officers in 1812 and were primarily assigned afloat.

Agents still provided valuable services at other shore stations, and the secretary remained mired in the morass of supply details. Navy yard commanders were ordered in 1821 to establish a regular and permanent mode of paying all the officers attached to navy yards in the United States. The commanders were told to direct the purser of the yard to pay salaries, subsistence, and allowances to all officers, including the commander.

Congress finally passed the stalled appropriations bill in May 1822. The settlement procedure was changed when the secretary reported that decreased appropriations required new accounting procedures, including monthly reports to him by navy agents. The secretary advised agents who lacked money because of the delayed appropriations that their requisitions for cash would be honored partially at once. He told them that the balance of money they requisitioned would be forthcoming when the agents used a new form, a sample of which he provided.

In April 1823 the secretary published a general order, chastising pursers who were paying navy yard employees in old currency that was not worth its face value despite the fact that the Navy was providing pursers with new currency, which was negotiable at par value. He ordered navy yard commanders to assure that the practice ended and that pursers who disregarded the order be reported.

Although the responsibilities of pursers of the yard and navy agents were distinctly different, there was some overlap. When the office of the agent in New York became vacant in March 1823, the secretary decided to assign the agent's duties to New York Navy Yard Purser Edward N. Coxe until the ensuing winter. But first, the secretary made certain that, inasmuch as the agent's business did not fall within the duties of a purser, Coxe would agree to assume the additional duties.

The secretary's office continued to be the focal point for the details of Navy supply and financial matters. In 1827 the secretary wrote to Richard Harris, agent at Boston, emphasizing the necessity of uniformity in requisitions made on the Navy Department. He also told Harris that each requisition form should be accompanied by a letter indicating the purpose for each item charged to each account.

Rules of the Civil Establishment of the Navy

In 1832 the Navy Department published a 70-page book, *Rules of the Navy Department Regarding the Civil Establishment of the Navy of the United States,* which gathered in one document the rules issued between 1808 and 1832 and then still in effect. A sampling of rules provides insight into the regulations governing such subjects as property accounts, advances, allowances, and uniform specifications for pursers:

> Chapter 2
> All commanders of vessels previous to leaving any port where supplies have been obtained, for which the accounts have not been regularly signed or certified, are required to fix upon a particular day with the agent, consul or other officer, for the express purpose of examining and signing such accounts.
> —*Regulation, 26 July 1808, Amended September 1831*
>
> All disbursing officers within every period of three months, if within the United States, and within each period of six months, if in foreign port, must settle their accounts.
> —*Act of Congress and Regulations, January 1823*
>
> When any officer is found indebted to the United States, his pay is to be stopped (but not his rations) until his accounts be balanced.
> —*Opinion of the Attorney General, 1830*
>
> The property accounts kept by the Navy Board with the different yards, vessels, stations, and officers must be kept in such manner as to show, not only the amount of all articles at the respective yards, etc., but also the balance of each description of articles due from each yard vessel, station and offices, together with the individual who is liable to the United States for each balance.
> —*Regulation, March 1832*

Chapter 3
The usual advance made by direction of the President to officers joining a vessel is two months pay on short voyages, and from three to four months pay on long voyages.
—Regulation, August 7, 1810

Advances cannot be made to Naval Officers except when ordered on foreign service—and in such cases the authority of the Secretary of the Navy is required under the direction of the President.
—Act of Congress, January 31, 1823

Chapter 5
The Navy Department has no authority to purchase arms, or to maintain Africans after delivery to the agent, beyond the limits of the United States, under the act of March 3, 1819.
—Opinion of the Attorney General, September 21, 1829

Chapter 6
The expenses of the protection of live oak timber are to be paid from the fund for the gradual improvement of the Navy, excepting the pay of the officers and seamen on board the vessels of the United States. The salaries of agents are to commence when they have received their appointments, and commenced their duties by leaving home to execute them.
—Regulation, May 1831

Chapter 7
Navy agents are required to deposit all public money in banks. they are not to draw checks for the same, excepting for services rendered, or supplies furnished the Navy.
—Regulation, May 1831

Chapter 8
The estimates for the wants of the squadron and navy yard at Pensacola, are to be made three months in advance by the Commander of the yard and squadron. A remittance of one third of the estimate is allowed in monthly requisitions vouched for by the pursers.
Allotments cannot exceed one half the pay and must be restricted to families or relations of the parties making them. Commanding Officers must ascertain these facts, and not sign allotment tickets for other purposes.
—Regulation, May 1831

Chapter 10
In lieu of cabin furniture, officers were allowed monthly:
Commodore of a squadron, $30
Captain of line of battle ship, $25

Captain of frigate, $20
Master commandant, in command of sloop of war, $15
Lieutenant, commanding, $10

Chapter 14
No transfer of appropriations can be made, except under the special direction of the President; and his power is confined to transfer to and from appropriations for provisions, for medicine and hospital stores, for repair of vessels, and for clothing.
—Act of Congress, March 1832

Chapter 53
The practice of paying the senior lieutenant at a station or navy yard, as a lieutenant commanding is ordered to cease. No such lieutenant will be allowed more pay than any other lieutenant.
—Regulation, May 12, 1820

Chapter 54
Officers aboard are to paid monthly, but not the men. The latter are allowed to be paid about one-third of their pay to buy slops, etc.
—Regulation, May 12, 1820

Chapter 61
Pursers must transmit to the Navy Commissioners a certified invoice of all articles provided for them for vessels bound on a cruise; including all articles procured to be sold for their own benefit.
—Regulation, October 20, 1830

Navy Agent Commissions and Ranks

The rules allowed navy agents a commission of 1 percent on all disbursements in the United States, not to exceed $2,000 per annum. No commission was allowed on the transfer of funds. The rules permitted the agents in London and at Gibraltar a commission of 2½ percent, but the agent at Gibraltar was subject to an annual limitation of $5,000.

The Navy Department recognized in 1832 that the commission of 2½ percent on payments by pursers was inadequate. The new rules allowed pursers an allowance of 5 percent on sales of clothing, 25 percent on articles of secondary necessity, and 50 percent on luxuries, regardless of whether sold to officers or crew.

Navy regulations also established the allowances to be paid at navy yards. Regulations required that officers attached to yards live at or near the yards, but where there were no quarters for them, they were allowed $2 a week. The rules further spelled out the allowances to be paid to clerks at the yards. Clerks to storekeepers at Boston, New York, and Norfolk were paid $500 a year, the clerk to the storekeeper at Washington received $450, but the clerks performing similar duties at Portsmouth, Philadelphia, and Pensacola received only $300.

The Navy also specified maximum amounts to be paid for furniture for Navy offices and quarters, for fire wood, for candles, for sugar cane, seeds and plants, and for pay and emoluments of school masters and mathematicians at navy yards and stations. The rules established allowances for travel and transportation of baggage overland at 15 cents a mile for captains, master commandants, and judge advocates and 12 cents for all others. When travel was by water, the amounts were 10 cents and 8 cents. Pursers had lobbied long and hard for officer rank commensurate with their responsibilities within the naval establishment. The matter was resolved in 1833 when Navy regulations first placed them below lieutenant (junior grade). A group of line captains took up the pursers' cause, and the Navy's supply officers were subsequently ranked with lieutenants. Pursers remained in that status until 1857, when those with more than 12 years of service were ranked with commanders, and those with less service remained ranked with lieutenants.

Before the Civil War, navy agents received four-year commissions from the president with the advice and consent of the Senate. They were paid a stated percentage of public monies disbursed. Throughout the first half of the nineteenth century, critics charged favoritism and political cronyism in appointment of navy agents. The critics also questioned the agents' methods of choosing and remunerating civilian contractors.

In 1841 Samuel Lowden, a New York blockmaker, complained to Commander Paulding at the New York Navy Yard that lower-quality supplies were being sold to the Navy at higher prices for the benefit of contractors' friends. A circular from the comptroller, dated 22 March 1842, called navy agents' attention to provisions of the 1809 legislation that required that all purchases and contracts for supplies or services must be made either by open purchase or by advertising for proposals.

The Navy Expands

In the years following the War of 1812 the United States extended its operations throughout the world to cast a protective net over American maritime interests. The U.S. Navy formed an African Squadron in 1820 to suppress the slave trade and aid in the settlement of Liberia by freed slaves from the United States. When American merchantmen ventured farther and more frequently into the Pacific, they required protection.

This led to formation of a Pacific Squadron in 1821, further expanding logistical requirements.

When Seminole Indians massacred a detachment of soldiers near Tampa in December 1835, the Army asked for assistance. The Navy sent a "mosquito fleet" of two schooners and a flotilla of flat-bottomed barges and canoes, manned by sailors and marines, to bolster Army forces pursuing the Indians into the Everglades. Supplying this assorted collection of fighting men was extremely difficult in nearly impenetrable swamps. Temperatures sometimes reached 120 degrees; food and water were always in short supply; and men were beset by disease, poisonous snakes, and alligators. It took six years for American military might to force the Seminoles out of Florida and to a reservation west of the Mississippi River.

Aside from these occasional assignments, the intervening years for the Navy were largely a period of tranquil cruising and sightseeing among the historic sites of Europe. In the leading ports of Europe, the officers and men of the established navies watched the upstart Yankee Navy closely. Spit and polish took on a new meaning as the American ships displayed impressive shining brasswork, immaculate holystoned decks, and spotless canvas. The local aristocracy, particularly along the Mediterranean, entertained the visiting American officers enthusiastically and lavishly.

Technological Progress and the Bureau System

During this period, the Navy lagged behind other maritime nations in technological progress. Senior uniformed and civilian Navy leaders were slow to recognize the advantage of steam propulsion, which other navies favored. Although Robert Fulton had developed the system, the U.S. Navy did not commission its first steamship, the *Demologos*—later renamed *Fulton*—until 1814. She was relegated to station ship status one year later and steam, for all its promise, had become a dead issue in Washington.

In 1835 Secretary of the Navy Mahlon Dickerson ordered a second *Fulton* to replace the first, which had been destroyed by explosion in 1829. The new *Fulton,* a twin-hulled side-wheeler, was designed as a harbor defense ship and not intended to be a seagoing vessel, but Captain Matthew Calbraith Perry sailed her from New York to Washington. In the nation's capital, President Martin Van Buren and congressional leaders were impressed by *Fulton*'s capabilities as well as Perry's dedication to development of a steam navy. However, neither Van Buren nor the cost-conscious Congress took action to advance conversion to the new method of propulsion.

With no one in a leadership position to make the case for steam to Congress, the cost of building and outfitting an entirely new type of ship was a deterrent. Also, the effort and cost to establish a wholly new supply system to source, store, and issue fuel—wood or coal—was a limiting factor. In 1837, the U.S. Navy had no steamships in active service, but the French had 23, and the Royal Navy had 21; even Sweden and Egypt had steamships in their navies.

Congress eventually developed interest in steam's potential and in 1839 authorized construction of two steam-propelled side-wheel frigates, *Missouri* and *Mississippi*. When completed in 1842, they were considered the equal of any European steamer. Meanwhile, Captain Robert F. Stockton enticed a Swedish engineer, John Ericcson, to come to America and demonstrate his screw propeller invention to the Navy.

The shift to steam was accelerated by threat of yet another war with Great Britain, this time over a border dispute between the state of Maine and the Canadian province of New Brunswick. An American Home Squadron was created in 1841 to patrol the Atlantic Ocean off the disputed territory, and the two new steam frigates joined the squadron.

Another border dispute soon broke out with Great Britain—this one concerning the Oregon territory. Meanwhile, mounting pressure over annexation of Texas threatened war with Mexico. These pressures, in areas far removed from the East Coast, clearly indicated the need for a larger, faster, more mobile, and more powerful Navy. This need obviously would require more sophisticated logistical support.

Continuing reform in several other areas was as important to the Navy as the conversion to steam. Foremost among the reforms was the need for higher-quality personnel to operate steamships and the need for an improved system of acquiring and training personnel. An important part of the reform movement was the recognition that decision by committee, as practiced by the Board of Navy Commissioners, was inefficient at best. It was even more difficult for the board to assign responsibility for carrying out its decisions.

Congress attempted to resolve these problems in 1842 by abolishing the Navy Board and dividing the administrative functions of the Navy into five technical bureaus. The bureau system took coordination and operational control out of the hands of inexperienced politicians and placed them in the hands of five experienced officers. The five bureaus, whose chiefs provided professional direction, were:

- Bureau of Navy Yards and Docks

- Bureau of Construction, Equipment and Repairs
- Bureau of Provisions and Clothing
- Bureau of Ordnance and Hydrography
- Bureau of Medicine and Surgery

The Bureau of Provisions and Clothing

In addition to rectifying a problem with the coordination and control of the Navy, the bureau system gave pursers an organizational structure in the Bureau of Provisions and Clothing that institutionalized their functions afloat, ashore, and at headquarters. The legislation charged the Bureau of Provisions and Clothing with handling "all provisions of every sort, whether solid or liquid; all clothing of every sort; all labor employed thereon; all contracts and accounts relating thereto." After 47 years, the supply organization of the Navy had become a separate, recognized entity.

The bureau system also boosted pursers' status within the Navy by giving them group identity for the first time. Their status advanced another important step in 1842, when they were placed on a standard pay scale. Complaints of purser profiteering and exploitation diminished noticeably when they were required to purchase all supplies with public funds. This brought to an end the often-criticized system of private purchases by pursers of necessaries and luxuries that were resold to the crew on a commission basis.

The enabling legislation required that the chief of the Bureau of Provisions and Clothing be a civilian, and Charles W. Goldsborough, the long-time former chief clerk of the Navy, was appointed to the position in 1842. Goldsborough was a veteran bureaucrat well versed in Washington politics and not a uniformed naval officer. He provided the Bureau with much-needed continuity in the implementation of the new system.

LORE OF THE CORPS

George Washington Goldsborough

Chief Clerk of the Navy, 1802–13; Chief, Bureau of Provisions and Clothing, 1842–43

Records of the Navy Department reveal two noteworthy distinctions attributed to Charles W. Goldsborough. He was the first chief clerk of the Navy and the first chief of the Bureau of Provisions and Clothing.

Goldsborough was born in 1777 at Cambridge, Maryland. At the age of 21 he became confidential secretary to Secretary of the Navy Benjamin Stoddert 1798. In 1802 Goldsborough succeeded Abishai Thomas, who had the title of principal clerk. He quickly demonstrated an astonishing capacity for paperwork. According to Christopher McKee:

> He was able to write easily, and with considerable rhetorical elegance, for hours on end—seemingly with little need to revise what he had written. The number of official papers in his beautifully clear handwriting on any given day would have exhausted an average clerk. On top of this, Goldsborough was able to maintain an extensive correspondence with individual officers of the Navy in which much of the real business of the Navy Office was transacted without it ever appearing on the official record.

During his 11 years as chief clerk, Goldsborough served two brief stints as acting secretary of the Navy, but by 1813, his reputation had diminished, and he had become a controversial figure. A new secretary of the Navy, William Jones, offered Goldsborough the option of resigning or being fired. The chief clerk selected the former option, but returned to the Navy Department in 1815 for staff duties with the Board of Navy Commissioners.

By working hard and avoiding the controversies which marked his final years as chief clerk, Goldsborough survived in Washington. Faced with growing criticism of the Board of Navy Commissioners, Congress enacted the Navy Reorganization Act of 1842 established five bureaus, including the Bureau of Provisions and Clothing. The act specified that the chief of the Bureau be a civilian, and Goldsborough was selected as its first chief.

When he assumed the office in 1842, Charles Goldsborough faced many complicated problems. The act charged the Bureau with a multitude of tasks, relative to the supply and fiscal support of the Fleet. Among the major responsibilities was to "administer all clothing and provisions and labor, contracts and accounts related thereto." Without a working model for guidance, he had to supervise the creation of the whole machinery of a supply system. He tackled the job with the same dedication he had shown earlier as the chief clerk.

Goldsborough did not approve of the issue of rum to sailors, and convinced the secretary of the Navy to restrict severely its issue to men in the Fleet. He also enforced a rigid and effective system for keeping and disposing of public property in Navy yards. He also issued "Invitations to Bid" similar to those currently in use, including sealed and endorsed bids.

Charles Goldsborough served as chief of the Bureau until his death in 1844. His son, Louis, became an admiral in the U.S. Navy.

Sources

McKee, Christopher. *A Gentlemanly and Honorable Profession: The Creation of the U.S. Naval Officer Corps, 1794–1815.* Annapolis: Naval Institute Press, 1991.

Official Biography. Naval Supply Systems Command, n.d.

Reactions to the Bureau System

The new system gave the bureaus broad responsibilities for handling matters in their areas of technical competence. Navy agents, however, were still on station and reported directly to the secretary of the Navy, giving rise to a new flood of letters. The agents were unhappy with the new bureau arrangement.

M. Jordan, the commandant of the Gosport Navy Yard, wrote to the secretary in early February 1843 to acquaint him with the problems the bureau system caused at his station. Jordan reported that Gosport had divided the returns for public stores on hand and complained about the extra correspondence the new arrangement caused him. Later, Jordan noted, "I keep my first and second clerks constantly employed in preparing those returns. The mere copying of the return is a trifle."

R. O. Witman, navy agent at New York, complained that the commanding officer of a ship wanted to deviate from the established order for procuring furniture, but he needed additional authority to eliminate the possibility of the auditing officer denying payment.

B. D. Hewitt, navy agent at Charleston, agreed to assume the duties of purser but required an additional clerk at an annual salary of $700 or $800. A civilian tailor refused to give the New York agent a statement of the kinds and quantities of material received, so Goldsborough concluded the issue by making a different bookkeeping entry. William Scott, navy agent at Washington, complained that his business had increased threefold over the preceding three years. Therefore, he justified the contested expense for keeping a horse as necessary by virtue of the many services he had to perform over great distances. Scott went on to request an increase in annual salary from $1,800 to $2,500, pointing out that the agents at New York and Boston received $3,000. The agent also requested that the purser of *USS Macedonian* be allowed to pay him any amount the secretary might determine to be proper to rent a suitable office for the purser's increased workload.

In March 1845 William Scott, agent at Washington, responded to accusations by G. V. Smith that he had been guilty of misconduct. Scott told the secretary that his conduct had already been investigated and that no wrongdoing had been found. He pointed out that he handled large amounts of money and the job carried considerable patronage that subjected him to attacks by bidders who failed to win contracts.

Joseph White, agent at Baltimore, requested another clerk, at a salary of $500 a year, because the duties of his office had increased to such an extent that one clerk could not handle them properly; William Brennan, naval storekeeper at Memphis, also requested permission to hire a clerk.

Financial matters continued to plague the Navy. The agent at New York complained to the secretary in August 1844 that his requisitions drawn on the Bureau of Provisions and Clothing and the Bureau of Construction on 20 July had not been filled. Until they were, he warned that his station would be literally without funds to meet the smallest demands presented to him. When the Army Engineers built a dry dock at the New York Navy Yard, they presented a bill for $40,000, and the agent asked the secretary for instructions regarding payment for materials. Purser Philo White of the frigate *Potomac* at Pensacola advised the secretary that he required $8,000 for pay, provisions, and medicine.

Although only the post of chief of the Bureau of Provisions and Clothing was designated to be filled by a civilian, many senior Navy officers coveted it. One of these was Commodore William B. Shubrick, a distinguished line officer for 38 years. In a purely political move, Admiral Shubrick resigned his commission and announced his candidacy.

LORE OF THE CORPS

William Branford Shubrick

Commodore, USN, 1807–44, 1846–62; Chief, Bureau of Provisions and Clothing, 1844–46
Period of Service: 1807–62

Having resigned his commission as a commodore, William Shubrick was appointed the second civilian chief of the Bureau of Provisions and Clothing in 1844. When he completed two years in office, his commission was reinstated and he returned to active duty.

Born on Bull's Island, South Carolina, in 1790, William Shubrick was one of 16 children. He attended schools in nearby Charleston and in Dedham, Massachusetts, spent a year at Harvard, and entered the Navy as a midshipman at the age of 16.

During his first assignment in 1807, he formed a strong and lasting friendship with one of his mates, James Fenimore Cooper, who dedicated two of his books, *The Pilot* and *The Red Rover,* to Shubrick. Over the next 30 years, Shubrick served successfully in a variety of assignments at sea and in ordnance duty. In 1839 he was promoted to commodore in command of a West India Squadron, and in 1840 he took command of the Norfolk Navy Yard.

As a civilian chief, Shubrick gave primary attention to clothing, food, and procurement in general. He reported to the secretary of the Navy that the Navy's clothing supply was "abundant and the quality is excellent." However, he recommended to the secretary that the 1844 Act be modified to replace commissioned or warrant officers in charge of naval stores for foreign squadrons with competent and experienced civil servants. Shubrick complained that few officers desired the duty, and, "It does not appear proper to require of an officer to enter into bond to perform duties under orders. I have no doubt that money could be saved by allowing the appointment of civilians."

After he completed two years in the Bureau at the start of the Mexican War, Shubrick applied to return to active duty and to go to sea. His commission was reinstated, and he sailed in *USS Independence* to the California coast to relieve Commodore John Drake Sloat in command of Navy forces there. Under Shubrick, the Navy successfully closed the Mexican War on the Pacific Coast, thus securing California for the United States.

In August 1852, Commodore Shubrick became chairman of the Lighthouse Board, a position he held for 19 years although on occasions his services were needed elsewhere. At one point the Navy sent him to Halifax, Nova Scotia, where he successfully negotiated temporary arrangements with the Royal Navy for a fisheries treaty. And in 1858, President Buchanan placed Shubrick in command of a 19-ship, 2,500-man expedition to settle commercial and other disputes with Paraguay. He and the American commissioner in Asuncion secured a treaty, settling all points of dispute satisfactorily for the United States.

As the Civil War approached, Shubrick was in the same painful position as many other native Southerners in federal service. Although as a Navy flag officer Shubrick was of importance to Confederate leaders, he remained at his post in Washington. After the Union defeat at the first Battle of Bull Run, he offered to return to active service. But his situation had been overtaken by events. In December 1861 Congress passed as law creating a retired list for Navy officers, but the Navy exercised its option of continuing his service as chairman of the Lighthouse Board. In July 1862 he was promoted to rear admiral and placed on the retired list. Shubrick died in Washington in May 1874 at the age of 83.

The Navy named four ships in Shubrick's honor. The first was a lighthouse steamer transferred from the Lighthouse Board to the Revenue Center Service in 1861. The second *USS Shubrick* was a torpedo boat laid down in 1899 and commissioned in 1901. In August 1918 she was renamed *Coast Torpedo Boat No. 15* to allow her name to be given to a new destroyer.

The third *USS Shubrick* (DD-268) was laid down in June 1918, commissioned in July 1919, decommissioned in June 1922, and recommissioned in December 1939. In November 1940 she was struck from the U.S. Navy list and recommissioned *HMS Ripley* in the Royal Navy. She was scrapped in March 1945. The fourth *USS Shubrick* (DD-639) was laid down in February 1942 and commissioned in February 1943. While *Shubrick* was on picket duty off Okinawa in May 1945 a Japanese plane crashed into her and its bomb blew a 30-foot hole in her side. Back in Bremerton, with the end of World War II, the Navy decided not to invest in repairs. She was decommissioned in November and sold for scrap in September 1947.

Sources

Cooper, Susan Fenimore. *Rear Admiral William Branford Shubrick: A Sketch*. Reprinted from *Harper's Magazine*, 1876.

Dictionary of American Naval Fighting Ships. Vol. 6. Washington, D.C.: Naval Historical Center, Department of the Navy, 1951.

Official Biography. Naval Supply Systems Command, n.d.

Agents and Storekeepers at Foreign Stations

Procuring supplies required by U.S. Navy ships arriving at foreign ports created special problems. The agent at Rio de Janeiro reported in February 1843 that when the local ship chandlery could not fill orders from its stock, a clerk would accompany a ship's officer to buy the items elsewhere. The officers rarely spoke Spanish, and the agent was concerned the prices included on bills presented to him by the chandler might be inflated.

In November 1843 the agent at Lima, Peru, noted that three U.S. Navy ships operating in the Pacific were due at that port in January 1844 and that no American storeship had called recently. In anticipation of the flotilla's needs, the agent advised the secretary that he had deposited 2,700 barrels of bread at Valparaiso, Chile. As the frequency of U.S. Navy cruises into the Western Pacific increased, agents were appointed to serve at stations on the coast of China. In January 1844 Storekeeper Thomas Waldron at Hong Kong acknowledged receipt of his bond.

A Navy Department order on 15 March 1844 required naval storekeepers at foreign stations to purchase all articles requisitioned by U.S. Navy ships calling at their ports. In September, the storekeeper at Honolulu requested that in view of the additional workload created by the order his salary be increased and that he be authorized to hire a clerk.

The following spring, Thomas Alexander, the agent at Port Prayo in the Cape Verde Islands, wrote new Navy Secretary George Bancroft to note the serious disadvantage of the location as a depot for the squadron and personnel. He reported that the United States had already lost one valuable cargo from exposure to the elements. Alexander recommended that the Navy anchor a storeship in the harbor of one of the other islands. In January 1846 he requested leave from his post for health reasons or, alternatively, that he be relieved.

Cooperage on the island of Macao in Hong Kong Harbor was not only expensive but also tedious according to the navy agent there. As a result, he requested in May 1846 that the Navy put at least two iron hoops on all barrels of beef, pork, whiskey, vinegar, and pickles sent to that island. In June, a Mr. Hormel arrived at Macao to take over as storekeeper. He reported that no U.S. Navy ship had arrived and, therefore, he did not have the money to defray the cost of running the office or to pay his salary or that of his clerk. Hormel wrote again in July to report that because he had not received a reply from the secretary to his June letter he had borrowed $500 on the credit of the Navy Department.

E. McCallum, special agent at Lima, Peru, wrote to Secretary Bancroft on 13 May to report that Commodore John D. Sloat had positioned his Pacific Squadron off Mazatlan on the west coast of Mexico in anticipation of war and that McCallum had received no stores from the United States for some time. McCallum pointed out that if the squadron stayed at the Mexican station much longer, it would need supplies, particularly bread. By early July, the ships were in a seriously deteriorated condition because of a shortage of supplies, and Sloat determined to send them home by way of Lima. Later in the month, Navy Agent White at Baltimore reported that a vessel was ready to take freight to Mazatlan, to California, or to any other port in the Pacific.

The Naval Academy

A series of highly publicized incidents involving midshipmen aroused public interest. Attention was focused on the haphazard and politically influenced appointment of midshipmen, who were given warrants without regard to age, education, or fitness and sent to sea immediately. Their training depended upon the whims and abilities of officers to whom they were assigned. As early as 1777 Captain John Paul Jones had recommended the establishment of a naval academy to train young officers. Between 1800 and 1845 Congress rejected 20 attempts to approve the institution.

Secretary Bancroft was convinced of the need for a naval school and asked a council of senior naval officers to prepare a plan for a more efficient system of instructing young officers. Faced with lack of congressional support, Bancroft bypassed the legislative branch and opened the U.S. Naval Academy on 10 October 1845 with 40 midshipmen in the first class.

The navy agent, designated on 10 September to pay bills for furniture for the new school at Annapolis, informed Secretary Bancroft the following day that he had not received the appropriate requisitions. On 14 November 1845 Joseph White, agent at Baltimore, was ordered to take over the duties of purser at the academy.

The Final Civilian Bureau Head

In 1846 Gideon Welles became the third—and last—civilian chief of the Bureau of Provisions and Clothing when he replaced William Branford Shubrick, who resigned to return to active duty. Records indicate that under Welles the Bureau served the Fleet well.

LORE OF THE CORPS

Gideon Welles

Chief, Bureau of Provisions and Clothing, 1846–49;
Secretary of the Navy, 1861–69

Gideon Welles, a well-connected New England politician, succeeded Shubrick in 1846. Welles continued to be the only civilian chief of a Navy bureau, whereas chiefs of the other four bureaus were military officers. When he was subsequently appointed secretary of the Navy, he became the only chief of the Bureau of Provisions and Clothing to head an executive department of the U.S. government.

Born in Glastonbury, Connecticut, in July 1802, Welles attended the Episcopal Academy at Cheshire and the American Literary, Scientific and Military Academy (later Norwich University) at Norwich, Vermont. He studied law, but turned to journalism and became editor and part owner of the Hartford *Times* in 1826 and continued as editor until he resigned to enter the Connecticut legislature in 1827 as its youngest member. A dedicated Democrat, Welles was a strong supporter of Andrew Jackson. He served in the legislature until 1835 and ran unsuccessfully for Congress in 1834, but was elected state comptroller three times—in 1835, 1842, and 1843. President Jackson appointed him postmaster of Hartford in 1836, a post he held until removed by President Harrison in 1841.

When President James K. Polk's nomination of Welles for the position of chief of the Bureau of Provisions and Clothing came before the Senate, Joseph Smith, chief of the Bureau of Yards and Docks, organized the Navy officer corps to oppose confirmation.

Although nominally a civilian, Welles's predecessor William Shubrick had been a member of the close-knit Navy community and was still called "admiral." The Senate confirmed Welles despite the senior Navy officer opposition, and in later years Smith became one of his closest advisers.

During his three years as the only civilian bureau chief, the other chiefs treated Welles politely, but there was no camaraderie. Senior professional Navy officers were accustomed to dealing with politicians as secretary of the Navy, but resented having to accept Welles as a professional associate. Resentment was intensified by his occupying one of the few senior positions in the Navy at a time when outstanding officers such as John A. Dahlgren and David Dixon Porter remained lieutenants for 20 years. Yet according to the historian John Niven, "There was not an officer in the Fleet who had a modicum of Welles' experiences in business, politics, or general administration. Few could match his industry or ability in areas other than in strictly naval affairs."

Despite resentment and virtual ostracism by many in the Navy and government, Welles's strong Puritan ethic stood him in good stead. He was determined to do a good job and would not let personal slights deter him from taking the corrective actions he felt the Bureau of Provisions and Clothing needed.

The Mexican War started within a year of Welles's taking over the Bureau, and he rose to the challenge of supplying the Fleet with provisions and clothing for semitropical regions. First, he scoured bureau records and noted past problems and then took corrective actions. He wrote specifications for naval stores in clear, understandable English and developed new, more efficient purchasing procedures.

Welles was a businesslike administrator whose services were invaluable during a war. He transformed a small, stodgy office into an efficient operation by instituting reforms where he found them necessary.

He demoted clerks who could not add and subtract. In doing so, he earned grudging admiration from his detractors, gained valuable experience as an administrator, and made many enduring friendships in the process. However the newly elected Whig president Zachary Taylor replaced him in June 1849. After an unsuccessful bid for a Senate seat in 1850, Welles left the Democratic party over the slavery question. He then resumed his journalistic endeavors, serving as one of the chief political writers of the *Hartford Evening Press,* a Republican paper he helped establish. He also wrote an important series of articles for the *New York Evening Post* and *National Intelligencer* in Washington during the tense days before the Civil War.

Welles was an unsuccessful candidate for governor of Connecticut in 1856, but was a member of the National Republican Executive Committee and head of the Connecticut delegation to that party's 1860 convention in Chicago. Upon his election as president, Abraham Lincoln called Welles back to Washington to take over direction of the Navy Department. Welles was secretary of the Navy through both the Lincoln and Johnson administrations (1861–69), longer than any previous incumbent.

Welles reorganized the Navy Department and in effect created a Navy out of a collection of ships where they lay throughout the world. With secession, many native southern officers defected to the Confederacy. By 1863 he recognized that the Civil War would be a long one and that reconciliation would at best require more than a generation. As secretary, he was both widely praised and often criticized. In December 1862, he warned the Naval Committee that only fast, ironclad cruisers could maintain the position of the Union against other naval powers. However, his approval of the building of light-draft monitors was largely believed to be a costly blunder that arose from his failure to supervise an assistant whose previous record gave Welles unwarranted confidence in him.

Despite the number of Welles's critics, President Lincoln, in July 1864 wrote to him, "Your department has been conducted with admirable success." In 1868 he returned to the Democratic party and retired from the Navy Department in 1869. He became a Liberal Republican in 1872. Welles published articles that remain important historical documents, and he continued to be politically active until his death in February 1878.

The U.S. Navy honored Gideon Welles by naming two destroyers for him. The first *USS Welles* (DD-257) was laid down on 13 November 1918—two days after the World War I armistice was signed—and commissioned in September 1919. She was decommissioned in June 1922 and recommissioned in November 1939. She was decommissioned again in September 1940 for the purpose of transfer to the Royal Navy, which renamed her *HMS Cameron*. She was severely damaged during a German air raid on Portsmouth in December 1940 and remained a hulk until broken up for scrap in November 1944.

The second *USS Welles* (DD-628) was laid down in September 1941 and commissioned in August 1943. She earned eight battle stars during World War II and was decommissioned in February 1946. *Welles* remained in the Reserve Fleet until February 1968 and was sold for scrap in July 1969.

Sources

Dictionary of American Naval Fighting Ships. Vol. 8. Washington, D.C.: Naval Historical Center, Department of the Navy, 1951.

Niven, John. *Gideon Welles, Lincoln's Secretary of the Navy*. New York: Oxford University Press, 1973.

Official Biography. Naval Supply Systems Command, n.d.

"Watchful Gideon." *United States Naval Institute Proceedings,* August 1936.

West, Richard S., Jr. *Gideon Welles, Lincoln's Navy Department*. Indianapolis: Bobbs-Merrill, 1943.

War with Mexico

Negotiations with the British over the Oregon border dispute resulted in a treaty satisfactory to both the United States and Great Britain. The Senate ratified it on 18 June 1846. On the other hand, relations with Mexico had deteriorated to the point that an undeclared war was already underway. In the summer of 1845, Navy Secretary John Y. Mason ordered Commodore David Conner to position his Home Squadron off the Mexican coast in the Western Gulf of Mexico and sent reinforcements. Mason also ordered Commodore Sloat, whose squadron was located off California, to seize the territory immediately, if he were certain that war with Mexico had begun.

The fundamental cause of war with America's southern neighbor was the proposed annexation of the independent Texas Republic by the United States. War probably could have been averted had President Polk not been determined to have California as well. The actual declaration of war came on 12 May 1846, and the U.S. Navy was already in position for the forthcoming conflict.

The Mexican War was essentially a land conflict, but the Navy, operating under highly unfavorable conditions, made several major contributions to the war's success. Conner's forces faced a shortage of light craft capable of operating in the shallow waters off the Gulf Coast. The crews of the few vessels that could operate in those waters suffered from malaria and yellow fever in the summer and from violent storms in the winter.

The Navy's young bureaus had difficulty providing the necessities of war, especially ammunition. The Bureau of Provisions and Clothing was the exception to the general unpreparedness of the other bureaus. As chief, Gideon Welles had shaken up the stodgy bureau and instituted many reforms, but Navy Secretary Bancroft failed to provide crucial details of planned enlargement of the Fleet, making Welles's planning efforts especially difficult. Despite their cool relationship, Welles made more than a dozen recommendations to simplify and strengthen procurement procedures, improve naval stores and transportation, and save money. His analyses were comprehensive, his figures were accurate, the estimates based on careful market research and comparisons of contractual performance over long periods. Bancroft eventually began to appreciate Welles's honesty and competence, but their relationship never warmed.

The chief put into place rigid specifications for all purchases by the Bureau of Provisions and Clothing. Butter had been a special and serious problem for the Navy. In going through the records of purchases, Welles had found that 59 percent of one prewar shipment of butter was condemned as useless. He ordered that higher-priced, expertly made Irish butter, which kept well under sea conditions even in tropical climates, be substituted for the lowest-priced butter manufactured domestically. He successfully defended his unauthorized practices to Congress and in the process influenced American suppliers to improve their manufacturing practices.

Welles's exacting specifications for flour, sugar, molasses, and whiskey—all staples aboard Navy ships—established new standards. He ordered that samples of pea jackets, blue flannel shirts and undershirts, red flannel drawers, linen frocks and trousers, woolen stockings, shoes, and blankets be kept at navy yards so inspectors would be familiar with standards acceptable to the Bureau.

When the war started, the nearest Navy supply base was at Pensacola, about 900 miles from Vera Cruz, where Commodore Conner established a blockade. Pensacola was poorly equipped with facilities and supplies. It took 30 days to bake sufficient bread at Pensacola to last Conner's flagship three months. It was difficult to obtain fresh water, and there was no coal at the Florida base for the steamships in Conner's force.

Under Welles's simplified procurement policies, the Bureau turned to civilian contractors at New Orleans. Wartime operations put a tremendous strain on the obsolete American military services. A shortage of tenders and storeships proved especially serious when hostilities were about to commence. To obtain support at Pensacola, the round trip for each vessel of the Home Squadron required a month or more, and they often had to wait for arrival of the needed equipment and supplies. Government supplies of fresh provisions were insufficient, and paymasters of the squadron had to eke out "eatables" from New Orleans huckster boats and European merchant ships. Fortunately, the reforms in purchasing instituted by Welles made things easier for afloat paymasters, but even then a serious outbreak of scurvy in the summer of 1846 disabled some of the largest and most efficient combatant ships for several months.

The Home Squadron subsequently established a blockade at the mouth of the Rio Grande River with a handful of station ships, although the balance of the ships remained at Pensacola until called upon to escort Army transports from New Orleans to Corpus Christi. Even though New Orleans is 150 miles closer to Mexico than Pensacola, logistics continued to be problem for Conner and his blockade strategy. Few storeships were available to transport supplies from either Pensacola or New Orleans to the advance base Conner had established on Anton Lizardo, an island about 12 miles south of Vera Cruz. Conner anchored one storeship at his Mexican base and also used the colliers sent to support his steamers for temporary storage.

Conner complained to Secretary Bancroft, who did little to resolve the logistical problems. The Home Squadron commander believed that the Bureau of Provisions and Clothing had performed well, but criticized the other material bureaus for their lack of support. In turn, Washington criticized Conner for not keeping the Navy Department informed of his needs.

Fortunately, the Mexicans were even less prepared. They could not prevent Conner's force from keeping the sea lanes open, maintaining the blockade, and supporting the advance of Taylor's army across the Rio Grande. Conner's blockade was concentrated on the ports of Vera Cruz, Alvarado, Tampico, and Matamoras. Two Mexican steamers, *Guadalupe* and *Montezuma,* managed to escape to Havana before Conner completely implemented the blockade. Shortly thereafter, the American force established such a preponderant presence that no other enemy vessel was able to go to sea. Home Squadron ships cruised slowly offshore, watching in vain for the Mexicans to come out and challenge them.

Serving in a squadron sailing leisurely up and down the Mexican coast provided few opportunities for pursers afloat in the Gulf of Mexico to do more than practice the routine chores of their trade. Living conditions in the ships, crowded with wartime complements, were routinely poor. Rations consisted almost entirely of salt beef or pork and hardtack, washed down by hot tea. The ships often went for months without fruit and vegetables, thus scurvy was a constant threat. Manning the ships was also a major problem. The Navy could not enlist sufficient men and boys to meet its authorized strength, which had been increased from 7,500 to 10,000. No more than 8,100 men served at any point during the Mexican War.

While Conner's squadron was engaged in blockading and raiding duties on the Gulf coast of Mexico, Commodore Sloat's squadron in the Pacific began the long-awaited conquest of California. American vessels had no base on the West Coast from which to operate, and long voyages were necessary to obtain provisions. In spite of the handicaps under which the Pacific Squadron operated, Sloat seized Monterey on 7 July 1846 and San Francisco on 8 July without bloodshed. Captain Robert F. Stockton on 29 July formed 200 marines into a strike force to conquer all of California, which he accomplished at the start of 1847.

Meanwhile, Taylor's army stalled about halfway to Mexico City and he needed relief. President Polk believed that a reinforced Army should strike into the heartland of Mexico from the Gulf Coast and capture Mexico City. Polk decided on an amphibious assault, and Conner chose a beach three miles south of Vera Cruz. In the late afternoon of 9 March 1847, American forces under General Winfield Scott came ashore in small boats. The Mexicans did not contest the landing, and the boats grounded about 100 yards from the beach. The soldiers waded ashore, holding guns and cartridge belts over their heads, accompanied by the Home Squadron band. Amazingly, 8,600 troops were landed on the beachhead in five hours without the loss of even one man.

Commander Matthew C. Perry, who relieved Conner, made several attacks on the strong fortifications at Vera Cruz from the sea and battered the city into submission on 29 March. A few weeks later, Scott's army, including 300 Marines, marched off to join Taylor's stalled army on the same route Cortez had taken three centuries earlier. Reinforced with fresh troops, the joint force, after several victories en route, took Mexico City on 13 September.

Perry made attacks on other, smaller Mexican ports along the Gulf, but the landing at Vera Cruz remained the Navy's most important accomplishment of the Mexican War. The day after capturing Mexico City, Scott lauded the Home Squadron and its two leaders, Conner and Perry, for their contribution to the success of the campaign, which ended on 8 February 1848.

Supply in the Postwar Navy

The implementation of new procedures growing out of logistical lessons learned in the Mexican War could not be implemented during the hostilities because of the war's short duration. During the period from the end of the Mexican War to the start of the Civil War, the Bureau of Provisions and Clothing codified and solidified its role in Navy supply.

Navy agents continued to complain about their diminished commissions as pursers assigned to shore stations purchased naval stores directly from suppliers rather than placing requisitions with the agents. The agents constantly bombarded Secretary of the Navy Mason with complaints about their loss of income. They requested that pursers be directed to make their purchases through the agents or that the agents' commissions be increased significantly. Agents at home and abroad besieged the secretary with requests for salary increases and for additional clerks to handle the increased paperwork caused by the bureau system.

Preservation of provisions remained a special problem for shipboard pursers as well as navy agents based in foreign lands. Spoilage took a large percent of food afloat and ashore. The secretary received almost as many suggestions for new methods of preservation as he did complaints of spoilage. In June 1847, for example, Horatio Crabb, naval storekeeper at Honolulu, recommended that the Bureau of Provisions and Clothing consider shipping bread in airtight stowage barrels rather than in whiskey hogsheads to prevent spoilage. The U.S. consul at Valparaiso wrote to the secretary in February 1848 to recommend that a few hundred barrels of Navy salted beef and pork be provided for the supply of U.S. government vessels calling at that port because it was impossible to procure good quality meat in the Chilean market. The consul reported that bread and biscuit of the best quality was available at Valparaiso at prices varying from $4.25 to $5 per hundred weight and warranted to remain sweet for 12 to 18 months. Naval Agent Samuel Patterson at Philadelphia complained that tea being used at the navy yard was unfit to drink, and he objected on moral grounds to selling surplus quantities, as required by law, because it was tainted.

The Supply Depot in Monterey

After the annexation of California, the secretary approved the Navy's decision to close the depot at Honolulu and relocate the supplies to Monterey. Naturally, the newly arrived Storekeeper Crabb at Honolulu objected in February 1848, arguing that facilities at Monterey were poor and inadequate.

The discovery of gold in California in 1848 created another problem for Navy pursers and agents. Thomas Larkin, the agent at Monterey, wrote to the secretary in July 1848, contending that it would be difficult to sell government drafts if the production of gold continued at the same rate. Larkin claimed that as, long as 22- to 24-carat gold could be purchased at $15 an ounce, few people would purchase drafts at par. In August, Larkin complained that he had received no instructions regarding the stores being transferred from Oahu. He indicated that he had paid for the transportation, rented a storehouse, and paid the salaries of the clerks. Meanwhile, Crabb reported from Honolulu that, following shipment of all Honolulu government stores to Monterey, the Hawaiian station would have difficulty supporting the squadron expected to call at the islands in October. He also reported that Great Britain and France were about to establish depots in Hawaii and warned against abandoning the U.S. depot.

In April 1849 Larkin predicted that 200 to 300 American ships in San Francisco would not be able to leave because of a shortage of available crewmen, a result of so many men having left their ships to join the search for gold. He reported that the steamer *Oregon* had succeeded in retaining a sufficient number of crewmen by paying the unheard of salary of $150 a month.

In a period of intense interservice rivalry, Army Captain Rufus Lyalls praised naval storekeeper efforts in California. In a letter to the secretary of the Navy, Lyalls reported that Army storehouses were frequently broken into and robbed, whereas Navy storehouses remained untouched.

The Apprentice System and a New Chief

Congress was slow to recognize the need for reform, but legislation in 1850 approved an apprentice system designed to enlist better recruits and end the reliance on foreigners to man the Navy's ships. On 30 June 1849 Welles was succeeded by Purser William Sinclair, the first commissioned Navy officer to serve as chief of the Bureau of Provisions and Clothing while still on active duty. A civilian was never again to head the Bureau.

LORE OF THE CORPS

Purser William Sinclair, USN

Chief, Bureau of Provisions and Clothing, 1849–54
Period of Service: 1809–58

Purser William Sinclair had the distinction of being the first commissioned officer to be appointed chief of the Bureau of Supplies and Accounts. He also was probably the only bureau chief to forget to include his salary in his first annual budget estimates.

Sinclair, a native New Englander, was born in 1789 at Salem, Massachusetts, and appointed a midshipman in 1809. He served in the Navy for 49 years, with five tours of sea duty interspersed with shore tours at various Navy yards.

When he made his first annual report as chief to the secretary of the Navy, Purser Sinclair made a number of significant recommendations for improving the system of naval stores to support the Fleet. He recommended that the naval depot at Honolulu be discontinued and the stores consolidated in a new station at San Francisco, with an obsolete sloop converted into a floating storehouse for safekeeping of supplies. He contended that this move would enable the Bureau to keep the station supplied better and more economically. He also recommended closing the depot at Monrovia, Liberia.

Sinclair anticipated that the western migration of settlers would eventually lead to the spot procurement of fresh provisions. However, until the area was more generally settled, the wide swings in prices would make spot purchases impractical. He recommended that the Bureau continue to make shipments from the East Coast to California. He also felt that the Navy would have a better and more perfect system of accountability with a more frequent interchange of communications among the Bureau, the West Coast commander, and the storekeeper of the California station.

The chief was concerned with tremendous losses incurred from the need to survey large quantities of bread and biscuits. He reported to the secretary, "For many years complaints have been made of bread furnished the Navy because of large quantities that have been condemned due to being moldy and wormy." He also complained that the Navy was not receiving the quality of bread it had a right to expect and proposed establishment of a Navy bakery at Brooklyn under the Bureau's control. He estimated a cost not to exceed $25,000 and pointed out that condemned bread cost the Navy $13,500 in 1845.

As his predecessors had done earlier, Sinclair continued to ask for additional clerks to handle the increased workload in the Bureau and for increased salaries for clerks at the Bureau and at navy yards. On his watch in 1854, Congress enacted legislation that advanced the pursers' fight for equality with line officers. The new law legalized the General Order of 1847 that provided for pursers of more than 12 years' service to rank with commanders, and those with fewer than 12 years' to rank with lieutenants.

Purser Sinclair left office in 1854 and was granted leave in 1855 and 1856 to visit Europe. He died in May 1858 while still awaiting new Navy orders.

Source

Official Biography. Naval Supply Systems Command, n.d.

Problems at Foreign Stations

Correspondence records of the secretary of the Navy reveal many interesting communications that reflect the problems that pursers and agents encountered. Navy agents and naval storekeepers at foreign stations were often the victims of new and strange diseases, causing many to give up lucrative posts and return to the United States. Agents reporting to or returning from a foreign station often were delayed for long periods when the ships in which they had embarked were detained in port. They were not reluctant to request that their pay include the time spent involuntarily in port. The cost of passage often exceeded the travel allowance.

In April 1851 Purser John Wilson wrote to the secretary that he had lost nearly all his belongings in "coming across the plains" to his new duty station at San Francisco. He also said that it was impossible to rent a suitable room for less than $150 a month when similar rooms in the East were $200 a year. In August, Wilson wrote again and said that he and his family could not live in San Francisco for less than $1,000 a month.

Another problem for agents was the growing number of pursers assigned ashore to displace agents, storekeepers, and their clerks. B. Wright, agent at Pensacola, complained in August 1851 that the maximum pay for agents was reduced from $2,000 annually in 1826 to $1,000 and requested that pursers be required to make their requisitions through the agents. In January 1852, the agent at Portsmouth made a similar request.

R. P. DeSilver, agent at Hong Kong, wrote that Purser Sinclair endorsed his suggestion to send out small and frequent shipments of supplies and to bake bread in Hong Kong. DeSilver claimed that if his suggestion were adopted, fewer stores would be condemned. He added that this would result in fewer sales of condemned goods, reducing available cash to take care of special needs of the squadron on station. DeSilver also reported in January 1854 that he was shifting stores from Macao to Hong Kong, where a future U.S. naval depot would be located for the East India Squadron. Responding to pressure, DeSilver expedited supplies to Commodore Perry's ships but complained that the necessary documentation made his duties "arduous in the extreme." DeSilver told the secretary that his clerk of six years, at a salary of $600, preferred not to move to Hong Kong but would do so at increased pay to $800.

Lieutenant Commander J. D. Johanes, storekeeper at Valparaiso, Chile, reported in January that he had purchased, at the direction of the chief of the Bureau of Provisions and Clothing, $3,793.90 worth of provisions. In accordance with instructions, he shipped the provisions to the Sandwich Islands to support a surveying party led by Commander C. Ringgold.

Coal, Reports, and Pay

The increasing use of coal-fired steamships introduced a new commodity into the supply system. In July 1854, Storekeeper DeSilver noted that six coal ships were in Hong Kong, awaiting the arrival of Perry's squadron. DeSilver preferred a direct transfer of the coal to squadron's ships, but their delayed arrival required putting 8,000 tons ashore. Bids for storage were $60 and $40 a month from two contractors at separate locations. In December 1855, DeSilver acknowledged receipt of orders not to sell any coal in storage at Hong Kong, but to save it for the arrival of *USS San Jacinto*.

With the expansion of the United States and the more distant deployment of the Fleet, compliance with regulations presented special problems. Pursers and navy agents did not always file their reports and returns on time and often gave the excuse that events over which they had little or no control made timely reporting impossible. The San Francisco agent, acting as purser in November 1854, noted that regulations required pursers within the United States to make monthly requisitions for funds with approval of their commanding officers. Because of the distance of San Francisco from the seat of government, he said, his requisitions reflected his estimates for three months' funds requirements.

In August 1855 the navy agent's office at Norfolk was closed for the month because of a "malignant epidemic," making it impossible to file required month-end reports. When a riot broke out in San Francisco in May 1856, the purser on station reported that he had removed all books, papers, and other records from his office and would be unable to complete his returns for April.

The problem of reduced navy agent income surfaced frequently. In March 1857 A. W. Maxwell, agent at Pensacola, asked that the secretary reinstate instructions to pursers to submit requisitions through agents rather than directly to the bureaus.

The matter of pay for those involved in Navy supply also continued to crop up. In November 1857 Anson Herrick, naval storekeeper at New York, wrote directly to both President James Buchanan and the secretary to request an increase in pay. In December, James Ferguson, storekeeper at Rio de Janeiro, advised the secretary that the $1,500 standard salary for foreign stations was inadequate because prices in Rio were so high.

Tight finances resulted in a retrenchment in 1858, which caused great concern among pursers, navy agents, and storekeepers who were ordered to reduce the number of clerks and storehouse workers. Several complained, but to no avail. Another result of the financial squeeze was banks' devaluation of government drafts, which were sold at a 7½ percent discount in May.

In November, James Filoe, storekeeper at Key West, reported that he had only gold and silver and no other currency. He informed the secretary that he paid his bills with a draft on a Washington bank, but recipients could only convert them to cash at a discount whereas a draft on a New York bank involved no discount. In a July 1859 letter, Storekeeper Filoe reported on the unfinished state of the Key West coal depot, the lack of storage space, and the need for a cistern. He added that Key West was an excellent port to supply the Navy's needs for provisions and water and that "the health of the city so far this summer is extremely good." In November, Filoe reported that he had sold 50 tons of anthracite coal to a British naval steamship and could replenish it from one of the local merchants.

From Purser to Paymaster

The status of Navy's supply officers was enhanced in 1858, when their title was changed from purser to paymaster in recognition of the importance of their duties as pay officers. In the same year, they were placed on a standard pay scale.

As war clouds were again gathering over the nation in 1860, significant change lay ahead for the Navy. Perhaps the most important development before the war was the rapidly accelerating introduction of steamships into the Fleet. The number grew from 6 in 1853 to 38 in 1860, and the number of sailing ships without auxiliary steam power declined from 59 to 44 in the same period.

The revolution in propulsion and other technological developments provided major opportunities for the Bureau of Provisions and Clothing and the men who provided the supplies and supported the operations of the Fleet. Definitive ranking with other commissioned officers, a place in the standard pay system, and a new name were important to the men who were responsible for Navy supply. It meant recognition for their professional contributions. At last they could concentrate on doing the job without concern for their status in the organization.

Sources

Sources for material used in this chapter and not cited earlier include:

Dudley, William S., ed. *The Naval War of 1812: A Documentary History*. Vols. 1 and 2. Washington, D.C.: Naval Historical Center, 1985.

Navy Supply Corps Newsletter, February 1970, September 1973.

Wellborn, Fred W. *The Growth of the American Nationality, 1492–1865*. New York: Macmillan, 1951.

Additional sources for material:

Letters Received by the Secretary of the Navy from Navy Agents and Storekeepers, 1843–1865. The original letters are on file at the National Archives in Washington and microfilm copies are on file at the U.S. Naval Academy Library.

Smith, Justin H. *The War with Mexico*. New York: Macmillan, 1919.

CHAPTER THREE

The Civil War

1861–65

Secession of Southern states in 1861 brought the young American nation face to face with its greatest challenge—the potential dissolution of the Union. The United States had survived an earlier crisis when the New England states threatened to secede during the War of 1812. This new threat from a more united group of Southern states posed a much greater problem.

U.S. forces and Southern militia began to engage in skirmishes in late 1860, as both sides strove to enhance their positions before the anticipated start of the war that neither side wanted. Democrat President James Buchanan was reluctant to react strongly to attacks on Union forces, reportedly because he did not want to start a war his recently elected Republican successor, Abraham Lincoln, would have to carry out.

Southerners in federal service were torn between their loyalty to their native region and to the federal government to which they had sworn allegiance. Thousands of officers and enlisted men in the U.S. Navy, Marine Corps, and Army faced the agonizing decision of whether to remain in service to the Union or to return to their native Southern states.

The ideals of family loyalty and love of their native regions were logical reasons, to Southerners, for leaving the federal military, but the Lincoln administration reacted with hostility. Resignations of some officers were accepted, and the men were discharged. Others resignations were rejected, and the petitioners summarily dismissed. Many of the resigned and dismissed officers were later to offer their services to the Confederacy, but others simply left federal service and returned to civilian life in their home states.

Lincoln took office in March 1861 and appointed Gideon Welles secretary of the Navy. Welles, who had been the third chief of the Bureau of Provisions and Clothing from 1846 to 1849, was just the experienced politician Lincoln needed for the job. By the time Welles took office, 70 Navy officers who were native Southerners, married to Southerners, or harbored sympathies for the South had already submitted resignations. The secretary had to deal with the question of loyalty of those who remained in federal service. He created the Office of Detail, which had responsibility for:

- weeding out Southern sympathizers,
- answering the loyalty question,
- investigating new applicants,
- assigning new officers to appropriate billets, and
- handling routine transfers caused by vacancies resulting from resignations.

Native Southerners were not the only military people who were confronted by this dilemma. Northerners who had married women from Southern states also had difficult decisions to make. What would happen to their families if they took up arms against their wives' states?

In the end, 373 commissioned and warrant officers of the Navy and Marine Corps—25 percent of the total U.S. Navy officer corps—elected to resign their U.S. commissions or warrants. Thirteen paymasters—20 percent of the Navy's total—were among the officers who resigned or were dismissed. Of the 13 paymasters who left, 4 were allowed to resign and 9 attempted to resign, but were dismissed instead. An accepted resignation was considered an honorable discharge. A dismissal was not.

The experience of one such paymaster is an example of a family with a heart-rendering choice to make when the Civil War began.

LORE OF THE CORPS

Paymaster John Story Gulick, USN

Paymaster, *USS Wabash,* 1861–62
Period of Service: 1851–59, 1861–79

One U.S. Navy supply officer who faced the dilemma of divided loyalty at the start of the Civil War was Paymaster John Story Gulick. Born near Kingston, New Jersey, he was educated at Lawrenceville School and was graduated from Princeton University in 1838. He was subsequently admitted to the New Jersey Bar. President Millard Filmore had appointed him a Navy purser in 1851, and he made two cruises on the Brazilian Station and one in the Pacific before the war. He married an artist, Elizabeth Milligan, in 1854, left the Navy in 1859, and took up residence in his wife's home state of Virginia.

When Virginia seceded in 1861, Gulick decided to return to federal service. He and his wife loaded their belongings in a covered wagon and escaped through the tight Confederate lines to reach his hometown in New Jersey. Shortly thereafter, the Navy accepted his application and assigned Paymaster Gulick to *USS Wabash,* a steam frigate operating with the South Atlantic Squadron. The following year, 1862, he served tours at the navy yards in Washington and Philadelphia.

Gulick was made fleet paymaster of the Mississippi Squadron in 1864. He returned to shore duty in 1865 at the Philadelphia Navy Yard and, in 1867, at the Naval Academy. He was made fleet paymaster of the European Squadron in 1869 and was promoted to pay director in March 1871. He returned for duty at both the Washington and Philadelphia navy yards. In 1879, at the mandatory retirement age of 62, Pay Director Gulick returned to civilian life at his hometown of Kingston, near Princeton University. He died in 1884.

Sources

Baker, Cecil Sherman, SC, USN. *A Collection of Abstracts Giving Historical Background for the Work of the Supply Corps* (ca. 1939).

Hamersly, Lewis. *Records of Living Officers of the U.S. Navy and Marine Corps.* 3d ed. Philadelphia: L. R. Hamersly, 1878.

Wartime Chief Experienced in Job

When the war began, COMO Horatio Bridge had been chief of the Bureau of Provisions and Clothing for seven years; he relieved Purser William Sinclair in 1854. Bridge is noted as an efficient chief who served longer than any other paymaster general or chief of Supply Corps in the 200-year history of the Corps.

LORE OF THE CORPS

Commodore Horatio Bridge, USN

Chief, Bureau of Provisions and Clothing, 1854–69
Period of Service: 1838–73

When the Civil War began, Horatio Bridge was chief of the Bureau of Provisions and Clothing and paymaster general. He served throughout the war and held that office for 15 years, the longest term of any individual before or since. Bridge is credited with being the first man to employ the idea of comprehensive fleet supply.

Horatio Bridge was born at Augusta, Maine, in April 1806. The son of a judge, he studied in private schools and was graduated from Bowdoin College in the famed class of 1825, which included Nathaniel Hawthorne and Henry Longfellow. His long and intimate friendship with Hawthorne had a profound influence on his life, and he wrote and later published several papers and a book about Hawthorne. Following graduation from Bowdoin, he studied law at Northampton Law School and was admitted to the bar in 1828. He practiced law for 10 years until it became distasteful to him and then entered the U.S. Navy in 1838 as a paymaster.

He served at sea for five of his first six years off Africa and in the Mediterranean. Paymaster Bridge wrote *Journal of an African Cruiser,* describing his cruises while on the African Station. This literary effort was edited by his close friend Hawthorne and published in 1845. Bridge sailed back to Africa and the Mediterranean in 1846 as fleet paymaster of the flagship *USS United States.* Following an 1849–51 tour at the Portsmouth Navy Yard, he sailed for the Pacific in the sloop *USS Portsmouth* in late 1851.

In 1854, the Navy ordered him home to serve as chief of the Bureau of Provisions and Clothing. In a debate on the floor of the Senate, a frequent Navy critic, Senator James W. Grimes said, "No bureau of this government has been more admirably and adequately managed than the Bureau of Provisions and Clothing." Senator John P. Hale added, "I think a great reason and a very important one, is because there is at the head of the Bureau an honest, vigilant, and faithful man."

During his long watch at the Bureau of Provisions of Clothing, Commodore Bridge instituted many significant innovations, including:

- changing the name "purser" to "paymaster";
- making advertising for competitive bids mandatoryexcept for personal services and in emergencies;
- requiring that promotions to the Corps of Paymasters be made from the list of assistant paymaster;
- permitting purchase of preserved meats, pickles, butter, cheese and desiccated vegetables without formal advertising and sealed bids;

- specifying that the chief of the Bureau, also known as the paymaster general, be appointed from the list of the paymasters of the Navy of not less than 10 years' standing (for the first time, it was legally impossible for the paymaster general to be a civilian); and
- eliminating the rum ration, effective 1 September 1862, with enlisted men's pay increased 5 cents a day.

Horatio Bridge resigned as chief of the Bureau in 1869 and shortly thereafter accepted the position of the first chief inspector of provisions and clothing. He held that position until he was required to retire in 1873, upon passage of legislation barring Navy officers from serving on active duty after reaching the age of 62. He returned to his country home in Athens, Pennsylvania, where he died in March 1893.

The Navy named the lead ship of a new class of refrigerated stores ships for him in recognition of his leadership and his many contributions. *USS Bridge* (AF-1) was launched in May 1916 and commissioned in June 1917. The new ship was assigned to the Naval Overseas Transportation Service, made four round trips across the Atlantic during World War I, and was a vital component of the Service Force in the Pacific during World War II.

Bridge escaped serious damage in both world wars, but suffered considerable damage when she struck a mine off Korea two months after World War II ended in 1945. The veteran support ship was decommissioned at Sasebo, Japan, in June 1946, sold in the Philippines in December 1947, and scrapped in March 1953.

Sources

Dictionary of American Naval Fighting Ships, vol. 1: *A-B.* Washington, D.C.: Naval Historical Center, Department of the Navy, 1964.

Hamersly, Lewis. *Records of Living Officers of the U.S. Navy and Marine Corps.* 3d ed. Philadelphia: L. R. Hamersly, 1878.

Official Biography. Naval Supply Systems Command, n.d.

The Anaconda Plan

The Lincoln administration adopted a two-part strategy in 1861. The Union Navy was to blockade the 3,500-mile coastline of the Confederate states and to cut the South in half by seizing control of the Mississippi River. Meanwhile, the Union Army was to crush the Confederacy on land. This strategy, recommended by General Winfield Scott, came to be known as the "Anaconda Plan." Secretary Welles believed the blockade would be the Navy's key contribution to the war. As a matter of fact, it was the one aspect of Scott's plan that politicians and the press did not widely criticize.

The blockade was strategically ineffective initially because of complex logistics. By 1862 each of the four blockading squadrons required an average of 3,000 tons of coal a week to fuel the Union steamers. Each blockading ship was required to break off from its station and put into one of two distant major coaling depots, Port Royal or Pensacola, to fill its bunkers. This process frequently necessitated additional time away from duty because of inadequate stocks of coal at the depots. The situation improved markedly in April 1862, when Union forces occupied New Orleans, where the Navy established a coal depot.

Communications problems also plagued the blockade. Officers had been promised cash prizes for captured Confederate vessels brought into port. The cash was to be paid by the resident navy agents at their respective ports. When Union Navy officers asked for their funds at New York, the navy agent balked at paying the bill. Secretary Welles had not advised his agents of their authority to make such payments, and the New York agent informed Welles that he would not honor payment requests until the Navy Department approved them. The cash was important to the prize officers, who usually had to purchase their own transportation back to the blockading squadron.

U.S. Navy Depots and Stations in the South

The U.S. Navy maintained several captured depots and stations in Southern states to support Union patrolling and blockading squadrons during the war. These bases stocked and issued ordnance, provisions, coal, and naval stores and were equipped to repair naval vessels. The retreating Confederates had attempted to destroy the base at Norfolk, but failed to do so completely. The U.S. Navy recognized the importance of Norfolk's strategic location and concentrated on restoring the base there. Pensacola, on the other hand, was considered less important, and few improvements were made after its recapture.

The Bureau of Provisions and Clothing had been criticized for a shortage of storage space and wharf facilities at the start of the war. This situation was rectified when the Navy took over recaptured yards along the Atlantic and Gulf coasts and funds were available to repair and expand facilities. The Navy operated former Confederate stations or depots at New Orleans, Ship Island (Mobile), Key West, Port Royal, and Beaufort at the end of the war. The base at Port Royal, South Carolina, was recaptured early in the war and became the main support facility for the South Atlantic Blockading Squadron. At one time, more than 200 vessels were anchored or docked at Port Royal. Key West was a major resupply point for ships going into or coming out of the Gulf of Mexico. Large quantities of coal and provisions continued to flow into Key West throughout the war.

Early in the war, the tough-minded COMO Horatio Bridge, challenged the Bureau of Provisions and Clothing to provide outstanding service in purchasing and supplying food and clothing to the Union Navy. The Bureau managed to supply clothing for a sixfold increase in Navy personnel with only a fourfold increase in expenditures, despite a doubling of the inflated average price of clothing. Bridge obtained congressional approval to adopt a revised procedure for supplying bread to the Navy. The old practice of purchasing bread from contractors frequently resulted in the Navy receiving poor-quality bread. This system was replaced by a new one in which the Navy purchased the flour and supervised baking by contract bakers, resulting in higher-quality bread for the Fleet.

Refrigerated Ships

The Navy experimented early in the war with the use of commercial supply ships with onboard refrigeration to deliver fresh meat and vegetables to the Fleet. Secretary Welles, whose earlier experience as chief of the Bureau of Provisions and Clothing gave him a unique perspective on the importance of logistics, issued an order to COMO Bridge on 19 July 1861: "You will proceed to New York and take the requisite means to placing on board the Steamer *Rhode Island* fresh beef, vegetables, and other supplies necessary for crews of blockading vessels south of Cape Hatteras. Your arrangements will be made with reference to supplying all the vessels with fresh beef and vegetables on the outward trip of the *Rhode Island,* and on returning."

Historian Charles O. Paullin reports that the system proved successful from the beginning and was quickly refined. Two such steamers, equipped with large "ice houses," operated regularly from New York, Boston, and Philadelphia to the Gulf of Mexico to supply the West Gulf Squadron with 12 to 17 tons of refrigerated fresh beef and 600 to 700 barrels of fresh vegetables. Other steamers supplied the East Gulf, North Atlantic, and South Atlantic squadrons on a regular basis. Paullin writes that these ships "ran almost with the regularity of packets" and also carried mail, dispatches, and passengers. Similar ships operated on the Mississippi River.

The Mississippi River Campaign

The Mississippi River naval campaign became an integral component of the Anaconda Plan, but was implemented more slowly than the coastal blockade. Lincoln knew that war support was weaker in the Midwest than in North Central and New England states, and General Scott recognized the vulnerability of the Confederacy's western flank.

The strategy of controlling the Mississippi and Tennessee rivers was significant because it would eliminate the Confederates' western supply route via the Mississippi as an alternate to the coastal route in the event the Union coastal blockade achieved its objectives. Lincoln moved ahead with the western campaign in the fall of 1861 despite Welles's preoccupation with the coastal blockade. Inasmuch as the extensive rail network could easily supply Union forces at river cities, logistics did not present the problems to river forces that the coastal blockading squadrons experienced. After the fall of Vicksburg, Mississippi, in July 1863, use of the Mississippi River was denied to the Confederacy, and Union commerce from the Midwest once again moved unimpeded to New Orleans.

Paymasters' Appointment Legislated

Meanwhile Congress enacted legislation in 1861 to make permanent COMO Bridge's ruling that appointments to the Corps of Paymasters could be made only from the list of assistant paymasters. In 1862 legislation required that future heads of the Bureau of Provisions and Clothing must be paymasters.

The number of paymasters on active duty increased dramatically during the war. As a group, their performance contributed significantly to the Union victory. The experiences of these paymasters illustrate their dedication to duty, heroism, and personal privation.

LORE OF THE CORPS

Paymaster Elisha W. Dunn, USN

Fleet Paymaster, Mississippi Blockading Squadron, 1862–65
Period of Service: 1858–69

Dunn was a key figure in the successful establishment of the Union blockade of the Mississippi River. He was born in Virginia and commissioned an assistant paymaster in March 1858. He was living in Washington when the Civil War broke out.

Fleet Paymaster Dunn operated out of an office at the U.S. Naval Depot, Cairo, Illinois, at the confluence of the Mississippi and Ohio rivers, when he reported to the Mississippi Squadron in 1862. It is obvious from official correspondence that Acting Rear Admiral C. H. Davis and Commandant and Fleet Captain A. M. Pennock had considerable confidence in Dunn. They frequently gave him special assignments, and Davis often asked Dunn to explain to the Navy Department why it was difficult to follow certain regulations. Pennock sent Dunn to St. Louis to sign up paymasters for two of his ships, the *Mound City* and the *Bragg*. In September 1862 the western flotilla was transferred from the War Department, and Paymaster Dunn was charged with instructing junior paymasters on their duties. Dunn later was placed in charge of the light-draft flotilla and various other craft.

The lack of coal for the Mississippi River Squadron's steamers had become a serious problem by the fall of 1863. Although the Navy continued to secure coal from Kentucky mines, the shortage was so acute that the Fleet was required to substitute less energy-efficient wood. Meanwhile, Paymaster Dunn was awaiting cash from Washington in order to make the necessary purchases. By May 1864 Dunn had money, but it soon ran out. In August, Fleet Captain Pennock again advised his superiors that Dunn was awaiting additional funds.

A fire aboard the naval wharf boat at Mound City destroyed Dunn's office and all his books, papers, and vouchers involving the large amounts for which he was responsible. RADM David D. Porter wrote to the chairmen of both the House and Senate Naval Affairs committees, explaining the situation and asking for "favorable attention to the case" Dunn would present to them.

Porter told the committee chairmen, "Fleet Paymaster Dunn has been with me from the time I took command of this fleet, and I have found him an honest, faithful and efficient officer, and such statements as he may make in regard to his affairs will be entirely reliable."

Available records do not reveal the disposition of this issue, but in 1867 *Hamersly's Records of Living Officers of the U.S. Navy and Marine Corps* shows that Dunn had duty in the receiving ship *New Hampshire* in 1867 and as inspector of provisions at New York in 1868. Dunn is not listed in the 1870 *Hamersly's Records,* and it can be assumed he was out of the Navy by that time.

Sources

Hamersly, Lewis. *Records of Living Officers of the U.S. Navy and Marine Corps.* Philadelphia: J. B. Lippincott, 1870.

Official Records of the Union and Confederate Navies in the War of the Rebellion. Vols. 24, 26, 27, and 29. Washington, D.C.: U.S. Government Printing Office, 1911, 1912, 1921.

Register of the Commissioned, Warrant and Volunteer Officers of the Navy of the United States, 1867, 1868, and 1870. Washington, D.C.: U.S. Government Printing Office, 1870.

The Purchase of Badly Needed Ships

Paymaster Augustus H. Gilman was assigned special duty with the Mississippi River Blockading Squadron from 1861 to 1865. During the war, the native of New Hampshire was provided with funds and sent out to acquire badly needed vessels for the Mississippi Squadron. His search for available ships took him up the Mississippi River to St. Louis and up the Ohio River to Cincinnati. Correspondence between Fleet Captain A. M. Pennock and RADM Porter reveals some of the obstacles Gilman faced in his special assignment. For the most part, he was able to overcome the obstacles and arrange the purchase of the required ships.

Augustus Gilman served on active duty for 28 years and retired as pay director with the rank of captain at Portland, Maine, in August 1886.

Heroic Actions

Acting Assistant Paymaster William W. Williams, a native of Ohio, served on an Army general's staff, commanded an Army gunboat, and performed gallantly in several naval engagements during the Civil War. Williams was attached to the steamer *Louisiana* on the North Atlantic Blockading Squadron. In 1862 he participated in a number of battles at North Carolina towns. At the siege of Washington, he was in command of an Army gunboat, the *Eagle,* and on the staff of General J. G. Foster. He was promoted to paymaster in March 1864.

While on duty with the Brazilian Squadron and in the steam sloop *Wachusett,* he participated in the capture of *CSS Florida* in October 1864. Williams was advanced 10 numbers in the Pay Corps in 1871 and promoted to pay inspector for gallant and meritorious service during the war. While on duty in the storeship *Fredonia* at Callao, Peru, the ship was capsized and wrecked by a tidal wave on 13 August 1868. Williams was one of three surviving officers.

Another hero was Acting Assistant Paymaster Luther G. Billings in his first assignment 18 months after the native New Yorker had been appointed acting assistant paymaster in October 1862. Billings performed heroically in hand-to-hand combat with Confederate soldiers when a large party of rebels boarded his ship, *USS Water Witch,* on the night of 4 June 1864 while she was on blockade duty at anchor in Ossabaw Sound, Georgia.

Billings was the first man on deck and took an active part in the combat. He killed the Confederate officer leading the boarding party and saved the life of his commanding officer by killing the man who cut him down. Billings was severely wounded and taken prisoner. He was moved to the Confederate Naval Hospital at Savannah for treatment. There, he incurred the displeasure of the hospital commander, and on 12 June was transferred, before his wounds had healed, to the Oglethorpe prison camp at Macon, Georgia.

On 20 July he and 1,500 other Union officer prisoners were taken by train to Charleston. En route, Billings and four other Union officers jumped from the fast-moving train and escaped in the darkness. It took a detachment of cavalry and 34 bloodhounds to track down and capture the fugitives on 25 July, only 4 miles from the coast. The tired and hungry escapees were nearly mangled by the hounds before being rescued by Confederate troopers.

The recaptured escapees finally arrived in Charleston two days later. On 1 September the original group of prisoners began a journey to the Libby Prison at Richmond. They were served only one ration en route, and a number of prisoners died from starvation, including four from *Water Witch.* Available records do not indicate whether Billings was in a prisoner exchange, or whether he escaped or was released, but he was back on duty in the steamer *USS Connecticut* before the end of 1864.

Connecticut participated in a special South Pacific Squadron cruise in 1864 and 1865, visiting all the forts in the West Indies and several on the Atlantic Coast. Billings was promoted to assistant paymaster during the special cruise in March 1865 and to paymaster in May 1866.

His Civil War experience was not the only time that unusual events interrupted his routine. His subsequent assignment in 1866 to the steamer *USS Wateree* of the South Pacific Squadron took him to many ports on the west coast of South America. He also witnessed the bombardment of Callao, Peru, by Spanish warships.

On 14 August 1868 a strong earthquake caused immense loss of life and utterly destroyed the town of Arica, Peru. The quake and resulting tidal wave sank all the ships in the harbor except for *Wateree,* which ended up about 500 yards inland. Assistant Paymaster Billings received a commendatory letter from Commander Gillis for his "cool and courageous bearing during the trying circumstances."

LORE OF THE CORPS

Paymaster John Henry Stevenson, USN

Paymaster, *Satellite,* 1862–63
Period of Service: 1862–93

One of the real heroes of American naval history is a competent but little-known paymaster who compiled an enviable record of daring and bravery during the Civil War.

John Henry Stevenson was born at New York City in 1839 and educated at the City College of New York, then known as the Free Academy. He was an ardent unionist and although employed in a well-paying job with the New York City Gas Company had a strong desire to fight for the Union. He was a good horseman and an excellent swimmer, abilities that would later prove to be invaluable.

A few days after the fall of Fort Sumter, Stevenson enlisted in the Army for 90 days as a private. He went proudly off to war, but when he fell ill in a troop encampment at Washington, he was sent home. While absent from his unit he missed the First Battle of Bull Run in which his unit was nearly decimated and many of the survivors taken prisoner.

Stevenson's heavy cough persisted when he was at home in New York. His doctor advised him to make a sea trip to recuperate in pure air, so he visited Ireland. He still had the urge to participate in the war when he returned to the United States. He shunned a return to the primitive life of an Army private and obtained an appointment as acting assistant paymaster in the Navy in September 1862. His first assignment was in *Satellite* of the Potomac Squadron.

Stevenson grew weary of waiting and watching Confederate activity along the shore, so he joined a company of sailors sent to take part in a battle near Fredericksburg, Virginia, under General Joe Hooker. The Navy unit managed to survive the disastrous fight at Fredericksburg, but the experience made a lasting impression on Paymaster Stevenson. He wanted to be a part of the action ashore in addition to outfitting, clothing, and paying sailors.

In December, Stevenson boasted that he could capture all the members of a group of Confederates on shore who were sending signals and also their equipment. He persuaded his C.O. to hold fire and delivered on his boast by going ashore, capturing the rebels, and breaking up the encampment. The young paymaster learned while ashore that a rebel cavalry unit had set up a recruiting station 10 or 12 miles from the river. Leaving four men to guard the small boats anchored just offshore, Stevenson and his party slipped safely past Confederate pickets, broke up the recruiting station, and captured the officer-in-charge along with several men. Stevenson and his charges returned safely to *Satellite* with their prisoners. In a masterpiece of understatement, his commanding officer wrote, "To the bravery and energy of Acting Assistant Paymaster Stevenson the success of the expedition was due. Mr. Stevenson frequently volunteered his services for other hazardous duty, and always performed it to my entire satisfaction."

The Confederates reaped revenge on *Satellite* nine months later on a dark night when they boarded and captured her while at anchor in the Rappahannock. But the hated Stevenson had been transferred to the *USS Princess Royal,* a unit of the Western Gulf Blockading Squadron, assisting General Ulysses S. Grant in clearing the Mississippi River. She was anchored off Donaldson, Louisiana, to protect the town, where wounded Union soldiers and sailors were recuperating. The town was soon besieged by a large Confederate force.

Paymaster Stevenson decided on his own to reconnoiter the Confederate camp to learn the enemy's plan for the final attack on the town. He went ashore on afternoon liberty and changed into the rags of a refugee. He then slipped past Union pickets in the dark but deliberately drew their fire by boldly dashing into the Confederate camp for "safety." He told the Confederate provost that he was an escaped rebel prisoner and was allowed to "enlist" in the Confederate Army.

He gathered information on the planned attack for two days before trying to return to *Princess Royal* without being detected by the Confederates or shot by Union pickets. He was rescued by a Union gunboat and returned to his ship. Captain Woolsey, the commanding officer, strongly reprimanded Stevenson for being absent without leave, but when Stevenson carefully apprised his C.O. of the Confederate attack plans in great detail Woolsey relented and suspended formal disciplinary action.

Armed with Stevenson's intelligence, Union forces inflicted severe casualties on the attacking rebels, who eventually gave up the siege of Donaldson. Woolsey cited Stevenson for "conspicuous bravery and risk of life in obtaining information that led to the Confederate defeat."

On 9 July 1863 Captain Woolsey sent the *USS New London* to New

Orleans with dispatches for Admiral David G. Farragut. She ran aground opposite Confederate-held territory. Once again, Paymaster Stevenson stepped forward and volunteered to retrieve and deliver the dispatches. Woolsey approved the mission, and Stevenson crept along the base of the levee in darkness to reach *New London* safely.

With the dispatches in hand, Stevenson started his 75-mile odyssey to New Orleans by crawling, floating, and swimming under cover of the levee at night and hiding in thickets during daylight. When Confederate sympathizers discovered him, he tried to convince them that he was merely a "swamp rat," but they decided to hang him. Before they could carry out the execution, a federal gunboat spotted the rebels and fired upon them while they scattered for cover. The paymaster escaped with the dispatches and signaled the gunboat, which took him aboard, outfitted him, and sent him on his way. Farragut congratulated Stevenson on his successful mission and, in the restrained wording of the times, commented in the paymaster's record, "I distinctly remember that this officer was very active and energetic in conveying dispatches on the Mississippi River in 1863, and I therefore cheerfully endorse his conduct during that period, as set forth by his commanding officer and consider him well qualified for Government recognition."

Rear Admiral David Porter was transferred from the Mississippi River Blockading Squadron to the North Atlantic Blockading Squadron in late 1864, when the blockade of the river was essentially accomplished. Porter took along the daring Stevenson, and the paymaster was assigned to the double-ended side-wheel gunboat *USS Massasoit.*

Paymaster Stevenson was not in a position for a year and a half to volunteer for another special mission. *Massasoit* was on detached duty in the James River when ships of the squadron participated in the capture of Fort Fisher at the mouth of the Cape Fear River near Wilmington, North Carolina. Stevenson missed the action, but another opportunity soon arose when *Massasoit* joined the main force off Wilmington.

Admiral Porter feared that General Sherman, whose army had completed its march across Georgia and was ready to fight its way north through the Carolinas to join Grant in Virginia, was unaware of the capture of Fort Fisher. Porter wanted Sherman to know that Fort Fisher was no longer a threat so that the Army forces could continue north without distraction. The admiral decided to send a messenger through enemy lines to Sherman with news of the capture of the fort.

Paymaster Stevenson once again stepped forward and volunteered. Well aware of the paymaster's previous daring deeds, Porter approved Stevenson for the mission. John Stevenson had an uneventful journey to Savannah, impersonating a Confederate straggler from Fort Fisher trying to get home. He delivered the dispatch to Sherman just as the Army was about to start north.

Paymaster Stevenson was reluctant to push his luck on a trip back to his ship through enemy lines, so he received permission to travel north with the Army. When the troops reached Fayetteville, North Carolina, he boarded the U.S. gunboat *Eolus,* which had fought its way up the Cape Fear. *Eolus* eventually returned him down river to *Massasoit.*

Admiral Porter's report of the incident included the following: "I called for a volunteer to carry dispatches through the enemy's country. Mr. Stevenson volunteered and carried the dispatches safely to General Sherman, through the enemy's country, at the risk of his neck, for had they caught him, they would have hung him."

The Civil War ended three months later, and temporary officers, including Stevenson, were quickly mustered out of the Navy before the end of 1865. President Andrew Johnson reviewed the young assistant paymaster's wartime record and was so impressed that he appointed Stevenson a passed assistant paymaster in the regular Navy. He returned to active duty in *USS Pawnee* in the South Atlantic Squadron from 1866 to 1869. In 1869, Stevenson was advanced 15 numbers for "extraordinary heroism in the Civil War" and promoted to paymaster. He had two other sea tours and three shore tours, including special duty at the Navy's exhibit in the Centennial Exposition at Philadelphia in 1876, and in charge of stores at Nagasaki, Japan. He reported for duty at the New York Navy Yard in 1877.

In June 1879 President Rutherford B. Hayes approved the advancement of Paymaster Stevenson another 15 numbers to date back to June 1863 in further recognition for "gallant and conspicuous conduct in battle and extraordinary heroism." This sequence of events brought him to the top of his pay grade, and in January 1881 he was promoted to pay inspector.

Stevenson was a man of uncompromising forthrightness and impatience with red tape. He was general storekeeper at the New York Navy Yard when a dispute arose with a board investigating irregularities in the sale of surplus material, and he was made a collateral defendant in a court of inquiry. However Navy Secretary William C. Whitney dismissed all charges for lack of evidence.

In 1889 Stevenson reported as commissary officer at the Naval Academy. He decided that the midshipmen deserved a better bill of fare than they had been receiving and took steps to improve it, drawing the ire of the Bureau of Supplies and Accounts. Stevenson's vigorous defense of his actions appears to have antagonized Paymaster General James

Fulton. Two years later, when he was examined for promotion to pay director, a majority of the board found him qualified, but the senior member dissented, citing the New York sales irregularities and the Naval Academy "extravagance." The reviewing authority disapproved his promotion.

Following a public outcry, a second board was appointed, but its promotion recommendation of Stevenson met the same fate. Further public indignation brought appointment of a third board, which, realizing the futility of attempting to promote Stevenson, recommended retirement for physical reasons. John Stevenson was placed on the retired list in September 1893, a fate he did not appeal.

Navy officials decided to establish a huge supply depot for the Atlantic Fleet on short notice when the Spanish-American War broke out in 1898. Assistant Secretary of the Navy Theodore Roosevelt knew that it was necessary to cut through red tape in order to expedite supplies to the Fleet. Roosevelt immediately selected Pay Inspector Stevenson for the job, ordered him recalled to active duty, and placed him in charge of the depot. Stevenson accomplished this demanding task in his usual outstanding manner. A quotation attributed to John Stevenson sums up his philosophy on service to the Fleet: "I would rather be court-martialed for failure to follow the regulations than for failure to supply the Fleet."

When the war was over in August 1898 he was again placed on the retired list. John Henry Stevenson's wartime duties further strained his precarious health, and he died on 14 June 1899.

Sources

Ellicott, J. S., USN (Ret.). "John H. Stevenson: Pay Corps Daredevil." *U.S. Naval Institute Proceedings,* August 1942.

Hamersly, Lewis. *Records of Living Officers of the U.S. Navy and Marine Corps.* 7th ed. Philadelphia: L. R. Hamersly, 1902. (Although this publication lists Stevenson as retired and still living, the *Proceedings* article notes his death as 1899. It appears that Hamersly was unaware of his death three years before publication of the seventh edition and therefore did not remove his listing.)

LORE OF THE CORPS

Paymaster Alexander W. Russell, USN

Paymaster, *USS Sacramento,* 1866–67
Period of Service: 1842–44, 1861–86

Paymaster Russell had broken Navy service. Between the two periods, he was a Texas Ranger, then served as a congressional staff member before returning to the Navy during the Civil War.

He was born in Maryland, entered the Navy in 1842 as captain's clerk, and served in the sloop-of-war *Saratoga* off Africa from 1842 to 1844. Afterward he left the Navy, joined Company C, Mounted Rifle Regiment of the Texas Rangers at the outbreak of the Mexican War, and served from 1858 to 1861 as clerk to the Committee on Naval Affairs, U.S. Senate.

Russell wanted to get into action when the Civil War started and secured an appointment as a Navy paymaster in February 1861. He was assigned to the steamer *Pocahontas,* serving in the Potomac River and Chesapeake Bay. In May, he was transferred to the sloop *Savannah,* which served on blockade duty with both the North and South Atlantic squadrons. He was placed in command of the Powder Division. From 1862 to 1864 he served in the ironclad steamer *New Ironsides*. Commodore Rowan, commanding *New Ironsides,* commended Russell in official dispatches "for great zeal and ability in command of the powder and shell divisions during the various [27] engagements with the forts and batteries of Charleston harbor."

Rear Admiral George E. Belknap wrote to Paymaster Russell, "Do you know that you supplied to the guns of *Ironsides,* in face of the enemy, 4,439 charges of powder, together with a like number of shells? That the aggregate weight of the shells was 258½ tons?"

Russell was serving in the receiving ship *North Carolina* at New York in 1864 and 1865 when he inaugurated the lasting reform of issuing to all recruits their needed outfit of clothing and small stores. Each recruit was furnished with "an itemized bill of the cost at government rates, instead of the scant and un-uniform [*sic*] supplies furnished to them by the shipper, at the most exorbitant cost."

He was ordered to duty in the steam sloop *Sacramento* in 1866. The ship ran aground and began to break up in the Bay of Bengal off the coast of India in 1867. The commanding officer ordered two life rafts constructed when it was apparent that the ship's boats could not survive the strong breakers. Russell was ordered to go on one of the rafts to seek relief. Before departing *Sacramento,* the paymaster carefully packed his most important books and vouchers in a tarpaulin bag he inserted into another bag for protection from water damage. He then took it upon himself to provide all officers, petty officers, and leading men with a liberal amount of money in the event that any of them became separated.

The men lashed themselves to the rafts and were towed through the violent surf by a whale boat. Once ashore, the paymaster spread his books in the sun to dry. Russell then took two men to set out on foot in search of relief, but he fell from sunstroke. The party soon reached a small village, and Russell was revived when the Americans were refreshed with water and boiled goat's milk. They rented a large canoe with six natives to sail to Coringa, where Paymaster Russell engaged three large wrecking boats and sent them to assist the foundering *Sacramento.*

Russell proceeded to Cocanada, where English officials were stationed, and rented a small steamer in customs service. Leaving orders for quartering and subsisting the officers and crew who had abandoned the ship, Russell returned to the battered ship and recovered his safe, which contained about $30,000. All of Paymaster Russell's accounts were subsequently settled without a loss of one cent, either to him or to the government.

Russell next had duty from 1868 to 1870 at Washington Navy Yard as inspector of provisions and clothing and from 1870 to 1873 at the Navy Pay Office in Philadelphia. While in the latter position, he was promoted to pay inspector in 1871. He had four other shore tours and was promoted to pay director in 1877. He returned to the Navy Pay Office in Philadelphia and retired in February 1886.

Source

Hamersly, Lewis. *Records of Living Officers of the U.S. Navy and Marine Corps.* 7th ed. Philadelphia: L. R. Hamersly, 1902.

Dealing with Adversity

Robert B. Rodney's career as a Navy paymaster was brief but distinguished. During August and September 1864, the blockader *USS J. S. Chambers* was moored alone off Indian River Inlet, Florida, when nearly the entire ship's complement of 70 men was stricken with yellow fever. About half the officers, including the commanding officer, and a fourth of the crew died, and the only medical officer became helpless. One officer, apparently still in good health, was reported to have been so overcome by the delirious shrieks of the sick and dying that he jumped overboard and drowned.

Paymaster Rodney had sole responsibility for duties involving provisions, clothing, and stores as both his clerk and steward died. He later assumed the additional duties of watch officer, chaplain, and nurse. He and the other survivors managed to sail the ship to Philadelphia. En route, the paymaster became the last member of the crew to be stricken with the disease.

Rodney was never fully cured of the ravages of yellow fever but was sufficiently recovered to return to duty in 1865. In July 1866 he was one of the few selected from more than 400 temporary acting assistant paymasters to be commissioned in the regular Navy and advanced to the grade of passed assistant paymaster. He later served in the storeship *USS Cyane* in Panama Bay from 1868 to 1869. When he surpassed all others in the examination for promotion to paymaster with relative rank of lieutenant commander in June 1869, the board noted, "Examination especially complimentary to Rodney."

A Pay Corps Officer and His Records

In a variety of circumstances, supply officers have been so dedicated that they have risked their lives to save their ships, their shipmates, or official records. One such dedicated officer was Assistant Paymaster Joseph Foster, a native of Massachusetts. Shortly after the Civil War, while attached to the steamer *USS Commodore McDonough,* he saved his official books and papers when his ship was wrecked in August 1865. Nothing else was saved from the wreck.

The record of his dedication probably was a major factor in his becoming one of the few Civil War temporary paymasters permitted to join the regular Navy. He was commissioned an assistant paymaster in July 1866. He served as fleet paymaster in the steamer *USS Monocacy* on the Asiatic Station from 1879 to 1882.

The fourth auditor of the Treasury Department specially mentioned Paymaster Foster in his 1882 annual report for negotiating a large amount of exchange in a satisfactory manner. Foster served at sea extensively during the balance of his career and was station paymaster at Key West, Florida, the key fleet support base during the Spanish-American War. Foster sent a personal letter to Paymaster General Edwin Stewart in May 1898 to report "the accounts at the Storehouse here [Naval Station Key West] are in a chaotic condition owing to the present war, and that it is impossible with the present help to do the clerical work of the General Storekeeper's Office. In addition, the Fleet Paymaster has transferred to me the accounts of a dozen tugs and vessels."

He was promoted to pay director in August 1901. Available records do not indicate the dates of his retirement or death.

LORE OF THE CORPS

Paymaster William Frederick Keeler, USN

Paymaster, *USS Monitor,* 1862–65
Period of Service: 1862–66

Officers who performed pay and supply duties during the Civil War came from a variety of civilian pursuits. Fortunately, one of them—William Keeler—had a working knowledge of machinery. Paymaster Keeler used this knowledge to prevent the famous ironclad *USS Monitor* from sinking when she nearly foundered at sea early in the war.

Letters written by Paymaster Keeler to his wife Anna chronicle several feats of personal bravery and compose the most comprehensive record of Civil War service by a Navy supply officer. These letters, published in two volumes in the 1960s, reveal a record of dedicated performance under trying circumstances and provide a graphic picture of the transformation of a civilian into an effective officer.

William Keeler was born in June 1821 at Utica, New York. In 1842 he purchased a lot and settled in LaSalle, Illinois. He married Elizabeth Dutton, daughter of the governor of Connecticut, in 1846.

Although nominally the head of a family venture with his younger brothers, William Keeler went to California to participate in the 1849 gold rush. When he failed to find a fortune, he sailed in the *SS Samuel Russell* to China and back to New York. Keeler returned to LaSalle and in 1853 set up a shop to sell watches, jewelry, silverware, clocks, guns, pistols, stationery, toys, and "sportsmen's material of every kind."

By 1857 Keeler had become the senior partner of Keeler, Bennigan Company, an ironworks, foundry, machine shop, and retail outlet for a wide variety of equipment. It was at this firm that he became familiar with operating machinery—knowledge he would put to good use in his first Navy assignment. As the war began, Congressman Owen Lovejoy secured an appointment for William Keeler as acting assistant paymaster and clerk in December 1861. Keeler was ordered to duty in the ironclad *USS Monitor* at the Brooklyn Navy Yard in 1862.

Keeler learned his job quickly and served on *Monitor* throughout her commissioned life, including during her famous battle with the ironclad *CSS Virginia* (or *Merrimac*). In heavy seas in the Atlantic, en route to that epic battle, engine-room blowers on *Monitor* failed, and the engineers were felled by fumes. Keeler rushed below, assessed the hazardous situation, and used his knowledge of engines to correct the problem. In the process, he climbed over heaps of coal to rescue an unconscious sailor. He then took charge of the engines until morning, when the engineers had recovered sufficiently to resume their duties.

Monitor eventually reached Hampton Roads, where Paymaster Keeler relayed orders from the captain to the chief gunner during the battle with *Virginia*. A Confederate shell struck the pilothouse, wounding and blinding the skipper, LT John L. Worden, and Keeler rendered aid to him. The night after the battle, the weary paymaster, who had experienced three consecutive sleepless nights, stood the mid watch for a line officer he thought was in greater need of sleep. A few days after the battle, Keeler sent the end of an unexploded shell to President Lincoln, "With the respects of the officers of the *Monitor*."

Monitor departed Hampton Roads on 29 December 1863 and headed south in tow of the side-wheel gunboat *Rhode Island*. The next day, the tranquil seas turned ugly as the little convoy was passing Cape Hatteras, the infamous "Graveyard of the Atlantic." *Monitor* was not the most seaworthy of vessels and began to take on water. The condition worsened, extinguishing the ironclad's furnaces and dooming her to sink.

Keeler went below to save his record books and the government cash, but could not open his safe, which was completely below water. With great difficulty he made his way on deck but was swept overboard by a huge wave, only to be returned by the back-set of the wave. He was rescued by a launch from *Rhode Island* and experienced a hazardous trip across a half-mile of sea. Because his hand had been smashed during the ordeal he could not grasp a lifeline. When a bight was passed down, he slipped it under his arms and was hauled aboard to safety, if not comfort.

While the saga of *Monitor* was playing out, the Navy was cutting orders for her new skipper, Captain Bankhead, to assume command of the blockader *USS Florida*. Bankhead requested that Paymaster Keeler be assigned to his new command. Keeler was delighted that his captain had asked for him and considered it approval of his performance in *Monitor*.

Keeler's experience in *Florida* was not as memorable as the glorified life in *Monitor*. Blockade duty involved several minor skirmishes as *Florida* encountered many blockade-runners, captured three of them, and assisted in destruction of several others. Paymaster Keeler was wounded twice. The first wound was serious enough to require three months to heal and earn him a pension of $10 a month. He characteristically chose to remain aboard ship throughout his recuperation.

William Keeler was detached from *Florida* and returned home to La-Salle and civilian life in November 1865. He received his official release from service in April 1866.

Sources

Aboard the USS Monitor, *1863: The Letters of Paymaster William Frederick Keel-*

er, U.S. Navy to His Wife, Anna. Vol. 1. Annapolis: Naval Institute Press, 1964.
Aboard the USS Florida, *1863–65: The Letters of Paymaster William Frederick Keeler, U.S. Navy to His Wife, Anna.* Vol. 2. Annapolis: Naval Institute Press, 1968.

Duties of Paymasters

The Civil War had been raging for more than three years when Louville H. Merrill, a resident of Cumberland Centre, Maine, secured an appointment as acting assistant paymaster in July 1864. He was assigned to the steamer *USS Yankee,* in which he served throughout his brief service as a navyman.

Merrill's service is notable for the two letterbooks he compiled while serving in *Yankee,* which was attached to the Potomac Flotilla and became part of the blockade system on station in the Chesapeake Bay. He provided detailed accounts of a paymaster's responsibilities for a ship on routine blockade duty with such limited combat as engaging in shore bombardments. *Yankee* occasionally was used as a transport, including ferrying Union troops and Confederate prisoners. The Louville H. Merrill letterbooks are in the East Carolina Manuscript Collection (no. 627.1) in the J. Y. Joyner Library, East Carolina University, Greenville, North Carolina.

Another supply officer who chronicled the day-to-day details of duty was Acting Assistant Paymaster Benjamin Franklin Munroe, who served four years—and only three of those as a commissioned officer. Munroe was clerk to Captain William Murine, flag officer of the Gulf Blockading Squadron, in the frigate *USS Colorado* and was present at the capture of New Orleans. Munroe passed an examination for acting assistant paymaster in August 1863 and was commissioned the following month. He posted bond and reported to *USS Supply,* a square-rigged sailing vessel (fourth-rate) assigned to the South Atlantic Blockading Squadron. In 1864 he was transferred on special duty to the screw steamer *USS Neurus,* assigned to the North Atlantic Blockading Squadron. He kept copies of much of his correspondence with Navy Secretary Welles. Eighty-one such items are in the archives of the Navy Supply Corps Museum at Athens, Georgia. They provide interesting insight into the routine of supplying fleet men-of-war from supply ships. After the war, Benjamin Franklin Munroe became a prominent stockbroker with Stearns and Beale in New York City.

Direct Purchases by Bureau Chiefs

As early as 1861 navy agents had complained to Secretary Welles about direct purchases by the bureau chiefs. J. S. Blood, agent at Norfolk, reminded Welles in late 1861 that, in addition to being the disbursing officer, he was also the purchasing officer of the station. He maintained that even the chief of the Bureau of Provisions and Clothing allegedly had "lately made in this city extensive purchases of navy beef and pork, flour, bread, tobacco, whiskey and arranged for freight." Inasmuch as the navy agents' compensation included a percentage of government funds disbursed, the Norfolk agent believed that the chief's actions substantially reduced his income. Other agents complained that line officers were purchasing goods directly and that "only the navy agent should be the buyer."

In early 1862 navy agents at Washington, New York, and Boston, noting the increased wartime activity at their respective stations, requested additional clerks to handle the workload. Shortly after assuming office, Secretary Welles issued a commission to his brother-in-law, George D. Morgan, as a navy agent and gave him broad powers to buy vessels for the Union Navy. In 1861 Morgan purchased 90 vessels at a personal gain of $70,000. In contrast, John M. Forbes, acquiring ships in New England, worked without compensation. Through the combined efforts of Morgan and Forbes, the Navy acquired 479 vessels by the end of the war in 1865.

Navy agents on overseas stations complained constantly about suffering financially because of the decline of business. Many Navy ships had been withdrawn from international stations to support the war effort on blockade duty. As a result, fewer Navy vessels were calling at foreign ports to draw supplies from the agents at those ports. Overseas agents also were having to deal with the problem—real or imagined—of Southern sympathizers. Agents at Rio de Janiero, Hong Kong, and Sardinia expressed their concerns to Secretary Welles.

H. McColley, naval storekeeper at Valparaiso, Chile, frequently complained that stores aboard the storeship *Fredonia* were "not in the condition that I would like." Of the commanding officer of *Fredonia,* McColley wrote, "I find Captain Watson a noble and strong Union man, although a Virginian." He recommended appointment of inspectors and storekeepers who knew the quality of provisions and what steps they should take to prevent spoilage in warm climates.

Establishing a Confederate Navy

The South had started out with no navy, no maritime tradition, no reserve of trained seamen, no major shipyard, and no marine engine-building capability. The Confederate Congress realized that a navy was a necessity and, on 20 February 1861, established a Navy Department. The rebel government issued a call for "all persons versed in naval affairs to consult with the Committee on Naval Affairs." President Jefferson Davis appointed Stephen R. Mallory of Florida, former chairman of the Naval Affairs Committee of the U.S. Senate, to be secretary of the Navy for the Confederate States of America.

Breaking the Union Blockade

Mallory knew that to have any chance of winning the war, the Confederacy had to break the Union blockade. Through his former chairmanship of the U.S. Senate's Naval Affairs Committee he was aware of the technological developments by the navies of major European nations. He was determined to make use of Old World technology to achieve his goals.

Mallory moved quickly to disrupt the maritime trade of the United States. He arranged to have fast and powerful commerce raiders constructed in England and France. The South also managed to build locally several powerful ironclads for defense. The Confederate commerce raiders *CSS Florida* and *CSS Alabama* had highly successful careers, taking prizes worth more than $8 million. However, their exploits were insufficient to turn the tide of war in favor of the Confederacy.

As for the blockade, Mallory's solution was to commission hundreds of small, fast blockade-runners to take advantage of the deficiencies in the Union effort. Although the blockade was politically and popularly well received in the North, it was strategically a failure. Southern blockade-runners pierced the Union line of ships time and time again along the Atlantic and Gulf coasts. These daring vessels were successful in avoiding interception and delivered 80 percent of the contraband arms they carried from Europe.

Even in the latter months of the war and despite the Union's continuing strengthening of its blockade force, the Confederacy was still receiving significant shipments through Wilmington. Between October 1864 and January 1865, blockade-runners brought 69,000 muskets, 43 cannon, 750 tons of lead, nearly 100 tons of saltpeter, 546,000 pairs of shoes, and 4,300 tons of meat into that North Carolina port city.

Confederate Navy Personnel

One of the first challenges for the new Confederate Navy was recruiting officers. The obvious source was the significant number of native Southerners serving in the U.S. Navy, many of whom had recently left Union service.

The Confederate Navy adopted the system of making purchases through civilian naval agents, who were representatives of the Office of Provisions and Clothing. Their duties were also similar to those of their U.S. Navy counterparts: to acquire items for use throughout the Navy. They had the power to make contracts with manufacturers and to pay contractors. Paymasters performed the agents' duties when there was no agent present at a specific location.

Material acquired by the naval agents was sent to storehouses or directly to commands that ordered or required it. The Confederacy maintained three naval storehouses under the charge of civilian naval storekeepers. The most important naval storehouse was inland at Charlotte, North Carolina, and the other two were at Albany, Georgia, and Mobile, Alabama. Curiously, the facility at Mobile was the only Confederate depot located adjacent to deep water.

The question of the loyalty of Union military personnel and civilian employees suspected of Southern sympathies was an issue for agents and storekeepers. One agent asked Secretary Welles to clarify whether instructions regarding the status of resigned officers applied equally to officers who had submitted resignations on which the U.S. Navy had not yet acted.

Navy Agent Austin E. Smith in San Francisco was a native Virginian and made no effort to hide his Southern sentiments. When Smith decided to return to the South, his successor, Richard Cheney, complained to Secretary Welles on 3 June 1861 that Smith had left no books or bills and not enough money to pay current accounts. Two weeks later, Cheney reported a conversation with Smith, who had $15,000 in U.S. funds in his possession and said he was going to turn the money over to Virginia. Cheney said that the U.S. district attorney in San Francisco had told him he could not force Smith to turn over the funds despite the fact that Smith was leaving shortly to return to Virginia.

The disruption of families caused by the war was a constant issue. For example, William Speiden, Jr., naval storekeeper at Hong Kong and son of retired Paymaster William Speiden, wrote to Secretary Welles in November 1861. A board was meeting at the Brooklyn Navy Yard to consider the status of senior and disabled U.S. Navy officers residing in Southern states. The younger Speiden expressed concern over the status of his father, then living in Fauquier County, Virginia. He pointed out to the secretary, "By examining the records of the Department, you will find that the mind of Paymaster Speiden failed him while in the active discharge of his duties on board the *USS Hartford* of the East India Squadron. He was condemned by a medical survey and sent home, since which time his mind has been entirely lost to him."

Storekeeper Speiden reported that his father was unable to return to Washington where his property was located and where he was to draw his retirement pay. Young Speiden also drew the secretary's attention to another complication: his brother, a surgeon in the Confederate Army, might try to "influence his father in negative ways."

U.S. Navy Paymasters in the Confederate Navy

The Confederacy adopted a smaller version of the U.S. Navy organization but set up offices instead of bureaus, including an Office of Provisions and Clothing and a pay branch. The choice of 11 of the 13 former U.S. Navy paymasters was to sign on as paymasters in the pay branch of the Confederate Navy. One of them, Paymaster John DeBree, a Virginian, became officer-in-charge of the Office of Provisions and Clothing of the Confederate Navy. Paymaster James A. Semple, another Virginian, became DeBree's deputy and eventually succeeded him. The other eight paymasters who came over to the Confederate Navy from the U.S. Navy and their states of citizenship were:

George W. Clark (Arkansas)
James K. Harwood (Maryland)
W. W. J. Kelly (Florida)
Henry Myers (Georgia)
John W. Nixon (Louisiana)
George Ritchie (Virginia)
Felix Senac (Florida)
Thomas R. Ware (Virginia)

Paymaster Richard T. Allison, a Marylander, left the U.S. Navy and became a paymaster in the Confederate Marine Corps. Paymasters John C. Johnston, an Irishman who was a naturalized citizen of North Carolina, and Miles H. Morris of Mississippi left the U.S. Navy, but did not join the Confederate Navy.

Ranks in the Confederate Pay Branch

According to the historian Tom H. Wells, there were two ranks of commissioned officers in the pay branch—paymaster and assistant paymaster. A paymaster with more than 12 years' service ranked with commanders, and those with fewer were ranked with lieutenants. They were assigned to major staffs and the most important shore stations.

Wells reports that none of the assistant paymasters had prior naval service. They were appointed upon successfully passing an examination before three paymasters, proving their ability to keep a ship's books, and presenting letters testifying to their good character. Assistant paymasters with five years' service ranked after lieutenants. and those with fewer than five years ranked after a master. Of course, regulations did not envision that the Confederacy would last a mere four years. Promotion from assistant paymaster to paymaster was by seniority. Paymasters and assistant paymasters were required to be bonded.

A third grade of pay officer was clerk to a paymaster, an appointed noncommissioned officer who ranked with midshipmen. Paymasters' clerks were appointed on the recommendation of paymasters with approval of their captains.

Duties of officers of the Confederate Pay Branch were similar to those of their U.S. Navy counterparts. Petty officers were the ship's stewards and ship's cooks.

Confederate Navy Supply Leaders

Paymaster John DeBree, a native of New Jersey, served in the U.S. Navy for 44 years before resigning his commission in June 1861 after his adopted state, Virginia, seceded. He was appointed paymaster in the Confederate States Navy in October 1862, to rank from March 1861.

Paymaster DeBree was an old man when he became officer-in-charge, Office of Provisions and Clothing of the CSN and head of the Confederacy's naval supply system. He was an accommodating man, but conservative. DeBree served in the position until April 1864, when he was replaced by Paymaster James Semple. DeBree then served in the Semmes Naval Brigade and was paroled at Greensboro, North Carolina, shortly after the Civil War ended in April 1865.

James A. Semple was another of the 11 U.S. Navy paymasters who defected to the South at the start of the Civil War. He had served in the Union Navy for 17 years before resigning in June 1861. A native Virginian, he was the son-in-law of former president John Tyler. His commission as paymaster in the Confederate Navy, issued in October 1862, ranked him from March 1861.

Semple participated in the Battle of Hampton Roads in *CSS Virginia* and at Drewrys Bluff, Virginia, from 1862 to 1864. He was brought into the Office of Provisions and Clothing by Paymaster DeBree, who became increasingly dependent upon the younger officer. Semple and DeBree were exact opposites. Semple was aggressive, admired by fellow naval officers, and considered thoroughly competent for the job. He served as officer-in-charge until the Confederacy collapsed in April 1865. He died in 1886.

A 700-Ship Navy

The end of the Civil War found the U.S. Navy with almost 700 ships in commission, including 65 ironclads. The men and ships of the U.S. Navy had been successful in carrying out Lincoln's Anaconda Plan to strangle the Confederacy from both east and west and had earned the respect of the world's sea powers.

The Confederate Navy was no longer in existence. The South's ships, long neglected as a result of both material and personnel shortages, were in poor condition and of little use. The Southern officers and men, who had made a proud and dedicated effort in vain, returned to civilian life. Their cause had been doomed to failure from the beginning in the face of overwhelming Union superiority in both manpower and resources. The Confederate Navy officers and sailors could take consolation, however, in the knowledge that they had put up a good fight and that their blockade-runners had achieved astonishing success in penetrating the Union's lines.

The experience of the Civil War led to the conclusion that making Navy purchases through civilian naval agents, a system in use by the U.S. Navy since 1776, led to abuses. The position of navy agent was abolished in 1865, and agents' duties were assigned to Navy paymasters.

Sources

Sources for material used in this chapter and not cited earlier include:

Dudley, William S. *Going South: U.S. Navy Officer Resignations and Dismissals on the Eve of the Civil War.* Washington, D.C.: Naval Historical Foundation, 1981.

McKee, Christopher. *A Gentlemanly and Honorable Profession: The Creation of the U.S. Naval Officer Corps, 1794–1815.* Annapolis: Naval Institute Press, 1991.

Miller, Nathan. *The U.S. Navy: An Illustrated History.* Annapolis: Naval Institute Press, and New York: American Heritage Publishing Co., 1977.

Miscellaneous Letters Received by the Secretary of the Navy, 1801–85. The original letters are on file at the National Archives in Washington, and microfilm copies are on file at the Naval Historical Center, Washington, D.C.

Navy Supply Corps Newsletter, February 1970.

Official Records of the Union and Confederate Navies in the War of the Rebellion. Vol. 26. Washington, D.C.: U.S. Government Printing Office.

Paullin, Charles O. *Paullin's History of Naval Administration, 1775–1911.* Annapolis: Naval Institute Press, 1968.

U.S. Naval Records and Library, comp. *Register of Officers of the Confederate*

States Navy. 1898, revised 1933. Reprint. Mattituck, N.Y.: J. M. Carroll, 1983.

Wells, Tom H. *The Confederate Navy: A Study in Organization*. University: University of Alabama Press, 1971.

The first *USS Supply,* 1846-79, a ship-rigged sailing vessel, was purchased by the Navy to support Commodore Perry's forces in the Mexican-American War. (Smithsonian Institution and *Navy Supply Corps Newsletter*)

Berth-deck cooks in *USS Powhatan* during the late 19th century. (Naval Historical Center)

Sailors of *USS Mohican* in 1888 illustrate the Navy's characterization as "iron men and wooden ships." (Official U.S. Navy photograph)

Recruits clean their mess gear at Naval Training Center Great Lakes in 1918. (*Navy Supply Corps Newsletter*)

Paymasters and medical officers, Naval Hospital, Memphis, 1863. (Official U.S. Navy photograph)

Shown together in 1918 are (left to right) Secretary of the Navy Josephus Daniels, Paymaster General Sam McGowan, and Assistant Secretary of the Navy Franklin D. Roosevelt. (Naval Historical Center)

Norfolk Naval Station Supply Department buildings under construction around the Old Pine Beach Hotel in 1919. (Official U.S. Navy photograph)

USS Sacramento (PG-19) is refueled from coal barge in San Diego harbor circa 1920. (*Navy Supply Corps Newsletter*)

The famous class of 1939-40, Naval Finance and Supply School Philadelphia, produced 4 flag officers, including 2 chiefs of the Corps, and many World War II heroes. (*Navy Supply Corps Newsletter*)

USS Cyclops (A-C-4) coals a battleship in the early 20th century. (*Navy Supply Corps Newsletter*)

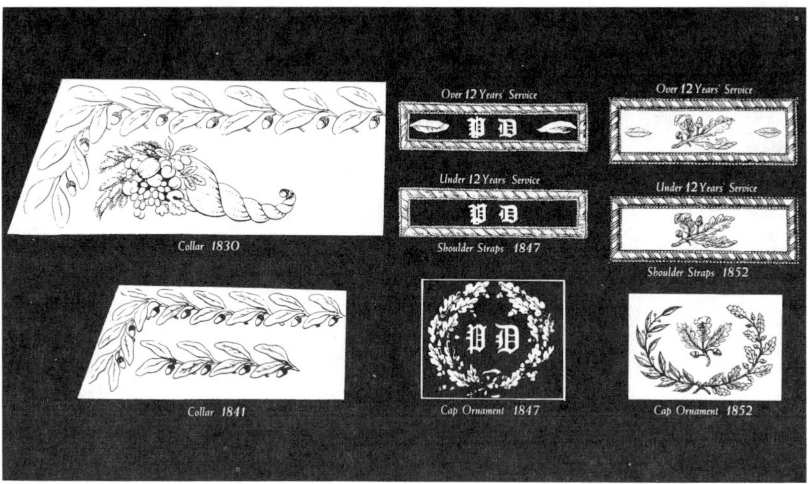

The evolution of the Supply Corps insignia. (*Navy Supply Corps Newsletter*)

CHAPTER FOUR

Reconstruction and Building a Modern Navy

1866–98

Reconciliation and reconstruction became the objectives of a nation that had suffered huge losses while winning the fight to keep the Union intact. The American public, preoccupied with recovery from the devastating war that left the nation saddled with massive debt, was not concerned that its Navy fell behind other seafaring nations in numbers of combatant ships. Patriotic civilians who had responded to their respective side's call resumed the lives they left when they went off to war.

As it had twice before—and several times since—the victorious Union began to dismantle its armed forces. With war over, the numbers of U.S. Navy ships far exceeded peacetime requirements. As a result, hundreds of vessels were decommissioned. Many of the disposed ships were merchantmen or hastily built vessels of little value, so their loss was of no real concern. However, powerful ironclads and fast cruisers, the essential components of a strategic reserve, were allowed to rust and rot. By 1880, the number of ships in the Fleet had dropped to 48 outmoded vessels. The U.S. Navy ranked twelfth—behind such powers as Chile, China, and Denmark. U.S. citizens were unaware that the Navy was failing to keep up with technological developments that were propelling France, England, Germany, and Russia into the forefront of the world's sea powers.

The Bureau of Provisions and Clothing and the Navy's paymasters faced new challenges, including how to continue to provide adequate supply with greatly reduced assets to a far-flung fleet. Members of Congress recognized the importance of an elite corps of dedicated officers to provide supply support of the Navy afloat and ashore and in 1865 had legislated discontinuance of the employment of navy agents. The agents' duties were assigned to navy paymasters.

COMO Horatio Bridge, who had served for 15 years as chief of the Bureau of Provisions and Clothing, retired in 1869. He was relieved by CAPT Edward T. Dunn, a Civil War veteran with 33 years of service in supply, who was given the additional title of paymaster general a year later.

LORE OF THE CORPS

Captain Edward Thomas Dunn, USN

Chief, Bureau of Provisions and Clothing, 1869–73;
Paymaster General, 1870–73
Period of Service: 1831–74

After the war, when Edward Dunn was paymaster general and chief of the Bureau of Provisions and Clothing, he campaigned for radical changes in feeding and clothing enlisted men in the Fleet. First, he recommended that a supply of clothing be given to each enlisted man at no cost to the individual. Second, he proposed that tea, coffee, and sugar rations be increased. In May 1872, Congress gave him part of what he requested when an act was passed increasing the sugar and coffee rations.

Born in the District of Columbia in 1812, Dunn was commissioned in the Navy in February 1831. His first assignment was in the sloop *John Adams,* Mediterranean Squadron, until 1834, when he reported to the Pacific Squadron, first aboard the schooner *Boxer* and in 1836 in the sloop *Vincennes.* He subsequently served in the frigate *Macedonian,* West India Squadron, from 1837 to 1840, then in the receiving ship *Norfolk* in 1845 and in the frigate *Columbus,* East India Squadron, in 1846. He was on duty in the Pacific Squadron during the Mexican War.

He came ashore for a brief tour at the New York Navy Yard before returning to *Columbus* for duty with the Home Squadron from 1852 to 1855. He spent the next three years at the Norfolk Navy Yard and then went back to sea in the sloop *St. Marys,* attached to the Pacific Squadron.

He served as fleet paymaster for the West Gulf Blockading Squadron from 1863 to 1865, when he became paymaster at Baltimore. In July 1869 he was promoted to captain and appointed chief of the Bureau of Provisions and Clothing. During his tour as chief, the Act of July 1870 officially established the Pay Corps of the Navy, and he was designated paymaster general. This designation remained in effect until the organization was renamed the Supply Corps nearly 50 years later.

PMG Dunn pleaded for the Navy to provide early-morning coffee or tea for the men, saying, "It is the practice on board vessels of the Navy to have the men called up at daylight in the morning, and not to have breakfast until 8 o'clock, and it is almost the universal custom and considered highly necessary to health, for persons in malarious and tropical climates, immediately upon rising to take a cup of tea or coffee." He was gratified when Congress enacted such legislation in May 1872, and the ration of coffee and sugar for Navy enlisted men was increased. In his annual report at year-end, he stated that the increase had given great satisfaction to the men and added much to their health and comfort.

Following detachment from the Bureau in February 1873, Captain Dunn was placed on the retired list and ordered to special duty at the Naval Station, New Orleans, and at navy yards at Pensacola, Florida, and Mare Island, California. He then returned to Washington in August 1873. He retired at the age of 62 in 1874 and died at Baltimore in September 1887.

Source

Official Biography. Naval Supply Systems Command, n.d.

The Pay Corps

In 1870 Congress established a separate Pay Corps, enhancing the status of paymasters. The legislation designated the chief of the Bureau of Provisions and Clothing as paymaster general to head the new corps. At last the Fleet's professional business men had an administrative home and an official Navy leader.

The *Virginius* Episode and a New Course

Naval historians speculate that the deterioration of the U.S. Navy would have continued indefinitely had not the captain of a Spanish warship injudiciously decided in October 1873 to seize a Cuban-owned ship, the

Virginius, that was illegally flying the flag of the United States. The Spaniards took the *Virginius,* which was loaded with Cuban revolutionaries, into the port of Santiago, Cuba, then a Spanish colony.

The Spaniards quickly held courts martial and shot 53 passengers and crewmen, some of them Americans. The American public was indignant, but, when the Spaniards released the *Virginius* and 102 survivors, war was averted for the next quarter century. The Cubans also paid an indemnity, although they proved conclusively that the ship had been sailing under false colors.

According to naval historian Nathan Miller, when the Navy used a fleet of Civil War relics to put on a show of power off Key West for the benefit of Spain, it was the largest armada gathered in one place since the war. But as the collection of "stubby monitors, graceful steam frigates, and sloops" puttered along at a barely perceptible 4.5 knots, Navy officers were appalled at the sight. A future admiral, CAPT Robley D. Evans, commented, "Two modern vessels of war would have done us up in 30 minutes." Evans did not blame the Navy. "We did the best we could with what Congress gave us."

Although steam ships had proved their superiority during the Civil War, a major logistical problem compelled the U.S. Navy to returned to sail after the war. The Navy did not have the necessary coaling capability to support a sizable steam fleet in foreign waters. Congress refused to appropriate the necessary funds to expand the Navy and its support facilities because the American public did not favor it. An 1865 general order required all Navy vessels to have "full sail power." The number of propeller blades on steamships was reduced from four to two to improve sailing qualities, and boilers on steamships were either removed or replaced by smaller ones.

Officers were embarrassed that their ships were ridiculed by foreigners. CAPT (later RADM) Alfred Thayer Mahan was stung when a Frenchman belittled the ancient muzzle-loading guns of an American warship. Meanwhile, in 1873 the British launched *Devastation,* the coal-fired steam prototype of the modern battleship, complete with heavy armor and powerful twin turrets. The Royal Navy claimed that she could sail from England to North America and back without recoaling. Many influential Navy and civilian officials believed that the United States should not adopt any of revolutionary developments until the Europeans had tested them thoroughly.

As discouraging as official actions were, the *Virginius* episode had set in motion developments that would eventually propel the United States and the Navy onto a new course that would take it into the top rank of international sea powers.

In July 1873, COMO John O. Bradford, another Civil War veteran, was appointed chief of the Bureau of Provisions and Clothing in relief of Captain Dunn.

Commodore John Otis Bradford, PC, USN

Chief, Bureau of Provisions and Clothing, and Paymaster General, 1873–77
Period of Service: 1845–77

Paymaster General John Bradford was the only incumbent of that position who left the Bureau in the hands of an acting chief during his incumbency.

He was born at Wilmington, Delaware, in 1815 and married the daughter of a well-known Boston minister named Taylor. Bradford was commissioned a purser from Pennsylvania in March 1845. During his first six years on active duty, he served at sea in three Navy sloops from 1845 to 1851: *Saratoga, Germantown,* and *Portsmouth*. Following shore duty at the Boston Navy Yard from 1854 to 1855, he returned to sea duty in 1855 in the steam frigate *San Jacinto* and was assigned to the receiving ship *Boston* from 1860 to 1861.

In 1862, he came ashore at the Boston Navy Yard then went back to sea briefly in 1863 with the West Coast Blockading Squadron before being assigned later in 1863 as fleet paymaster, South Atlantic Blockading Squadron. He served as inspector of provisions at New York from 1865 to 1867, when he returned to sea as fleet paymaster, European Squadron. In 1869 he was assigned as paymaster at New York and promoted to pay director in 1871.

Bradford was appointed chief of the Bureau of Provisions and Clothing in January 1873, with the rank of commodore, and immediately turned over the helm to Acting Chief James H. Watmough. Although available records do not provide details of his reason for this action, Bradford spent nearly two years in Great Britain. The trip was widely believed to be for the purpose of conducting financial negotiations with the British government. He returned to Washington in the fall of 1874 and only then did he assume the normal duties of chief of the Bureau.

One of Bradford's first reports to the secretary of the Navy promoted the idea of giving enlisted men a credit of three months' pay in lieu of the outfit of clothing that several of his predecessors had recommended. Bradford concluded, "It would be more effectual to prevent desertion than an outfit of clothing to each man upon shipment." He later recommended adoption of a plan similar to the Army's to encourage thrift among sailors by which any balance on the paymaster's books for individual sailors should bear interest at the rate of 4 percent a year.

He also recommended in 1875 that appointments to the Pay Corps be made from graduates of the Naval Academy, citing the favorable experience of the Engineering Corps of academy appointments. Bradford told the secretary that the "proposed change would tend to promote unity of feeling between line and staff officers and add materially to the efficiency of the Naval service."

Commodore Bradford retired upon completion of his tour as paymaster general in February 1877. When he died in June 1879 in New York City *The New York Times* gave pneumonia as the cause of his death. The *Washington Evening Star* reported that he died "on account of old age." Both newspapers agreed that COMO Bradford was "a genial companion and a kind friend" to his large circle of acquaintances.

Sources

Hamersly, Lewis. *Records of Living Officers of the U.S. Navy and Marine Corps.* 4th ed. Philadelphia: L. R. Hamersly, 1890.

Official Biography. Naval Supply Systems Command, n.d.

A Navy Paymaster in the Imperial Japanese Navy

No duty performed by a Pay Corps officer was more unusual than the mission Paymaster Jonathan Q. Barton undertook in 1874, when he was granted a leave of absence to serve in the Imperial Japanese Navy.

LORE OF THE CORPS

Paymaster Jonathan Q. Barton, PC, USN

Special Duty, Japanese Imperial Navy, 1874–77
Period of Service: 1864–93

Well known to naval historians is Commodore Matthew C. Perry's role in opening Japan to the Western world in the mid-nineteenth Century. Less well known is the fact that a U.S. Navy paymaster—Jonathan Q. Barton—was granted a leave of absence in 1874 to serve for three years in the Imperial Japanese Navy, the only American to have done so voluntarily.

Born in Maine, Jonathan Barton was appointed acting assistant paymaster in January 1864 and posted his bond the following month. He was assigned to *USS Relief,* a storeship that sailed from America, delivered supplies to the Rio de Janiero Station, and then continued through the Straits of Magellan to China. Barton remained aboard *Relief* in the East Indies and Asiatic Station for two years. He was commissioned as assistant paymaster in March 1867 and ordered to duty in *USS Saco* on the North Atlantic Station. He was promoted to passed assistant paymaster in 1870.

In 1873, Paymaster Barton reported again to *Relief,* which had become the receiving ship at the Washington Navy Yard. While in that assignment, the Navy granted him leave in October 1874 to go to Japan to organize a pay department and "be the instructor of accounts for Japanese youth." He completed his assignment in October 1877.

Barton obviously did an excellent job in his unusual assignment. The Japanese government requested that he be allowed to stay in Japan and continue his service, but the U.S. Navy denied the request, and Barton returned to the United States. In 1878 the emperor of Japan conferred upon Paymaster Barton the Fourth Class of the Order of the Rising Sun in recognition of his unique service to that nation.

Once home, Barton became a member of the Navy Board of Inspection in 1878 and then went back to sea in *Nipsic* to the West Indies, Mediterranean, and North Africa from 1879 to 1883. He was promoted to paymaster in May 1882 and served three tours of shore duty before returning to sea duty in 1891. Barton retired in August 1893 for a disability unrelated to his naval service.

Sources

Hamersly, Lewis. *Records of Living Officers of the U.S. Navy and Marine Corps.* 5th ed. Philadelphia: L. R. Hamersly, 1902.

Miscellaneous Papers and Documents of Paymaster Jonathan Q. Barton, 1887–92. Navy Supply Corps Museum, Athens, Ga.

Official Biography. Naval Supply Systems Command, n.d.

Paymasters in Varied Assignments

The business orientation and training of Navy paymasters produced a corps of officers uniquely qualified to undertake a wide variety of assignments, often in severe crises. For example, in the summer of 1885 Passed Assistant Paymaster (later Pay Director) John R. Martin undertook a special assignment when he was detailed as commissary officer ashore at Aspinwall, Colombia, during the Colombian Revolution.

While Paymaster Bradford was overseas at the start of his tour of duty, Pay Director James H. Watmough was acting chief of the Bureau of Provisions and Clothing. Then, with two apparently satisfactory years of administrative experience in Bradford's absence, Watmough was appointed to the position when John Bradford retired.

LORE OF THE CORPS

Pay Director James Horatio Watmough, PC, USN

Chief, Bureau of Provisions and Clothing, and Paymaster General, 1877
Period of Service: 1843–84

James H. Watmough is best remembered for two distinctions: He is the only chief of the Bureau who studied to be a medical doctor before entering the Navy, and he served as chief for only one year. He was acting chief for nearly two years while his predecessor, RADM John O. Bradford, served on a special assignment in Great Britain from early 1873 to the fall of 1874.

Rear Admiral Watmough was born at Whitemarsh, Pennsylvania, in 1822 and attended the University of Pennsylvania. He was appointed an acting midshipman in November 1843 and appointed to the Naval Academy in December 1844. He became a purser in 1844 and served in the Pacific Squadron from 1844 to 1848. During the Mexican War, he participated in most of the actions in California. He then served in several ships, including *USS Constitution,* off the coast of Africa from 1849 to 1855, followed by duty on the Great Lakes and Gulf of Mexico from 1857 to 1860, when he was promoted to paymaster. Two Spanish steamers were captured during his tour in *USS Saratoga* in the Gulf.

Watmough was paymaster of the Philadelphia Navy Yard at the start of the Civil War, but he soon went back to sea. He was fleet paymaster, South Atlantic Blockading Squadron, from 1864 to 1865 and participated in most of the operations of the squadron. Following postwar duty ashore he was promoted to pay director in 1871 and became general inspector of the Bureau before assuming its temporary charge in January 1873. In February 1877 Watmough became chief in his own right but served only through mid-November of that year. He retired in July 1884 and was promoted to rear admiral in 1906. He continued to live in

Washington and was 95 when he died in January 1917— the oldest Navy officer on the retired list.

Sources

Hamersly, Lewis. *Records of Living Officers of the U.S. Navy and Marine Corps.* 7th ed. Philadelphia: L. R. Hamersly, 1902.

Official Biography. Naval Supply Systems Command, n.d.

The Apprentice System for Seamen

The quality and quantity of American seamen declined in the decade following the Civil War. Many sailors serving in U.S. Navy ships were foreigners who had been enlisted at ports around the world on an as-needed basis. When an officer surveyed the citizenship of 128 men aboard his ship in 1876, he counted 47 Americans, 21 Chinese, 20 Irish, 9 British, and representatives of 22 other nations. At the gangway of a ship, Commodore Stephen B. Luce spotted a sign that read, "Ici on parle Anglais" [English spoken here]. Although the sign had been a jest, Luce thought it properly reflected a condition in which foreigners had for years been maintaining the "honor and integrity of the American flag."

Luce developed a plan for training American seamen for both the Navy and the Merchant Marine. He recommended a system for training apprentices similar to one Commodore Perry had proposed 30 years earlier. In April 1875, Congress authorized the enlistment of 750 youths between 16 and 18 to serve in the Navy until they reached the age of 21. Luce's proposal was that the youths be given preliminary instruction on station ships and then transferred to training ships to be taught seamanship, gunnery, and other nautical skills. Commodore Luce later objected when it was suggested that new recruits be trained at boot camps because he strongly favored that training be exclusively at sea.

When Pay Director Watmough completed his tour as chief in November 1877, he was succeeded by Pay Inspector George Cutter, who had been inspector of provisions and clothing at Washington since March.

LORE OF THE CORPS

Pay Inspector George Francis Cutter, PC, USN

Chief, Bureau of Provisions and Clothing, and Paymaster General, 1877–81
Period of Service: 1838–81

George F. Cutter served as chief of the Bureau for nearly four years and is best remembered for the establishment of a Naval Clothing Factory at Brooklyn, New York.

He was born in August 1819 in Massachusetts and commenced his Navy career in 1838 as captain's clerk in *USS Cayne,* serving with the Mediterranean Squadron until 1841. He was commissioned a purser in June 1844 and went to sea in *USS Truxtun* of the African Squadron. Later, while operating in the Gulf of Mexico in August 1846, *Truxtun* was wrecked. Purser Cutter was taken prisoner by the Mexicans, but he was released on parole and exchanged the following month. He served in the receiving ship *Franklin* at Boston from December 1846 to April 1847 and married Mary Louisa Forster of Somerville, Massachusetts, in June 1847.

Cutter reported to *USS Albany* in the Gulf of Mexico in August 1847 and returned to Boston in 1851 for duty in the receiving ship *Ohio.* His next duty was in *USS Massachusetts* with the Pacific Squadron until April 1854. In October 1857 he reported to duty at the Portsmouth Navy Yard. He went back to sea at the start in 1860 in the steamer *Richmond,* attached to the Mediterranean Squadron.

Richmond transferred to the Western Gulf Squadron at the start of the Civil War and participated in operations leading to the capture of New Orleans, Vicksburg, and Port Hudson. From April to December 1863, Cutter was assigned to the flagship *San Jacinto* as fleet paymaster, East Coast Blockading Squadron. He served as inspector of provisions and clothing, Boston Navy Yard, for three years to December 1866. He was purchasing paymaster, New York, for two months in the summer of 1867 and in October 1867 became fleet paymaster, Asiatic Squadron, serving in that position until July 1869.

After several tours of shore duty at Boston and New York, Cutter was made general inspector of provisions and clothing at Washington in March 1877. Eight months later, he was appointed paymaster general and chief of the Bureau.

In a report to the secretary of the Navy in 1870 on the completion of the Navy Clothing Factory, Cutter claimed, "Here clothing can be made at a lesser rate than could be obtained by the contract system, besides being of better workmanship and more strictly in accordance with prescribed uniforms."

Cutter was also concerned with the professional status of paymasters and recommended that "assistant paymasters of the Navy be placed on the same footing as assistant surgeons and be made eligible for promotion after three years service."

He retired in 1881 and remained in Washington, where he died in September 1890. He was buried at Boston, but his remains were moved to Arlington National Cemetery in 1894.

Sources

Hamersly, Lewis. *Records of Living Officers of the U.S. Navy and Marine Corps.* 4th ed. Philadelphia: L. R. Hamersly, 1890.

Official Biography. Naval Supply Systems Command, n.d.

A Decline in Ships

The number and condition of U.S. Navy ships continued to reflect the reluctance of Congress to appropriate funds for modernization. From 203 ships in 1869, the Navy declined to 139 in 1881, although only about 50 were actually in commission, The decline, largely from 1869 to 1877, was caused by losses at sea and sale or by the breaking up of obsolete or worthless vessels. Those that remained were approaching obsolescence. For example, flagships of Navy squadrons in 1876 were all wooden, screw-propelled steamers with auxiliary sail power. Between 1869 and 1877, Congress appropriated funds for only 10 small naval craft.

It was in this atmosphere of limited resources that Rear Admiral Joseph A. Smith relieved Pay Inspector Cutter in June 1882 as chief of the Bureau of Provisions and Clothing and paymaster general of the Pay Corps.

LORE OF THE CORPS

Rear Admiral Joseph Adams Smith, PC, USN

Chief, Bureau of Provisions and Clothing, and Paymaster General, 1882–86
Period of Service: 1861–99

RADM J. Adams Smith, a lawyer who entered the Navy at the start of the Civil War, participated in one of the great battles in U.S. Navy history. While an assistant paymaster in the steam sloop *USS Kearsarge,* he commanded her powder division during the epic battle with the Confederate cruiser *CSS Alabama,* resulting in the sinking of the *Alabama* off Cherbourg, France, on 19 June 1864.

Born at Machais, Maine, in September 1837, Smith received his LL.D. from Harvard University Law School. He offered his services to his country when the Civil War broke out and was appointed assistant paymaster in October 1861. His first assignment was in special service in *Kearsarge,* and he was promoted to paymaster in 1862. After the Civil War, Paymaster Smith decided not to return to the practice of law, but to stay in the Navy. He was assigned to the receiving ship *USS Constellation* in February 1865, with collateral duty in charge of accounts for a number of seagoing ships. He was fleet paymaster, Gulf Squadron, from 1866 to 1867. Following duty at Boston at the end of the decade, he became judge advocate general court martial, in March 1870 and again in February 1871.

He completed a cruise through the Straits of Magellan to California in *USS California* in July 1870. After a series of routine sea and shore duties, he reported to duty at the Naval Academy in October 1874. In August 1875, he became fleet paymaster of the Asiatic Station until July 1878. He was promoted to pay inspector in May 1879 and appointed paymaster general and chief of the Bureau in June 1882.

Smith presided over the Bureau during a quiet period in history and completed his tour in 1886. He then continued on active duty, including tours as general storekeeper at Portsmouth from 1889 to 1892, and was promoted to pay director in November 1891. He was general storekeeper at Washington from 1892 to 1895, served a short tour on the Naval Examining Board in 1895, and was general storekeeper at League Island from 1895 to 1896. He was general storekeeper, purchasing paymaster, and paymaster at Havana from 1891 to 1899, and his last tour was as general storekeeper at Philadelphia. He was a rear admiral when he retired in September 1899 and died in 1907.

Sources

Hamersly, Lewis. *Records of Living Officers of the U.S. Navy and Marine Corps.* 4th ed. Philadelphia: L. R. Hamersly, 1890.

Official Biography. Naval Supply Systems Command, n.d.

The Transformation into a Modern Sea Power

Transformation of the U.S. Navy from the age of sail into a modern sea power began in 1881 when newly elected President James A. Garfield appointed William H. Hunt as secretary of the Navy. Hunt, an experienced and capable politician, believed that bickering among senior officers ruined any chance of support for increased appropriations from Congress, and he convened a Naval Advisory Board to develop a comprehensive plan for a modern Navy.

The board came up with a plan to construct 68 modern steam-propelled vessels, including 18 steel cruisers. Hunt was unable to implement the plan before President Garfield was assassinated and his successor, Chester A. Arthur, replaced Hunt with William F. Chandler. However, Chandler pleasantly surprised proponents of a modern Navy when he proceeded with a modernization program.

Further impetus was given to modernization in July 1882 when a British fleet reduced to rubble the fortifications around Alexandria, Egypt—stronger than any protecting major American ports. Witness to the successful Royal Navy bombardment was the steam sloop *USS Lancaster,* whose officers described the awesome destruction. Navy officials in Washington were duly impressed. At about the same time, the Chilean navy ordered the protected cruiser *Esmeralda* to be constructed in Great Britain. She would incorporate an armored deck, 10-inch breech-loading guns, a speed of 18 knots, and be clearly superior to any U.S. Navy combatant. Proponents of a strong Navy used these two events to press for a strong, modern American presence at sea.

The new, modern steel U.S. Navy became an eventual reality when Congress appropriated $1.3 million for the construction of the "ABCD" ships—the protected cruisers *Atlanta* and *Boston* (3,000 tons each), *Chicago* (4,500 tons), and the 1,500-ton dispatch vessel *Dolphin*. Despite construction delays, charges of fraud in the award of contracts, problems with procurement of the new high-quality steel, and their odd combination of steam and full sail rigging, the ABCD ships eventually were completed and gave good service.

Two more 4,000-ton protected cruisers—*Charleston,* built from British plans, and *Newark,* the last American cruiser to be fitted with full sail rigging—were authorized in 1885. The next year, Congress and the Navy took a major step by ordering two second-class battleships: *Texas* and *Maine*.

Secretary Whitney reported that large private purchases had traditionally been made by the bureau chiefs, but he intended that contracts should be awarded to the lowest bidder. Much of the business of the Navy was controlled by brokers instead of suppliers. During the fiscal year ending 30 June 1885, bureaus, acting independently, took the following actions: 7 bureaus expended $138,000 for 166 open purchases of coal, without competition; 8 bureaus made 299 open purchases of stationery; 6 bureaus bought lumber and hardware for $121,315 in 499 open purchases; 7 bureaus spent $46,000 for oils and paints in 269 purchases; 8 bureaus supplied ships with stationery; and 3 bureaus furnished lamps and lanterns.

Whitney stipulated that domestic steel and machinery must be used in construction of the two new ships, and to ensure a continuous supply of armor and forgings. He pooled all the requirements into a single $4.4 million contract. Concurrently, the Navy ordered its first high-speed torpedo boat. New, more powerful ships began to join the Fleet each year, and the Naval War College, established in 1884, provided a professional forum for developing the strategies and tactics of the future.

In 1886 the Bureau of Provisions and Clothing was organized into two divisions: Purchase and Supplies, and Accounts and Audit. That same year, the Bureau also sponsored an experiment in *USS Independence* to eliminate berth-deck messing in favor of a consolidated general mess. The Navy's financial system was revamped and the Bureau given responsibility for all Navy accounting. The concept of keeping records by classes of receipts and expenditures of material was developed.

Bureau chief Commodore James Fulton implemented an improved accounting system and centralized responsibility of purchasing of naval stores in 1886. Navy Secretary William C. Whitney, who appointed Fulton to succeed Smith, was in favor of simplified purchasing. The move to centralized purchasing was an important factor in assuaging congressional concerns over proper accounting, for the requested significantly increased appropriations for the new shipbuilding program.

LORE OF THE CORPS

Commodore James Fulton, PC, USN

Chief, Bureau of Provisions and Clothing, and Paymaster General, 1886–90
Period of Service: 1858–90

Paymaster General Fulton is alleged to have "told off" the newly appointed secretary of the Navy, Benjamin Tracy, in May 1890, when the latter challenged his authority to centralize Navy purchasing as authorized by Tracy's predecessor. While an exact quotation could not be documented, the fact remains that Commodore James Fulton is the only paymaster general to quit under fire.

A native of Tennessee and one of 13 children, Fulton received an appointment to the U.S. Naval Academy in November 1858. When he was graduated, he was commissioned a purser and reported to the storeship *Relief,* serving with the Home Squadron. He later served in the steamer *Saginaw,* with the East India Squadron, from 1859 to 1862 and temporarily in the flagship *Hartford* in 1860. He then reported to the steam sloop *Adirondack* on special service until she was wrecked in August 1862 near Abaco Island.

He next served in the steam sloop *USS Lackawana* on the West Gulf Blockading Squadron in 1863 and 1864 and participated in the Battle of Mobile Bay in August 1864. In 1865 Paymaster Fulton was transferred to the Washington Navy Yard; was a member of the Board of Examiners from 1866 to 1867 and ordered to special service in the steam frigate *Minnesota* from 1867 to 1868, when he returned to shore duty at the Philadelphia Navy Yard. He was promoted to pay inspector in March 1871 and ordered to duty as fleet paymaster, European Station, attached to the flagship *Wabash,* on which he served until 1873. In 1874 he was on temporary duty at the Navy Pay Office, Philadelphia.

Fulton was promoted to pay director in August 1876. He served as inspector of provisions and clothing, Mare Island Navy Yard and was promoted to pay director in August 1876. After another tour of temporary duty as naval storekeeper at Villefranche on the French Mediterranean coast in 1877, he returned to the San Francisco area, where he served as pay officer for the area from 1878 to 1880. He was ordered to Washington in 1880 for a series of special assignments, including inspection and examination of the accounts of disbursing officers at the Bureau of Provisions and Clothing in January 1885. He was appointed chief of the Bureau in November 1886 and promoted to commodore.

Fulton encountered many problems when he took over as head of the Bureau because the various bureaus operated independently in the matter of purchases, keeping accounts, and caring for and issuing material under their cognizance. This independence created different accounting systems and led to large and unnecessary accumulation of stores.

Fulton's tour as chief is cloaked in controversy, apparently not of his own making. Shortly after assuming the office in November 1886, then-secretary of the Navy William C. Whitney called Fulton to his office and gave him a special assignment. The secretary was convinced that there were widespread irregularities in the purchase of Navy stores as a result of each bureau of the Navy having authority to make its own purchases.

In a move designed to correct the situation, Secretary Whitney gave COMO Fulton and the Bureau of Provisions and Clothing responsibility for purchasing all Navy stores. Chiefs of the other bureaus, all line officers, balked at giving up their authority over purchases for their own fiefdoms. They accused Fulton, whom they derisively dubbed head of the Bureau of "Spuds and Duds," of empire-building. In December 1886, Secretary Whitney issued General Order 355, which specified that a complete inventory of all naval stores be taken on the first day of January 1887. The other chiefs dragged their feet on cooperation with the inventories designed to ascertain the volume and value of supplies then in the various storehouses under their control.

Although effectively ostracized by his peers, Fulton carried out his assignment and Whitney backed him completely. Fulton made considerable progress in correcting the situation through 1888, but the zeal with which he carried out Whitney's wishes made enemies among the line community. Fulton put Pay Corps inspectors on location to inventory and inspect incoming shipments to assure that other bureaus were complying with the maximum purchase threshold of $500 allowed them under new Navy Department regulations.

Fulton issued General Order 373 in June 1889, establishing the office of general inspector of the Pay Corps for the purpose of inspecting the accounts of Pay Corps officers. He also recommended that the number of assistant paymasters be increased to 25 and that future appointments be made from the graduates of the Naval Academy, subject to examination by a board of paymasters, as was then required by law.

COMO Fulton's problems increased when Secretary Tracy came into office with the new administration of President Benjamin Harrison in 1889. Tracy did not share Whitney's reform goals. Fulton's abrupt departure came after he had fired off a strong letter of reprimand to a commanding officer for violating the law and not following established purchasing requirements as spelled out in the Naval Appropriations Act of 1889. According to several written accounts, the letter was the last straw, and Tracy called Fulton on the carpet in November 1890. Fulton had also been vilified by chiefs of the other bureaus, whose friends in the press had attacked him unmercifully. The secretary purportedly had been wanting to replace the chief since taking over the office and allegedly was looking for an issue. Fulton was no longer willing to take the abuse and seized the initiative to sever the relationship.

COMO Fulton had been in the Navy 31 years at the time of his confrontation with Secretary Tracy, but his abrupt resignation as chief did not end his Navy career. He accepted an assignment at the Naval Academy in Annapolis and served as an instructor until 1894, with additional duty as a member of the Naval Examining Board in 1893.

Commodore Fulton was married twice. His first wife had died when he had taken her to Europe for health reasons. Their only child died at birth. He later remarried, and his only son died during a trip to Italy.

Commodore Fulton died at the Naval Academy in March 1895, and classes were suspended out of respect for him.

Sources

Hamersly, Lewis. *Records of Living Officers of the U.S. Navy and Marine Corps.* 4th ed. Philadelphia: L. R. Hamersly, 1890.
Official Biography. Naval Supply Systems Command, n.d.

General Inspector of Pay Corps

The Bureau of Provisions and Clothing was made purchasing agent for the entire Navy in 1889, taking over responsibility from the individual bureaus. In the same year, the Office of General Inspector of Pay Corps was established to inspect accounts of pay officers. Pay Director Thomas H. Looker was appointed to the post.

A Promise to Fulton

There was considerable speculation in the press over who would succeed Commodore Fulton. *The Army and Navy Register* reported that Secretary Tracy wanted to appoint Pay Director Edwin Stewart, but President Harrison insisted on Pay Director Thomas H. Looker. Meanwhile, Fulton remained on the job until Harrison's choice prevailed. *The Register* also reported that former President Hayes, another Ohioan, was a strong influence in the decision. Thomas Looker was promoted to commodore and confirmed as chief of the Bureau of Provisions and Clothing in March 1890. Shortly after he took office, Looker went to Fulton's quarters to assure him that he, too, would fight for the highest businesslike ethics in all Navy purchasing negotiations. Obviously, Looker's call greatly pleased Fulton. His successor's assurances vindicated Fulton's policies, if not his temper.

LORE OF THE CORPS

Rear Admiral Thomas Henry Looker, PC, USN

Chief, Bureau of Clothing and Provisions, and Paymaster General, 1890
Periods of Service: 1846–52, 1853–91

RADM Looker was chief of the Bureau and paymaster general for the shortest period of any incumbent—three months. Apparently, the short tour was due to chronic illness, which was also the reason he resigned his commission early in his career only to be recommissioned less than a year later. Looker had taken over the Bureau on short notice in March 1890 when RADM James Fulton resigned abruptly.

Thomas Looker was born in November 1829 at Cincinnati, Ohio, the son of the publisher of the *Cincinnati Gazette* and the grandson of a governor of Ohio, Othneil Looker. He entered the Naval Academy in 1846 and served through the Mexican War at sea in fleet actions in *USS Germantown* and the schooner *Flirt* and on expeditions ashore in small boats. A protracted illness, attributable to exposure in the line of duty, caused him to resign his commission in November 1852. He recovered and was reappointed a purser in August 1853.

Purser Looker's first assignment after reappointment was in the brig *Bainbridge,* followed by the sloop of war *Portsmouth.* He served during the years immediately before the Civil War in the steamer *Brooklyn,* conveying troops and instituting a blockade at the mouth of the Mississippi River. He was paymaster in charge of supplies for the North Atlantic Blockading Squadron from 1861 to 1863 and volunteered for action in the battle between *Monitor* and *Virginia* in May 1862. Looker was fleet paymaster, South Pacific Squadron, from 1866 to 1868. He was promoted to pay director in March 1871 and appointed assistant to the secretary of the Navy in 1877. He subsequently served two tours as general inspector of the Pay Corps: from 1878 to 1882 and from 1889 to 1890. Between those tours, he headed the Pay Office at Washington.

When COMO Looker was appointed chief of the Bureau and paymaster general in March 1890, *The Army and Navy Register* reported, "His record of integrity and faithful service entitled the Navy to regard him as the man who should be selected as Chief of the Bureau. He was the senior officer of the of the Corps at the time and had the support of many of the older officers of the Navy."

COMO Looker had promised his predecessor, COMO Fulton, that he would continue the reorganization of the Bureau and the purchasing reforms that Fulton had instituted and were the cause of the dispute with Secretary Tracy. However, Looker's service was too short for him to fulfill that pledge or to make any significant mark on the office.

A nervous ailment prompted COMO Looker to resign as chief in May 1890, and he resigned his Navy commission in November 1891. A more calm and tranquil life apparently had a salutary effect upon his health. He lived for almost 19 years after retirement and died at Washington in July 1910. He was buried in Cincinnati.

Sources

Hamersly, Lewis. *Records of Living Officers of the U.S. Navy and Marine Corps.* 7th ed. Philadelphia: L. R. Hamersly, 1902.
Official Biography. Naval Supply Systems Command, n.d.

Edwin Stewart

Secretary Benjamin Tracy's choice, RADM Edwin Stewart eventually became paymaster general and chief, Bureau of Provisions and Clothing, in May 1890, three months after he was passed over in favor of COMO Thomas Looker. Stewart was promoted to rear admiral and served as bureau chief for nine years.

LORE OF THE CORPS

Rear Admiral Edwin Stewart, PC, USN

Chief, Bureau of Provisions and Clothing, 1890–92;
Chief, Bureau of Supplies and Accounts, and Paymaster General, 1892–99
Period of Service: 1861–99

Edwin Stewart was chief of the Bureau when the Spanish-American War commenced, and he served throughout the hostilities. His tenure in the post—nine years—was second only to that of Horatio Bridge. Stewart presided over the reorganization of the Bureau of Provisions and Clothing, which was renamed the Bureau of Supplies and Accounts in 1892.

Stewart was a political survivor. Appointed first to the office by President Benjamin Harrison, a Republican, in May 1890, he was subsequently reappointed by Grover Cleveland, a Democrat, in May 1894 and then by the Republican William McKinley in May 1898. His visionary actions in the handling of supply problems before the start of the Spanish-American War were important to the spectacular success the United States achieved in that short conflict. The secretary of the Navy declared, "His work was performed with the most gratifying efficiency and promptness."

Edwin Stewart was born into a well-to-do family at New York City in 1837. He was educated at Andover Academy, Yale University, and Williams College, Williamstown, Massachusetts. He left Williams after only three years to join the Civil War effort. He was appointed assistant paymaster in September 1861 and ordered to duty in the steam gunboat

USS Pembina on the South Atlantic Station. Paymaster Stewart was commended for valor in operations preceding the capture of Port Royal, South Carolina. He was promoted to paymaster in April 1862. After the war, he served on the Great Lakes and at the Navy Pay Office in Washington before becoming fleet paymaster of the Asiatic Station from 1872 to 1875. He was promoted to pay inspector in March 1879 and ordered to duty as fleet paymaster, European Station from 1883 to 1885.

His last duty before his appointment as chief of the Bureau was chief pay officer at the Navy Pay Office in New York. In this post, while COMO James Fulton was chief, Stewart was largely instrumental in accomplishing the major reform in purchasing that Fulton and Secretary Whitney had begun earlier.

Stewart was a logical candidate to succeed RADM Thomas Looker, who resigned suddenly in May 1890, because Whitney had wanted Stewart in the first place, but had been overruled by President Benjamin Harrison. In addition to overseeing the reorganization and renaming of the Bureau, the new chief was a proponent of enacting into law strong professional prerequisites for appointment to the Pay Corps. When in 1897 a Reorganization Board for Personnel of the Navy sought his views, the chief made it clear that the duties of Pay Corps officers could not automatically be assumed by line officers, no matter how experienced they were. He pointed out the need for accounting expertise and suggested that raising the age limit for assistant paymasters from 25 to 30 and holding competitive examinations would produce better results. Many of his recommendations were adopted and subsequently became law.

Stewart was a rear admiral when he retired in May 1899. Williams College granted him three degrees: bachelor of arts in 1862, master of arts in 1882, and doctor of letters and laws in 1898. He died at South Orange, New Jersey, in 1933.

Sources

Hamersly, Lewis. *Records of Living Officers of the U.S. Navy and Marine Corps.* 7th ed. Philadelphia: L. R. Hamersly, 1902.

Official Biography. Naval Supply Systems Command, n.d.

A Controversial Procurement Act and New Regulations

The issue that had driven COMO James Fulton out of office was resolved when Congress enacted legislation in 1890 that included the following provision: "All supplies purchased with moneys appropriated for any branch of the naval establishment shall be deemed to be purchased for the Navy and not for any bureau thereof."

With the issue of centralized procurement and accounting for acquired material settled, and the threat of war increasing, RADM Stewart began to prepare the Bureau of Provisions and Clothing and the Pay Corps for forthcoming hostilities with Spain. Growth of the Pacific Northwest and the increasing importance of Alaska emphasized the need for a major Navy facility to serve forces operating in that area and led to the establishment of the Puget Sound Naval Shipyard.

The Bureau of Provisions and Clothing was renamed the Bureau of Supplies and Accounts in 1892 to reflect more properly the expanded responsibilities of the organization. In the following year, the Naval Supply Fund—to be administered by the Pay Corps—was established to be used in the purchase of ordinary commercial supplies. The fund was later renamed the Navy Stock Fund.

Regulations issued in 1893 authorized a pay department aboard Navy ships. The regulations also gave the title of general storekeeper to pay officers assigned duty as head of the supply department of yards and stations. In 1894 Paymaster General Stewart called attention to confusion over nonstandard stock system, and work was begun on formulating specifications covering all ordinary commercial articles used by the Navy. The office of Auditor of the Navy Department was established in the same year.

The first Navy ship's store was established in *USS Indiana* in 1896. A board was convened, also in 1896, to examine Navy specifications and simplify them to bring them into conformity with commercial practices.

War with Spain Begins

By 1898 the inevitability of war with Spain had increased dramatically. RADM Stewart believed that much of the combat would take place in the Far East, putting a great strain on logistical pipelines, particularly fresh provisions. Stewart pioneered the use of refrigerator ships in support of American forces in the Cuban and Philippine theaters.

The paymaster general prepared a memorandum in early 1898 that enabled Admiral Dewey to obtain the funds needed to purchase, within 48 hours, the collier *Nanshan* and the supply ship *Zafro* and load them with five months' supply of coal and stores. These actions, taken in advance of the start of the shooting, were major factors in decisive U.S. victories at both Manila Bay and Santiago. The startling American success against a recognized naval power resulted in the shortest war in American history--four months, from April to August 1898.

The seeds of war had been germinating throughout the 25 years since the *Virginius* affair. The United States considered purchasing or annexing Cuba. Although nothing came of the idea, Americans made significant investments in Cuba, not out of any imperialistic objective, but to help the people achieve independence from Spain. The Cubans revolted against Spanish rule in 1895.

Charles W. Littlefield was paymaster of the battleship *USS Maine,* which was sent to Havana to protect American interests. He was relieved by Paymaster (later COMO) Charles M. Ray ten days before the lid finally blew off. The catalyst was the spectacular explosion and sinking of *Maine* in Havana harbor in February 1898. Although the "yellow press" immediately charged Spaniards with sabotaging the *Maine,* the cause of the explosion has never been fully determined. Ray was aboard at that time and was reputed to be the last officer to leave the wardroom before the explosion. He suffered serious psychological injury and was ordered to duty at the Coast Survey and Pay Office, Baltimore.

Spain wanted to avoid war, but the press whipped U.S. public opinion to a frenzy, and on 25 April Congress declared war. The strength of the Spanish navy was vastly overrated. European naval observers predicted a long war, but Mahan predicted an American victory in "about three months." The Navy assembled a fleet of three first-line battleships, a smaller battleship, and two armored cruisers in the Western Atlantic and Caribbean. The battleship *Oregon* (BB-3) was ordered from the West Coast to join this fleet and raced around Cape Horn, covering the 13,000 miles from California to Key West in 66 days. The feat dramatized the need for a shorter route between the Atlantic and the Pacific. Many Americans, Theodore Roosevelt among them, vocally advocated construction of a canal across the Panamanian isthmus, which was then a part of Colombia, as the answer to speeding commerce.

The Spanish Fleet and Admiral Dewey

The Spanish fleet was ill-prepared for the imminent war, and Spaniards clearly did not want to fight. The ships, although equal in number, could not match the material condition or the morale of the Americans crews. After surveying his ships upon sailing for the Americas, Spanish Admiral Pascual Cervera y Topete gloomily commented, "Nothing can be expected . . .except the total destruction of the fleet or its hasty and demoralized return."

The U.S. Navy, on the other hand, led by the aggressive and dynamic Assistant Secretary Theodore Roosevelt, was eager to prove its superiority. The first opportunity came to Commodore Dewey's Asiatic

Squadron, consisting of the battle cruiser *USS Olympia,* three other cruisers, two gunboats, and a revenue cutter. Already in Hong Kong and under orders from Roosevelt to be ready for immediate action, Dewey honed his ships to fighting sharpness. Sailors filled the bunkers with coal, restocked magazines and storerooms, repaired engines, and repainted hulls from white to slate gray to make detection more difficult.

On 27 April, already in the China Sea to avoid compromising British neutrality, Dewey set sail for Manila Bay to confront the Spanish squadron in the Philippines as soon as he was notified that Congress had declared war. Admiral Patricio Nomtojo y Pasaron's Pacific squadron consisted of only one modern cruiser with a leaky hull, five small steel cruisers, one larger wooden cruiser, and three gunboats. This motley collection was no match for the Americans. Slipping into Manila Bay nearly undetected, Dewey's squadron raked Pasaron's demoralized forces with murderous fire. By noon, the Spanish squadron had been annihilated.

Americans were thrilled when news of the sensational victory reached home. The Navy's next task was to locate Cervera's Atlantic squadron, which had sailed from Spain in late April. Fear swept the East Coast as "Spanish galleons" were reported to be off Boston and New York. To quell public concerns, the U.S. Atlantic Fleet was split into three squadrons: the main body under RADM W. T. Sampson at Key West, a strong "Flying Squadron" of fast ships under RADM Winfield Scott Schley at Hampton Roads, and a token force patrolling north of the Delaware Capes.

Cervera's strategy took his fleet on a circuitous route to Cuba, coaling at Curacao after the French had refused him badly needed fuel at Martinique. In the process, he managed to avoid Sampson's main force on watch in the waters off Puerto Rico and among the Windward Islands. The Spanish ships made it safely into Santiago harbor in mid-May without discovery by the Americans.

Logistical Restraints

The search for the elusive Spanish forces was hampered by U.S. Navy logistical restraints. Replenishment of coal and provisions was the major supply challenge. Concern over availability of these supplies limited the range of Sampson's search efforts.

Schley's squadron was ordered into the Caribbean to join Sampson's force. His four scout ships each burned 75 to 100 tons of coal a day. The ships' base of supply at Hampton Roads was 1,000 miles away, and Schley had only a small collier to replenish his needs at sea. When heavy seas were running—and they often were—it was difficult and dangerous for the collier to go alongside the larger warships for at-sea replenishment. Damage often occurred when the small collier came alongside the combatants and was battered by the larger and heavier ships in even moderately rough seas.

As a result of the dependence upon coal supplies, Schley ordered his ships to operate only at slow, cruising speeds to conserve fuel. On one occasion, he ignored Sampson's orders to deploy to the south side of Cuba and sailed to Key West to refuel. Fortunately, en route north he encountered smooth waters and was able to refuel his fighting ships from the collier in a slow procedure. With bunkers full of coal, Schley's squadron rejoined the search effort.

American forces did not locate the Spanish forces for several weeks. After a brief look at Cienfuegos on the southwest side of the island, the Americans finally stumbled upon the Spaniards at Santiago de Cuba, some 350 miles to the east. Sampson and Schley set up a blockade and waited out Cervera for more than a month. The Spanish finally attempted to break out and, in a battle lasting three hours, the Americans sank or drove aground all the Spanish ships. It was a glorious victory which, coupled with Dewey's success at Manila, eliminated Spain from the ranks of major sea powers.

The balance of the war was anticlimactic. After Santiago fell to the U.S. Army on 14 July, an American expeditionary force met little opposition in Puerto Rico and secured the island quickly. Hostilities ended on 12 August. As a result of two brilliant victories, the Navy attained national popularity greater than any since the War of 1812. More important, Cuba had gained independence; the United States had acquired Puerto Rico, Guam, and the Philippines; and Spain was no longer a factor in the Northern Pacific.

Supplying the Fleet

Through the foresight of Paymaster General Stewart and the efforts of his BuSandA staff, supply support for the Fleet had been refined and contributed to America's success in the four-month war. Stewart's supply plans, developed in peacetime, were put into practice at the start of hostilities, honed in battle, and proved in the successful support of Sampson's and Dewey's battle forces.

A major factor was the development of an early version of a consolidated allowance list for ships. According to Paymaster Ichabod G. Hobbs of Admiral Winfield Scott Schley's flagship *USS Brooklyn,* whose complement in 1898 was 427 men, 20 chief petty officers, and 33 officers, the paymaster was responsible for an average monthly payroll of $20,000.

Brooklyn's supply department made average monthly issues of 2,000 pounds of soap, 300 yards of flannel, 100 cap ribbons, 50 suits of underwear, 50 pairs of shoes, 25 pairs of trousers, and 25 overshirts. In addition, the crew purchased 500 pounds of tobacco each month.

Because Navy paymasters came from a variety of backgrounds, they often had hidden talents. An example is Pay Director William H. Galt, a native Virginian, who was appointed an assistant paymaster with relative rank of ensign in January 1871 and was a firsthand observer in *USS Raleigh* at the Battle of Manila Bay in May 1898. He wrote a poem, "The Battle of Manila Bay," in 1900 and published it in 1904.

If you will listen, I'll portray
The Battle of Manila Bay.
I ought to tell the tale aright,
As I was there, and in the fight:
And thankful I shall ever be
That fortune thus so favored me!

The dash was bold, the deed was great—
We seemed the instruments of fate.
No matter what events occur
In future, human hearts to stir,
The glory of the first of May
Will shine forever and a day!

The final stanza of his poem paid tribute to Commodore Dewey:

THE HERO OF THE SPANISH WAR!
In every great emergency,
When we have fought on land or sea,
A man has come to meet the hour,
And show the world our latent power.
George Dewey is the living peer
Of those great heroes of the past,
Whose fame will through all ages last,
Who taught our foes our flag to fear,
And us, THE STARS AND STRIPES revere!
When this most glorious fight was done,
With cable cut, he stood alone.
Whenever called upon to act,
He showed the most consummate tact.
Excelling in diplomacy,
A statesman wise, he proved to be;

And though the task he had was vast,
Made no mistake from first to last;
But, with demeanor firm and bland,
Shaped all things with a master hand.
All hail him VICTOR near and far.

Galt served his last tour of active duty at the Norfolk Navy yard in 1899. He retired from the Navy in 1902.

The Spanish-American War and a Popular Navy

Americans love winners, and the successful conclusion of the Spanish-American War found the U.S. Navy more popular than it had been with the American public since the War of 1812. U.S. victory and the acquisition of territories across the Pacific and in the Caribbean brought increased responsibilities for the Navy in carrying out national policy, however. It was during this period of euphoria that Albert S. Kenny became the chief of the renamed Bureau of Supplies and Accounts in May 1899.

LORE OF THE CORPS

Rear Admiral Albert Seawall Kenny, PC, USN

Chief, Bureau of Supplies and Accounts, and Paymaster General, 1899–1903
Period of Service: 1862–1903

In one century, the U.S. Navy had gone from being a nuisance to Great Britain to the most powerful maritime force in the world. Now, the new paymaster general, who had developed a revolutionary new Navy accounting system 15 years earlier, could turn his attention to improved food service and other living conditions for the Navy of the twentieth century. Kenny is often remembered because publication of the Navy's first cookbook occurred on his watch.

Albert Kenny was born at Pittsburgh, Iowa, in January 1841. He might never have entered the Navy had the Civil War not broken out. He was graduated from the University of Vermont in 1861 and began the study of law. When the war began, he abandoned his legal studies and obtained an appointment as an assistant paymaster in March 1862. Kenny was assigned to duty in the steamer *USS South Carolina* attached to the South Atlantic Blockading Squadron. In 1864 he was transferred to the steamer *USS Santiago de Cuba* attached to the North Atlantic Blockading Squadron. He was promoted to paymaster in March 1865 and elected to remain in the Navy after the war ended. He was in charge of stores at Loando in 1866 and returned to the United States as paymaster at San Francisco in 1868, where he served until 1871.

From 1872 to 1880, Paymaster Kenny served in *USS Plymouth,* in the ironclad *Roanoke,* and at the Naval Academy. He was on special duty at the Navy Department in 1881 and was fleet paymaster on the North Atlantic Station from 1881 to 1884.

Kenny was promoted to pay inspector with rank of commander in July 1884 and made a study of improved methods of accounting. In 1884 he also was a member of a board of officers to consider and report upon the Navy's accounting system. As a result of that study, the board recommended adoption of a plan Kenny advanced. Secretary of the Navy Benjamin Tracy wrote to President Chester A. Arthur, "Paymaster Kenny is the virtual author of one of the greatest executive reforms of the Navy. These reforms, introduced a new and radically different method of purchasing, handling, and distributing supplies, transporting men and supplies, and a different system of keeping the account and returns or purchases of supplies."

CDR Kenny was again ordered to special duty in the Navy Department. He had duty at the Boston Navy Yard from 1885 to 1887 and in the Bureau of Provisions and Clothing until 1890. He was general storekeeper, New York Navy Yard, from 1890 to 1893. His next duty was in *Chicago* on the European Station from 1893 to 1895. He took a leave of absence in May 1895, returning to active duty in January 1896 at the Navy Pay Office, New York. In June 1896, he became general storekeeper at the New York Navy Yard and then was summoned to Washington to become chief of the Bureau of Supplies and Accounts with the rank of rear admiral in May 1899.

RADM Kenny retired in January 1903 and remained in the nation's capital until his death in May 1930.

Sources

Hamersly, Lewis. *Records of Living Officers of the U.S. Navy and Marine Corps.* 7th ed. Philadelphia: L. R. Hamersly, 1902.

Official Biography. Naval Supply Systems Command, n.d.

A Century of Progress for the Navy

By the end of the century, the U.S. Navy had grown up. With enhanced popular support and logistical capability, along with improved administrative procedures, it had become a major sea power with which to be reckoned. Most important, the Navy had a technologically modern, armored fleet that had achieved resounding success in the short war with Spain. Suddenly, traditional naval powers throughout the world took notice that they no longer had a monopoly on the sea lanes. Uncle Sam had arrived as a world-class sea power!

Sources

Sources for material used in this chapter and not cited earlier include:

Galt, William W. *The Battle of Manila Bay.* New York: Home Publishing, 1909.

Graham, George Edward. *Schley and Santiago.* New York: Home Publishing, 1902. (The source of the discussion of providing provisions and coaling the Fleet during the Spanish-American War.)

Miller, Nathan. *The U.S. Navy: An Illustrated History.* Annapolis: Naval Institute Press, and New York: American Heritage Press, 1977.

CHAPTER FIVE

The United States Becomes a World Sea Power

1899–1913

The Spanish-American War had proved the importance of a strong Navy to project American power in both the Atlantic and Pacific oceans. Buoyed by American wartime success and popular support, Congress provided the Navy increased funding for construction, including authorization of 20 new battleships.

The war also had given the Pay Corps ample opportunities to demonstrate its ability to provide fresh and dry provisions, clothing, fuel, ammunition, and spare parts to two widely separated fighting squadrons in the Caribbean and the Pacific. However, the prolonged cruises of U.S. Navy ships did point out the need for additional advances in supply.

The Navy had considered the idea of replacing coal with oil as fuel for its steamships in the nineteenth century, but did not undertake serious testing until the twentieth century. The decision was made in 1903 to approve oil for use as fuel in Navy vessels, a move that created another area of logistical responsibility for the Pay Corps. First, the engineers had to solve the problem of smoke control from the newly authorized fuel and then, in conjunction with the Pay Corps, determine how to receive, stow, and issue a large volume of liquid fuel. It would take more than a decade to resolve the physical and political problems in order to make a complete changeover from coal to oil.

Messing in Fleet Ships

The Navy also was ready to turn its attention to improving shipboard living. From the time men first went to the sea in ships, crewmen had taken their meals in small berth-deck messes. Under the old messing system, each berth-deck mess had its own mess caterer and mess cook (frequently the same man). Mess caterers purchased provisions with ration money and supervised feeding of the men. The system was severely lacking in cleanliness, and there was a wide variance in food quality. Although tested at sea earlier, centralization of food preparation was not achieved until the start of the twentieth century.

Paymaster John S. Carpenter, supply officer of the battleship *USS Texas,* was intent upon improving shipboard messing. He received authorization to take over the commuted ration money from the individual messes in order to supervise the purchase and preparation of food for the entire crew. Carpenter's experiment was such a success that the Navy adopted the general mess system for all ships through General Order 68, issued on 26 November 1901.

Before that time, Pay Corps officers had been responsible for procuring and storing food, but administration of messing was under jurisdiction of the executive officers. Adoption of the general mess system greatly increased the amount of time required to supervise messing functions, and the responsibility was turned over to supply officers.

Meanwhile, Assistant Paymaster Thomas J. Cowie, commissary officer of the training ship *New Hampshire* and a future paymaster general, decided to expand the Navy ration established in 1861. He broadened the Navy definition of *meat* from beef and pork to include veal, mutton, and sausage. He also decided that lettuce, cabbage, radishes, and tomatoes, not just beans, peas, and beets, were also vegetables. In another departure from custom, he bought fresh bread from local bakeries when in port for extended periods.

Paymaster George P. Dyer, supply officer, *USS Missouri,* was concerned about cleanliness and introduced the first shipboard dish-washing machine in 1901. He also wrote a set of instructions for pantrymen to follow, including covering containers for butter, syrup, catsup, and other condiments to ward off flies. Another Dyer rule was to insist that warm dishes be served hot and cold dishes cold instead of being allowed to adjust to ambient temperatures before being served. Other Dyer innovations included using shipboard electricity to operate 40-quart ice cream makers, dough mixers, potato mashers and peelers, and meat grinders and slicers. The first ship's laundry and fresh-water cooling plant were installed in Dewey's flagship, *USS Olympia,* around the turn of the century.

The Boxer Rebellion

The U.S. Navy had been firmly established as one of the world's leading sea powers at the turn of the century when the Boxer Rebellion, China's first large-scale popular uprising against the imperialism of Japan and western nations, broke out. The rebellion, named for a form of shadowboxing practiced as calisthenics, was entering its second year in 1900. The Boxers were opposed to changes brought by foreigners and Christian missionaries and challenged the Chinese government and its pro-foreign policies. Boxer gangs went on the rampage in early 1900, sacking Christian missions and killing Chinese converts.

In June, ships of the U.S. Navy's Asiatic Squadron were deployed. Other foreign powers also sent ships and troops to protect their interests. On 14 June, the Boxers besieged foreign legations in Tientsin. On 20 June, they began their siege of legations in Peking, where nearly 1,000 foreigners and 3,000 Chinese Christians had taken refuge. The next day, the Dowager Empress Tz'u Hsi declared war on the foreign powers, and 250 foreigners and many Chinese Christians were massacred outside Peking.

An international force, numbering about 20,000, left Tientsin on 4 August and moved on Peking, arriving on 14 August. They proceeded to pacify Peking and the surrounding area of North China. The dowager empress fled the area, and remaining Chinese officials reorganized the government. By December the new government had worked out a settlement, the Boxer Protocol, with the foreign powers. The terms of this settlement, signed on 7 September 1901, were harsh. The United States fostered the Open Door Policy, which promoted the maintenance of a balance of the interests of the foreign powers while preserving the sovereignty of China. Without this policy, China might well have been partitioned in the manner some Western nations had proposed.

LORE OF THE CORPS

Paymaster Henry Erhardt Jewett, PC, USN

Period of Service: 1892–?

Henry Jewett resided in New Jersey when appointed assistant paymaster in May 1892. His first assignment was in *USS Yantic* from 1892 to

1895. He served three consecutive shore tours in Navy yards at Washington, Pensacola, and Key West from 1895 to 1898. After the Spanish-American War, he returned to sea in *USS Monterey*.

Paymaster Jewett was assigned to *USS Newark*, one of the ships dispatched to protect American interests during the Boxer Rebellion. He was a member of an armed contingent of 200 to 300 members of *Newark*'s crew, under Captain Bowman H. McCalla, commanding officer, which landed at Tangku, the port city for Tientsin. Once ashore, the Americans joined other armed naval units, largely British. The international force was ordered to move the roughly 100 miles by rail from Tientsin to Peking to relieve the beleaguered legations at Peking.

Advance of the rescue force was hampered when Boxers destroyed the railroad, forcing the main body to fight its way northwest on foot. After several days, the American vanguard element of the international force moved forward and lost contact with the main body. McCalla advised his men of the danger of the mission and called for a volunteer to restore communications with the other units. Paymaster Jewett stepped forward and offered to risk his life to travel alone back along the railroad right-of-way to contact the main body. Well aware of the odds against his completing the mission successfully, Jewett moved through several miles of territory held by the Boxers and succeeded in reaching the main body. The intrepid paymaster remained a member of the relief force throughout the 10-day fight into Peking.

CAPT McCalla later called Jewett "one of the most gallant men I have ever known." Several years later, Paymaster Jewett was advanced several numbers in seniority for conspicuous gallantry. Details of his subsequent service were unavailable.

Sources

Baker, Sherman, SC, USN. *A Collection of Abstracts Giving Historical Background for the Work of the Supply Corps* (ca. 1939).

The Encyclopedia Americana, International Edition. New York: Americana Corporation, 1970.

Hamersly, Lewis. *Records of Living Officers in the U.S. Navy and Marine Corps*. 7th ed. Philadelphia: L. R. Hamersly, 1902.

Jewett, H. S., SC, USN. Memorandum to CAPT Sherman Baker from RADM David Potter, SC, USN, 12 August 1937.

The First Navy Cookbook

The U.S. Army had just published a cookbook when the chief of the

Bureau of Medicine and Surgery suggested to Paymaster General Albert S. Kenny in August 1902 that a Navy cookbook would be of benefit aboard ship. Kenny concurred and assigned Paymaster Frank T. Arms the task of preparing the publication.

LORE OF THE CORPS

Rear Admiral Frank Thornton Arms, PC, USN

Director, Navy Cooks and Bakers School, 1902–3
Period of Service: 1892–25

RADM Arms was the son of Paymaster Frank H. Arms (1835–87). The younger Arms prepared and published a 32-page cookbook with three chapters—"General Mess," "Commissary Stores," and "Preparation of Food"—and 68 recipes.

Frank T. Arms was born at New London, Connecticut, in December 1866. His father was serving as a Navy paymaster and gave his young son the middle name Thornton as a compliment to a paymaster friend, Gilbert E. Thornton. Frank Arms had a diverse education because his family moved frequently during his father's Navy duty.

The younger Arms was appointed, in March 1886, a paymaster's clerk by his father, but his appointment expired in April 1887, when his father went to sea. Young Arms then went to Johns Hopkins University, Baltimore, and later to St. John's, when his father was lost at sea in March 1887 during a storm. He went to New York to work with Turner and Seymour Manufacturing Company, but contacted typhoid fever in November 1891. Following 70 days in the hospital and a period of recuperation at home, he accepted an appointment as assistant paymaster in March 1892. He served at sea in *USS Ranger* from 1892 to 1896. He was promoted to passed assistant paymaster in 1894 and to paymaster in 1898 while serving in *USS Indiana*.

Ranger lost her medical officer to yellow fever while off the coast of Central America in 1893. A native doctor was retained temporarily, and he prescribed a rum ration with a dash of quinine daily. Thereafter, Paymaster Arms had the rum barrel broken daily on the quarterdeck and, in the presence of the commanding officer, served up the doctor's prescribed preventative to each officer and enlisted man. Assistant Paymaster Arms was one of the last Pay Corps officer to dole out rum officially on the quarterdeck of a ship.

In 1900 Arms was serving in the receiving ship at New York. He was carrying 500 deserters' accounts on his pay rolls, and many of those were duplicated on the rolls of the ships from which they had deserted—some as many as four times. The frustrated paymaster decided that action was needed to remedy this confusion. He convinced the Navy Department to convene a board to address the question despite considerable opposition. Arms managed to get himself appointed to the board, where he drew up and typed the final report, which, among other things, recommended concentration of all deserters' accounts in the Bureau of Supplies and Accounts. The recommendation was accepted, thus standardizing procedures, centralizing deserters' accounts, and permitting the Bureau to handle them expeditiously. Paymaster General Albert S. Kenny complimented Arms for this work.

In 1902 Paymaster General Kenny assigned Arms, who had already shown interest in general messes, the task of producing a Navy cookbook. An earlier Army cookbook was in general use by the Navy, but it was deemed insufficient. For example, it provided such illuminating information as, "The presence of worm holes in coffee should not occasion its rejection unless it is of inferior quality and strength, since they generally indicate age, weigh nothing, and disappear when the coffee is ground." Arms admitted that he was unable to decide if the writer of that sage bit of advice was being witty or if his incompetence had escaped the attention of the Army's Quartermaster General.

In making the Arms assignment, Kenny wrote, "This officer has more experience with the commissary system and the feeding of enlisted men than any other officer in the Navy." The assignment also required Arms to write a manual for management of general messes throughout the Navy. He dictated recipes submitted by his chief cook and commented upon by his chief commissary steward to a stenographer at the paymaster's quarters in the evenings. Arms indicated that all of the recipes had been tried out and "had proved excellent" at the Cob Dock galley near where the New York receiving ship was tied up.

The assumption was that—unless men came to quarters hungry—mess caterers or berth-deck messes were honest and crew members were being fed properly. On one occasion, Arms was summoned by the officer of the deck, where crew members requested a tin of hardtack because they had eaten nothing that day. Arms gave each man two tins of hardtack. The "emergency rations" satisfied the men, but the experience made a strong and lasting impression on the paymaster. He was determined to correct the inequitable system.

Shortly thereafter, Paymaster Arms was appointed to a board to consider a general messing system, such as the one successfully instituted by Paymaster Carpenter, supply officer of *USS Texas*. The board members agreed unanimously to recommend such a system, which was put into effect virtually immediately and, with relatively minor modifications, remains in effect today.

The Navy Ration Board established the new enlisted ratings of commissary steward, cook, and baker in order to implement the new messing system. The board also established procedures for obtaining mess gear and the soap necessary for washing it. In 1902 Arms took over the school for training the Navy's cooks and bakers at Cob Dock.

Arms left Cob Dock in 1903 to become fleet paymaster in *USS Minneapolis* and took with him a young man who had demonstrated great proficiency in stenography and typing, appointing him fleet paymaster's clerk. When *Minneapolis* was at Fortress Monroe, Virginia, a soldier slashed the upholstery of Arms's automobile. His clerk asked whether Arms would like for him to go to the Army base and arrest the offender, but Arms advised him that he could not go on an Army base and make an arrest. The young man astounded Arms by revealing that he was an undercover Secret Service operative and could indeed do so. The agent went to the fort, where he apprehended the culprit, who was court-martialed, fined, and sent to prison. Although Arms did not receive cash restitution and had to pay for repairs to his car, he was pleased to learn that Secret Service man had selected his office for a base of operations and that he had not been "pinched."

RADM Arms later was assigned as officer-in-charge, Naval Supply Station, Hampton Roads, Virginia. He was detached from that duty in March 1925 and retired two months later. In 1937 Paymaster General Charles Conard asked RADM Arms for material to be used in a proposed history of the Navy Supply Corps. In response, Admiral Arms wrote an interesting and entertaining paper on supply in 1895. His paper was published in the *Navy Supply Corps Newsletter* on the 175th anniversary of the Corps in February 1970. RADM Arms died at New London in April 1945.

Sources

Baker, Cecil S., SC, USN. *A Collection of Abstracts Giving Historical Background for the Work of the Supply Corps* (ca. 1939).

Hamersly, Lewis. *Records of Living Officers of the U.S. Navy and Marine Corps.* 3d ed. Philadelphia: L. R. Hamersly, 1878.

Official Biography. Naval Supply Systems Command, n.d.

"Supply in 1895." *Navy Supply Corps Newsletter,* February 1970.

Domestic and Foreign Duties

In the early part of the twentieth century, the newly respected U.S. Navy was assigned to show the flag and protect the lives of American citizens abroad. These assignments presented many unusual challenges for Pay Corps officers, who were called upon to render assistance in natural disasters throughout the world and in special situations where their special talents were needed.

When the dormant volcano Mt. Pelee near the north tip of the island of Martinique exploded in a violent eruption on 8 May 1902, the destruction was unbelievable. The town of Saint Pierre was literally wiped out, and 30,000 people died. There remained a single survivor—a prisoner in the dungeon of the town jail. Paymaster Baron P. Du Bois was dispatched to Martinique to render all assistance to the government and to the survivors.

Paymaster (later Captain) Eugene C. Tobey and Paymaster G. C. Schafer were dispatched to the new Panama Canal Zone in 1905 to establish the first supply system and the first disbursing office in support of construction of the new canal across the Panamanian isthmus.

When a terrifying earthquake, measuring 8.3 on the Richter scale, struck San Francisco in April 1906, killing 452 people and causing $30 million in damage, the Navy swung into action again. The Pay Corps took over responsibility for feeding homeless survivors and assigned Assistant Paymaster James F. Kutz to spearhead the effort.

LORE OF THE CORPS

Assistant Paymaster James Fulton Kutz, PC, USN

Paymaster, *USS Independence,* 1905–8; Commissary Officer,
Marine Battalion, San Francisco, 1906
Period of Service: 1904–?

Paymaster Kutz was serving in *USS Independence* at San Francisco in April 1906 when a strong earthquake and ensuing fire devastated the city. Kutz was promptly ordered to duty as commissary officer for a battalion of Marines patrolling the northwest section of the city to save lives and prevent looting.

James Fulton Kutz was born in June 1880 at the Mare Island Navy Yard in San Francisco, the son of RADM George F. Kutz, Engineer Corps, USN. His parents gave the young Kutz his middle name in honor of Paymaster James Fulton. He attended public schools in Oakland, attended the University of California, and was graduated from Oakland Polytechnic Business College in 1903.

Kutz entered the Navy as assistant paymaster in July 1903 and was assigned to the ancient *USS Independence.* In 1904, while serving in *USS Petrel* in Panamanian waters, he was ordered to command a small naval expedition up the Tuira River in the jungles of Darien. He successfully completed a harrowing mission in an uncharted, alligator-filled river, where his craft grounded on several occasions, and received the Navy Expeditionary Medal for the achievement.

Kutz's duty in connection with the San Francisco earthquake required the feeding of Marines in four camps around that part of the city as well as thousands of destitute civilians. Public transportation was out of service and the streets in shambles, so Kutz used a sedate Army cavalry horse to make his rounds and supervise the emergency feeding.

The monitor *USS Wyoming,* the first oil-fired U.S. Navy warship, was commissioned at Mare Island Navy Yard in October 1908 with a crew marched from *Independence,* two miles away. After the commissioning ceremonies, the crew discovered that there was no fuel oil for the galley and none available at Mare Island. There were no stores, provisions, clothing and small stores, or pay accounts aboard. The crew was marched three times a day—a total of 12 miles—to *Independence* for their meals. When *Wyoming*'s commanding officer realized that no paymaster had been assigned to his ship, he fired off a dispatch to Washington, advising the Navy Department of the omission. Kutz was eventually ordered as paymaster of *Wyoming,* whose name was later changed to *USS Cheyenne.* One of his first duties was to arrange for a supply of fuel oil for his ship.

Paymaster Kutz served in *USS Princeton* and *USS Albany* during 1909 and 1910 as part of the Nicaraguan Expeditionary Squadron. *Albany,* with Kutz as paymaster, became flagship on the Asiatic Station in 1911. When in port at Chinkiang, China, later that year during one of the frequent revolutions, a large induction coil on *Albany*'s radio was disabled. The paymaster used a Chinese compradore (agent), to obtain bids for a replacement coil from Chinese merchants. He traveled by train from Nanking to Shanghai, where he purchased the required replacement part. The heavy box was delivered to the railroad station for transportation to Chinkiang station, located several miles from the river, where it was to be moved to the ship. Kutz arranged for half a dozen laborers, a two-wheeled hand truck, and a rickshaw for himself to make the trip to the river. He recalled that the journey was accompanied by high-pitched squeaks of rusty wheels and the dismal work chants of the men.

From 1915 to 1917 Kutz was paymaster of the Third Division in the battleship *USS Virginia,* flagship of the division. He later was paymaster of the new *USS Maine,* namesake of the battleship sunk at Havana in 1898. He served ashore with a Marine expedition force sent to protect American interests during a 1917 revolution in Cuba. During World War I, he made eight round trips between Hoboken, New Jersey, and Brest, France, in the troop transport *USS Mount Vernon* (the former German liner *Kronprinsessen Cecile*).

Paymaster Kutz had duty at Norfolk Navy Yard in 1918 and at the Naval Training Station, San Francisco, from 1918 to 1921. He then became supply officer in the battleship *USS New York* (BB-34), division flagship of the U.S. Battle Force, before returning ashore as supply and accounting officer at the Naval Training Station, Great Lakes, Illinois, in 1923. He served as supply officer of the flagship of the Battle Force, *USS California* (BB-44), from 1926 to 1927.

LCDR Kutz was senior assistant supply officer at the Puget Sound Navy Yard from 1927 to 1930 before completing the senior course at the Naval War College in 1931. As a commander, Kutz was fleet supply officer and fleet paymaster of the Asiatic Fleet in *USS Houston* (CA-30) and in *USS Augusta* (CA-31) from 1930 to 1934, at the Naval Training Station, Newport, Rhode Island Station, and U.S. Fuel Depot Melville, Rhode Island. Available records do not indicate the date of his retirement, but according to the *Official Register of Commissioned Officers* he was a pay director, with rank of captain, on duty as accounting officer at the Philadelphia Navy Yard in 1940. Records suggest that Kutz died in October 1945.

Sources

Baker, Sherman, SC, USN. *A Collection of Abstracts Giving Historical Background for the Work of the Supply Corps* (ca. 1939).

Official Biography. Naval Historical Center, July 1942.

Register of Commissioned and Warrant Officers of the United States Navy and Marine Corps. Washington, D.C.: U.S. Government Printing Office, 1 July 1940.

Duty at Argentina

In 1910 two Atlantic Fleet armored cruisers and a scout cruiser formed a special service squadron and were sent to Puerto Militar, Argentina, for the celebration of the Argentine centennial. They were joined by two armored cruisers from the Pacific Fleet and a Japanese cruiser.

Leaving the five large ships at Puerto Militar, *USS Chester* went upriver to Buenos Aires for the centennial parade, and crewmen of the U.S. and Japanese cruisers were formed into the Brigade Argentina (B.A.) and went by special train to Buenos Aires. Paymaster (later Captain) A. F. Huntington was assigned as brigade commissary. Members of the brigade were assigned billeting and messing in an Argentine naval barracks for several days, but were dissatisfied with the thin soup and bread served them after they had paraded.

Huntington convinced the men that, as guests of the Argentine government, they should "put a good face on it." He went to *Chester*, tied up in the Rio de la Plata, whose paymaster, F. T. Watrous, agreed to work his galley staff nearly all night during the period to prepare substantial sandwiches for the brigade. Huntington knew that transporting the sandwiches to the barracks would embarrass their hosts, so the men were sent in squads to *Chester*, where they were fed good Navy chow, and the Argentines were none the wiser.

The Great White Fleet

Convinced that the wealth and strength of the United States warranted greater influence among the major world powers, President Theodore Roosevelt determined to give an impressive demonstration of American sea power. The vehicle he chose was called the "Great White Fleet," comprised of 16 modern, powerful battleships.

When the Fleet steamed out of Hampton Roads on its around-the-globe mission on 16 December 1907, it did so with a comprehensive logistical plan put together by the brilliant young Pay Inspector Samuel McGowan (chapter 6).

The Panama Canal was under construction while the Fleet was on its tour. Roosevelt wanted to determine his options if war broke out with Japan before the canal could be completed, making it difficult for America to reinforce the Pacific Fleet quickly. Roosevelt believed it would be important for American interests to impress Japan with American naval power. This was especially important in light of the Japanese fleet's spectacular success over the Russian fleet, which had sailed halfway around the world only to meet ignominious defeat at Tsushima in 1905. The tour by the assemblage of mighty American warships was a great success, and thousands gathered to view and cheer the Yankees in every port at which they called.

The battleships were dispersed to major ports to show the flag when the Great White Fleet reached the Mediterranean in late fall of 1908. On 28 December, an earthquake struck Italy, centered at Messina, Sicily, with a force of 7.5. Eighty-three thousand people were killed. Roosevelt ordered RADM Robley D. Evans, fleet commander, to render all possible assistance to the Italian government and the earthquake survivors. Evans dispatched Fleet Paymaster McGowan to Rome to offer the Navy's help. McGowan met with King Vittorio Emmanuel III, who quickly accepted the offer of aid. However, McGowan insisted on one caveat. Suspecting the potential for waste, fraud, and abuse on the part of civilian authorities, the fleet paymaster stipulated that all aid be distributed by Italian military officers.

Celtic, a 6,750-ton freighter built for trade between England and Australia and found adrift off Newfoundland in 1898, was taken over by the Navy. She served as the cold storage ship at Manila following the Spanish-American War. From 1898 to 1917, *Celtic, Culoga,* and *Glacier* were the only U.S. Navy supply ships.

In late December 1908, while *Culoga* was accompanying the Great White Fleet, *Celtic* was loading provisions to sail from New York on 5 January 1909 to meet the Fleet at Ceuta Bay, North Africa, opposite Gibraltar. As a result of the earthquake, her orders were modified, and Paymaster (later CAPT) John N. Jordan supervised taking on shoes, clothing, and 200 tents. She sailed on 28 December and after a stormy Atlantic crossing and recoaling at Gibraltar, *Celtic* arrived at Naples on 19 January, where her cargo was turned over to Paymaster McGowan for distribution to earthquake survivors. In all, $144,000 in humanitarian aid was drawn from stocks aboard the *Culoga* and *USS Celtic,* and distributed according to plans developed by McGowan and Paymaster Byron D. Rogers.

McGowan was concerned over the impact of readiness on the Fleet as a result of the humanitarian drawdown of *Culoga* supplies. He called paymasters of all fleet ships to the flagship and required them to bring complete inventories of parts and provisions. He and his staff then analyzed each ship's supplies and instituted an informal afloat inventory control point to assure that no hoarding took place and that needed supplies could be provided to meet each ship's real needs.

The Naval Supply Account

Paymaster Charles Conard became interested in revising forms used on board ship when serving in *USS Franklin* from 1904 to 1906. When his suggestions became known at BuSandA, Conard was ordered into the Bureau on temporary duty in 1907 to review all forms for shipboard use. He observed that the other bureaus, particularly Yards and Docks, had large quantities of stores deliberately left over at the end of the fiscal year, apparently so the bureaus might use them in the next fiscal year without additional cost.

There was no general naval supply account in existence at the time, but there was a general account for stores and special accounts for stores purchased with special appropriations. Conard recognized that if all of the stores in the Yards and Docks general account were placed in a single account and made available for everybody, each bureau would benefit. He visited each of the Navy's yards, talked with the appropriate officers, and eventually convinced each bureau that it would be better off with a new system. He was successful in prompting the Navy Department to sponsor legislation that resulted in the establishment of a single fund, which became the Navy supply account fund.

Paymaster General Kenny, who had successfully ushered the Bureau of Supplies and Accounts and the Pay Corps into the twentieth century, retired at the mandatory age of 62. He was relieved by RADM Henry T. B. Harris in January 1903.

LORE OF THE CORPS

Rear Admiral Henry Tudor Brownell Harris, PC, USN

Chief, Bureau of Supplies and Accounts, and Paymaster General, 1903–6
Period of Service: 1867–1906

As paymaster general, RADM Harris undertook a vigorous campaign to rid the Pay Corps of "all undesirable members." He was obviously concerned that not all officers were performing in a satisfactory manner.

Henry Harris was born at Hartford, Connecticut, in March 1843, and was appointed acting assistant paymaster from New York in November 1864. He was commissioned assistant paymaster in 1867. His first sea duty was in Nyack, South Pacific Station, from 1867 to 1869. He then reported for duty in the first *USS Supply* in 1870 and 1871. From 1875 to 1877, he was in charge of naval stores at Honolulu and was in charge of naval stores at Rio de Janiero from 1878 to 1879.

Harris served in *Swatara* on the Asiatic Station, from 1880 to 1883 and was promoted to paymaster in January 1881. Paymaster Harris reported to the training ship *Minnesota* in 1884 and for special duty at the New York Navy Yard in 1886. He later served in *Galena,* on the North Atlantic Station, and at the Naval Academy from 1886 to 1889. Paymaster Harris served in *Boston* at the New York Navy Yard, and in *Miantonomah* from 1892 to 1894; was general storekeeper at Norfolk Navy Yard in 1895; and reported in 1897 to the receiving ship *Vermont.*

There he also had the accounts of *Dolphin* and torpedo boats. He was ordered to the armored cruiser *USS Boston,* Asiatic Fleet, in 1900 and took part in the North China campaign and the Philippine insurrection. He was transferred to the European Fleet in 1901 and remained there until 1903. As a pay director, Harris was then ordered to duty at the League Island Navy Yard, Philadelphia, where he served until called to Washington in July 1903. There he assumed duties as chief of the Bureau of Supplies and Accounts.

RADM Harris was dedicated to reform of Navy purchasing and supply administration. He established a concept of unrestricted public competition in the Navy's purchase system and created a comprehensive supply system run by experienced Pay Corps officers.

He was not satisfied with clearing the Corps of deadwood. He also took steps to assure that candidates for the Pay Corps were fully qualified to be paymasters and not commissioned solely as a result of political influence. Harris inaugurated a plan to subject all "respectable and properly accredited young men" to compete for appointment to the Pay Corps through comprehensive examinations. The decision brought to the Navy Pay Corps a cadre that was intelligent and dedicated. The move was popular with Navy leaders and Congress and hailed widely throughout the United States. Before Harris inaugurated his plan, he was careful to notify all Pay Corps officers that the time of dilatory and careless performance had passed and that he expected "constant, energetic, and serious work." He warned all who were tempted by delinquency and dereliction of duty what was expected of them if they wished to remain in the Pay Corps.

When the Naval Committee of the House of Representatives was considering the question of enlarging the Navy General Board into a general staff, the chairman asked Admiral Harris for his thoughts on the subject. He studied the issue and prepared two thoughtful papers that proved useful to both the House and the Senate.

Harris assigned paymasters to assume responsibility for management of the fiscal affairs of the customs of the Republic of San Domingo. He also assigned Paymaster (later Captain) Eugene C. Tobey and Paymaster G. C. Schafer to establish the first supply system and first disbursing office in the Panama Canal Zone. The first Navy Pay Officers School was established at Washington in 1905 on his watch.

Henry Harris was placed on the retired list in March 1905, but was retained on active duty as chief of the Bureau until he retired in November 1906. He became ill while on a transatlantic crossing and died in July 1920, shortly after arriving in England.

Sources

Hamersly, Lewis. *Records of Living Officers of the U.S. Navy and Marine Corps.* 7th ed. Philadelphia: L. R. Hamersly, 1902.

Official Biography. Naval Supply Sustems Command, n.d.

A Spanish-American War Vet at Helm of BuSandA

When RADM Harris retired in November 1906, he was relieved as chief of the Bureau of Supplies and Accounts and paymaster general by Pay Director Eustace B. Rogers, who had served with Dewey at the Battle of Manila in 1898. Rogers was promoted to rear admiral upon taking office.

LORE OF THE CORPS

Rear Admiral Eustace Barrow Rogers, PC, USN

Chief, Bureau of Supplies and Accounts, and Paymaster General, 1906–10
Period of Service: 1879–1910, 1917–19

Rear Admiral Rogers was a renowned fisherman and is remembered principally for having resigned his post in a dispute with the secretary of the Navy.

He was born in San Francisco in May 1855, the son of Robert Clay Rogers, who served with distinction as a midshipman in the Mexican War. The future chief traveled east to attend Lehigh University and later returned to the Bay Area to complete his education at the University of California.

Eustace Rogers was appointed an assistant paymaster in March 1879 and had an early taste of Navy Department life when he served a short first tour in the Bureau of Supplies and Accounts before going to sea in *USS Tennessee* later in the year. He was promoted to passed assistant paymaster in 1884, served another, longer tour at BuSandA, and was promoted to paymaster in 1894.

He was in charge of the Naval Clothing Factory, Brooklyn, from 1895 to 1897. He next served in *USS Monterey,* present at the capture of Manila in the Spanish-American War in 1898, and later in *USS Oregon.* He returned to Brooklyn in 1900 to serve a second tour in charge of the Naval Clothing Factory.

Rogers's tour as chief of the Bureau was generally uneventful until his abrupt retirement at his own request in 1910. According to newspaper accounts, "He resigned because of a dispute with the Secretary of the Navy, George Von L. Myers [*sic*]." Although the news reports did not provide details of the disagreement, it was known throughout the Navy that the dispute arose over a statement Rogers made to a congressional committee. The admiral had advocated industrial management at navy yards and added that the industrial manager should be a constructor because they were the smartest people in the Navy. His statement infuriated both the secretary and Navy line officers.

Rogers was always proud of his California heritage and returned to the Pacific Coast when he retired. His reputation as a fisherman was recognized by an article in *Outdoors* magazine, in which he was called a "skilled and veteran angler." A popular fishing fly, the admiral, is named after him.

In retirement, Rogers lived in Tacoma, Washington, was secretary of the Pacific Steamship Company, and played a role in the 1915–16 merger of the fleets of that firm and the Pacific-Alaska Navigation Company. According to the *Lehigh Alumni Bulletin,* the merger involved 22 vessels carrying practically all of the passenger business and a majority of the freight business between the northern and southern ports on the Pacific Coast.

RADM Rogers was recalled to active duty in January 1917 as general inspector of the Supply Corps, a position he held until January 1918. He had temporary duty at the Thirteenth Naval District from April to August 1917 and as Pacific Coast representative of the Emergency Fleet Corporation from August 1917 to January 1918. He retired again in 1919.

After return to civilian life and retirement from business, Eustace Rogers lived abroad for several years before returning to Washington in 1928. He died at League Island Naval Hospital, Philadelphia, in 1929 and was buried at Arlington National Cemetery.

Sources

Hamersly, Lewis. *Records of Living Officers of the U.S. Navy and Marine Corps.* 7th ed. Philadelphia: L. R. Hamersly, 1902.

Official Biography. Naval Supply Systems Command, n.d.

A Veteran Pay Director as Assistant Chief

Supply Corps archives contain details of the service of all paymasters general and chiefs of Supply Corps, but there is little beyond bare-bones biographies of those who served as assistant chiefs. One notable exception is Pay Director John S. Carpenter, who was on duty in *USS Texas* when she participated in the defeat of a Spanish fleet off Santiago, Cuba, during the Spanish-American War. Carpenter's outstanding performance in a variety of sea and shore assignments came to the attention of Pay Corps flag officers. When Rear Admiral Eustace Rogers became chief of BuSandA in 1906, he brought Carpenter into the Bureau as assistant chief.

LORE OF THE CORPS

Pay Director John Slaughter Carpenter, PC, USN

Assistant Chief, Bureau of Supplies and Accounts, 1906–9
Period of Service: 1881–1924

Paymaster Carpenter served as assistant chief of BuSandA for about three years. He is credited with having distinguished himself by his unusual knowledge of official duties and being what is today called a quick study. He played an important role in the establishment of the general mess in the Navy and of the Supply Corps School of Application in BuSandA.

John Carpenter was born at Louisville, Kentucky, in May 1860 and saw preliminary Navy service as a clerk to his uncle, Pay Inspector (later RADM) Frank C. Cosby, fleet paymaster in the flagship *Trenton*. He accepted a commission as assistant paymaster in October 1881. His first tour of duty was in the Bureau of Provisions and Clothing from 1881 to 1882.

Carpenter reported to *USS Montauk* in 1882, then transferred to *USS Yantic* in 1883 and served until 1886. His next duty was at the Washington Navy Yard from 1887 to 1889. Carpenter returned to sea in *USS Michigan* in 1889 and served until 1891, when he was ordered to *USS Albatross* and promoted to passed assistant paymaster. He went on sick leave and entered the hospital in April 1893 but was released at year-end. He returned to duty at the Washington Navy Yard in January 1894 and moved across town to the Bureau of Supplies and Accounts in May. Pay Director Carpenter was appointed acting assistant chief of the Bureau in May 1897 and served until November.

In January 1898, he reported as supply officer of the battleship *USS Texas* and served there throughout the Spanish-American War. He was on hand for the destruction of the Spanish Atlantic fleet off Santiago in July. Carpenter remained in *Texas* until November 1900 and is best remembered for establishing the general mess system and for his many innovations in food preparation. *Texas* messmen were particularly impressed with the dishwashing machine he installed.

Carpenter then was on special duty in the Navy Department until detached in 1903 to return to sea as fleet paymaster, Pacific Fleet, in *USS Chicago.* He went back to the Bureau of Supplies and Accounts in December 1906 as assistant chief. In 1909 he reported to the Boston Navy Yard, where he held several positions, including aide for supply during World War I. In 1919 he transferred to the Third Naval District as aide for supply.

During a tour of duty in the Navy Department from 1921 to 1924, he was officer-in-charge of the Supply Officer's School of Application. While in that position, he was promoted to rear admiral in July 1921. Carpenter retired in May 1924 after 43 years of commissioned service; he died in June 1929.

Sources

Baker, CAPT Cecil, SC, USN. *A Collection of Abstracts Giving Historical Background for the Work of the Supply Corps* (ca. 1939).

Hamersly, Lewis. *Official Records of Officers of the U.S. Navy and Marine Corps.* 7th ed. Philadelphia: L. R. Hamersly, 1902.

Experiments with Aviation

The first successful flight by the Wright Brothers in 1903 made a lasting impression on President Theodore Roosevelt. He encouraged the government to investigate the feasibility of aviation for future military use, but little came of his suggestion at that time. In 1908 Roosevelt prodded the Army into testing an advanced version of flying machines, and the Navy sent an observer to the test flight. Despite the crash of the test plane, the observer saw future potential in aircraft in scouting and gunfire spotting.

Navy pilots were successful in demonstrating the feasibility of shore-ship-shore flight in tests at Hampton Roads in 1910 and in 1911 at San Francisco. Congress approved the formation of a naval aviation unit, which was deployed to Guantanamo Bay, Cuba, in 1913, and supported the Mexican incursion in 1914. Just as it had with the first usable submarine, *USS Holland,* in 1900, the onset of naval aviation provided new, challenging opportunities for BuSandA and the Pay Corps.

New Colliers Improve Recoaling

From the time steamships were incorporated into the U.S. Navy, the process of manual recoaling its steamships had changed little at the turn of the century. A Navy collier purchased during the Spanish-American War required 100 men to bag coal in its hold and could discharge a maximum of 50 tons of bagged coal per hatch in an hour. This ship normally required 10 hours to discharge 1,200 tons from its 4 hatches.

The Navy realized that rapid coaling was essential to fleet efficiency and that manual labor must be reduced substantially. Increased sailing speed and decreased time spent in recoaling fleet ships was an important factor in supply planning in the first decade of the century. The solution was for the Navy Department to build its own colliers from Navy designs.

The new Navy-designed collier *USS Hector* could discharge 190 tons per hatch per hour through use of a self-filling bucket operated by 2 men. *Hector* was a 12-knot ship with a capacity of 7,500 tons. Improved colliers under construction in 1910 were capable of 14 knots and were rated at a capacity of 12,500 tons.

While the transition was underway from coal to oil as the principal fuel for Navy ships, coal was still a major supply problem. The primary Navy coaling stations were located on both coasts, at Honolulu, and at Olangapo in the Philippines. The costs of transporting and storing coal escalated rapidly. These costs became a major budgetary concern of the Bureau of Supplies and Accounts. When RADM Rogers resigned as chief of BuSandA as a result of his dispute with Secretary Meyer, he was succeeded by RADM Thomas J. Cowie in July 1910.

LORE OF THE CORPS

Rear Admiral Thomas Jefferson Cowie, PC, USN

Chief, Bureau of Supplies and Accounts, and Paymaster General, 1910–14
Period of Service: 1879–1921

Paymaster General Cowie served nearly two years of enlisted service before being commissioned in the Pay Corps. His early experiences as a sailor had a strong influence on his later service. Throughout his administration of the Corps, he showed great interest in, and sympathy for, the well-being of naval personnel.

He was known as a shrewd and likable man and had great influence with Congress. These traits served him well when he undertook the task of convincing legislators of the necessity of correcting long-standing injustices in the Navy's pay system by passing remedial pay legislation.

Born at Montezuma, Iowa, in February 1857 and educated in Washington, D.C., Cowie served as a civilian engineer's yeoman at sea from January 1877 to October 1878. Two days after completing his contract, he enlisted in the U.S. Navy at Constantinople, Turkey, and served in *USS Despatch* until honorably discharged in August 1879. Cowie remained out of federal service for less than a year and then returned to the Navy in June 1880, when he was commissioned assistant paymaster and ordered to duty at the Navy Yard in Washington.

He was promoted to passed assistant paymaster in March 1889. After several tours of sea duty, including service in *USS Monocacy* as intelligence officer during the Sino-Japanese War (1893–95), Cowie made paymaster in 1895.

Paymaster Cowie served two subsequent sea tours of duty and in July 1903 became fleet paymaster of the European Squadron. In January 1905, he commenced a tour of five and a half years at Annapolis as general store keeper for the Naval Academy.

Cowie was appointed chief of the Bureau and paymaster general in July 1910 with the rank of rear admiral. During his administration of the office, a system of Navy allotments was established, and responsibility for administering it was placed under BuSandA. In this period, the first Navy commissary store was opened. The Navy standard stock catalog also was developed under Cowie and published in 1914.

After he was succeeded by RADM Sam McGowan in July 1914, RADM Cowie remained on active duty as president of the Naval Examining Board at the Washington Navy Yard. He reported to the Naval War College at Newport, Rhode Island, in November 1914. When the United States entered World War I in 1917, he assumed duty as disbursing officer for the Second Naval District at Newport. He returned to the Bureau of Supplies and Accounts, where, from February 1918 through the balance of the war, he served as disbursing officer. In Washington, he was placed in charge of the Voluntary Allotment, War Risk Insurance, and Naval Reserve divisions. A month after reporting back to BuSandA, he was given additional duty as the Bureau's contracting officer.

In February 1919 Cowie assumed charge of the Navy Pay Office at Baltimore, but a month later was recalled to Washington for duty in connection with the Fifth Liberty Loan. Treasury officials told Cowie that it would be impossible to fulfill the Navy's assigned quota. Cowie determined to succeed. And, he did! In May 1919 he became head of the Navy Allotment Office but remained in charge of the Navy's drive to achieve Liberty Loan goals. He also continued his liaison with Treasury on War Risk Insurance.

Stating that the admiral had achieved the impossible, the Treasury Department presented him the first Liberty Loan Medal (made from captured German cannon metal). He was awarded the Navy Cross in 1919 in recognition of his exceptional and meritorious service during the war and his extraordinary success with the Liberty Loan program.

RADM Cowie became secretary and treasurer of the Navy Mutual Aid Association in 1920. He was placed on the retired list in February 1921, but continued his duties with Navy Mutual Aid, a position he held with distinction for 15 years. Rear Admiral Thomas J. Cowie died in Washington in July 1936.

Sources

Baker, CAPT Cecil, SC, USN. *A Collection of Abstracts Giving Historical Background for the Work of the Supply Corps* (ca. 1939).

Hamersly, Lewis. *Records of Living Officers of the U.S. Navy and Marine Corps.* 7th ed. Philadelphia: L. R. Hamersly, 1902.

Official Biography. Naval Supply Systems Command, 1953.

From Coal to Oil

The move to convert the U.S. Navy from coal to oil began to accelerate in the second decade of the century. At the same time, the Royal Navy moved forward more rapidly toward solving the two major obstacles to total conversion from coal to oil: smoke control and onboard storage of oil.

By 1910 the United States had two battleships capable of burning oil, but only as an emergency supplement to coal. In addition, four destroyers and four submarines were equipped to burn oil. Battleships under construction would also use oil only as an auxiliary to coal.

The British were building 56 destroyers and 74 submarines to be powered solely by oil when Winston Churchill became first lord of the Admiralty in 1911. Most Royal Navy vessels in commission were already equipped with oil sprayers to increase the efficiency of coal-fired shipboard plants, relying on oil imported from the United States. Because British battleships still used coal, a reliable supply of petroleum had not yet become a problem.

Fleet commanders had, for a half century, been hampered by steamers having to return to distant stations to replenish coal supplies. The advocates of oil pointed out that being absent from the Fleet while shuttling back and forth to recoal was a tactical disadvantage as well as a waste of fuel. They pointed out that oil-burning fleets could be much more easily refueled at sea than their coal-burning counterparts and would mean increased speed and steaming radius. Churchill also noted that battle efficiency of coal-burning ships was impaired because crews became exhausted by the laborious manhandling of coal sacks.

The U.S. Navy moved slowly on the universal transition to oil despite the large U.S. domestic petroleum reserves, which Navy officials feared would be exhausted. They believed that the Navy should have its own petroleum reserves, but that the government's reserves should not be used as long as sufficient oil could be purchased on the open market.

When Josephus Daniels took office as secretary of the Navy in 1913, he immediately faced the question of whether the newly authorized battleship *Nevada* would be coal- or oil-fired. Daniels consulted the Department of the Interior, then ordered that *Nevada* be oil-fired. His decision had far-reaching effects. The Navy was committed to a future battle fleet that would operate solely on oil. Never again did the United States authorize a new, coal-fired Navy ship.

By the end of 1913, the Navy was operating or had under construction 4 battleships, 41 destroyers, 30 submarines, and several smaller ships—all oil-burners. In addition, eight American battleships, a transport, and a supply ship were equipped to burn both oil and coal.

With the demand for fuel oil on the increase, oil prices began to rise alarmingly. Paymaster General Cowie reported to the House Naval Affairs Committee in early 1913 that "fuel oil prices at the present time have increased 50 percent over the prices paid in 1912 and a further increase in price is expected, due to increased demand." By year-end 1913, Navy Secretary Daniels reported that prices of oil the Navy paid had doubled since 1911.

Daniels proposed the construction and operation of a government pipe line from midcontinent oil fields to the Gulf of Mexico and a government refinery to assure adequate supplies at lower costs. The Daniels proposal failed to win congressional approval, but the Supreme Court solved the problem in June 1914 by breaking the oil monopoly's hold on prices. Domestic oil prices declined significantly in 1914 and 1915.

The British, who had been the leaders in conversion to oil, also felt the pain of rising fuel-oil prices. Navies throughout the world struggled to determine how to obtain adequate supplies of oil at reasonable prices for the increasing number of oil-fired ships in their fleets and new warships on the building ways.

Relief to Flood Victims

From 25 to 27 March 1913, the Pay Corps responded to a human tragedy caused by the devastating flood that took 732 lives on the Ohio River. Paymaster Leon N. Wertenbaker and Paymaster Donald W. Nesbit were given responsibility for delivering relief supplies to 42 towns in Ohio, Indiana, Illinois, and Kentucky. The Navy Department paid a bill of nearly $127,000 for food and clothing supplies.

LORE OF THE CORPS

Paymaster Leon Norris Wertenbaker, PC, USN

Assistant Supply Officer, New York Navy Yard, 1915–21
Period of Service: 1899–1935

Paymaster Wertenbaker was a hero to thousands of victims of a devastating Ohio River flood in 1913, when he led the effort of the U.S. Navy to deliver relief supplies.

Leon Wertenbaker was born at Washington, D.C., in June 1884 and entered the Navy in July 1899 at the age of 15. He was appointed to the Pay Corps as an interim assistant paymaster from Ohio in July 1905 and attended the first Navy Paymasters' School at the Bureau of Supplies and Accounts. He went to sea as pay officer in *USS Supply,* station ship at Guam, in December of the same year. In May 1907 he was ordered as pay officer for four ships in reserve at Norfolk, including two famed veterans of the Spanish-American War, *RS Brooklyn,* and *RS Texas.*

In December 1907 he transferred, as pay officer of *RS Franklin.* He was promoted to lieutenant, junior grade, in March 1908, and was assigned as assistant to the general storekeeper at Norfolk Navy Yard with similar duty at the Portsmouth Navy Yard in April 1909. In October 1909 he reported to the New York Navy Yard for loading *USS Culoga* and was commissioned a passed assistant paymaster in November.

He was ordered back to the New York Navy Yard in September 1910 as assistant to the officer-in-charge of the Provisions and Clothing Depot. In March 1913 he volunteered to organize relief efforts for flood victims along the Ohio River from Marietta to its junction with the Mississippi River. Although the flood inundated land as far north as Dayton, Paymaster Wertenbaker succeeded in getting the first train loaded with relief supplies through to Columbus, where it was loaded on trucks and wagons and taken down to the river.

There, Paymaster Wertenbaker commandeered an old Mississippi side-wheel steamer and pushed a loaded barge downriver. Sailors and civilian volunteers distributed food and clothing to every home and group of houses on both sides of the Ohio from Marietta to Louisville. When his relief mission was completed, Wertenbaker returned to New York.

In June 1915 he reported for duty at the New York Shipbuilding Company, Camden, New Jersey, as prospective supply officer, *USS Melville,* and was promoted to paymaster with rank of lieutenant commander in August 1916. He next served as supply officer, *USS Florida,* in January 1917 and was commissioned a Regular Navy paymaster in January 1918. He had subsequent duty as supply officer, Fleet Supply Base, Brooklyn, and supply officer, *USS Alert.* LCDR Wertenbaker went to the Bureau of Supplies and Accounts in December 1921. He reported for duty in the armored cruiser number 4, *USS Pittsburgh,* as supply officer, in May 1925 with additional duty as force supply officer, Naval Forces, Europe. He reported again to BuSandA in July 1926 and was promoted to interim pay inspector with rank of commander in October 1926, back-dated to December 1920. He was commissioned pay director with rank of captain in March 1927.

CAPT Wertenbaker reported to the Pearl Harbor Navy Yard in May 1929 and to the staff, commander, Base Force, in June 1932. He retired from the Navy in May 1935.

Sources

Baker, CAPT Cecil, SC, USN. *A Collection of Abstracts Giving Historical Background for the Work of the Supply Corps* (ca. 1939).

Bureau of Naval Personnel. *Transcript of Naval Service.* July 1942.

Register of Commissioned and Warrant Officers of the United States Navy and Marine Corps. Various dates, 1914–35.

War on the Horizon

With another war in Europe on the horizon, the Navy was committed to total conversion to oil, but had not solved the problems of petroleum supply and prices. These problems continued to challenge two successive paymasters general—RADMs Cowie and McGowan—and dominated supply considerations when the war commenced in Europe.

Sources

The source for material used in this chapter and not cited earlier is primarily

Nathan Miller, *The U.S. Navy: An Illustrated History* (Annapolis: Naval Institute Press, and New York: American Heritage Press, 1977).

Additional sources for material:

Crumpacker, John W., Jr., SC, USN. "Supplying the Fleet for 150 Years." *U.S. Naval Institute Proceedings*. June 1945.

Long, John D. *The New American Navy*. Vol. 2. N.p.: Outlook Company, 1903.

"Petroleum and the United States Navy before World War I." *Mississippi Valley Historical Review*, June 1954–March 1955.

CHAPTER SIX

World War I

1914–18

The outbreak of war in Europe caused little alarm in the United States; military experts expected the war to be short, and President Woodrow Wilson called for impartiality. The U.S. Navy was still growing, and *USS Nevada* (BB-36), the first American battleship to be powered by oil instead of coal, was launched in 1914. Congress appropriated funds for the Naval Act of 1916, which included a powerful new class of 4 32,000-ton battleships, each with a main battery of 8 16-inch guns and oil-powered.

Secretary of the Navy Josephus Daniels shocked the naval establishment in July 1914 with the surprise appointment of 43-year-old Pay Inspector Samuel McGowan as chief of the Bureau of Supplies and Accounts and paymaster general. With the appointment, the talented McGowan assumed the temporary rank of rear admiral. Daniels's surprising move proved to be a stroke of genius.

McGowan had compiled an outstanding service record, including tours as assistant chief of the Bureau, director of the Navy Pay Officers' School, and fleet paymaster for the Great White Fleet. For his new challenge, he carefully selected a strong cadre of able and trusted associates who would apply fresh approaches to age-old supply problems.

Paymaster General McGowan put his associates to work to prepare a wartime logistical plan. When the plans were drawn up, he wanted to compare his assumptions with the actual circumstances in which the British were operating. He sent a BuSandA representative to London to review the wartime logistical record that the Royal Navy had experienced between 1914 and 1916. McGowan's decision to prepare the

Navy Pay Corps for probable entry into the war in Europe led to a degree of preparedness unknown at the start of either the Civil or Spanish-American wars.

LORE OF THE CORPS

Rear Admiral Samuel McGowan, PC, USN

Chief, Bureau of Supplies and Accounts, and Chief of Pay Corps, 1914–19;
Chief of Supply Corps, 1919–20
Period of Service: 1894–1920

Probably more has been written about Sam McGowan than about any other chief of the Supply Corps. His exploits were widely reported, and he was quoted extensively in the press of the day. One newspaper dubbed him the "live wire of the Navy." Sam McGowan revolutionized Navy supply, and the Supply Corps even now bears McGowan's strong imprint.

Samuel McGowan was born at Laurens, South Carolina, in September 1870, the son of a lawyer who had served as a major in the Confederate Army. Young Sammy, named for his grandfather, a Confederate general, was graduated from the University of South Carolina and the university's law school, but he never practiced law because his mother talked him out of doing so. She feared, she said, that if he ever lost a case he would volunteer to serve his client's sentence. He chose instead a journalistic career before winning appointment as an assistant paymaster in March 1894. He served for the next three years in *USS Minnesota, USS Dolphin, USS Marblehead, USS Michigan, USS Kearsarge,* and *USS Alabama.*

Early in his career, McGowan demonstrated characteristics of which legends are made. An example of his unusual talents is a sequence of events that could have destroyed his career had he not been so resourceful. He reported for duty at the Naval Station, Port Royal, South Carolina in 1897. He had attended a friend's wedding in Charleston the night before an important appointment with the inspector general of the Pay Corps. The morning after the wedding, McGowan overslept and missed the last scheduled train that could get him back to his duty station in time for his appointment. He chartered a railroad locomotive and passenger coach for an unscheduled, high-speed, 60-mile dash across the South Carolina lowlands to Port Royal and was seated in his office when the inspector general arrived at the appointed time. By the time the inspection was concluded, it was too late for the I.G. to catch a train to Charleston. McGowan came to his superior's rescue with an easy solution: return with the chartered train to its home terminal.

Paymaster McGowan reported to the New York Navy Yard in 1903 as assistant in charge of the Naval Clothing Factory. He became the youngest ever assistant paymaster general—next to the top man in the Bureau of Supplies and Accounts—in 1904. Following that tour, he was promoted to pay inspector with the rank of commander and in 1905 became officer-in-charge of the newly formed Navy Pay Officers School in BuSandA.

McGowan played a key role in supply organization and planning for the worldwide cruise of the Great White Fleet from 1907 to 1909. He joined the armada as fleet paymaster at San Francisco in early 1908, six months after the cruise began at Hampton Roads, and remained in that post for the balance of the cruise. Roosevelt attributed the great success of the cruise largely to advance preparations in which McGowan participated and for which he received a presidential commendation.

While the Fleet was dispersed among a number of Mediterranean ports, Sam McGowan was the key official in directing the Navy's humanitarian relief role to victims of a strong earthquake that devastated Messina, on the Italian island of Sicily, in December 1908. The chief of staff notified his fleet paymaster to render all possible aid. McGowan rushed to the scene with food, clothing, and other supplies from the flagship *USS Connecticut* and the supply ship *USS Celtic* (AF-2) and directed distribution to survivors. McGowan then went to Rome and met with King Vittorio Emmanuel III to offer further Navy assistance but insisted that he deal directly with Italian military and naval authorities.

The aid seriously depleted the Fleet's stores, and a loaded relief ship sank in a storm en route to its rendezvous with the Fleet. McGowan called paymasters from all the American ships together and set up a central inventory system of all supplies within the Fleet. He then ordered transfer of stocks among the ships to balance the inventories. A crisis was thus avoided by the impromptu establishment of an at-sea inventory control point.

The fleet paymaster also had to deal with the problem of acquiring locally fresh meat and vegetables in place of the lost replenishment load. McGowan resisted the urge to rush into contracts for the perishable food items and made purchases after review of sealed bids from French suppliers.

After the triumphant Great White Fleet returned to Hampton Roads in September 1909, Paymaster McGowan returned to shore duty as pay officer at the Charleston Navy Yard and in October 1910 reported for similar duty at the Philadelphia Navy Yard. He returned to sea duty in

December 1912 as fleet paymaster in *USS Wyoming* (twice), *USS Connecticut,* and *USS Arkansas.*

By 1914 McGowan's accomplishments were widely recognized by senior naval and civilian leaders. RADM Charles H. Badger wanted him in 1914 as fleet paymaster of the Fleet operating off Mexico, but Secretary of the Navy Daniels had other ideas. When McGowan was appointed paymaster general in April 1914, he was the youngest paymaster ever to be so recognized. McGowan was a humble man and recognized that true leaders could not do it all alone. He delegated significant authority to RADM Christian J. Peoples, his "strong right arm," and to CDRs John M. Hancock and James C. Hilton.

Lessons learned from the Great White Fleet's voyage around the world proved valuable for future war planning. The experience reinforced McGowan's belief that a more uniform method of shipboard stocking was needed, and that there was a lack of uniformity in the pay system among ships on the cruise. Sam McGowan strongly believed that a wartime supply system must be based upon readiness to meet the needs of operating forces at a moment's notice, and that the Navy needed its own supply and store ships. He constantly thought about ways to improve the Navy's supply and pay systems. McGowan was not hesitant to share his radical concept with the chief of naval operations and other top Navy officials. They realized that he was right and often accepted his proposals.

The young chief firmly believed that the sole reason for the existence of the shore establishment was to contribute to the Fleet's efficiency. World War I broke out only a month after McGowan took office. He was convinced that the Navy's 1914 peacetime supply and logistical plans should be no different from those necessary in the war in which the United States would surely soon be involved.

Under McGowan's direction, BuSandA drew up lists of food, clothing, and other consumable supplies for ships' complements of various sizes. McGowan's planners also compiled fuel needs, sources of supply, and available rail and water transportation data for all supplies needed by the Fleet.

When the United States entered the war on 17 April 1917, it had little effect on BuSandA. The Navy wartime supply system was already up and running. On the day war was declared, McGowan gathered the key officers and civilians in the Bureau and announced, "While the war of 1917 will be fought in France and in Belgium, and in Italy, and in Germany, it must be won in Washington." His prewar planning had been wise.

Paymaster General McGowan decided that the ideal way for BuSandA to make its contribution would be to follow the Fleet's administrative methods. He introduced intrabureau orders to parallel fleet regulations and intrasection orders to parallel those of a ship. McGowan developed a formal set of policies and procedures by which prompt, concentrated, and coordinated action could be taken in support of the Fleet.

There was no supply problem that the energetic McGowan did not study in great detail and determine the corrective actions needed. For example, he became concerned that the number of items being carried were turning ship's stores into miniature department stores and in 1915 issued new regulations specifying the items that could be carried.

He was totally imbued with the idea of service to the Fleet and felt that providing good food in ample quantities for the Fleet's sailors should be the Navy's primary focus. The U.S. Navy was the best fed in the world and, through wise buying practices, maintained excellent food quality. In 1917 ration costs increased only 20 percent, despite a 40 percent rise in the U.S. wholesale food index costs. The war proved the idea that supplies—especially those that required long lead times and those not carried in sufficient quantities by commercial firms—are military assets whose value could not be measured solely in dollars and cents.

During Sam McGowan's six-year administration, the motto of BuSandA was, "It can't be done, but here it is." In 1919 he orchestrated changing the name of the Pay Corps to the Supply Corps to reflect the broader scope of paymasters' duties. By 1920 the peripatetic McGowan had become a tired man and asked to be retired after 26 years of service rather than the customary 30. A grateful and admiring Congress enacted special legislation that allowed him to do so, and he retired in the permanent grade of rear admiral. Upon retirement, he was awarded the Distinguished Service Medal.

McGowan was widely praised in Congress and the press for his foresight and the Bureau's exceptional performance during the war. Among his most vociferous supporters were President Theodore Roosevelt and Admiral George Dewey.

In retirement, Sam McGowan, a life-long bachelor, remained involved in a variety of civic and volunteer activities. He returned to South Carolina, and the Red Cross sought him out in 1921 to direct the distribution of relief and rehabilitation supplies in Greece. Later, he served voluntarily as South Carolina highway commissioner before moving to New York City from where he wrote a weekly column for his hometown newspaper in Laurens. He suffered a series of colds during the winter of 1934, returned home to recuperate, and died of pneumonia in November 1935.

The Navy remembered the contributions of this legendary Supply

Corps figure and named a destroyer for him. The *USS McGowan* (DD-678) was commissioned in December 1943 and served with distinction during World War II and the Korean War. She was later sold to Spain and served as the *Jorge Juan* until stricken from the list of active naval vessels in 1988.

Sources

Bell, CAPT Lewis Baker, SC, USN (Ret.). "Samuel H. McGowan." Master's thesis, Princeton University, 1947.

Dictionary of American Naval Fighting Ships. Vol 4. Washington, D.C.: Naval Historical Center, Department of the Navy, 1969.

Official Biography. Naval Supply Systems Command, n.d.

New Strategic Options

Work on the gargantuan Panama Canal project took more than eight years and was finally opened on 15 August 1914. Completion of the long-awaited short cut between the Atlantic and Pacific oceans provided the United States with enormous commercial as well as military benefits. The huge locks, with individual chambers measuring 1,000 feet long by 110 feet wide, could accommodate any ship then afloat.

For the Navy, the ordeal experienced in the frantic 66-day dash of *USS Oregon* (BB-3) around Cape Horn from the Pacific to join Sampson's squadron off Cuba in 1898 would never have to be repeated. Every U.S. Navy ship could navigate the Panama Canal. The width its locks (as well as the clearance beneath the Brooklyn Bridge) governed maximum dimensions of Navy ship construction for nearly a half-century.

The war in Europe did not end quickly, but dragged on. Although the Wilson administration was officially neutral, the sympathies of the American public gradually moved toward the Allies. Past tensions between the United States and Germany in the Western Hemisphere, reports of German intervention in Mexico, and a large volume of Allied propaganda were all important factors in turning American public opinion against Germany. When a German submarine sank the Cunard liner *Lusitania* off Ireland in 1915, with the loss of 128 American citizens, Wilson decided on a course of preparedness while maintaining neutrality.

Official support for Great Britain was only thinly veiled by late 1916. British and French purchases of American products lifted the United States out of economic doldrums and were welcomed by a grateful public. In return, American financial institutions invested heavily in Britain and France.

Trouble in the Caribbean

Meanwhile, Americans were greatly concerned over threats to U.S. citizens and their investments in Mexico when the dictator Victoriano Huerta took office through the power of arms. President Wilson sent a squadron to show the flag off the Mexican Gulf Coast and to demonstrate American unwillingness to tolerate any actions against unarmed Americans.

On 9 April 1914, unarmed American seaman went ashore at Tampico in search of gasoline and were arrested by Mexicans. The sailors were released after a short time, but RADM Henry T. Mayo, squadron commander, demanded an apology and a 21-gun salute. Huerta authorized profuse apologies, but refused to render the salute.

At the time of the Tampico incident, a destroyer flotilla was anchored at Pensacola, Florida, awaiting orders, which came the following day. The flotilla, with 18 destroyers including *USS Ammen,* the scout cruiser *USS Birmingham,* the battleship *USS Mississippi,* and the tender *USS Dixie,* was ordered to fuel and provision to capacity and leave for service in Mexican waters. As the flotilla raced toward Tampico, each destroyer was ordered to have 20 of its 82-man crew armed, equipped, and ready to land. Paymasters of the ships devised a Civil War-type substitute for knapsacks by rolling individual blankets around a suit of blues, a suit of whites, a suit of underwear, a towel, and toilet articles. This rudimentary pack fitted over either shoulder, and the two ends made fast under the opposite arm at the waist. Each man was issued a rifle and a belt with 90 rounds of ammunition.

En route to Mexican waters, the destroyers, never intended for the purpose of embarking landing forces, made the best of the situation by drilling their designated forces of mostly senior petty officers into shape for any contingency. Charles W. Fox, a yeoman, third class and later a Supply Corps vice admiral, wrote years later that his skipper in *Ammen* noticed that the landing party on one of the other destroyers was dressed in what appeared to be khaki uniforms. Because the only uniforms the crews had were blues and whites, the skipper decided that the white uniforms must have been dyed in coffee and ordered his landing party to do likewise. Fox, a member of the party, reported later that he had firsthand knowledge that there is "absolutely no comfort" in wearing a uniform soaked from having been dipped in a pot of coffee dregs. The flotilla arrived off Vera Cruz on 20 April.

A force of 800 armed sailors and marines went ashore the following day to seize the customhouse in order to prevent the unloading of weapons from a German ship. The American landing force was reinforced two days later by an additional 3,000 men who went ashore from newly arrived transports to overcome stubborn Mexican resistance. Two U.S. ships provided shore bombardment in support of the landing force. The naval brigade fought a bitter house-to-house action and succeeded in capturing Vera Cruz at a cost of 17 American dead and 63 wounded.

Ammen's landing party was held in reserve, so Charlie Fox did not get into the land action. *Ammen* and other destroyers made mail and reprovisioning runs back to Galveston, Texas, and escorted troop transports to Mexico. *Ammen* and Fox left Mexican waters and returned to Norfolk on 19 June.

The San Juan de Ulua Fortress

American naval and Marine forces at Vera Cruz occupied the supposedly invincible fortress of San Juan de Ulua on 27 April, when the commandante surrendered his demoralized and isolated post. Paymaster (later RADM) Fred McMillen was serving as pay officer in the newly commissioned *USS Vestal* (AR-4) and chronicled the events in *U.S. Naval Institute Proceedings* (August 1936). *Vestal*'s skipper, Commander Edward L. Beach, was ordered to take command of the fort, which had been serving primarily as a prison with 872 Mexican inhabitants, including 515 inmates. McMillen recalls that the fortress unofficially became the U.S. Naval Station, Vera Cruz.

CDR Beach, along with McMillen and the other department heads, made a "searching tour of inspection to survey the resources and facilities of the station and to adopt measures for the preservation of Mexican property, as had been specifically enjoined by the commander-in-chief." They found evidence of vandalism and looting everywhere. McMillen reports further that "instruments and equipment of the government meteorological station had been destroyed and removed. The interiors of both the dispensary and the prison infirmary were completely wrecked and the floors strewn with broken bottles, surgical dressings, drugs, and medicines."

Paymaster McMillen reported that *Vestal*'s sanitary squad found unimaginable filth and squalor in the dungeons of the fortress. U.S. personnel directed washing and disinfecting of all prisoners and a complete disinfection and fumigation of the area, using "unbelievable quantities of sulphur, creosote, and other disinfectants."

A critical shortage of food for the fortress garrison and prisoners had become desperate in the final days before surrender. Malnutrition among the Mexicans—prisoners and captors alike—was an overriding concern of CDR Beach. McMillen immediately rounded up 1,000 Navy rations to feed the starving Mexicans. Kitchen police were assigned, the kitchen cleaned and disinfected, and a huge cauldron of beef stew prepared under Paymaster McMillen's direction. It was the first hearty meal that the occupants of the fortress had eaten in many days.

McMillen reported that the Mexican officers cooperated completely with the Americans, and the prisoners were overwhelmed by their treatment, especially when compared with the filth and brutality of their Mexican jailers. They became willing volunteers for all the dirty jobs in the prison area. The occupation at Vera Cruz ended in August 1914.

The Navy and Marines in Haiti

Between 1914 and 1916 unrest in Cuba, Haiti, Nicaragua, and Santo Domingo, and the possibility of danger to Americans, resulted in Navy and Marine expeditions and the subsequent occupation of Haiti, Nicaragua, and Santo Domingo. The president of Haiti was murdered on 27 July 1915, and chaos ensued. A force of American bluejackets and Marines was landed at Port-au-Prince to restore order. On 19 August, the Navy Department directed RADM W. B. Caperton to assume charge of customhouses at Port-au-Prince and nine other locations in Haiti. He took over the facility at Port-au-Prince on 2 September.

A group of 11 Pay Corps officers had already been dispatched to Haiti in the old cruiser *USS Tennessee*. RADM Caperton designated Paymaster Charles Conard as administrator of customs and fiscal officer in general charge of collection of customs duties at all the Haitian ports. The other paymasters were deeply involved in directing customs and financial institutions throughout the island.

Paymaster McMillen was dispatched to the customhouse at Petit Goave, with complete authority over all port activities and coastwise trade in the arrondissement of Petit Goave. The Pay Corps officer arrived at his new post as collector of customs and captain of the Port of Petit Goave in September 1915.

LORE OF THE CORPS

Paymaster Fred Ewing McMillen, PC, USN

Collector of Customs and Captain of the Port, Petit Goave, Haiti, 1915–16
Period of Service: 1907–46

Fred McMillen served in Mexico in 1914 and was one of 11 Navy paymasters sent to take over Haitian financial institutions in 1915. He was on duty at Boston both times the United States entered a world war, was involved in development of war plans for World War II, rose to Flag rank, and became the first commanding officer of the Bureau of Supplies and Accounts Field Branch in Cleveland, Ohio.

He was born at Springfield, Wisconsin, in April 1882. McMillen attended Wisconsin State Normal College before appointment to the Naval Academy in 1900. He resigned from the naval service upon graduation in 1904, then reentered it in June 1907 and was appointed assistant paymaster with rank of ensign. McMillen's first active duty was at the Norfolk Navy Yard for practical training. From December 1907 to March 1909, he served as assistant to the pay officer in *USS Virginia,* assistant to the flotilla pay officer in *USS Hopkins,* and assistant to the pay officer and commissary officer in *USS Connecticut.* He then served briefly on the board at the New York Navy Yard before becoming assistant to the supply officer.

Paymaster McMillen reported to the Bureau of Supplies and Accounts in February 1911 and to *USS Panther* as pay officer in June 1912. He returned to Boston in May 1913 for fitting out of *USS Vestal* (AR-4) and as her supply officer upon commissioning. McMillen was *Vestal*'s pay officer at Vera Cruz during the capture and occupation of the fortress of San Juan de Ulua, where he played a major role in feeding the starving occupants and rehabilitating the facilities.

Detached from *Vestal* in August 1915, he joined a group of 11 paymasters sent to handle financial matters in Haiti after the assassination of that country's president and resultant riots. Paymaster McMillen was appointed collector of customs and captain for the Port of Petit Goave.

McMillen found conditions decidedly primitive when he arrived at his Haitian post. A hurricane had roared through Petit Goave a few days earlier, so his first task was to rehabilitate the customs warehouse filled with coffee and other exports awaiting shipment. The only means of communication were an unreliable field radio set in the hands of Marine occupiers and the even more unreliable Haitian telephone system. McMillen described the roads as miserable and mountain trails as entirely impassable during the rainy season. Navy ships called only every two or three weeks.

He finally was able to have the warehouse's roof repaired, but had to supply the materials to do so. After that problem was corrected, McMillen turned to organizing the functions of weighing, checking, witnessing, appraising, and fixing the tariffs for all imports and exports and preparing the necessary paperwork. He soon scrapped a system of recording all papers "of every description" in large ledgers and adopted a simple system with new records. As a result, piles of useless papers were thrown out, reducing the process of approving imports and exports to three working days from the three to four weeks it had been taking.

Fortunately, the number of regular steamships calling at Petit Goave had declined as a result of war in Europe. On the other hand, the U.S. Navy and Marine Corps were unable to patrol the harbor and adjoining coastline; smuggling to avoid Haitian duties continued unabated, especially at the smaller nearby port of Miragoane.

Bad as the customhouse, office, warehouse, and infrastructure conditions were, living conditions were worse. Initially, the three officers at Petit Goave shared the barracks of the enlisted men, located at the market place. The lower floor of the frame building had a paved floor, and the Americans quickly screened the structure for use as a galley and messroom. Living quarters were on the second floor, which was surrounded by a wide gallery. Eventually, Paymaster McMillen rented a house for $13 a month that had been formerly occupied by a French chef, but the building had to be renovated extensively and fumigated before it was habitable.

A native boy and his burro, which had two casks strapped on its back, supplied potable water from a nearby mountain spring for the officers' quarters and the barracks. The Americans could obtain no local food except seasonally available bitter citrus fruit, custard apples, and mangoes. Occasional live fish and purchases of cheese and other pantry food from visiting ships supplemented the standard fare from tin cans.

Paymaster McMillen finally was rescued from his arduous tour at Petit Goave in March 1916, when he was ordered to duty at Port-au-Prince. There, Paymaster Conard, senior member of the Pay Corps team in Haiti, assigned McMillen as a member of a board to draw up an auditing system for the Haitian Customs Service and recommend changes in laws and procedures to simplify administration. Before the board completed its work, all Navy Pay Corps officers on special duty in Haiti, except for Paymaster Conard, were relieved.

McMillen returned to the United States in May 1916 and was serving as assistant to the supply officer, Boston Navy Yard, when America entered World War I. He moved to the Headquarters, First Naval District, as supply officer in November 1917 and was transferred a year later to New York as supply officer, Third Naval District. He was supply officer, Destroyer Force, U.S. Fleet, from April to July 1919 and squadron supply officer, Destroyer Squadron 3, Atlantic Fleet, with additional duty as aide to commander, Destroyer Force, Atlantic Fleet, until May 1921.

McMillen reported for a second tour of duty at BuSandA in charge of the fleet division until ordered to *USS Henderson* (AP-1) in May 1925. He returned to the Bureau in November 1926 as assistant chief of the Planning Division. He was promoted to pay director with rank of captain in July 1929 and went back to sea in May 1930 as supply officer of Aircraft Squadrons, Scouting Fleet, which was later renamed twice—first to Carrier Division 1 and then to Aircraft, Scouting Force, U.S. Fleet. CAPT McMillen served from July 1931 to March 1936 in the War Plans Division, Office of the Chief of Naval Operations, after which he had duty at the Naval Supply Depot Norfolk.

McMillen was sent back to Boston in July 1940 as officer-in-charge, supplies and accounts, First Naval District, and was ordered to additional duty as supply officer, Boston Navy Yard in November 1940. He was serving in that post when the Japanese attacked Pearl Harbor and the United States entered World War II. He was promoted to rear admiral in 1942 and reported as the first commanding officer of the BuSandA Field Branch at Cleveland in December 1942. RADM McMillen headed the Field Branch until January 1946, when he was awarded the Legion of Merit for "displaying exceptional initiative, a broad knowledge of maintenance and brilliant administrative ability." Fred McMillen then returned to BuSandA headquarters, from which he retired in August 1946. He died at New Hartford, New York, in September 1959.

Sources

McMillen, Fred E., SC, USN. "Some Haitian Reflections." *U.S. Naval Institute Proceedings,* April 1936.

Official Biography. Naval Office of Information, September 1959.

Latin American Service

General unrest, including revolutionary activity throughout Latin America, caused serious concern in 1915 and 1916 over the lives of American citizens and property of U.S. firms. Fear of harm and expropriation prompted the government to send Navy units and Marine troops to the area.

Navy paymasters were assigned a variety of duties in Latin American countries from Mexico to islands in the Caribbean. Although these assignments usually involved supply and fiscal duties, Pay Corps officers were not immune to coming under hostile fire. One of those was Ensign Charles L. (Chub) Austin, who served his country in uniform for 40 years, 38 of them in the Pay Corps and Supply Corps, and eventually attained Flag rank.

Ensign Charles Linnell Austin, PC, USN

Special Duty, Mexico and Santo Domingo, 1915–16
Period of Service: 1913–53

Supply Corps officers who attended Navy Supply Corps School at Bayonne, New Jersey, probably recall "Chub" Austin as the jolly, rope-climbing rear admiral who served as commanding officer of NSCS following World War II. But as a young ensign he served heroically in the Caribbean in 1915 and 1916.

Born at Moorestown, New Jersey, in October 1891, he attended Georgetown Academy in Philadelphia for 10 years before entering the Naval Academy in 1909. An avid athlete, he played football and baseball and was a member of the boxing team all four years at the academy. Upon graduation in June 1913, he was adjudged to be color blind, so he resigned from the Navy and was commissioned a second lieutenant in the Army Coast Artillery Corps.

He transferred to the Navy as an assistant paymaster with the rank of ensign in February 1915. After instruction at the Navy Pay Officers School in Washington, he was assigned to the *USS Sacramento,* from which he participated in the Mexican, Haitian, and Dominican campaigns.

In August 1915, Ensign Austin was placed in charge of 10 Mexican soldiers and a guide put ashore on Cozumel Island off the coast of Yucatan. Their assignment was to conduct a search for a Navy family, allegedly living on the island after having been lost when a hurricane sunk a United Fruit steamer in which they were embarked. According to ENS Austin, the rescue party spent three frantic days living on turtle eggs, fresh and otherwise, and tea made from stagnant, smelly water, searching futilely before returning to their ship.

In June 1916, Ensign Austin was a member of a Joint Navy-Marine Corps landing party at Puerto Plata, Santo Domingo. When the American group started up the hill beyond the beachhead, the Marine captain in charge was shot and killed. As the senior surviving officer, young Austin, who had learned to handle weapons as a midshipman, took charge of a machine gun. He scrambled up the hill and sprayed the enemy position with fire, driving the defenders into the bushes and permitting the hill to be secured for the landing party. He then was assigned as quartermaster for the Marines who remained in Santo Domingo. Later, RADM Austin maintained that his machine-gun exploits were far less dangerous and interesting than his six-month duty with the Marines.

Austin was promoted to lieutenant in 1917 and had early experience in the instruction of paymasters for four months as assistant to the officer-in-charge of the Navy Pay Officers School. In December 1917, LT Austin was assigned to the American naval base at Queenstown, Ireland, where 36 destroyers and two tenders were based. He was later ordered to London, where one of his principal duties there was to pay crews of U.S. minesweepers tasked to assist the Royal Navy in clearing German and British mines.

The ships were based at ports throughout Great Britain, and Austin was required to undertake heavy travel to hold pay days. He devised a plan, in cooperation with several large British banks, to moderate his burdensome travel schedule. He would wire money lists for ships to the bank branch at each port where a U.S. Navy ship was located. Branches would allow crew members to withdraw money up to the authorized amount on the list and send pay receipts to the head offices in London, which would notify Austin. The paymaster would immediately issue checks for the total obligation to the respective banks. This arrangement significantly reduced travel requirements and gave Chub Austin time to enjoy the abundant social life of London.

LT Austin served tours between the two world wars as supply officer of a submarine division, ashore at Norfolk, at BuSandA, at two air stations, and three tours at sea, including *USS Whitney* (AD-4), *USS Arkansas* (BB-33), and *USS Memphis* (CL-13). He was promoted to lieutenant commander during this period and to commander in June 1935. He returned to the Naval Academy in the summer of 1939 for a two-year tour in charge of the Midshipmen's Store.

CDR Austin went back to London as assistant naval attaché in September 1941 and later as special U.S. naval observer at the American Embassy. In May 1942 he became supply officer on the staff of the commander, Naval Forces, Europe. He later was assigned additional duty with the Joint General Purchasing Board in Europe. He returned to the United States in February 1944 and served tours as supply officer of the Naval Torpedo Station, Newport, on the staff of commander, Amphibious Forces, Pacific Fleet, and at the Naval Academy.

RADM Austin assumed command of NSCS Bayonne in January 1947 and remained in that post for six and a half years. He played tennis and softball well into his sixties. When the author of this volume was an NSCS student, he recalls sliding into home plate and colliding with RADM Austin, catcher of the NSCS staff team. The admiral shook off the collision, the game proceeded, and, by giving it his all, the author avoided being put on report.

Austin regularly hosted a late-morning gathering in his office for a small group of NSCS officer students scheduled to give obligatory short speeches at the wardroom luncheon that day. He had a rope rigged to the overhead in his office and would challenge students to beat his time in climbing to the top. A number of officer students tried, but there are no reports of any accomplishing it.

Chub Austin strove to assure that his frequent public speeches would not always sound the same, so he enlisted faculty and staff officers to write them for him. He usually had several drafts from which to select, including those written by LTJG (later CAPT) Thomas J. Ingram, III, disbursing instructor, who was also the source of some of the data included in this account. Ingram also recalls that Chub Austin encouraged religion at NSCS and always read the Christmas story at chapel services on Christmas Eve.

Rear Admiral Austin retired in 1953. In a final message to the officer students at NSCS he said, "Whether you like it or not, you are an officer and a gentleman, As such, you will inspire the highest devotion, loyalty and respect from your men. At the same time, you will arouse the lesser resentment for those occasional lapses to which you may be given. . . . if your manner to juniors is indistinguishable from your manner to seniors." In retirement, he accepted employment with States Marine Ship Lines. He died of cancer in May 1963 in Scotch Plains, New Jersy.

Sources

Baker, Cecil S., SC, USN. *A Collection of Abstracts Giving Historical Background for the Work of the Supply Corps* (ca. 1939).

CAPT Austin to CAPT Henry De F. Mel, SC, USN, 10 June 1939.

Details of the arrangements with British banks in 1918 to pay crews of Navy minesweepers were told by RADM Austin to LTJG Thomas J. Ingram, III, NSCS Bayonne, 1953. CAPT Ingram provided these details in May 1994.

Official Biography. Navy Biographics Section, 1953.

"RADM Charles L. Austin, CO at NSCS Bayonne, Retires." *Navy Supply Corps Newsletter,* July 1953.

The Naval Act of 1916 and Preparedness for War

War was well underway in Europe when Congress backed up the Wilson preparedness program by passing the Naval Act of 1916, authorizing the construction of a new class of four battleships more powerful than anything in the world. It was in this environment that the Office of the Chief of Naval Operations was established to provide centralized strategic planning. Rear Admiral William S. Benson was appointed to the post.

Secretary Daniels asked his bureau chiefs to comment on aspects of preparedness in supply and logistics. Paymaster General McGowan responded with a 55-item, 12-page memorandum on 19 June 1916. McGowan's first point was that the shore establishment was of use only to the extent that it contributed to Fleet efficiency.

He went on to emphasize that there should be no difference in ship supply between peacetime and wartime and between peace footing and war footing. McGowan believed that American involvement in the European war was increasingly inevitable. He criticized the Navy's peacetime proclivity for supplying the active fleet symmetrically. He told the secretary that new inventions, rapid transport, and quick communication were important, but that the primary lesson he had learned was that "things, not men, lose wars."

McGowan reported that BuSandA had accumulated a reserve stock of general materials in order to assure a regular and reliable flow of supplies to the Fleet when the United States inevitably became involved in the war. The Bureau had drawn up allowance lists and expanded the Navy Standard Stock Catalog, which had been introduced in 1914. The revised and expanded catalog was issued in loose-leaf form for the first time to facilitate revisions when stocked items or prices changed.

Procurement Reform

RADM McGowan was also behind reform of procurement practices which, under retail contracts, provided for deliveries of as many items as required. During 1917, he stated that all such items would be purchased in large quantities and kept in storehouses for delivery to shipyards and Navy vessels requiring them.

The permanent Logistics Committee, comprised of the chiefs of the six bureaus—Supplies and Accounts, Steam Engineering, Ordnance, Medicine and Surgery, Yards and Docks, and Construction and Repair—agreed with McGowan's recommendation. In a memorandum to the chief of naval operations on 1 November 1916, the committee recommended that "to meet the initial requirements of the Navy in the event of war, a very substantial increase must be made in the quantity of supplies carried. Now is the time to provide for their storage." The committee called for a significant increase in storage facilities, particularly at New York, Philadelphia, Norfolk, Puget Sound, and Mare Island. Not surprisingly, Paymaster General McGowan was chairman of the committee.

Profiteering by commercial firms at the expense of the U.S. government, and the Navy in particular, was always a major concern of Sam McGowan. He had been successful in combating attempted profiteering by French firms when he was fleet paymaster of the Great White Fleet in 1908, and he had learned the lesson well. In addition to substantial increases in coal and petroleum prices, the Navy was experiencing rapid price rises in a wide variety of other commodities.

Storehouse Adequacy

Where to stow war reserve material authorized for purchase by the Navy was also a major problem overseas. Questions concerning perishable and nonperishable provisions and general supplies became a matter of discussion between the United States and Great Britain in 1916. The adequacy of available storehouses was also a concern of Vice Admiral William Sowden Sims, the senior U.S. Navy officer in Great Britain. Sims noted that all the storage space at Queenstown and Passage had been used. He pointed out the additional need to carry stock for the U.S. Aviation Forces in Ireland and for the Grand Fleet would necessitate acquisition of additional facilities. He emphasized that existing buildings had been used wherever possible and that no new warehouses had been constructed at Queenstown. However, he had requested a sum not exceed 10,000 pounds sterling to build a shed structure. Without it, he predicted that a "very acute situation will develop" that might require diverting shipments of provisions, clothing, and general supplies to Liverpool or other ports.

Sims also noted that it had been necessary to remove large quantities of stores and equipment from U.S. battleships based in Scotland. The Royal Navy agreed to stow the material at Rosyth and Aberdeen, but that space was limited. Sims reported that arrangements were "being made to secure temporary use of a large shed conveniently located on the water front." He believed that supplies at the U.S. Navy base at Brest, France, were ample, and that if en route shipments arrived safely, "Brest in the near future will be in all respects as well off as Queenstown." As Sims viewed matters,

> On the whole, the general supply situation is very satisfactory indeed. A safe supply is in hand. The loss of a supply vessel at this time would, of course, be seriously regarded, yet it would not complicate our operations in any way, as the amount of material on hand is sufficient to last until a replacement could arrive. Considering the multiplicity of our demands, and the distribution of our forces, the force commander considers it quite remarkable that there has been no occasion of complaint of delays in receipt of important items of supplies.

That was quite a compliment coming from the commander of American Naval Forces, Europe. The wisdom of Sam McGowan's planning and his placement of the Bureau of Supplies and Accounts on a wartime basis as early as 1914 had paid off.

Supply Readiness in 1916

In his June 1916 memorandum to the secretary, Sam McGowan reported that:

- In April 1914, all Navy fuel depots had been well stocked with coal purchased at prices substantially lower than those charged in early 1915. The availability of these coal reserves forced suppliers to lower their prices for sales in 1915 and 1916.
- The use of Navy ships to transport coal to the West Coast drove down "excessively high" rates charged by commercial carriers.
- BuSandA also had laid in a large supply of fuel oil, gasoline, and other petroleum products under an existing contract at one-third the forthcoming prices announced by oil companies.
- A purchase of five million pounds of sodium nitrate in Antofagasta, Chile, saved the Navy approximately $60,000 over the lowest price available in the United States. By coincidence, an empty collier held up in the Pacific by an interruption of traffic through the Panama Canal had been diverted to Antofagasta, where she was loaded with the sodium nitrate. "A further saving results from the employment of a naval collier, due to the present excessive ocean freight rates."
- When the Navy needed to purchase 1.5 million pounds of shellac, an Indian firm in Calcutta bid $67,000 less for delivery in Manila than a U.S. company. "It is the intention to ship this shellac from Calcutta by commercial vessel to Manila, and then to the United States in a naval collier." McGowan knew that granting contracts for quality material to foreign low-bidders would bring lower bids from American suppliers, a source that would be needed when the United States entered the war.

- BuSandA established a system of operating accounts, plant and cost records, and financial statements "essential to the proper direction of an industrial establishment, whether private or governmental."
- By paying special attention to the purchase of quality provisions at the lowest possible cost and through adoption of a cafeteria system aboard ship, BuSandA had assured that "the U.S. Navy is the best fed Navy in the world."
- The Navy Pay Officers School, established in 1905 and subsequently abolished, had been reopened.

The Allied Blockade

The Allied blockade of the German coast had a strong impact on the Central Powers, who recognized in early 1917 that they could not open their supply lanes solely through use of conventional naval power. Their solution was to wage unrestricted submarine warfare against all neutral and belligerent merchant shipping contacted in the war zone. The German High Command understood that this policy risked bringing the United States into the war. However, the Germans gambled on starving Britain into submission by cutting off its vital sea lanes before American power could be unleashed.

The German submarine campaign to interdict the British lifeline nearly succeeded when the British supply of grain dropped to the three-week level. Sims had been sent to London initially to open contacts with the British well before American entry into the war. The British were reluctant to implement a convoy system, as Sims strongly recommended. According to historian Nathan Miller, senior Royal Navy officers considered convoying a defensive measure and they preferred to use such offensive measures as sending destroyers out to hunt down U-boats, arming merchant ships, and blocking approaches to submarine bases. However, Sims continued to advocate convoys and ultimately convinced the Royal Navy to adopt the system. His persistent pressure resulted in an emergency deployment of American destroyers to the war zone to combat the submarine threat. Use of American destroyers and convoys broke the back of the German submarine threat and staved off disaster.

Although the United States managed to stay officially neutral through the first two and a half years of the war, open submarine warfare, including attacks on American-flag ships, forced President Wilson and Congress to act. Public opinion had shifted markedly toward support of the Allies.

BuSandA and Pay Corps on a Wartime Basis

When Congress declared war on 6 April 1917, Paymaster General McGowan was organized and took steps to assure that everyone in BuSandA and in the field understood that Vice Admiral Sims's mission in Europe had changed from that of observer to operational commander. McGowan issued orders that any requirement Sims laid on the Bureau of Supplies and Accounts was to be filled—without question and on the same day it was received.

In 1917, Great Britain was suffering from a severe fuel shortage. The lack of oil was most critical and resulted in the U.S. Navy sending five older, coal-burning battleships to reinforce the British Grand Fleet rather than newer, more powerful, oil-fired "battlewagons." Coal supplies were only marginally better than oil and continued to dwindle. Coal soon became one of the major logistical challenges of the war for American forces in Europe.

Commander John Hancock was not only the BuSandA purchasing authority, he was also Sam McGowan's unofficial righthand man. Apparently, the chief took few major steps without calling Hancock into counsel.

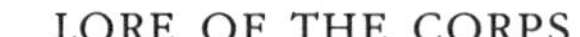

LORE OF THE CORPS

Lieutenant Commander John Milton Hancock, PC, USN

Purchasing Director, Bureau of Supplies and Accounts, 1914–19
Period of Service: 1904–19

John Hancock was one of RADM Sam McGowan's most trusted associates. On one occasion, when Bernard Baruch asked how the purchases of the Bureau had gone the previous day, McGowan responded, "I do not know; I haven't asked Hancock yet."

John M. Hancock was born at Emerado, North Dakota, in February 1883. He attended the University of North Dakota, where he was a lineman on the football team and editor-in-chief of the student publication. He was graduated in 1903 and was principal of a high school for a year before he accepted a commission as an assistant paymaster in the Navy in June 1904.

Following three months of instruction afloat and ashore, Hancock reported to the Bureau of Supplies and Accounts for the first time. He became general storekeeper at the Naval Station, Olongapo in the Philippines, in August 1906; was promoted to lieutenant, junior grade, in

May 1907; and then to passed assistant paymaster in October 1907 while serving in *USS Galveston*. This duty was followed by accounting tours at Boston, Philadelphia, and Puget Sound navy yards and Cavite Naval Station in the Philippines from October 1909 to March 1914.

Hancock returned to the Bureau of Supplies and Accounts in October 1914 as a paymaster and remained there throughout the war. He attained the rank of lieutenant commander in October 1916 and pay inspector with rank of commander in January 1918.

Hancock was the Navy's principal purchasing agent during the war. The Navy and Army often competed for many of the same resources, which each claimed it needed to carry out its respective mission. Hancock's orders were to get what the Navy needed, "come hell or high water," and worry about the Army later. He commented that the Army's plans for industrial mobilization were largely due to the Navy's success in wartime procurement. He believed that the Army feared it would lose to the Navy in competition for commonly desired items—fears that were well-founded. Hancock often succeeded in obtaining such things first, then let McGowan, Secretary Daniels, or the War Industries Board—on which Hancock served—decide whether the Navy should keep them.

Hancock's Purchasing Division performed phenomenal feats in purchasing $2 million worth of needed materials for the Navy each day during the war. He also served as chairman of the War Industries Board. The citation accompanying the Navy Cross he was awarded in 1919 read: "For exceptionally meritorious service in a duty of great responsibility in connection with the expansion and administration of the Bureau of Supplies Accounts and in maintaining liaison with outside organizations associated with the Bureau in the work of supplying the Navy."

When the United States entered World War I, existing Navy procedure called for the secretary of the Navy to sign much of the official paperwork personally. Officers serving in the Navy Department often experienced frustrating difficulty in obtaining the secretary's signature. Josephus Daniels seemed far less impressed with paperwork than did the bearers, who considered it to be more important than anything else.

Hancock, who routinely went to the secretary's office with important papers for Daniels to sign, waited all afternoon to see the secretary on one such occasion. It was almost 1800 hours when he entered Daniels's office, only to be told to return the following morning. Hancock replied that he had been waiting all afternoon. Daniels asked whether Hancock could not provide additional information, but the young officer replied that he would have no more information the next day than he already had.

Impressed with Hancock's assurance, Daniels started to sign his name. After putting his first name on the paper, he looked up at Hancock and asked whether he was sure of his arguments in the paper. Had he not been certain of his ground, Hancock assured Daniels, he would not have come to the office. Daniels completed his signature and, from that time on, Commander Hancock reportedly had no difficulty in obtaining the secretary's signature promptly.

CDR Hancock resigned in July 1919 and accepted the vice-presidency of the Jewel Tea Company in Winnetka, Illinois, one of 23 positions reportedly offered to him when he left the Navy. Lehman Brothers, the respected New York investment banking firm, was a major investor in Jewel. Hancock's success in turning around the situation at Jewel led to an offer of the presidency of Sears Roebuck and Company, but he became a partner in Lehman Brothers instead. Hancock also became a member of the boards of directors of a dozen major American businesses.

Hancock was called in 1939 to serve on the War Resources Board involved in developing a U.S. preparedness program for World War II. He worked with his old friend and World War I associate Bernard Baruch on a rubber survey, and the two served as advisers to the World War II Office of War Mobilization Board. John M. Hancock lived in Scarsdale, New York, and died in September 1956.

Sources

Baker, CAPT Cecil S., SC, USN. *A Collection of Abstracts Giving Historical Background for the Work of the Supply Corps* (ca. 1939).

Official Biography. Naval Historical Center, May 1932.

Who's Who in America (1948–49).

Provisioning a Flotilla

A flotilla of six U.S. destroyers was ordered to England in April 1917, a week after the United States officially entered the war. They were underway within 10 days and were followed, on roughly a weekly basis, by 5 additional flotillas of 6 destroyers each. Initially, supply support was on a somewhat ad hoc basis, but McGowan put his staff to work immediately on a long-term program to provide provisioning support for the destroyers based in Europe. On 14 May, ENS (later CAPT) William R. Ryan provided the paymaster general with a memorandum containing a comprehensive proposal for supporting the destroyers.

The BuSandA staff recommendation was based on a total of 36 destroyers in two squadrons and supported by two tenders, *USS Melville* and *USS Dixie*. Calculations of provisions requirements were based upon the assumption that each destroyer sailed with 45 days of provisions, as specified in the BuSandA provision list. Using this information, a common date was calculated on which the destroyers in each squadron should exhaust their provisions. This technique required that the entire squadron would pool its provisions among the 18 destroyers.

Having determined the date on which the provisions for each squadron would run out, the Bureau turned to determining how many additional days could be added through reprovisioning from the two tenders, *Melville* and *Dixie*. Three days were added to each destroyer squadrons' projected date of exhaustion to determine the number of transatlantic crossings required to support each.

Ryan concluded his recommendation with the suggestion that "I might be able to work out a schedule whereby the *Melville* and the *Dixie* could return here, fill up and go back again without the necessity of sending a supply ship if you care to consider such a method of supplying the destroyers. They would not, of course, get nearly so much fresh stuff as they would by supply ship." McGowan wrote across the bottom of the memorandum, "Excellentissimo! So be it."

LORE OF THE CORPS

Ensign William Russell Ryan, PC, USN

Special Assistant, Bureau of Supplies and Accounts, 1914–20
Period of Service: 1912–49

Ryan was an ensign when he wrote the plan for supporting destroyers in Europe, but he had been on Sam McGowan's staff since 1914, when he reported to BuSandA as a pay clerk.

William R. Ryan was born at Norristown, Pennsylvania, in April 1890, attended public schools there, and the Schissler Business College in Philadelphia. He was appointed a paymaster's clerk in November 1912 and assigned to the Naval Home, Philadelphia. He then went to sea in *USS Wyoming* as assistant to the fleet paymaster from 1913 to 1914. In October 1914, he reported to BuSandA as assistant to the general inspector of the Pay Corps and was promoted to pay clerk in July 1915. Ryan was commissioned a temporary ensign in October 1917.

He also had additional duty as special assistant to Paymaster General McGowan, a position he held until McGowan retired in 1920. McGowan was highly complimentary of the program Ryan developed for the loading and scheduling of provisions ships in support of U.S. Naval Forces in Europe. Ryan was promoted to lieutenant in September 1918. He was detached in December 1920 and received a letter of commendation for his services that said: "As the Officer in Charge of all administrative matters pertaining to provisions and ship-store stock for the entire service and subsistence in the Fleet, and in the Naval Districts, and to troop transport subsistence, he rendered highly meritorious service."

LT Ryan was ordered to duty as supply officer on the staff of commander, Train (forerunner of the modern Service Force), Atlantic Fleet, in the flagship *USS Columbia* in 1920. He was given a permanent commission in the Regular Navy in September 1921 and served as officer-in-charge, Navy Motion Picture Exchange, New York, from 1922 to 1926. In March 1926, he reported for duty as assistant government secretary and aide to the governor (a Navy officer), St. Thomas, U.S. Virgin Islands.

Ryan returned to CONUS in September 1928 as supply officer of the Philadelphia Navy Yard. He was promoted to lieutenant commander in June 1931 and ordered back to sea in *USS Omaha* (CL-4), Battle Force, Pacific Fleet, from 1931 to 1934. LCDR Ryan had duty at the Charleston and Mare Island navy yards and was promoted to commander in June 1938. He had sea duty as supply officer in *USS Mississippi* (BB-41) from 1938 to 1940 and returned to Mare Island in January 1940.

CDR Ryan served as executive assistant at the Naval Supply Depot Oakland, California, from May to October 1942 and was promoted to captain in June. He next reported for duty as the commissioning supply officer in command, Naval Supply Depot Scotia, New York. He was promoted to commodore and reported for temporary duty in October 1944 to the Bureau of Supplies and Accounts. In March 1945, he was ordered to duty as supply officer on the staff of commander, U.S. Naval Forces in Europe with additional duty as special naval observer, American Embassy, London.

COMO Ryan returned to BuSandA in January 1946 as fiscal director. In April 1947, authority for his temporary rank expired, and he reverted to the rank of captain. In April 1947, he reported for duty as supply officer in command, Naval Supply Depot Clearfield, Utah. He retired 1 June 1949 at Jacksonville, Florida.

Sources

Official Biography. Naval Historical Center, 1949.

Ryan, W. R., to S. McGowan. "Provisioning Destroyers in Europe." Memorandum. 14 May 1917. Navy Supply Corps Museum, Athens, Ga.

Food Shipments from America

U.S. forces in Europe continued to rely on shipments of fresh meat and vegetables from the American side of the Atlantic because of wartime food shortages in Britain and France. In December 1917, McGowan endorsed a letter from the commanding officer of the "reefer" *USS Bridge* (AF-1), requesting the installation of additional refrigeration equipment in order to increase the carrying capacity for fresh vegetables. The paymaster general concurred, but only if *Bridge,* which was a vital link in the supply of U.S. forces in Europe, could be spared for the six to eights months required for the alterations.

McGowan recommended in his endorsement that the matter be referred to the commander-in-chief of the Atlantic Fleet, with further reference to the commander of the Train for specific comments. He went on to point out that there was no need to provide additional refrigerated space for potatoes from the United States to be transported to Europe. "Potatoes are available over there at a much less price than what they can be obtained for in this country. On a recent trip of one of the supply ships to European waters with a cargo of fresh vegetables, about 170,000 pounds of potatoes were brought back for this very reason."

Apparently, the request for expansion was denied, and *Bridge* remained in service. During 1917–18, she made four transatlantic round trips while attached to the Naval Overseas Transportation Service. In July 1918, *Bridge* was assigned to the Train, Atlantic Fleet.

Deployment of the U.S. Navy Sixth Battle Squadron, comprised of the newer, oil-fired battleships, also involved considerable logistic decisions. The ships were first sent to Scapa Flow in the Orkney Islands north of Scotland, where the British Grand Fleet was deployed to conduct operations against the German fleet in the North Sea. The American and British battleships later returned to the Firth of Forth. In March 1918, Pay Inspector W. J. Glick, the on-site naval stores officer, recommended that certain supply support for the Sixth Battle Squadron be drawn from British sources in order "to save tonnage and transportation from the United States."

Glick pointed out that the squadron had, or would soon have, sufficient stores to last until November 1918. He reported that American naval authorities proposed to maintain supplies by means of a supply ship that would arrive at four-to-six-month intervals. The intention of this scheme was to maintain stocks on board these ships at a level of about six months, but the weight of such loading would reduce speed of the supply ship. Flour and dry provisions were the big problems. As a result, Glick indicated that, after replenishing ships of the squadron, the balance of stocks would be transferred to a storehouse at Aberdeen to support American forces. In addition, Glick proposed that certain bulky naval stores, flour, and dry provisions also be obtained from the British.

Pay Inspector Eugene C. Tobey, on the staff of the commander, Naval Forces Europe, was responsible for determining which provisions were more logically obtained in Great Britain and which should be imported from the United States.

LORE OF THE CORPS

Pay Inspector Eugene Cameron Tobey, PC, USN

Assistant to U.S. Naval Attaché, London, 1916–18; Aide, Staff, Commander, U.S. Naval Forces Europe, 1918–19
Period of Service: 1898–20

Pay Inspector Tobey served throughout World War I as a key link in command relationships between the U.S. Navy and the Royal Navy, for which he was awarded the Distinguished Service Medal.

Eugene Tobey was born in Maine in August 1870, was appointed temporary assistant paymaster in May 1898, and served in *USS Montauk* and *USS Marcellus*. At the end of the Spanish-American War, he was detached and returned home to settle his accounts. He was released from active duty in March 1899, but reentered the Navy in April 1899 with a regular commission as assistant paymaster. He was assigned first to the Naval Station, Bremerton, Washington, and, in October 1900, to the Mare Island Navy Yard.

Tobey was ordered the following month to *USS Don Juan de Austria* in Asiatic waters, where he served until ordered to the New York Navy Yard in 1903. He became the general storekeeper there in 1904 and later that year reported as paymaster, Panama Canal Commission, and served in that post until 1906. One of his duties was setting up and operating the Panama Canal Commission postal service and thus became, in effect, the Canal Zone's postmaster general.

Official records are sparse on his subsequent duties, but they do indicate that he was promoted to pay director with rank of commander in July 1917 and pay inspector with rank of captain in January 1919. CAPT Tobey completed his assignment with U.S. Naval Forces Europe in August 1919 and was ordered to Paris for special duty in connection with the Shipping Board. He resigned his commission in April 1920.

Sources

Director of Victualling, Royal Navy to Pay Inspector E. C. Tobey. Memorandum. 30 March 1918. Navy Supply Corps Museum, Athens, Ga.
Official Biography. Naval Historical Center, n.d.

Fresh Meat to Forces in Europe

The commander, Train, Atlantic Fleet, estimated that the 80,000 men of the American Naval Forces Europe required 9.33 million pounds of fresh meat every three months. The three older refrigerated supply ships then in the Train—*Culoga, Glacier,* and *Celtic*—had a combined refrigerated capacity of 1.93 million pounds of fresh meat. Making 2 trips each every 3 months, the 3 ships could move 3.86 million pounds to Europe, leaving a balance of 5.47 million pounds to be supplied by other means. To transport the total requirement from America would require 14½ ships of comparable capacity. The recently commissioned *Bridge,* with a capacity of 1.2 million pounds, had been transporting only frozen meats because vegetables, eggs, and butter were preferably obtainable in Europe.

The commander, Train, using available requirement and capacity data, forecast that three additional ships of the Bridge-class would be required to provide the necessary fresh meats. Four and one-half *Bridges* would be required should it be necessary for the ships to carry a balanced cargo to supply 27,000 men for 30 days' meat and 21 days' fresh vegetables. The commander noted that ships going abroad spent a great deal of time in going from port to port to discharge their loads. He recommended that, should future terminal facilities be available, each ship could unload at only one port on each trip, returning sooner for another load. Smaller ships or overland transportation would distribute cargo to the ultimate destination, thereby saving much time and increasing the number of trips each ship could make quarterly.

Petroleum Supply

The supply of petroleum products for American and British forces continued to be a major concern of the U.S. Navy and the Royal Navy. On 3 July 1917, a conference of American and British officers was convened at the Bureau of Supplies and Accounts to discuss Allied requirements.

Following the conference, Paymaster General McGowan advised Secretary Daniels that, based on British estimates, combined monthly fuel-oil requirements of American and British forces would be 200,000 tons by August. Because U.S. tankers could transport only about half the requirements, McGowan pointed out that additional American or British tankers would be required to make up the deficit. While awaiting information on tanker tonnage the British could supply, he requested all American tanker owners to advise him of U.S. tankers available for charter.

Daniels cabled Sims on 20 July with information that arrangements had been made to deliver an additional 105,000 tons of fuel oil by 30 September and an additional 25,000 tons a month thereafter. The secretary pointed out that meeting this schedule was contingent upon the release of tankers as soon after arrival in theater as possible in order to assure that each made one round trip a month. Daniels went on to point out that plans were being formulated to assure additional deliveries, for a total of 280,000 tons by 30 September 1917 and 75,000 tons a month thereafter. To accomplish this would require additional tanker resources from the British Admiralty, but the British had not yet confirmed these resources.

Secretary Daniels reported in March 1918 that the Commerce Department expected new American tankers, with a combined capacity of 161,649 tons, to be completed by September. At the time, the Navy building program called for an increase of 130 percent in the number of destroyers by 30 September, but Daniels questioned whether all would be completed before the end of hostilities. Assuming that fuel requirements of the new destroyers would double, he projected that the new tankers could provide the capacity to meet the petroleum requirements of U.S. naval forces in Europe, with a surplus of 45,000 tons by 30 September 1918.

The Army was already operating two tankers, but its needs were expected to increase significantly when the Army aviation units were deployed on the Continent. Daniels told the Bureau chiefs that to support Army needs, "Steps will immediately be taken to undertake the building of 12 tankers in order that they may be put into service as soon as possible without delaying the destroyer program."

Special and Unusual Fuel Demands

The paymaster general shared with all concerned agencies the assumptions that had been used in March 1918 to project the fuel-oil and coal tonnage necessary to sustain the entire Fleet in European waters. McGowan said that all Navy vessels should be self-sustaining insofar as their fuel needs were concerned. He also emphasized that fuel-carrying colliers must be considered available for delivery of cargoes alongside ships, as well as into shore storage. The average time required for the Atlantic round trip, therefore, would be an estimated 40 days.

Troop transports and cargo carriers operated by the Navy in transatlantic service would be required to bunker on the Atlantic seaboard for the round trip. The schedule of operation for all fighting vessels would be 18 days underway and 12 days at anchor.

McGowan reported a monthly estimate for the Fleet of 390,289 tons of coal for the 250 coal-fired Navy ships in foreign service. Based upon a need for 193 colliers and 102 available, an additional 91 vessels would be required. McGowan's estimate for the 142 oil-burning ships in foreign service was 91,957 tons. To meet the need, he suggested that 8 tankers be obtained in addition to the 12 scheduled to be delivered in the summer.

Poised for Action

The anticipated epic sea battles, reminiscent of the War of 1812, never happened. The British Grand Fleet, reinforced by American battleships, waited for the Germans to venture forth again. However, the Berlin High Command hesitated to chance a repeat of the debacle at Jutland in May 1915. As a result of stalemates both on the ocean and in the trenches of France, British and American naval strategy concentrated on combating the remaining German submarine threat and moving fresh American troops to Europe.

By the summer of 1918, an American fleet of troop transports and converted passenger liners successfully moved 10,000 "doughboys" daily to French ports. Before hostilities ended in November, this armada had transported more than two million American troops to France without the loss of a single ship or man.

Supplying fuel oil for operating forces was not the only issue for U.S. naval forces Europe. In March 1918, American and French authorities disputed which of them was to place orders through the British Admiralty for a supply of fuel oil for the U.S. Naval Station at Brest, France. The dispute arose when the French minister of marine sought to abrogate a December 1917 agreement between Captain Richard H. Jackson, a line officer who was staff representative of U.S. Naval Forces Europe in Paris, and the ministry. Under this agreement, U.S. naval forces at Brest were to place fuel-oil requisitions directly on the British Admiralty, but the French would handle and issue the fuel until additional tanks were erected.

Communications between American and French officials continued for more than a month in an attempt to resolve the issue. Finally, in a 29 April memorandum, CDR John F. Hatch, aide for material and supplies in London, advised the commander, U.S. Naval Forces France, that "under the agreement now in force with the French Ministry of Marine, the U.S. Navy will not concern itself with obtaining a supply of fuel oil for the French fuel-oil station at Brest. In order, however, that there may be no possible misunderstanding and resultant shortage of fuel oil, I suggest that the Naval Base Brest inform me monthly of the fuel oil on hand and the estimated requirements for the U.S. Naval Forces for the following month."

A side issue concerned the accounting for receipts and issues of fuel oil at Brest. The matter was the subject of many dispatches between Europe and Washington in 1918 and 1919 and was still being discussed as late as February 1920 in communications between BuSandA and Navy representatives remaining in Europe.

LORE OF THE CORPS

Commander John F. Hatch, PC, USN

Assistant Aide for Material, Supplies and Repairs, U.S. Naval Forces in France, 1917–19
Period of Service: 1901–45

CDR Hatch was ordered to Paris as the second-ranking supply officer on the staff of the commander, U.S. Naval Forces France shortly after the United States entered World War I. He succeeded in achieving a compromise between U.S. and French naval commands in a dispute over the procurement, issue, and accounting for petroleum on the Atlantic coast port of Brest. Secretary of the Navy Josephus Daniels recognized CDR Hatch's contributions with a letter of commendation.

John Hatch was born at St. Albans, Vermont, in December 1879. He was educated in public schools in St. Albans and Des Moines, Iowa, and attended Wesleyan University for a year before receiving an appointment as assistant paymaster with the rank of ensign in January 1901. He reported for duty on the Asiatic Station with consecutive tours in *USS Manila, USS Isla de Luzon, USS Don Juan de Austria, USS Glacier,* and *USS Chattanooga.*

Between 1905 and 1915 Hatch served ashore as general storekeeper at the Boston Navy Yard, the Mare Island Navy Yard, the Naval Station at Cavite, the New York Navy Yard, and the Philadelphia Navy Yard. He reported as fleet supply officer, *USS Vestal* (AR-4), flagship of the Train, Atlantic Fleet, in December 1915, and in August 1917 to wartime staff duty as assistant aide for material, supplies, and repairs, U.S. Naval Forces in France.

CDR Hatch returned to the United States in November 1919 and had consecutive duty at New York, Boston, and Puget Sound navy yards, then returned to the Philippines for duty at the Naval Station, Cavite. He served as aide and fleet paymaster on the staff of commander-in-chief, U.S. Pacific Fleet from 1925 to 1927. Returning once again to America, he reported as officer-in-charge, Navy Purchasing Office, Newport, Rhode Island and was transferred to duty at the Naval Supply Office, Brooklyn, in July 1928.

He was supply officer, Puget Sound Navy Yard, from 1933 to 1935, when he reported to the Third Naval District, New York City. As a pay inspector with rank of captain, Hatch served as general inspector, Supply Corps, East Coast, Washington, D.C., between 1936 and 1938. His next duty was as supply officer-in-command, Naval Supply Depot San Diego, with additional duty as district supply officer, Eleventh Naval District, where he was serving when the United States entered World War II.

One of the junior officers in his department was LTJG (later RADM) Bernie Bieri, who recalls that Hatch was a smart, dedicated, no-nonsense officer who wanted no excuses, just performance. Bieri recalled, "When he got that [performance], you were on his side forever." Bieri also remembers that the Hatches were quite nonsocial. On one occasion when Bernie and Peggy Bieri attempted to make the customary courtesy call on his reporting senior, "It was after 4PM, the authorized hour, and they [the Hatches] sat in the living room, reading the paper, and wouldn't answer the door bell."

Hatch was promoted to rear admiral in 1942 and became district supply officer, Twelfth Naval District, San Francisco. He had additional duty as administrator of the Petroleum Pool, Pacific Coast. RADM Hatch reached mandatory retirement age in January 1944 and was placed on the retired list, but he remained on active duty at San Francisco until the war ended in August 1945. He is believed to have remained in San Francisco after retirement and to have died there shortly after World War II.

Hatch received the Chevalier of the Legion d'Honneur from the French government for his service during World War I. He was also awarded the Legion of Merit.

Sources

Hatch, J. F., to Commander, U.S. Naval Forces in France. "Supply of Oil at Brest." Memorandum. 29 April 1918. Navy Supply Corps Museum, Athens, Ga.
Official Biography. Naval Historical Center, 1946.

British Fuel to U.S. Ships

Standing orders were issued in June 1918 by the commanding officer, *USS Leonidas,* relative to the supply of fuel oil and coal at U.S. Naval Base 25 at Corfu in the Adriatic. The orders stated that "fuel oil and coal may be obtained from the British. All fuel oil and coal is in charge of the Senior British Naval Officer on board *Latona.* As he must be communicated with before any vessel go for these stores, it is necessary that the senior U.S. naval officer have complete data as to the amounts required before making a request."

The standing orders also laid out the procedures for coaling and gave locations for other supplies, including gasoline. Fresh water could be obtained from *Leonidas, HMS Aquaris,* or *HM Fleet Auxiliary Bacchus.* Fresh provisions would be issued daily from *Leonidas.*

Fuel requirements were not the sole supply matter to require attention at Brest. In September, VADM Sims sent a dispatch to McGowan in which he recommended a revised delivery schedule for *Celtic* and *Glacier.* He called for one supply ship to be routed to Brest and the Pauillac Naval Air Station in France. Another would go to Southampton first and then to Plymouth. Sims spelled out the specific quantities required at each place. He also pointed out that Brest had reported that the U.S. Army needed 400 tons of frozen meat and needed to know immediately whether this amount could be sent.

McGowan Strikes Back at Misinformation

The paymaster general was proud of the performance of the Pay Corps and the Bureau of Supplies and Accounts during the war. He was quick to react at even a hint that American sailors did not enjoy the best treatment of any navymen in the world. In August 1918, he sent a memorandum to Secretary Daniels regarding a solicitation of funds to supply British and American sailors with fresh fruits and vegetables, jams, and preserves. A solicitation letter being circulated by one well-intentioned but misinformed Benjamin Guiness of New York stated that crews of

British and American warships "get practically no fresh vegetables and no fresh fruit whatever, except what they pay for out of their own pockets."

The indignant McGowan asked the Office of Naval Intelligence to investigate Guiness. ONI reported that Guiness was a respectable man who had merely mistakenly assumed that sailors had to purchase their own fresh vegetables and fruit. When he was apprised of the facts, Guiness immediately destroyed his remaining letters and enclosures and said that he intended to write an unconditional letter of apology to McGowan.

Sam McGowan, ever alert to the advantages of positive public relations, suggested to Secretary Daniels that, without mentioning the name of the offending author, he issue an official statement to the press. The statement should set out the facts and warn the public against similar efforts "to collect funds for purposes which the Government amply provides for."

Wartime Contributions

When the war ended in November 1918, the U.S. Navy was not only the strongest it had ever been, but also the most powerful in the world. Although historians have largely characterized World War I as a land war, naval forces played a major role, and naval logistics was a significant factor in the success of the Allied effort on both land and sea.

After the war, Admiral William V. Pratt, vice chief of naval operations, said, "Our total naval effort in this war consisted less in the operation of forces at the front than in a logistics effort in the rear, in which the greatest problems we had to contend with originated and had to be solved here at home." It should be remembered that Paymaster General Sam McGowan had told his associates, when the United States entered the fighting in 1917, that although the war would be waged in France, Germany, and Belgium, it would be won in Washington.

Navy purchases, largely the responsibility of the Bureau of Supplies and Accounts, illustrate the dimensions of the logistics effort. In 1914, three years before the United States entered the war, McGowan recommended a substantial increase in the Navy's material account for 1915. The increase made it possible to build war reserve stocks of Navy-specific items that could not be quickly obtained from commercial stocks. Also in 1914, BuSandA developed the Navy Standard Stock Catalog, which was of great value when the Navy purchased more than $500 million of equipment and supplies in 1918. The importance of the catalog to the Navy's successful war effort led to authorization for McGowan to establish a Federal Standard Stock Catalog based upon the Navy's catalog system.

For the fiscal year 1916, before the United States entered the war, the paymaster general reported that the Navy purchased $27 million in equipment and supplies. In a single day in 1918, Navy purchases were more than $30 million.

Secretary Daniels reported in his annual report for 1918 that "there has been no confusion, no relaxation of any of the established safeguards against imposition and fraud. So far as practicable, everything has been bought—just as it always was—after open and public competition among manufacturers and regular dealers (and where this was impossible) the transaction was nevertheless open to the public."

A wartime need arose for 24-inch nickel steel billets (bars). BuSandA had determined in 1915 that it was important to have a supply of these billets on hand, even though no specific identifiable need existed before the United States entered the War. The Bureau had authorized purchase of a large quantity of the billets and stocked them at Mare Island Shipyard in California. The yard later received orders to construct destroyers, but the supplier of shafting material could not make delivery on time. The nickel billets were withdrawn from stock and forged into shafts for *USS Fairfax* two months earlier than possible had the yard waited for shafting supplied from commercial sources. The ready availability of the billets allowed expedited completion of the ship to join the hunt for German submarines.

Expansion rather than change characterized the wartime operations of BuSandA. The number of Pay Corps officers grew from 232 to 3,315, and the number of civilian employees from 120 to 1,645. This talented group of military and civilian personnel generated many innovative ideas, the most widely publicized of which was the Eyes of the Navy Program. The war had cut off the foreign supply of binoculars, long glasses, and telescopes when the German submarine threat created a need for these instruments. BuSandA appealed to patriotic Americans to furnish the needed "eyes." Under this program, 51,217 instruments were sent in, and 31,000 were deemed suitable for use in U.S. Navy ships. Each owner received a letter of thanks and a sales or rental check for one dollar. Each instrument supplied to the Navy was engraved with a serial number, and a permanent record was established. At the end of the war, BuSandA returned the instruments to their owners, along with documentation of how each was employed.

Under wartime restrictions on shipping, commercial shippers were hampered in moving nonmilitary shipments. The shippers began to resort to consigning carload shipments to a naval officer at a commercial firm, although the Navy was not involved in the transactions. BuSandA issued an alert order to shippers, and the Justice Department secured indictments against several firms that engaged in this illegal practice.

McGowan and Equal Status for Staff Officers

Sam McGowan had worked tirelessly to eliminate the second-class status of Navy staff officers. Assistant Secretary Franklin Roosevelt was supportive, but he was not confident that he could convince Secretary Daniels to issue an order that would give Staff Corps officers equal status with line officers. Roosevelt and McGowan agreed on a strategy to obtain Daniels's agreement. McGowan capitalized on Daniels's trust of CDR John Hancock by enlisting that talented officer in a plan to obtain the secretary's consent.

McGowan drew up a proposed regulation to accomplish his objective and waited patiently for the right time to present his case. The opportunity came in August 1919, when Daniels called Commanders Hancock and James Hilton into his office late one afternoon to commend them for their wartime accomplishments. Hancock went with McGowan's draft order in his hands. Roosevelt, McGowan, other senior Supply Corps officers, and Sue Dorsey, McGowan's trusted secretary, waited in the paymaster general's office for Hancock and Hilton to return. They finally returned at 1915 hours. Hancock was all smiles, but Hilton was unaware of the nature of the document Hancock had casually convinced Daniels to sign. The paymaster general already had the order printed and in preaddressed envelopes, ready to be placed in the mail immediately. The order, requiring that all officers of the Navy be addressed by rank rather than such functional titles as *doctor* and *paymaster* went out that night. It also called for the elimination of the white band between gold stripes on uniform sleeves of staff officers.

Line officers were indignant and strongly resented Sam McGowan's coup. They protested vigorously, but Daniels refused to rescind the order. McGowan had accomplished his mission and struck a welcome blow for all Navy staff officers.

During the war, the Bureau of Supplies and Accounts and the Pay Corps had experienced an unprecedented level of demand on its services and facilities. Led by Paymaster General McGowan, BuSandA had met the challenges of wartime service to the Fleet and put into place many of the practices and procedures that would guide Navy logistics for decades to come. Members of the Pay Corps could not only take pride in their wartime accomplishments but also in their officially attained status as full-fledged officers of the U.S. Navy alongside their line brethren.

Sources

Sources for material used in this chapter and not cited earlier include:

Miller, Nathan. *The U.S. Navy: An Illustrated History*. Annapolis: Naval Institute Press, and New York: American Heritage Press, 1977. (Discussions of historic events.)

Carter, Worrall R., and Elmer E. Duvall. *Ships, Salvage, and Sinews of War: The Story of Fleet Logistics Afloat in the Atlantic and Mediterraanean Waters during World War II*. Washington: U.S. Government Printing Office, 1954. (Passages dealing with Navy supply depots from 1940 through 1942.)

Copies of the dispatches, memoranda, and other official Navy communications during World War I quoted and otherwise referenced were provided by William N. Still, Jr., former director, Program in Maritime History and Nautical Archeology, Department of History, East Carolina University, Greenville, N.C. These copies are now on file at the Navy Supply Corps Museum, Athens, Ga.

Additional sources for material:

"The Bureau in World War I." *Navy Supply Corps Newsletter*, February 1970.

Dictionary of American Fighting Ships, vol. 1: *A-B*. Washington, D.C.: Naval Historical Center, Department of the Navy, 1954.

The second *USS Supply*, 1895-1921, a schooner-rigged iron-steamer, served as a fleet replenishment ship during the Spanish-American War. (*Navy Supply Corps Newsletter*)

Burning and sinking U.S. battleships are shown at Pearl Harbor immediately following the sneak Japanese attack on 7 December 1941. Two Supply Corps ensigns died in their ships. (*Navy Supply Corps Newsletter*)

Supplies accumulate on a World War II beachhead as Marine and Army troops move inland. (*Navy Supply Corps Newsletter*)

CAPT George Bauernschmidt, C.O., and CDR Bill Nelson, X.O., inspect enlisted personnel at Naval Supply Depot, Oran, Algeria, January 1944. (CAPT Sam Meyer, SC, USNR-Ret.)

Warehouses and open storage, Naval Supply Depot Guam, May 1948. (Official U.S. Navy photograph)

Pier 91, Naval Supply Depot Seattle before consolidation into NSC Puget Sound. (*Navy Supply Corps Newsletter*)

Naval Supply Center Norfolk Building W-143 was the largest building south of the Pentagon in 1970. (Official U.S. Navy photograph)

Fleet Air Wing 16 supply officers from detachments throughout Brazil attended a conference at NAS Recife in May 1943. (CAPT Ernest F. Williams, SC, USNR-Ret.)

Supply Corps officers stationed at Charleston and guests celebrate the sesquicentennial of the Supply Corps in 1945. The speaker is CAPT Eddie Hunt; CDR Hersh Goldberg is second from left. (Official U.S. Navy photograph)

Two World War II chiefs of the Supply Corps—RADM Nick Carter (seated, center left) and RADM Brent Young (seated, center right)—are shown with officers on BuSandA staff, including a future chief, RADM Murrey Royar (standing, fourth from right). (*Navy Supply Corps Newsletter*)

Future chief of the Supply Corps and DLA director ENS Gene Grinstead, a member of Underwater Demolition Team 12, with a group of recently liberated Chinese in October 1945. (VADM Eugene A. Grinstead, SC, USN-Ret.)

A portion of the nearly 11 tons in cash shipped to San Francisco and accompanied by LTJG Ed Goddard being loaded aboard *USS General William Mitchell* (AP-114) at Guam in 1946. (Edward Goddard)

CAPT Kenneth McIntosh, C.O., NSCS Harvard, inspects room of four WAVE ensigns (left to right) Jane Staiger, Mary Day, Sally Bronson, and Marie Gartner. (Navy Supply Corps Museum)

President Harry Truman presents photos of the Yalta Conference to Prime Minister Winston Churchill aboard the presidential yacht *USS Williamsburg* in January 1952. LCDR Leo Roberts, supply officer, stands by in left background. (CAPT Leo Roberts, SC, USN-Ret.)

Eggburt cartoons by LCDR Earle Chesney, with verses by LT Lowell Lawrence, were conceived to get important messages across to new Supply Corps officers during World War II in a light and unofficial manner. (RADM Charles A. Blick, SC, USN-Ret.)

CHAPTER SEVEN

Between the World Wars

1919–38

Paymaster General Sam McGowan had proved the wisdom of adherence to the century-old philosophy of another South Carolinian, John C. Calhoun. In 1820 Calhoun wrote, "The only difference between peace and war formation ought to be in magnitude; and the only change in passing from the former to the latter should consist in giving to it the augmentation which will then be necessary."

The Bureau of Supplies and Accounts had been ready for the war. The organization and procedures were in place, and the only change in passing from the peace of 1914–16 to the war of 1917–18 was in the augmentation of the Bureau with the additional Pay Corps officers and civilian employees necessary to address the increased magnitude of activity.

Officers of the Pay Corps had gained new respect from their line brethren. Legislation in 1916 had fixed the authorized strength of the Pay Corps at 12 percent of the line, and a 1918 general order gave Pay Corps officers full equality with line officers. The Pay Corps was redesignated Supply Corps in 1919 in recognition of the expanded scope of supply responsibilities.

Sam McGowan had led the Bureau of Supplies and Accounts through its greatest challenge and had emerged with the admiration of both government and the press. He was a national hero, but by the end of 1919 he was worn out. Although 30 years of service was customarily required for an officer to retire under the then-existing regulations, an admiring Congress passed special legislation allowing McGowan to retire with only 26 years of service, effective 31 January 1920.

RADM Christian J. Peoples, SC, USN, another of McGowan's trusted comrades, who was awarded the Navy Cross for his wartime service, was appointed acting chief of the Bureau of Supplies and Accounts and paymaster general.

LORE OF THE CORPS

Rear Admiral Christian J. Peoples, SC, USN

Acting Chief, Bureau of Supplies and Accounts, 1920–21; Chief, Bureau of Supplies and Accounts, 1933–35
Period of Service: 1900–1940

When Secretary of the Navy Josephus Daniels decided to appoint RADM Peoples, acting chief of BuSandA from January to May 1921, permanently to the position, Peoples surprised the secretary and fellow officers by declining. Such an opportunity rarely comes to an individual twice, but in Peoples's case it did—12 years later. The second time—in 1933—he accepted.

Christian J. Peoples was born at Creston, Iowa, in October 1876, and was educated in California at St. Ignatius College, Sacred Heart College, and the University of California. In 1900 he was appointed assistant paymaster in the Pay Corps with relative rank of lieutenant, junior grade, and assigned for a short time as assistant general storekeeper at the Puget Sound Naval Station. He went to sea briefly in the hospital ship *Solace* in 1901, then to *USS Wilmington* on the Asiatic Station. He was promoted to passed assistant paymaster in March 1903 and to paymaster in December.

Paymaster Peoples came ashore in February 1904 to settle accounts and reported as general storekeeper, Norfolk Navy Yard, for a brief tour. He was ordered for duty later in 1904 at the Bureau of Supplies and Accounts, where he served for nearly seven years and developed improvements to the centralized purchasing system. This system included a complete change in methods of delivery, an increase in the number of Navy standard specifications, and new procedures for storage and conditions of payment. He was promoted to lieutenant commander in February 1910.

LCDR Peoples returned to sea as supply officer of the battleship *USS Utah* with the Atlantic Fleet from 1910 to 1914. During this tour, Peoples took a special Naval War College course for officers afloat. In 1914 he was ordered to duty as general inspector of the Pay Corps and assistant chief of the Bureau of Supplies and Accounts. He remained in that billet throughout World War I and received wartime promotions to commander and captain. He was promoted to the rank of rear admiral in July 1917.

His earlier experience in development of a modern purchasing system was an important factor in the outstanding record compiled by BuSandA in supplying the Fleet during World War I. Among the wartime projects for which Peoples was responsible was the design and implementation of standardized systems for providing steaming coal and fuel oil for American naval forces overseas. He also recommended the creation of the emergency Export Control Committee, was the Navy's representative on the War Industries Board, and a member of the Navy Yard Development Board.

While Peoples was serving as assistant chief of the Bureau, an urgent need arose for foul-weather gear for navymen serving in destroyers on convoy and antisubmarine warfare duty in the North Atlantic. Secretary Daniels asked him to appear before congressional committees to secure a $4 million supplemental appropriation for the protective clothing. Peoples had the Naval Clothing Factory at Brooklyn make up "suitable clothing" and provide him with photographs of sailors wearing it. When he went before the House Naval Affairs Committee, he argued the case forcefully and at length and showed the committee the photographs. The committee approved the $4 million appropriation, and deployed sailors promptly received the warm, waterproof clothing.

When RADM Peoples declined the offer of permanent appointment as chief, Secretary Daniels wrote to him, "The reason you give that you prefer not to stand in other people's way, especially since you are already a senior Rear Admiral, indicates a spirit of unselfishness worthy of the highest commendation." Admiral Peoples was awarded the Navy Cross. When he left BuSandA, RADM Peoples became general inspector of the Supply Corps for the Pacific Coast from May 1921 to March 1930 and then officer-in-charge, Naval Supply Depot Brooklyn, from 1930 to 1933.

In July 1933, he finally agreed to accept nomination as chief of the Bureau of Supplies and Accounts and paymaster general of the Supply Corps. Four months later, at the request of Treasury Secretary Henry Morgantheau, he was appointed concurrently to the additional post of director of procurement, Department of the Treasury. Because of the pressure of public business in both offices and at the direction of President Franklin D. Roosevelt, Peoples resigned as chief of BuSandA in 1935, but remained as Treasury's chief of procurement until October 1939. In 1939 the Procurement Division was renamed the Bureau of Federal Supply and, in 1949, evolved into the present federal supply service, the General Services Administration.

When RADM Peoples left Washington in October 1939, he once again became general inspector of the Supply Corps on the Pacific Coast until he retired from the Navy in November 1940. In retirement he became special representative of the Todd Shipbuilding Corporation in Washington. He died of pneumonia in February 1941 and was buried in Arlington National Cemetery.

Sources

"Adm. Peoples Dies; Headed U.S. Purchasing." *Washington Post,* 4 February 1941.

Daniero, Roger D., Commissioner, Federal Supply Service, General Services Administration to Commander Naval Supply Systems Command, 8 January 1991.

Official Biography. Naval Supply Systems Command, n.d.

Who's Who in America, n.d.

The Atlantic and Pacific Fleets

With opening of the Panama Canal in 1914 and scuttling of the German fleet at Scappa Flow in 1918, Navy strategists turned their attention to the Pacific and the rising Japanese threat. In the summer of 1919, the U.S. Navy was divided into two fleets, with the newest and most powerful ships assigned to the Pacific Fleet.

Naval strategists, noting that Japan had undertaken significant expansion of its navy, were suspicious of that nation's interests in the Pacific. They pointed out that during the war Japan had seized German properties in China and taken over the Mariana, Marshall, and Caroline islands, which were astride the American line of communications between Hawaii and the Philippines. The Japanese had also aggressively pressed demands upon China in complete disregard of the Open Door policy that the United States had fostered there. Building upon its considerable experience gained during the war, BuSandA and members of the Supply Corps turned to expansion of the Navy's logistics capabilities in the Pacific.

Only 4 of the 10 U.S. 32,600-ton battleships, authorized in 1916, had been laid down when work was halted during the war in order to concentrate on destroyer construction to combat the submarine menace. With the war over, President Wilson startled the nation with a proposal not only to resume the program but to also expand it. He proposed a program to give the U.S. Navy an unmatched fleet of 39 dreadnoughts and 12 battle cruisers.

Speculation arose that Wilson's proposal was not serious, but rather intended to gain Britain's support of his pet project, the League of Nations. His proposal worried and angered the British and caused a rift between the former allies that lasted for a decade. In the end, the British supported the League of Nations, but the U.S. Senate did not.

Ashore, the Navy Catalog Office was established at the Naval Supply Depot Brooklyn in 1920. Formal training of Supply Corps officers was resumed with establishment of the Navy Supply Corps School of Application at BuSandA in 1921, which had been closed in May 1918 when the decision was made to send Pay Corps officers to the Naval Academy for training of a more nautical nature. The school offered a four-month course of instruction in business economics, banking, accounting, manufacturing, and practical phases of the naval profession.

When Rear Admiral Christian Peoples retired in July 1921, RADM David Potter, a veteran of Mexican service in 1914, became chief of the Bureau of Supplies and Accounts and paymaster general.

LORE OF THE CORPS

Rear Admiral David Potter, SC, USN

Chief, Bureau of Supplies and Accounts, and Paymaster General, 1921–25
Period of Service: 1898–1939

David Potter boldly maintained that the methods of business administration of the Navy should serve as models for the methods of industry. He first took this audacious position publicly in an article entitled "The Pay Corps of the Navy: A Sketch" in the December 1917 issue of the *United States Naval Institute Proceedings*. During his administration, he gave lectures at colleges and universities throughout the nation.

David Potter was born at Bridgeton, New Jersey, in December 1874, and was graduated from Princeton University in 1896. He practiced law briefly before accepting a commission as an assistant paymaster with rank of ensign in 1898. His first duty was in *USS Katahdin*, an unusual, low-freeboard, 2,155-ton vessel known as *Old Half-Seas Under* intended to ram and sink enemy ships. He served in *Katahdin* throughout the Spanish-American War on coastal patrol off New England, a time when citizens were concerned about potential attacks by the Spanish fleet. He then served in *USS Buffalo* during the Philippine campaign, and served seven sea tours during the early part of the century, mostly in battleships.

Potter was serving in *USS Washington* when sent ashore at Vera Cruz,

Mexico, in 1914 as fiscal officer of customs during the brief American occupation. Widespread and uncontrolled printing of paper money by Pancho Villa's revolutionaries had seriously undermined currency values. When Potter arrived at the customhouse in Vera Cruz in April, he found the place in shambles, with furniture and equipment destroyed and the floors knee deep with records and papers.

Mexican legal officials, who did not trust the Yankees, had disappeared. Potter, accompanied by armed Marines, convinced them to return and open the vaults for an inventory of cash on hand. There was $40,000 in gold, $15,000 in silver, and $30,000 in revenue stamps. Fortunately, a search of the pile of papers on the floor uncovered a small piece of paper that verified the amount of cash in the vault as being the official count on the day before the Americans arrived. Potter's persistence eventually uncovered the local controller of currency, who assisted him in restoring order to a thoroughly disorganized customs organization. With a Mexican statement that confirmed the cash found in the vault and with order restored, Potter had abundant proof of Yankee honesty. All was in order when the American Navy and Army returned Vera Cruz to the Mexican constitutional authorities.

Captain Potter went on the road in 1917 to lecture at Harvard and New York universities on "Fiscal Adventures of an Officer of the U.S. Navy" and to describe the important role he had played as fiscal officer of customs at Vera Cruz.

Potter served as a member of the Navy Compensation Board during the World War I, handling details of vessels constructed in civilian shipyards. He was given a temporary promotion to the rank of rear admiral when he relieved RADM Christian J. Peoples as chief of the Bureau of Supplies and Accounts in 1921. In his new role as head of both BuSandA and the Supply Corps, Potter reopened the Navy Supply Corps School of Application at Washington in July 1921. As chief, he also was a member of the Board for Settlement of Claims Arising from the Treaty Limiting Naval Armament.

It was customary for chiefs of Navy bureaus to revert from their temporary rank of rear admiral to their permanent rank of captain when relieved. Potter, who was relieved by RADM Charles Morris in 1925, became a member of the Naval War Claims Board from 1926 to 1930. Captain Potter's next assignment was as general inspector of the Supply Corps for the West Coast until 1934. His article "The Annual Naval Appropriations Bill" was published in the December 1932 issue of the *United States Naval Institute Proceedings*. He relinquished the general inspector post in 1934 to establish the Navy Finance and Supply School at the Philadelphia Navy Yard. Potter remained at the head of the school until 1938. He then had temporary duty at Headquarters, Twelfth Naval District, San Francisco, until he retired on 1 January 1939 at San Francisco after 42 years of naval service.

Potter continued to write for publication in *Proceedings;* "The Naval Finance and Supply School" was published in the August 1939 issue.

Sources

Official Biography. Naval Supply Systems Command, n.d.

Potter, David, CAPT USN. "The Annual Naval Appropriations Bill." *U.S. Naval Institute Proceedings,* December 1932.

———. "The Naval Finance and Supply School." *U.S. Naval Institute Proceedings,* August 1939.

———. "The Pay Corps of the Navy: A Sketch." *U.S. Naval Institute Proceedings,* December 1917.

Who's Who in America, 1916–17.

The Naval Armaments Conference

The United States did not join the League of Nations, but President Warren G. Harding was eager to demonstrate that he favored peace, and he accepted a British proposal for a disarmament conference. The British had accepted the reality of the U.S. Navy's emergence as a naval power the equal of the Royal Navy and agreed to accept parity between their respective navies.

The Harding administration invited Great Britain, Japan, France, and Italy to a conference in Washington in November 1922 to seek limitations on naval armaments and to resolve problems in the Pacific. The conference recognized that tensions in the Pacific were factors in a naval armaments race. China, Belgium, the Netherlands, and Portugal, as full participants, were invited to take part in discussions of the Far East, where they had interests.

Secretary of State Charles Evans Hughes opened the conference by making startling proposals that the nations cease building capital ships. He also proposed a naval tonnage ratio of the United States (5), Great Britain (5), Japan (3), France (1.7), and Italy (1.7) for battleships, aircraft carriers, cruisers, destroyers, and submarines. Foreign diplomats and American naval officers were stunned. However, no nation was willing to be blamed for sinking the conference, so the conferees eventually accepted the American proposal. They also reached two additional agreements:

- The Nine-Power Treaty, signed by all participants, was aimed at preserving the territorial integrity of China.
- The Four-Power Treaty, among the United States, Britain, France, and Japan, was an agreement for the signatories to respect each other's rights in the Pacific.

An Increased Role in the Pacific

The increasing emphasis on the U.S. Navy's role in the Pacific highlighted the need for expanded logistical support. The Naval Supply Depot San Diego, was commissioned in 1922 as the West Coast counterpart of the Naval Supply Station, Norfolk, which had opened in 1919.

Throughout the 200 years of Supply Corps history, supply officers—and their predecessors—often volunteered to undertake unusual tasks, many hazardous and not normally associated with their assigned duties. In 1919 LTJG Thomas S. Wylly, supply officer, *USS Wilmington,* a gunboat of the Asiatic Squadron, undertook a secret mission to deliver a special message to an Asian exile in China.

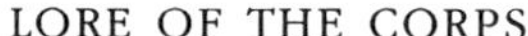

LORE OF THE CORPS

Lieutenant (junior grade) Thomas S. Wylly, SC, USN

Supply Officer, *USS Wilmington,* 1919–21
Period of Service: 1917–45

Tom Wylly had an unusual Supply Corps career and undertook two volunteer special assignments during his 28 years of service. He delivered a secret government message in China in 1919 and was an unofficial cartographer in Panama in the early 1920s.

Wylly was born at Darien, Georgia, in May 1893, where he attended public schools. When the United States went to war in 1917, he selected the Navy and went to Washington for additional schooling. He passed a competitive examination for a Pay Corps commission, was commissioned an assistant paymaster with rank of ensign, and attended the Navy Pay Corps School at the Washington Navy Yard. He requested sea duty and was assigned to the troop transport *USS Finland.*

Tom Wylly was one of four newly commissioned ensigns ordered to *Finland* in dry dock at the Brooklyn Navy Yard. Wylly was the oldest of the four, so he became supply officer and the other three became his assistants. The shipyard was repairing a torpedo hole, Wylly later recalled, "big enough to drive a train through."

He was supply officer of *Finland* when she made 24 Atlantic round trips, taking American troops to Europe during World War I and bringing them back after. In addition to his three Supply Corps assistants, Wylly had 150 enlisted men in the Supply Department to serve 3,600 military people on each loaded crossing. As he was once quoted, "With girls in France and girls and shows in New York and dodging German submarines in between, life was never dull for a newly caught young naval officer."

When interviewed in 1986, however, he admitted that "most of it was very monotonous" except the time that his ship collided with another transport crossing *Finland*'s bow as a result of a malfunctioning rudder. Both transports remained afloat, but *Finland*'s bow was bent at a right angle. French shipyard workers made temporary repairs, and Brooklyn shipyard workers later fitted a new bow. German submarines never sank a loaded troop transport en route to France, but an empty one was lost westbound after a successful eastbound crossing in a convoy with *Finland*.

Tom Wylly was bored with his duty in a troop transport returning soldiers after the war. He wanted "something more exciting, or at least interesting." At that time, junior officers did not make requests directly to the Navy Department. Wylly was not shy, so he requested two days leave in 1919, went to Washington and asked Paymaster General Sam McGowan to transfer him to the Asiatic Station. McGowan granted his request, and Wylly was ordered to report to the commander-in-chief, Asiatic Station, in the flagship *USS Brooklyn* (AC-3). He reported aboard the flagship at Olongapo in the Philippines for several weeks before being ordered to the gunboat *USS Wilmington* as supply officer. *Wilmington* was based at Shanghai and assigned to patrol the lower Yangtze River.

Wylly was departing *Brooklyn* for his new duty when the commander-in-chief, VADM William L. Rodgers, invited him to his cabin, where the Chief of Staff CAPT Thomas A. Kearney asked if Wylly would be willing to locate a man in Shanghai and deliver a message to him. The young LTJG assured his superiors that he would be happy to do so. They then told Wylly that the man's name was Sze Ching Wong; the message was "No." They told him to see the U.S. consul general at Shanghai, where *Wilmington* was anchored off the Bund, in order to find Sze.

Tom Wylly called on the consul general, whom he found pleasant and cooperative when he explained his mission. The consul thought that he would be able to contact Sze in a shabby part of the native Chinese section of the city. Several sampans appeared alongside *Wilming-*

ton over the next several days with messages from the consul to Wylly. Wylly went to the consul's office and met a mysterious American expatriate, George Sokolsky, who volunteered to help locate Sze. Wylly went ashore again several days later to an address provided by Sokolsky, where a woman said she had never heard of Sze, but agreed to help when Wylly mentioned the consul general and Sokolsky.

The next day, the consul requested that Wylly meet Sokolsky at the same address. There, he was promptly invited in to find Sokolsky and two young daughters of a Chinese businessman, who spoke excellent English. After an extensive discussion of world affairs and many questions about Wylly took place, they invited him to return for a third time a few days later.

On his return, he was introduced to Sze. Wylly delivered his message and returned to his ship. A few days later, CAPT Kearney went aboard *Wilmington* to assume command of the Yangtze Patrol. One day he told Wylly in confidence that Sze was actually Syngman Rhee, a Korean in exile who became the first president of democratic Korea 29 years later. Rhee had asked President Wilson whether he would send American troops to support him in the event that Rhee could mobilize the populace to overthrow the Japanese, occupants of his homeland.

In 1921 Wylly was ordered to the Special Service Squadron, a group of small gunboats homeported in Panama and supported by *USS Cleveland* (CA-19). The gunboats cruised the Caribbean and the west coast of South America, where Tom Wylly visited countries in Central and South America, including Chile, Bolivia, and Peru.

Wylly's supply duties were not overtaxing, so he volunteered to learn to draw maps. He borrowed instruments from a U.S. Coast and Geodetic Survey ship and became adept at map-making. When the teams sent out in small boats to survey the Panamanian Pacific coast returned each day, he used their notebooks and the borrowed instruments to make detailed maps. The Navy Hydrographic Office put the finishing touches on his maps and published them.

Tom Wylly had made lieutenant commander when he finally drew shore duty, reporting to the Boston Navy Yard in 1926 as one of four assistant supply officers. The submarine *S-4* was rammed and sunk by a rum-runner, but was raised and brought into the Boston Yard about a month later. Wylly was assigned to board the submarine to recover the bodies and personal possessions. He had the bodies embalmed and sent home and inventoried personal possessions and distributed them to surviving relatives. That experience was the downside of his Boston duty, but the upside was meeting his future wife, Edith, in 1927 and marrying her in 1928.

LCDR Wylly was outfitting supply officer of *USS Northampton* (CA-26), launched in 1929. *Northampton* served in both the Atlantic and Pacific fleets during Wylly's two and a half years aboard. In 1932 he was transferred to the Mare Island Navy Yard, and in 1935 was assigned as comptroller and cashier of the Bank of Guam. Wylly went to the Naval Powder Factory, Indian Head, Maryland, in 1937 as supply officer for two years. He was promoted to commander in 1939 and assigned as supply officer of the *USS Enterprise* (CV-6). Wylly did not care for carrier duty because he lacked an aviation background. He developed a medical problem in 1940 and retired on disability in early 1941.

Tom Wylly applied for recall to active duty when the United States entered World War II. A medical board found him fit for limited duty on the mainland only, so he was ordered to the Supply Department of the Naval Hospital, San Diego. He retired again in 1945. He died in Coronado, California in 1989, a week short of his 96th birthday.

Sources

Interview of Thomas S. Wylly, Coronado, Calif., March 1986.
"Intrigue." *Shipmate Magazine,* December 1983.

Carriers and Naval Aviation Supply

Aviation supply took on a new dimension in 1922 with the decision to convert the collier *USS Jupiter* into the U.S. Navy's first aircraft carrier the *USS Langley* (CV-1). *Langley* was commissioned in August 1924.

The Bureau of Supplies and Accounts took several actions to increase the efficiency of its operations in the early 1920s. Ship's service instructions were formally incorporated into Navy regulations in 1923. The Navy Freight Office, San Pedro, California, was established in 1924 to provide improved coordination of the movement of Navy freight in the Pacific. In 1925 Rear Admiral Charles Morris relieved RADM Potter as chief of the Bureau of Supplies and Accounts and paymaster general.

LORE OF THE CORPS

Rear Admiral Charles Morris, SC, USN

Chief, Bureau of Supplies and Accounts, and Paymaster General, 1925–29
Period of Service: 1898–1929

Charles Morris was the first chief of the Bureau to earn an engineering degree. He was a veteran of the Spanish-American War, had duty in Haiti, and was a crusader for administrative reform.

He was born at Newport, Rhode Island, in August 1873 and attended the Massachusetts Institute of Technology, from which he was graduated with a bachelor's degree in electrical engineering. His thesis was entitled "Efficiency of Incandescent Lamps."

Morris was commissioned an assistant paymaster in May 1898, shortly after the Spanish-American War began. His first duty was in *USS Hist,* and he was onboard during the American takeover of Samoa. From 1901 to 1915, he served three tours at sea in *USS Bennington, USS North Carolina,* and *USS Montana;* four navy yard tours—at Puget Sound, Norfolk, Boston, and New York—and in the Bureau of Supplies and Accounts.

He was with Admiral Caperton in *USS Washington* later in 1915 at the occupation of Port-au-Prince. He developed a system for the collection of, and accounting for, customs duties when the customhouses of Haiti were taken over.

Paymaster Morris served as fleet supply officer in *USS Texas* in the early days of World War I and later at the Navy Yard, New York. After the war, he was fleet paymaster, on the staff of commander-in-chief, Battle Fleet. He was ordered to duty for a second time at BuSandA as assistant chief in 1923 and became chief in 1925.

RADM Morris recommended early adoption of a simpler form of appropriations. He convinced Secretary of the Navy Curtis D. Wilbur that merging administrative and financial management would increase efficiency. Morris reminded the secretary that field agencies were grouped under administrative agencies within the Navy Department. He gave as examples the administration of ordnance and armament plants under the Bureau of Ordnance, air stations under the Bureau of Aeronautics, and hospitals and medicine under the Bureau of Medicine and Surgery. Morris continued to promote his program with lectures and articles, including one entitled "The Business Organization of the Navy" in the *United State Naval Institute Proceedings.*

Morris retired in April 1929 and was relieved by RADM Joseph J. Cheatham in 1929. He moved to Stamford, Connecticut, where he died in October 1934.

Sources

Morris, Charles, SC, USN. "The Business Organization of the Navy." *United States Naval Institute Proceedings,* n.d.

Official Biography. Naval Supply Systems Command, n.d.

The Naval Reserve as Part of the Regular Navy

During World War I, 60 percent of Navy men on active duty were Reservists, a fact that motivated Congress to review the entire defense organization and pass several new laws to strengthen the Navy and Army. One such law was the Naval Reserve Act of 1925, which repealed all previous Reserve laws. This law established the Naval Reserve as part of the Regular Navy.

The act also authorized Reserve commissions of indefinite duration, subject to existing legislation regarding age and time in grade. It also authorized a limited number of officers up to the grade of commander, drill pay, and active duty for training with pay.

Subsequent acts of Congress required that Reservists in organized units undergo annual training and provided for them to attain the ranks of captain and rear admiral. The cumulative effect of these acts was to provide a cadre of trained and qualified Naval Reserve officers ready to step into important roles when the United States began to mobilize for World War II in 1940.

Training Inactive Supply Corps Officers

Enhancing professional qualifications of inactive duty Reserve officers had plagued the Navy since the Naval Reserve Act of 1925. During the early 1930s, because of the unique work of the Navy Supply Corps, attention was directed to the professional training of Supply Corps Reservists. Reserve line officers could be assigned to ships, and Medical Corps and Dental Corps officers could relieve their regular counterparts at hospitals and shore stations. Each year, Navy officers in charge of Reserve training assignments asked what to do about paymasters.

The answer to that question, at least in the Third Naval District, came out of a conference between district and New York Naval Militia leaders in 1933. Their solution: a two-week program of carefully planned group instruction. According to an article in the May 1934 issue of the *U.S. Naval Institute Proceedings* by LTJG Joseph J. Lennox, a Supply Corps Reservist, 15 Fleet Reserve and 3 volunteer officers attended the program from 19 August through 1 September 1933. The seven-part course, conducted at Third Naval District headquarters in Manhattan, consisted of lectures by Supply Corps officers on duty in the area, line officers on allied subjects, and civilian authorities on economic issues.

The program included field trips to the Brooklyn Navy Yard, the Naval Supply Depot Brooklyn, the Navy Purchasing Office in New York, and *USS Seattle* (IX-39). LTJG Lennox reported that there was a general feeling that this form of active training duty was a success. Reserve Supply Corps officers, most of whom were veterans of Reserve cruises, were unanimous in praising the program as the most valuable type of shore duty.

The Norfolk Naval Supply Station

Little changed at the Norfolk Naval Supply Station after World War I. Supply functions had supported the Fleet at Gosport Navy Yard (now a part of the City of Portsmouth, Virginia) since the outfitting of *USS Chesapeake,* one of six frigates authorized under the first Naval Armament Act in 1794. The Norfolk Supply Station was established in 1919, but there was no official stocking point for spare parts in the 1920s. Ships were severely handicapped in obtaining needed spares. The facility was designated a Naval Supply Depot in 1927 in recognition of its strategic location and the growing realization of the need for a major stocking point for the Atlantic Fleet.

In 1929 work was completed on a Federal Standard Stock Catalog for common items required by the various government agencies. The catalog was based upon the model of the Navy Standard Stock Catalog developed by BuSandA in 1914.

Also in 1929, at the request of General M. K. Record, captain of the U.S. Rifle Team, the secretary of the Navy approved the detail of LCDR James M. McComb as quartermaster for the team's participation in international matches in Stockholm. According to a collection of Supply Corps abstracts compiled by CAPT Cecil S. Baker, this was the first time that a Supply Corps officer had performed such a duty. General Record is reported to have stated that "it was the only time the financial affairs of the U.S. Rifle Team had ever been kept in an accurate and comprehensive manner."

CAPT Joseph J. Cheatham took the reins of the Bureau of Supplies and Accounts in July 1929 from RADM Charles Morris.

LORE OF THE CORPS

Rear Admiral Joseph Johnston Cheatham, SC, USN

Chief, Bureau of Supplies and Accounts, and Paymaster General, 1929–33
Period of Service: 1894–1936

Joseph J. Cheatham was appointed chief of the Bureau of Supplies and Accounts in 1929. At the time his brother, MAJGEN B. Frank Cheatham, was quartermaster general, the Army's counterpart to paymaster general. This was the only time that brothers simultaneously headed the supply branches of both services.

Joe Cheatham was born at Beach Grove, Tennessee, in 1872. His father, Confederate General B. Frank Cheatham, named his son for a friend, Confederate General Joseph E. Johnston. Joe Cheatham was educated in Nashville and worked in the local post office. He served as an officer in the Tennessee National Guard before he was appointed assistant paymaster in the Navy in August 1894 at the age of 22. He served four tours of sea duty in *USS Minnesota, USS Alliance, USS Wilmington,* and *USS Maine* and ashore at the Naval Station, Cavite in the Philippines from 1894 to 1899. He reported to the Bureau of Supplies and Accounts in 1899 and to the New York Navy Yard in 1900. Also in 1900, he married Alice Eldridge Arms, the daughter of Paymaster Frank Hiram Arms and sister of Paymaster Frank Thornton Arms.

Cheatham served a second tour in BuSandA and then was fleet paymaster, U.S. Atlantic Fleet. He returned to shore duty as supply officer, Mare Island Navy Yard. In 1922 he sailed for Rio de Janeiro to serve as a member of the U.S. Naval Mission to Brazil. Cheatham came back to the United States in 1926 and enrolled at the Army Industrial College at Washington.

CAPT Cheatham was appointed chief of the Bureau of Supplies and Accounts in April 1929 and was promoted to rear admiral in May 1933. He was outspoken in his recommendations for modernizing the Navy supply system. His first report to the secretary of the Navy included a bold statement that the Navy needed a businesslike system to eliminate conflicts among appropriation acts and to permit the best use of aggregate funds. He emphasized that the Bureau's main function was "service of supply to the Fleet."

RADM Cheatham told the secretary in another report that the Navy was entitled to all the advantages that experience, skill, study, and research could bring to bear in support of the Fleet. He added, "There can be no justification for retention of antiquated methods, with only the halo of tradition to justify their existence." The chief was willing to fight for the legislation needed to implement his programs in BuSandA and was not hesitant to fault language in Navy appropriation bills.

In November 1931 he delivered a lecture, "Naval Methods of Supply," at the Army War College in Washington. RADM Cheatham told the Army officers that 75 to 80 percent of Navy procurement took place in BuSandA. He said that the remaining 20 to 25 percent was accomplished by the Bureau's field agencies, including Navy purchasing and disbursing offices, supply officers at Navy yards and naval stations, and supply officers of ships afloat. He described BuSandA as essentially a service bureau whose function was to serve the Fleet and other units of the shore establishment that support the Fleet.

He summarized his talk by giving an example of Navy supply efficiency at the Naval Supply Depot Brooklyn for the year beginning 1 July 1929. He told the Army officers that the aggregate of business transacted during the year was about $36 million and the net stock handling errors were $11,870.76. That amounted to 3/100ths of 1 percent of the value of business done. He also reported that the net results of the inventories was a gain of approximately $1,600—or 4/1,000ths of 1 percent. This was not an isolated case, results experienced at other yards and stations were "quite comparable with those obtained at Brooklyn."

The chief wrote in 1931, "In the final analysis, the success of any organization depends largely upon the type of men of which it is composed, the principles by which they are guided, and the ideals they uphold. The whole structure of the Navy is based upon the sound principle of service to the nation and its final position in the scale of success will be armed by the consistency with which this principle is held in view and uninterruptedly followed."

RADM Cheatham was relieved by RADM Christian J. Peoples in May 1933 and became supply officer, Fifth Naval District, and officer-in-charge, Naval Supply Depot Norfolk. He retired in March 1936 and moved to Kalispell, Montana, where he died in September 1942. At the time of his death, the Navy was constructing new supply and fuel facilities on the York River between Yorktown and Williamsburg, Virginia, to supplement the overburdened facilities at Norfolk. RADM Brent Young, then chief of BuSandA, announced in November 1942 that the new facility would be officially commissioned as Cheatham Annex. Cheatham House at the Norfolk Naval Base also is named in honor of RADM Cheatham.

Sources

BuSandA Monthly Newsletter, October 1942, November 1942.

Cheatham, Joseph H. "Naval Methods of Supply." Lecture given at the Army War College, 10 November 1931.

Losson, Christopher. *Tennessee's Forgotten Warriors: Frank Cheatham and His Confederate Division.* Knoxville: University of Tennessee Press, 1989.

Obituary. *Nashville Banner,* 9 September 1942.

Official Biography. Naval Supply Systems Command, 1970.

A New Ration Law

Feeding sailors continued to be a major area of emphasis for the Navy and a major area of concern for Congress. In 1933 Congress revised the Navy Ration Law, which, with a few additions such as allowing the use of margarine instead of butter, has remained basically unchanged since then. Before the new ration law was passed, messing of crews afloat featured such items as hardtack, molasses, salt horse (salted beef or pork), corn pone, beans, plum duff, coffee, tea, and scouse (hardtack soaked in leftover soup). In port, the crew fared slightly better with fresh meat and some vegetables.

The new law recognized the need for more vegetables and milk and less meat. The 1933 Ration Law required general messes to price locally the value of food items consumed against the new law, using a complex quantitative system that was both cumbersome and time-consuming.

RADM Christian J. Peoples, who had served briefly as chief of BuSandA in 1920 and 1921, returned as chief in 1933. During the Peoples administration, two other significant operations were established in 1933. The Naval Clothing Depot was opened at Brooklyn, concentrating Naval Clothing Factory manufacturing there with a centralized distribution facility. The growing size and importance of Navy aviation made it prudent to establish a Stock Control Section to coordinate all aeronautical material at the Naval Aircraft Factory, Philadelphia. This latter operation was the forerunner of today's Aviation Supply Office.

The First Permanent Supply School

Training of Navy Supply Corps officers continued to be an important concern of BuSandA, but formal schooling had been an off-and-on thing under a variety of names, length of classes, and in several locations. Finally, in 1934 the first permanent supply school, the Naval Finance and Supply School (NF&SS), was established at the Philadelphia Navy Yard.

The Vinson Act, providing limitation of profits on specified types of government contracts, was enacted by Congress in 1934. It provided for the enlargement of the Navy's cost inspection function. A Navy Disbursing and Transportation Office was established at San Pedro, California, in 1935.

RADM Charles Conard, a veteran of service in Haiti and the author of legislation leading to establishment of the Navy Supply Account Fund, relieved RADM Peoples as chief of the Bureau in August 1935.

LORE OF THE CORPS

Rear Admiral Charles Conard, SC, USN

Chief of Bureau of Supplies and Accounts, and Paymaster General, 1935–39
Period of Service: 1898–1939

Throughout his naval career, Conard was at the center of controversy, but always managed to emerge with his career intact. He was one of many Supply Corps officers who undertook special assignments for which Pay Officers School did not specifically prepare them.

Charles Conard was born in March 1875 in Washington, D.C. He attended Rockville Academy in Maryland and was graduated from Cornell University with an electrical engineering degree in 1896. He was appointed an assistant paymaster with rank of ensign in May 1898, a month after the Spanish-American War started.

He served sea tours during that war in *USS Franklin* and *USS Alliance* before being ordered to duty in the Bureau of Supplies and Accounts in 1900. He next was supply officer, *USS New Orleans,* where he was involved in his first run-in with a superior. Conard was without funds to pay the crew and arranged with a local company in Yokohama, Japan, to exchange nine U.S. Treasury checks for about $3,000 in gold. The skipper called him to task by letter, asking in especially offensive language why he failed to follow regulations. The young paymaster took offense and replied by letter, calling the C.O.'s attention to a regulation permitting such a transaction. His skipper agreed that the regulation did indeed permit the transaction, but that it had been superseded. The incident ended when the C.O. suggested destroying the correspondence, which was apparently causing him discomfort.

Paymaster Conard had duty at the Naval Station, Cavite, the Philippines, in 1904 and 1905, then served again in *USS Franklin,* where he determined that there was a strong need for revising some of the forms used aboard ship. He made several suggestions to BuSandA and was called to duty in the Bureau in 1906, where he revised all the shipboard forms. While on this duty in Washington in 1908, he noticed that some of the bureaus, particularly Yards and Docks, had a large amount of stock on hand. Conard suggested that the Navy would benefit if all the stores were in one account and available to all bureaus. It would be necessary to convince each bureau of the wisdom of this approach in order to realize its benefits, so he convinced the Navy Department to propose legislation that resulted in what became the Navy Supply Account Fund in 1909.

Paymaster General Eustace Rogers had a serious disagreement with

Secretary of the Navy George Von L. Meyer as a result of a statement Meyer made before Congress. Some of the resultant animosity migrated to Conard, who was thought to be the brains of the Bureau. Conard was suddenly detached from special duty in BuSandA and ordered to sea in *USS Nebraska* in 1910. He then served in *USS New York, USS Florida, USS North Carolina,* and *USS Wyoming,* and at the Portsmouth Navy Yard.

Conard was fiscal officer of the Port of Vera Cruz, Mexico, during the Mexican campaign in 1914, when his article, "Navy Yard Economy," was published in the *United States Naval Institute Proceedings* and won an annual Naval Institute Prize. After the article was brought to Secretary Meyer's attention it was probably no coincidence that Conard was ordered back to Washington for duty in the secretary's office. His report on a survey of U.S. industrial plants convinced Secretary Meyer that additional studies were necessary. Meyer then appointed a board to examine existing U.S. industrial management and cost-accounting practices.

Conard was ordered to Port-au-Prince in 1915 for duty as financial advisor and administrator of customs for the Republic of Haiti. He improved the collection of customs and succeeded in the apparently impossible task of reforming Haiti's currency. The paymaster returned to the United States in October 1916 and had additional duty consulting with the Latin-American Division at the State Department, where he continued to work on rehabilitation of Haiti's economic matters. Conard's draft of an operating system was used until a treaty was signed by the two governments and ratified by the Senate. He received commendations from both the State and Treasury departments for his service in connection with Haitian financial matters.

Conard reported to the Naval Gun Factory at the Washington Navy Yard in July 1917 and in October 1919 was on duty with the general comptroller, Shipping Board, Washington. Also in 1919, he proposed a new method of preparing the naval appropriation bill by means of a single fund, with estimates for various activities, instead of separate appropriations for each project.

In November 1922, CAPT Conard had duty with the chief coordinator, Bureau of the Budget, Treasury Department. He was drawn into the controversy involving the great public hue and cry of support for a bonus to be given Americans who had fought overseas in World War I. The Bureau of the Budget determined to present the fiscal facts to President Calvin Coolidge, who had not made his position on the bonus clear.

Conard was assigned to furnish the president with material, both pro and con. He went to the president's office with two drafts of a speech—one for and one against the issue. Conard informed Coolidge that there were two ways to look at the momentous fiscal and political problem. The president blurted out, "I'm opposed to the bonus," and Conard handed him the draft outlining the fiscal hazards of such an act. Conrad did not let on that he had come also with a speech supporting a bonus.

In 1925 Conard served as supply officer of the Naval Academy and, in 1928 he became general inspector of the Supply Corps, East Coast, at BuSandA. He prepared and submitted a memorandum on budgeting limitations of naval armament to the Navy General Board. The chief, Bureau of Navigation, requested in 1930 that CAPT Conard be assigned duty as naval attaché, Mexico City. He was next ordered to duty in 1932 as supply officer, Pearl Harbor Navy Yard. He was ordered in May 1935 for similar duty at the Puget Sound Navy Yard, but the duty was short-lived. He was called to Washington three months later to become chief, BuSandA, and paymaster general.

RADM Conard completed his tour as chief in April 1939, but was recalled to active duty in March 1941. His first duty was as Navy liaison officer in the Division of Purchase, Office of Production Management, and then he was head of the Office of Production Management. President Franklin D. Roosevelt signed an executive order in April 1942 designating him chairman of the Interdepartmental War Savings Bond Committee. Conard was awarded the Legion of Merit for his outstanding performance on the committee. He retired again in Washington in July 1943.

Sources

Baker, CAPT Cecil S., SC, USN. *A Collection of Abstracts Giving Historical Background for the Work of the Supply Corps* (ca. 1939).

Conard, Charles, SC, USN. "Navy Yard Economy." *United States Naval Institute Proceedings,* n.d.

Official Biography. Navy Biographies Section, 1952.

War Clouds in Europe Again

None of the Western powers moved to stop Germany's rise to power during the mid-1930s, leaving Adolf Hitler's Nazi forces free to pick off Eastern European democracies one by one: the Saar in 1935, the Rhineland in 1936, and Austria in 1938. Britain and France failed to challenge Hitler at Munich in September 1938. The Anglo-French inability to rein in Germany assured the dismemberment of Czechoslovakia and emboldened Hitler to plan the political or military conquest of Poland, Hungary, Romania, Bulgaria, and Yugoslavia.

American military planners realized that war was coming in Europe and superseded their Orange Plan (Pacific war with Japan) with the Rainbow Plan. This new plan dealt with America's possible involvement in simultaneous conflicts in both the Atlantic and the Pacific. The war planners concluded that it would be difficult for the United States to hold the Philippines and the other U.S. possessions in the face of a Japanese all-out offensive. One of the key features of Rainbow was the expectation that war would begin in the Far East with a surprise Japanese attack.

The Importance of Destroyers

During the 1930s, the U.S. Navy had increasingly relied upon destroyers, a class of ships that had first come into the Fleet in 1902. The *USS Bainbridge* (DD-1) was a 450-ton vessel capable of 29 knots and armed with a pair of 3-inch guns and a pair of 18-inch torpedo tubes. Another 36 of the four-stackers joined the Fleet over the following decade. By the end of the war, they had become the mainstays of the Navy's worldwide operations, but Supply Corps officers were not regularly assigned. The function of supply fell to junior line officers—usually "George," as the most junior officer was known. In addition to his primary duties as assistant engineer, the junior officer was assigned as stores officer. Another junior line officer was usually in charge of the general mess.

The earliest record of a Supply Corps officer assigned to a destroyer was LTJG (later CAPT) Walter R. Wright, who reported to *USS Hatfield* (DD-231) at Brooklyn in August 1936. *Hatfield* had been sent to Gibraltar and several Spanish ports to evacuate American, British, Swiss, and Spanish nationals during the Spanish Civil War. Wright drew $11,000 from Barclay's Bank of Gibraltar in order to feed the refugees while aboard *Hatfield*.

LTJG Allen M. (Gus) Gray became the first Supply Corps officer assigned to a Pacific Fleet destroyer in January 1937. He reported aboard *USS Preston* (DD-379) for temporary duty in conjunction with a lengthy shakedown cruise to Australia in company with *USS Smith* (DD-378). When the ships were about to depart 10 days later, he bought nearly $10,000 in government funds for anticipated needs during the cruise. Despite the fact that he was frequently seasick, records show he kept all accounts straight and in good order.

When other destroyers were deployed in the Eastern Atlantic and

Mediterranean, a Supply Corps officer was embarked as disbursing officer in each. These officers also took charge of commissary and supplies aboard.

LTJG (later CAPT) Robert R. (Bob) Bowstrom, a Naval Academy classmate of Wright's, was assigned as disbursing officer in *USS Kane* (DD-235) during the Spanish civil war in January 1937. His predecessor had returned to the United States and taken all funds with him, requiring Bowstrom to buy funds at Cook's Tours and the Bank of Gibraltar. He also had to trust that enough American tourists would come to Spain during the hostilities and leave behind sufficient American currency to meet his needs. By 1940, Supply Corps officers were routinely assigned to destroyer divisions, usually composed of four ships.

The Roosevelt Naval Expansion Plan

Congress fended off isolationist pressure and narrowly enacted President Roosevelt's naval expansion proposals as the Naval Act of 1936, which provided greatly increased funds for shipbuilding and aircraft purchases. Work began immediately on a major shipbuilding program, including the North Carolina class of battleships. Four more battleships were authorized in 1938.

Tensions in the Pacific dramatically demonstrated the urgent need for a major base in the San Francisco Bay area to support the Pacific Fleet. The Navy, with a Supply Corps officer, CAPT A. H. Mayo, playing a major role, pressed the issue, which had been awaiting congressional approval for three decades. In 1939 Congress finally approved a proposal to convert the former site of the San Francisco World's Fair, on man-made Treasure Island adjacent to Yerba Buena Island, for Navy use. Also in 1939, the first joint service audits of cost-plus-fixed-fee contractors holding both Navy and Army contracts were conducted.

RADM Ray Spear, a 39-year Navy veteran who served during the Spanish-American War, relieved RADM Conard in April 1939.

LORE OF THE CORPS

Rear Admiral Ray Spear, SC, USN

Chief, Bureau of Supplies and Accounts, and Paymaster General, 1939–42
Period of Service: 1900–1945

Ray Spear enjoyed a long and illustrious career in the Navy's supply business and was strongly praised by Representative Ditter of Pennsylvania when he relinquished the command of BuSandA and the Supply Corps in 1942. Rep. Ditter said of RADM Spear: "His record is replete with signal accomplishments. . . . He has performed magnificently, without any furor or fanfare, in his own quiet, modest, determined, inimitable way, and the nation owes him much."

Spear was born at Springfield, Illinois, in September 1878. He enlisted in the Army in April 1898 at the start of the Spanish-American War and served as an infantry private during that short conflict. He was honorably discharged in August of the same year. He was commissioned an assistant paymaster in March 1900 and reported to *USS Independence* for two months of instruction. He then served in *USS Iris* on the Asiatic Station from June to October of that year. He next reported to the Naval Station, San Francisco, as pay officer for *USS Pensacola, USS Albatross,* and *USS Alert.* It was in this assignment that his career nearly ended.

He discovered that his predecessor had been incorrectly crediting sea duty pay to officers attached to the local receiving ship but living in government quarters. He immediately corrected the officers' records and began paying them the proper shore duty pay.

The commandant, Rear Admiral Bowman McCalla, called the young paymaster on the carpet and told him that he was to make no changes on payrolls of officers without consent of the commandant. Spear told McCalla that he was astonished at his interpretation of the law. The commandant ordered Spear arrested, but before Spear could reach his quarters, McCalla sent a Marine orderly after him with instructions for the paymaster to return to his office. McCalla demanded, "Paymaster, what is this all about?"

When Spear had again explained the law, McCalla replied, "Well, I guess you're right after all. Paymaster, you are released from arrest." From that point on, Ray Spear could do no wrong in McCalla's eyes. The commandant became so convinced of Spear's ability that, when he learned that he was to be ordered to command the Mare Island Navy Yard, McCalla called the Mare Island general storekeeper and his assistant to Yerba Buena to see how a supply department should be administered.

Spear went on to serve sea tours in *USS Tacoma* and *USS Iowa.* In 1907 he was assigned as assistant to the general storekeeper at Mare Island Navy Yard. He then served three consecutive shore tours at the Puget Sound Navy Yard (1908–10), the Naval Station, Cavite, the Philippines (1910–12), and Norfolk Navy Yard (1912–16).

Paymaster Spear reported for duty in 1916 in *USS Milwaukee,* with additional duty as supply officer, Torpedo Flotilla, Pacific Fleet, at the

Naval Station, Guam. In April 1917, he was transferred to *USS Washington.* Six months later, he became aide on the staff of commander, Cruiser Force, Atlantic Fleet, a post he held until September 1919. He was awarded the Navy Cross for distinguished service and also received the Distinguished Service Medal from the War Department. The citation reads in part: "For exceptionally meritorious and conscientious service as Force Supply Officer, the efficient performance of which contributed greatly to the successful provisioning of ships engaged in the transportation of troops and supplies overseas."

Ray Spear had additional duty during the last three months of his Atlantic Fleet tour as aide for supply, Third Naval District, in connection with bunkering Navy vessels and the development of fueling projects. Spear was detached in September 1919 to report for duty as purchasing pay officer in charge of the San Francisco Pay Office, and in 1920 was given additional duty as general inspector of the Supply Corps for the West Coast. He became coordinator, General Supply, Ninth Corps Area, San Francisco, in 1921. He was aide on the staff, commander, Scouting Fleet, with additional duty as fleet paymaster, Scouting Fleet, from April 1923 to May 1924.

He reported in May 1924 as disbursing officer, Naval Home, Philadelphia, and in September became supply officer of the Philadelphia Navy Yard. In 1925 he assumed additional duty as district supply officer, Fourth Naval District. Spear had two other tours as supply officer, first at the Washington Navy Yard in 1925 and later at the U.S. Naval Academy in 1928.

Captain Spear reported in 1936 for duty in the Office of Director of Shore Establishments in the Navy Department, where he served until selected to be the chief of the Bureau of Supplies and Accounts and paymaster general with rank of rear admiral on 1 April 1939.

The war in Europe broke out five months after he took office. RADM Spear presided over the buildup of the Navy supply system and a huge increase in the number of Supply Corps officers as the inevitability of U.S. involvement became apparent. He commissioned the Naval Supply Depot in Mechanicsburg, Pennsylvania, the Naval Supply Depot in Philadelphia, and the BuSandA Field Branch in Cleveland.

America had been at war for more than six months when Spear was relieved by RADM William B. Young in July 1942. Upon relief, Spear again became general inspector, Supply Corps, Pacific Coast, a post he held until he was released from active duty in July 1945. Spear and his wife Emille lived in Diablo, California, in retirement.

Sources

Baker, CAPT Cecil S., SC, USN. *A Collection of Abstracts Giving Historical Background for the Work of the Supply Corps* (ca. 1939).
Official Biography. Naval Supply Systems Command, 1950.

The End of a Tenuous Peace

America was divided as it watched with horror news reports of the Nazis gradually absorbing the democratic republics of Eastern Europe and blatant Japanese aggression in the Far East. The League of Nations rhetoric and British Prime Minister Neville Chamberlain's plan of appeasement proved to be ineffective. Isolationists such as Charles Lindbergh and Gerald L. K. Smith spoke out against American involvement. The American Navy and Army were certainly unprepared for war between 1939 and 1941. Ships authorized in 1938 would not be available before 1942. Both services were short of men, machines, fuel, and other essentials. Many members of Congress believed they had authorized sufficient funds in 1938 and were in no mood to appropriate additional money, even to stay abreast of rising costs. Yet military planners, despite woefully inadequate financial and physical resources, worked long and hard throughout the second half of the 1930s to increase readiness. At this point, Europe exploded into a major war.

Sources

Sources for material used in this chapter and not cited earlier include:

Miller, Nathan. *The United States Navy: An Illustrated History*. Annapolis: Naval Institute Press, and New York: American Heritage Press, 1977.
Navy Supply Corps Newsletter, February 1970, September 1973
The World Almanac and Book of Facts. 1981.

CHAPTER EIGHT

World War II: The Early Years

1939–42

World tensions continued to build throughout the 1930s. American naval planners envisioned a probable war against the fictitious Orange power, a thinly veiled reference to Japan, but the full-scale war actually broke out in Europe. Germany, under the Nazis, absorbed Austria and much of Czechoslovakia in 1938, and the German dictator Adolf Hitler sent his blitzkrieg into Poland on 1 September, despite a 10-year nonaggression pact the Germans had signed with the Poles in 1934.

France and Great Britain, which had guaranteed Poland's independence, declared war on Germany two days later. However, the two were unable to assist Poland effectively. The United States reemphasized the Neutrality Act of 1937, but it was obvious that the sympathies of the Roosevelt administration—and many Americans—were with the democracies of Europe.

The U.S. Navy had, since 1922, relied on the Royal Navy to dominate the North Atlantic, thereby freeing America to deploy the majority of its naval forces to the Pacific to deal with any Japanese threat. Early German victories over British and French forces in 1940 seriously concerned the president. A British defeat would mean that the United States would either have to fight a war in two oceans without a viable ally or make major concessions to Germany and Japan.

To shore up British prospects, President Roosevelt decided to render all assistance "short of war." The French surrendered to the Germans on 17 June 1940, and on the following day Roosevelt sent the chief of naval operations, Admiral Harold R. Stark, to Congress to present a $4 billion proposal for an expanded two-ocean navy. The authorization request virtually sailed through and became law on 22 June. The legislation provided for 257 new ships, including 2 fast, modern battleships, 20 Essex- and Independence-class aircraft carriers, 15,000 Navy aircraft, and a shipyard at Long Beach, California. Roosevelt also ordered deployment of significant Navy forces back to the Atlantic.

New Supply Depots

The Navy had two supply depots in 1940, at Norfolk and at San Diego. Each navy yard also had a supply department, but the range of stock carried at the shipyard retail level was severely limited. The growing probability of war, coupled with the unprecedented major shipbuilding program, put substantial pressure on the Navy supply system to increase the level, range, and location of its inventory.

BuSandA determined that new supply depots were needed, especially to support operating forces in the North Atlantic and farther north on the Pacific Coast. Work was begun in 1940 on two depots, one at Bayonne, New Jersey, and the other at Oakland, California. The new depot at Oakland became operational a week after the United States entered the war, and the Bayonne depot early in 1942.

The Navy also moved forward with establishing smaller depots in 1941 at Argentia, Newfoundland, Canada, and Balboa, Canal Zone, Panama.

The Reserve Supply Corps School

A school was established in 1940 at Georgetown University to train the large number of Naval Reserve Supply Corps officers who would be required in the event the United States was drawn into the war. The new school complemented the Navy Finance and Supply School (NF&SS), already in operation at Philadelphia, providing supply training for Naval Academy and Naval Reserve Officer Training Corps (NROTC) graduates.

The class of 1939–40 at NF&SS Philadelphia has been called the "transition class" because its members made major contributions to the Supply Corps' evolution into the modern business organization it is today. This class was comprised of two categories of officers. The first consisted of 22 LTJGs from the Naval Academy Class of 1937 who, for physical reasons (mostly eyesight), transferred from the line to the Supply Corps. The second group was comprised of 18 ensigns from the 5 NROTC units around the nation.

The newly qualified U.S. Navy Supply Corps officers were graduated from NF&SS in the spring of 1940 and were ordered to duty in the Pacific. Five left together with orders directing them to report to the Commander Asiatic Fleet at Manila for further assignment. They departed San Francisco aboard the *SS President Adams* in late May 1940. When they reached Manila, they were given their first fleet operational assignments.

- LTJG Lewis O. (Lew) Davis had orders to the oiler *USS Pecos* (AO-6).
- ENS Allan Jack Fisher's ship, *USS Pope* (DD-225), was at Manila.
- ENS Harold L. (Wooze) Usher, Jr., was to report to the Yangtze Patrol at Shanghai.
- ENS Kenneth R. (Ken) Wheeler stayed at Manila for duty at the Navy Yard, Cavite.
- ENS Clifford W. (Hacker) Wilson was to find his new duty assignment in *USS Black Hawk* (AD-9) at a port in the Netherlands East Indies.

All five would see extensive combat action in the forthcoming war in the South Pacific. Another of the graduates, ENS Charles L. (Lin) Loring, went first to the Pacific, but his ship was transferred to the Atlantic Fleet in the spring of 1941.

LORE OF THE CORPS

Ensign Charles Linwood Loring, SC, USN

Assistant Supply Officer, *USS Wasp* (CV-7), 1940–42
Period of Service: 1939–59

Ensign Loring was ordered to duty with the Pacific Fleet in 1940 but was soon assigned to the Atlantic Fleet, serving on the Neutrality Patrol before the United States entered World War II.

Lin Loring was born at Berkeley, California, in May 1916, and attended the University of California, where he was a member of the Naval Reserve Officer Training Corps. He was ordered to active duty in 1939 and reported to NF&SS Philadelphia, where he roomed with his Cal classmate, Ken Wheeler.

From NF&SS, ENS Loring reported to duty in June 1940 as disbursing officer, *USS Yorktown* (CV-5), in the Pacific Fleet. In the spring of 1941, *Yorktown* was ordered to the Atlantic Fleet for participation in Neutrality Patrol. In July 1941, ENS Loring was ordered to duty as assistant supply officer in *USS Wasp* (CV-7). The *Wasp* task force routinely steamed from Norfolk out to the Azores and back to Bermuda, performing unofficial scouting duties for the Royal Navy in the Caribbean. *Wasp* and her escorts were in Bermuda on 7 December 1941. Loring recalls that, two or three days later, the task force sailed for Martinique to strike the Vichy French fleet at Fort-de-France. According to Loring, the bomb-laden planes were poised for take off when the attack was called off in Washington. The task force blockaded Fort-de-France for five days before being called back to Bermuda.

In addition to convoy duty, *Wasp* made two trips from England to Malta to deliver Spitfire fighters. Loring was promoted to LTJG in January 1942, and the carrier was ordered to the Pacific in mid-1942 to bolster the hard-pressed American carrier force that was down to four flat-tops after *Yorktown* was torpedoed and lost in June following the Battle of Midway. On 15 September, *Wasp* was torpedoed and sunk in the Coral Sea while protecting a convoy of six transports taking Marine reinforcements to Guadalcanal. Of the five Supply Corps officers aboard, LCDR John Wyman and Chief Pay Clerk John Wood were lost, but LT (later CAPT) John Burkhardt, ENS Martin Earlinger, and Loring, who had made lieutenant in May, survived. Earlinger, the disbursing officer, and Wood, the clothing, small stores, and ship's store officer, were on the flaming flight deck. They both wanted to go below to save their records, but Loring told them not to. Wood went anyway and was not seen again.

John Burkhardt was evacuated with the air group on a different transport, leaving Loring as the senior surviving member of the Supply Department to arrange to outfit *Wasp* crew members with replacement clothing and personal items when they reached New Caledonia. *Wasp*'s skipper, CAPT (Later ADM) Forrest P. Sherman, obtained a motor whaleboat for Loring to go from ship to ship in the harbor to ask for clothing, shoes, toilet articles, blankets, and tobacco for survivors.

Upon return to the United States, Loring was ordered to BuSandA to make a report on the supply problems of a sunken ship, the second carrier loss of the war. LT Loring reported to the Navy Supply Depot Oakland, where he was made outgoing stores officer and promoted to lieutenant commander. He later became senior assistant to the OIC, General Supply Branch, which earlier had turned down *Wasp*'s request for additional life jackets because they were not on her allowance list. After his arrival, he was the only officer who could turn down a requisition from a ship in the Fleet.

LCDR Loring returned to sea in August 1944 as supply officer, *USS New Mexico* (BB-40). He found that his predecessor would not serve bread until all the hardtack had been eaten and would not allow coffee on the bridge. His first two actions were to throw all the hardtack overboard and order coffee makers for the bridge.

New Mexico's skipper always allowed his department heads to review any operating plans. On reviewing the plans to operate in the Linguyen Gulf, Loring believed that the accompanying destroyers and smaller ships did not carry enough food to last through the operation. The skipper sent Loring to the flagship, where he was made acting force supply officer. LCDR Loring arranged a hasty meeting of all supply officers in the task force to plan the transfer of provisions from the capital ships to the smaller ships. When Kamikaze attacks severely damaged *New Mexico* and she was released to return for repairs, Loring transferred his remaining provisions stocks to the smaller ships. He had just enough food left for the noon meal when the battleship sailed into Kossol Roads and caught up with a supply ship.

He next went to Admiral Nimitz's CinCPac staff in September 1945 to work on logistics plans for the invasion of Japan. He recalls that the plan envisioned a large number of American casualties. He is convinced that "lots more [American] lives were saved by 'the bomb' than the bomb killed."

From CinCPac, Loring went as stock control officer, Naval Gun Factory, Washington, from November 1945 to June 1948. He was offered a career-enhancing captain's billet as supply officer at Kodiak, or a LCDR billet as supply officer at NAS Bermuda. He chose Bermuda, where he served for two and a half years and was promoted to commander. Next, he attended the Armed Forces Staff College at Norfolk from January to June 1950, when he reported as assistant supply officer at NAS Jacksonville. He fleeted up to supply officer when his boss retired.

CDR Loring admits that he continued to be a rebel as assistant district supply officer, Eleventh Naval District, San Diego, from December 1952 to June 1954. His next two duties were as chief of supply and transportation for CinCAlaska in June 1954 and as assistant supply officer, New York Naval Shipyard, Brooklyn, in February 1956.

Lin Loring recalls that "the selection board hinted that I should retire." He had come full circle. His first Navy commanding officer was CAPT (later RADM) Frederick G. Pyne, at NF&SS Philadelphia, and his last C.O. was line CAPT S. N. Pyne, son of the first. CDR Loring retired at Treasure Island, California, in September 1959 and then spent nearly 17 years with the Missile and Space Division, Lockheed Aircraft Company, retiring again in June 1976. A widower, he lives in Lompoc, California.

Source

Telephone interview of CDR Charles Linwood Loring, April 1994, and subsequent notes provided by CDR Loring, May 1994.

The Submarine War in the Atlantic

German submarine warfare was virtually forcing Britain into starvation in 1940, just as it had threatened to do in 1917. France had been defeated, and President Roosevelt and ADM Stark were well aware that Britain was "sinking fast." They also knew that the U.S. ships under construction would not be available in time to help Great Britain.

British Prime Minister Winston Churchill pleaded with Franklin Roosevelt to let the Royal Navy have 50 of the old World War I "four-piper" destroyers being overhauled for patrol duty. Roosevelt faced a hostile Congress and an American public deeply divided between anti-war isolationists and those who favored providing assistance. In September 1940, Roosevelt signed an order that transferred the 50 ships to the British in return for 99-year leases on British bases in the Atlantic from Canada to the Caribbean.

The Naval Attaché Staff in London

The United States decided in 1940 to expand the staff of the naval attaché in London by ordering in additional communications officers and, for the first time, a Supply Corps officer to handle disbursing duties. LTJG (later CAPT) John B. Kackley was detached from his duty in *USS Pennsylvania* (BB-38) and ordered to the London duty.

LORE OF THE CORPS

Lieutenant, junior grade, John Baile Kackley, SC, USN

Disbursing Officer, American Embassy, London, 1940–42
Period of Service: 1937–67

LTJG Kackley served in London and in the Pacific during World War II, was aide to an assistant secretary of the Navy, and was involved in establishing the Office of the Comptroller of the Navy during his 30-year Supply Corps career.

John Kackley was born at Miami, Florida, in November 1915 and was graduated from Georgia Tech with a bachelor's of science in civil engineering and a Naval Reserve commission in June 1937. In August, he was commissioned assistant paymaster with rank of ensign in the Regular Navy. Upon completion of NF&SS Philadelphia, he was ordered to *USS Pennsylvania* (BB-38) as assistant supply and disbursing officer.

ENS Kackley was given an unusual assignment in early 1940 when the Fleet, deployed to Hawaiian waters for maneuvers, was anchored in Lahaina Roads, off Maui. Kackley was called to the office of the Flag secretary and instructed to fly to Pearl Harbor to obtain tickets for a Pan American Airways Clipper flight to San Francisco for two civilian passengers. ADM James O. Richardson, Commander-in-Chief, U.S. Fleet, and CAPT Vincent R. Murphy, war plans officer, were traveling in civilian clothes to Washington to plead with President Roosevelt for an increased state of readiness for the Fleet. The mission was unsuccessful. Richardson was unceremoniously removed from office and replaced by ADM Husband E. Kimmel.

Kackley was promoted to LTJG in June 1940 and was the first Supply Corps officer ordered to duty at the U.S. embassy in London as assistant naval attaché and supply officer. He was briefed at BuSandA and the Office of Naval Intelligence (ONI), which oversaw U.S. naval attachés around the world. ONI provided LTJG Kackley an inflatable life jacket, a World War I-type steel helmet, and a gas mask.

While in New York City, LTJG Kackley had gone to the Navy Purchasing Office, where he and CAPT Henry de F. Mel, the NPO chief, discussed problems that the Navy Clothing Office was encountering in obtaining gold braid and embroidered cap and sleeve devices. The war in Europe had cut off the primary sources of these uniform items, which were in France. Kackley agreed to explore alternate sources in the United Kingdom. *RMS Scythia,* a Cunard liner sailing independently across the Atlantic. Aboard, he encountered three other officers also headed for embassy duty at London.

John Kackley arrived at London during an air raid and was put up temporarily at the exclusive Claridge's Hotel, whose $8 a day rate seemed a bargain, even on $6 per diem. During lunch on his first day at work, a German bomb destroyed a large house only four doors from the embassy in Grosvenor Square.

Disbursing was LTJG Kackley's primary duty for the staff, which had grown from 7 or 8 officers and civilians before the war to 30 with arrival of the 4 additional officers. Jack Kackley found bills piled up, records in poor shape, quarterly returns not yet prepared, and much catching up to do. He had the embassy's duty watch on the nights of the four worst air raids on London. He escaped the air raids at Christmas 1940 when he was the guest of Lord and Lady Astor at Cliveden, their country estate.

The number of U.S. Navy officers in England to observe Royal Navy operations and oversee development of a destroyer base at Londonderry in Northern Ireland and two submarine bases in Scotland swelled steadily in 1941. The financial workload also increased, and there was a commensurate expansion of the disbursing office. In addition to his other duties, by January 1941 Kackley had notified CAPT Mel that he had located six potential British suppliers of gold lace.

On the night of 7 December 1941, LTJG Kackley was having dinner at a London club when he was attracted by the clatter of the teletype machine in the lobby. His curiosity led to discovery of the news that unidentified planes had attacked Pearl Harbor. At 0245, he was awakened by the embassy duty officer, who provided official confirmation of the Japanese attack and passed the word that uniforms had been ordered for all hands. Up to that time, the noncombat diplomatic status of neutral American personnel had dictated wearing civilian clothes.

Kackley reported as a lieutenant in May 1942 for duty at the Bureau of Supplies and Accounts, where he was officer-in-charge, Disbursing Instructions Section, and *the* authority on Navy pay and allowances. Later, he was officer-in-charge, Field Branch Liaison Division.

LCDR Kackley went to sea in November 1944 as supply officer in the two-year-old battleship *USS Alabama* (BB-60), deployed with Fast Carrier Task Forces 38 and 58 in the Western Pacific. One of his duties was to remain on the *Alabama*'s bridge when escorts would come alongside to refuel after dawn alert. Often, the smaller ships would have additional supply needs that he would take over the bridge-to-bridge telephone and relay to a storekeeper outside on the deck. The storekeeper would then have the items brought up on deck for transfer.

Alabama was a big ship, displacing 35,000 tons, with a large amount of sophisticated electrical and electronic equipment, many of which used common parts. The spare parts for each system were kept in metal boxes designated for that particular system. Kackley devised a system of centralized parts control, which he implemented when *Alabama* went into the Puget Sound Navy Yard for refit, replacing spare parts boxes with bin stowage.

Alabama participated in the assault on Okinawa in May 1945. LCDR Kackley was assigned as battle announcer advising personnel throughout the ship of the actions taking place above them. On 14 May, a large formation of kamikazes circled the fast carrier task force from all points of the compass, but were concealed by low-hanging clouds.

The first plane crashed into *USS Enterprise* (CV-6), off *Alabama*'s port side, but firefighters quickly controlled the fire and the carrier was able to resume flight operations. The battleship's gunners shot down the second and third attackers. Fire from *Alabama* and nearby ships also shot down the fourth and fifth planes. (A synopsis of LCDR Kackley's report on the actions of that day is on file at the Navy Supply Corps Museum, Athens, Georgia.)

Kackley was promoted to commander in July 1945 and received an M.B.A. with distinction from the Graduate School of Business at Harvard University in September 1947. He next was sent to Rochester, New York, to observe industry practices at Stromberg-Carlson Co. from October 1947 to January 1948 and he reported to the Naval Supply Depot Bayonne, New Jersey, as planning officer and later as executive officer. When CDR Kackley arrived at Bayonne, Yoh Company was just starting a contract to receive spare-parts boxes from throughout the Navy and employ the same concept he had implemented in *Alabama* three years before.

During the Korean War between 1950 and 1952, CDR Kackley was involved in setting up the new Office of Comptroller of the Navy. Recognizing the need to simplify afloat accounting requirements for ships during wartime rather than just to drop the requirements as had been done during World War II, Kackley developed a new concept, equally applicable in peacetime and wartime. The Navy bureaus, the chief of naval operations, and the Fleet commanders accepted his proposal, and Kackley traveled to the West Coast, Hawaii, and Japan in 1951 to hold seminars for ship's supply and fleet support officers on the new concept.

In August 1952, he reported for duty as aide and special assistant to the assistant secretary of the Navy for installation and logistics. CDR Kackley accompanied his boss on many trips to Navy activities where the assistant secretary's interests were primarily material logistics and military construction matters, including meetings of the Navy Ship's Store Office Advisory Committee.

CDR Kackley reported in December 1954 as force supply officer, Commander Naval Forces Far East, located at Chinhae, Korea, where he was also briefer for the Navy's program of assistance for the Republic of Korea Navy. He was promoted to captain in July 1955 and reported as officer-in-charge, Navy Audit Office, New York.

CAPT Kackley returned to Washington and the Office of the Comptroller of the Navy, this time as assistant comptroller and auditor general, from September 1958 to August 1962. He next was ordered as commanding officer, Naval Supply Center Subic Bay in the Philippines. In August 1964, he reported as executive officer, NSC Oakland, and in June

1966 as comptroller, Naval Shipyard, Charleston, South Carolina. He retired a year later.

In July 1967, newly retired Jack Kackley accepted a senior financial position with the United Nations Food and Agriculture Organization (FAO) at its headquarters in Rome, Italy. He retired again in 1972 and returned to the United States with his wife, Eleanor, to establish residence at Naples, Florida.

Sources

Biographical notes. *Insights*. Georgia Institute of Technology, Fall 1993.
LTJG Kackley to CAPT H. de F. Mel, 14 January 1941.
Telephone interview of CAPT John Baile Kackley, June, October, 1994.

The Lend-Lease Act and New Supply Depots

Roosevelt waited until after he had been sworn in for his third term to render further aid to the Allies. In March 1941, he won a close congressional vote to replace the cash-and-carry provisions of the Neutrality Act of 1937 with the Lend-Lease Act. The act authorized lending arms, munitions, and supplies to nations whose defense the president considered vital to the United States.

American forces seized Greenland in early 1941 to prevent its capture by the Germans. Soon, the U.S. Navy was escorting convoys to Greenland, where the Royal Navy took over. German submarines began to attack escorting American ships in September, sinking *USS Reuben James* (DD-245), badly damaging *USS Greer* (DD-145) and *USS Salinas* (AO-20), and attacking but failing to hit *USS Kearny* (DD-432). The U.S. Navy was in the Atlantic war even without a formal declaration.

Expansion of the Navy supply system continued at an accelerated pace in 1941, creating a demand for large numbers of additional Supply Corps officers, more than the Navy Finance and Supply School could produce. NF&SS Philadelphia graduated its final class in March 1941. A study of suitable sites for relocation of the school was launched, and the school was moved from Philadelphia to Boston. A new Navy Supply Corps School (NSCS) was opened at the Graduate School of Business, Harvard University on 2 June 1941.

The new supply depots at Oakland, Argentia, and Balboa highlighted the need for expanded use of transport aircraft to move a growing volume of men and material. The Naval Air Transport Service (NATS) was created in 1941 to meet this need. Construction of an additional Navy supply depot was begun at Oakland, California, in September 1941. Another large Navy supply depot at Mechanicsburg, Pennsylvania, was authorized in December. Two more large depots at Scotia, New York, and Clearfield, Utah, were proposed by RADM Ray Spear, the BuSandA chief, in January 1942 and approved in February.

The United States continued to maintain an embassy at Berlin as an important listening post within the heart of the growing Nazi empire despite growing enmity between the two nations. A member of the staff of the naval attaché was a Supply Corps officer, LT Onnie P. Lattu, a naturalized citizen who had been born in Finland, a German ally since the Russo-Finnish War began in November 1939. Lattu reported to duty in Berlin in the summer of 1940.

LORE OF THE CORPS

Lieutenant Onnie Peter Lattu, SC, USN

Assistant Naval Attaché, Berlin, 1940–42;
Diplomatic Internee of Germany, 1941–42
Period of Service: 1930–65

Onnie Lattu had an especially unusual career in the Supply Corps. He served on the Asiatic Station in the late 1930s, was a member of the U.S. embassy staff in Berlin when the United States entered World War II, was interned by the Gestapo, and later rose to Flag rank.

He was born at Nehvola, Karjala Province, Finland, in August 1906. His family emigrated to the United States, and young Lattu attended high school at Fort Bragg, California. He attended the University of California, Berkeley, in 1926, where he was selected as a member of the first NROTC unit in the United States. Through an administrative oversight, his selection occurred a few days before his citizenship papers came through. Onnie Lattu survived a potential disenrollment as an alien and remained in the NROTC unit, which CAPT Chester Nimitz had started at Berkeley. The young Finnish-American became a favorite of the Nimitzes, in whose home he was a frequent guest. He graduated in June 1930 with a bachelor of arts degree and a commission as ensign, Supply Corps, U.S. Naval Reserve.

ENS Lattu reported as assistant supply officer in *USS New York* in February 1931, and in November of that year was transferred to *USS Saratoga* (CV-3). Lattu moved on to *USS Augusta* (CA-31), flagship of the Scouting Force, as disbursing officer from January 1932 to September

1933. He was at the Puget Sound Navy Yard until 1935, when he went to the Navy Yard, Cavite, in the Philippines.

In September 1936, he returned to *Augusta*, then flagship of the Asiatic Squadron. LT Lattu was ordered to the Bureau of Supplies and Accounts in January 1938 with additional duty as White House aide.

He was sent to Europe in August 1940 as assistant naval attaché, U.S. embassy, Berlin, with additional duty at the American legations in Madrid, Rome, Stockholm, and Vichy, France. Onnie Lattu's attempt to reach his new duty at Berlin was an adventure in itself. He went by ocean liner to Lisbon, intending to go to Berlin via occupied Paris, where he planned to purchase an automobile from a fellow Supply Corps officer, LT (later RADM) Charles (Count) deKay.

Officials at the legation in Lisbon advised against the Paris route because gasoline was scarce and the Nazis unlikely to permit a drive into Germany. All travel in Europe had been disrupted and seemed to be, in Lattu's words, "a mess." He accompanied a courier to Bern, Switzerland, via Spain and France, encountering bureaucratic delays at every border crossing. After several weeks, he finally reached Berlin and reported to his new post.

Lattu spent a month learning German at the University of Berlin. He and other Americans—Army officers and members of the press—moved from their dreary hotels and pensions into an apartment. The Americans pooled their rations and elected Lattu mess treasurer. The young, single Supply Corps officer took weekend trips within the permitted 70 miles of Berlin. He found the people in the villages happier, better fed, and less concerned with the war than Berliners. He also made several official visits to the other legations where he had collateral duties. Lattu had planned to go to Sweden and then go to Finland to look up relatives. He traveled by train and ferry to Stockholm, arriving on 6 December 1941. When he learned the following evening of the Japanese attack on Pearl Harbor, he changed his plans. Although Lattu was not authorized to travel by air, he managed to book passage and flew back to Berlin the following morning. He arrived in Berlin only two days before the Germans declared war on the United States on 11 December.

LT Lattu was interned, with other embassy personnel, for more than four months in a rundown resort at Bad Nauheim. They were finally repatriated in May 1942. Lattu returned to duty at the Bureau of Supplies and Accounts and was responsible for the Navy's leadership in materials handling, packaging, and preservation. He then went to the Naval Supply Depot Oakland, California, in April 1944, and in May 1945 served briefly as assistant supply officer, Service Squadron TEN. In September of that year, he joined the staff of Commander Fifth Fleet, under

Admiral Ray Spruance, with additional duty as assistant logistics officer.

CDR Lattu returned to BuSandA in June 1946 as director of material and supply. He attended the strategy and logistics course at the Naval War College, Newport, Rhode Island, in 1948 and 1949. He then reported in June 1949 for duty on the staff of the Commander-in-Chief Pacific Fleet and force supply officer under Admiral William A. Radford, with additional duty on the staff of Commander Service Force Pacific. These two commands provided logistics support of the Fleet and overseas bases during the Korean War.

He returned stateside to assume command of the Naval Supply Depot Newport, in September 1952, with collateral duty as supply officer of the Newport Naval Base. His next duty, in November 1954, was as commanding officer, Ships Parts Control Center Mechanicsburg, Pennsylvania.

He was promoted to rear admiral in 1956 and became executive director of the Military Petroleum Supply Agency (now the Defense Fuel Supply Center). In September 1961, he was ordered to duty as assistant chief, Bureau of Supplies and Accounts for Transportation and Facilities. He was detailed to the Department of the Interior in May 1964, where he was appointed director of the Office of Oil and Gas.

RADM Lattu retired from the Navy in November 1965 but remained the director of the Office of Oil and Gas as a civilian. He retired from the Interior Department in March 1969. In May of that year, he became director of the Washington office of Cities Service Company, a position he held until retiring for a third time in 1974. Onnie and Arlene Lattu lived at Washington, D.C. He died in January 1995.

Sources

Burdick, Charles B. *An American Island in Hitler's Reich*. N.p.: Markgraf Publications Group, 1987.

Interview of RADM Onnie P. Lattu. Washington, D.C., 12 April 1988.

"Journal: Guests of the Gestapo." *Foreign Service Journal*, American Foreign Service Association, May 1986.

Official Biography. Naval Supply Systems Command, n.d.

Potter, E. B. *Nimitz*. Annapolis: Naval Institute Press, 1976.

Tensions in the Pacific

Japanese forces occupied Indochina in July 1941 without opposition from the Vichy French, and the United States demanded that the Japanese withdraw immediately. Japan refused, so the Roosevelt administration froze that nation's assets in America and tightened an existing embargo on vitally needed shipments of oil and scrap metal. These moves further exacerbated relations between the two countries and brought war even closer.

The Japanese had a history of striking first before formal declarations of war, a strategy that was effective against both Russia and China. The British were barely hanging on and trying to defend the Suez Canal. The Netherlands were already occupied. With those two potential obstacles downgraded, Japan's military government set its sights on the British and Dutch petroleum and mineral resources in Southeast Asia and the East Indies.

The stage was thus set for the inevitable confrontation between the United States and the Japanese empire. The U.S. Navy and Army reinforced major bases in Hawaii and the Philippine Islands and other outposts throughout the Pacific as best they could. As a result of the prewar buildup of the Navy throughout 1940 and 1941, the Supply Corps had grown to 800 Regular and 1,400 Reserve officers on active duty in early December 1941.

Pearl Harbor

The United States had conducted fleet exercises in 1932 in which American carrier planes launched a mock attack on Pearl Harbor. The lessons learned from that exercise were not lost on Japanese Admiral Isoroku Yamamoto, who knew that only by using Japan's capital ship numerical superiority to knock out the U.S. Pacific Fleet in a single blow could Japan win a Pacific war. Eight U.S. battleships were moored in the close quarters of Pearl Harbor on the weekend of 6-7 December 1941. Expecting two Pacific Fleet carriers to be there also, Yamamoto launched the attack from his six carriers at a day and time when he knew the American guard would be down.

The Hawaiian sky was typically clear and bright blue when the sun rose over the island of Oahu on Sunday, 7 December 1941. A few minutes before 0800, the U.S. Navy at Pearl Harbor, as in other locations around the world, was settling into a normal Sunday routine. Half the crews of the ships of the Pacific Fleet were on liberty, and those aboard were either sleeping in or were preparing for morning colors and divine services. On this quiet light-duty day, there was no indication that their world was about to change forever.

LTJG Joseph M. Lyle, duty officer in the Supply Department at the Pearl Harbor Navy Yard, had just finished breakfast. He was walking into the duty office when he heard and felt a series of explosions. He quickly ascertained that an attack was underway on Pearl Harbor and the moored Navy ships. Lyle immediately notified the Yard's supply officer, CAPT John Gaffney, who was dressing in his quarters for church services. Lyle then called the senior assistant, LCDR Howard M. Shaffer, and LCDR M. N. Gilbert, the stores officer, at their quarters. Lyle's fourth call was to the senior Supply Department watch officer, LTJG Thomas A. Brown, who was asleep at home.

Most Honolulu-area Supply Corps officers were relaxing in contemplation of a normal "Sunday in paradise." ENS John Burrill was doing his daily pushups while his bride was preparing breakfast. LTJG Lincoln Letterman was working on his automobile at his quarters. ENS J. Patrick Quinn was asleep at the Honolulu YMCA. LTJG O. B. Patterson, officer-in-charge, Stores Section, Kuahua, had reported to his post in Building KD at 0700, nearly an hour before the start of the attack. Patterson and his key civilian, a Mr. Miller, had given employees their assignments for the day's work, which was well underway when the attack began.

Howard Shaffer hung up from Joe Lyle's call, dressed, and headed for the office, driving through heavy traffic that thinned out as he neared the yard. He was at his desk by 0820. His first duty involved the issuance of steel helmets and sidearms at Building 71, where he found officers busily engaged in checking pistols and adjusting gunbelts. Tom Brown had also dressed immediately when Joe Lyle called. He picked up his next-door neighbor, a Navy chaplain, and drove to the navy yard. Brown insists that he took the chaplain with him not for divine protection but merely as a neighborly gesture.

Meanwhile, John Gast, a yeoman third class, had the duty at the Office of Naval Intelligence in the shipyard. His application for a commission in the Supply Corps was pending.

ENS Vance Fowler, disbursing officer, *USS West Virginia* (BB-48), which was moored in "Battleship Row," had conducted a large payday on Saturday. He had the duty Sunday morning and was about to balance his cashbook. He was scheduled to be relieved at 1200 hours and was looking forward to a round of golf at the Oahu Country Club in the afternoon with his NF&SS classmate, ENS Stan Parker, disbursing officer, Destroyer Division FIVE.

ENS Joseph L. (Joe) Howard, disbursing officer, Destroyer Division 80, also had a golf date that day. He was to meet ENS Verdi D. Sederstrom, a NF&SS classmate and disbursing officer of the battleship *USS Oklahoma* (BB-37), shortly after 0800. When the attack began, Joe Howard was standing on the quarterdeck of *USS Sacramento* (PG-19), in which he was temporarily quartered while his ship, *USS Chew* (DD-106), was in for overhaul. He ran to his stateroom, changed from his golf togs into uniform, and then went to his temporary office in a shack on the dock.

Wounded and badly burned sailors, many covered with oil and grease, were soon brought in from ships on Battleship Row and landed on the dock. ENS Howard and some of his storekeepers turned their attention to assisting the casualties by washing them with a cold-water hose and using towels to wipe off the worst of the grease and grime before sending them on to the dispensary. A doctor came by and told them not to send any more men to the overloaded dispensary but commandeered a truck to take the worst cases with him.

Stan Parker was shaving aboard *USS Conyngham* (DD-371), which was in tender overhaul, when the attack started, ending his plans to play golf with Fowler.

ENS Paul (Dixie) Howell, then a line officer in *USS Neosho* (AO-26), had just finished gauging the Ford Island fuel tanks into which *Neosho* had completed an overnight transfer of aviation gasoline. Howell relaxed at the rail on deck while a mess steward prepared breakfast. *Neosho* was tied up at Fox 4 berth between the battleships *USS California* (BB-44), which was 300 feet off the bow, and the nested *Oklahoma* and *USS Maryland* (BB-46) immediately astern.

At approximately 0755, Howell was astonished to see a low-flying aircraft with Japanese markings heading past the battleships toward the Ford Island seaplane base. The first plane was followed by torpedo planes, which he witnessed launching their lethal "fish" and scoring hits on both *California* and *Maryland.* A major aerial assault was underway.

A Supply Officer Prepares for War

CAPT Gaffney had warned Supply Department officers in August that war could start as early as mid-October. He insisted that his department and "customers" make preparations to operate as if a war already were underway. Navy officials had already determined in mid-1941 to establish a new supply depot at Pearl Harbor, separate from the Navy Yard Supply Department, and had given CAPT Gaffney responsibility for setting up an organization for it. Gaffney wanted a former associate from his days at BuSandA, LCDR (later CAPT) Norman A. Helfrich, to tackle the administrative task. He arranged to have Helfrich's orders to *USS Trenton* (CL-11) canceled and new orders issued for him to report to the Supply Department at Pearl Harbor.

Helfrich reported on 24 November and went to work immediately on the project, segregating functions, writing job descriptions for both supply activities, and reassigning and moving personnel. He had completed job sheets for more than 500 new civilian positions late on Saturday, 6 December. He asked for a copy of the watch, quarter and station bill and was advised that there was none. It was too late in the evening to begin to structure one, so Helfrich returned to the Donna Hotel, where he, his wife, and 13-year-old son were temporarily residing until they could move into quarters. In the meantime, Navy Yard Supply Department personnel completed provisioning of the battleships, which were scheduled to go to sea on Monday to make room for the returning carriers and escorts.

The first order of business when the attack commenced was to secure the base and its facilities against possible enemy incursions, either by direct assault or through clandestine moves by individuals in the large Japanese population residing in Hawaii. John Gaffney had issued a memorandum on 12 November to all officers in his department, requiring them to report to the Marines for instruction in handling the .45 caliber service automatic pistol. This was another example of the farsighted Gaffney preparing his department for the inevitable war that everyone expected—but not on that particular Sunday morning.

Dozens of Supply Corps officers assigned to the various Navy installations throughout the Hawaiian Islands rushed to their duty stations on 7 December to implement contingency plans carefully made during October and November. LCDR Julian J. Levasseur, supply officer of *Oklahoma,* was also staying at the Donna Hotel. He and LCDR Helfrich sped to Pearl Harbor when the attack commenced. Helfrich reported to the Supply Department and Levasseur rushed to the officers' club landing in order to return to his ship. When he reached the landing, he saw that *Oklahoma* had capsized as a result of the sneak attack. He immediately reported for duty to the Navy Yard Supply Department. Two enlisted *Oklahoma* survivors also arrived at the Supply Department later in the morning and offered their assistance.

The Supply Department Toll

The Supply Department suffered two casualties in the rush to duty stations. While en route to his post at the Merry Point Provisions Depot, Linc Letterman was struck on the elbow by gunfire from a plane that strafed his car. David H. Kahookele, a civilian laborer, was killed when the car in which he was riding to work was struck by a bomb from a Japanese plane. Letterman, who was to stand by at Merry Point for response to possible incendiary bombing, continued on to his duty post after being wounded but was soon removed to the dispensary for treatment.

Helfrich knew that loss and serious damage to battleships, other vessels, and shore stations meant that it was necessary to arrange alternate messing for thousands of sailors and Marines who normally subsisted aboard ships no longer afloat. He also knew that it would be necessary to draw extra provisions from limited Supply Department stocks to replace those destroyed in the attack. He volunteered to take over the Merry Point cold-storage plant and ration provisions on a daily basis from stocks already depleted by the loading of the battleships fewer than 24 hours earlier. CAPT Gaffney readily agreed to Helfrich's plans, including the issue of ready-to-eat food to units without cooking facilities.

LTJG Phillip D. Chubb, commissary officer of the submarine base at Pearl Harbor, also rushed to Merry Point to assist in the issue of provisions and arrived before Helfrich could get there. The wounded Letterman soon returned from treatment of his wound and opened the cold-storage section to make the issues. LCDRs Helfrich and Landregan arrived at the Provisions Depot and gave instructions to prepare 25 pallets of emergency dry-stores items in case of the need for emergency issues, especially to cruisers and destroyers.

Helfrich, assisted by Chubb, Landregan, and Lettermen, made the emergency issues, but conditions were too hectic to adhere strictly to prescribed accounting procedures. Instead, Helfrich instituted a temporary plan to have quantities issued to each unit listed on a notepad, to be signed by the unit's authorized representative to draw the items.

ENS Gardner T. (Whitey) Pollich was with his wife, who was pregnant, in their apartment in Waikiki when he heard strange noises and load bursts. Joe Lyle called and told him to report in immediately, so Pollich rushed to Pearl Harbor. He recalls that a Marine sentry was firing his pistol at the attacking planes but managed to wave the supply officer through the gate with his free hand. Pollich went directly to Building 9 and secured the front door to keep workers inside and out of line of strafing aircraft. CAPT Gaffney then sent Pollich and four other officers to the officers' club, recreation center, hospital, and other support activities to ascertain needs for food, cots, blankets, and medical equipment.

Pat Quinn was awakened by the YMCA desk clerk, who advised him of the attack on Pearl Harbor and the order that all Navy personnel report to their duty stations. Quinn hailed a taxi for the trip to Pearl Harbor, along with several enlisted personnel. He reported to the Supply Department, where he later relieved Joe Lyle as duty officer, on schedule.

ENS Wallace F. Millson went to Kualua and had storekeepers review the files of undelivered stores to determine the quantity of steel helmets, medical stores, and gun mounts that had been packed to await pickup by personnel from ships in the harbor. Millson ordered space cleared in his warehouse for possible emergency use. Four ships sent working parties to pick up emergency stores Sunday afternoon, but none showed up on Monday.

ENS W. J. Peterson opened Building KA and checked ships' papers to determine whether urgently needed materials were in the building. He then positioned the material for quick issue to ships that had requisitioned it.

LTJG John Vinn, Jr., was one of the last Supply Corps officers to learn of the attack, but he, too, rushed to his duty station. He was directed to make an emergency issue of 200 outfits of clothing to the Naval Air Station for survivors of the sunk *USS Utah* (AG-16), a target ship and former battleship.

The First Wartime Contract

LTJG Lyle alerted the Honolulu purchasing office of an urgent need for blankets for men who had been burned while swimming from their battered ships through blazing oil. John Burrill contacted the manager of Liberty House, a local department store, and arranged what was probably the first contract of the war—for the needed blankets.

CAPT Gaffney directed LT Errett R. Feeney to ascertain needs for food, bedding, cots, and mattresses at the naval hospital, where medical personnel told him that they were fully equipped to handle all anticipated demands on the hospital's facilities. Gaffney then ordered Feeney to Merry Point to take charge of handling ammunition.

LTJG George L. Bennett was at Oahu on temporary duty with the Fourteenth Naval District material officer to assemble equipment and supplies for his regular duty station on Johnston Atoll, 750 miles southwest of Hawaii. He was awakened at his Oahu home by explosions, and antiaircraft fire alerted him that something was amiss. Bennett was turning on his radio when his brother, an officer attached to a minelayer, knocked on his door to tell him of the attack and the call for Navy personnel to report for duty.

The two brothers started to drive to Pearl Harbor, picking up a chief petty officer and a nonrated enlisted man on the way, but were delayed by traffic jams and did not reach the District Supply Office until about 0930. Bennett's request for orders to the navy yard supply officer for temporary duty was approved. CAPT Gaffney welcomed the extra help.

At 1100, Gaffney assigned Bennett to duty with the Marines to handle their requirements for additional supplies, but the Marines indicated there was no immediate need for such supplies so Bennett returned to the supply office. At 1330, the Marines called for 500 cots and mattresses to be sent immediately to NAS Pearl Harbor on Ford Island. While trucks were en route to the storehouse to pick up the requested material, the requirement was upped to 1,500 cots and mattresses. Bennett authorized the increased issue. The following day, he was assigned as liaison between the supply officer and the Marine's post quartermaster.

Under Attack

Five inactive Naval Reserve Supply Corps officers residing in the Honolulu area heard the radio call for all U.S. Navy personnel to report to their duty stations. The Reservists, without written orders of any kind, instinctively reported for duty at the Supply Department. CAPT Gaffney immediately briefed the newly arrived reinforcements and assigned them duties.

- ENS William M. Armstrong was sent to Ford Island to make delivery of the emergency clothing issued by John Vinn.
- ENS J. James (Jerry) Condran, Jr., assumed the telephone watch in the Supply Department duty officer's room.
- ENS Frank V. Gandola was assigned as officer-in-charge of Building 71 to continue the issue of steel helmets and sidearms.
- ENS Maynard B. Hasselquist filled in at Merry Point for ENS Letterman while he was at the dispensary for treatment of his wound.
- LTJG J. B. Andrade was ordered to drive into Honolulu to purchase five tons of Kona coffee.

CAPT Gaffney also put the five Reservists on the expanded 7-day, 24-hour watch bill. The paperwork officially recalling them to active duty would have to wait until things calmed down. Tom Brown (who retired as a captain) proudly recalls that within two days the performance of the Reservists was indistinguishable from that of their USN counterparts.

Bill Armstrong commandeered two trucks to take the clothing Vinn had initially issued to Ford Island, but they were delayed at the ferry slip when the second wave of enemy planes strafed the area. Armstrong eventually issued clothing to survivors of *Utah* and other sunken or damaged ships. Captain Gaffney then appointed Armstrong to supervise Supply Department construction, engineering, and transportation, which increased greatly with repair, reconstruction, and alteration of area supply facilities.

Condran assumed the telephone watch in the duty officer's room, relieving Pat Quinn to make entries in the official log. The young Reserve officer reported a steady high rate of incoming calls and was impressed by the calmness and businesslike manner of military and civilian personnel in the Supply Department.

Frank Gandola and his associates in Building 71 issued:

- 165 .45-caliber service automatic pistols and holsters,
- 612 steel helmets,
- 125 rifles,
- 55 machine guns,
- 18 machine gun mounts, and
- spare parts for machine guns.

His supply of helmets was gradually diminishing, and he feared he would run out, so he ordered all helmets collected at the main gate as civilian workers left the yard. He used his own automobile to shuttle back and forth between Building 71 and the main gate to return helmets for reissue to the next shift of shipyard workers.

Hasselquist immediately conducted an inspection of the cold-storage area at Merry Point Provisions Depot to determine damage and to prepare to fight possible fires.

J. B. Andrade found that Honolulu wholesale firms could not provide the full five tons of Kona coffee, and Gaffney approved substitution of standard commercial brands. Andrade arranged truck transportation to move the coffee from wholesalers to the navy yard. Blue paint, needed to darken vehicle headlights in compliance with hastily ordered regulations, was in short supply, but Andrade improvised by taping blue paper over headlights. All the coffee was delivered by late evening.

John Gast's ONI office was on the first deck of the Pearl Harbor Navy Yard administration building, which was spared in the aerial assault. The Japanese pilots concentrated their attacks on the ships of the Pacific Fleet, Navy planes on Ford Island and Kanehoe Bay, and Army Air Corps planes at Hickham Field. Gast quickly recovered from the initial shock and was kept busy for days in processing reports of spies in the area by well-intentioned individuals. Most of the reports proved to be false.

Back on Battleship Row, the first torpedo hit *West Virginia* as Vance Fowler tried to reach his battle station three decks below; the area was already being evacuated as water rushed through a huge hole caused by the torpedo. Fowler then went to the disbursing office and retrieved his cash book and a few other records. *West Virginia* was already listing at least five degrees when he reached the quarterdeck. The battle raged around him, and the explosion that ripped apart the *USS Arizona* (BB-39), moored only 75 yards behind *West Virginia,* knocked Fowler off his feet. He slid into the water. Luck was with the young officer despite the frightening experience of sliding overboard. Another torpedo struck the ship directly below the disbursing office. Had Fowler still been there, he certainly would have been killed.

He climbed back aboard *West Virginia* and was hit by numerous fireballs of bits of powder bags from *Arizona*'s exploding magazines. He sought refuge from the debris behind a 16-inch gun turret that a 1,500-pound bomb soon hit 10 feet from where he was crouched. He had his second close call when the bomb proved to be a dud and failed to detonate. (Although it looked like a bomb, fell from the sky like a bomb, and hit the ship like a bomb, it later proved to be a 15-inch armor-piercing shell equipped with fins. See volume 8 of *Dictionary of American Fighting Ships.*)

When the order was given to abandon ship, Fowler went over the side into a life raft with no paddles, still clutching his cash book. While the other occupants used their hands to propel the raft toward a motor launch, Vance Fowler dug in with his carefully preserved cash book. They raced to reach safety in the launch before being overtaken by a rapidly advancing burning oil slick or struck by bullets from strafing Japanese aircraft. Fortunately, they made it.

Ensigns Walter S. (Red) Savage, Jr., assistant paymaster in *Arizona,* and Verdi D. Sederstrom, assistant paymaster in *Oklahoma* (BB-37), were not so fortunate. Savage had reported in late October and had been aboard for only two pay periods when Japanese bombs destroyed his ship, entombing him forever in the sunken hull. Sederstrom had also been on duty for a short period when bombs caused his ship to explode and capsize. He was declared missing and presumed dead. They are believed to be the first two Supply Corps officers to die in World War II. Joe Howard did not learn until several days later that his friend and golf partner Verdi Sederstrom had gone down with *Oklahoma.*

ENS John P. (Pat) Wolfe, then a line officer and assistant gunnery officer of *USS Blue* (DD-387), was one of four ensigns comprising the duty watch and relieving duty watch. The four were eating breakfast in the wardroom when the attack started. ENS Nathan Asher, senior officer aboard, gave orders to sound general quarters, man battle stations, and prepare to get the ship underway. Pat Wolfe recalls that it took 45 minutes before the ships' engines had sufficient steam to do so. Meanwhile, ENS Wolfe was in the gun director and coordinated the firing by crews manning 4 5-inch, .38-caliber gun mounts that succeeded in shooting down five enemy planes. *Blue* was also credited with sinking a Japanese submarine and driving off another during the attack.

The capsized *Oklahoma* held the inboard *Maryland* captive. Her only escape route was blocked by *Neosho,* moored across the angled Fox 4 pier. *Maryland* frantically signalled *Neosho* to abandon her berth and allow the battleship to get underway. *Neosho*'s skipper realized that the attackers had become aware that an unexpected tanker was moored among the battleships, presenting an inviting target. No tugs were available, but *Neosho* managed to get underway in the main channel just as the second attack began.

The *USS Nevada* (BB-36) had been torpedoed trying to exit the harbor to gain maneuvering room in the Pacific, so her C.O. swung her damaged rudder over hard and grounded the battleship to avoid being sunk in the main channel. Enemy planes then swarmed toward *Neosho* in an attempt to sink her in the channel to bottle up the surviving American ships. Dixie Howell reports that *Neosho* put up an effective antiaircraft defense aided by guns on shore and managed to reach the open sea. She eventually tied up at a Merry Point pier just as the last Japanese planes were departing the area. Destroyers, scheduled for refueling at Merry Point in the early hours of 8 December, did not dock as originally planned, so Errett Feeney had to arrange transfer of 50 depth charges by Whitney and Dobbins boats to the ships anchored in the harbor.

On Alert at NAS Supply Department

Over at Ford Island, CDR Charles J. Harter, supply officer at the Naval Air Station Pearl Harbor, had 11 junior Supply Corps officers on his staff. Harter, a hard-driving, stern taskmaster, had told the young officers on Monday, 1 December, that war could start at any time.

ENS (later LT) John McCormack, a recent NF&SS graduate, had reported to NAS from *USS Maryland* only a week before. At the time of the attack, he was asleep at the bachelor officers' quarters, but dressed quickly and reported for duty. McCormack, a Reservist, remained on duty until May 1945, when he was retired on physical disability.

Rolland Helsel had been detached from *USS Pennsylvania* (BB-38) on Thanksgiving Day 1941 and reported to NAS Pearl Harbor the next week. He was assigned as incoming stores officer and had the duty on 7 December. During and after the attack, Helsel supplemented his security duties by helping the wounded from ships moored alongside Ford Island. NAS Alameda had been directed shortly after the attack to expedite shipment of half the material in each supply bin to NAS Pearl Harbor, which received considerable damage during the attack. Helsel and his associates lacked covered storage for the shipload of parts that arrived three weeks later. However, working parties toiled long hours and managed to get most of the costly aviation items under cover, if only covered by tarpaulins.

Nine-year-old Ted Walker, whose father was operations officer on the staff of Commander Submarines United States Fleet at Pearl Harbor, climbed on the roof of his Honolulu home when he heard the first explosions from the attack. He remained on the roof for the rest of the morning, watching events unfold. Forty-three years later, RADM Ted Walker became the 35th chief of Supply Corps.

CAPT Gaffney called a meeting of all shipyard Supply Department officers at 1800—10 hours after the last Japanese bombing run. He stressed that although there had been no formal declaration of war, the nation was in fact at war, and the situation was serious. He pointed out that the department's stocks of required items were high, but the emergency issues made that day and subsequent demands would reduce stock levels significantly. Replenishment of many items would be expedited, but Gaffney decreed that hoarding must be discouraged.

After the Attack

Pearl Harbor was warned to be on the alert for additional air raids. Jittery military and civilian personnel were alarmed Sunday night, when American airplanes returning to flattops flew in low over the area to land on Ford Island. Several were shot down by defending gunners.

On Monday, Congress declared war on Japan. At Pearl Harbor, Joe Lyle instructed storekeepers to resume regular routines. He composed a dispatch to be sent to the chief of naval operations and the Bureau of Supplies and Accounts, stating emergency needs for small arms, helmets, blankets, and cots. Another dispatch was sent to the Puget Sound Navy Yard, requesting that all unfilled requisitions for lumber be filled immediately and shipped by first available transportation. Requisitions for additional lumber to double Pearl Harbor stocks were airmailed to Puget Sound.

Available stocks of critical material available in Honolulu were purchased on 8 and 9 December using oral awards by authority of CAPT John Gaffney. Requisitions were airmailed to Mare Island Navy Yard for a year's requirements of those items most likely to be needed, based on stock usage and stockmen's estimates, but not available in the Honolulu area.

Whitey Pollich was assigned the task of collecting all the U.S. paper currency from the banks in Hawaii for shipment back to the Federal Reserve Bank in San Francisco to keep it from falling into Japanese hands in the event of an invasion. Immediate implementation of the shipment was ordered, leaving time only to collect the greenbacks and not enough to count it. CAPT Gaffney instructed ENS Pollich to make out the bill of lading with such entries as "5 cubic feet of U.S. currency." The U.S. military government then issued new currency with the word *Hawaii* imprinted on each certificate to keep potential invaders from possessing any true U.S. bills should they seize the banks.

Expanded Operations

CAPT Gaffney took many steps in the days immediately following the outbreak of hostilities to expand his department's operations to meet anticipated wartime demands. He established the office of Coordinator for Naval Procurement in downtown Honolulu on 12 December, with ENS Richard S. Balch as assistant coordinator for naval procurement in charge of the office.

Gaffney reached an agreement on 13 December with the Army at Camp Punahou to permit the Navy and the Marine Corps to have 25 percent of any Army frozen food stocks without question. Gaffney's stamp or that of any of the assistant coordinators for naval procurement would be sufficient to authorize purchases of more than 25 percent of the Army's frozen stock.

By the time the first resupply reefer ship arrived from CONUS nearly a month after the attack, the Supply Department was thousands of dollars over-issued, with only nonaccountable signatures for issues made. LCDR Helfrich decided, on his own, to increase invoice prices on all future receipts by 10 percent before issue to make up the shortage.

CAPT Gaffney was concerned that his April 1942 quarterly returns would show significant losses in provisions, but LCDR Helfrich eased his boss's concern by advising him of the earlier action to adjust invoice prices. A subsequent inventory revealed that the Supply Department was thousands of dollars above what it had issued free. BuSandA authorized Gaffney to continue the increasing price program to cover losses by sinking and other causes.

On 14 December, Gaffney executed a contract with the Hawaiian Pineapple Company to rent, as required, 10-ton trucks, with drivers, through 30 June 1942. The contractor was to have at least 50 trucks available at all times. The contract rate for a truck and driver was $3.65 an hour.

Gaffney directed the local agents for the Dutch Motor Ship *Rosevale,* laying over at Honolulu en route to the Netherlands East Indies, to unload and dispose of her cargo for credit to the account of the ship's owners. Gaffney ordered nine cases of Royal Air Force aviation items on board retained for Navy disposition. These actions, taken on 17 December, were warranted because the Dutch East Indies were already under attack and being invaded by Japanese troops.

Fuel Controls for Hawaii

The Pearl Harbor supply officer appointed C. W. Turner, Honolulu branch manager for Standard Oil Company, as assistant to the coordinator for naval procurement for the Fourteenth Naval District on 19 December. He directed Turner to control bunkering of Navy, Army, and all commercially registered vessels in order to conserve the supply of fuel in Hawaii and minimize withdrawal from local storage facilities. Gaffney further directed Turner to meet with officials of other oil companies, public utilities, and local corporations that controlled bulk storage and arrange for conservation of all petroleum products they held.

Turner made arrangements with the harbor master on 21 December to board all vessels arriving at the port of Honolulu and obtain from their masters an inventory of onboard fuel oil. He also ascertained whether they required refueling.

CAPT Gaffney convened a fuel conference of Navy, Army, and civilian officials on 26 December to discuss further the critical fuel situation in the Territory of Hawaii. He pointed out the need for increased storage of aviation fuels and proposed two steps to meet this need:

- reduce motor-grade gasoline storage from 16.5 million gallons to a maximum of 10 million gallons, and
- import only a single grade of motor gasoline into the territory.

Gaffney emphasized that by adopting this plan they could increase storage capacity of aviation fuels to 8.5 million gallons. Gaffney's plan was promptly implemented.

Back at Encinal Terminal, Alameda, California, *USS Procyn* (AK-17) was preparing to sail for Pearl Harbor on the day of the attack. Her supply officer, LT (later RADM) Charles A. (Charlie) Blick, recalls that "insane confusion" reigned in the Bay Area when news of the disaster spread. *Procyn* was directed immediately to Mare Island Navy Yard to load medical supplies, including vaccines, injectables, and anti-infection sulfa drugs, for Hawaiian medical and hospital facilities, which were sorely overtaxed with thousands of burned and wounded personnel. *Procyn* sailed for Pearl on or about 13 December and arrived five days later. Charlie Blick remembers that he was aghast at the damage done to the battleships and shore facilities. "People were in a state of shock and clean-up was minimal," he recalls.

Also at Pearl Harbor at the time of the attack were LCDR William H. (Bill) Abbey, supply officer, *USS Oglala* (ARG-1), and LCDR Charles F. (Charlie) House, supply officer, *USS Vestal* (AR-4). The two had enlisted in 1902 and 1903, respectively, and both had been pay clerks at Pearl Harbor when the United States entered World War I. *Vestal* had been alongside *Arizona* during the 1941 attack and was damaged, but not sunk. *Oglala,* tied up at a pier, escaped damage.

After Pearl Harbor

It is obvious that John Gaffney's foresight and decisive actions before, during, and after the sneak attack on Pearl Harbor were important contributions to the war effort. They were typical of his 35 years of Supply Corps service, and he was promoted to rear admiral in September 1942.

Joe Lyle went on to an illustrious Navy career. He became one of only 13 Supply Corps officers to reach the rank of vice admiral, as director, Defense Supply Agency (now the Defense Logistics Agency).

Paul Howell later transferred to the Supply Corps and rose to the rank of rear admiral in the Naval Reserve, but almost did not make it. He had a close call when *Neosho*'s luck ran out five months after Pearl Harbor. Japanese planes found and sunk her and the escorting destroyer *USS Sims* (DD-409) in the Coral Sea the day before planes located the U.S. task force *Neosho* had been sent to refuel. Howell was one of the few aboard *Neosho* and *Sims* to survive. He spent four days adrift in the open ocean before being rescued. Paul Howell is proud that *Neosho* shot down several Japanese planes in six hours of attacks at Pearl Harbor and in the Coral Sea. Howard M. Shaffer also became a rear admiral in 1958. Joe Howard was promoted to Flag rank in 1967.

At least 26 Supply Corps officers who were at Pearl Harbor on 7 December achieved the rank of captain, including Richard Balch, George Bennett, Tom Brown, John Burrill, Phillip Chubb, Vance Fowler, Frank Gandola, Norman Helfrich, R. S. Hill, William Hyland, Linc Letterman, Wallace Millson, Whitey Pollich, Pat Quinn, and John Gast, whose commission in the Supply Corps was approved in 1942.

Eight of those who made captain were among 12 Supply Corps officers on duty at NAS Pearl Harbor on 7 December 1941: CDR Harter, LT Raymond Cope, LTJG Wallace L. Atkinson, and Ensigns Norton J. Arst, Paul Cosgrove, Rolland Helsel, Daniel F. Logan, and Gilbert M. Rice. In addition to Lyle, Shaffer, Howard, and Howell, Cosgrove also went on to achieve Flag rank. Pat Wolfe transferred to the Supply Corps in 1946, and he, too, made captain.

A Bold Telephone Call

Back in Washington, where Japanese diplomats were playing out a charade of negotiations even while the Pearl Harbor attack was underway, another graduate of the NF&SS class of 1939–40, LTJG (later RADM) Robert (Bob) Northwood, was the BuSandA duty officer. An urgent message came in from Pearl Harbor shortly after the attack for mine detonators stored at Yorktown, Virginia.

Without hesitation, Northwood called the president of United Airlines and asked that the two nearest United planes—whether on the ground or in the air—be diverted to a landing strip near Yorktown. The United executive responded with equal promptness, and two of the airline's planes were dispatched, their passengers off-loaded, and the seats removed. The detonators were soon on their way to Hawaii. Northwood later was amazed as he reflected on how a mere lieutenant was able, in a single unconfirmed telephone call, to mobilize one of the nation's leading air carriers.

In Retrospect

The brilliantly conceived and executed Japanese attack rendered the near fatal blow Yamamoto wanted, but luck and the American spirit combined to moderate the full impact of the attack. First, the carriers were not in Pearl Harbor that day. Fortunately, RADM William F. (Bull) Halsey had taken two U.S. aircraft carriers, *USS Enterprise* (CV-6) and *USS Lexington* (CV-2), to sea the previous week to deliver fighters to Wake Island, thus escaping the surprise air raid on Pearl Harbor.

Second, the American response was quick and effective. Some historians reason that although Americans and the nation itself were seriously divided before 7 December over whether the United States should enter the war, the sneak attack united Americans in a manner that no amount of political rhetoric could have done.

Although the proud U.S. Pacific Fleet had sustained terrible damage on 7 December 1941, the response of the officers and sailors to the devastating attack was outstanding. The sound planning and advance preparations that the Pearl Harbor Shipyard Supply Department made under CAPT John J. Gaffney were major factors in the Fleet's prompt rebound from the costly losses of that day.

LORE OF THE CORPS

Captain John Jerome Gaffney, SC, USN

Supply Officer, Pearl Harbor Navy Yard, 1941–42
Period of Service: 1912–47

John Gaffney was a farsighted and imaginative Supply Corps officer, and the Navy was fortunate to have him in charge of the Pearl Harbor Navy Yard Supply Department on the day of the Japanese sneak attack. He had first warned of impending war with Japan as soon as he assumed his new duties at Pearl Harbor, and in October 1941 he put his department on a wartime footing.

Gaffney was born at Charleston, South Carolina, in March 1891. He was educated at the College of Charleston and at St. Lawrence University, where he played baseball and was president of both his class and the student body. He was commissioned assistant paymaster with rank of ensign in September 1912, reported to the old *USS Salem* later that year, and subsequently had duty in *USS Pompey* and *USS Cincinnati* (CL-6) from 1913 to 1916.

When he and CAPT Robert R. (Bob) Campbell, SC, USN (Ret.) served together after World War II, Gaffney recalled a story about his first encounter with the famous RADM Sam McGowan around 1912. At the time, Pay Inspector McGowan was on duty at the Philadelphia Navy Yard when Gaffney's ship put into port. According to Campbell, Gaffney made a trip via streetcar to the Philadelphia Federal Reserve Bank to obtain a large amount of cash, taking along a Navy satchel and his sidearm. On his return trip to the Yard, Gaffney sat next to a distinguished-looking gentleman wearing a dress hat and carrying a cane. He carefully put the loaded satchel under his seat and began to read the daily newspaper. He soon became aware of the cane reaching under the seat and hooking the handles of the satchel. Instantly alerted, Gaffney warned the man to remove the cane or be shot. The cane was retracted. Only then did Gaffney learn that the apparent thief was none other than McGowan, who had been sizing up the young paymaster and wanted to teach him a lesson in the care of cash.

Gaffney was ordered from sea duty to the Charleston Navy Yard, where he was officer-in-charge, Experimental Clothing Factory, with additional duty as Charleston Navy Yard accounting officer. He earned a special letter of commendation from the secretary of the Navy for this duty.

The incident with McGowan may have played a part in Gaffney's being ordered to BuSandA in 1918. There, he was a trusted advisor to Paymaster General McGowan during World War I. LT Gaffney then reported in 1919 for duty as aide on the staff and financial advisor to the governor of the Virgin Islands, which the United States had purchased from Denmark in 1917 for defensive purposes.

He returned to the United States in 1923 as senior assistant supply officer, New York Navy Yard, and went to Headquarters, Sixth Naval District, at Charleston as accounting officer. Subsequently, he served successive sea tours from 1926 to 1928 as supply officer first of *USS Dobbin* (AD-3), then of *USS California* (BB-44). He later served as supply officer, *USS Saratoga* (CV-3) before joining the staff of VADM William F. Halsey, Jr., Commander Aircraft Battle Force, as supply officer, *USS Yorktown* (CV-5) in 1939.

CAPT Gaffney reported as supply officer of the Pearl Harbor Navy Yard in the summer of 1941. He was given the additional duty as Fourteenth Naval District supply officer and supply officer in command, Naval Supply Depot Pearl Harbor, in 1942. Wartime supply activities increased a thousandfold under his direction.

Gaffney's superiors credited his ability to foresee logistics problems well in advance as a major factor in the Pacific Fleet's success throughout the war. He was rewarded with promotion to rear admiral in July 1943, to rank from 15 September 1942, and was awarded the Legion of Merit in 1945.

RADM Gaffney reported as supply officer in command, Naval Supply Depot Oakland, California, in August 1945. He died after a brief illness while still on that duty in November 1947.

Sources

Brown, Thomas A., SC, USN. "I Remember It Well." *Navy Supply Corps Newsletter,* December 1959; reprinted February 1970.

Obituary. *Navy Supply Corps Newsletter,* December 1947.

"Reminiscences of CAPT John J. Gaffney." Prepared by CAPT Robert R. Campbell, SC, USN (Ret.), April 1994.

SACO in China

Navy planners had long realized the value of accurate weather forecasting in the Pacific when the seemingly inevitable war between the United States and Japan began. Because air currents move from west to east in the temperate zones of the earth, the weather in the Gobi Desert of Mongolia one day will probably be the next day's weather over Japan and the day after that over U.S. possessions in the Pacific. The Japanese, with weather stations on their home islands supplemented by stations in Manchuria and China, had a strong tactical advantage over a potential foe, whose forecasts would be largely the result of guesswork. Japan could forecast weather in the Pacific with a great deal more accuracy than the United States could.

Negating this advantage became a critical U.S. Navy objective. The framework of a super-secret organization, the Sino-American Cooperative Organization (SACO)—or U.S. Naval Group China—was formed. RADM (later VADM) Willis A. (Ching) Lee, Jr., was given responsibility for putting it into motion in the event of war in the Pacific. On 8 December 1941, as America was still reeling from the sneak attack on Pearl Harbor, Lee reviewed records of officers on duty in the Navy Department and found his candidate to lead the difficult and hazardous mission: Line CDR Milton Edward (Mary) Miles. Lee briefed Miles, an eight-year veteran of service in China, on the need and the hazards of the proposed SACO operation. Miles volunteered immediately.

The SACO team, which eventually grew to almost 3,000 Navy, Army, Marine, and Coast Guard personnel, had three objectives in a quid pro quo arrangement with Generalissimo Chiang Kai-Shek:

- to station U.S. Navy aerologists and meteorologists at strategic locations in the west and southwest of China with sufficient Nationalist Chinese troops and loyalist guerrillas to protect them;
- to position U.S. Navy coast-watchers to report Japanese ship movements with similar Chinese protection; and
- to equip and train Nationalist Chinese regular and guerrilla forces to carry out sabotage against Japanese forces and participate with Chinese forces in joint attacks.

SACO Logistics

Because of the super-secret nature of the operation, supply and logistics of American and Chinese personnel in the "Rice Paddy Navy" were extremely difficult and uncertain. Navy Supply Corps officers, both Regular and Reserve, assigned to SACO had their work cut out for them. The operation could not be revealed to anyone—including U.S., British, and Indian personnel at Calcutta, the southern terminus of Army Air Corps flights over "the Hump" via C-46 aircraft. Most of these Supply Corps officers were quite junior and unhampered by the experience of doing everything by the book. Their initiative and creativity were exceeded only by their courage and dedication.

Miles was forced to travel by commercial steamship and arrived at Chungking in May 1942 to meet with Chiang Kai-Shek and to reach a definitive agreement on the SACO mission. Navy personnel ordered to SACO duty in China traveled independently and could seek no special priority for fear of compromising security of the operation. By the end of 1942, the Americans and Chinese both came to recognize the importance of SACO succeeding. It would be necessary for the small but efficient intelligence force to be expanded into a full-fledged secret army.

Early Japanese Successess

Buoyed by their startling success at Pearl Harbor, Japanese forces swept through Southeast Asia and the Pacific in late 1941 and early 1942. Hong Kong, the Dutch East Indies (now Indonesia), Malaya (now Malaysia), Singapore, Thailand, Guam, and Wake Island fell to the Japanese onslaught with unparalleled swiftness. The Philippines held out a little longer, but the challenge to the U.S. Navy was never greater nor the outlook more bleak.

One young Supply Corps junior officer destined for greatness was ENS (later VADM) Ken Wheeler, who reported for duty in the summer of 1940 at the Cavite Navy Yard in the Philippines. Wheeler was assigned to work with a veteran Supply Corps officer, LCDR George Williams. The two were to share experiences at Manila and on Bataan, Corregidor, until the fortunes of war sent Williams to Australia via submarine and Wheeler to Japanese POW camps when Corregidor fell.

LORE OF THE CORPS

Lieutenant Commander George Henry Williams, SC, USN

Assistant Supply Officer, Cavite Navy Yard, P.I., 1940–41
Period of Service: 1908–46

George Williams served in the original *USS Constellation,* was an acting pay clerk in World War I, was on duty in the Philippines when the Japanese attacked, and was evacuated to Australia in 1942.

He was born in May 1888 on a farm at Boonville, Indiana. He was graduated from Indiana Common School in 1904 and followed his brother into the Navy. He enlisted as a landsman in July 1908. His first cruise was in *USS Franklin*. In January 1909, he joined *USS Constellation* (IX-20), a full-rigged frigate commissioned in 1797, and was immediately promoted to yeoman, third class. He subsequently served in the old *Franklin,* the old *USS Hancock,* and the gunboat *USS Paducah* (PG-18), on which he made chief yeoman in April 1912. He joined the fabled supply ship *USS Celtic,* where he completed his enlistment and was discharged in October 1916.

He was recalled to active duty for World War I service in September 1917 as an acting temporary pay clerk in *USS Pennsylvania* (BB-38) and was made a temporary ensign in September 1919. He almost did not become an officer because of his short stature, but his captain ordered four sailors to take him by the arms and legs and stretch him and then informed the doctor to remeasure him and that Williams had better be tall enough or the doctor would have trouble. He was commissioned a regular ensign in April 1921, ordered to the Bureau of Supplies and Accounts, and entered the Navy Supply Corps School of Application at BuSandA in April 1922. Williams was ordered to duty at NAS San Diego as a LTJG. He next had duty at Guam and Great Lakes Naval Station and attended the Army Quartermaster School in Chicago from August 1926 to September 1927. Then LT Williams had duty with Destroyer Division 15, *USS Melville* (AD-2), where he made lieutenant commander, and with the receiving station at the Washington Navy Yard.

LCDR Williams reported as senior assistant supply officer, Navy Yard, Cavite, in May 1940, where he was in charge of Navy provisions stowage for the Asiatic Fleet and area bases when the Japanese attacked the Philippines on 8 December 1941. The veteran supply officer was deeply involved in requisitioning and maintaining sufficient fresh, frozen, and dry provisions in keeping with existing war plans. In the months preceding the attack, LCDR Williams laid in large quantities of provisions when Fleet units were relocated from China to the Manila area.

According to a report prepared by Williams in early 1942 while still in the Philippines, stocks of provisions on 8 December 1941 were estimated to supply 8,000 men for four months in the Fleet and 2,000 ashore for a like period. These provisions were stowed in both government-owned and leased private facilities throughout the Manila area. A fleet of 20 small barges was used to transport provisions to the base at Mariveles on Bataan and to the heavily fortified Corregidor Island. When hostilities commenced, the Asiatic Fleet consisted of 2 cruisers, 13 destroyers and a tender, 6 submarines and a tender, 6 or 8 gunboats, a repair ship, an oiler, 12 PBY Catalina flying boats, and a few tugs and other yard craft.

LCDR Williams and his junior assistant, ENS Ken Wheeler, supervised loading barges and shipping hundreds of tons across the harbor to Mariveles and Corregidor in late December as the Japanese army advanced on Manila. These food stocks sustained U.S. military personnel during the long siege of Bataan and Corregidor, the final U.S. outposts in the Philippines. When they had shipped all the food they could, Williams and Wheeler opened the food storehouses and told civilian employees to take any and all the food they wanted. When they had done so, the storehouses were doused with gasoline and set afire. Williams then drove his car around to Mariveles on Bataan.

Ken Wheeler says that George Williams was his mentor. LCDR Williams was promoted to commander on 19 April 1942 while on Corregidor. Wheeler had been told in early April that he was to be evacuated from Corregidor by submarine, but he recalls that his boss and friend came to him one day and tearfully told him that he, not Wheeler, was being evacuated. So it was that on 29 April 1942 CDR George Williams escaped from the Philippines. He arrived at Fremantle, Australia, on 2 May. The Japanese overran Corregidor before Wheeler could be evacuated, and he spent more than three years as a POW.

CDR Williams returned to America as a passenger in *SS Isle de France,* arriving at San Francisco in early January 1943. He was inspector for the Eleventh Naval District on Treasure Island in San Francisco Bay when he was promoted to captain in August 1944. He was retired in April 1946 at San Diego, where he lived until his death in December 1986 at the age of 98.

Sources

Papers of CAPT George H. Williams, provided by family members, 1988, 1994.

Williams, George H. "Trials and Errors in Provisioning—Cavite—Mariveles—Corregidor," n.d. Navy Supply Corps Museum, Athens, Ga.

LORE OF THE CORPS

Ensign Kenneth Ray Wheeler, SC, USN

Assistant Supply Officer, Cavite Navy Yard, 1940–41; Prisoner of War, 1942–45
Period of Service: 1939–74

Ken Wheeler's career in the Navy Supply Corps took him from the depths of wartime privation as a Japanese prisoner of war to the heights of Navy achievement as the 31st chief of Supply Corps, a rear admiral, and vice chief of naval material, vice admiral. In the process, he showed the amazing courage and fortitude that exemplify the "can do" spirit of the Supply Corps. He was awarded three Bronze Star medals for unselfish acts of heroism during World War II.

He was born at Huntsville, Arkansas, in June 1918, but his family moved to Fullerton, California, when he was quite young. He enrolled at the University of California in 1935, where he was advised to join ROTC. Wheeler chose the Navy's four-year active duty commitment over the Army's two-year requirement. He was graduated in May 1939, received a Reserve commission as a line ensign, and assigned immediately as assistant gunnery officer and navigator in *USS Hull* (DD-350).

Soon after reporting to *Hull,* he learned that regular USN commissions were available to NROTC graduates who opted for transfer to the Supply Corps. He was a successful applicant and in August was ordered to the Navy Finance and Supply School at the Philadelphia Navy Yard. Wheeler was impressed by a guest lecturer, LT James Boundy (later a rear admiral and chief of the Corps), who had come in from duty with the Yangtze Patrol on the Asiatic Station. His presentation led ENS Wheeler to determine to get duty with the Asiatic Fleet. Upon graduation, most of the class went to the Pacific.

ENS Ken Wheeler reported to duty as an assistant supply officer, Navy Yard, Cavite, the Philippines, in July 1940. He was assigned as officer-in-charge of a branch purchasing office in Manila. On 7 December 1941 (6 December in the United States), Wheeler had gone to the Army-Navy Club in Manila and stayed overnight. He was awakened at about 0300 and told that the Japanese had bombed Pearl Harbor. He and all other officers were to report immediately to their respective ships and stations.

The Japanese attacked the Philippines within hours of the Pearl Harbor raid, when it was already 8 December west of the International Date Line. Routine peacetime duties rapidly evolved into wartime activity. Naval personnel knew reinforcement or resupply was months away, but they dug in and fought desperately to hold off the aggressors while awaiting the relief that never arrived.

Wheeler reported to his duty station on the first day of the war at the cold-storage plant, which was flooded with emergency communications and orders from all ships in the harbor anxious to comply with orders to get underway immediately. The actual attack on the Philippines came later in the morning.

The Cavite Supply Department immediately began an "all hands" emergency issue of supplies to U.S. and Allied ships and to land-based U.S. military installations. The Japanese attack was rapidly destroying Manila, which was declared an open city. ENS Wheeler was instructed to ship all foodstuffs he could to the Bataan peninsula, then to open the warehouses to the Filipino population. He was evacuated to Bataan on the last truck out. It was Christmas Day.

When he arrived at Mariveles, ENS Wheeler was first assigned to the disabled but still afloat *USS Canopus* (AS-9). Later, along with other Navy personnel, he was assigned to the Provisional Naval Infantry Battalion, Bataan. The new infantry recruits—officer and enlisted—were issued English Enfield rifles of World War I heritage. Then they underwent brief training and formed a beach defense unit at the lower end of Bataan. The unit had been in place only a day or two when 600 Japanese marines landed in its sector in an attempt to cut the last U.S.-held road around the Bataan peninsula.

The naval unit held off the aggressors, took heavy casualties, and was relieved by a regular Army unit six days later. Wheeler, who had been promoted to lieutenant, junior grade, was ordered to Corregidor in early April to relieve two senior Supply Corps officers, including LCDR George Williams, who were evacuated to Australia by submarine.

After the fall of Bataan in early April, American survivors huddled on Corregidor, where they experienced unmerciful air-sea pounding from the Japanese. Corregidor's final hours came on the night of 5 May. All available hands were sent to reinforce the east end of the island, where the enemy was attempting to land.

Corregidor fended off five waves of Japanese from Bataan until a sixth wave, with tanks and heavy tracked armor, overwhelmed the Americans. Following surrender of U.S. personnel, the Japanese rounded up their prisoners in a "very rough and vicious way," strip searching them and confiscating rings, watches, glasses, and false teeth and knocking out gold teeth with rifle butts and pistols.

Wheeler remembers that it took several days for their captors to assemble everybody. In the meantime, the prisoners were forced to sit in the sun with no food, no water, no attention of any kind. Eventually the Americans were allowed to move. They started putting their organizations back together, burying their dead, taking care of their wounded and sick, and arranging for water and food. The Japanese made the Americans forage for food and water among the debris of the battlefield. They found little.

Wheeler describes the next three-and-a-half years as the most trying and difficult times of his life, "In the final analysis, however, it may have been the most important positive experience of my life as well. I think, at a very early age, I was able to arrive at some firm decisions about the philosophy that I wanted to live by."

After a month in the sun on Corregidor's concrete, the prisoners were moved to their first prison. Wheeler reports that survivors were transferred by ship to Manila, put ashore south of the city, and marched on a dirty, dusty unpaved road to Manila some 5 to 10 miles away. They were pushed, shoved, and beaten into a filthy, muddy disheveled state and marched past thousands of sober, quiet and, extremely sympathetic-looking Filipino civilians.

The prisoners spent about a month in the damp dungeon of an old Spanish prison. Then they were taken through Central Luzon Island in railroad boxcars to a former Philippine army training base at Cabanatuan that had been converted into a concentration camp. The POWs stayed there for several months while malaria and dysentery took a heavy toll. On average, about 30 died each day—nearly 3,000 in 3 months.

In December 1942, a group of the prisoners, including LTJG Wheeler, was put aboard a Japanese transport at Manila and taken to Davao on Mindanao Island. They were marched through an unexplored area of rain forests to a maximum security penal colony, where 2,000 American prisoners were held for 18 months. In early 1943 the Japanese told the Americans that they had to leave Mindanao Island because of American pressure. They put the Americans on old, cramped, dirty, flea-infested ships and returned them to Cabanatuan via Manila.

The prisoners sighted two flights of about 100 U.S. fighters and bombers one day while being forced to labor in rice fields at Cabanatuan. The sightings, the first indication that U.S. forces had returned to the area, lifted spirits of the prisoners. That spirit emboldened the prisoners as they returned to camp from working in the rice fields on Christmas Eve 1943 to sing Christmas carols spontaneously. Their guards made no effort to stop them, so they concluded the impromptu sing-along with "God Bless America."

The POWs were moved yet again—this time their destination was to be Japan. The prisoners drew up last wills and testaments and were loaded aboard two unmarked transports that left on the night of 12 December 1943 in a seven-ship convoy. Around dawn the next day, the convoy was attacked by American carrier aircraft. When his unmarked POW ship was torpedoed and abandoned, LTJG Wheeler assisted a seriously wounded Supply Corps officer friend, Bill Elliott, in getting off the ship, using skills he had sharpened as a varsity swimmer in high school and college. He swam back twice to rescue fellow prisoners, an act for which he was awarded his first Bronze Star Medal.

Japanese guards used machine guns to force the survivors to swim to the beach at the old Olongapo Naval Station on Subic Bay, where they were recaptured. They were kept in the sun on a tennis court for several days without food, shelter, or clothing. Eventually, they were taken by truck to a large barrio—San Fernando Pampanga—where they were put into the decrepit Spanish jail.

The Japanese offered to take a group of seriously wounded to a hospital for treatment to avoid gas gangrene. They first agreed to take 3, but eventually took 13. Wheeler's friend Bill Elliott was one them. It was not until the Yokohama War Crimes Trial after the war that Ken Wheeler learned that the wounded prisoners had been driven a short distance to a mass grave site where they were decapitated. The Japanese sergeant in charge of the massacre was found guilty and executed.

The remaining prisoners were taken north again in small, narrow-gauge boxcars. They spent Christmas Day 1944 on the beach at San Fernando la Union at the northern end of Luzon. Wheeler recounts another horrible experience: "We were there for a couple of days, until a transport with cavalry horses was unloaded in the harbor. They then loaded the surviving prisoners aboard that ship. No one had cleaned up after the horses, so it was a very uncomfortable trip from that point on."

The ship left on New Year's Day 1945 for Tako, Formosa, where it tied up alongside an oiler for refueling only to be caught in the process by attacking U.S. Navy aircraft. A salvo of rockets hit the ship, which again was unmarked as a POW vessel. More than 300 of the 400 prisoners held in the same hold with Wheeler were killed, and virtually all the rest injured.

The Japanese offered no first aid or made any attempt to free those trapped as the ship sank. Slightly injured, LTJG Wheeler again swam to shore, rescuing several of his wounded comrades, an act for which he was later awarded his second Bronze Star and the Purple Heart for his wounds. The dead POWs were buried on the beach, and the survivors finally reached Japan a month after leaving Manila.

The remaining prisoners first went to a camp at Fukuoka on Kyusha Island, where Ken Wheeler braved subfreezing temperatures in the unheated barracks to treat the sick and wounded. All the time he kept up tireless efforts to sustain morale and maintain order among the desperate and starving prisoners. B-29 bombings of Japan increased, and the prisoners could sense that the end of their ordeal was approaching.

At Fukuoka, Wheeler suffered a wracking cough and severe chest pains, which he thought was pneumonia. He credits an Army doctor who slipped him some sulfa pills with saving his life. In his weakened condition, it took nearly a month for him to recover.

On a morning in April 1945, when the prisoners were lined up to go to forced labor in the fields, one of the guards came by to say, "A friend of yours died yesterday. Roosevelt is dead. Now the war will soon be over." It was inconceivable to the prisoners that the only president they had known in their adult years was gone. The shocked Americans were not surprised when the Japanese scheduled a celebration that evening. Wheeler remembers that the discomfort and sadness of the prisoners apparently added to the joy of their captors. Suddenly, from the rear of the prison ranks, an American bugler sounded taps. The prisoners removed their tattered caps and stood at attention. Their shocked and uncomprehending guards made no move to interfere.

In all, the prisoners had been in Japan only a few months when, in spring, they were moved by ferry to the Korean port of Jinsen, now called Inchon. Ken Wheeler recalls:

> They put us into a prison camp there and that was the camp from which I was to be liberated in October 1945. Great things happened then, just like bad things had happened before. When the 7th Army landed at Inchon, tanks came up through the town, burst down the gates to the prison camp and young GIs came in, carried us all bodily out to the trucks and down to the beach. Landing craft were there and took us out to a hospital ship where we saw real American women—or women of any kind, really—for the first time in about four years. We were reintroduced to clean white bedsheets, to doctors who cared and understood, and just all kinds of good things, including some good Supply Corps chow.

Ken Wheeler's actions during World War II demonstrate his extreme courage in the face of unparalleled privation. Following his liberation at the end of hostilities, he was promoted immediately to lieutenant, returned to active duty, and was hospitalized until January 1946, when he was ordered to duty in the Bureau of Supplies and Accounts. He was soon promoted to lieutenant commander and, in April 1946, he was assigned as supply and accounting officer, Naval Training Center Bainbridge, Maryland. He returned to BuSandA in July 1947 as detail officer.

In July 1949, CDR Wheeler reported as supply officer of *USS Boxer* (CV-21), assigned to the Seventh Fleet in the Far East. He was supply and fiscal officer, Naval Air Station Moffett Field, California, from 1950 to 1953 before reporting to the Aviation Supply Office, Philadelphia, where he was provisioning coordinator until 1956. Next he attended the Naval War College at Newport. He was promoted to captain and reported as supply officer, Naval Air Station, Jacksonville, Florida, in 1957.

CAPT Wheeler returned to BuSandA in 1960 as director of Supply Corps personnel until he was ordered as commanding officer, Naval Ordnance Supply Office, Mechanicsburg, Pennsylvania, in 1963. He attended the 46th Advanced Management Program at the Graduate School of Business Administration, Harvard University.

He was promoted to Flag rank in June 1965 and reported in July as force supply officer, Commander Service Force, U.S. Atlantic Fleet, with additional duty as fleet supply officer, Commander-in-Chief, Atlantic. He became fleet supply officer and assistant chief of staff for supply, U.S. Atlantic Fleet, in June 1967. One month later, RADM Wheeler again returned to Washington as director of financial services in the Navy Office of the Comptroller. His title was changed in May 1969 to assistant comptroller of financial management, with additional duty as Commander Navy Accounting and Finance Center Washington. He was awarded Legion of Merit medals for both his Atlantic Fleet and comptroller tours.

RADM Wheeler reported as Vice Commander Naval Supply Systems Command in July 1969 and was designated Commander Naval Supply Systems Command and chief of Supply Corps in June 1970. As commander of NAVSUP, RADM Wheeler was credited with devising and directing new and better ways of doing business through advanced management techniques. He was promoted to vice admiral and designated vice chief of naval material in January 1973. As principal assistant and advisor to ADM Isaac Kidd, Jr., chief of naval material, VADM Wheeler directed the Navy's acquisition and logistics programs in providing material support to operating forces. The six systems commanders reported to him.

VADM Wheeler retired in September 1974, first to Jacksonville, Florida, and later to Statesville, North Carolina. Ken and Marilyn Wheeler live in Statesville, where he is active in the Rotary Club, in civic affairs, and in both the Navy Supply Corps Association and the Navy Supply Corps Foundation.

Sources

Interview of VADM Kenneth Ray Wheeler. Statesville, N.C., 1 August 1987.

Official Biography. Navy Office of Information, September 1970.

"VADM K. R. Wheeler Retires." *Navy Supply Corps Newsletter,* September 1974.

Arrest and Repatriation

While Congress enacted the official declaration of war on Japan on 8 December, Germany and Italy, Japan's partners, declared war on the United States on 11 December. Congress reciprocated with formal declarations of war on the two Axis nations hours later.

In Berlin, LT Onnie P. Lattu, assistant naval attaché of the American embassy at Berlin, recalls that there were no cheers, smiles, or angry looks when the Nazis declared war. Lattu believes that the average German did not like the idea of fighting the Americans again, and many felt that it was the beginning of the end for Germany. The Gestapo took control of the embassy and placed staff and employees under house arrest. The internees were sent by train to Bad Nauheim, north of Frankfurt au Main and about 250 miles southwest of Berlin. They were interned at the old Jeschke's Grand Hotel, an unheated former summer resort that had been closed for two years.

The internees had been told that they would be repatriated in two weeks to a month, but that time soon passed with no action. The "guests" were treated with stiff correctness by their Gestapo captors in the shabby Jeschke's, but the food was adequate. Winter cold soon made the inside temperature drop below freezing. The long-expected repatriation process finally began on 12 May 1942. The Swedish liner *SS Drottningholm* was designated as the transfer vessel, with Lisbon as the transfer point. LT Lattu and his 131 fellow internees traveled by train to Lisbon via Paris and Biarritz. The newly liberated Americans finally left Lisbon for home on 22 May and entered New York harbor on 30 May.

The comptroller general's office curiously ruled that the internees' pay would cease as of 14 December 1941 because they were no longer working. The repatriated Americans also learned that they would accrue no leave because of the "luxurious" nature of their internment. The former internees were astonished at the rulings. The pettiness of their treatment contrasts sharply with the benevolent treatment accorded the staff of the U.S. embassy in Tehran, Iran, upon release of its internees in 1981.

Many of the military and diplomatic personnel repatriated in 1942 from Germany and occupied European nations did not return home. They were ordered directly to new assignments in Europe, Africa, and the Middle East.

Expanded Facilities

The Supply Corps had already expanded when the United States entered World War II, but the demand for additional officers became so great that the Navy Supply Corps School rapidly grew beyond the capacity of Harvard's facilities. The Navy entered into agreements in 1942 with nearby Babson Institute and two women's colleges, Radcliffe and Wellesley, to become NSCS training sites.

Allied Forces in the East Indies

The rapid Japanese advance in early 1942 deprived Admiral Thomas C. Hart's Asiatic Fleet of its Philippine bases, so he moved the Fleet south to the Dutch East Indies in accordance with existing plans. The U.S. forces joined with Allied naval units to form the ABDA Fleet, so named because American, British, Dutch, and Australian ships composed the force. ADM Hart, a competent and experienced officer who had been kept on active duty past retirement age, was placed in command.

The ABDA Fleet was a strong force, with 9 cruisers, 26 destroyers and 39 submarines, and prospects of Royal Navy reinforcements. Japanese carrier planes doomed the fleet before it could be assembled, however, by sinking the battleship *HMS Prince of Wales* and the battle cruiser *HMS Repulse* off Malaya on 10 December. The aircraft carrier *HMS Indomitable,* ordered to Java, never made it to the Pacific when she ran aground in the West Indies. Japanese bombers caught most of the Allied planes on Java in December and destroyed them before they were airborne, depriving the ABDA Fleet of badly needed air cover.

The gallant collection of Allied ships had no carrier-based air support and no time to exercise and to develop the coordinated communications and operating procedures needed for effective joint tactics. They nevertheless took on the well-trained and well-armed Japanese Imperial Fleet.

Four U.S. four-stack destroyers—*USS John D. Ford* (DD-228), *USS Pope* (DD-225), *USS Parrott* (DD-218), and *USS Paul Jones* (DD-230)—initiated the first U.S. Navy surface action against the enemy since the Spanish-American War. These badly outgunned ships dashed among the ships of a large Japanese convoy anchored off Balikpapan, Borneo, in the Makassar Strait on the night of 24 January. The Americans ships had a field day among the enemy silhouetted by blazing Dutch oil tanks, and they sank three transports and a patrol boat before escaping safely.

Another Allied force, composed of two U.S. and two Dutch cruisers and seven destroyers, attempted to blast a second Japanese convoy in the Makassar Strait on 4 February. Japanese bombers badly damaged *USS Marblehead* (CL-12), but she was able to limp back to the United States. *USS Houston* (CA-30) remained in the area despite the destruction of her after 8-inch turret in an air attack. She was the last American cruiser left in the Java Sea when *USS Boise* (CL-47) was disabled by striking a reef and left the area for repairs.

The Last Java Sea Battles

Under RADM Karel W. F. M. Doorman, Royal Netherlands Navy, the remnants of the ABDA Fleet, with five cruisers, including Doorman's flagship *HMNS De Ruyter, HMNS Java,* the British *HMS Exeter,* the Australian *HMAS Perth,* and the badly damaged *Houston,* attacked a large convoy headed for Java. Doorman also had nine destroyers, including the four U.S. four-pipers, when he sailed from his base at Soerabaja on 27 February. The Allied force could not get past the Japanese escorts and supporting air cover, but after a torpedo run by the Allies, the Japanese withdrew to check damage.

That night, Japanese planes dropped flares that illuminated the Allied fleet. *De Ruyter* and *Java* were severely damaged and sinking, but Doorman ordered *Houston* and *Perth* to escape and not to risk being hit by stopping to pick up survivors. This brave and unselfish action cost the lives of 344 Dutch navy officers and men, including the admiral.

The two surviving cruisers, short of ammunition and seriously impaired, swept into Banten Bay and caught the Japanese by surprise. One transport was sunk and three others so badly damaged that they were beached, but the gallant ABDA ships had reached the end of the line. Both went down under withering enemy fire.

Two heroes of the last Java Sea battles were Supply Corps officers, ENS Allan Jack Fisher, supply officer of *Pope,* and ENS Preston R. Clark, disbursing officer of *Houston.* They survived the sinking of their ships, were captured by Japanese forces, and spent the rest of the war in prisoner-of-war camps.

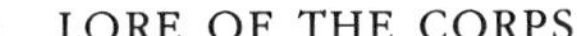

LORE OF THE CORPS

Ensign Allan Jack Fisher, SC, USN

Disbursing Officer, Destroyer Division 59, 1940–42; Prisoner of War, 1942–45
Period of Service: 1939–69

Allan Jack Fisher was another member of the highly successful and much-decorated Navy Finance and Supply School Class of 1939-40, most of whom saw considerable action in the Far East during World War II. He was one of five members of the class who were captured and held prisoner by the Japanese.

Jack Fisher was a native Californian, born at Los Angeles in October 1916, and reared in Bishop and Ontario. He entered the University of California as a junior in 1936 and applied for the NROTC program. Fisher had only two years left to complete college, but the NROTC director gave him three years to complete his four-year Navy studies. He remained at Berkeley an extra year after graduation and was commissioned an ensign in 1939.

ENS Fisher reported to NF&SS at the Philadelphia Navy Yard in August 1939, two weeks before war broke out in Europe. When he was graduated in the spring of 1940, he requested duty with the Asiatic Fleet and was assigned as disbursing officer of Destroyer Division 59 in *USS Pope* (DD-225). He reported to his ship at Manila at the end of June.

Pope had just returned from exercises in the Sulu Sea when Jack Fisher visited overnight with his classmate, ENS Ken Wheeler, in Wheeler's large quarters at the Manila Army-Navy Club. Another classmate, ENS Chuck Osborne, disbursing officer, *USS Canopus* (AS-9), was also there. At 0300 (Philippine time) on Monday, 8 December, Wheeler awakened his friends, advised them of the attack on Pearl Harbor, and told them that they must return to their ships.

Fisher was back aboard *Pope* by dawn. The ship went to battle stations and was quickly underway, with *USS John D. Ford* (DD-228), convoying commercial ships in Manila Bay to a location south of Mindanao. There they turned over their charges to a Navy group, including the cruiser *Houston,* for escort to the Dutch East Indies. *Pope* then returned to Manila, but she was running low on fuel and went to Sangley Point to refuel. She was tied up and taking on fuel on 10 December when Japanese bombers made another attack on the Cavite Navy Yard and ships in the harbor. *Pope* broke all fuel lines and headed out into the harbor, where Japanese planes were strafing individual ships.

The attack devastated Cavite and damaged a number of ships, including *USS Peary* (DD-226), a DesDiv 59 destroyer, but *Pope* escaped. Fisher had volunteered for gunnery duty and was battery officer on the galley deck. He took over a .50-caliber machine gun in the heat of the battle and believes that he damaged a Japanese plane, although he received no official credit for doing so.

Pope completed a second escort mission, delivering another convoy safely to Darwin, Australia. *Peary* also arrived in Darwin shortly thereafter. Fisher had paid *Peary*'s officers and crew their overdue pay shortly before she was sunk during a Japanese air raid. There were only six survivors.

Pope left Darwin in January 1942 in company with two cruisers and three other destroyers for Menado, Celebes. They were diverted to Balikpappan, Borneo, a major Dutch fuel distribution point that was targeted by the Japanese. The two cruisers, *USS Boise* (CL-47) and *USS Marblehead* (CL-12), were forced to drop out because of noncombat problems. The four destroyers pushed ahead and sank at least six enemy ships while damaging several others in the first American naval surface action since the Spanish-American War and the first American victory of World War II. Fisher believes the successful attack may have caused a significant delay in Japan's advance.

DesDiv 59 was involved in another successful venture on 18 February, accompanying Dutch naval forces in a night attack on Japanese forces in the Badoeng Strait who were attempting to land on Bali. The Dutch lost some ships, but the U.S. destroyers escaped without significant damage. *Pope* and *Ford* were awarded the Presidential Unit Citation for their highly successful efforts at Balikpappan and the Badoeng Strait.

In the victorious night action *Ford* lost a motor whaleboat that was shot out of its davits and floated free. Meanwhile, Japanese cruiser fire blew up the Dutch destroyer *HMNS Piet Hein,* whose survivors were thrown into the water, where they encountered *Ford*'s whaleboat, which was without oars or gasoline. Shortly thereafter, they bumped into a full 50-gallon gasoline drum jettisoned by *Pope*. The Dutch sailors poured the gasoline into the boat's engine and sailed safely off into the night to Java, where they became prisoners of war.

Pope accompanied two British ships, the cruiser *HMS Exeter* and the destroyer *HMS Encounter,* on 1 March in an attempt to reach Ceylon via the Sundra Straits. Fisher, who had been promoted to LTJG, recalls that during a five-hour battle, the three Allied ships were sunk by Japanese cruisers and aircraft in early morning. Fisher was thrown against one of *Pope*'s stacks by a bomb blast that severely damaged his ears. He was one of the last to leave when the abandon ship order was given. The survivors had been in the water nearly 57 hours when a Japanese destroyer rescued them about 2200 on 3 March and they were taken to Makassar in the Celebes.

The Americans were taken to an old, native jail, and 40 were put in cells designed for 10. They were later moved to a former Dutch naval barracks, where they joined about 2,000 Dutch, British, native, and other American prisoners, including the entire crew of the submarine *USS Perch* (SS-176). The Americans also met the Dutch sailors who survived in *Ford*'s whaleboat.

The prisoners were poorly fed, suffered dysentery, and were beaten frequently over the next three and a half years. Jack Fisher was often singled out. The prisoners were moved to a malarial swamp south of Makassar, where they were required to build camp buildings out of bamboo. American prisoners, especially commanding and communications officers, were taken periodically to other camps in Japan, Korea, and Java. In 1942 each prisoner was allowed to compose a 10-word message, limited to the fact he was alive and "all right," to his next of kin. The messages were ultimately transmitted via "Tokyo Rose" broadcasts in April 1943, their relatives' first word about the fate of missing loved ones.

All the other U.S. officers had been sent to other prison camps by October 1942, leaving LTJG Fisher as the senior American with 167 U.S. Navy enlisted men and 1 from the Army Air Corps. By January 1945, every prisoner—American, British, and Dutch—had malaria, beriberi, edema, pellagra, and other tropical diseases. The POWs began to die at a rate of 2 to 12 daily. Each day brought more of the simple burial services. LTJG Fisher secretly kept a roster of each American's name, cause of death, and location of burial.

Later in 1945, 200 of the prisoners were put topside on a small oil tanker, along with 200 wounded Japanese soldiers. The only rations they had were a cup of water and a handful of rice a day. After five days, Army Air Corps P-38 fighters attacked the tanker as it approached an anchorage in a Soerabaja estuary, but the prisoners survived and were put in another camp at Soerabaja and subjected to the same poor food and rough treatment as they had received at Makassar.

On or about 8 August, the Japanese took them in boxcars to Batavia, some 400 miles to the west and put them in a native jail. The prisoners were let out of jail on or about 25 August and taken to a camp with Australian, British, New Zealand, and other American prisoners.

The Japanese told their prisoners on 7 September that the war had ended and that the area Allied commander, Admiral Lord Louis Mountbatten, had directed them to ensure the prisoners' safety, to hold them in camp, and to feed them properly. On 18 September, an OSS team arrived and selected Fisher for a group of 30 officers and enlisted men to be sent to Calcutta for treatment and tests at a U.S. Army hospital before their return home.

In early October, Jack Fisher and several of his fellow prisoners were advised by Army nurses to visit the Calcutta Officers' Club for a relaxing change from the hospital routine. There he spotted one of his NF&SS classmates, LCDR Bill Durant, and spoke to him. Durant, the senior U.S. Navy officer in the area, did not recognize the emaciated former prisoner at first, but soon the two had a pleasant reunion. LCDR Durant was in charge of logistics for a planned invasion of China that was negated by the end of the war. When he learned that the repatriated officers had only ragged clothing and old Japanese army boots, Bill Durant told Fisher that they could come down to his warehouse and get anything they needed. The hospitalized officers and enlisted men soon were wearing the best uniform items in the clothing warehouse. Still, there were no shoes to fit Fisher. Durant called in an Indian shoemaker to make a pair of Jodhpur boots, which Fisher wore for the next 15 years.

The American officers were flown home via the Taj Mahal, over the Pyramids and to Cairo, Tripoli, and Casablanca, where they spent a night. In Tripoli, a Red Cross nurse sent the first word of his release to his mother and father.

After treatment and more tests at Bethesda Naval Hospital, near Washington, Jack Fisher flew west on 10 October 1945 and arrived at his parents' home at Ontario, California, the following day. Although he had been away five years and five months, his fiancée, Genevieve, had faith that he was still alive and would return. She had waited for him, and they were married six weeks after he reached home.

One of Fisher's first actions upon his return home was to contact the next of kin of the prisoners who had died in camp and provide the details of their death, information he had secretly kept throughout his imprisonment. In February 1946, following hospitalization at Norco Naval Hospital, Fisher returned to active duty, as a lieutenant commander, with other ex-POWs for a reorientation course in Washington. He was awarded the Bronze Star Medal with a combat V and the Purple Heart for his part in the Navy's first successful surface action of the war at Balikpappan. He was awarded the Legion of Merit for working "untiringly for the welfare of those under his charge" while the senior American officer prisoner, and a second Purple Heart for injuries suffered in beatings by Japanese captors.

LCDR Fisher was ordered from Washington to the Naval Supply Depot San Diego in February 1946. He next went to *USS Missouri* (BB-63) as supply officer for 15 months and was aboard when she ran aground in a much publicized incident at Hampton Roads in January 1950. As a commander, he reported as senior assistant district supply officer, Eleventh Naval District, in the fall of 1950. Among his duties was bringing Reserve Supply Corps officers and enlisted personnel in supply ratings on active duty during the Korean War. His next duty was as a student at the Armed Forces Staff College.

In May 1953 he had duty as logistics officer, Commander Service Force Sixth Fleet, for two years. During that tour, he developed significant expertise in underway replenishment. In 1955 Fisher was ordered to duty as executive officer, General Stores Supply Office, Philadelphia, for 10 months when RADM John Crumpacker was commanding officer. When Crumpacker was relieved, Fisher served for three months as acting C.O. until another NF&SS classmate, CAPT (later RADM) Robert Northwood, arrived.

Fisher served for two years in the Bureau of Supplies and Accounts as head of supply operations. He was promoted to captain in 1958, and in 1960 he was sent to the Industrial College of the Armed Forces, Washington. From there, he went to the Naval Shipyard, San Francisco as supply officer from 1961 to 1964. At San Francisco, one of the young officers on CAPT Fisher's staff was LTJG James E. (Jim) Miller, shipyard stores officer. Fisher recalls that, even then, it was obvious that the future chief of Supply Corps "was an outstanding, sterling officer."

CAPT Fisher was ordered as the deputy commander of the Defense Depot Ogden, Utah, in 1964. After only 10 months as second in command, he relieved an Army general as commander of the depot. CAPT Fisher was the first Navy officer to command a major DOD distribution center. In 1967 he reported as officer-in-charge of the Navy Area Audit Office, San Diego, where he headed teams conducting audits from Texas to Vietnam.

The Fishers retired to Coronado, California, in October 1969; Genevieve Fisher died in October 1994.

Sources

Citation. Bronze Star Medal, 1945
Citation. Legion of Merit, 1945
Interview of CAPT Allan Jack Fisher. Asheville, N.C., 8–9 May 1993.

LORE OF THE CORPS

Ensign Preston Richter Clark, SC, USN

Disbursing Officer, *USS Houston* (CA-30), 1940–42; Prisoner of War, 1942–45
Period of Service: 1940–60

Press Clark is another of the graduates of the famous NF&SS class of 1939–40. He survived the sinking of the cruiser *USS Houston* and also the harrowing experience of POW slave labor in building the famous bridge over the River Kwai in Burma.

Clark was born at Beverly, Massachusetts, in January 1917, and was graduated in 1938 from Harvard College, where he participated in the NROTC program. He was commissioned a line ensign in the Naval Reserve upon graduation. In February 1940, he received a Regular Navy commission as assistant paymaster with rank of ensign. Upon graduation from NF&SS, he was ordered to duty as disbursing officer of *USS Houston* (CA-30), then in dry dock at the Mare Island Navy Yard.

Houston sailed for Manila in late October 1940 to relieve *USS Augus-*

ta (CA-31) as flagship, Asiatic Fleet, in mid-November. Clark enjoyed duty on the Asiatic Station and liked the Manila Army-Navy Club. He would occasionally "bunk down" on the floor of the club's brewery, under the jurisdiction of his classmate ENS Ken Wheeler.

By the summer of 1941, however, tensions had increased to the point that Admiral Thomas Hart, Commander-in-Chief Asiatic Fleet, ordered Navy dependents home. The Army soon followed suit. *Houston* went south to Tawitawi, a small island group off the east coast of Borneo, to determine how long the defenders could last without the logistical and subsistence support from Manila.

When the war began, *Houston* was in the Philippine port at Iloilo, about 300 miles south of Manila, taking on oil at a small fuel pier. She left Iloilo after Japanese planes came over, apparently in search of the American cruiser, and bombed the fuel depot. *Houston* set course for Soerabaja on the island of Java, where she was involved in a few small convoys before being ordered to Darwin in Northern Australia. *Houston,* in company with four other cruisers—*HMS Exeter, HMNS De Ruyter* and *Java,* and *HMAS Perth,* and a few destroyers—sailed for Soerabaja on 27 February to join the hastily assembled ABDA task force. The task force then headed north to intercept a large Japanese invasion fleet bound for Java.

The commanding officer of *Houston* sent a U.S. signalman to *De Ruyter,* flagship of RADM Karel W. F. M. Doorman, RNN, the task force commander, to compensate for possible communication problems that might arise from language differences. According to Clark, the only message *Houston* received before the battle was "follow me." The Allied ships inflicted some damage on the Japanese fleet, but the British cruiser and two Dutch cruisers were sunk.

The American and Australian cruisers escaped to fight again, which turned out to be the next day—28 February—when they were sunk in a midnight battle with superior enemy forces in the Sunda Strait. The Japanese had finally made good on their often-reported destruction of *Houston,* known as the "Galloping Ghost of the Java Coast" because she was involved in so many actions after enemy broadcasts claimed she had been sunk.

With only a kapok life jackets for flotation, Clark and other survivors managed to reach a coral beach, where Japanese troops soon captured them. The 30 POWs were marched barefoot to a native jail at Serang in Western Java. About two months later, they were moved to a former Dutch army barracks, where they stayed from late March until October 1942. They were then taken to Singapore, where they joined a group of nearly 80,000 British prisoners.

Clark was put in charge of a group of about 50 sailors and soldiers who had to pull a railroad flatcar up a hill to load rubber-tree logs for cooking fuel. Two British Royal Engineer sergeants controlled the car's handbrakes for the loaded downhill trip. Their instructions were to control the speed so as not to kill Japanese on the intersecting road. The group took great pleasure in running their car at faster and faster speeds on return trips and watching the Japanese scurry for safety.

The Americans were sent to Thailand by rail and ship in January 1943 to join British POWs in building a railroad from Tajnburzateir, Thailand, to Moulmein, Burma, including a bridge over the Kwai River. The Japanese were in great haste to complete the line, so they ignored an existing British survey and went over the hills instead of around them, forcing old steam engines to labor up the steep grades on the new line.

The prisoners, despite physical abuse and inadequate diets, completed the line in August or September 1944 and were transferred on the railroad they had built to a camp at Chanthaburi. "Not very," Clark responded when questioned about the accuracy of the film *The Bridge on the River Kwai*. No British colonel, he maintains, was stupid enough to want to build the best possible bridge. He says the prisoners took every opportunity to sabotage the project by making small, undectable errors in implementing construction plans. He recalls that the POWs composed special, highly uncomplimentary, lyrics to the tune of the "Colonel Bogie March."

The Japanese attitude and treatment changed drastically in August 1945 as the end of the war neared. It took nearly a month after the surrender on 2 September to get all the U.S., British, and Australian former POWs out of Thailand.

Press Clark had been promoted to LTJG during his ordeal in the South Pacific but did not know it. He was promoted to lieutenant in October 1945. After he was repatriated, he recalls that a young Navy dentist at Bethesda Naval Hospital found that he had nine cavities and planned to fill one each day. LT Clark would have none of that and informed the dentist that he would fill five on one side then and there and four on the other side the next day. That settled, he received three months' rehabilitation, but the POWs were given no back pay. An order signed by President Harry S. Truman ruled that back pay was "not in the national interest." The former prisoners winced, saluted with a firm "aye, aye," and moved on.

Clark's first return to duty was at the Bureau of Supplies and Accounts, where he, along with a group of other ex-POWs, reviewed a new BuSandA manual in October 1945. They were told that if they, who had endured more than three years in prison, could understand the new system, then Supply Corps officers in the Fleet probably would have no trouble doing so. LT Clark then asked to be sent to the Boston Navy Yard and reported there in June 1946 as an assistant in the Material Department. From March 1947 to July 1948 he was on duty at the First Naval District, involved in supply inspections. He reported in August 1948 to the General Stores Supply Office, Philadelphia, where an NF&SS classmate, LCDR (later RADM) Bernie Bieri, was executive officer.

From GSSO, CDR Clark was sent in January 1951 to serve on the recommissioning detail of *USS Wisconsin* (BB-64), becoming her supply officer when she went to the Pacific for duty in Korean waters. He returned to the Boston Navy Yard in November 1952 and had subsequent duty at the Military Sea Transportation Service in Washington as assistant supply officer from 1955 to 1958; he then was ordered as supply officer, Navy Supply Depot Rodman, Canal Zone, from 1958 to 1960. He retired from the Navy in June 1960.

Press Clark was employed by the Smithsonian Astrophysical Observatory and retired a second time in 1982. A bachelor, he lives in Wenham, Massachusetts.

Source

Interview of CDR Preston Richter Clark. Asheville, N.C., 8 May 1993.

LORE OF THE CORPS

Ensign Charles Spurgeon Osborne, Jr., SC, USN

Disbursing Officer, *USS Canopus* (AS-9)
Period of Service: 1939–63

Another member of the famous NF&SS Philadelphia class of 1939–40 was Charles S. (Chuck) Osborne. He was ordered to duty with the Submarine Force, U.S. Asiatic Fleet, and managed to stay one step ahead of the advancing Japanese through duty stations in the Philippines and the Netherlands East Indies, until eventually reaching Australia.

Chuck Osborne was born at Hondo, New Mexico, in June 1918. He attended the University of California, where he was a roommate, fraternity brother, and NROTC comrade of another future Supply Corps officer, VADM Ken Wheeler. He was graduated and commissioned a Naval Reserve line ensign in June 1939. He worked in San Francisco briefly and volunteered for active duty in November. He served briefly in *USS Mississippi* (BB-41) before transferring to the Supply Corps in February 1940 and entering NF&SS Philadelphia. Osborne reported to the submarine tender *USS Canopus* (AS-9) at Manila in September 1940 as disbursing officer. The tender was supporting 33 submarines of the Submarine Force, Asiatic Fleet.

Chuck Osborne, Ken Wheeler, Jack Fisher, and three fellow Cal alumni serving in the Army had planned a reunion at the Manila Army-Navy Club on Saturday, 6 December. The Army officers were called away on an emergency alert, so the three Navy Supply Corps officers went ahead with the reunion and played golf on Sunday. They were staying overnight in Wheeler's room when the Japanese attacked Pearl Harbor early on Monday morning (Philippine time).

Canopus was moved to Mariveles on the southern tip of Bataan shortly after the first Japanese attack on Manila, where she was subjected to air attacks. Osborne next encountered Wheeler washing clothes in a small stream near Mariveles. The two agreed to stick together, and that they would get out of the seemingly hopeless situation somehow. Osborne was unaware that superiors had something else in mind for him.

ENS Osborne was sent to Corregidor on 31 December 1942, ostensibly to obtain cash for *Canopus*. He was told not to take anyone with him. When he reached the island stronghold, he was advised that he had been transferred to the staff, Submarine Force, Asiatic Fleet, and was being evacuated immediately with the rest of the staff by submarine. He spent New Year's Day 1942 in *USS Swordfish* (SS-193) en route to the Dutch East Indies. The staff relocated temporarily at Soerabaja on the north coast of Java, where Osborne was promoted to LTJG, but he never wore the stripes because he made lieutenant before he heard about JG. Later, the staff went to Tjilatjap on the south coast. As the Japanese advance was about to engulf Java, the Submarine Force staff again relocated, this time to Fremantle, Australia, for the balance of the war.

Chuck Osborne was promoted to lieutenant in Australia. He had started back to the United States in May 1943 for reassignment, and when he reached Sydney he was diverted to Brisbane for duty on an LST serving temporarily as a hospital ship. He resumed his journey back to the United States in December and was ordered to the commissioning crew of *USS Shamrock Bay* (CVE-84) in February 1944. He served aboard the escort carrier throughout the Okinawa campaign in August 1945, during which he was promoted to lieutenant commander. He returned to the United States for a tour at the Naval Aviation Training Center at Chincoteague Island, Virginia.

His next tour was at the New York Naval Shipyard in September 1947. He made commander, was ordered to the precommissioning detail of *USS Oriskany* (CV-34) in June 1950, and served as supply officer after *Oriskany* joined the Fleet. In March 1952, he reported to the Naval Supply Depot Mechanicsburg, Pennsylvania, where he was operations officer and later planning officer. In late 1953 he went to the newly established Military Advisory Assistance Group for Germany, located temporarily at Heidelberg, but moved to Bonn in early 1954.

CDR Osborne and CDR Ken Wheeler were reunited at the Naval War College in 1956. Osborne then reported to the Office of Chief of Naval Material in July 1957. While there, he was promoted to captain. His final tour was with the Navy Area Audit Office, San Diego, from June 1960 to July 1963, when he was retired on medical disability. Chuck and Magi Osborne live in Kelseyville, California.

Source

Interview of CAPT Charles Spurgeon Osborne, Jr. Asheville, N.C., 8 May 1993.

The First U.S. Offensive Actions

Buffeted by spectacular early Japanese advances and heart-wrenching American and Allied losses, Admiral Ernest J. King, Commander-in-Chief U.S. Fleet, adopted a defensive strategy in the Pacific while the Allies concentrated on winning the war in Europe. King ordered Nimitz to hold a line running from Midway through Samoa and Fiji to Australia. On 1 February 1942, Halsey's carriers struck Japanese bases in the Pacific to stop the enemy's eastward advance. U.S. task forces pounded the Marshall, Gilbert, Wake, Marcus, and New Britain islands.

These raids helped, but President Roosevelt wanted something more spectacular to boost American morale and ordered an air attack on the Japanese homeland. The Navy and the Army Air Corps teamed up to launch a flight of Army B-25 bombers from the deck of the *USS Hornet* (CV-8) to bomb Tokyo, more than 650 miles away, on 18 April. The "Doolittle Raid" did minimal physical damage compared to that inflicted by the Japanese at Pearl Harbor, but it was a major psychological victory back home.

Corregidor finally surrendered to overwhelming Japanese forces on 6 May 1942, after holding out for five months of incessant pounding. The last American bastion in the Far East had fallen. The next day, in the Coral Sea, an American task force intercepted a Japanese force headed for Port Moresby in eastern New Guinea. In a two-day battle, costly for both sides, the Japanese extracted the greater toll in tonnage. But the Navy scored a strategic victory when the Japanese forces turned back. America's Australia and New Zealand allies could breathe a sigh of relief because their homelands were spared invasion.

Expansion and Reorganization

The Bureau of Supplies and Accounts established new Navy supply depots in order to improve its ability to provide effective support to deployed Navy and Marine forces, overseas bases, and facilities in the United States. The new depots were located in Seattle, New Orleans, Bayonne, San Pedro, Newport, and Mechanicsburg, Pennsylvania.

A field branch was established at Cleveland in 1942, and two new functions were established within BuSandA—the Central Office of General Inspector of Supply Corps and the Office of Procurement and Material. Also in 1942, the Compensation Board was abolished, its duties consolidated into the BuSandA Cost Inspection Service. A BuSandA directive decentralized procurement.

The BuSandA Accounting Group, the largest centralized accounting system in the world, was charged with keeping the Navy's property and financial accounts, and it controlled the financial structure of the Navy. It employed nearly 600,000 civilian personnel in 1,500 field activities ashore. As the demands of World War II continued to build, the efficiency of the group suffered from a shortage of qualified personnel. The Bureau of Supplies and Accounts established a committee in 1942 to investigate modernization of the Navy's accounting system. As a result of this effort, called the Grady Report, the Office of the Comptroller of the Navy, reporting directly to the chief of BuSandA, was established.

A new Chief, RADM W. Brent Young, took over from RADM Ray Spear in June 1942.

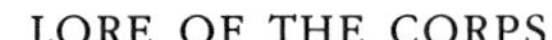

LORE OF THE CORPS

Rear Admiral William Brent Young, SC, USN

Chief, Bureau of Supplies and Accounts, and Paymaster General, 1942–45
Period of Service: 1912–46

Brent Young was a commander when he had the distinction of being the first officer originally appointed to the Naval Reserve to attain the rank of rear admiral and one of only four Supply Corps officers advanced two grades to Flag rank. He was chosen over dozens of senior officers for promotion to rear admiral and appointment as chief of the Bureau of Supplies and Accounts on 1 June 1942.

Brent Young was born at Washington, D.C., in June 1888. He was educated in local schools, and attended Georgetown University, where he was a track star. After receiving his bachelor of laws degree from the Georgetown Law School in 1915, he practiced law in the District of Columbia for two years and wrote sports articles for the *Washington Evening Star.* When the United States entered World War I, he was appointed a Pay Corps ensign in the Naval Reserve and ordered to active duty.

He exhibited extraordinary leadership qualities and advanced rapidly. A year later, he was assigned to the Philadelphia Navy Yard Supply Department as outside superintendent, War Material Section, and was promoted to lieutenant. In this position, he was responsible for shipment of war material to the American Expeditionary Force in Europe.

After the war, he left active duty and returned to the inactive Naval Reserve. In 1921 he took a competitive examination and was commissioned in the Regular Navy. Lieutenant Young served for the next 10 years in typical assignments with the Atlantic and Asiatic fleets and ashore. In 1931 he was a student at the Army Industrial College, and in June 1932 he reported for duty at the Bureau of Supplies and Accounts.

Commander Young became supply officer, U.S. Atlantic Fleet, in early 1941. His outstanding performance during a period of unprecedented expansion of the Fleet and supply support facilities earned him the Legion of Merit. The citation read, in part: "During this period of intense activity in the Atlantic, the establishment of numerous new bases, and the ever increasing overseas movements of troops and supplies, Commander William B. Young displayed remarkable ability and foresight in the overall planning of the logistics phases of the Atlantic operations."

Young's performance with the Atlantic Fleet proved that he was just the man Secretary of the Navy Frank Knox needed to head the Navy's logistical effort as America went on the offensive in the Pacific. Hence, much as Secretary Josephus Daniels had done with Sam McGowan during World War I, Knox reached deep into the ranks and made the surprise appointment of Young as chief of the Bureau of Supplies and Accounts.

BuSandA, under RADM Young, played a major role in the successful logistical support of the two-ocean U.S. Navy. Young continued to hammer home the need for senior officers to remind junior officers and civilians that the shore establishment existed solely to serve the Fleet. He urged that "this rule of conduct not be obscured by a routine type of thinking."

RADM Young was known to be impatient with red tape. He believed strongly that the only purpose of U.S. Navy forces ashore was to support the Fleet at sea. He was fond of saying, "We can account with the Fleet or we can fight with it, and I say we fight with it."

He traveled throughout the Atlantic, the Pacific, and the Caribbean to assure that supplies were being rushed to the fighting forces as quickly as possible. Victory over both Germany and Japan was virtually assured by March 1944 when RADM Young completed his tour as paymaster general. For his efforts in the war he was awarded a gold star in lieu of a second Legion of Merit. He also was honored by the Order of the British Empire, the French Legion of Honor, and the Norwegian Order of St. Olaf.

RADM Young was appointed assistant commissioner, Foreign Liquidation Commission, when he left BuSandA. The commission had been established by Secretary of the Navy James V. Forrestal and Secretary of War Henry L. Stimson to handle disposal of surplus property in the United States, territories, and possessions. RADM Young served with the commission until his retirement from the Navy in October 1946. He died in August 1959.

Sources

Letter from the Chief. *Paymaster General Newsletter,* December 1942.
Official Biography. Naval Supply Systems Command, n.d.
"RADM Walter B. Young Dies." *BuSandA Monthly Newsletter,* September 1959.

An All-out Attack

Admiral Yamamoto had declared in 1941, "I shall run wild for the first six months, but I have no confidence in the second and third years of the fighting." Accordingly, he was obsessed with winning an all-out victory for Japan during the first year of the war. Subsequent events were to prove him prescient. Yamamoto sent the most powerful surface fleet that had ever been assembled to launch a crippling attack on American facilities at Midway Island in early June 1942. He took along transports with 5,000 troops to invade the U.S. base. The anticipated success was to be followed by another attack on Hawaii, and the powerful fleet was then to sail on and attack the West Coast of the United States to force a peace treaty favorable to Japan.

Yamamoto first ordered a diversionary attack on the Aleutian Islands on 3 June to disguise his primary objective, but the U.S. Navy had broken the Japanese code and knew that Midway was the real target. U.S. carrier planes scored a spectacular victory against Yamamoto's main force west of Midway the next day, sinking three large Japanese carriers and so severely damaging the fourth that it was scuttled the next day. The United States lost the *Yorktown,* the badly damaged survivor of the Battle of the Coral Sea, to a Japanese submarine on 6 June, while she was under tow back to Pearl Harbor after suffering additional damage from Japanese carrier planes. The stunning victory was the watershed point of the war. From that point on, the initiative belonged to the United States.

American forces went on the offensive in August 1942, when U.S. Marines landed on Guadalcanal, in the Solomon Islands, with the primary objective of capturing a Japanese landing strip and turning it into an American air base. The Japanese realized the strategic importance of Guadalcanal, and the struggle raged for more than three months. Japanese naval forces, called "Tokyo Express" by Americans, roared down Savo Sound, scene of seven major battles. Losses by both sides were so great that Savo became known as "Iron Bottom Sound." Two valiant and dedicated Naval Reserve Supply Corps officers—LTJG Alfred Naifeh in *Meredith* (DD-434) and ENS Neal A. Scott in *USS Smith* (DD-378)—were killed when Japanese carrier-based planes attacked and sunk their ships in the seas around the Solomons in October 1942.

LORE OF THE CORPS

Lieutenant, junior grade, Alfred Naifeh, SC, USNR

Disbursing Officer, *USS Meredith* (DD-434), 1942
Period of Service: 1941–42

LTJG Alfred Naifeh was born at Covington, Tennessee, in 1919 and was graduated from the University of Oklahoma and the university's Law School. He became a law clerk for a federal judge, and in July 1941 was commissioned ensign in the Supply Corps, U.S. Naval Reserve.

Following graduation from Supply Corps School at Harvard, he reported in February 1942 as disbursing officer, *USS Meredith* (DD-434), operating in the Solomon Seas. He was promoted to lieutenant, junior grade, on 1 October 1942.

Two weeks later, the destroyer was part of a small convoy sent to Lunga, Guadalcanal, with two cargo ships, several smaller vessels, and the destroyer *USS Nicholas* (DD-449) to deliver badly needed fuel and ammunition to beleaguered Marines. The two destroyers were towing barges loaded with highly volatile cargo. They were spotted around noon on 15 October and attacked by Japanese carrier-based planes.

Meredith pressed on and was soon sunk amid fierce explosions and blazing fuel.

Horribly burned survivors lay on rafts, and those who were able clung to raft lifelines while fighting off frenzied sharks. After the order was given to abandon ship, LTJG Naifeh and others worked tirelessly throughout the night of 15-16 October to locate severely wounded and burned crew members and help them into rafts and onto floating wreckage. Utterly exhausted, Naifeh died on the sixteenth. He had been on Pacific duty only seven and a half months.

For his heroic actions LTJG Naifeh was awarded the Navy and Marine Corps Medal posthumously, and a ship was named for him. *USS Naifeh* (DE-532) was commissioned on 4 July 1944 by his mother, Rathia Naifeh, and served in both the Atlantic and Pacific fleets during World War II. *Naifeh* was recalled from the Pacific Reserve Fleet in January 1951 and returned to action during the Korean War. She was sunk in 1966 while being used as a target ship.

Sources

"Alfred Naifeh: A Supply Corps Hero and His Ship." *Navy Supply Corps Newsletter,* March-April 1983.

Dictionary of American Naval Fighting Ships. Vol. 5. Washington, D.C.: Naval Historical Center, Department of the Navy, n.d.

LORE OF THE CORPS

Ensign Neal Anderson Scott, SC, USNR

Disbursing Officer, *USS Smith* (DD-378), 1942
Period of Service: 1942

Ensign Neal Scott had served in the South Pacific less than a month before he was killed in action. He was born in May 1919 at Montgomery, Alabama, the son of a Presbyterian minister, and grew up in Valdosta, Georgia. He attended Davidson College and was graduated from the University of North Carolina. He was employed by the Equitable Life Insurance Company before being appointed assistant paymaster with rank of ensign in the Naval Reserve in April 1942. ENS Scott was graduated from Navy Supply Corps School at Harvard University in July.

Scott reported for duty as disbursing officer, *USS Smith* (DD-378), on 10 October 1942. *Smith,* operating in the seas around the Solomon Islands, was escorting *USS Enterprise* (CV-6) during the Battle of Santa

Cruz Islands 16 days later when a Japanese torpedo plane crashed into her. The crash caused *Smith*'s entire forward topside to burst into flames, engulfing the No. 2 gun Scott commanded. The young Supply Corps officer was mortally wounded. As he was being carried below, he exhorted crew members, "Keep those guns firing, mates."

Smith survived, but ENS Scott died on 26 October and was awarded the Navy Cross posthumously. The citation included, "His gallant fighting spirit and remarkable courage served as an inspiration to the crew of the ship." A new escort ship was named for him. *USS Neal A. Scott* (DE-769) was commissioned on 31 July 1944 and decommissioned in April 1946. A new academic building at the Navy Supply Corps School, Athens, Georgia, was dedicated to the memory of ENS Scott on 21 December 1967.

Sources

Dedication of Scott Hall Program. Navy Supply Corps School, Athens, Ga., 21 December 1967.

Dictionary of American Naval Fighting Ships. Vol. 5. Washington, D.C.: Naval Historical Center, Department of the Navy, n.d.

Obituary. *Savannah Evening Press,* 20 November 1942.

The End of the Guadalcanal Campaign

A Navy victory in an Iron Bottom Sound battle on 14 November 1942 eliminated the last major threat to the American position on Guadalcanal. The Tokyo Express made its final run on 30 November and inflicted damage on U.S. ships, but the Japanese were beaten off. U.S. Army troops, who relieved Marines on Guadalcanal in December 1942, took over the task of mopping up the 12,000 starving Japanese survivors and securing the island.

The Submarine War with Germany

The Germans had been just as surprised as the Americans by the Japanese attack on Pearl Harbor. Germany was engaged in a major expansion of its underseas forces and not ready to take on the United States. Only six of its long-range submarines were capable of reaching the U.S. coast to commit to a new front in the Western Atlantic in early 1942. The U.S. Atlantic Fleet was concentrated on the transatlantic routes to Great Britain and Russia to protect merchant shipping. This situation permitted considerable initial success by a few German U-boats against coastal shipping targets, including sinking a significant amount of the existing U.S. coastal tanker tonnage. A severe shortage of escorts and other antisubmarine resources contributed to the Navy's inability to curtail the Atlantic carnage early in 1942.

The Q-ship Project

During the first 18 days of 1942 German submarines sank 35 merchant ships operating off the Atlantic Coast. On 19 January, President Roosevelt and ADM King discussed the havoc German U-boats were wreaking on the American Lend-Lease supply line. The conversation turned to the Q-ship operation that the British had used during World War I. They employed heavily armed ships disguised as merchantmen. Roosevelt said, "Let's have a few of our merchant vessels converted into Q-ships and send them against the U-boats until we have something better to throw at them."

Thus, the secret Project LQ was born. King chose VADM Frederick J. Horne and RADM William S. Farber, both in OPNAV, and RADM Ray Spear, chief of BuSandA, to plan, implement, and manage the project. The trio had to work out the details of financing, procurement, conversion, manning, and providing logistical support promptly and in extreme secrecy. Two 30-year-old steamships, *SS Carolyn* and *SS Evelyn,* were purchased from the A. H. Bull Steamship Company and delivered to the Navy Yard at Portsmouth, New Hampshire, for conversion to antisubmarine combatants.

Personnel selection was an unusual challenge. All officers and men had to be volunteers, and each had to be qualified for the assigned billet. Only a few key officers of the two ships were to know the true nature of the mission: luring German submarines to the surface, where hidden guns would open fire.

Two Reserve Supply Corps officers with Merchant Marine backgrounds were selected for important roles in Project LQ. The two were ordered to report to the chief, BuSandA. ENS Kenneth M. Beyer was detached from *USS North Carolina* (BB-55), and LTJG Edgar T. Joyce, a United Fruit Steamship Company employee, was called to active duty.

Beyer and Joyce met for the first time outside RADM Spear's office on 4 February 1942 and recognized each others's last names. They confirmed that the ENS Beyer's father was a senior master with United Fruit and LTJG Joyce's father was United Fruit's senior medical officer. They were interviewed in the chief's conference room by CDR (later VADM and chief, BuSandA) William J. (Nick) Carter and LCDR (later RADM)

Walter Honaker. They told the two young paymasters that they had been selected for a secret project that was strictly voluntary, required initiative, integrity, and imagination, and involved considerable personal risk in a combat environment. They were also told that they could decline the assignment with no adverse comments in their official records, but both accepted immediately.

They were then told the nature of the assignment, including the fact that the two merchantmen would be converted into heavily armed submarine decoys. They would be commissioned as *USS Asterion* (AA-100) and *USS Atik* (AA-101) but would operate as *Evelyn,* with ENS Beyer as supply officer, and *Carolyn,* with LTJG Joyce as supply officer.

Accounts of $100,000 each were established in the names of Asterion Shipping Co., K. M. Beyer, treasurer, and Atik Shipping Co., E. J. Joyce, treasurer, at Riggs National Bank, Washington. Work on converting, heavily arming, and fitting out the two former merchantmen, along with meticulous crew selection, proceeded on a crash basis. Both supply officers arrived at Portsmouth on 9 February 1942. Close coordination was required to assure adequacy of supply space, loading of the ships, and preparation of meals, all to an extremely tight schedule.

Armament of the two ships consisted of four 4-inch, .50-caliber guns concealed in the deck house, four .50-caliber machine guns, and six single depth-charge throwers. Small arms included Lewis machine guns, shotguns, and hand grenades. The ships also were equipped with echo-ranging and listening devices. There were a limited number of officers on each ship, so all, including the supply officers, were qualified as deck watch and combat officers.

The crews were assembled at the Navy Receiving Station, Brooklyn, and reported aboard on 4 March for secret commissioning ceremonies. The two ships departed on their four-day sea trials on 23 March, with orders to avoid normal shipping lanes. The ships flew the flags of neutral countries, and all officers and crew members wore civilian shipboard clothing.

Carolyn/Atik had fewer than four days of life as a Q-ship. An SOS on 27 March indicated that she had been torpedoed. Another SOS indicated she was sinking as the result of a second torpedo hit. Ships in the area raced to the location radioed by *Carolyn* to pick up survivors, but none was found. Listed as missing in action for more than two years, all hands were officially declared dead in May 1944. It was not until after the war's end that the Navy had access to German submarine records and could learn details of *Carolyn/Atik*'s fate. The Germans recorded that U-123 was caught on the surface after torpedoing the Q-ship and was raked by machine gun fire from the Americans. The German U-boat retreated out of range of *Atik*'s guns and launched the second torpedo that doomed the damaged American vessel.

Evelyn/Asterion completed six deployments, ranging from the Grand Banks off Nova Scotia to Trinidad. Beyer recalls that his ship had numerous active and passive contacts with U-boats, but was unsuccessful in luring any of them to the surface. He was relieved in October 1943 before *Asterion*'s seventh deployment and later transferred to the Regular Navy, from which he retired as a captain in 1968.

The LQ Project was a costly effort that produced no tangible benefits. However, to those who knew of it, the Q-ship effort lifted spirits as an offensive gesture when every other U.S. Navy operation in the Atlantic was purely defensive.

U-boat Attacks in the Gulf

In May 1942, when Allied antisubmarine warfare became more efficient in the Atlantic, Germany shifted its attacks to the Gulf of Mexico. The Germans were relatively unchallenged in the Gulf and sank 41 ships, most of them tankers and bauxite carriers, totaling nearly 220,000 tons. American railroads responded by moving substantially increased volumes of petroleum products from the Southwest to the Northeast to keep America's war machine fueled.

Navy blimps and planes borrowed from the Army were pressed into the fight until increased antisubmarine resources became available. As 1942 wore on, the U.S. Navy antisubmarine forces, augmented by Coast Guard units, became increasingly more effective in the Gulf of Mexico. Faced with growing losses, the Germans shifted their efforts back to the more lucrative North Atlantic. In the 5 months from August to December 1942, U-boats sank two-and-a-half million tons of merchant shipping in convoys—700,000 tons in November alone. The Allies again found themselves in a situation similar to that they had faced in April 1917. A major commitment of additional assets was required to fight the increasingly devastating threat as 1942 ended.

New Communications Efforts

During the fall of 1942, BuSandA decided to improve its major communications medium by transforming the mimeographed sheets comprising the *Paymaster General's Newsletter* into a typeset and printed magazine and to add illustrations to break up the copy. LT (later CAPT) Lowell Lawrance, a Reservist and former Kansas City newspaperman, was appointed editor.

Another objective of BuSandA was to find a semiofficial way of passing the word about Navy regulations, customs, and traditions to the many Reserve Supply Corps officers who had been commissioned directly from civilian life. These new members of the family had trained in the supply curriculum so intently in so short a period that little time was left for orientation in other important aspects of the Navy. This lack was noticeable in the Fleet, and Paymaster General RADM Ray Spear wanted something done.

Lawrance was frustrated by security regulations, which prohibited the use of most wartime photographs. He turned to LCDR (later CAPT) Earle D. Chesney, another Reserve Supply Corps officer and BuSandA's legislative liaison. Chesney's hobby was cartooning, and he and Lawrance came up with a solution: a cartoon character named Eggburt would be the vehicle for accomplishing both objectives. Chesney would draw the cartoons to break up the solid type, and Lawrance would compose the accompanying verses to reinforce the essence of naval customs, traditions, and regulations. The pair delivered what Spear and his successors wanted.

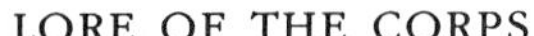

LORE OF THE CORPS

Lieutenant Commander Earle D. Chesney, SC, USNR

Legislative Liaison Officer, BuSandA, 1942–45

Earle Chesney served American presidents in the White House from Herbert Hoover to Dwight Eisenhower, with time out for service in two wars.

He was born at Swanton, Nebraska in 1900 and was a well-known high school athlete in his home state and later at George Washington University in Washington, D.C. He worked his way through college to an engineering degree by drawing and selling political cartoons. Chesney also studied law at GWU. When the United States entered World War I in 1917, he enlisted in the Army. After the war he returned to Washington to complete his college studies and then worked for the federal government. In 1924 Chesney was assigned by the Veterans Administration as the first congressional liaison representative to Congress. He was detailed to the White House during the Hoover administration, served as head usher for two years, and then returned to the Veterans Administration.

He was commissioned a lieutenant commander in the Naval Reserve Supply Corps in July 1942 and ordered to active duty as BuSandA's legislative liaison. His hobby was cartooning, and in the fall of 1942 he was called upon to solve a communications problem. The result was the birth of Eggburt, a Chesney cartoon character which appeared in the pages of the *Newsletter* during the balance of World War II. Earle Chesney served on active duty for three-and-a-half years, the last as a commander. He returned to government service as a civilian at year-end 1945 and remained in the Naval Reserve. While on two weeks of active duty at BuSandA in 1948 he gave a series of lectures, "Know Your Congress."

When the Korean War broke out in 1950 Chesney was recalled to active duty as a captain and served as director, Technical Information Division, at BuSandA. Eggburt, the hero of his Supply Corps cartoons, was also resurrected as a Korean War recallee in the pages of the *Supply Corps Newsletter.* CAPT Chesney was released again to inactive duty in December 1953 and joined the Eisenhower administration as assistant to the deputy assistant for legislative programs. He was placed on the Naval Reserve retired list in July 1960 and left the White House in January 1961.

Earle Chesney was elected to the board of directors of the Home Casualty and Surety Company and later became President of Underwater Storage Operations Company. He died in his sleep in April 1966.

Sources

Navy Supply Corps Monthly Newsletter, December 1948, June 1952, August 1958, May 1966.

Supply Line, Navy Supply Corps School, Bayonne, N.J., August 1952.

Seizing the Initiative

The United States and her allies had lost significant territory in the Pacific during the first six months of the war, and the Japanese still held the captured lands as 1942 drew to a close. German U-boats continued to be a major hazard for Allied shipping in the Atlantic. But there were positive signs for the Allies. Stopping the Japanese invasion fleet in the Coral Sea, a stunning U.S. Navy victory in the Battle of Midway, the Marine/Army conquest of Guadalcanal, and the Allied landings in North Africa were all strong evidence that the tide was turning. The United States and her allies had seized the initiative. As 1943 arrived, the pendulum had swung, and Allied military forces were solidly on track for a march toward victory and the eventual unconditional surrender of the Axis powers.

Sources

Sources for material used in this chapter and not cited earlier include:

Baker, CAPT Cecil S., SC, USN. *A Collection of Abstracts Giving Historical Background for the Work of the Supply Corps* (ca. 1939).

Miller, Nathan. *The United States Navy: An Illustrated History*. Annapolis: Naval Institute Press, and New York: American Heritage Press, 1977.

Navy Supply Corps Newsletter, February 1970, September 1973.

The World Almanac and Book of Facts. 1981.

Additional sources for material:

Principal sources of material concerning actions of Supply Corps officers at Pearl Harbor on 7 December 1941 are Navy messages, instructions, and logs, and individual reports prepared by Supply Corps officers describing their duties ashore and afloat on that day. Articles using portions of this same material appeared in the December 1959 issue of the *Navy Supply Corps Newsletter* and were reprinted in the February 1970 issue on the Corps' 175th anniversary. This material is on file at the Navy Supply Corps Museum, Athens, Ga.

The principal source of material on the Q-ships *Atik* and *Asterion* is CAPT Kenneth M. Beyer, SC, USN (Ret.), whose December 1989 paper "Project LQ, a Very Unorthodox Operation" was copyrighted in 1994. Parts of that paper were incorporated into "Desperate Measures" in the *Navy Supply Corps Newsletter,* July-August 1992.

An additional source of the discussion of World War II logistics has been *Ships, Salvage and Sinews of War* by Worral Reed Carter and Elmer Ellsworth Duvall (Washington: U.S. Government Printing Office, 1954).

CHAPTER NINE

World War II: The Road to Victory

1943–45

The Europe First strategy of the Allies meant that only limited resources were available for the war against Japan. In November 1942 a joint Navy-Army amphibious operation had succeeded in landing American troops ashore in North Africa to secure bases for the protection of Allied shipping in the Mediterranean Sea. U.S. Army forces in North Africa, led by the flamboyant General George S. Patton, were in ferocious tank battles with Nazi troops under the equally flamboyant General Erwin Rommel as 1943 dawned.

By early 1943, American industry had completed the conversion from peacetime to wartime production and was turning out the weapons of war at a pace that allowed the United States to begin to increase significantly the resources allocated to war in the Pacific. The U.S. Navy had been hard pressed to have two aircraft carriers available for a task force in 1942, but by mid-1943 task forces could have as many as 12 carriers, 6 battleships, and a like number of cruisers and destroyers to pummel the Japanese. Despite huge initial losses early in the war, the Navy had some 18,000 aircraft by July 1943, and 30,000 by year-end.

The great increase in ships and planes placed even greater demands upon the Navy supply system. The conflict with Japan truly had become a war of logistics. Keeping the Fleet supplied with fuel, ammunition, spare parts, food, and clothing was possible only through the outstanding and dedicated contributions of thousands of Supply Corps officers, sailors in supply rates, and Civil Service associates.

New supply bases established as atoll after atoll was captured provided primary logistical support for U.S. Navy task forces driving relentlessly across the Pacific. As the new bases came on line, they reduced the distance combatants were required to travel for repairs, replenishment, and rest and relaxation. However, this resulted in a concomitant lengthening of the logistical pipeline. Although underway replenishment was far from a perfected practice, floating logistics bases—composed of tenders, fleet oilers, and ammunition, refrigerated, and dry-stores ships—trailed the task forces to replenish combatants.

Logistics Problems and Submarines

From the start of hostilities, submarines proved to be the vital American offensive weapons in the Pacific, wreaking havoc on Japanese shipping lanes even in the early days of the war when the Allies were losing most of their bases in the Far East. However, only about 13 of the 67 U.S. submarines in the Pacific could be kept on station at any one time during early 1942 because of difficult logistical requirements. The huge Pacific distances meant that half of each sub's time at sea was spent on the journey to and from its station.

The submarine supply pipeline was from Mare Island through Pearl Harbor to tenders and advance bases. As increasing numbers of submarines were built and assigned to the Pacific, the complex support system became inefficient, and operations suffered. Further complicating supply support was the fact that engine spare parts were not interchangeable among submarines constructed at three major shipyards. Similar situations existed for other hull, electrical, and mechanical systems, including electric-drive motors, radio, radar, and sonar. Standardization had not yet become a prime thrust of Navy design and procurement. Allowance lists for onboard submarine spares, tender spares, and base spares came largely with parts-peculiar stock numbers. Initially, submarine tenders were outfitted with only one manufacturer's parts. Submarines requiring spares could not draw support from the nearest tender, but had to locate and go to a tender that stocked its parts.

The magnitude of the war called for fundamental change in submarine supply support. A decision was reached in early 1943 to set up a new submarine supply center (SSC) at Pearl Harbor, cutting the supply pipeline in half from the Submarine Supply Center at Mare Island. As a start, all repair and spare parts were given new stock numbers.

When the newly constructed *USS Proteus* (AS-19) arrived at Pearl Harbor in 1943, all onboard spare parts, tools, and accessories peculiar to one manufacturer, in the familiar gray steel boxes, were offloaded. A new composite load, already in bins, that contained a spread of all manufacturers' parts, was substituted and loaded aboard. *Proteus* sailed west from Pearl, ready to support any submarine in the Fleet.

Each new submarine tender had the new system, and those returning from Pacific deployment to Hawaii for resupply were also converted. Quantities of all parts, tools, and accessories were calculated for each ship in advance of reloading. SUBPAC's supply flexibility was suddenly and dramatically improved.

SSC Pearl Harbor was staffed totally with uniformed Navy personnel. No civilian employees were involved in its operation. Lieutenant (later CAPT) William G. (Bill) Tonner, Jr., a member of the famed NF&SS Philadelphia Class of 1939, was ordered to duty as supply officer at the newly established inventory control point for submarine parts. He later became officer-in-charge when the original line commander officer-in-charge was given command of a tender.

LORE OF THE CORPS

Lieutenant William Gregory Tonner, Jr., SC, USN

Supply Officer, Submarine Supply Office, Pearl Harbor, 1943–45
Period of Service: 1939–70

As an ensign, Bill Tonner was sent south to the Special Service Squadron headquartered in Panama rather than west when he was graduated from the Navy Finance and Supply Corps School Philadelphia in May 1940. He was assigned as disbursing officer, *USS J. Fred Talbot* (DD-156), but soon went to duty with the submarine service.

William G. Tonner, Jr., was born in March 1917 at Boston and had never ventured beyond the East Coast until he joined the Navy. He enrolled in the NROTC program at Harvard University and was graduated in the summer of 1939 with an A.B. in history and economics and a Reserve commission as a line ensign. With war on the horizon in Europe, he applied for a Regular Navy Supply Corps commission. In August 1939 he was sworn in and reported to the Navy Finance and Supply School at Philadelphia. ENS Tonner completed the NF&SS course in May 1940 and was ordered to duty with the Special Service Squadron in Panama as disbursing officer in the World War I-era, four-pipe *Talbot.*

More than a year before the United States was officially in the War, *Talbot* was patrolling off the west coast of Central America. *Talbot* and a Canadian ship located two German and two Italian ships loading coffee at Puntarenas, Costa Rica. The Canadian warship, waiting outside the Golfo de Nicaya and monitoring the four Axis ships, was suddenly withdrawn for other duties before the quarry was ready to depart. When the four Axis ships left Puntarenas, the helpful *Talbot* sent a plain language dispatch to the commandant of the Fifteenth Naval District. As a result, the world learned that the ships had sailed and on what course they headed. None of the Axis ships was able to go more than 500 to 600 miles before the Canadians found and sank it.

The Special Service Squadron was disbanded in October 1940, and the ships were combined into a new squadron with U.S. destroyers formerly stationed in Spain and Portugal. ENS Tonner's new duty was division disbursing officer for four destroyers, including the *USS Tattnall* (DD-125). When *Tattnall*'s disbursing officer brought his account records to *Talbot,* he "accidentally" dropped them overboard. The soggy documents were fished out of the water and given to Tonner, who refused to take responsibility for them because the accounts were illegible but put them into an unused fire room to dry. The coxswain of *Talbot*'s boat that had brought the officer and accounts from *Tattnall* told Tonner that the accounts had been dropped overboard intentionally.

Tonner's ship left Panama for Puerto Rico the following day, with *Tattnall*'s wet and illegible accounts still aboard. Bill Tonner later learned that the disbursing officer was tried by court martial and sentenced to four years in prison for purposeful destruction of government records and theft of funds.

ENS Tonner reported to the Portsmouth Navy Yard as assistant supply officer and was promoted to LTJG in January 1942. He was promoted to lieutenant in June 1942 and in March 1943 reported to the supervisor of shipbuilding, Bethlehem Steel Company, San Francisco, for duty in connection with fitting out of the antiaircraft cruiser *USS Reno* (CL-96) at Mare Island. He was to be the supply officer upon commissioning. A decision to switch the location of oil and water tanks to reduce *Reno*'s vulnerability to enemy attack meant a year's delay getting into action. At the urging of friends in the Submarine Force, Tonner succeeded in having his cruiser orders canceled and replaced with orders to the new Submarine Supply Center at Pearl Harbor.

After spending 45 days with CDR (later CAPT) Ed Metzger, OIC, SSC Mare Island, learning the ropes, Tonner reported to SUBPAC as supply officer in May 1943. The Submarine Supply Center at Pearl Harbor was still in its infancy. VADM Charles A. Lockwood, Commander Submarine Force, Pacific Fleet, told Tonner that he doubted that a Supply Corps officer could handle the job, but gave Tonner a chance because so many of his sub skipper friends had recommended him.

Tonner spent three years—from 1943 to 1945—setting up and running the Pacific Submarine Supply Center and during that time became Lockwood's close friend. Bill Tonner proved to Lockwood that a junior officer could succeed in the unusual challenges of the new operation. While Tonner was in the job, the center had total responsibility over submarine supply, including inventory control, stock numbering, and stock integration on tenders. A smoothly functioning SSC gave Lockwood the flexibility he needed for maximum operational availability of his submarines, and Bill Tonner was promoted to lieutenant commander in April 1945.

The young Supply Corps officer lived at Pearl Harbor's Makalapa housing complex near the quarters of Fleet Admiral Nimitz, who took exercise walks through the area every day he was not out in the Pacific. On several occasions when Tonner came home from work, the admiral invited the young officer to accompany him. The two also occasionally swam together in the Pacific off Waikiki Beach from the Royal Hawaiian Hotel, the designated R&R location for submarine crews returning from deployments. Bill Tonner recalls that once he thought the admiral was going to swim all the way to San Francisco. When Nimitz asked him if he were getting tired, Tonner admitted that he was, so the two climbed into an accompanying boat. That ended the day's swimming.

In May 1945 LCDR Tonner was ordered back to the Bureau of Supplies and Accounts and was assigned as OIC, Materials Handling, Packaging, and Preservation Division. He found that many senior Supply Corps officers in BuSandA were unaware of the stock integration and absolute control SSC Pearl Harbor had of submarine spares. He wanted to expand the concept throughout the Navy supply system.

In late 1945 and early 1946, LCDR Tonner found an ally in CAPT Charles (Chuck) Stein, Jr., an NF&SS classmate. Tonner recalls that a paper by Stein laid out the philosophy and rationale for BuSandA to be the inventory manager of almost all technical repair parts throughout the Navy. In March 1946, Tonner was given additional duty as OIC, Automotive Branch, and chairman, Automotive Procurement Coordinating Committee. He was detached from BuSandA in February 1947 and reported to the Ordnance Stock Office at the Naval Gun Factory, Washington, as planning officer. In March 1949, he reported to the general inspector of the Supply Corps as assistant general inspector for ordnance. He was promoted to commander in July 1949.

CDR Tonner next was under instruction for six months at the Armed Forces Staff College. He reported, in March 1951, to the Commander Naval Forces Far East at Tokyo, where he was logistics plans officer.

Tonner was the logistics briefer when Secretary of the Navy Dan A. Kimball visited COMNAVFE in March 1952. Tonner explained the constraints under which Navy ships operated in the Far East, but emphasized that supply support remained strong and effective.

Tonner went back to BuSandA in October 1952 as director, Stock Coordination Division, and went back to sea in October 1955 as supply officer, *USS Valley Forge* (CVS-45) and staff supply officer, Commander Carrier Division 16. His next tour was as supervising inspector of naval material, Upper Darby, Pennsylvania, from October 1957 to July 1960. He was promoted to captain in July 1958.

CAPT Tonner returned to the Armed Forces Staff College at Norfolk in July 1960 as an instructor and spent five years in that assignment. He reported in July 1965 as commanding officer, U.S. Navy Clothing and Textile Office at Philadelphia. Tonner's final tour of duty was as supply and fiscal officer, Naval Station, Washington, D.C., from which he retired in July 1970.

In retirement, he was employed at the Government Printing Office from 1970 to 1981. He and his wife, Helen, live in Bethesda, Maryland.

Sources

Interview with CAPT William G. Tonner, Jr. Asheville, N.C., 9 May 1993.

The Navy's Role in Korea. Report by Staff Naval Forces, Far East, to SECNAV Dan A. Kimball, March 1952.

Organization and Administrative Instructions, Spare Parts. Submarine Supply Center, Pearl Harbor, November 1943.

Roscoe, Theodore. *United States Submarine Operations in World War II.* Annapolis: United States Naval Institute, 1949.

Fleet Air Wing and Brazilian Operations

Bad winter weather on the Atlantic shipping lanes sharply reduced Allied shipping losses in January and February 1943. Many of the German U-boats were moved south, where eastbound convoy movements could not rely on protection from bad weather.

As one way to meet the increased challenge of German submarines in the South Atlantic, the Commander Air Force, U.S. Atlantic Fleet, set up a new unit. Fleet Air Wing (FLAW) 16 was tasked to intensify aerial attacks on the submarine menace. Headquarters of the new unit, the air arm of Fourth Fleet, would be located at Recife, Brazil.

LCDR (later RADM) Emory D. Stanley, Jr., was designated supply officer of the wing and the Headquarters Squadron (HEDRON), and LT (later CAPT) Ernest F. Williams was assistant supply officer. Ernie Williams was ordered to the seaplane tender *USS Albemarle* (AV-5) on 31 March 1943 to accompany the first shipload of 500 tons of supplies from NAS Norfolk to Natal, Brazil, where the supplies were to be unloaded and transported to bases being set up at three locations.

The plan was to set up separate bases for conventional aircraft, blimps, and seaplanes at Recife with a good connecting road built by Brazilians under supervision of U.S. Army Engineers. En route to Natal, *Albemarle*'s orders were changed, and she steamed past Natal and went directly to Recife. Williams and his associates had expected an orderly unloading and stowage of the offload. Upon arrival at Recife, *Albemarle* was ordered to unload and depart as soon as possible, leaving a jumble of equipment on the dock. Because of a shortage of trained drivers, LT Williams learned to drive a tractor-trailer rig in order to move the supplies to Ibura Field outside Recife. There was no covered storage space at Ibura, and tents, tarps, and shipping crates were used to protect the equipment.

FLAW 16 operations were expanded to 17 bases along the Brazilian coast from Amapa, 1,300 miles northwest of Recife, to Rio Grande, nearly 2,000 miles south. The bases were designated naval air facilities. Each had a commanding officer who provided all personnel support services, including berthing, messing, and clothing. Aviation supply items and maintenance were the responsibility of the assistant wing supply officer or assistant HEDRON supply officers at the various aviation facilities.

Complicated Logistics

Supporting so many different types of conventional planes, seaplanes, and blimps spread over such great distances created enormous logistical challenges. The supply pipeline included Aviation Supply Annex, NAS Norfolk; Aviation Supply Depot Philadelphia; and direct support from manufacturers. Supplies also were drawn occasionally from NAS Trinidad or Fleet Air Wing 7, Key West via ship, combat aircraft, and eventually the Naval Air Transport Service. According to Ernie Williams, COMAIRLANT supply officers were the key individuals for many requisitions from Brazil.

Eventually the complex logistical challenges and scarcity of aviation supplies became critical in Brazil in 1942 as the planned invasion of North Africa demanded priorities in shipping. Tight control of critical items was necessary, and the Wing Stock Control Office was established at Recife with LT Williams in charge. FLAW 16 personnel subsisted on

Spam, vienna sausages, powdered eggs and similar military food items until the supply lines loosened up later in the year. LT Williams was detached from FLAW 16 in May 1944 and was relieved by LT Frey. Earlier in the year, LCDR Em Stanley was relieved by LT (later RADM) Jack J. Appleby.

Fleet Air Wing 16 planes fanned out over the South Atlantic and as far east as Ascension Island. They scored many successes against German U-boats, but they suffered some losses.

A Shift in Submarine Warfare

Meanwhile, as weather conditions improved in the North Atlantic, the German submarines shifted their major emphasis back north. In March, Allied shipping losses increased to nearly 600,000 tons. The Germans lost only six of their U-boats. They appeared to be on the verge of totally disrupting the flow of war materials from the United States to Europe just as the Allies were struggling to build up the assets needed to return the war to the European land mass.

Even as the U.S. Navy was pressing its growing advantage in the Pacific, the primary goal of the Allies remained winning the war in Europe. At the end of 1942, with American troops already on the African continent, the Allies were preparing to liberate the occupied countries of Western Europe.

The Navy's role in the Atlantic arena throughout 1942 had been largely confined to antisubmarine warfare in an attempt to assure safe passage of transports, landing craft, and supply ships and to providing offshore gunfire support for amphibious operations. The successful North African landing provided valuable tactical lessons, including the identification of serious problems with procedures and equipment.

The United States, Great Britain, and the Free French had agreed in a conference at Casablanca in January 1943 that the initial effort to free Western Europe from Nazi occupation should be on the weakest Axis partner—Italy—the key to the soft underbelly of Europe.

The Navy Supply Depot North Africa

Before February 1943 U.S. Navy forces on both sides of Gibraltar had drawn support from the United States or from ships departing the area to return home. Senior naval officers of the three countries stressed the need for a base on the north coast of Africa to support fleet operations in the Mediterranean Sea and the forthcoming landings in Europe. American theater commanders recommended the establishment of a complete naval operating base at Oran, Algeria. The British, however, wanted only a pool of repair materials at Oran and a small supply organization to operate it.

The conflicting ideas stymied action until late March 1943 except for preparation of a bill of material for repair parts in a pool and their initial procurement. By that time, Sicily had been targeted as the key to Italy and tactical plans were drawn up for the invasion, but the exact date of the landing awaited only defeat of the last German army units in North Africa.

Commander (later RADM) George W. Bauernschmidt was ordered as prospective supply officer in command of the planned Naval Supply Depot Oran. (At the time, the Navy still would not permit staff corps officers to be given the title *commanding officer.*) Bauernschmidt's orders were to plan and obtain equipment for an industrial supply depot to receive, store, and issue the material required to support U.S., British, and French ships in the Western Mediterranean.

He was advised that he need do nothing about obtaining the materials. They were being ordered and would arrive at Oran with him. A staff of 10 Supply Corps officers was assigned to him in Washington to assist in planning. Additional officers and enlisted men would be drawn, as needed, from personnel already in Africa.

LORE OF THE CORPS

Commander George William Bauernschmidt, SC, USN

Supply Officer in Command, Naval Supply Depot Oran, 1943
Period of Service: 1922–55

Bauernschmidt brought a unique perspective to the Supply Corps. He served as a line officer before transferring to the Corps and served in the Pacific before being assigned to establish a supply base in North Africa.

George William Bauernschmidt was born at Baltimore, Maryland, in March 1899. He attended Gilman County School, Severn School, and Princeton University before being appointed to the Naval Academy in 1918, and in June 1922 he was commissioned an ensign in the line. He served in the battleship *USS North Dakota,* in *USS New Mexico* (BB-40), and was a submariner, including a tour as commanding officer of *R-2.* LT Bauernschmidt returned to the Naval Academy in July 1929 as an instructor and December 1930 was ordered to the Naval Station, Tutuila, American Samoa, as assistant captain of the yard and chief customs officer. He served in the hospital ship *USS Relief* (AH-1) and in *USS Nevada* (BB-36) from September 1932 to June 1935.

When he was found to be color blind, he opted for the Supply Corps. He excelled in logistics at the Navy Finance and Supply School at Philadelphia but admits that disbursing and accounting were "somewhat of a chore." He was graduated in May 1936, first in his class of 25, as a passed assistant paymaster with rank of lieutenant.

LT Bauernschmidt was ordered to the submarine tender *USS Beaver* (AS-5) as assistant to the supply officer, and because of his extensive line background he had additional duty as squadron intelligence officer. His next duty was as supply, disbursing, and accounting officer of the Naval Research Laboratory, Anacostia Station, Washington, in July 1937 and was promoted to lieutenant commander.

During an official visit to NRL, the Supply Corps inspector general chided Bauernschmidt for giving away garbage to a farmer who hauled it for nothing in return for obtaining food for his pigs. The I.G. told the supply officer that he had no right to give away anything. LCDR Bauernschmidt advertised for competitive bids to haul the garbage but received only one response. The farmer then offered $5 a year. Bauernschmidt had spent a large amount of money to advertise but ended up taking a pittance. He had conformed to the letter of the law.

From Anacostia, LCDR Bauernschmidt went as supply officer, *USS New York* (BB-34) with additional duty as staff supply officer of the Battleship Division in July 1939. He set up an after-hours food service for sailors returning from liberty to encourage them not to stop for a last drink and sandwich before they reached their ships. At first, returning sailors ate more than the supply officer's ration allowance but that soon tapered off. His experiment resulted in a significant reduction in masts for sailors having to answer for liberty infractions.

George Bauernschmidt was another one of those perceptive officers who believed that involvement in the war was inevitable, and the size of the Navy would increase greatly. He set up an onboard school based on the BuSandA manual to prepare storekeepers, disbursing clerks, cooks, and mess attendants for greater responsibility. As a result of this educational enterprise, many of his students were appointed Supply Corps officers or pay clerk warrant officers during the war.

New York participated in Marine amphibious exercises at Culebra Island off the east coast of Puerto Rico in the winters of 1940 and 1941. According to Bauernschmidt, the Army sent a force to the 1941 operation, but it was virtually a wasted effort. The Marines started their landings from Navy ships at dawn, but the Army came in its own ships and the civilian crews would not turn a hand until after 0730. By that time of the day, the Marines had invariably completed the exercise.

Taking a break from Neutrality Patrol duties, *New York* was anchored off Argentia, Newfoundland, Canada, where contractors were building an American naval and air station. On a visit ashore to the prospective new naval facilities, LCDR Bauernschmidt discovered a stack of accounting documents piled on a table. He then assigned some his best storekeepers ashore to set up accounts, straighten out the documents, order the necessary supplies, and arrange their stowage for the expected Argentia supply officer, who eventually reported aboard.

New York during the fall of 1941 struck a submerged rock pinnacle off Argentia, opening up a 110-foot hole in the hull. The battleship was ordered to Norfolk for repairs, but shoring was unavailable in Argentia. LCDR Bauernschmidt made an unofficial deal with the civilian contractor to swap some of the ship's ample supply of electrical cable for lumber.

His ship made the trip safely in early December and went into dry dock at the Norfolk Navy Yard. Bauernschmidt went home to Baltimore to visit relatives. On Sunday afternoon, his aunt expressed surprise that her relaxed nephew was so calm despite the fact that the Japanese had attacked Pearl Harbor. He had not heard about the attack and immediately rushed back to Norfolk.

George Bauernschmidt was selected for commander and ordered to duty as assistant to the supply officer at the Philadelphia Navy Yard in January 1942. With the United States in the war and the Philadelphia yard anticipating a large volume of repair activity, CDR Bauernschmidt ordered half a trainload of welding rods. BuSandA ordered him to cease and desist further ordering except in accordance with War Production Board procedures.

He had been at Philadelphia only nine months when he received orders to the staff of Commander Cruisers and Destroyers Pacific, in *USS Dixie* (AD-14) located at Pearl Harbor, with additional duty as staff personnel officer. In this collateral duty he was responsible for a pool of 40 to 50 Supply Corps officers, mostly Reservists, who had been sent to the Pacific. He made individual assignments to cruisers and destroyers in the Pacific Fleet as needed. Often, the young officers had to wait at Honolulu for their ships to return, so CDR Bauernschmidt arranged for them to attend line schools at Pearl Harbor. Thus, to the delight of their commanding officers, many new Supply Corps ensigns reported aboard trained in such valuable skills as gunnery, deck watch standing, coding, and fire fighting.

In early 1943 he received proceed immediately orders to Washington, where he assembled the staff, equipment, and supplies for a new supply depot in North Africa. Although he had been rushed by plane to Washington in 30 hours, he was sent to Africa by LST, which took 31 days. CDR Bauernschmidt arrived at Oran, Algiera in April 1943. In May he was made assistant to CAPT David P. Polatty, the supply officer in command, Naval Supply Depot, whom he relieved in June when promoted to captain. CAPT Bauernschmidt was given additional duty as supply officer, Naval Operating Base, Oran.

When 400 Italian prisoners of war were assigned to work at NSD Oran, CAPT Bauernschmidt fed them essentially the same bill of fare he served his own enlisted men. The Army told him to feed the Italians the same POW rations that Army prisoners received—an order to which Bauernschmidt agreed only when the Army threatened to prefer charges. He then arranged to serve the Italians leftovers from the crew's galley, and the appreciative prisoners ate nearly as well as they had before. CAPT Bauernschmidt was awarded the Legion of Merit for his exceptionally meritorious service before and during amphibious invasions of Sicily in July 1943 and the Italian mainland in September.

CAPT Bauernschmidt was ordered as staff supply officer, Commander Naval Forces in Europe, London in January 1944 as relief of CAPT (later RADM) Charles L. Austin. Just getting to his new duty was a challenge. He left Oran for London, but his plane was commandeered at Marrakech, Morocco, by Winston Churchill, who had been recovering from pneumonia in a hotel there. The movement of Churchill's whole staff took two days and forced George Bauernschmidt to hitch a ride in a plane being ferried from the States to England.

In London, he was assigned to a group planning the logistics needs for the forthcoming invasion of France. CAPT Bauernschmidt had LTs Spencer Hall and Ernest I. Steinberg ordered from Oran for duty with him to develop loading plans for the ships moving supplies from England to the Normandy coast. He was detached in early June for a month's duty on the staff of Commander Naval Ports and Bases, France. This duty required shuttling back and forth between London and Plymouth and involved plans to set up a supply depot in France as soon as possible after the landings.

When Cherbourg was liberated, Bauernschmidt was instructed to turn a French chateau into staff headquarters. He accomplished that job as ordered, but was involved in a controversy when the chief of staff ordered him to have the flagstone floors carpeted. He submitted a requisition to the British, who were reluctant to fill it from their sparse supplies and passed it up the line to higher American authorities, who returned it for justification. The chief of staff then told Bauernschmidt to cancel *his* requisition. The flagstone floors of the chateau, which had been a museum, were worn into deep hollows from four centuries of use. When carpeting could not be supplied, Bauernschmidt was told to fill the hollows with cement. George Bauernschmidt says that although he was not an antiquarian, he thought that was a sacrilege.

The chateau had a large pool occupied by a solitary swan, which became a favorite of the American staff. When the staff moved forward from the beachhead behind the advancing Allied armies, a new headquarters site was selected at Calais. CAPT Bauernschmidt was ordered to arrange transportation of the swan to the new headquarters. He had a Seabee pontoon set aboard a large flatbed trailer to transport the swan to a new home at Calais. An uproar arose over the transfer, and SHAPE headquarters ordered the swan returned to the chateau. Once again, Bauernschmidt directed movement of this delicate cargo—back to Cherbourg—and "Operation Swan" was concluded successfully.

CAPT Bauernschmidt returned to London to deal with final details in the supply plan for Europe. He did not get into the details of supply in France, he recalls, because he was returned to the United States in July 1944 for brief tours in the Bureau of Naval Personnel and in the Bureau of Supplies and Accounts. In January 1945 he reported as executive officer, Naval Supply Depot Mechanicsburg, Pennsylvania, and in August of that year became supply officer in command, Naval Supply Depot Guam.

At Guam, in addition to continuing to provide service to the Fleet, Bauernschmidt dealt successfully with a number of social problems that were later to become major national issues. He set up an integrated officers' club, arranged for a Negro Red Cross unit to be sent to Guam, and settled a dispute with chaplains of various faiths over the timing of religious services. Although he had fed Japanese POWs American-style food, they wanted fish and rice. Bauernschmidt used canned salmon to satisfy their request, and in the process kept the POWs happily fed while reducing the daily ration cost by about 70 percent.

Bauernschmidt went back to Washington in April 1946 and served as a member of the Navy Regulations Board, convened to rewrite Navy Regs, a subject on which he had made a number of recommendations over the years. When the Board completed its work in July 1947 he again went to BuSandA. He became assistant chief for logistics plans coordination in February 1948 and deputy chief to RADM Charles W. Fox in October 1949. In his new assignment Bauernschmidt made many inspection trips to supply activities around the world. He was assigned additional duty as Navy member of the Advisory Council of the Military

Traffic Service. Bauernschmidt believes that the comptrollership function was assigned to line officers while he was deputy chief because the essentially accounting function was pronounced *controllership,* and *control* was the sole province of the Line.

Selected for Flag rank near the end of his BuSandA tour, RADM Bauernschmidt reported in December 1951 as commanding officer, Naval Supply Center Pearl Harbor, the major provider of support for Navy and Marine forces in the Pacific during the Korean War. He had suspected there were wide discrepancies between the stock on hand and what was carried on the books throughout the supply system as a result of frantic issues during the hectic days of World War II. The new C.O. ordered inventories conducted in each of the depots and surveyed all missing items amounting to more than a million dollars, but the stock records finally reflected the actual inventory in the warehouses.

Bauernschmidt was also a strong and early advocate for equal treatment of women officers and assigned them identical duties to those of male officers. He did stipulate, however, that when women officers patroled the waterfront at night, they must do so in pairs.

Bauernschmidt thought it was absurd to buy fresh vegetables in California and then ship them to Pearl Harbor for repacking and reshipping to Midway, Kwajalein, and other Pacific islands. Often lettuce and other highly perishable items would rot during the laborious transit. The admiral unilaterally offered contracts to Hawaiian farmers before they put seed into the ground. He guaranteed the farmers that the Navy would buy a specific quantity of their crops at an agreed price. This idea was quite foreign to BuSandA, but his proposal was accepted reluctantly. The first contracts to implement his program were let shortly after he left Pearl Harbor to assume command of the Navy Supply Depot Clearfield, Utah, in February 1954.

The Clearfield location, between Salt Lake City and Ogden, was roughly equidistant from San Diego, Long Beach, San Francisco, and Seattle, and had excellent transportation to naval activities all along the Pacific Coast. NSD Clearfield had eight million square feet of covered storage and was designated the area disposal agency for all three services. RADM Bauernschmidt wanted to clear an area and accumulate scrap iron from such sources as surplus Army tanks and artillery pieces until the market price went from the then current $6 a ton to the anticipated $18 a ton and was unhappy when told to sell it immediately. Two years later, Bauernschmidt says, prime scrap metal prices rose to $60 a ton. He believes this decision cost the government a significant revenue loss.

George Bauernschmidt grew tired of BuSandA's constant rejection of his requests, ideas, and recommendations in areas of organization, personnel management, and surplus disposal, and his early retirement request was honored effective 30 April 1955. He now lives at Annapolis, Maryland.

Sources

Bauernschmidt, G. W. *The Early History of NSD Oran (Glen 73) with Lessons in Logistics*. Bureau of Supplies and Accounts, September 1951.

Official Biography. Navy Office of Information, August 1955.

Oral Autobiography, RADM George H. Bauernschmidt. Annapolis: United States Naval Institute, 1969–70.

Stillwell, Paul, ed. *Assault on Normandy, First-person Accounts From the Sea Services*. Annapolis: Naval Institute Press, 1994.

Effective Antisubmarine Efforts

German U-boats sank 567,000 tons of Allied shipping in the first 20 days of March 1943, but from that point on the effectiveness of the U-boats began to decline. The Allies used advanced technology to develop new and improved equipment and tactics. More effective radar and high-frequency radio direction-finders led American and British land-based bombers to the submarines. A nautical version of the Army Air Corps four-engine, long-range B-24 bomber, called "Privateer" by the Navy, was armed with depth charges. New destroyer escorts equipped with the more effective forward-firing hedgehog depth charges joined the Fleet in increasing numbers. U.S. shipyards were also turning out merchant ships faster than the Germans could locate and sink them. In May, 41 underseas raiders—one-third of Germany's deployed U-boats—failed to return from patrol.

Meanwhile, more tempting targets attracted attention of the U-boats farther south. The U.S. Navy force protecting the supply lines to the Mediterranean was ready for repositioning of the U-boats with four hunter-killer groups built around escort aircraft carriers. The four groups sank 13 U-boats in two months, and two destroyer escorts sank another three German subs.

The Development of NSD Oran

The new Naval Supply Depot at Oran received material from the United States at an accelerated rate. Start of construction had been delayed by indecision over the mission of the base, and material was arriving faster than the facilities to hold them could be completed.

CDR Bauernschmidt asked for 500 additional experienced, rated men to handle the enormous workload, and they began to trickle in. Living conditions were primitive, but Bauernschmidt fought for improved facilities. The commissary officer at NSD Oran, ENS (later CAPT) Sam Meyer, recalls that his boss was a dedicated Supply Corps officer whose line background gave him unusual insights into supporting the Fleet. Meyer reports that George Bauernschmidt was not reluctant to stand up to his superiors, including those at BuSandA, for what he thought was right. That tendency was to bring him grief several times during his distinguished career.

As the time approached for the invasion of Sicily, CAPT Bauernschmidt's depot staff had worked 70 to 100 hours a week and had made great progress toward overcoming the handicap of having arrived too late with too little in establishing NSD Oran. They had developed a plan for the systematized trans-shipment of freight to the new battlefronts scheduled to be opened in Europe soon thereafter. They had satisfied the Royal Navy's demand for a pool of repair parts. Depot sections had been set up to handle provisions, general stores, clothing, ship's store stock, electronics material, engine repair parts, and ordnance material. NSD Oran was ready to give full support for the Allied invasion of Southern Europe that began in July 1943 at Sicily and at Salerno, Italy, 30 miles below Naples, two months later.

In February 1943 detailed planning for the invasion of France was well underway. CAPT (later RADM) Robert F. Batchelder, senior assistant to the supply officer, Philadelphia Naval Shipyard was ordered to duty as force supply officer on the staff of the Commander Amphibious Force, U.S. Atlantic Fleet. In November 1943, CAPT Batchelder was reassigned as force supply officer, U.S. Task Force 122 and the Western Allied Task Forces.

With NSD Oran fully operational and American troops in Italy, CAPT Bauernschmidt was transferred to England in January 1944 on the staff of Commander Naval Forces in Europe headquartered in London. In June, he became staff supply officer for the Commander Naval Ports and Bases, France.

The Landing in Northern France

Historical accounts give lesser attention to the role of naval forces on 6 June 1944 at Normandy than to Army land and air forces, yet the U.S. Navy and the Royal Navy, supported by the Free French, performed major services in support of the D-Day landings. The vast majority of invading soldiers crossed the turbulent English Channel in an armada of 5,000 naval craft of every size and description. Three U.S. battleships, two cruisers, and nine destroyers provided heavy bombardment at Utah Beach supported by British and French battleships and cruisers. When a German counterattack threatened to repel the invading troops on the beaches, the Allied ships moved in close to the beach and eliminated individual German gun emplacements to quell the threat.

LTJG (later CDR) Russell K. Wood, Jr., assistant supply officer of *USS Arkansas* (BB-33), kept a 19-page log of events from 5 to 17 June. After 31 years of having never fired a shot in anger, *Arkansas,* the oldest battleship in the Fleet, began to fire on German shore positions with her 5-inch and 12-inch guns. Throughout the morning, Higgins boats brought wounded Allied personnel to *Arkansas* for treatment. According to Wood's report, by evening of 7 June U.S. Navy ships had begun to exhaust their ammunition supplies, requiring them to return to Plymouth for replenishment.

Combat Decoration for Supply Corps Officer

While CAPT Batchelder was deeply involved in the landing operations, CAPT Bauernschmidt was denied the opportunity to be involved directly. He had intended to be a part of the support forces that followed closely behind the Normandy landings on D-Day. He also planned to take along LTs Hall and Steinberg, who had supervised loading of invasion supplies at Channel ports; however, the Commander Naval Ports and Bases, France, denied all three permission to accompany the invasion force. He commandeered Bauernschmidt's boat, insisting that there was no need for Supply Corps officers in an assault.

The effect of precluding the three London-based Supply Corps officers from the initial invasion armada was immediately felt in France. High-priority dispatches poured in to London, requesting urgent delivery of material which had been loaded in ships that accompanied assault forces and were already in France. However, there was nobody in France to tell the beachmasters precisely which ships had the needed material. Those people were still in England. Bauernschmidt recalls that there was a tremendous early cross-Channel movement of emergency freight.

CAPT Bauernschmidt did finally get to Normandy several days later on an inspection trip, and he was able to take his two lieutenants with him and placed them aboard the supply ships. He then informed the beachmasters of the presence of the two supply officers who knew where the supplies were located and could assist in getting them into the hands of those who needed them. Shortly thereafter, properly supplied Allied troops broke out of the beachhead areas to begin their final attack on Nazi Germany's army and to liberate Western Europe.

CAPT Batchelder was decorated by both the American and French governments for his planning efforts and logistical support of the landings.

LORE OF THE CORPS

Captain Robert Fred Batchelder, SC, USN

Force Supply Officer, Task Force 122, and
Western Allied Naval Task Force, 1943–44
Period of Service: 1917–57

Robert Batchelder's distinguished 40-year Navy career spanned three major wars. His memory is perpetuated by the annual Vice Admiral Robert F. Batchelder Awards, originated by the Navy League of the United States in 1983.

Batchelder was born at Worcester, Massachusetts, in March 1895 and attended Worcester Polytechnic Institute. He was appointed an ensign, Supply Corps, U.S. Naval Reserve in October 1917 and ordered to active duty at the Navy Pay Officers School at Washington in December. In January 1918 he reported for duty in connection with the fitting out of the *USS Elinor,* but was detached the following month for duty in the Bureau of Supplies and Accounts until November 1918, when he joined *USS Antigone*. ENS Batchelder was released from active duty in October 1919.

He returned to active duty with a regular commission in October 1921 and attended the Supply Corps School of Application, Washington, and the Boston Navy Yard until May 1922. He went to sea as assistant for disbursing and assistant supply officer, *USS Chaumont* (AP-5) from May 1922 to July 1924, when he reported to Harvard University Graduate School of Business, from which he received an M.B.A. degree in 1926.

LT Batchelder remained in Massachusetts for his next two tours of duty, first at the Navy Yard from July 1926 to September 1927. He traveled a short distance south to report to the Bethlehem Shipbuilding Corporation at nearby Quincy, Massachusetts, for duty in conjunction with fitting out *USS Lexington* (CV-2), originally laid down as a battle cruiser. Upon commissioning of *Lexington* in December 1927, he served as assistant for disbursing and senior assistant supply officer until January 1930.

From March 1930 to September 1933 he again had duty at BuSandA and returned to sea as supply officer, *USS Nitro* (AE-2), in October. In August 1936 CDR Batchelder reported to duty on the staff, Navy Finance and Supply School Philadelphia. He joined *USS California* (BB-44) as supply officer and was promoted to pay inspector with rank of captain in July 1940. In December he reported again to NF&SS as executive officer, and he was appointed officer-in-charge three months later. The school was moved to Harvard University and consolidated with the newly established Navy Supply Corps School in August 1941. CAPT Batchelder became the first executive officer of the expanded school for the training of a growing group of future fleet Supply Corps officers.

In January 1942 he was transferred to duty as senior assistant to the supply officer, Philadelphia Navy Yard. CAPT Batchelder became force supply officer on the staff of the Commander Amphibious Force, U.S. Atlantic Fleet in January 1943 and participated in the Sicilian landings in July 1943. He was ordered to duty as force supply officer on the staff of VADM (later ADM) Alan G. Kirk, Commander Task Force 12 and the Western Allied Naval Task Force in November 1943. For his service in that assignment during the Normandy landings in June 1944, he was awarded the Legion of Merit with Combat V with the following citation: "Captain Batchelder, Force Supply officer, Western Naval Task Force, planned for and provided for the necessary supplies during the planning and operational phases of the amphibious assault landing on the coast of Normandy, France, commencing on 6 June 1944. His professional skill and tireless devotion to duty contributed immeasurably to the success of the Normandy Campaign." CAPT Batchelder was also awarded the Croix de Guerre with Palm by the French government. The citation stated that the award was for "exceptional war services rendered in the course of the operations of the liberation of France."

CAPT Batchelder returned to the United States in August 1944 and was assigned duty as senior assistant to the director, Naval Material Redistribution and Disposal Administration and became director in April 1945. For his services with that agency, he was awarded a gold star in lieu of a second Legion of Merit. In November 1945 he was promoted to the temporary rank of commodore and appointed chief, Property Disposition Branch, Office of Naval Material. He continued in that assignment until June 1946, when he was detailed to duty as deputy administrator of the War Assets Administration.

COMO Batchelder left the WAA in February 1947 to return to Navy duty in the Bureau of Supplies and Accounts, where he was designated assistant chief (administrative and planning) in March 1947. In December of that year, he reverted to his permanent rank of captain. From February 1948 to December 1951, he commanded the Naval Supply Depot San Diego, with additional duty as district supply officer, Eleventh Naval District. He was promoted to rear admiral in January 1951.

In January 1952, RADM Batchelder became commanding officer, Naval Supply Activities, Brooklyn, New York, and in January 1955 he assumed duty as inspector general of the Supply Corps in BuSandA. He served in that capacity until transferred to the retired list effective April 1957 and was advanced to the honorary rank of vice admiral on the basis of a combat award.

VADM Batchelder's first wife, the former Elsie C. Allison, died in April 1954. He married Norma M. Brown, a Naval Reserve Supply Corps officer, in Boston in 1959. VADM Batchelder died in May 1973 at La Jolla, California. CAPT Norma M. Batchelder died in March 1982 and left a bequest to the Navy League of the United States in honor of her husband. A trust agreement was established between her estate and the Navy League, specifying that "the award is to be included in the existing national annual recognition awards presented by the Navy League of the United States to active duty personnel and shall be designated to honor and recognize an outstanding Supply Corps officer of the United States Navy."

In 1983 the Naval Supply Systems Command determined that the Batchelder Award would go to those Supply Corps officers who had "made the most significant personal contribution to the supply readiness of our operating forces." The first awards were made in October 1984.

Sources

"Captain Batchelder Receives Legion of Merit." *BuSandA Monthly Newsletter,* January 1945.

"Inspector General Batchelder Retires." *Navy Supply Corps Newsletter,* April 1957.

Obituary, CAPT Norma M. Batchelder. *Navy Supply Corps Newsletter,* September 1982.

Official Biography. Navy Biographies Branch, April 1957.

Official correspondence on VADM Robert F. Batchelder Award between Navy League and Naval Supply Systems Command, February, August, December 1983. Navy Supply Corps Museum, Athens, Ga.

"Smooth Sailing Admirals! CAPT Batchelder Promoted." *BuSandA Monthly Newsletter,* February 1951.

"VADM R. F. Batchelder Dies." *Navy Supply Corps Newsletter,* September 1973.

The Rice Paddy Navy

While the war was raging throughout Southeast Asia, the British enlarged their major bases in India and the Americans soon set one up in Calcutta. The ranking Supply Corps officer stationed in India initially was LTJG (later CAPT) William B. (Bill) Durant, Jr., another member of the NF&SS Class of 1939-40. One of his assignments was to support the Sino-American Cooperative Organization (SACO), operating in China to provide weather data for the Fleet and to train Chinese guerillas. It was obvious that the secret, young, and efficient U.S. Navy-Chinese operation should be turned into a full-fledged, well-trained force. The Chinese required more Navy personnel and supplies for their guerrilla army as part of the bargain.

SACO was a successful endeavor for the U.S. Navy almost from the start, and that was a matter of serious concern for the Japanese, who sent an agent to eliminate CAPT Milton Miles, head of SACO. The agent attacked him on a railroad platform at Allahabad, inflicting serious knife wounds, but Miles survived.

Competition was fierce for passenger and cargo space on each U.S. Army Air Corps flight, primarily in Curtis C-46 twin-engine cargo planes, and priority bumping was a way of life. There was no strict schedule of flights. While they waited at Camp Knox in Calcutta for space in one of the sporadic flights to the interior of China, Navy personnel were indoctrinated in Chinese customs and conditions behind the Japanese lines.

LT (later CDR) Roy O. Stratton, a Supply Corps officer who had come up through the ranks, served with SACO and wrote two books about the operation: *SACO—The Rice Paddy Navy* and *The Army-Navy Game*. In his first book, Stratton commented: "Sunglasses were a must. Formality of military dress was completely disregarded. GI Army field shoes were fashionable. Once in your quarters, you stripped to your skivvies [shorts]. Book matches melted in your pocket."

BuSandA and the Bureau of Personnel (BuPers) had little knowledge of the conditions under which SACO Navy personnel worked. SACO was initially the Far Eastern branch of the Army's Office of Strategic Services (OSS), which was responsible for all procurement of supplies and services until May 1943. No Supply Corps officers were assigned to SACO until LT Ernest S. Tharpe departed for the supply base in China via Calcutta on 5 April 1943. The first shipment of Navy stores reached him in August. The SACO Agreement called for the U.S. Navy to deliver materials and equipment to Chungking for further delivery by the Chinese to bases within China.

Navy Supply Corps officers constantly battled to get their supplies from the United States to China via India. The stumbling blocks erected by the U.S. Army became so severe that support was sought from the Joint Chiefs of Staff to assure movement of SACO freight into China. The JCS authorized the movement of 150 tons a month from India to China by air.

According to Stratton, on one occasion, GEN Joseph Stillwell ignored the JCS authorization and held up SACO supplies for six months. Lengthy negotiations led to the signing of a formal agreement by Secretary of the Navy Frank Knox, BGEN William J. (Wild Bill) Donovan, director of OSS, CAPT Miles, and Chinese officials on 15 April 1943. The agreement solved the supply problems, but other troubles cropped up. The OSS had been set up to do much the same kind of work that SACO was doing in China, and, despite the critical need for weather information, Army officials were not supportive.

Navy personnel considered for assignment to SACO were first sent to Washington for screening. Candidates were required to be physically rugged and have at least two technical skills and one useful hobby. To assure that they did not consider the Chinese weak and ineffective—a popular belief held by many Americans—the candidates must never have been in China before.

Stratton reported that because of the highly secretive nature of the operation, supply organization and operations were unlike any other in the Navy. There were no initial outfitting lists and no usage factors on which to base requisitioning. Palletization and materials handling equipment was unheard of in China. The physical brawn of Chinese coolies, worn-out, ancient trucks fueled by a mixture of gasoline and alcohol or vegetable and pine oil, and ox carts had to suffice. Chinese drivers were used to move stores between locations and often stopped along the way for indefinite periods until U.S. Navy riders were assigned to accompany the trucks and to keep the drivers moving.

Administrative and technical cognizance became a major problem. Who had responsibility for what? What kind of materials were needed and in what quantities? Typical Navy planning did not apply, and BuSandA manuals were of no use. Decisions were necessarily made on the spot to reflect tactical operations deep inside a country whose industry, business, financial, and transportation infrastructure was, in large part, controlled by the Japanese invaders. Detail officers back in Washington were unable to describe the duty to Supply Corps officers, pay clerks, and storekeepers. "The majority of them learned what was expected of them only after they arrived at Calcutta. All of them turned in excellent job performances," Stratton wrote.

The SACO Supply Department

A Naval Group China Supply Department was established on 1 January 1944, at Chungking, with LCDR (later CAPT) Alfred C. Jackson as the first staff supply officer and LT Robert M. Crumley was disbursing officer. Jackson eventually convinced Miles that he and Crumley should be located at Kunming. Supply departments, established at Kweiyang, Chungking, and Keinyang, gradually became good-sized activities, with several warehouses, general stores, and disbursing offices and a full complement of storekeepers. Each of the outlying bases had its own supply department, but relied on the three major supply departments for support.

U.S. Navy personnel trained young, inexperienced Chinese soldiers as storekeeper assistants, and they were then assigned to bases and transshipment points. Despite language problems, the training program was successful and continued until the end of the war. Ultimately, SACO grew to 2,000 U.S. Navy personnel, including 42 Supply Corps officers and 2 pay clerks in China and another 6 Supply Corps officers in India.

SACO supply officers developed procedures at Calcutta to obtain as much material and stores as possible from the Royal Indian and British armies and from the Royal Navy through reciprocal aid. This reduced the demand on ocean transportation from the United States. The British continued to supply material up to the war's end.

In February 1944 SACO received its first modern military vehicles: two jeeps and a weapons carrier. It had become apparent that effective supply support was only possible if a screening and requisitioning agency were set up in the States. This need was met on 18 February 1944, when LTJG Gether O. Covington reported to the SACO Washington office to set up a procurement operation. Requirements were fed to Chungking or Calcutta and then passed to Washington for processing. Covington requisitioned standard stock items from the Navy Supply Depot Bayonne. Nonstandard items were procured through the cognizant Navy bureaus. Files were maintained and bills of lading were prepared with advance copies sent to the appropriate SACO supply officer.

Pilferage and Poles

American supply personnel were constantly concerned with safeguarding stores from pilferage. The problem arose because the Chinese Nationalist Government encouraged its people to steal or destroy enemy stores and commended them for doing so. It was difficult to convince illiterate coolies not to steal from a foreign ally when it was all right to take the belongings of another foreigner. The problem continued throughout the war.

Procurement of supplies locally was often frustrating to Supply Corps officers. When SACO was tasked to construct a radio station at Chungking, it was necessary to purchase 75 telephone poles. The supply officer located some poles along a river bank about an hour's walk from headquarters. They had been floated down the river from the upper provinces. When he found one pile that contained 75 poles, no one was interested in selling them, and so he left word he would return the following day.

The supposed owner showed up the next morning, but he only owned six of the poles. Each pole had a Chinese character written on its end to designate the owner. It took three days for one man to gain complete control of 75 poles, either by acting as agent for the owners or by buying up the individual lots. A deal was finally made, and the supply officer was handed a pot of ink and a brush and asked to affix his name to each pole he had purchased. The buyer and seller then retired to a nearby tea shop to complete the transaction, taking two hours to prepare an invoice and affix the required tax stamps. It had taken nearly five days to purchase 75 pieces of timber.

SACO Operations and Currency Inflation

Not until mid-1944 did SACO operations really begin to pay off in a big way. From 1 June 1944 to 1 July 1945, SACO guerrillas, led frequently by Navy and Marine Corps personnel, killed 23,540 Japanese, wounded 9,166, and captured 291; they also destroyed 209 bridges, 84 locomotives, and 1,412 ships and river craft. Meanwhile, the Fleet benefited from the weather data SACO stations compiled and transmitted.

In July 1944 CAPT (later RADM) George F. Yoran flew to China on a BuSandA inspection trip of supply facilities in central and coastal China. Navy carrier air strikes were stepped up against targets in Formosa and mainland China in 1944, and SACO was ordered to obtain 25 million in Chinese Farmers' Bank dollars to prepare escape packs for downed aviators. Yoran and LCDR Jackson were designated as couriers to take the money to Washington, where Jackson remained, and LT Crumley replaced him as staff supply officer pending LT Stratton's arrival.

The Japanese occupied Nanking in November 1944, posing a threat to Kunming. SACO personnel were mobilized to transport demolition material and ammunition to the threatened city in December. The Japanese thrust in late 1944 and early 1945 marked their final expansion in China, but it had an adverse impact on the value of Chinese currency and greatly complicated procurement. In January 1944 the official Chinese government rate of exchange was 20 Chinese dollars to 1 U.S. dollar. The rate reached 2,900 to 1 in July 1945. SACO used the official rate in obtaining Chinese dollars until February 1944, when permission was granted to purchase currency requirements in the open market. From that point, all transactions were for cash and no credit was extended.

Disbursing officers of the various SACO units carried the currency on their books at various rates, reflecting the individual transactions. In May 1945 the SACO Disbursing Office (Dochina) took over responsibility for procuring all currency needs for the Navy in China.

The First over Ledo Road

LTJG Conrad Bradshaw, SACO supply officer at Jorhat, India, was sent to China to deliver a jeep over the new Ledo Road (also known as the Stillwell Road), the first land route from India to China. When it was completed in January 1945, and while the Army was setting up a photograph of its first convoy to China at the Burma-China border, Bradshaw decided he would be first over the route. He drove his lone jeep across the starting line and sped full tilt down the new 500-mile road. He arrived at the Chinese end of the road four days ahead of the convoy, although the official Army news release made no mention of the fact.

Bill Durant had been promoted to lieutenant commander and reported as supply officer, SACO India Unit in May 1945. LT Stratton reported as Jackson's relief, although Jackson had already departed for the United States. Durant and CDR McCarthy went back to the States in July or early August for a conference at Washington, where McCarthy remained, but Durant returned to Calcutta. CDR Chubb fleeted up as McCarthy's successor as SACO staff supply officer on 1 September.

When news of the Japanese surrender was received in China, SACO units broke camp and reported to designated occupation centers, equipment was transferred to the Chinese, and supply personnel in western China moved east to Hankow and Shanghai. The Navy Purchasing Office Shanghai was reactivated when CDR Chubb reported and was fully functional when the first units arrived on 19 September 1945.

Dochina opened shop at Shanghai in September with Stratton in charge, and in October SACO's rear echelons at Calcutta and Jorhat were deactivated. Material at those locations was loaded aboard ships and sent around to Shanghai for turnover to the Chinese during the period from November 1945 to January 1946. Stratton relieved Chubb as SACO staff supply officer in November 1945. By December, the only remaining SACO operations in China were the disbursing office and two storehouses at Shanghai.

Throughout the first half of 1946 the transfer of all SACO equipment and stores either to the Chinese government or to U.S. Navy ships and shore stations was completed. LCDR Stratton was detached in April 1946 and ordered to Tsingtao as supply and accounting officer. Naval Group China and SACO were deactivated on 30 June 1946, ending an amazing but little known chapter in U.S. Navy history.

LORE OF THE CORPS

Lieutenant Roy Olin Stratton, SC, USN

Naval Group China, 1945–46
Period of Service: 1917–46, 1951–53

Roy Stratton spent 12 years as an enlisted man, made warrant in 1930, was commissioned in 1942, served in China both before and during World War II, and wrote two books and numerous published articles on Navy subjects as well as several mystery novels.

Born at Richmond, Indiana, in August 1900, he enlisted in the Navy in April 1917. During World War I he served in *USS North Dakota* and *USS Maddox* with a destroyer flotilla and remained on the European Station during 1919 and 1920. He had duty in *USS Flusser* at Vera Cruz, Mexico, during an epidemic of bubonic plague in 1920. Stratton was next assigned to the Asiatic Fleet, first in *USS Sacramento* (PG-19), then in *USS Black Hawk* (AD-9). During his Asiatic service, he participated in the joint U.S.-British expedition at Vladivostok in 1919 in support of the White Russians. He rose through the ranks as a storekeeper to chief.

In October 1930 Stratton was appointed acting pay clerk and then pay clerk one year later. He participated in the 1932 landing at Shanghai and was on the staff of Commander Aircraft, Battle Force before reporting to the Naval Air Station, Lakehurst, New Jersey, in 1936. He was promoted to chief pay clerk in October and was serving as Supply Department duty officer on May 6, 1937 when the German zeppelin *Hindenburg* exploded and burned as she was preparing to dock at the NAS dirigible mooring mast. He received a letter of commendation for his part in the rescue of *Hindenburg* personnel.

Stratton reported in June 1937 to *USS Astoria* (CA-34), Cruiser Division 6, Scouting Force, U.S. Pacific Fleet, as assistant supply officer and in July 1940 was assigned to the Disbursing Department, Ninth Naval District. In February 1942 he was ordered to duty as supply officer, U.S. Naval Base, Rosneath, Scotland. Stratton was commissioned as a lieutenant, junior grade, in August 1942. He received a letter of commendation for his service at Rosneath. He had similar duty at U.S. Naval Base No. 2 at Londonderry, Northern Ireland, and at other locations in Great Britain. In November 1943 he returned to Washington and reported to the Bureau of Supplies and Accounts. LT Stratton next had duty with the Advanced Base Supply Unit, Naval Operating Base, Norfolk, in January 1944.

When a large volume of supplies and equipment had arrived in China, CAPT Miles was concerned and wanted an accurate accounting of amounts and their location. LT Stratton was identified as an old China hand and was ordered to duty as disbursing officer for the United States Naval Group China in November 1944. He had additional duty as international aid and disbursing officer, China, in connection with SACO operations. Stratton was promoted to lieutenant commander in 1945 and served as senior staff supply officer until April 1946. He remained in China as supply and accounting officer at the U.S. Naval Port Facility, Tsingtao. He received a second letter of commendation for his service with SACO.

LCDR Stratton returned again to the Bureau of Supplies and Accounts in November 1946, where he served in the Fiscal Division until relieved of active duty on 1 April 1948 and placed on the retired list with the rank of commander. In retirement, he served as corporate secretary-treasurer of the Harvey School at Hawthorne, New York. CDR Stratton was recalled to active duty in January 1951 and reported to the Bureau of Supplies and Accounts. After temporary assignments at various East Coast naval facilities, he was ordered to special duty with the Commander Naval Forces Eastern Atlantic and Mediterranean at London. He conducted a classified research and writing project in Europe and the Far East. In this duty, he interviewed former German naval officers to assess their logistics operations in World War II. He later went to the Admiralty at London to undertake a similar assessment of the Royal Navy's World War II logistics. His wife, Arlene, accompanied him to England and died there in May 1952.

In addition to providing official reports to BuSandA, CDR Stratton wrote a three-part series, "The Supply Corps of the British Navy," published in the *Navy Supply Corps Newsletter* in 1954. He also was author of "Navy Guerrilla," an article that appeared in the *U.S. Naval Institute Proceedings* in 1963.

Roy Stratton later met and married Monica Dickens, a descendant of the famous British author Charles Dickens. He retired from the Navy a second time in 1953, and he and his wife settled in North Falmouth, Massachusetts. Over the next 32 years he was active in a wide variety of civic, political, and military organizations. In addition to the two books about his duties in China during World War II, he wrote several mystery novels; *One Among None* was a Mystery Book of the Month selection. He suffered a stroke in February 1985 and died at the age of 84.

Sources

"Navy Guerrilla." *U.S. Naval Institute Proceedings,* July 1963.
Obituary. *The Enterprise,* Falmouth, Mass., 27 February 1985.
Official Biography. Naval Historical Center, 9 May 1951.
Stratton, Roy. *The Army-Navy Game.* N.p.: Volta Company, 1977.
———. *SACO: The Rice Paddy Navy.* N.p.: C. S. Palmer Publishing Co., 1950.
"The Supply Corps of the British Navy." *BuSandA Monthly Newsletter,* May, June, July 1954.

Expanding to Meet Wartime Demands

As the wartime demands upon the Navy supply system increased in both the Atlantic and Pacific theaters, the Bureau of Supplies and Accounts also expanded. In 1943 the Aviation Supply Depot was established at Philadelphia, an Aviation Storekeeper School was established at NAS Jacksonville, and a Navy Packaging School was established at the University of Wisconsin at Madison.

Significant changes were made in procurement, and the technical bureaus regained certain procurement authority from BuSandA. Another major change came in 1943, when the Committee on Accounting Changes issued the Grady Report, which modernized the Navy accounting system.

Inland Navy Supply Bases

With full-scale war raging in both the Atlantic and the Pacific, demands upon the Navy supply system increased at an accelerated rate. Inland Navy supply depots, originally designed to provide protection for valuable inventories against possible enemy attack from the sea, were established in 1943 at Scotia, New York; Spokane, Washington; and

Clearfield, Utah. Their strategic location, however, provided other advantages as well. Supplies now could be sent directly to any port on either coast rather than being routed through seaboard rail centers and up and down the coasts. A naval supply depot was also established in 1943 at Guantanamo Bay, Cuba, to support fleet operations in the Gulf of Mexico and the Caribbean.

Aviation Supply Problems

The Bureau of Aeronautics and the Bureau of Supplies and Accounts had recognized in early 1941 the need to resolve the continuing problem of spare parts for aircraft. Until that time, BuAer was responsible for procuring the airplanes, and BuSandA was responsible for procuring spare parts. Each worked independently.

When the two bureaus decided that the time had come to work together more closely, they set up a team to work out the problems jointly. LT (later RADM) Charles Shattuck, a naval aviator, was given responsibility for this effort, and he eventually transferred to the Supply Corps.

LORE OF THE CORPS

Lieutenant Charles W. Shattuck, USNR

Head, Technical Supply Division, Aviation Supply Office, 1943
Period of Service: 1932–71

Lieutenant Shattuck, an aeronautical engineer and a naval aviator, worked on a supply team during the early days of World War II. He saw action in the Pacific as C.O. of a torpedo squadron, transferred to the Supply Corps as a commander, and retired as a rear admiral in the Naval Reserve.

Charlie Shattuck was born in Oklahoma in August 1911 and became a pilot in 1927. He was graduated from Los Angeles City College in 1933, where he studied aeronautical engineering. He joined the Naval Reserve as a seaman in July 1936 and the following month was enrolled in the Aviation Cadet Program (AVCAD).

Shattuck reported for flight training at Pensacola in December 1936 and qualified as an aviation cadet in 1937. He then spent three years in the Fleet and was promoted to ensign in July 1939. He was on duty at NAS Pearl Harbor in 1939 and 1940. ENS Shattuck returned to Pensacola as an instructor in April 1940 and was promoted to LTJG in December of that year.

In March 1941 he responded to a call for junior aviators who had an aeronautical engineering background to apply for duty at the Bureau of Aeronautics in Washington. He was appointed the senior of two volunteer junior aviators, BuAer's representatives on a joint team with BuSandA, to develop a system that would provide more effective aviation supply support. Shattuck and LTJG Warren Lenerauth were given an intensive briefing on aviation supply by CDR (later VADM) E. Dorsey Foster. Newly promoted, LT Shattuck set up an office, with 34 young military and civilian engineering graduates reporting to him. Transferred personnel from the two bureaus formed an effective team; those from BuAer made the purchase decisions and those from BuSandA handled the paperwork. By the spring of 1943 the team had grown to more than 200 members, with Dorsey Foster as the initial Supply Corps liaison officer.

The new organization had absolute control over the manufacture, allocation, and distribution of aircraft spare parts during the war. According to Charlie Shattuck, in addition to the Navy, the office also exercised authority over the allocation of common aviation spare parts to the Army Air Corps and commercial airlines. Shattuck was promoted to lieutenant commander. In May 1943 LCDR Shattuck and his team—now 300 members—moved to the newly established Aviation Supply Office at Philadelphia. The team became ASO's Technical Supply Division, with Shattuck, still a line officer and aviator, as division head. The division developed the "Quarterly Stock Status Report" and an aviation supply syllabus for the Navy Supply Corps School at Harvard.

Charlie Shattuck was a flier at heart, and he asked to be returned to flying duties with the Fleet. He reported in October 1943 as commanding officer of a torpedo squadron at NAS Westerly, Rhode Island, comprised of 27 ensigns fresh out of Pensacola.

In February 1944 he became C.O. of Torpedo Squadron 80 in *USS Ticonderoga* (CV-14), later transferred to *USS Hancock* (CV-19) after *Ticonderoga* was heavily damaged by kamikaze attacks. In March 1945 he was ordered as air officer in *USS Saratoga* (CV-3). After two months learning the job as assistant air officer, he took over as air boss in May and was promoted to commander.

Following the war, CDR Shattuck served for 18 months as inspection officer, NAS Corpus Christi, Texas, with 137 inspectors, most of them civilians, working for him. After leaving active duty in 1947, he went to work as special assistant to the commanding general of the Panama Air Depot in the Canal Zone.

When RADM Dorsey Foster became chief of BuSandA in 1948, he offered to bring his old friend, Charlie Shattuck, back on active duty as a Supply Corps officer. CDR Shattuck agreed, providing he could retain the right to fly as a naval aviator. Foster worked out the details, and Shattuck was sent back to ASO as head of the Planning Division. In 1949 he was appointed officer-in-charge, Naval Aviation Supply Depot Philadelphia, and in 1950 went to the Philadelphia Naval Shipyard. When his father became ill in July 1950, CDR Shattuck asked to be released to inactive duty again.

Back in California, he accepted an executive position with Douglas Aircraft Corporation. He was subsequently promoted to captain and Flag rank in the Naval Reserve and retired in 1971. He lived in Bonsall, California, until his death in March 1994.

Sources

Correspondence and documents provided by RADM Charles W. Shattuck, 1991–92.

Oral history of reminiscences of RADM Charles W. Shattuck, SC, USN (Ret.). Navy Supply Corps Museum, Athens, Ga., June 1989.

Fresh Food for the Fleet

In the early days of the war, before fleet issue ships were available in the Pacific, Supply Corps officers were tested severely in order to provide fresh food for the crews of their ships. For example, one who recalls the trials and tribulations he faced in the South Pacific in 1944 is RADM Jack F. Pearse, then an ensign. He reported for duty in December 1943 as commissioning supply officer of *USS Mobjack* (AGP-7), an 1,870-ton motor torpedo boat tender supporting 30 of the fast boats.

At various times *Mobjack* was located at Woendi, Manus, Treasury Island, and Morotai Island. ENS Pearse would fly to Espiritu Santo, Guadalcanal, Hollandia, or Tulagi to obtain perishables, which were delivered to *Mobjack* by old tuna boats. "It was a real exercise in scrounging supplies before fleet issue ships came into being," he recalls.

RADM Pearse observed that independent supply duty in the Pacific during World War II taught young Supply Corps officers quickly to stand on their own two feet. "They made the wheels turn when they needed to turn." Once fleet issue ships came on line, supply officers developed a quick appreciation of the support policies put into effect to help those at the end of the line.

Pearse left active duty after World War II, affiliated with the Reserve, and was promoted to Flag rank in 1970. He owns and operates an export firm in San Francisco and lives with his wife Helen Earle in Burlingame, California. He believes that his World War II experiences are helpful in his business even today.

The Pincers Strategy in the Pacific

Buoyed by improved techniques of stretching the logistics chain through advance bases and improved underway replenishment, the American strategy in the Pacific developed into a kind of pincers movement. Halsey's air and amphibious forces, along with General Douglas MacArthur's air and ground units, moved northward from New Guinea and by December 1943 were poised to begin the effort to liberate the Philippine islands.

However, ADM Nimitz's major objective was to drive against the Japanese homeland directly across the Central Pacific through the Gilbert, Marshall, and Mariana island chains. He planned to use the captured, liberated islands as bases for submarine and long-range air attacks on Japan. Nimitz decided to bypass and isolate the heavily fortified Japanese base at Truk, where American carrier strikes had destroyed most of the planes, to liberate Guam, and to capture Tinian and Saipan.

The Japanese chose to make a stand on Saipan in June 1944 and sent nine carriers to attack the American beachhead and supporting naval forces. The Battle of the Philippine Sea, more commonly called the "Great Marianas Turkey Shoot," began on 19 June. The 12 U.S. and Japanese battleships did not engage in surface action, and when fanatical yet unskilled Japanese carrier pilots pressed the attack, they were no match for the veteran U.S. Navy fliers. At the end of the day, American fighter pilots had shot down a staggering 373 Japanese airplanes. Navy bombers and submarines also had sunk three enemy carriers and badly damaged a fourth.

Improved Support Efficiency

VADM Lockwood's strategy called for his submarines to sever Japan's lifeline by attacking her commercial ocean and inter-island trade, on which she relied heavily, as well as her warships. New submarines were added to the Fleet each month and were supported by the improved submarine supply system. A record was set in October 1944, when 68 U.S. submarines sunk 320,900 tons of Japanese merchant ships, one-third of them tankers.

The Bureau of Supplies and Accounts took a number of steps in 1944 to improve the efficiency of support to the Fleet. A Navy Inventory Control Office was established under CNO to provide guidance to Navy bureaus and inventory control points. CINCPAC commissioned Service Squadron Six, the first force devoted solely to providing logistical support to fleet units at sea. The Western Sea Frontier Command was established to coordinate the work of 15 separate agencies on the West Coast involved in logistical planning and the flow of materials into the Pacific.

BuSandA established a Naval Supply Operational Center at Bayonne, New Jersey, to provide practical training in mechanized materials handling. Merger of ship's store and ship's service functions was made mandatory aboard ships with supply officers and was permitted on other ships. The prewar Navy accounting and finance system had been adequate for a Navy of about 200,000 officers and men, but rapid expansion of the Navy after the attack on Pearl Harbor put an enormous strain on the system. Finally, a new, streamlined Navy payroll system was put into effect on July 1, 1944, with a resultant increase in efficiency and reduction of forms, waste of labor, surplus clerical routines, and lost pay records. The new system also made it possible to reconstruct lost or destroyed individual pay records.

The Ensign and His Fleet

Often, young Reserve Supply Corps officers, who suddenly found themselves in the unaccustomed role of warriors, had to be creative in carrying out their missions. In January 1944 young ENS Robert A. Stevenson was assigned to the staff of AIRPAC on Ford Island, Pearl Harbor, as booking and shipping officer. His principal duty was to arrange the unloading of damaged or inoperative aircraft (called "duds") from carriers, mostly CVEs with newly qualified aviators, who engaged in training exercises en route to Pearl Harbor, and loading replacements. Stevenson reports that each inbound carrier would have three to seven duds because of damaged equipment.

At a Ford Island berth, unloading and loading was no problem, using the ship's crane. Soon, the number of carriers arriving at Pearl exceeded the capacity of Ford Island berths, which delayed deployment of carriers to the war zone. A jury-rigged self-propelled pontoon lighter proved to be an unsatisfactory solution to servicing the carriers at moorings. ENS Stevenson located 13 out-of-service, 100-ton YCK lighters that could accommodate four planes each, had their own cranes, and better operating characteristics. He eventually was able to get 11 of them in operation, and he arranged to line up crews on an as-needed basis. He became the most junior "fleet commander" in the Navy.

Eventually, responsibility for replacing aircraft was turned over to NAS Ford Island. Stevenson remained on active duty until 1947, when he entered the Foreign Service. He served primarily in Latin America, but was ambassador to the African nation of Malawi from 1974 to 1978. Ambassador Stevenson retired from the State Department in 1978 and lives with his wife Dorothy in Vienna, Virginia, with a winter home in Naples, Florida.

Commanding a British Carrier

Another unusual duty undertaken by a Supply Corps officer during World War II involved LCDR Walter Reierson, who had the "con" of a British escort aircraft carrier. Reierson was a passenger riding *HMS Patroller* from Australia to NAS Alameda in March 1944 when the commanding officer ordered him to take over the bridge watch.

LCDR Reierson took over at 0945 as *Patroller* steamed across the Pacific while the skipper posed for a picture of the ship's officers. He was relieved 35 minutes later and resumed his passenger status. Reierson left active duty in September of 1948, retired from the Naval Reserve as a commander in 1958, and lives with his wife Margaret at Gig Harbor, Washington.

A Supply Mixup

Yet another officer who faced an unusual challenge was LTJG (later LCDR) Thomas O. C. Murray, supply officer, *USS John D. Henley* (DD-553).

Henley's allowance list called for a maximum of five gallons of non-medical alcohol. Murray had submitted his requisitions, including one for the allowable five gallons of alcohol, and took a working party ashore at Guam in late 1944 to obtain the needed supplies. After picking up the bulk of the supplies at various locations around the advance base he arrived at a quonset hut where valuable items were kept in secure storage.

The alcohol for *Henley* had been set aside in a bin, but the amount was 50 gallons not the 5 gallons Murray had ordered. The chief storekeeper in charge of the alcohol supplies was perplexed. LTJG Murray decided to capitalize on his bonanza, so he and the chief reached a compromise. Murray believed 10 gallons would be more than sufficient, so he did his best to erase the cipher, signed the requisition for 5 gallons, took 10, and told the chief to adjust his own inventory to fit.

Murray reports that the officers had a party later at Ulithi Atoll in the

Palau Islands. There were no repercussions from the illegal alcohol issue. Murray left the Navy in the summer of 1947, but was recalled for the Korean War from 1951 to 1953. He then was employed in business and academia, and he retired from the Naval Reserve as a lieutenant commander in 1979. He lives with his wife Marie in West Roxbury, Massachusetts.

The Kamikaze Horror

The last major American amphibious operation of the war took place on Easter Sunday, 1 April 1945, when a Marine-Army force landed on Okinawa, largest of the Ryukyu Island chain, only 350 miles from Kyushu, the southernmost island of Japan. From the beginning, it was obvious the Japanese would make an all-out effort to hold Okinawa in an attempt to deny Americans its use as a staging base.

The huge U.S. Fleet, composed primarily of ships constructed through the massive mobilization of American industry, was poised off Okinawa to support the invasion. Suddenly, a new force focused its attention on ships of the U.S. Navy. Japan had lost most of its experienced pilots to earlier American action, and this unique weapon, called "kamikaze" (divine wind), was composed of inexperienced pilots who volunteered to crash their bomb-laden planes into American ships. They wreaked havoc among U.S. vessels, sinking 30 ships and damaging 233 others between 1 April and 21 June 1945. Of the 30 ships sunk, 22 were destroyer types.

Destroyers were assigned to radar picket duty off Okinawa to detect incoming Japanese planes and to alert the great mass of ships supporting the invasion. Two Supply Corps officers who survived vicious suicide attacks on their ships on 6 April 1945, lived to tell their stories.

LTJG (later RADM) Robert H. (Bob) Spiro, Jr., was supply officer, *USS Morris* (DD-417), a prewar Sims-class vessel and one of a group of six destroyers assigned to picket duty. As the sun was setting, a lone Japanese Kate bomber approached low over the water and crashed into *Morris* forward of the superstructure. A bomb or torpedo carried by the plane exploded after passing through the ship, nearly breaking it in two.

Spiro was engaged in fire fighting and assisted the wounded when the order was given to abandon ship, but the skipper decided the ship could be saved and ordered all able-bodied men back aboard. *Morris* limped into the harbor at Kerama Rotto, a small island west of Okinawa.

Efforts were made to make the ship safe and habitable for open ocean passage back to the States for repairs. LTJG Spiro reorganized the mess aft, borrowed supplies, and reopened the ship's store and laundry. His safe, located in the flooded mess decks, was finally recovered weeks later when diesel fuel and salt water were pumped out. Currency amounting to $65,000 was soaked and caked in smelly muck.

LTJG Spiro put $20,000 of wet $20 bills in the ship's drier, but the smell of burning paper quickly caused him to remove it. The money was brown around the edges—but dry and negotiable. After smoothing out and verification, the money was transferred to the disbursing officer of a tender, who held payday.

Morris eventually made it back to Hunter's Point Navy Yard at San Francisco, where she was decommissioned and scrapped in 1947. LT Spiro left active duty and embarked on a career in academia with a concurrent career in the Naval Reserve. Spiro rose to the presidency of Jacksonville University and rear admiral in the Reserve, from which he retired in 1978. He also served as undersecretary of the Army. He is chairman of the Board of Sports 2000, Inc. and vice president of the American Security Council. He and his wife Terri Gay live in Alexandria, Virginia.

Ensign (later CAPT) Robert G. (Bob) Whitacre had been a Reserve Supply Corps officer for just under a year when he experienced "two hours of pure hell on earth" as supply officer of *USS Colhoun* (DD-801), also on picket duty during the unrelenting kamikaze attack. *Colhoun,* too, had been commissioned less than a year when she sailed to war. The new destroyer was assigned to screen transports unloading at Iwo Jima and provide fire support. On 1 March 1945, while supporting Marines at Iwo Jima, *Colhoun* was struck by an enemy shell, causing a torpedo flask to explode.

Whitacre recalls that after brief repairs at Saipan *Colhoun* reported for radar picket duty off the coast of Okinawa on 6 April. *Colhoun* was soon involved in a ferocious air-sea battle when 12 kamikazes converged on the destroyer and *USS Bush* (DD-529). *Colhoun* received four kamikaze hits, one of which broke her keel, but she shot down six of the Japanese suicide planes. The order was given to abandon the battered and twisted hulk, and the crew transferred to the rescue vessel *USS Wayne* (APA-54).

ENS Whitacre went to his midships stateroom and recovered about $200,000 in U.S. currency from his safe, as well as the crew's safe deposits and the crew's pay records, which were preserved in a 5-inch, .38-caliber shell casing. He then abandoned *Colhoun* off the fantail. The doomed ship was taken under tow by another destroyer, *USS Casin Young* (DD-739), but the damage was too great, and *Young* was forced to sink *Colhoun.*

The following day, ENS Whitacre turned over the money and records to the supply officer of *USS Wayne* for safekeeping and secured a receipt. Whitacre was able to return most of the safe deposits to the owners, and, because he had saved the pay records, he could pay the crew.

After his kamikaze ordeal, Bob Whitacre was assigned stateside duty and returned to civilian life in the accounting profession after the war. He served as commanding officer of three Naval Reserve units and retired in 1984 as a captain. He and his wife Kay live in Lombard, Illinois, where he conducts his own financial consulting business.

The Victorious Conclusion in Sight

By early 1945 Navy strategists concluded that the war could be won in the Pacific during that year. The Bureau of Supplies and Accounts and its sister Navy technical bureaus fine-tuned their organizations and procedures to maximum efficiency in support of the final thrust. A Ships Parts Control Center was established at NSD Mechanicsburg as the Navy supply system's primary inventory control point for nonaviation material. The Radio Supply Annex, established in 1944 at Long Island City, New York, was redesignated the Electronic Supply Annex and given responsibility for controlling stock numbers assigned to electronic repair parts throughout the U.S. Navy.

In 1945 BuSandA authorized installation of electronic accounting machines at NSD Norfolk and NSD Oakland to test the viability of automated data processing in supply applications. A Navy Central Disbursing Office was established, and a resale committee recommended establishment of a central office to assure businesslike and professional aspects of Navy resale activities. The Naval Supply Depot Pearl Harbor and the Naval Supply Annex Stockton, California, were established. A joint Army-Navy Petroleum Purchase Agency commenced operations.

By the spring of 1945 the Naval Supply Depot Pearl Harbor was supplying more than a ton of supplies for each sailor in the Fleet, up from 1,400 pounds in 1941, according to CAPT John Gaffney, supply officer, Fourteenth Naval District. NSD Pearl was issuing a million pounds of perishable goods each day. Balancing the huge flow of materials, including fuel oil, to Hawaii with limited storage space was a continuing challenge.

RADM Brent Young had been at the head of the Supply Corps for more than three years when he relinquished the job to his righthand man, RADM Nick Carter, on 8 March 1945.

LORE OF THE CORPS

Vice Admiral William Joseph Carter, SC, USN

Chief, Bureau of Supplies and Accounts, and Paymaster General, 1945–46
Period of Service: 1917–46

Nick Carter is reported to have been personally recruited by his fellow South Carolinian RADM Sam McGowan during World War I when the two were introduced at the Navy Department by Carter's brother. Carter went on to become the first Supply Corps officer to attain the rank of vice admiral.

William J. Carter was born at Dillon, South Carolina, in April 1893 and was graduated from Wofford College in 1913. He also attended Cornell University. Carter was commissioned assistant paymaster with the rank of ensign in June 1917, two months after the United States entered the war.

During the war he served as assistant supply officer in troop transports, first the *USS Leviathan,* where he was promoted to LTJG in October 1917, and later in *USS Pocahontas,* where he was promoted to lieutenant in July 1918. He returned from sea duty and served as disbursing officer, Office of the Assistant Secretary of the Navy at New York City in 1919 and became assistant supply officer, Boston Navy Yard, from 1920 to 1921. He served a brief tour of duty at the Norfolk Navy Yard, another as senior member, Board of Survey, Appraisal and Sale, Fifth Naval District in 1921, and was officer-in-charge, Commissary Store Philadelphia Navy Yard from 1921 to 1923.

LT Carter returned to sea in May 1923 as supply officer, *USS Capella* (AK-13) and in September 1924 reported to Harvard University, from which he received an M.B.A. in 1926. He went back to Norfolk as supply and accounting officer, Naval Air Station from 1926 to 1928. This was followed by duty in *USS Altair* (AD-11) from 1928 to 1930 before he completed a course at the Philadelphia Textile Institute in June 1932. While attending school at Philadelphia, he was promoted to lieutenant commander.

Carter next had duty at the Naval Supply Depot New York and at the Naval Clothing Depot Brooklyn from 1931 to 1934. He then had a two-year tour as supply officer, *USS California* (BB-44) from 1935 to 1937. Carter reported to the Bureau of Supplies and Accounts in August 1937 and was not to leave BuSandA until he retired nine years later.

His first position in the Bureau was head of the Provisions and Clothing Division, were he served as member of the Permanent Uniform Board and was promoted to commander in 1938. CDR Carter was selected to fill President Roosevelt's request for a unique uniform design for the Civilian Conservation Corps (CCC). He headed BuSandA's Officer Personnel Division from 1939 to 1942, became assistant chief of the Bureau, and was promoted to captain in June 1942. In September of that year, he was promoted to the temporary rank of rear admiral while serving as assistant chief.

In March 1945 he was confirmed as rear admiral and appointed chief. He was awarded the Distinguished Service Medal for duty from June 1942 to the cessation of hostilities. During the war, RADM Carter was present at the invasion of the Marshall Islands to "evaluate at first hand the flow of supplies from advanced bases to beachheads."

Carter was an advocate of planning for a strong postwar Supply Corps. He announced the assignment of 80 Supply Corps officers to the Graduate School of Business at Harvard University in February 1946 to "provide the Corps with a group of trained officers who are experts in the functional fields which were the true specialities of the Supply Corps."

In August of 1946, Carter was advanced to the rank of vice admiral and retired in that rank on October 1, 1946. In retirement, he was director of public relations at the Washington office of Boston Gear Works.

Sources

BuSandA Monthly Newsletter, March 1944, June 1946.

Memorandum from Chief, Bureau of Supplies and Accounts, 1 February 1946. Navy Supply Corps Museum, Athens, Ga.

Official Biography. Naval Supply Systems Command, 2 October 1946.

The End of the War in Europe

President Roosevelt died on 12 April 1945, and a shocked America and the Allies wondered what effect his death would have on the war effort. Roosevelt's vice president, Harry S. Truman, was promptly sworn in as president, and he made it clear that the drive for unconditional surrender of Germany and Japan would go forward as planned.

The final land assault on Nazi Germany continued through the winter months of 1945, and advance elements of the American and Russian armies applied massive pressure on Berlin from both east and west. The Nazis abandoned their dream of world domination and surrendered on May 7, 1945.

With the fighting concluded in Europe, the Allies were free to turn the full brunt of their combined might on Japan. B-29s continued their incessant pounding of Japan as American forces were gearing up for the final assault from the sea.

Back in the United States, scientists were working feverishly on the "ultimate weapon," packing the unimaginable explosive force of nuclear fission into a bomb that could reduce entire cities to rubble. Their super-secret project was unknown to the Pacific planners marshaling resources at new American bases on Okinawa for the planned large-scale, conventional amphibious landings on the Japanese home islands.

The Potsdam Conference

With the war over in Europe, the final Big Three conference was convened at the Berlin suburb of Potsdam from 17 July to 2 August 1945. In December 1943 Premier Joseph Stalin had committed the Soviet Union to declare war on Japan after the defeat of Germany, but when the Nazis capitulated the Soviets reneged.

Nuclear weapons were ready for deployment in August, but Harry Truman wrestled with the decision of whether to authorize their use to shorten the war and save thousands of American lives that would be at risk in a costly amphibious assault on Japan. The Allies gave a final warning, which Japan ignored. President Truman then authorized the first use of atomic weapons. Two nuclear bombs were dropped—one at Hiroshima on 6 August 1945 and a second at Nagasaki on 9 August. Two days after the first bomb was dropped, the Russians declared war on Japan. The day the second bomb was dropped, Soviet troops invaded Manchuria. It was obvious that the Soviet Union fulfilled its bargain only to be in a position to share the spoils of victory.

The Japanese announced unconditional surrender on 14 August. The formal document was signed on 2 September 1945 aboard the battleship *USS Missouri* (BB-63) anchored in Tokyo Bay only a short distance from where Commodore Perry had opened Japan to the Western world 92 years earlier. The most destructive war in history had been brought to a dramatic close.

End of War, Changes in Plans

The end of the war changed a special assignment of one Navy Supply Corps officer on Okinawa. ENS (later CDR) Emil W. (Bill) Wickert had been selected for a unique special mission when a land assault of Japan was still anticipated.

Bill Wickert was a professional baseball player who volunteered for

Navy service in 1942. He was selected for the Supply Corps and commissioned in 1944. ENS Wickert's orders out of NSCS were to report to Western Sea Frontier, San Francisco for further assignment to a merchant ship in the Pacific. He was en route to Pearl Harbor when he learned that the ship had been sunk, so he returned to San Francisco. There, the former professional athlete was assigned as supply and disbursing officer of a newly formed unit that was to deploy to a small Pacific island and assigned both R&R and antichemical warfare roles. The unit, given the secret code name BIVE 65, LION 8, was commanded by a line lieutenant named Caldwell, who was an all-American football player, and it had 20 chief athletic specialists.

Before atomic bombs were dropped on Japan, large numbers of American casualties were anticipated from the impending invasion of Japan. Use of chemical weapons by the Japanese was considered a real possibility. ENS Wickert qualified as the unit's gas officer at the Navy Chemical Warfare Instructors Course at Treasure Island and also went to the Army Chemical Warfare School near Denver.

By the time Wickert completed training and other preparations for his new assignment, the war was over. At this point, the R&R phase of his duty took precedence as hundreds of U.S. Navy combatant ships suddenly no longer had combat missions. ENS Wickert left the San Francisco area by air and the athletic equipment left by ship.

The island of Tsuken Shima off Okinawa, undamaged by war, had been chosen as the site of the base and was ready for fleet ships to send their sailors for R&R. Unfortunately, two typhoons hit the island shortly after the camp began functioning, and all facilities were destroyed. During the first one, ENS Wickert was ferrying supplies in an LCM from Okinawa to the small island when the landing craft took on water and sank. Wickert and his two enlisted assistants were washed ashore and all three survived. The staff survived the second typhoon by taking refuge in caves in the hills. The two officers were promoted on Christmas Day 1945. LTJG Wickert received orders to relieve Caldwell as officer-in-charge, effective 1 January 1946, and he continued to provide R&R services to fleet ships for a month, when he was ordered to Okinawa for transportation home.

Bill Wickert was never officially relieved of his command, but he was released from active duty in February 1946 and returned to baseball. However, an injury he had incurred while undergoing chemical warfare training during the war caused a serious deterioration of his eyesight, and he was moved into a front office job by the New York Yankees. He later moved to Chicago, where he was active in the Supply Corps of the Naval Reserve and retired as a commander in July 1971. His wartime injuries eventually resulted in his being declared legally blind. He and his wife Betty live at Kerrville, Texas.

The Postwar Drawdown

The war ended with such suddenness that it was difficult for logisticians to slow the flow of supplies from the United States to the Pacific. Huge shipments of war materials were still arriving at ports throughout the Pacific weeks after hostilities ceased.

As early as 1943 the Navy had begun to cancel orders for major capital ships because eventual victory was anticipated before they could be completed. The first cancellation had been one of six of the new, larger, Midway-class carriers in January 1943. Three of six Alaska-class battle cruisers were canceled in June 1943, the five battleships of the projected Montana-class were canceled in July, and six Essex-class and two additional Midway-class carriers were canceled in March 1945.

The Supply Corps had grown from 800 to 2,900 USN officers and 14,900 Reserve officers—a total of 17,800—on active duty at the end of the war. A point system was used to determine the order of priority for American military personnel to return home and for Reservists to be released from active duty. Those who had served in combat areas the longest earned the most points and thus went home first. Token forces were left at key points in the Pacific, but most American ships returned to home ports.

As service men and women reached the United States, Reservists were promptly released back to civilian life. Signs reading "Reserves Won the War" began to appear widely, reflecting the fact that 95 percent of America's military personnel in World War II were Reserve citizen sailors and soldiers.

As 1945 drew to a close, the euphoria of total victory, so prevalent in September, was on the wane. The peace so nobly desired and so costly achieved was beginning to appear as distant as it had during the hostilities.

Sources

Sources for material used in this chapter and not cited earlier include:

Miller, Nathan. *The United States Navy: An Illustrated History*. Annapolis: Naval Institute Press, and New York: American Heritage Press, 1977.

Navy Supply Corps Newsletter, February 1970, September 1973.

The World Almanac and Book of Facts. 1981.

Additional sources for material:

The incident concerning LTJG Conrad Bradshaw and the Ledo Road was reported in the *BuSandA Monthly Newsletter,* April 1945. *USS Colhoun*'s saga was reported in "The Pickets Paid Off," *All Hands,* Navy Department, May 1946. Further details of the Pacific experiences of RADM Spiro, CAPT Whitacre, and CDR Wickert were provided over a period of years to the author, a long-time Reserve shipmate of the three.

Third *USS Supply* (AVS-1), 1944-46, was launched as *SS Ward* in 1921, purchased by the Navy, recommissioned as an aviation support ship at Pearl Harbor in 1944, and scrapped in 1946. (*Navy Supply Corps Newsletter*)

RADM John Crumpacker, Chief of BuSandA (fourth from left) and Navy Department officials visit Supply Department, Guantanamo Bay, Cuba, May 1963. (Official U.S. Navy photograph)

From left: CAPT Cliff Messenheimer, Sixth Fleet logistics officer; RADM Jimmy Boundy, Chief of Supply Corps; Deputy Assistant SECDEF C. P. Milne; SECNAV Thomas Gates; and VADM C. R. Brown, COMSIXTHFLT aboard *USS Des Moines* (CA-132), circa 1959. (*Navy Supply Corps Newsletter*)

RADM James Dietz, C.O., Naval Supply Center, Norfolk, presents Assistant SECNAV commendation to CDR Betty Brown, NSC, Director, Comptroller Division, January 1968. Brown was the first woman Supply Corps officer to achieve the rank of captain. (Official U.S. Navy photograph)

The cover of the August 1954 issue of the *Newsletter* features Supply Corps officers, MAAG France, in the shadow of the Eiffel Tower. Left to right: LT Bill Dorion, LTJG Frank Allston (*Newsletter* associate editor), LCDR Bill Gilbert, CDR Dick Cobb, LCDR George Iber, LT Roland Breault, and LT Jackson Schultz. (*Navy Supply Corps Newsletter*)

Shipment of provisions procured under contract from Navy Purchasing Office Los Angeles is inspected before delivery. (*Navy Supply Corps Newsletter*)

Original main entrance to Navy Supply Corps School, Athens, Georgia, as it appeared shortly after opening in 1953. (*Navy Supply Corps Newsletter*)

Coat of arms, Navy Supply Corps. (Navy Supply Corps Association)

Crewman were forced to take meals on deck of *USS E. G. Small* (DD-838) when she struck a North Korean mine in 1951, losing her bow and destroying the galley and mess decks. (Official U.S. Navy photograph by CDR Albert Ristan, SC, USN-Ret.)

"GOSH! --WHAT A SUPPLY OFFICER SHE'D MAKE!"

I STILL DON'T WANT ANY SPAM!!

Eggburt cartoons were originated during World War II to break up solid pages of *BuSandA Newsletter* type when publication of photographs was prohibited for security reasons. (RADM Charles A. Blick, SC, USN-Ret.)

CHAPTER TEN

The Cold War Years

1946–60

The Allies had achieved total victory over the Axis, but all the combatants had suffered tremendous losses in the most bloody of all wars. People throughout the world looked forward to a new period of peace, but there was a threat of a different kind: communism. When World War II ended, the Soviets turned their backs on their wartime allies and remained on occupation duty in the countries of Eastern Europe. The Soviets similarly occupied Korea, north of the 38th parallel, and gave their support to the growing communist movement in China.

The U.S. military responded to the American public's clamor to "bring the boys home." The U.S. Navy launched Operation Magic Carpet and pressed many combatant ships, including aircraft carriers and battleships, into service as temporary troopships. The huge influx of passengers on ships not designed for that purpose presented major berthing and messing problems for Navy supply officers, who were equal to the challenge and "made do." In the seven months from October 1945 through April 1946, the Navy brought more than two million people back to America. Proper manning of the ships was a major challenge to the Navy because the sea service itself was mustering out large numbers of men as a substantial part of the overall demobilization.

Navy leaders were aware of the problems caused by too-rapid drawdowns after previous wars, but their calls for restraint went unheeded. Within a year of the Japanese surrender, 2,000 U.S. Navy ships were decommissioned, and more than 3 million Navy men and women on active duty had declined to about 500,000. Contracts for another 9,800 Navy ships and boats under construction were canceled.

Surplus War Material

When the war ended suddenly, the logistical pipeline was still full, and shipments of material continued to accumulate at U.S. military posts throughout the world, especially at bases in the Pacific. CAPT George Bauernschmidt, Commanding Officer, NSD Guam, decided to take immediate action to return some of his extensive surplus material. He sent a shipload of steel barrels back to the States. When the barrels arrived in CONUS, Bauernschmidt was advised pointedly that he was to make no further shipment of surplus material. Although he received no explanation, he surmised the policy was intended to protect small manufacturers, who had geared up to meet wartime needs and might be harmed financially if the postwar domestic market were flooded with low-priced surplus goods.

The word went out from Washington that there would be no return of surplus material. Recycling was not a national imperative in 1946, and indiscriminate dumping of unreturnable expensive equipment and supplies became routine. Soon, press reports of the wasteful dumping triggered howls of indignation from Congress and the press.

The Armed Services were in a quandary. There was insufficient secure inside storage space in which to move valuable equipment and supplies from temporary outdoor storage. Quick disposal had been ruled out. The rapid demobilization left many bases severely undermanned, and valuable equipment suffered from lack of proper care. The State, War, and Navy departments met and decided to enter into a contract with the Nationalist Chinese to take all surplus property located at U.S. bases in the Pacific, except in the Philippines and Japan and on Truk. Any classified or combat material would first be demilitarized. The contract, effective 1 July 1946 to 30 June 1948, called for the Chinese to pay about 10 cents on the dollar for the purchases.

In 1946 LCDR Tyler R. (Ty) Matthew reported to the staff of Commander Fleet Air Western Pacific, headquartered at NAS Orote, Guam. The new Supply Corps officer was assigned as surplus property disposal officer and liaison officer to the Office of the Foreign Liquidation Commissioner (OFLC).

Matthew received orders, in May 1947, to take a 15-man working party to Iwo Jima in the admiral's personal transport aircraft to correct a situation of costly Navy material exposed to the elements and subject to pilferage. Matthew's team went to the site of a former Navy carrier aircraft service unit (CASU) and found aircraft engines on outdoor service stands, flight jackets, and machine guns deteriorating in the open, and wearable shoes rotting in an open shed, which had lost its roof to a typhoon. Borrowing a bulldozer from the Army and a Hyster lifter from the Air Force, they took two weeks to scrap all combat material and sorted and inventoried the nonmilitary material, which was then stored indoors. On return to Guam, Matthew declared surplus the material placed in secure storage. He was sent back to Iwo Jima in the fall to turn the material over to a Chinese representative.

Matthew resigned from the Navy in 1955, affiliated with the Naval Reserve, and became an aerospace logistician. A widower living at Seattle, he retired as a captain, USNR, in 1978.

Five Peace Treaties

On 15 September 1947, five peace treaties—with Italy, Finland, Bulgaria, Hungary, and Romania—became effective. The treaties gave the Soviet Union the excuse to continue domination over the three Eastern European states. Through efficient espionage, the Soviets stole vast amounts of Western technology and other resources. In a few short years, the Soviets managed to turn a peasant-oriented society into a state-controlled military super-power. Thus, the cold war replaced the hot one concluded in 1945.

These aggressive movements in Europe forced the United States to adopt a foreign policy aimed at blocking further Soviet expansion. The U.S. Navy remained a significantly deployed force despite continuing postwar downsizing by returning to its prewar policy of maintaining a presence on distant stations, notably in the Mediterranean and South China seas, albeit with fewer ships.

This overseas deployment policy brought with it a continued need for extended supply support. The Naval Supply Depot Guam was recommissioned as a naval supply center in 1946. American forces had taken control of the Japanese naval base at Yokosuka when Japan was occupied in August 1945 and established a new command, Commander Fleet Activities, Yokosuka. The new permanent U.S. advance base included an operating supply department to provide forward support for U.S. fleet operations in the Western Pacific.

As the downsizing of the Navy continued in early 1946, certain functions were pulled back from forward areas to the continental United States. The Federal Reserve decided to reduce significantly cash reserves held by the Navy for the account of the Bank of Guam. A young Supply Corps officer drew the assignment to deliver more than $26 million in cash from Guam to San Francisco.

LORE OF THE CORPS

Lieutenant, junior grade, Edwin E. Goddard, SC, USNR

Officer-in-Charge, Central Funding Agency, 1945–46
Period of Service: 1942–46

Ed Goddard was a young businessman in Brooklyn when he was commissioned as a Supply Corps ensign in 1942. He never dreamed the Navy would one day entrust him with transporting $26.5 million more than 6,000 miles across the Pacific.

Goddard was born in Urbana, Ohio, in April 1919, and was graduated from Wittenberg College with a bachelor of arts degree in 1941. He was called up by Selective Service, but he was turned down for medical reasons. New York University offered him a scholarship, and he earned a master's degree in retailing in 1942. Young Goddard then went to work for Namm's Department Store in Brooklyn.

When his medical condition cleared up, Ed Goddard was commissioned as an ensign in the Supply Corps, U.S. Naval Reserve, and ordered to active duty at the Boston Navy Yard. He purchased a uniform at Macy's Department Store and went off to war in November 1943.

He completed the course at Navy Supply Corps School at Harvard University in April 1944 and was ordered to supply and disbursing duty with the Seabees at Eastport, Maine. After a six-month tour, he was sent to the Norfolk Naval Base to await further orders. Two weeks later, he received orders in October 1944 to temporary duty at the Naval Operating Base, Guam. NOB had no billet for him, so he awaited a permanent assignment as the island struggled back to normal following liberation from Japanese occupation. ENS Goddard was given temporary custody of half a million dollars to facilitate reopening of the Bank of Guam. He was never sure why the Navy chose him as custodian of so much money; he had only a year in service, and six months of that had been in school.

The Bank of Guam, nominally a private organization, was to be operated by the Navy for the convenience of the large number of U.S. military personnel on Guam. ENS Goddard took custody of the cash about two weeks before arrival of officials designated to operate the bank. The young Supply Corps officer found that there were no suitable vault or safe facilities available, but the NOB disbursing officer provided a Quonset hut in which to store the money. Goddard set up an armed guard and waited for the bank officers to arrive and "take the cash off my hands." When they did, ENS Goddard was ordered as disbursing officer for a small boat unit where he served for several months and made lieutenant, junior grade, in February 1945.

In early 1945 the Central Funding Agency (CFA) for U.S. services in the Pacific was relocated from Hawaii to Guam. LTJG Goddard was designated as officer-in-charge of CFA, reporting to the supply officer of the Guam Naval Base, and obtained an old communications vault for storage of the funds. The Federal Reserve decided that CFA should be the depository for the Bank of Guam rather then for the bank to remit its excess cash to the Federal Reserve Bank in Hawaii or San Francisco. Suddenly, LTJG Goddard found himself designated as permanent rather than temporary custodian of large amounts of bank cash in addition to the CFA funds.

Bank deposits exceeded $500,000 each month, but the Bank of Guam required only $200,000 to $300,000 for its monthly cash flow. After using necessary operating capital for expenses and required reserves, the bank transferred substantial amounts of cash to Goddard weekly. "Being good bankers, they turned over all their mutilated, mildewed and stained money to me to account for," Goddard remembers. The amount of cash in Goddard's Quonset hut grew rapidly, and at one time he had in his custody more than $35 million in U.S. currency and coin.

In May 1946 Goddard was ordered to transfer the money then in his custody—less that needed to continue CFA funding—to the Federal Reserve Bank in San Francisco. At that point, the cash on hand totaled more than $31 million. Holding back $5 million for CFA purposes, LTJG Goddard supervised the loading of $26,526,400 in 642 packages and pouches of currency and 146 cartons of coin for shipment.

The young Supply Corps officer shouldered great responsibility as depository for the Bank of Guam, but that was a "piece of cake" compared to what was to follow. The weight of the currency and coin to be shipped was nearly 11 tons, according to Goddard. The first task in carrying out his orders for transfer of the treasure was to arrange transportation. The NOB Supply Department trucks could not handle the sheer weight of so much money. Ever the enterprising Supply Corps officer, Goddard obtained a lowboy trailer from his Seabee friends for the transfer from the Quonset vault under guard to dockside for loading aboard the transport *USS General William Mitchell* (AP-114).

LTJG Goddard secured use of cells in the ship's brig on the upper deck for safe storage of the money during the voyage to San Francisco. Once the cash hoard was in the brig, crew members welded iron straps across the entrance. A problem arose when the weight of the money caused a pronounced list, but that was corrected by shifting ballast to restore *Mitchell*'s seaworthiness.

Goddard turned over duties at the Central Finance Agency to his assistant, Ensign Larry Harrison, and accompanied the money to San Francisco. During a largely uneventful ocean trip, Goddard learned that *Mitchell* would be anchored in San Francisco Bay and the money would be transferred ashore in small boats. When he informed the skipper that such a transfer could only be made if each of the hundreds of money pouches were attached to a separate buoy in the event of being dropped into the water, the captain quickly initiated message traffic which resulted in pier space at San Francisco being assigned to the transport.

Mitchell arrived in San Francisco on Primary Election Day, a public holiday in California, but the Federal Reserve Bank remained open to receive the unusually large deposit. Bank officials were unable to locate sufficient armored cars to transport all that money from pier to bank, so they rented a large semitrailer from a moving company for the job.

LTJG Goddard remained responsible for the huge money shipment until it was officially counted and accepted by the Federal Reserve Bank. He "rode shotgun" in the van with his .45-caliber service automatic at the ready. The van had no windows, so Goddard could see no other security for the movement of his valuable cargo. Federal Reserve officials advised him only after he arrived at the bank that a plainclothes officer had been on every street corner during the 12-block journey.

Goddard describes the situation when he arrived at the Federal Reserve Bank with all that money: "It was nerve-racking. I always wondered if it would all balance out with what was supposed to be there. I knew what was going to happen when they verified this. There had to be errors and I told them that if it amounted to $50 or less, send me the wrappers that were incorrect and I would remit anything up to $50. If over $50, I would come back on active duty and stand a board of inquiry."

LTJG Goddard completed transfer of the money to the Federal Reserve on 4 June 1946. He was detached from active duty and returned home. He received a telegram from the Federal Reserve Bank of San Francisco 17 days later that read, "Piece verification of coin and currency deposit made by you June 4 completed today and deposit contained a net shortage of $12.23. To avoid any possible criticism by delaying credit for full amount to Treasurer of the United States, please forward by airmail remittance for $12.23 made payable this bank."

Goddard promptly forwarded a check for the requested amount to San Francisco and breathed a sigh of relief. The 26-year-old Goddard resumed his retailing career in New York City, followed by 30 years as personnel director at Penn Traffic Company in Johnstown, Pennsylvania, and 7 years in county services for youth and the aging before retiring in 1984.

Ed Goddard credits his Navy service as a factor in his learning responsibility and truthfulness for his success in the business world. "It was marvelous for future development, but I wouldn't have wanted to go through it again. The Navy experience did much to enable me to accept some major responsibilities in the business in the business world—early on."

Sources

Correspondence and notes provided by LTJG Edwin E. Goddard, January, February, May 1993.

"Other People's Money." *The Tribune-Democrat* [Johnstown, Pa.], 16 January 1993.

"War and Remembrance." *Modern Maturity,* December 1992-January 1993.

Postwar Reorganization

The Navy Supply Corps School, which had turned out thousands of new supply officers, most of them Reservists, during its wartime domicile at Harvard, Radcliff, Wellesley, and Babson Institute, was moved from the Boston area to Bayonne, New Jersey, as a tenant of the Naval Supply Depot in July 1946. Most of the Reserve Supply Corps officers trained during the war began to return to civilian status in late 1945. Their expertise would be a valuable asset to the United States in the event of another war. To assure continued updating of this cadre in current supply practices, BuSandA developed the Naval Reserve Supply Corps Program, an all-volunteer force to be called upon as needed. Before year-end in 1946, the chief of naval personnel authorized commissioning of the Supply Corps component of the Naval Reserve.

With the redefinition of logistics missions, the Naval Supply Depot New Orleans and the Electronic Supply Annex were decommissioned in 1946. Responsibility for ship's stores was transferred from BuPers to BuSandA, which established a Ship's Store Office at Brooklyn in April 1946 to coordinate worldwide operation of ship's stores ashore.

The outstanding record of support compiled by the Submarine Supply Center at Pearl Harbor during World War II led BuSandA to separate the control of submarine parts from surface ship parts. The Submarine Supply Office was established at the Naval Base, Philadelphia, in September.

In the BuSandA fiscal year 1946 annual report to the secretary of the Navy, Assistant Chief RADM Walter A. Buck reported that the year was marked by cutbacks occasioned by the end of the war. Many wartime functions were closed down. As a result, Buck reported, BuSandA turned to other functions as a result of demobilization, such as contract terminations, property disposal, and a return to peacetime accounting. The report indicated that the Bureau immediately canceled $253.6 million of contracts for general stock upon the termination of hostilities. On 1 October 1946, RADM Buck relieved VADM William J. Carter as chief of the Bureau of Supplies and Accounts and paymaster general.

LORE OF THE CORPS

Rear Admiral Walter Albert Buck, SC, USN

Chief, Bureau of Supplies and Accounts, and Paymaster General, 1946–48
Period of Service: 1917–48

Walter Buck was an electrical engineer by training. He entered the Navy Supply Corps during World War I and compiled a distinguished record in World War II.

Buck was born in Oskaloosa, Kansas, in June 1895 and was graduated from Kansas State College of Agriculture and Applied Science with a bachelor of science in electrical engineering in 1913. He received a master of science degree from Kansas State in 1916, and he was commissioned an assistant paymaster with rank of ensign in July 1917. ENS Buck completed Navy Pay Officers School at Washington in September and had temporary duty in the Bureau of Supplies and Accounts. He reported for duty in connection with fitting out of *USS Canandaigua* and served as her supply officer from commissioning in March 1918 until July 1919, operating with the Mine Force in the North Sea. He received temporary promotions to LTJG and lieutenant during the war and permanent commissions as LTJG in March 1920 and lieutenant in July 1920.

From 1920 to 1922, LT Buck served in two destroyers, the old *USS O'Brien* and *USS Satterlee* (DD-190), and at the Naval Training Station, Newport. He was graduated from the Harvard Graduate School of Business Administration with a master's degree in July 1924. He then reported for duty fitting out *USS Marblehead* (CL-12) and served as her supply officer from September 1924 to June 1926. For the next four years he was back in BuSandA and served in the Planning Division. He was promoted to lieutenant commander and returned to sea duty in July 1930 as supply officer of the seaplane tender *USS Wright* (AV-1). He completed the Army Industrial College course in 1933 and remained as an instructor for the next three years. He was assistant supply officer,

Pearl Harbor Navy Yard, from June 1936 to July 1938 and promoted to commander during that time.

CDR Buck was executive officer of the Navy Finance and Supply School at the Philadelphia Navy Yard from August 1938 to February 1941, when he reported as force supply officer, Commander Support Force, U.S. Atlantic Fleet, in the flagship *USS Prairie* (AD-15). He was detached in February 1942, was awarded the Legion of Merit, and reported to the Office of Procurement and Material in the Bureau of Supplies and Accounts and was promoted to captain in June 1942. CAPT Buck next reported as supply officer, Philadelphia Navy Yard, in January 1943 and returned to Washington in May 1944 as director of the Navy Material Redistribution and Disposal Administration and chief of the Property Disposition Branch in the Office of Assistant Secretary of the Navy. He was awarded his second Legion of Merit for that duty and reported again to BuSandA in October 1945. He was appointed assistant chief in February 1946.

He became chief and paymaster general with the rank of rear admiral on 1 October 1946. The Buck administration was marked by the continued demobilization, downsizing of the infrastructure, and disposition of a huge amount of excess war material. He retired from the Navy on 1 March 1948 after 30 years of service.

Walter Buck became president of the Radiomarine Corporation of America, a subsidiary of the Radio Corporation of America (RCA), just days after he left the Navy. He rose rapidly in the RAC hierarchy, becoming operating vice president. He was elected an RCA director in 1949 and vice president, Operating Services on the RCA corporate staff in 1950. He resigned as a director in 1954 and retired from RCA in June 1955.

In addition to two Legion of Merit awards and several other Navy awards, he received the RCA Victor Award of Merit in 1950. He lived at Wynnewood, Bucks County, Pennsylvania, and died on 13 June 1955.

Sources

Annual Report to the Secretary of the Navy. Bureau of Supplies and Accounts, 1946, 1947.

Obituary. *Washington Post and Times-Herald,* 14 June 1955.

Official Biography. Naval Supply Systems Command, 21 April 1948.

The National Security Act

Buoyed by the existence of the atomic bomb and the decisive role it played in shortening the war, Army Air Corps generals and other advocates pushed for a growing air warfare role largely at the expenses of the Navy. General Carl A. Spaatz, architect of the massive bombing of Germany, spoke for air warfare proponents when he asked, "Why should we have a Navy at all?" Fleet Admiral Nimitz and others countered that the Army's challenge was nothing new. They pointed out that critics had written off the Navy when the submarine, torpedo, and airplane had been adapted for military use.

Meanwhile, the Navy's program to develop nuclear-powered ships was gathering momentum. The first application of nuclear power given serious consideration was for submarines, capable of carrying large nuclear-armed weapons that were previously the sole responsibility of the Army Air Corps.

As the verbal battle continued and the National Security Act of 1947 worked its way through Congress, Secretary of the Navy James V. Forrestal navigated a compromise. The compromise gave the Marine Corps statutory protection and the Navy assurance that its land-based antisubmarine warfare capability would not migrate to the planned spinoff of the Air Corps from the Army and the establishment of the U.S. Air Force.

In 1947 Congress enacted the National Security Act, which authorized a new cabinet-level executive organization, the Department of Defense. The act also changed the names of the War and Navy departments to the Department of the Army and the Department of the Navy, respectively. A new uniformed service, the United States Air Force, was authorized, along with a Department of the Air Force, whose secretary enjoyed equal status with the secretaries of the Navy and Army.

The Importance of Logistics

Two significant developments in 1947 highlighted the Navy's formal recognition of the importance of logistics. The first was creation of the Office of Chief of Naval Material, reporting directly to CNO. Second, BuSandA established the Integrated Navy Supply System and committed to a formal, comprehensive plan for supply support of the Fleet. The plan included a new system of procurement of all line items. The system was based upon the principle of decentralized control of policy and operations and incorporated several methods of contracting, including an expanded use of contract negotiations and advertising for bids. The plan, built upon BuSandA's experience in World War II, recognized the importance of technical functions in procurement and the economic feasibility of joint purchasing under specified circumstances.

Supply depots at Norfolk and Oakland were redesignated as naval supply centers on 1 August 1947 in recognition of their primary roles in support of the Atlantic and Pacific Fleets. The supply center concept centralized all aspects of supply support in a single operational unit. A new Naval Supply Depot was established at Great Lakes, Illinois, to support the Naval Training Center and other midwestern Navy facilities as well as an expanded Naval Reserve program.

Four new inventory control points were established in 1947: the General Stores Supply Office at Philadelphia; the Yards and Docks Supply Office at Port Hueneme, California; the Clothing Supply Office at Brooklyn; and the Electronic Supply Office at Great Lakes.

For many years, Navy Central Disbursing offices throughout the country were responsible for disbursing Navy funds at the local level. In keeping with the BuSandA plan to decentralize operations, these disbursing offices were given expanded functions and responsibilities and renamed Navy Regional Accounts offices.

The Department of Defense and Congress conducted studies in 1948 into duplicate functions performed by more than one armed service to determine where coordination of such functions could be more effective and reduce costs. The Armed Forces Procurement Act of 1947 contained provisions governing all purchases and contracts made by the Department of Defense in the procurement of supplies and services and the obligation of appropriated funds.

Supply officers afloat had been providing, maintaining, and stowing provisions afloat and ashore since the turn of the century. In 1948 they assumed from executive officers primary responsibility for food service afloat.

The Supply Corps Officer and Ghandi's Assassin

LCDR Herbert (Tom) Reiner, a former SACO economic intelligence assistant, reported for duty at the U.S. embassy, New Delhi, India, in January 1948. According to a report in the July 1948 issue of the *BuSandA Monthly Newsletter,* he planned to visit one of Mohandas Ghandi's prayer meetings at Birla House on the last day of the month.

LCDR Reiner reported that the Indian nationalist leader arrived in late afternoon with his customary minimum security. As Ghandi passed directly in front of Reiner, a man stepped from the crowd and fired four quick shots. The American officer made no effort to "proffer aid," but moved toward the gunman. "Under the circumstances, it was not difficult and no act of heroism to apprehend this misguided nationalist."

Reiner attempted to seize the man's gun hand, but hit his shoulder instead, spinning the culprit into the hands of members of the Royal Indian Air Force. When he ascertained the assassin could not escape, Reiner withdrew.

The Berlin Blockade and Airlift

At the end of World War II, Germany and the capital city of Berlin, located in the Soviet zone, had been divided into four sectors and occupied by American, British, French, and Soviet troops. The Soviets controlled all land access into the city, including narrow railroad and highway corridors from the three western sectors to Berlin. A four-power agreement guaranteed the Allies free access through the corridors, but from the beginning Soviet guards harassed their former allies, and on 24 June 1948 they blockaded the three corridors. President Harry Truman and British Prime Minister Clement Atlee immediately lodged official protests.

The U.S. Air Force and the Royal Air Force quickly formed the Combined Airlift Task Force (CALTF) to provide an air pipeline to transport food, clothing, fuel, and other essential material to Allied forces and civilian residents of Berlin. The Berlin airlift, dubbed Operation Vittles, was also the only method by which thousands of Allied military personnel, government officials, and German business people could move between West Germany and the western zones of Berlin.

The primary workhorses of the fleet were the four-engine USAF Douglas C-54 Skymaster and the RAF's York and Lancaster bombers, which were converted into cargo planes and flying tankers. They were supplemented by chartered commercial airliners. Although the French were not able to provide significant air transport assets, they provided men and ground equipment at both ends of the airlift.

The U.S. Air Force had committed virtually all its transports to Operation Vittles and could not support the rapidly expanding American bases in Europe over the lengthy North Atlantic run to Germany. Navy Supply Corps officers became involved when the Navy Air Transport Service (NATS), fighting for its life politically, stepped in to establish an extended supply pipeline between NAS Patuxent River, Maryland, and Rhein-Main and Wiesbaden Air Force bases in Germany. The transatlantic flow of material was maintained throughout the Berlin Airlift by R5D aircraft (Navy version of the C-54) from Navy Transport Squadron VR-3.

LCDR (later VADM) George E. (Rhythm) Moore, then serving in a dual capacity in BuSandA and BuAer, was assigned the task of developing Navy supply operations in Germany at whatever facilities the Air Force provided. At Rhein-Main, these facilities were located at the far end of the apron.

Moore's first chore was locating a Supply Corps officer who was familiar with transport spare parts support. The man he chose was LCDR Chuck Ernst, who had served at NATS but was then at the Naval War College. With the concurrence of his bosses in BuSandA and BuAer, Moore convinced Ernst to leave NWC and go to Germany to become Navy liaison officer at headquarters of U.S. Air Force Forces in Europe, located at Wiesbaden.

When Air Force communications channels could not accommodate Navy supply business transactions, Ernst turned to ham radio to get information back to Moore in Washington for relay to ASO and stock points. Business transmissions via ham radio violated regulations of the Federal Communications Commission (FCC), which issued two warnings, but a switch to baseball talk bridged the gap until regular military channels became available to the Navy.

Fuel was supplied to Navy squadrons from the start through Air Force channels and was not a major problem, but tires and landing gear became critical issues. Goodyear Tire & Rubber Company was able to provide the tires, and Ernst and the squadron supply officers found an Air Force interchangeable landing gear strut in long supply in Germany.

While Rhythm Moore was concerned with spare parts in Washington, LTJG (later CAPT) Carl L. Henn, Jr., SC, USN, former supply officer, VR-8, was assigned to the staff, First Airlift Task Force. Henn traveled around Germany to assure the flow of Navy parts to loadout points.

Navy Air and the Berlin Airlift

In October 1948, as winter approached, CALTF realized that additional four-engine transports were needed, especially to handle a large increase in sacked coal. NATS again stepped up to provide the extra assets and assigned two squadrons of its Pacific Division to depart Guam and Honolulu on 27 October 1948 and to deploy to Rhein-Main not later than 15 November. The pressure on the two squadron supply officers, LT Russ Haag, VR-6, and LTJG C. A. Smith, VR-8, was enormous.

According to LTJG Henn, every plane of the two squadrons was loaded to its limit with aircraft spares and personal gear for the trip to Germany. As Navy transports touched down on naval air stations at Alameda, Moffett Field, and Jacksonville, supply departments placed high priority on rendering maximum support. BuSandA and its field activities rushed additional support equipment to Westover AFB for airlift to Wiesbaden.

The first Navy R5D landed at Rhein-Main AFB on the morning of 9 November, nearly a week ahead of schedule, and made its first trip to Berlin that night. As the other transports landed, they, too, were pressed into service within 24 hours of arrival. From its arrival, VR-8 held first place among all American and British squadrons of CALTF in rated efficiency, as measured by the tons carried and trips made. On 16 December 1948, the 18 planes of VR-8 flew a record 51 sorties, only to be topped by VR-6's new record of 60 sorties a few days later. Normally, NATS planes throughout the Navy flew an average of 5 to 6 hours per day, but VR-6 and VR-8 planes averaged between 9 and 13 hours daily. On 30 April 1949, VR-6 planes in Germany averaged 17.6 out of 24 hours in the air. The CALTF operation, with the significant contribution of the two Navy squadrons, flew approximately 250 million ton miles in the 9 months ending 31 March 1949. That exceeded the total freight and express ton miles flown by U.S. domestic commercial airlines during the 20 years from the start of 1928 through 1947.

The Navy Supply Corps learned many vital logistical lessons from participation in Operation Vittles. The two Navy squadrons, operating under Air Force procedures and command, used Air Force supply channels almost exclusively for common items. Not one Navy aircraft was prevented from meeting its schedule for lack of parts during the deployment.

Navy Supply Corps and Army Quartermaster Corps personnel worked together in procuring and transporting the cargo on precise schedules to the Allied airheads. Outstanding Supply Corps support was an important factor in the success of the two Navy squadrons in proving that extensive interservice operations were possible. ENS Dick Rainey, one of the squadron disbursing officers, broke his leg shortly after arriving in Germany but stayed on the job in his hangar office, his leg in a full-length cast. LT Haag and LTJG Smith and the Navy supply system had performed well under conditions never encountered before.

After 17 months of around-the-clock operations, including flights through fog, ice, and snow of the vicious winter of 1948–49, the Soviets finally lifted their blockade on 30 September 1949. The success of the operation and the role of the Bureau of Supplies and Accounts was of great satisfaction to RADM Dorsey Foster, deputy chief since January 1947, who had been closely identified with Navy aviation throughout his career. He relieved RADM Walter A. Buck as chief of the Bureau and paymaster general on 1 March 1948.

LORE OF THE CORPS

Rear Admiral Ewing Dorsey Foster, SC, USN

Chief, Bureau of Supplies and Accounts, and Paymaster General, 1948–49
Period of Service: 1917–50

RADM Dorsey Foster could rightfully be called the "father of naval aviation supply." He was one of the pioneers in the development of naval aviation and served for half of his Navy career in aviation supply billets before becoming chief in 1948. He also was the first Navy Supply Corps officer promoted to the wartime rank of commodore.

Edwin Dorsey Foster was born in Cape May Court House, New Jersey, in February 1896. He attended Princeton University, where he played baseball. He was commissioned an assistant paymaster with rank of ensign in June 1917. Ensign Foster was ordered to duty in Europe in November 1917 with the U.S. Naval Aviation Forces, Paris, and later as supply officer, Naval Air Station, Queenstown, Ireland.

After the war, he served as supply officer of the old cruiser *USS Savannah* from 1919 to 1920 and then returned to naval aviation as supply officer, Naval Air Station, Norfolk, from 1920 to 1924. In 1924 he belatedly received an A.B. degree from Princeton. He served subsequently as cashier, Bank of Samoa; disbursing officer and commissary officer, Tutuila; officer-in-charge, commissary store, San Diego; supply officer, *USS Langley* (CV-1); assistant to the supply officer, Naval Aircraft Factory; assistant supply officer, *USS Ranger* (CV-4); Philadelphia Navy Yard; and a student at the Industrial College of the Armed Forces. He also had assignments in the Bureau of Supplies and Accounts.

LCDR Foster was graduated with an M.B.A. degree from Harvard University with distinction in a class of 600 in 1933. While at Harvard, Foster worked with Clarence Birdseye, the frozen food pioneer, and was responsible for introducing frozen foods in U.S. Navy ships at sea.

LCDR Foster also was concerned with improving the operation of messes aboard ship. In an article in the January 1937 issue of *U.S. Naval Institute Proceedings,* he explained the advantages of the cafeteria system on *Ranger* over the food-carrier (waiter) system afloat. These advantages, according to Foster, included sailors' choice in food selection, a better use of the ration, improved sanitary and hygienic control, reduced food service manpower, and more efficient utilization of messing space. "*Ranger*'s system for a period of over two years' trial has contributed more to crew contentment and morale than could any other system of messing yet devised," he wrote.

In 1938, while on duty as a commander in the BuSandA War Plans Division, he served on a presidential panel to develop a wartime price control system. From BuSanda, Foster returned to sea in 1940 on the staff, Commander Aircraft Patrol Force, U.S. Fleet. When the attack on Pearl Harbor took place, CDR Foster was back in BuSandA as officer-in-charge, Aviation Supply Division, working on plans to build aviation supply annexes at Norfolk and Oakland. He publicly stated that he was one of three officers in BuSandA and BuAer who would have been retired as commanders had hostilities not broken out. Promoted to captain, Dorsey Foster was ordered to duty as aviation supply officer at Philadelphia in December 1942, and to additional duty as supply officer in command, Naval Aviation Supply Depot Philadelphia in June 1943. In October 1944 he was the first Supply Corps officer promoted temporarily to commodore and was promoted to rear admiral in April 1945.

RADM Foster reported that by March 1945 the Aviation Supply Office was managing 400,000 line items, with daily purchases exceeding $1.5 million. When he was relieved in January 1947, he was awarded the Legion of Merit, and Great Britain designated him an Honorary Commander of the Most Excellent Order of the British Empire (Military Division).

RADM Foster reported as deputy and assistant chief of the Bureau of Supplies and Accounts on 21 January 1947 and became chief and paymaster general on 1 March 1948. He was assigned additional duty as Navy member of the Munitions Board Petroleum Committee in June 1949. He was ordered to duty as vice chief of naval material and promoted to vice admiral in October 1949.

Dorsey Foster retired in January 1951 and accepted the post of vice president of planning, RCA Victor Division, Radio Corporation of America at Camden, New Jersey. In 1958 he became vice president in charge of RCA's Electronic Data Processing Division. He retired from RCA in March 1963 and died in June 1979 at the age of 83.

Sources

"Cafeteria Afloat." *U.S. Naval Institute Proceedings,* January 1937.

Navy Supply Corps Newsletter, December 1944, February 1947, March 1948, May 1948, February 1951, August 1979.

Official Biography. Naval Supply Systems Command, n.d.

"Philadelphia Is Hub of Navy's Aviation Supply." *Everybody's Weekly,* 18 March 1945.

LORE OF THE CORPS

Lieutenant Commander George Everett Moore II, SC, USN

Deputy Director, Supply Division, Bureau of Aeronautics, and
Assistant to Director, Aviation Supply Division,
Bureau of Supplies and Accounts, 1947–49
Period of Service: 1939–73

As drummer in the NA-10 midshipman dance band at the Naval Academy, George Moore was called "Rhythm," a name that stuck with him throughout his Navy career. He played a key role in supplying the Navy transport squadrons that participated in the Berlin Airlift and went on to become deputy chief of naval material with the rank of vice admiral.

George E. Moore II was born in Westbrook, Maine, in January 1918. He attended high school at Lebanon, New Hampshire, and entered the Naval Academy in July 1935. He was graduated in June 1939 with a bachelor of science degree and a commission as a line ensign. His first assignment involved gunnery and communications duties in *USS Pennsylvania* (BB-38).

When an eyesight deficiency was detected, he transferred to the Supply Corps and reported to NSCS Harvard University in August 1941. He was promoted to lieutenant, junior grade, and was graduated from NSCS in February 1942. LTJG Moore was ordered to NAS Seattle, where he was assigned storage, procurement, and stock control duties and was promoted to lieutenant. In the summer of 1943, he reported as supply officer, *USS St. Louis* (CL-49), when she returned to Mare Island Navy Yard for repairs to damage suffered in the Battle of Kula Gulf. He was aboard during the Battle of Leyte Gulf, for which *St. Louis* received the Presidential Unit Commendation. He was promoted to lieutenant commander while serving in *St. Louis*.

LCDR Moore was ordered to the Naval Air Development Center Johnsville, Pennsylvania, where he served from March 1945 to November 1947, when he reported to unusual double duty in Washington. He was assigned as deputy director, Supply Division, Bureau of Supplies and Accounts, and as assistant to the director, Aviation Supply Liaison, Bureau of Aeronautics.

During this period, the Navy became deeply involved in the Berlin Airlift. First, a Navy transport squadron, VR-3, based at NAS Patuxent River, Maryland, took over the supply pipeline from the United States to Germany in support of U.S. Air Force transport aircraft deployed for the Berlin airlift. VR-3 became the only air resupply means to support all Air Force personnel and operations in Europe. In November 1948 two other Navy squadrons, VR-6 and VR-8, were ordered to supplement USAF planes when the German winter dictated additional lift requirements.

Supplying Navy personnel and operations involved in supporting the Air Force soon became a problem. LCDR Moore reports the Air Force located the Navy people at a site too far removed from the scene of action, and communications were a problem that Moore and his associates solved by resorting to unauthorized ham radio until official channels became available.

LCDR Moore was given a set of "do anything, go anywhere" orders to set up a special Navy supply system to maintain the flow of material to VR-3, VR-6, and VR-8. Rhythm Moore is proud of the Navy's performance in the Berlin Airlift, which saved thousands of lives and gave Germans confidence that the free world would not abandon the country to Soviet domination and communist rule.

LCDR Moore returned to NAS Seattle in November 1949 as supply and fiscal officer and was subsequently promoted to commander. In February 1952 CDR Moore joined *USS Princeton* (CVS-37) as supply officer and made two deployments to Korean waters. *Princeton* was retained on the line for a record 80 consecutive days, including the final truce negotiation period. Moore wears a second Presidential Unit Commendation ribbon that connotes the award to *Princeton* for "exceptionally meritorious service during operations against aggressor forces in Korea."

In November 1953 he was ordered as supply and accounting officer, Naval Air Material Center Philadelphia, where he served until April 1956. His next duty, in May 1956, was on the staff, Commander Naval Air Force, Pacific Fleet, first as assistant supply officer and later as supply officer and comptroller. He was promoted to captain at AIRPAC.

CAPT Moore attended the Naval War College, Newport, from August 1960 to June 1961. Upon graduation, he reported as operations officer at ASO and in January 1964 moved from Philadelphia over to Mechanicsburg as commanding officer of SPCC. In October 1964 he assumed additional duty as OIC, Maintenance Support Office, Mechanicsburg. He was selected for Flag rank and in February 1966 reported as assistant chief for supply operations, Bureau of Supplies and Accounts, and in May 1966 as Vice Commander Naval Supply Systems Command. When he completed his tour at BuSandA/NAVSUP, RADM Moore was awarded the Legion of Merit, the citation for which reads, in part, "An acknowledged leader in the science of management, he has succeeded in placing the Navy Supply Systems Command in the vanguard of Defense management."

In July 1969 RADM Moore reported as deputy chief of naval material for logistic support and became vice chief of naval material in July 1970. He was promoted to vice admiral in November 1970. His managerial expertise at CNM was recognized upon his retirement in February 1973 with award of the Navy Distinguished Service Medal.

Upon retirement, Rhythm Moore served as president of W. R. Systems, Inc., a small business concern in the logistic service field, and as a consultant in the accounting firm of Cooper & Lybrand. VADM Moore has been active in church work and Virginia politics and is deeply involved in volunteer work. The city of Alexandria recognized him as volunteer of the year for 1982-83. In the early 1980s he was the color man for local cable telecasts of baseball games in Alexandria. The team relocated to another city in 1984, but Moore believes that the move was unrelated to his performance as a broadcaster. Rhythm Moore also is still drumming in a dance band and says he manages "about a gig a week." He and his wife Peggy Jean live in Alexandria.

Sources

Documents supplied by VADM George Everett Moore II, July, August 1994.

Official Biography. Navy Office of Information, March 1973.

"RADM G. E. Moore II, Appointed for VADM Billet." *Navy Supply Corps Newsletter,* December 1970.

The Department of Defense

A variety of interpretations accompanied the National Security Act of 1947. Although a wide body of military opinion held that the act had merely established a small Department of Defense staff, it was clear that other officials conceived of the department as a super-level organization. They believed the act envisioned that DOD was established to assume many of the functions held by the former War and Navy departments. The issue was resolved in 1949 with the passage of the National Security Act Amendments of 1949, which made the secretary of defense the principal assistant to the president on the subject of national defense. The act also downgraded the three service secretaries to sub-cabinet level and changed the DOD concept from coordination to centralization.

The concept of centralization of military functions quickly spread to the area of supply and logistics. Secretary Johnson issued an order to establish a DOD supply system in November 1949. The three services were given additional logistical assignments to furnish supplies to one another in a cross-servicing arrangement to be overseen by the Munitions Board.

The chief of the Bureau of Supplies and Accounts, RADM Dorsey Foster, was appointed Navy member on the Munitions Board Petroleum Committee in June 1949. When RADM Foster was promoted to vice admiral and moved on to become the chief of naval material in March 1949, RADM Charlie Fox succeeded him as chief of BuSandA and paymaster general.

LORE OF THE CORPS

Rear Admiral Charles Welford Fox, SC, USN

Chief, Bureau of Supplies and Accounts, and Paymaster General, 1949–51
Period of Service: 1913–53

Charlie Fox enlisted in the Navy before World War I and rose to the rank of vice admiral during his 40-year career. Along the way, he became an expert in Navy aviation supply, compiled an outstanding record during World War II, became paymaster general, and completed his active service as chief of naval material.

Charlie Fox was born in Baltimore, Maryland, in December 1894. He choose to forego high school and enlisted in the Navy in 1913. He was a yeoman, third class, in *USS Ammen,* a four-piper assigned to the Atlantic Destroyer Flotilla, when it was ordered to duty in Mexican waters. YN3 Fox was one of 20 men selected as part of an *Ammen* landing party to go ashore at Vera Cruz to seize the town when Mexican rebels fired on U.S. sailors and Marines.

Ammen's party was held in reserve while similar parties from other ships captured the city. Charlie Fox's participation in the Mexican incursion was limited to serving on escort and provisioning runs between Mexico and Galveston, Texas.

During the early phase of World War I, Fox had duty at Queenstown, Ireland, where U.S. Navy destroyers were based. In January 1918 he was appointed acting pay clerk and assigned to the U.S. Naval Air Station, Moutchic Lacanau (Gironde), France, and in July was assigned to the Northern Bombing Group, Antigues, Pas de Calais, France.

Fox was commissioned an ensign in the Supply Corps in June 1919 and had subsequent duty at Naval Station, St. Thomas, Virgin Islands, and as secretary to the governor of the Virgin Islands for St. Croix. In 1922 he attended the Navy Supply Corps School at Washington and then reported to the Naval Aircraft Factory at Philadelphia. While at NAF, he had a special assignment as supply officer of the Navy Schneider Cup Seaplane Race at Cowes, England, in 1923.

As a LTJG and later as a lieutenant, Fox served in typical Supply Corps officer assignments afloat and ashore, culminating in his assignment as supply officer, Naval Air Station, Norfolk. LT Fox received national publicity in April 1924 when he led a convoy of Navy trucks on a cross-country journey from San Diego to Norfolk to reestablish the Stores Section of the Aircraft Battle Force at NAS Norfolk.

The unusual trip was conceived when railroad freight space was not available for 10 of 32 small motor trucks used to service the Aircraft Battle Force when it was reassigned from the Pacific Fleet to the Atlantic Fleet. The 22 trucks were sent ahead by rail to be in Norfolk when the planes arrived there. The other 10 trucks remained to service planes at San Diego until the flyaway. The unusual journey took 15½ days and was made without any problems. LT Fox reported that the trucks were underway over the rudimentary paved highways for 118½ hours, averaged 24.9 miles an hour, and consumed 4,420 gallons of gasoline carried in 9 tank trucks.

He returned to sea in *USS San Francisco* (CA-38) and, after a stint at the Mare Island Navy Yard, CDR Fox reported in July 1940 as supply officer, *USS Enterprise* (CV-6). The Presidential Unit Citation was awarded to *Enterprise* for "consistently outstanding performance and distinguished achievement during repeated action against enemy Japanese forces in the Pacific war area, 7 December 1941 to 15 November 1942."

In September 1942 CAPT Fox reported as officer-in-charge, Aviation Supply Division, Bureau of Supplies and Accounts, and went to the Aviation Supply Office at Philadelphia as assistant aviation supply officer in June 1944. At ASO, he collaborated with COMO E. Dorsey Foster to set up a new concept for control of aviation repair parts. Fox was promoted to commodore and ordered as supply officer-in-command, NSD Mechanicsburg, Pennsylvania, in April 1945. He was promoted to rear admiral in January 1946. RADM Fox was awarded the Legion of Merit for his service at ASO and NSD Mechanicsburg.

In March 1948 RADM Fox joined his mentor, RADM Dorsey Foster, at BuSandA as assistant chief of the Bureau. When Foster left to become chief of naval material, Fox succeeded him as chief of BuSandA and paymaster general.

RADM Fox facetiously gave himself the pseudonym "Oyster Fork Charlie" during a congressional inquiry to defuse the issue of the generous oversupply of oyster forks remaining in Navy inventory at the end of World War II. Early in the war, the Navy had purchased the forks for use in officer messes. They turned out to be of such inferior quality that supply officers refused to requisition them, and the resultant oversupply later drew the attention of congressional staff members. Admiral Fox's self-deprecating nickname cleverly eased tensions while exposing the ridiculousness of one subject of the committee devoting so much time to such a minor subject. The members of Congress had a good laugh, and proceedings moved on to more important issues of the day.

Charlie Fox was promoted to vice admiral and became chief of naval material in October 1951, upon retirement of Dorsey Foster. VADM Fox, in his new CNM role, also served as a member of a special board, appointed by CNO, to study all phases of operations in the naval aeronautical organization. He played a key part in the board's findings, which led to a new official Navy policy: the integrated Aeronautical Supply, Maintenance and Material Program.

VADM Fox retired after 40 years of naval service in August 1953 and was elected a vice president of the Slater Division of A.R.A. Services. He died in November 1975.

Sources

"Charles W. Fox, Only Active SC Vice Admiral, Retires 1 Aug." *Navy Supply Corps Newsletter,* August 1953.

"Dog Goned! The Navy's Here on Wheels!" *U.S. Navy Review,* August 1934; reprinted in *Navy Supply Corps Newsletter,* February 1970.

"1914—The Battle of Vera Cruz." *Navy Supply Corps Newsletter,* October 1968.

Obituary. *Navy Supply Corps Newsletter,* December 1975.

Official Biography. Naval Supply Systems Command, n.d.

The Bureau of Supplies and Accounts Reorganization

The Bureau of Supplies and Accounts was reorganized in the spring of 1950 to reflect the changed environment in which the Navy supply system was required to operate. The new BuSandA organization included the Office of the Chief, the operating divisions, and the staff divisions.

Early in 1950 the Naval Supply Center Guam reverted to a naval supply depot, and BuSandA was given responsibility for disposition of all Navy surplus property. A Naval Supply Research and Development Facility was established at the Naval Supply Depot Bayonne, New Jersey, with major emphasis on more efficient uniform materials, improved foul weather gear, and preservation of fresh food.

The Naval Supply Depot San Pedro was moved across the channel onto the Long Beach Naval Station/Shipyard complex and redesignated

NSD Long Beach. The secretary of the Navy approved the charter of the comptroller of the Navy, and accounting responsibilities were transferred from BuSandA to NAVCOMPT. The charter of the Navy Ship's Store Office was broadened to include retail exchanges of the newly established Military Sea Transportation Service (MSTS).

Attack on South Korea

Tensions had been mounting in the divided Korea since the end of World War II. A Russian-backed communist regime ruled in the North, and an American-backed democratic regime held power in the South. On 25 June 1950, North Korean troops poured across the border, threatening to overrun all of the Korean peninsula. The United States quickly presented a resolution before the United Nations Security Council, branding the invasion a breach of international peace and demanding an immediate North Korean withdrawal. The Russians were boycotting the UN and were absent and thus could not veto the resolution, which was adopted. On 27 June, the Security Council directed UN member states to "furnish such assistance as may be necessary to repel the armed attack."

President Harry Truman ordered General Douglas MacArthur, Commander in Chief Far East, to deploy naval and air units to stop the invasion. Truman subsequently authorized use of ground troops. Other nations did likewise, notably Great Britain, Australia, Greece, and Turkey. The president also ordered the Seventh Fleet, with a carrier, a heavy cruiser, an antiaircraft cruiser, and 12 destroyers, to take position in the Formosa Straits to prevent the Korean and Chinese protagonists from widening the conflict. President Truman decreed that the interdiction of the North Koreans was not a war, and it was to be called a "police action." To those involved in the shooting in Korea, it clearly was a war.

The North Korean army was eventually halted outside Pusan, at the south end of the Korean peninsula, and nearly three years of combat ensued. With most North Korean targets beyond the range of Air Force jets based in Japan, air attacks on North Korea and on its army's supply lines were launched from *USS Valley Forge* (CV-45) and the British light carrier *HMS Triumph*. Once again, the versatility of aircraft carriers had vividly contradicted the advocates of land-based air as the sole national defense need.

On 15 September 1950, General MacArthur chose to cut off the North Koreans with a daring Marine amphibious operation at Inchon, on the Yellow Sea about 15 miles southwest of then occupied Seoul. Coordinating their action with the successful Inchon landing, the Eighth Army troops broke out of the Pusan pocket. Facing entrapment by the rapidly advancing Marines and Army troops, the North Koreans beat a hasty retreat back across the 38th parallel. The UN force drove them and their Chinese allies all the way back to the border of China.

Navy Supply Support

Navy forces afloat in the Far East received their support from the Logistics Support Force, Task Force 92, which had developed the capability to replenish a fast carrier task force completely in nine hours. This extended the force's ability to remain on line at maximum sustained efficiency of periods averaging 45 to 55 days.

CDR (later CAPT) William G. Tonner briefed SECNAV Dan A. Kimball, who visited Korea in March 1952. Tonner reported that the Navy's shore facilities in the Far East were restricted to Navy fleet activities at Sasebo and Yokosuka, Japan. The total U.S. Navy personnel strength at the two former Japanese naval bases was about 13,000, while there were about 70,00 afloat in theater. There were no huge stockpiles of material nor well-equipped advance bases, but the Navy was well supplied by using existing stowage facilities in Japan, reliance on MSTS ships for resupply from CONUS, and workable interservice agreements.

Ships under Fire

American and Allied Navy ships dominated the seas around Korea throughout the war, from 1950 through 1954. However, the North Koreans were able to inflict serious damage by firing on ships from shore batteries and by employing large numbers of old, but effective, mines.

USS E. G. Small (DD-838) struck a submerged mine and was severely damaged off Korea in October 1951. Shipboard operations were significantly disrupted when the explosion blew out a section of the port side at the waterline. It destroyed the mess deck, galley, and forward living compartments, along with all of *Small's* refrigerated spaces.

LTJG Albert Ristan, supply officer, and the enlisted members of his department had to improvise with the mess deck, galley, and refrigerated capacity gone. *Small's* cooks prepared meals in the wardroom galley from dry supplies and served them to surviving crew members on deck, who ate wherever they could find space to sit. Without refrigerated space, it was also impossible to care for the remains of the sailors recovered from the blast, requiring their burial at sea.

Small was forced to steam into rough waters which caused a pronounced bounce, lifting her bow out of the waves and putting a severe strain on her already badly damaged hull. The ship eventually lost power and became dead in the water. LTJG Ristan was on deck and took photographs of the bow of the ship beginning to bend backward on every bounce. It eventually broke off completely and floated free. Crew members were able to move off the bow before it broke away. *Small* was ordered immediately to Kure, Japan, the closest port with dry dock facilities but still 215 miles away. An escorting tug took the badly damaged destroyer under tow—stern first—to Kure.

Al Ristan turned his film over to a board of investigation on *Small*'s arrival, and prints made from the film were used in the fact-finding. At Kure a false bow was constructed for *Small*. LTJG Ristan again faced a new range of challenges. The port of Kure was controlled by the Australian Navy, who, Ristan remembers, "couldn't have been more cooperative. We did have plenty of mutton and beef, but it came in bulk and the sides had to be broken down, a task not normally performed by ship's cooks, but they tried."

Fortunately, one of the members of the deck crew had worked in a slaughterhouse, and he was quickly transferred to the S Division and put to work as a butcher. Refrigeration was supplied ashore by the Aussies. "The crew was delighted with steaks for breakfast, lunch, and dinner until the novelty wore off," Ristan recalls.

Two days after arriving at Kure and with repairs to the ship underway, a typhoon struck with winds in excess of 100 miles per hour. All the other ships left port, but the bowless *Small* had to remain. In Al Ristan's words, "We weren't going anywhere in our condition." *Small* escaped further major damage thanks to the efforts of two Japanese tugs that held her fast to the dock.

The bob-nosed destroyer sailed for home via Yokosuka and Pearl Harbor on 14 November. During the Pearl Harbor stopover, the negatives of the photographs that he took as *Small* was losing her bow were returned to LTJG Ristan. *Small*'s unique experience and appearance was featured the week after arrival at Long Beach in *Life* magazine, which used Al Ristan's photos, now labeled "Official U.S. Navy Photograph."

LORE OF THE CORPS

Lieutenant Commander Leo W. Roberts, SC, USN

Supply Officer, Presidential Yacht *USS Williamsburg*, and
Presidential Mess Officer, 1950–52
Period of Service: 1941–62

Leo Roberts served a two-year tour in the presidential yacht *Williamsburg* and at the White House, bringing him into close contact with President Truman and his family.

Roberts was born at St. Albans, West Virginia, in May 1916. He was graduated in 1940 from nearby Fairmont State College with a bachelor of arts degree in physical science and spent a year at Duke University Law School. In June 1941 he was commissioned and ordered to the Navy Supply Corps School at Harvard University. In September ENS Roberts reported to the Philadelphia Navy yard as assistant supply officer.

He received orders in June 1942 to report immediately to BuSandA and then to Key West for duty as supply, commissary, disbursing, and accounting officer at advanced bases outside continental limits of the United States. At Key West, he learned that his duty would be with a new squadron, VS-2D7, being formed to operate from an airfield owned by Pan American Airlines at San Julian, Province of Pinar del Rio, about 90 miles southwest of Havana, Cuba. LTJG Roberts found it necessary to ship everything to the new base by railcar and auto ferry to Havana, thence to the nearest railhead, and by truck over the last five, unpaved miles to San Julian. Officer and enlisted personnel slept on cots in tents, worked and ate in hastily built, thatched-roof temporary buildings, generated their own electric power, and had no plumbing. The squadron flew patrol missions over the waters around Cuba, providing antisubmarine watch over American ships moving through the Gulf of Mexico. Keeping aircraft supplied with fuel, ammunition, and spare parts was especially trying under the primitive conditions at the advance base until a new, modern base was built.

In January 1944 LT Roberts received orders to attend a special course in industrial accounting at the Harvard University Graduate School of Business. At the conclusion of Harvard training, LT Roberts reported to the Accounting Division, Bureau of Supplies and Accounts. He subsequently was assigned as assistant to the staff supply officer, Commandant Seventh Naval District, at Miami, Florida, to prepare detailed property accounting records at installations in the district.

In 1945 LT Roberts reported as supply officer, *USS Starlight* (AP-175), operating in the Pacific Theater, and was promoted to lieutenant commander. When the war ended, the commanding officer froze Roberts in his *Starlight* billet, despite Roberts having sufficient points to come home, until his relief arrived. As a Reserve officer, he had 120 days from his release to apply for a Regular Navy commission, which he did after three months. He was assigned in 1946 as staff supply officer, Chief of Naval Air Training, at NAS Pensacola.

After tours at NAS Norfolk and the Aviation Supply Office, he reported to Stanford University in September 1949 for a special graduate course in personnel administration and training. Shortly before graduation with a master of arts degree in September 1950, LCDR Roberts was advised that he was to be the supply officer, *USS Williamsburg,* President Truman's yacht, with additional duty as presidential mess officer. Leo Roberts skipped the graduation ceremonies and left immediately to drive to Washington.

LCDR Roberts's reporting senior was *Williamsburg*'s captain, but his duties ranged far beyond those of a typical ship's supply officer. He kept his skipper advised of his activities even though shipboard duties took up only about 10 percent of his time. It was not always an easy task, because Bess Truman and RADM Robert Denison, chief naval aide to the president, frequently called him directly with orders or requests for special assignments. Leo Roberts was also one of seven Navy and Marine presidential aides. *Williamsburg,* home-ported at the Naval Gun Factory, Washington, was used frequently to entertain national and international government leaders and other special presidential guests on Potomac River cruises. Three times during Roberts's tour the yacht was sailed to Key West in order to meet the needs of the Trumans, who flew down to the "Little White House" there.

The presidential mess at the White House, conducted by the Army for the benefit of senior staff members, had been a sparse operation in an unappealing basement room. RADM Denison asked LCDR Roberts whether he could set up a Navy-style wardroom mess. "I can indeed," Roberts responded. He could have it operating in three weeks, he said.

Roberts kept his C.O. and X.O., CAPT (later RADM) Jimmy Boundy, Gun Factory supply officer, and RADM Ralph J. (Bear) Arnold, chief, BuSandA, advised of all developments. Arnold told LCDR Roberts that he had the full support of the Bureau and not to worry about expenses, but to do the job well. Leo Roberts had the basement space completely renovated and decorated, acquired new furniture, and installed a complete new stainless steel kitchen. He also obtained Navy-issue kitchen utensils, china service, stemware, linens, and sterling silver table service and service pieces. Finally, he arranged for the Naval Gun Factory to print menus. The new mess, seating 28 people, was an instant hit. The mess members soon voted to expand from 12 to 20 in number, with LCDR Roberts as treasurer. It was still operation in 1994.

LCDR Roberts's White House mess responsibilities included the Shangri-La getaway camp in the Catoctin Mountains northwest of Washington, although the president went there only once during Roberts's tour. During one of the Key West trips, Truman signed a promotion list. He called in LCDR Roberts and said, "I just made you a commander."

CDR Roberts left *Williamsburg* and his White House duties in June 1952 and reported as senior assistant supply officer, Naval Ordnance

Test Station, China Lake, California. In November 1955 he was ordered to duty as supply officer, *USS Randolph* (CVA-15), attached to the Atlantic Fleet. The air group was ashore at NAS Cecil Field, Jacksonville, Florida, while the ship was in dry dock at the Norfolk Naval Shipyard. Roberts sent his aviation supply officer and chief aviation storekeeper on temporary duty to Cecil Field to work with the four squadron material officers in tailoring their aircraft allowance lists against usage data.

One of CDR Robert's assistants in *Randolph* was a young Reserve LTJG whose family was in the hotel business. Leo Roberts decided to unburden him of his duties involving the ship's stores, laundry, tailor, cobbler, and barber shops and assigned him to operate the ship's "hotel"—staterooms, wardroom, and wardroom galley. According to Roberts, LTJG J. Willard Marriott, Jr., did "an outstanding job, in all respects." *Randolph* made two full cruises to the Mediterranean during CDR Roberts's two years aboard and won the prized battle efficiency award among the four carriers rotating on Sixth Fleet duty on both cruises.

CDR Roberts left *Randolph* in November 1957 and reported to BuSandA as director, Household Goods Division, and later as director, Management Control Division. As a captain he reported as a student at the Industrial College of the Armed Forces during the 1960-61 academic year. In the fall of 1961 he was ordered to the Navy Supply Corps School, Bayonne, New Jersey, where he was assistant executive officer and later served as X.O. before retiring from the Navy in May 1962.

In retirement he was employed in public relations with American Telephone and Telegraph Company until he retired again in 1981. He and his wife Beatrice live in Jacksonville, Florida.

Sources

Roberts, CAPT Leo W. *Three Tours of Duty*. N.p., n.d.

Reports and correspondence from, and telephone interviews of, CAPT Leo W. Roberts, 1991–94.

The Disestablished Facilities in the Korean War

In 1951 the conflict in Korea required reversal of some of the downsizing actions taken less than a year before. NSD San Pedro was reactivated in only recently abandoned buildings located adjacent to NSD Long Beach. A Surplus Materials Division was established in BuSandA to ensure maximum utilization of all items excess to requirements of material control points of Army, Navy, Air Force, and other federal agencies. Cross-service disbursing instructions were issued by BuSandA to all

Navy disbursing officers and facilities. BuSandA established the Quicktrans Program and entered into contracts with civilian air freight firms to expedite priority freight that could not be delayed pending available space in military aircraft.

In October 1951 RADM Murrey L. Royar relieved RADM Charles W. Fox as chief, Bureau of Supplies and Accounts and paymaster general.

LORE OF THE CORPS

Rear Admiral Murrey Levering Royar, SC, USN

Chief, Bureau of Supplies and Accounts, and Paymaster General, 1951–54
Period of Service: 1917–56

Murph Royar served in the Supply Corps for 39 years, including two world wars. He went on to become chief of BuSandA and the fifth Supply Corps officer to attain the rank of vice admiral and the third to serve as chief of naval material.

He was born in Los Angeles in November 1894. His father died when he was 12, and young Royar carried newspapers to supplement the family income. To earn money for continuing his education, he worked for a clothing company for two years before entering the University of California in 1914. He worked his way through school by waiting on tables, working as a milk tester, and serving as manager of his fraternity house.

Murph Royar left Cal during his final semester to take a 10-day, 10-part examination for the Navy Pay Corps. Royar worked at the Mare Island Navy Yard while awaiting results of the examination. The foreman took a dim view of "college boys" as workers, assigned young Royar to the toughest job in his domain, chipping rust from ships' hulls, and made life in general miserable for his young charge. Royar was accepted for the Pay Corps and sworn in as assistant paymaster with rank of ensign in June 1917. Despite not having completed the curriculum, the university granted him a bachelor of science degree in absentia in 1918.

He reported in July 1917 to the Bureau of Supplies and Accounts for enrollment as one of 125 new Pay Corps ensigns under instruction in the Navy Pay Officers School at Catholic University, Washington, D.C. Royar's parents had immigrated from Alsace-Lorraine, and that almost cost him a commission. Paymaster General Sam McGowan intervened and told Royar to go out and be a good supply officer.

In October 1917 Murph Royar was ordered to Norfolk for duty in the coal-burning cruiser *USS Columbia,* assigned to North Atlantic convoy duty. When the young ensign checked off the loading of stores prior to sailing, he noted that three sides of beef were missing. The veteran captain soothed his young paymaster's ruffled dignity by predicting, "Those sides of beef will turn up." One evening as *Columbia* zig-zagged its way across the Atlantic, a water tender invited Royar to the engine room he had not seen before. A half-dozen grimy, sweaty, shirtless firemen were enjoying thick, juicy steaks. One of the men placed a raw steak on a coal shovel and pushed it into an open furnace door. LTJG Royar asked where the men obtained the steaks and was offered a hot sample. Murph Royar insisted on knowing its origin first. The firemen showed Royar the remainder of the missing sides of beef, which were buried under the coal pile next to the side of the ship, where the cold water outside the hull kept the meat from spoiling and aged it in the process.

ENS Royar made three convoy trips in *Columbia,* but never set foot in Europe because their escorted charges were turned over about 200 miles from shore to destroyers based in Ireland. He was at sea when the Armistice was signed in November 1918. Young Royar wanted to visit Asia, but *Columbia* was to go to the Caribbean.

Royar convinced his detailer to order him to the cruiser *USS New Orleans* as a replacement for a supply officer who did not want to deploy to the Far East. Young Royar reported to *New Orleans* in January 1919, in time for deployment to the Pacific. After an extensive cruise through the Southwest Pacific, showing the flag from Yokohama to Singapore, *New Orleans* relieved *USS Albany* as station ship at Vladivostok. There, she also provided support for the "Lost Army," composed of detachments of American, British, Japanese, French, Italian, Spanish, and other World War I allies. Their primary mission was to take over responsibility for a huge group of German POWs who had been captured by Czarist Russians and to operate the Trans-Siberian Railroad. An additional assignment was to protect the Germans from being caught in the crossfire between the red Bolsheviks and white Czarist Russians.

One of the first people Murph Royar met upon arrival at Vladivostok was Mabel Lillian McVey, a Canadian from Ontario who served in the U.S. Army Nurse Corps. They met during a dance sponsored by *Albany* on its quarterdeck for the officers of *New Orleans*. Royar was immediately interested in the attractive young woman and proceeded to court her, using the skipper's steam launch to travel back and forth across the harbor to the Army hospital. One night, when he was returning from a visit, a Russian gunboat fired a shot across the bow of the launch. Royar identified himself as *Amerikanski,* and a response came back in pure Brooklynese, "Oh! Well, get the hell out of here."

There was also a group of Czechs at Vladivostok led by General Gaida. The group had marched across Siberia in an attempt to set up an independent republic. According to Royar, the general wanted a copy of the U.S. Constitution in order to draw up a similar one for his republic. Finding a copy of the Constitution on a deployed cruiser was quite a challenge, but ENS Royar located one. It was given to Gaida, who next asked for uniforms. Royar reminded his C.O. that they were not authorized to sell clothing, but agreed to a sale when the captain signed a statement of necessity. All identifying marks were removed from 40 to 50 uniforms that were then sold to the Czechs, who manned a couple of tugs and called them the Czech navy.

The Royar-McVey romance flourished when circumstances brought the two together in the Philippines in May 1920. *New Orleans* went to Olongapo for overhaul, and Mabel McVey was passing through Manila on her way to the States. The dashing paymaster persuaded her to skip the sailing of her ship, arranged a special discharge from the Army Nurse Corps for her, and they were married at Manila.

ENS Royar next reported in February 1921 as accounting officer, U.S. Naval Station, Cavite, in the Philippines, followed by a brief tour as supply officer, Naval Station, Olongapo. In April, still a temporary ensign, he took examinations for LTJG and lieutenant at the same time and later learned that he had made permanent LTJG in June 1920 and lieutenant the following month. In November 1921 he was ordered as supply officer of the repair ship *USS Panther,* scheduled to sail for New York and decommissioning. He was detached at New York in May 1922 and then went to BuSandA to settle accounts.

In September he reported to the Harvard University Graduate School of Business in the second group of Navy Supply Corps officers enrolled in the M.B.A. program, which he completed in June 1924. In July he returned to the Mare Island Navy Yard, Vallejo, California, as assistant accounting officer.

In October 1925 he reported to the hospital ship *USS Relief* (AH-1) as supply officer. The storekeeper in charge of the ship's canteen asked for an insulated ice cream storage cabinet, but such equipment was not authorized and Royar turned down the request. The storekeeper countered with the suggestion that Royar ask the executive officer to approve purchase of the storage cabinet with money from the ship's recreation fund. Royar supported the idea, the X.O. agreed, and several days later, after purchase of the ice cream cabinet, Royar's canteen operator announced, "I got my ice cream." When Royar asked where his ice cream supply was stored, the storekeeper invited him to see for himself. The two went to the ship's refrigerated morgue, which had been unused during a peaceful period. The eight compartments held no bodies, but were packed with five-gallon cans of ice cream. Admiral Royar recalls, "We had plenty of ice cream on that voyage, but I didn't eat any."

He was assistant supply officer, Twelfth Naval District, from 1927 to

1930. In December 1930 he was ordered back to the Mare Island Navy Yard for fitting out of *USS Chicago* (CA-29) and served as her supply officer from commissioning in March 1931 to June 1934. In September 1933 *Chicago* was en route from San Diego to San Francisco through heavy fog for the Navy Day celebration. LCDR Royar was having breakfast when he heard the collision alarm and felt a heavy bump forward. The fog was thick on deck, and he was just in time to see the British freighter *Silver Palm* backing out of *Chicago*'s bow. Two officers died in the collision and *Chicago*'s bow was severely damaged. A board of inquiry found *Chicago* and her officers blameless, but Royar said, "That was the most serious accident that I've been in, and I tell you I've had a lot of respect for fogs since that time."

After a four-year tour in BuSandA, in the Clothing and Stock divisions, CDR Royar returned to sea in June 1938 as supply officer, *USS Saratoga* (CV-3). He was ordered back to Washington in May 1940 as senior assistant to the supply officer, Washington Navy Yard. In May 1942 CAPT Royar again reported to BuSandA as officer-in-charge, Maintenance Division, with additional responsibility for the BuSandA Lend-Lease Program. In February 1944 he was appointed officer-in-charge of the Bureau's Accounting Group. He was appointed general inspector of the Supply Corps in November 1944, requiring inspection of supply activities in the States and overseas. In early 1945 CAPT Royar was appointed senior member of a Navy group sent to reopen the Bank of Guam. "When the Japanese left Guam in July 1944," he said, "they carefully boxed up every record, every voucher, everything that belonged to the Bank and stowed them away, apparently in the belief that they'd still own Guam after the War." The Washington group had anticipated months of work, but all they had to do was to unpack the records, validate their accuracy, and open the doors.

Royar was promoted to rear admiral in April 1945 and reported in February 1948 as supply officer in command, Naval Supply Center Oakland, where he served until September 1951. RADM Royar considered retiring from the Navy to accept one of several civilian offers, but instead became chief of the Bureau of Supplies and Accounts and paymaster general.

RADM Royar put aside his retirement plans and took office in October 1951. He led BuSandA and the Supply Corps through the balance of the Korean War, when the Navy procured much of the same material it had been required to dispose in the aftermath of World War II.

Frank Allston was a Reserve ensign, fresh out of NSCS Bayonne, when he reported to the Bureau of Supplies and Accounts as associate editor of the *Navy Supply Corps Newsletter* during the administration of

RADM Royar in 1953 and 1954. Royar was an impressive, patrician, soft-spoken, and immaculately groomed individual with a wry sense of humor. He frequently wore a white handkerchief in the pocket beneath his ribbons in much the same manner as Sam McGowan had done.

RADM Royar took a fatherly interest in the only ensign in the BuSandA front office and urged him to augment to the Regular Navy. The *Newsletter* assignment involved researching and writing articles about lesser-known Supply Corps billets to assist the Office of Supply Corps Personnel (OP) in generating applications from the field for those billets. The assignment originally was limited to articles on CONUS activities. OP had a great many requests for duty in prestigious European billets, but few for smaller, less visible yet important, posts in that theater.

In 1954 Royar approved a proposal to send the author on month-long temporary duty to visit and write about the duties of Supply Corps officers in both major and minor U.S. Navy posts in England, France, Germany, and Italy. The articles continued to run for several months after the author left active duty in August 1954. No member of the *Newsletter* staff ever had such an editorial assignment before or since.

As chief of BuSandA, RADM Royar led a move to streamline the Navy supply system through a program of stratification and fractionation of line items. He also worked hard to improve esprit de corps and emphasize to Supply Corps officers that it was an honor to serve in such a capacity.

One contentious subject that arose during his tour concerned a proposal to form a single service of supply. Royar was against the concept and recalled that his Royal Navy friends had said, "For God's sake keep out of that. We have it in England and it's the worst thing ever. You never know what you're going to get."

RADM Royar became chief of Naval Material in October 1954, but it was several months before the Senate confirmed him as vice admiral. He was succeeded at BuSandA by his deputy, RADM Ralph J. (Bear) Arnold, to whom Royar had already turned over much of the details of operations in the bureau.

VADM Royar had a relatively quiet tour as chief of naval material and enjoyed working with the heads of all the Navy bureaus. When floods hit New England in the summer of 1955, crippling much of the area's industrial base, VADM Royar conceived a plan for the government to participate in rehabilitation of New England industry, critical to the nation's mobilization readiness potential. This program was later extended to California, Oregon, and Nevada when they, too, were ravaged by floods.

As CNM, VADM Royar exercised authority over almost $450 million worth of Navy contracts, all on a competitive basis. He also urged prime contractors to let subcontracts to firms in distressed labor surplus areas. Murrey Royar served as CNM until February 1956. When he reached 62 years of age in November, he retired. On retirement, he told the *Navy Supply Corps Newsletter*:

> I was as proud of my uniform when a lieutenant, junior grade, as I was when I received my third star. If I were a young man starting out again and afforded the same opportunity to become a Navy officer as I had back in 1917, I wouldn't hesitate a minute.
>
> I learned that the first thing to do is get the facts, make sure they are correct, and then use the common sense God gave me before taking any action. I learned, too, that nothing is impossible as long as nobody cares who gets the credit. I learned that a man needs friends in the Navy to get along the same as he does in civilian life.

VADM Royar was awarded the Legion of Merit for outstanding World War II service, the Military Order of the British Empire (Commander), the Legion of Honor (Officer) from the French government, and the Haakon VII Liberation Medal from the Norwegian government.

Murph Royar accepted an offer by the National Radio Company as the company's representative in Washington. He later agreed to represent the Oakland Chamber of Commerce, City of Oakland, Alameda County, and the Port of Oakland. Royar also played an important role in introducing major league baseball to Northern California's East Bay area, to play in the Oakland-Alameda County Stadium. At the suggestion of a San Francisco acquaintance, Joe Cronin, the American League's president, Royar contacted Charlie Finley, owner of the Kansas City Athletics. Finley was unhappy with Kansas City and told Royar that he might move his team, depending upon the offer. So, Royar wound up, delivered the Oakland pitch, and Finley moved his team west.

By 1971 Murrey Royar was ready to spend time on his farm in West Virginia. He resigned the Oakland-Alameda job, but later agreed to work for the Californians on an as-needed basis. VADM Royar also served on the board of directors of the First National Bank of Arlington, Virginia. He was a resident of Vinson Hall, McLean, Virginia, when he died, at the age of 91, in December 1985.

Sources

Interview of VADM Murrey L. Royar. McLean, Va., 23 November 1985.

News release. RADM Murrey L. Royar, Paymaster General, Bureau of Supplies and Accounts, March 1954

"Obituary—Murrey L. Royar." *Washington Post*, December 1985.

Official Biography. Navy Biographies Section, March 1956.
Oral Autobiography. VADM Murrey L. Royar. U.S. Naval Institute, 1972–73.
"VADM M. L. Royar Retires." *Navy Supply Crops Newsletter,* March, 1956.

LORE OF THE CORPS

Ensign Wayman G. Caliman, Jr.

Officer Student, Navy Supply Corps School, Bayonne, 1952
Period of Service: 1950–79

Wayman G. Caliman served as an enlisted man before becoming the first African American to receive a commission in the Supply Corps of the U.S. Navy. A specialist in resale, he rose to the rank of captain.

He was born in New York City in September 1928, and was graduated from Williams College, Williamstown, Massachusetts in 1947, with a B.A. degree in economics. He received an M.A. in economics from Columbia University in 1948. He then spent two years as a merchandising executive for Macy's in New York City. Caliman enlisted in the Navy in October 1950, and, after recruit training, Seaman Apprentice Caliman attended Storekeeper Class A School at NSCS Bayonne from December 1950 to February 1951, when he reported for duty in *USS Cascade* (AD-16). As a storekeeper, third class, Caliman entered Officer Candidate School, Newport, Rhode Island, in April 1952. He was graduated among the top five in his OCS class and commissioned on 6 June 1952. He reported later that month to NSCS Bayonne, from which he was graduated in November 1952.

ENS Caliman reported for duty as assistant planning officer in the Navy Ship's Store Office, Brooklyn, New York. He was promoted to LTJG in December 1953. LTJG Caliman went back to sea in November 1955 as stores and sales officer in *USS Saratoga* (CVA-60), which became the first aircraft carrier to achieve annual retail sales volume in excess of $2 million. This record led to an article (in which Caliman was featured) on shipboard sales in the July 1957 issue of *Merchandising Age*.

He was promoted to lieutenant in December and reported as navy exchange officer, Military Sea Transportation Service, Pacific Area, at San Francisco. In this billet, he was responsible for retail sales in 60 MSTS ships operating in the Pacific Ocean area. LT Caliman's next duty was at the Naval Supply Depot Yokosuka, Japan, in June 1960, as assistant storage officer and was promoted to lieutenant commander in 1963. LCDR Caliman returned to the United States in July 1963 as supply officer of the staff of Commander Eastern Sea Frontier, New York City, and alternate maintenance and repair fund administrator, Atlantic Reserve Fleet, berthed in the Hudson River north of the city.

Caliman reported as supply officer and comptroller, Naval Air Station, Floyd Bennett Field, New York, in January 1966 and was promoted to commander in July. CDR Caliman became supply officer, *USS Cascade* (AD-16) in September 1967. In August 1969 he was ordered to duty at the Naval Supply Center Oakland, where he served as director, Material Department. CDR Caliman was promoted to captain in July 1972 and reported the following month as Navy exchange officer, Norfolk Naval Base. The Norfolk exchange complex had an annual sales volume of $60 million and employed 1,400 civilians.

CAPT Caliman reported in July 1976 as executive officer, Navy Resale and Services Support Operation, Brooklyn, renamed and expanded from the Navy Ship's Store Office, as it had been known. He served as acting commanding officer for a month in 1978 and retired from the Navy in July 1979.

Wayne Caliman remained in the retail business after his Navy retirement. He accepted employment with the Pathmark Division of Supermarkets General Corporation. He and his wife Shirley lived in Hazlet, New Jersey, until he died in September 1986.

Sources

Official Biography. Navy Resale and Services Support Office, 1978.

"Rear Admiral William J. Ryan Heads NAVRESO." *Navy Supply Corps Newsletter,* November 1978.

"Retirements—CAPT Wayman G. Caliman, Jr." *Navy Supply Corps Newsletter,* October 1979.

The Supply Corps and Nuclear Propulsion

In the years before World War II, the Naval Research Laboratory had studied the potential of nuclear propulsion, but the onset of war delayed further development activities. When hostilities ended, serious discussions about producing an American nuclear-powered naval vessel took place. One of many obstacles to progress in breaching technological barriers was the lack of Navy personnel with nuclear training. The Navy had assigned a small group of officers, including CAPT (later ADM) Hyman G. Rickover, to the government's laboratory at Oak Ridge, Tennessee, to develop the needed expertise.

By 1952 Rickover, who had become director for naval reactors, Atomic Energy Commission, realized that he needed officers with contracting experience in order to complete development of his program. Paymaster General Royar and Hyman Rickover had been good friends, but Rickover did not care for the way NSD Mechanicsburg was being run, especially as it affected control of nuclear submarine spare parts. Royar recalled in his oral autobiography that Rickover would ask for a list of five or six Supply Corps officers and pick one for his operation. The paymaster general insisted that he knew his officers better than Rickover did and would make the selection. Royar took the matter directly to Secretary of the Navy Charles Thomas, who overruled Royar.

CDR (later VADM) Vincent A. Lascara was the first Supply Corps officer chosen for the Navy nuclear program in 1953 when he became staff assistant to Rickover. Lascara was the first director, Nuclear Supply and Comptroller Department. He was later joined by LT Edward (Ren) Renfro, LT Mel Greer, and LT Thomas L. (Tim) Foster.

LORE OF THE CORPS

Lieutenant Commander Vincent Alfred Lascara, SC, USN

Director, Supply and Comptroller Dept., Naval Reactors Branch,
Atomic Energy Commission, 1953–60
Period of Service: 1941–79

Vince Lascara was another line officer who transferred to the Supply Corps and went on to a distinguished naval career. He was the first Supply Corps officer to join Rickover's staff and eventually rose to the rank of vice admiral.

Vincent A. Lascara was born in Norfolk, Virginia, in December 1919. He went on to Belmont Abbey Junior College, Belmont, North Carolina, where he lettered in basketball and baseball. Less than two months after the United States entered World War II, he enlisted in the Naval Reserve. He then attended the College of William and Mary, Williamsburg, Virginia, and was graduated in May 1942 with a bachelor of arts degree in economics and accounting.

He was commissioned an ensign in 1942 and trained in mine warfare and in gunnery. In May 1943 he joined LST-378 in time for the landings at Gela and Licate during the invasion of Sicily, then remained on Sicily from June 1943 to July 1944.

LTJG Lascara reported to the staff, Commander Naval Advanced Bases, U.S. Eighth Fleet in July and to the Naval Detachment, Marseille, France, and participated in the landings in Southern France before becoming communications watch officer on the staff of Commander Eighth Fleet at Naples, Italy.

He returned to his native Norfolk in December 1944 as communication and personnel officer in the Port Director's Office, Norfolk Naval Base. In October 1946 he transferred as a lieutenant to the Supply Corps Reserve, reported to Navy Supply Corps School, Bayonne, New Jersey, and was augmented in the U.S. Navy in November. From NSCS, he went back to sea as supply officer, *USS Olympus* (AGC-8) in April 1947. He reported to the Naval Academy in October 1948 as an instructor in navigation and antisubmarine warfare, with additional duty as assistant varsity baseball coach.

In August 1949 LT Lascara was ordered to duty under instruction at Stanford University, Palo Alto, California, and he received an M.B.A. degree in June 1951. He reported as planning officer of the Navy Ship's Store Office, Brooklyn, from June to December 1951, when he became administrative officer on the staff of the inspector general, Supply Corps, Pacific Coast. He was promoted to lieutenant commander in February 1952.

In March 1953 he was selected for a pioneering role in the Navy nuclear program. In his position as head of supply and comptroller functions in the Naval Reactors Branch, he was the principal business advisor to Hyman Rickover. Lascara was responsible for establishment of criteria for all Atomic Energy Commission and Navy supply, budgetary, fiscal, contractual, and logistics planning for design, development, construction, and operation of naval nuclear power plants. Vince Lascara was promoted to commander in February 1957, but retained his key position in the Rickover organization until relieved in September 1960 by CDR (later RADM) Kenneth L. Woodfin. CDR Lascara was awarded the Navy Commendation Medal for outstanding performance in the Navy Nuclear Propulsion Program.

Lascara reported as prospective supply officer of the first U.S. Navy nuclear-powered surface ship, *USS Enterprise* (CVN-65), in February 1961 at Newport News, Virginia. In September of that year, he was also designated staff supply officer, Commander Carrier Division 2. He was promoted to captain in July 1963.

In May 1964 CAPT Lascara returned once again to Norfolk, to head the Inventory Control Department, NSC Norfolk. He was awarded a second Navy Commendation Medal for meritorious service in the implementation of the Uniform Automatic Data Processing System for Navy stock points and for markedly improving NSC Norfolk's overall material availability.

CAPT Lascara then spent a year at the Naval War College, and in June 1967 he reported as executive officer, Navy Ships Parts Control Center

Mechanicsburg, Pennsylvania. In September 1968 he became commanding officer, Fleet Material Support Office at Mechanicsburg.

Less than a year later, in July 1969, he was ordered to duty as assistant comptroller, Financial Management Services, with additional duty as commanding officer, Naval Accounting and Finance Center Washington. He was promoted to rear admiral in July 1970, and in 1973 he went back to NSC Norfolk as commanding officer.

Three years later, in June 1976, he was promoted to vice admiral and named vice chief of naval material. VADM Lascara retired on 1 July 1979 to his native Norfolk, where he remained active in local business and civic affairs until his death in February 1994.

Sources

Official Biography. Navy Office of Information, 12 July 1973.
Rockwell, Theodore. *The Rickover Effect*. Annapolis: Naval Institute Press, 1992.
Transcript of Naval Service. Bureau of Naval Personnel, July 1978, as annotated June 1994.

Managing the System

In 1952 four new inventory control points were established by BuSandA: Provisions Supply Office, Medical and Dental Supply Office, Fuel Supply Office, and Ordnance Supply Office.

The continuing emphasis on improving messing in the Navy led to two changes—one semantic and the other practical. The name for feeding Navy personnel became *food service,* and the first Field Food Service Team began operating at NSC Norfolk to provide on-site assistance to food service officers in the fleet and ashore.

Warrant Payclerk Van Watts, assistant supply officer, *USS Sierra* (AD-18), is credited with instituting a pilot program in 1952 to recognize his ship's outstanding sailors. Under the Watts program, sailors were selected by their peers on a weekly, monthly, quarterly, and annual basis and honored by the commanding officer. This idea grew into a fleetwide program that is still conducted. Watts also instigated a series of Navy-oriented radio and television programs in the Tidewater area of Virginia during the 1950s. He retired from the Navy in 1962 and operates the Van Watts Studio in North Hollywood, California.

A Permanent Home for Navy Supply Corps School

The Navy Supply Corps School led a nomadic existence from the founding, in 1905, of its original predecessor, the Navy Pay Officers School in the Bureau of Supplies and Accounts at Washington. In the interim, the school had been disestablished and reestablished several times and located at Annapolis, Philadelphia, Boston, and finally at Bayonne, New Jersey. In 1953 NSCS finally found a permanent home and left Bayonne. Following extensive study, the site of the Old Georgia Normal School at Athens, Georgia, was selected, and the Navy purchased the property. The newly renovated facility was commissioned on 15 January 1954 and has been the site of Navy supply, fiscal, and logistical training ever since.

Also in 1953, the Ships Parts Control Center was established as a separate entity from NSD Mechanicsburg. The Naval Clothing Factory, Brooklyn, was disestablished, and contractor audit functions were transferred from BuSandA to the Office of the Comptroller of the Navy.

Finally, after more than three years of warfare, a truce was signed on 27 July 1953 to end the Korean War. BuSandA continued to apply its expertise in electronic data processing to areas other than strictly accounting functions, and in 1954 an EDP system for processing logistical data was installed at the Aviation Supply Office. Meanwhile, the Cost Inspection Service was transferred from BuSandA to NAVCOMPT. RADM Bear Arnold, deputy and assistant chief, BuSandA, was selected to relieve RADM Murph Royar.

LORE OF THE CORPS

Rear Admiral Ralph Judd Arnold, SC, USN

Chief, Bureau of Supplies and Accounts, and Paymaster General, 1954–58
Period of Service: 1923–60

Rear Admiral Arnold commanded a seaplane tender as a line officer, transferred to the Supply Corps, and won the Navy Cross for heroic service in World War II. He subsequently advanced to Flag rank and presided over the Bureau of Supplies and Accounts for more than four years.

Ralph Arnold was born in Garden Grove, Iowa, on 6 July 1902, and entered the U.S. Naval Academy in 1919. According to Alice Arnold, his widow, he had been of slight build, and at the Academy ate everything put on the table to increase his weight. The resultant fattening of his cheeks caused his midshipmen peers to nickname him "Bruno," "Honey Bear," and—the name that stuck throughout his Navy career—"Bear."

Upon graduation from the Academy in 1923, he was commissioned an ensign in the line and reported to *USS California* (BB-44). He then was on the staff of Commander Battle Fleet. In 1925 he was ordered for flight training at the Naval Air Station, Pensacola, Florida. He was disqualified for flight duty by a deficiency in his eyesight, but ENS Arnold was commended for his work in cryptography during fleet maneuvers in 1925. He served in *USS Brazos* (AO-4) from 1926 to 1927. In September 1927 he reported to Quincy, Massachusetts, for fitting out of *USS Lexington* (CV-2) and, upon commissioning in December, became a member of the ship's company.

In May 1930 he returned to Pensacola for six-month's instruction and was promoted to lieutenant, junior grade, in 1931. He remained at NAS Pensacola until April 1932, when he was sent to Pearl Harbor for duty in connection with the fitting out of the seaplane tender *USS Lapwing* (AVP-1) and assumed command when she was commissioned.

LT Arnold was detached from command in July 1935 and transferred to the Supply Corps in September. He was promoted to passed assistant paymaster with rank of lieutenant and entered Navy Finance and Supply School. In May 1936 Arnold was ordered to duty as assistant to the supply officer, Naval Aircraft Factory, Navy Yard, Philadelphia. Six months later, he was transferred to duty in the same capacity at the Naval Air Station, San Diego, California.

His next duty, in October 1937, was as supply officer of *USS Canopus* (AS-9) on the Asiatic Station at Manila. He was promoted to lieutenant commander in June 1938 and reported as assistant to the supply officer, Naval Air Station, Norfolk, in November 1939, where he was serving when the Japanese attacked Pearl Harbor in December 1941.

LCDR Arnold itched to leave shore duty and get into action, and his opportunity soon sailed into Norfolk. *USS Yorktown* (CV-5) had been called in the fall of 1941 from the Pacific Fleet to reinforce the Atlantic Fleet's defenses against the German U-boat menace. When *Yorktown* put into Norfolk, Arnold learned that he and her supply officer, LCDR Sterling Yates III, were both scheduled for rotation in six months. The carrier was en route back to the Pacific, so LCDR Arnold sent a dispatch to BuSandA requesting and receiving verbal orders to relieve Yates. Arnold and the carrier sailed off to their destiny shortly thereafter, and in early January 1942 her new supply officer was promoted to commander.

Yorktown reached the South Pacific in early 1942 to bolster thin American forces valiantly attempting to halt the Japanese advance. She suffered extensive damage in the Battle of the Coral Sea and was ordered to Pearl harbor for repairs. The shipyard work, expected to take weeks, was accomplished overnight, and *Yorktown* was quickly dispatched to participate in the defense of Midway Island. On 4 June 1942, *Yorktown*'s planes attacked and extensively damaged the Japanese invasion fleet, but Japanese bombs and torpedoes wounded the ship mortally. When the order to abandon ship was given, CDR Arnold slid over the side, keeping his shoes on to protect his feet. With his cap and glasses intact, Bear Arnold and other survivors were taken aboard *USS Hammann* (DD-412).

The destroyer was ordered to search for remaining Japanese forces the following day, but on 6 June returned to *Yorktown,* which was dead in the water, and a salvage party was put aboard. Arnold volunteered to go aboard to assist in recovering bodies, attempt to get a boiler on line to restore power, and prepare hot food for members of the salvage party. A powerful ocean tug had been dispatched to take *Yorktown* in tow back to Pearl Harbor for repairs.

While deep in the interior of the powerless ship with only battle lanterns for lighting, Bear Arnold had just located two gasoline stoves. He was about to move them up to the hangar deck to set up a temporary messing facility when two more torpedoes slammed into *Yorktown*. The explosions knocked him against a ladder and also caused him to lose the cap he had worn while swimming to safety two days before. He made his way up on deck and once again abandoned his ship. A third torpedo had struck *Hammann,* which was alongside the doomed carrier. The destroyer sank almost immediately, but other destroyers picked up survivors of both ships.

CDR Arnold received the Navy Cross for extraordinary heroism in preparation for action on 4 June and for the salvage attempt of 6 June. He was ordered to duty as supply and accounting officer, Naval Air Station, Seattle, in July, where he served for a year. He was promoted to captain in May 1943 and had a year of duty on the staff of Commander Fleet Air, South Pacific, located at Espiritu Santo in the New Hebrides Islands. He later served on the staff of Commander Aircraft, South Pacific Air Force until October 1944. He received the Bronze Star for meritorious service in offensive aerial operations against the Japanese in the Solomon Islands and Bismarck Archipelago campaigns.

CAPT Arnold reported as supply and accounting officer, Naval Air Training Base, Pensacola, in November 1944. He was assigned in October 1945 to the Office of the Secretary of the Navy, and from January to December 1946 had additional duty as Navy member of the Army and Navy Munitions Board. He reported as officer-in-charge of the Stock Office at the Naval Gun Factory in January 1947.

In October 1948 he became assistant chief for material and supply, Bureau of Supplies and Accounts, and was promoted to Flag rank in

August 1949. RADM Arnold reported as aviation supply officer and commanding officer, Naval Aviation Supply Depot Philadelphia in April 1951. He assumed duty briefly as vice chief of naval material in March 1954, and in May returned to Bureau of Supplies and Accounts as deputy and assistant chief. In October 1954 he relieved RADM Murrey Royar as chief of BuSandA. One of the major initiatives of RADM Arnold's tour as chief was adoption of the Ney Memorial Food Service Awards Program, created to encourage improvements in the food service field afloat and ashore through competition.

When he was relieved by RADM James W. Boundy in October 1958, he reported as commanding officer, Naval Supply Center Oakland, California. RADM Arnold retired on 1 July 1960 and worked briefly for Beckman Instruments and Lockheed Corporation. After retiring from the business world, he was active with the Children's Home Society in San Jose, California, near Los Altos, where he and Alice lived in retirement. He died on 1 July 1985 at the age of 83.

Sources

Arnold, CDR Ralph J. *The Last Sixty Hours of the Yorktown*. N.p., n.d.

Biography of Present Commanding Officer. Naval Supply Center Oakland, 1958, with telephone comments by Alice Arnold to the author, June 1994.

Obituary. *Navy Supply Corps Newsletter*, September-October 1985.

Nuclear Power at Sea

The event that propelled the U.S. Navy's nuclear propulsion program into national headlines was the maiden voyage in January 1955 of *USS Nautilus* (SSN-571). In true naval tradition, her skipper, CDR Eugene P. Wilkinson, sent a succinct message: "underway on nuclear power."

Having proved to a doubting world that the power of the atom could be harnessed for something other than bombs, Rickover's team was granted additional funds to expand the program. LT (later RADM) Edward E. Renfro, serving in the BuSandA Purchasing Division, was selected for a key role in the program in March 1955. He was followed by LCDR (later RADM) Kenneth L. Woodfin in the fall of 1957, and subsequently by LTs Mel C. Greer and Thomas L. (Tim) Foster. Renfro went to Schenectady, New York, as contracting officer at a General Electric plant, and Woodfin went first to the Bureau of Ships and later to Pittsburgh, Pennsylvania, as contacting officer at a Westinghouse facility.

LORE OF THE CORPS

Lieutenant Edward Eugene Renfro, SC, USN

Navy/AEC Contracting Officer, Schenectady, New York, 1955–61
Period of Service: 1943–75

Ren Renfro was an ensign when the Navy selected him for the M.B.A. program at the Graduate School of Business, Harvard University. He was an early Supply Corps participant in the U.S. Navy nuclear propulsion program and later rose to Flag rank.

Edward E. Renfro was born in Portland, Oregon, in 1925, and tried to enlist in the Navy the day after the Japanese attack on Pearl Harbor but was turned down because he was only 16. He entered the University of Portland while working full time. When he reached 17, he joined the Navy, and in March 1943 he entered the V-12 program, in which he spent two years, the first at Carroll College, Helena, Montana, and the second at the University of Washington, Seattle.

In October 1944 he was ordered to the Naval Amphibious Training Center at Port Washington, Long Island, New York, to be screened for further assignment. Young Renfro had been taking business courses in college and so was selected for the Supply Corps. He was sent to NSCS Harvard as a midshipman. In March 1945 he was commissioned an ensign in the Supply Corps, U. S. Naval Reserve, but remained at Harvard for another six months to complete the school year.

ENS Renfro reported to *USS Rendova* (CVE-114) as assistant supply officer in October 1945. With World War II over, Ren Renfro was contemplating leaving the Navy and had applied for admission to Harvard to complete requirements for an M.B.A. degree on the GI Bill. At the same time, BuSandA was planning to resume the prewar program of sending commanders and senior lieutenant commanders for the two-year course of study at the Harvard Graduate School of Business. The fact that Renfro had already completed a year of the Harvard graduate course led to his selection for the program, even though he was still an ensign. He figured that it would pay him to continue getting a Regular Navy paycheck while attending school rather than to enroll at Harvard as a civilian on a GI Bill shoestring.

From Harvard, ENS Renfro and six other Supply Corps officers went on temporary duty to the Navy Ship's Store Office at Brooklyn and to train for a new ship's stores management program. Under the new management scheme, Renfro and his associates were assigned to major locations to provide on-site assistance to the Supply Corps officers-in-charge, who had replaced line officers at all Navy ship's stores. Ren

Renfro's assignment was at the ship's store, Charleston, with five branches in Georgia, but he spent five months ironing out problems at the ship's store, Naval Hospital, Dublin, Georgia.

The next phase of the ship's store consolidation involved overseas stores, and LTJG Renfro was ordered to the Naval Air Station, Cocosola, Panama. About a year into the tour, he was assigned as commissary store officer. There was a shortage of fresh meat, so Renfro negotiated contracts with local suppliers. To solve the transportation needs, he convinced the commanding officer to permit station pilots to make food runs to Costa Rica rather than just "punch holes in clouds" to maintain flight proficiency.

Success with the meat program led to expansion to include Navy Exchange merchandise. Renfro contracted for textiles from Guatemala and wood products from Haiti. Eventually, he contracted with the Bacardi distillery in Havana to provide rum in 55-gallon drums, which fit into the bomb bay of PBY aircraft and training bomb racks on other aircraft. Such innovative ideas made Ren Renfro a popular individual with military people in Panama.

When the decision was made to set up a ship's store operation in the Military Sea Transportation Service, Renfro and his group started with the MSTS Brooklyn. They wrote the training manual for the MSTS ship's store operations. As the five young Supply Corps officers fanned out across the country to implement of the program in the field, Ren Renfro went to the MSTS office at New Orleans. From there, he went to run the San Francisco MSTS ship's store.

LTJG Renfro reported as supply officer, *USS Magoffin* (APA-199), at Bremerton Naval Shipyard in 1952, just as the ship was preparing to deploy to the Far East. He inherited a troubled department with many problems and was also assigned to straighten out problems with the wardroom mess. He improved food service, mess bills came down, and he became a hero with the other officers. *Magoffin* was involved in landing both Marine and Army troops in Korea, and Renfro was assigned collateral duty as debarkation officer. While in *Magoffin,* he was promoted to lieutenant.

In October 1953 LT Renfro reported to the Bureau of Supplies and Accounts. He was assigned to the Purchasing Branch and placed in charge of improving purchasing methods throughout the Navy. The Imprest Fund Purchasing Procedure grew out of this endeavor. Ren Renfro traveled extensively in setting up these funds at local commands. He and the author played in the outfield of the BuSandA softball team.

He returned from one trip to find a message that Rear Admiral Rickover wanted to see him. Renfro was unaware he was one of 10 Supply

Corps officers chosen to be interviewed for a special assignment in the Navy's nuclear power program. He missed the first scheduled interview because he was out of town. When he returned to Washington, his secretary informed him that he was to be at Rickover's office at 0800 the next morning, a Saturday. No excuses. Period.

Tired from extensive travel, Ren Renfro arose late and went to Rickover's office, where he was interviewed by seven members of Rickover's staff and then by the boss. Neither food facilities nor vending machines were available, and the interviewees were hungry and frustrated as they waited. Renfro, who had missed both breakfast and lunch and had a date that night, finally was ushered into Rickover's office at 1400.

Renfro found the interview challenging and characterized it "as a set of steady arguments with him bringing things up and I responding, and he disagreeing with my response and my disagreement with his disagreement." The 55-minute session ended with Rickover telling Renfro, "Ah hell, Lieutenant, you don't know what you're talking about. Get your ass out of here." Renfro responded, "Admiral, that's fine with me because I don't want anything to do with your damn program." On Monday morning, when LT Renfro told his boss what had happened on Saturday, he was told to forget about it, but he was astounded to learn in the early afternoon that he was to report for duty at Rickover's office at 0800 on Friday.

The job for which LT Renfro was chosen was in Schenectady, New York, where he was officially "double-hatted" in Atomic Energy Commission and Navy roles. He was director of contract administration for the AEC's Schenectady Operation and the Navy Bureau of Ships technical representative at General Electric Company. He was, in effect, a program manager as well as business manager of the Schenectady operation, which had nothing to do with bomb production, but was engaged in developing state-of-the-art nuclear power. Renfro believes that quality assurance, so often attributed to postwar Japanese industry, actually was started by Rickover.

LT Renfro was the only naval officer at the Schenectady Navy office when he reported, but eventually six additional officers—all engineering duty only—were assigned. In this unique position, Ren Renfro had contracting authority for both AEC and Navy funds and was responsible for the proper utilization of the funds. He remembers that his group worked well together and was frequently involved in all technical aspects of development and production of nuclear propulsion equipment.

He also confirms, from personal experience, Rickover's often-reported distrust of bureaucracy. As a result, Rickover set up two channels of business communications to permit flexibility in going around obstacles set up in either the AEC or Navy. Renfro believes that Admiral Rickover respected Supply Corps officers and recognized that they had certain talents and business capabilities that his program needed.

Ren Renfro went into the Rickover program as a lieutenant and came out seven years later as a commander. When he left the Nuclear Propulsion Program in late 1961, he was relieved by LT Mel Greer, whom Rickover transferred from Washington to Schenectady. CDR Renfro went to the Armed Forces Staff College. In early 1962, when American foreign policy shifted focus to Latin America, he was ordered to the U.S. Southern Command headquartered in Panama under the new joint commander, General Andrew Piomiera, U.S. Army. Renfro says Piomiera had characteristics similar to Rickover's and selected him because of the belief that anybody who could succeed under Rickover could do a good job in his command. Renfro was assigned as head of the Applications Division of the Navy Military Assistance Group, working with U.S. embassies in 22 countries in Central and South America, some of which he had worked with in his previous Panama duty.

When a line captain serving as head of the Navy Group died suddenly 18 months into Renfro's two-year tour, GEN Piomiera selected the Supply Corps commander as a replacement. As a result, Renfro's normal rotation date was extended. He accompanied GEN Piomiera to Washington for testimony before Congress and to work with headquarters of the three armed services. Ren Renfro spent four years in Panama.

In the fall of 1965 he was ordered to the Naval War College, Newport, Rhode Island. He and his wife Shirley had looked forward to a career-enhancing Washington tour of duty in 1966, but fate and American commitments in Southeast Asia intervened. NSD Subic Bay was gearing up to provide logistical support for U.S. Navy and Marine involvement in Vietnam. When CAPT (later RADM) Roland Rieve was ordered as C.O. of Subic, he selected CDR Renfro as his executive officer although the two had never met. It became necessary for Renfro to leave the War College early, but he was selected for captain and later was certified as having completed the course.

When CAPT Renfro arrived in mid-1966, NSD Subic was supporting U.S. naval forces operating in the Western Pacific, Navy and Marine forces in Vietnam, and an Australian task force. Renfro recalls that there were always 20 to 30 ships at Subic, and sometimes as many as 100. The huge supply operation also supported NAS Cubi Point, a large naval hospital, and a newly established off-shore patrol boat base. As exec, CAPT Renfro supported the establishment of bases in the I Corps area of Vietnam through the Naval Support Activity, Saigon. The principal focus, however, was with the U.S. Vietnam Command headed by ADM (later CNO) Elmo Zumwalt. On many of his frequent trips to Vietnam Renfro would be invited to stay in Zumwalt's quarters.

While Renfro was at Subic, NSD was awarded a Navy Unit Commendation for support under wartime conditions. Renfro also served as the senior shore patrol officer for the Subic Bay-Olongapo area. There were sometimes as many as 100,000 sailors on the streets or in the business establishments at Olongapo. He terms it "one of the most interesting collateral duties I've ever had in my life."

His next duty was as Commander Defense Contract Administration Service Region, Chicago, with responsibility for administration of defense contracts throughout the DCAS Midwest Region, with sub-offices at Milwaukee, Indianapolis, Fort Wayne, and South Bend. When he reported to DCASR Chicago, the operation was rated Number 11, last as measured by the Defense Logistics Agency. Within a year, DCASR Chicago was first. One day in spring 1971, after traveling around the Indianapolis DCAS District on official visits to a number of contractor plants, he and a DCAS civilian went to the Indianapolis Speedway to watch speed trials. CAPT Renfro was paged over the public address system and took a call from RADM (later VADM) Ken Wheeler, chief of Supply Corps, who informed Renfro that he had been attempting to reach him all day to inform him that he had been selected for Flag rank.

Renfro's next assignment in June 1971 was as deputy commander for supply operations, Naval Supply Systems Command. His major challenge was the introduction of a new, Navy-wide automated material management system, starting with the inventory control points and adding supply centers and depots within one year.

In 1973 RADM Renfro wanted a Navy assignment outside of Washington, but Admiral Rickover intervened and convinced RADM Wheeler to assign him to the Naval Ships Systems Command in the Contract Division. Although Ren Renfro was on the same line on the organization chart as ADM Rickover, there was no question of equality. The relationship with Rickover, recalls Renfro, was reminiscent of his days as a lieutenant. He provided the support Rickover needed when the Navy was undergoing severe shipbuilding problems dating back to the "Whiz Kids," who changed the Navy's traditional successful cooperation with industry to an adversarial fixed-price relationship. When Renfro arrived, claims of nearly $5 billion were outstanding, and construction programs were far behind schedule. Renfro and his division were able to turn the situation around and demonstrate how the Whiz Kid system was clearly not the way to build ships.

After spending two intense years dealing with members of Congress interested in having some of the $6 to 8 billion in shipbuilding contracts spent in their districts, Ren Renfro once again turned to introspection at the age of 49. He felt he was not going to get a major Supply Corps command outside Washington and that Rickover was going to insist that he remain with his program. Renfro also did not want to enter the postretirement employment market at the age of 50. He removed himself as a candidate for selection to rear admiral, upper half, and retired from the Navy in May 1975.

He became a faculty member and director of research at the Georgia Institute of Technology, intending to develop a significant research program to support Georgia Tech's academic program. He purchased a second home at Crystal River, Florida. The Florida Power Company had a nuclear plant nearby, and FPC officials were concerned about the implications of the 1980 accident at the Three Mile River nuclear plant in Pennsylvania. FPC was making many management changes and enticed Renfro away from Georgia Tech in September 1980. He was made director of nuclear operations for FPC, and Ren and Shirley became full-time residents of Crystal River.

He retired from Florida Power in 1991 and the next year became vice president for operations of a Crystal River marina recreation and residential development. He has also been active in civic affairs and remains a member of the board of directors of Georgia Tech.

Source

Interview of RADM Edward D. Renfro. Crystal River, Fla., February 1992.

A Supply Corps Aide to a Line Admiral

LTJG (later RADM) Philip A. (Phil) Whitacre, a native of San Diego and a graduate of San Diego State University and OCS, was another Supply Corps officer who served in an unusual assignment. After his inaugural tour of sea duty in *USS Sperry* (AS-12) from November 1955 to February 1957, he was ordered to the Naval Training Center at his hometown San Diego as assistant commissary officer.

In April 1957 the NTC commander, RADM Ralph C. Lynch, chose the young Supply Corps officer to be his Flag lieutenant and aide. In this position, Whitacre was associated with the guest dignitaries who participated in the weekly NTC recruit graduation reviews. Many three- and four-star Flag and general officers took the reviews, including Admiral Lord Louis Mountbatten, Royal Navy. Phil Whitacre was promoted to lieutenant while at NTC. Senior officers at BuSandA and BuPers questioned why a Supply Corps officer was in that billet, but Lynch kept Whitacre by his side until he retired in June 1959.

In midcareer, while checking his records at BuPers, then LCDR Whitacre found a fitness report that RADM Lynch had written. In what he probably considered a high compliment Lynch wrote, "This officer is too good to be a Supply Corps officer; we should make him a line officer now." Phil Whitacre never fully comprehended the significance of that comment, other than thinking that Lynch must have had a myopic idea of what a Supply Corps officer was and did.

LT Whitacre later managed six Navy exchanges on the Hawaiian islands of Oahu and Kauai. He completed his active duty in May 1961 and went on to a successful career in aerospace management before undertaking a subsequent career in performing arts management. He became one of the nation's foremost experts in this field. Concurrently with his business endeavors, he was active in the Naval Reserve and served as commanding officer of two Supply Corps Reserve units in the Chicago area before attaining Flag rank. As a Flag officer he was program director for Naval Reserve DLA, Navy Regional Contracting Center, and NAVSUP headquarters units. He retired as a rear admiral in May 1992 and lives in West Palm Beach, Florida, where he is executive director of the Palm Beach United Way. He is past president of the Navy Supply Corps Association and a founder and chairman emeritus of the Navy Supply Corps Foundation.

The Supply Corps Officer and Creativity

Supply Corps officers afloat often have to deal with the unusual, sometimes highly unorthodox, ideas of their skippers. In the summer of 1956 ENS (later RADM) Delbert H. (Del) Beumer was confronted by two such ideas within a week.

USS Edmonds (DE-406) left Pearl Harbor for Guam and a routine patrol of the U.S. trust territory of the Marianas Islands. ENS Beumer had reported aboard as supply officer just in time for the deployment, which was expected to be routine, boring, and scheduled to conclude just before Thanksgiving. Almost every crew member drew pay and left it home for support of families in Hawaii. Upon arrival at Guam, the skipper and crew learned *Edmonds* was to be refueled quickly and leave immediately for Yokosuka. The ship was to remain in Japan only four days and then return to Guam—all before the next pay day.

En route to Yokosuka, his skipper directed ENS Beumer to hold a pay day the following morning. The supply officer protested that pay day had just been held a few days before. The captain, however, was more interested in crew morale than in Navy pay regulations, which restrict the number of pay days allowed monthly. Besides, he, too, had only pocket change. Del Beumer held a quick conference with his disbursing clerk, and they came up with a solution that gave crew members money for their brief liberty in Japan.

Having achieved his special pay day, the captain pushed ahead. Why not have the ship's store load up on Japanese merchandise such as Noritake china, Mikimoto pearls, and glass-domed clocks, and the crew could do its Christmas shopping? ENS Beumer was in a quandary. All the regulations prohibited the idea. Many of the desired items were not authorized for the ship's store nor authorized for import into the U.S. in inventory, but the skipper insisted that Beumer find a way for the crew to shop in July for delivery in Hawaii in December. The next dilemma was how much of what would the sailors want to buy from the ship's store.

Beumer and his supply personnel devised a scheme to provide catalogs of available merchandise on the mess decks, and each man was permitted to order merchandise at a cost not to exceed 75 days' pay. The ordered merchandise would be stored onboard for delivery upon arrival back in Hawaii. Supply took orders from nearly 200 men, converted each into summary purchase documents in accordance with ship's store ashore regulations, and convinced Japanese suppliers to deliver onboard by noon the next day.

Del Beumer survived a crisis when two key storekeepers, who had worked long and hard on the ship's store special evolution, overstayed liberty and were delivered dockside by the Shore Patrol barely 15 minutes before *Edmonds* shoved off. *Edmonds*'s ship's store return showed one purchase of material and six payments of an equal amount for each sailor, all paid at sea and duly collected at the payline. The shortages were well within the allowable limits, and the store profit was small but acceptable. Nobody attempted to pilfer the valuable merchandise stored wherever space, most of it unsecure, could be found. The return to Baker Docks at Pearl Harbor was especially happy for crew and loved ones alike.

Del Beumer left the Navy upon completion of his obligated service in 1959 and embarked on a successful career in the securities field. He also had a distinguished career in the Naval Reserve and was promoted to Flag rank in 1982. He was program director for Naval Reserve fuel and transportation units until his retirement in 1989. He is still active in business. He and his wife Marlene live at Los Altos, California.

The Suez Canal and Logistics Problems

In 1956 the Suez crisis required NATO planners to reexamine carefully their petroleum contingency plans. CDR (later CAPT) James J. (Jack) Lynch, a Supply Corps officer assigned to the Joint Petroleum Office, Deputy CINCEUR, in 1955 at Paris, assumed a key role in the NATO petroleum planning process. On one occasion, he and a staff member of the United States Representation to Regional Organizations Overseas (USRO) compared notes on the number of tankers needed to move Middle East oil around the tip of Africa if Nasser shut down the Suez Canal. USRO had concluded that it would take 300 additional T-2 tanker equivalents—600 if the Trans-Arabian Pipeline were also shut down—just to meet civilian requirements in the United States and Europe. There were not that many available tankers in the world. Lynch pointed out to USRO that its calculations completely ignored NATO military needs.

When Israel invaded the Sinai peninsula in October 1956 with British and French support for a drive on the canal, Nasser had ships scuttled over the length of the canal and it was closed for the duration. The in-coming NATO commander, USAF General Lauris Norstad, wanted an immediate assessment of the canal's closing on his forces' ability to fight. It was lunch hour, but CDR Lynch was in his office and was thrown into the breach to brief the four-star NATO commander on the magnitude of the petroleum problem.

President Eisenhower became so upset with events that he issued an executive order withholding all U.S. oil from Europe. The situation became tense there, with a severe oil shortage in the midst of the coldest winter ever recorded. The Joint Petroleum Office (JPO) was called to brief the U.S. ambassador to France, and CDR Lynch was sent to London to gather data from the branch office at CINCNELM headquarters.

Jack Lynch and his associates at JPO soon were involved in determining if U.S. military forces in Europe could rely on European refineries for their petroleum needs. A visit to ESSO (later Exxon) European headquarters in London was most informative. ESSO had attempted just the day before to purchase 33 tankship cargoes and only 3 were offered. On the day of the visit, ESSO was surprised to succeed in purchasing sufficient stocks for their needs when oil hoarders determined that it was time to sell.

While the European commercial petroleum situation was resolved temporarily, the military fuel situation continued to deteriorate. NATO military commanders, with a wary eye on the Soviet crackdown on rebellious Hungary, were essentially cut off. Turkey and Greece were down to 45 minutes of jet fuel. Italy was only slightly better off.

Eisenhower was finally persuaded to restore the flow of petroleum from the United States. The Suez Canal remained closed, but war in Europe was averted. Ship salvagers made millions, and oil companies quickly found it economical to build huge tankers to move Middle East oil around Africa. CDR Lynch was awarded the Commendation Medal for his NATO service.

In 1957 Lynch was ordered to duty as director of planning, Military Petroleum Supply Agency at Washington. He played a key role in supplying special support to the U.S. Air Force in the Mediterranean during the Lebanon crisis in 1958, for which he received a Letter of Commendation. The experience of petroleum shortages during the Suez and Lebanon crises led President Eisenhower to issue a proclamation to limit foreign petroleum products imports.

In 1965 CAPT Lynch, then joint petroleum officer on the staff of the Commander-in-Chief Pacific, was sent to Vietnam to survey coastal harbors in South Vietnam and determine their ability to handle larger oil tankers. Air Force engineers had planned to construct a harbor at Tuy Hoa, subject to continuing extensive silting from a river that emptied into it and to the strong onshore currents of the South China Sea. The plan would require multimillions for repetitive dredging and construction of a shoreline breakwater.

Meanwhile, Army engineers were in the process of installing ship-handling facilities at the edge of Vung Ro Bay, a deep-water harbor just a few miles to the south. When the Air Force went ahead with a turnkey contract for the Tuy Hoa project, Jack Lynch set out to convince them of the sites's limitations. To visit and assess the two locations, he assembled a team of Army, Air Force, and COMUSMACV engineers and an MSTS skipper who had experienced a near grounding of his T-1 tanker while crossing the Tuy Hoa bar.

The team arrived at Tuy Hoa to find a contractor's dredge attempting to extricate itself from silt freshly deposited by recent heavy rains. A flight over the deep blue, sheltered waters of Vung Ro demonstrated that a proper port could be made available to the Air Force much more quickly with only moderate additions to the Army facility. All team members, including the Air Force engineers, agreed with the Supply Corps officer's proposal. Washington soon approved the change.

Fortune magazine featured CAPT Lynch's contributions to Vietnam POL logistics in April 1967. Jack Lynch retired from the Navy in September 1968. In retirement, he remained in Hawaii for some time, where he taught and consulted, but returned to his native California in 1986. He is an author and lives in Paso Robles.

Single Service Managers

The Department of Defense continued to move toward centralization of selected functions in 1956. The Navy was selected as the single service manager for petroleum products and medical supplies. The Bureau of Supplies and Accounts established the Military Petroleum Supply Agency and the Military Medical Supply Agency.

When the Army was designated as the single service manager for provisions, the Navy Provisions Supply Office was disestablished on 30 June 1956. A new Navy Subsistence Office was established with a new mission, responsible for administering the overall Navy Food Service Program and exercising technical direction and financial control of Navy general messes. The inventory control functions formerly performed by PSO were decentralized and individual Navy commands were charged with maintaining local subsistence stocks. With improved contract, purchase, inventory, and quality control procedures in place, Navy coffee-roasting plants at New York and Oakland were closed. The Navy commenced using commercial sources for the huge amount of coffee it consumed around the world each day.

BuSandA pushed ahead in 1956 with its program to automate inventory and stock control functions at the customer level, and the first major stock point computer installation went on line at NSC Norfolk. A Shipboard Supply Availability Program was established at major coastal ship concentrations in 1956 to provide on-site assistance to afloat supply officers.

As the Navy supply system furthered its program of streamlining its operations, the concept of coordinated shipboard allowance lists (COSAL) was developed in 1957. For the first time, COSAL provided the supply system, the Bureau of Ships, and others concerned with initial provisioning of ships with a single document that listed authorized equipment and parts.

In 1957 BuSandA reduced to partial maintenance status two field operations—NSD Scotia and Naval Aviation Supply Depot Philadelphia. Four new activities were also established, including two inventory control points: Navy Clothing and Textile Office and Navy Forms and Publications Supply Office. A Navy Overseas Air Cargo Terminal was established at Norfolk, and Navy Transportation Control offices were established at Norfolk and Oakland. At BuSandA, a Fleet Ballistic Missile Program Division was established.

Also in 1957, Chief of Naval Operations ADM Arleigh A. (Thirty-one-knot) Burke called upon a Supply Corps commander, with whom he had served eight years earlier, for a special assignment in his Pentagon office. That officer, CDR (later RADM) Joseph L. (Joe) Howard, had one of the most unusual and prestigious assignments ever entrusted to a member of the Supply Corps.

LORE OF THE CORPS

Commander Joseph Leon Howard, SC, USN

Special Assistant to Chief of Naval Operations, 1957–59
Period of Service: 1941–72

"The subsequent outstanding performance of Joe Howard . . . proved that strategic knowledge and the ability to express the need for naval power was not restricted to line officers. Joe Howard, particularly, had a better grasp of strategy than almost any other officer I had known." These are the words of the famous Navy World War II hero and later a chief of naval operations and are found in his autobiography, *Reminiscences of Admiral Arleigh Burke.* Joe Howard had two tours of duty with ADM Burke, went on to achieve Flag rank in the Supply Corps, and became a prolific author.

Joseph L. Howard was born in New Haven, Connecticut, in December 1917, and two years later his family moved to San Diego. He started his college education at San Diego State College in 1935, but transferred to the University of California in 1938. He was graduated in 1940 with an A.B. degree in economics and was employed by Consolidated Aircraft Company in San Diego.

In September 1940 Joe Howard decided to go into the Navy, and was commissioned an ensign, Supply Corps, U.S. Naval Reserve, in December 1940. He reported to the Navy Finance and Supply School at Philadelphia in March 1941.

ENS Howard was ordered as disbursing officer for Destroyer Division 80, based at Pearl Harbor, in July 1941 and assigned to *USS Chew* (DD-106), which was in overhaul on 7 December. Howard had a golf date that morning with ENS Verdi D. Sederstrom, an NF&SS classmate who was assistant supply officer, *USS Oklahoma* (BB-37). The two were to meet at 0800, but their outing became a victim of the Japanese bombing. When the attack started, ENS Howard, having no assigned battle station, rushed to his temporary office in a corrugated shack on a pier.

He and two enlisted men began treating casualties who came ashore from the sunken and damaged ships. Most of the survivors were badly burned and covered with oil and grease. ENS Howard and his men did their best for the survivors. They were hampered by lack of proper equipment and began to move the wounded to the dispensary, but a Navy doctor asked them to stop, because the facility was already overloaded. The doctor told them that they were handling the casualties properly and to keep dousing the wounded with cold water, the colder the better. Several days later, Joe Howard learned that Sederstrom was missing and presumed killed in the attack on *Oklahoma*.

Howard was promoted to lieutenant, junior grade, in June 1942 and reported in October as supply, commissary, and disbursing officer, Naval Section Base, Port Angeles, Washington. LTJG Howard was assigned duty as boarding officer for all ships entering the harbor to refuel. He determined their other supply needs.

On one occasion, the young LTJG, wearing a raincoat that obscured his Supply Corps device, boarded ship, when the skipper assumed he was a harbor pilot and immediately summoned Howard to the bridge. Before he could speak, the captain began throwing navigational questions at him, keeping up a steady line of chatter between questions. The fuel dock required careful maneuvering to come alongside. Howard was reluctant to become involved in ship handling, but knew they were headed for the dock at too sharp an angle. He warned the captain, who nonetheless held a steady course. The port anchor crashed onto the fueling pier, breaking the guard rail as they came alongside.

Howard wanted to get off the ship as quickly as possible, but the captain insisted they have coffee with the other officers in the wardroom. The skipper emphasized the importance of always listening to the pilot and insisted that the Howard take off his raincoat. Howard reluctantly complied. When the captain spotted the Supply Corps device, he slammed his fist on the table, uttered an oath, and stormed out of the wardroom. The rest of the officers stared at Joe Howard, straining to stifle laughter. The exec finally spoke up and introduced him to the stores officer, who handed Howard a sheaf of requisitions, with which he quickly departed.

LTJG Howard met many more ships in his nearly two years at Port Angeles, but from that time on he made it a point to yell up to the bridge that he was the supply officer, *not* the pilot. He was augmented into the Regular Navy in June 1942 and was promoted to lieutenant in December.

The focus of the war began to shift farther west, and the four section bases in the Pacific Northwest—Neah Bay, Port Angeles, and Port Townsend, all in Washington, and Coos Bay in Oregon—were closed. LT Howard became the settlement officer for the four bases. His duties included closing all accounts, reconciling all accounting and disbursing documents, and turning over the facilities to caretaker commands. He completed the task in July 1944 and reported as staff supply officer, Fourth Naval Construction Brigade, composed of 3 regimental staffs and 12 construction battalions, located at Manus Island in the Admiralty Islands, 3,500 miles west of Pearl Harbor. The brigade was redesignated the Eleventh Brigade, greatly expanded to 50,000 men, and positioned at Noumea, New Guinea, in early spring to prepare for the invasion of Okinawa and Japan. LT Howard was designated brigade supply and material officer and also took responsibility for Bureau of Yards and Docks material.

The Seabees went ashore on Okinawa under fire in April 1945, following the Marines and the Army, to set up construction dumps and to begin building roads, airfields, piers, bridges, and other needed facilities. Joe Howard was promoted to lieutenant commander in July 1945 and was awarded the Bronze Star with Combat V for his meritorious service in support of the Seabees on Okinawa. The citation says, "Lieutenant Commander Howard contributed immeasurably to the efficient manner in which the brigade completed its assigned tasks of building vitally needed roads, airfields, hospitals, supply depots, piers and personnel facilities despite the continuing threat of hostile attacks and the obstacles of climate, disease and difficult terrain."

First, LCDR Howard studied all the intelligence books and everything available about Okinawa, including the island's flora and fauna, indigenous people, village structures, and main city of Naha in order to plan where shiploads of material to support the Seabee landings could best be offloaded.

He arranged with Seabee battalion supply officers to create self-propelled barges from pontoons in order to speed up offloading of ships in Kotchin Honto, later renamed Buckner Bay. LCDR Howard visited ships carrying food and emptied them first over the objections of the island quartermaster, an Army colonel. Howard convinced the colonel, with aid of a few boxes of cigars, a case of beer, and a couple of pith helmets, to let him offload Navy provisions before a typhoon hit. The harbor was emptied when all ships weighed anchor to beat the storm. Howard also had the battalion supply officers allocate portions of their refrigerated spaces for the fresh provisions. As a result of Joe Howard's efforts, the Navy ate well while the Army subsisted on C-rations in the aftermath of the typhoon.

LCDR Howard solved a problem of identifying spare parts for the bulldozers, cranes, trucks, backloaders, and other Seabee equipment, which frequently arrived on Okinawa in large boxes that yielded no clue as to their intended use. Howard assembled a group of hand-picked technicians from each battalion to develop a parts-identification system to position the material shipped overseas directly from manufacturers.

He wrote an article for the *BuSandA Monthly Newsletter* in 1945 about how Supply Corps officers assigned to Seabee battalions exercised notable initiative and ingenuity in solving operational problems, often under fire. They used civilian interests such as ham radio experience, lessons learned from previous service as enlisted men, and the skills of the Seabees to meet challenges not covered by BuSandA manuals and not taught at NSCS.

As brigade supply officer, Joe Howard was retained on Okinawa when the war ended in order to consolidate the supplies, material, and equipment left behind as departing battalions were demobilized. He was also involved in setting up an advance base supply depot on Okinawa. Howard was ordered to the States in January 1946.

Back in San Diego, Howard received dispatch orders to report as supply, commissary, and disbursing officer of the newly formed Operational Development Center at Solomons, Maryland. He knew, from his experience at the Section Base at Port Angeles early in the war, that he could not handle supply, commissary, and disbursing alone, so he asked BuSandA to assign two more officers. A lieutenant was assigned as assistant supply and ship's store officer and a LTJG as disbursing officer. LCDR Howard was at the development center only until October 1946, but long enough to set up the postwar accounting system on the base and train the disbursing officer and some the enlisted personnel in the new system.

Howard's article "Doing Business with Uncle Sam," based on his dismay at how things were sent out to Okinawa during the war, was published in *All Hands* in 1947. He had asked RADM Mort Ring to look over the article, which presented views also held by some important people in Washington, and Ring decided that Howard should join his staff. In October 1946 Howard was ordered to Washington as special assistant to Ring, who was director, Material Division, Procurement Policy Branch, Office of the Assistant Secretary of the Navy.

The article launched Howard on a concurrent career as a writer. Three more of his articles were published in the *Naval Institute Proceedings,* including "Seabee Supply Was Big Business" (1947), "Staging Is No Holiday Frolic" (1949), and "The Navy and National Security" (1951).

LCDR Howard had no formal training in procurement. His knowledge of the field was limited to his active duty experience and the research talent he demonstrated in preparing his *All Hands* article. These talents were valuable to RADM Ring in developing the Armed Forces Procurement Act of 1948. While preparing research for the act, Howard became a student of naval procurement.

LCDR Howard reported for duty at the Naval War College in June 1948 in the second logistics class. The 150 students in the three NWC courses were required to write year-end term papers. Joe Howard's paper, on his concept of a possible future war and how the United States should deal with it, was one of six chosen for publication.

The immediate postwar period saw serious competition among the services for primacy in the emerging defense establishment. The Air Force proposed to take over everything that flies, including Navy and Marine aviation, and the Army wanted to expand the General Staff System to the U.S. defense establishment. The CNO, ADM Louis E. Denfeld, set up the Organizational Research and Policy Division to develop the Navy positions on strategic concepts and the organization for future military operations. Denfeld picked then CAPT Arleigh Burke to head the new division. Burke had been a member of the Naval Academy Class of 1923 and had led Destroyer Division 23—the "Little Beavers"—in World War II. His OPNAV division became OP-23, and he chose 23 officers for his staff.

Burke asked Naval War College Chief of Staff RADM C. R. (Cat) Brown and RADM George Bauernschmidt, Deputy Chief of BuSandA, for recommendations on officers for his organization. Burke was intrigued that Howard's name appeared on both lists and was impressed with Howard's War College paper. He invited Howard to Washington for an interview.

The interview lasted about an hour, at the end of which Burke invited LCDR Howard to join his staff. When Joe Howard told him that he had finally achieved his goal of assignment as supply officer of a carrier, Burke responded, "You can do more good right here on my staff than sitting out there on a carrier."

Howard was graduated from the Naval War College in June 1949 and reported immediately to OP-23 at Washington as the junior man. Howard sent frequent memos to Burke, who normally approved them but at times would call to discuss them. Burke and his staff worked on both the B-36 controversy with the Air Force and the Army's general staff proposal. Howard set up the sequence of Navy witnesses to testify before congressional committees, the point at which, he surmises, he impressed Burke with his strategic thinking. Joe Howard maintained a correspondence with his OP-23 boss over the following years.

In November 1949 LCDR Howard left OPNAV and reported to BuSandA as assistant director, Purchasing Division, where he reorganized the division and established the Navy Purchase Training Course. He remained in the position for two and a half years and was promoted to commander in July 1951. CDR Howard was assigned to organize the

Operations Department and assist in the establishment of the Naval Supply Depot Yokosuka, Japan, in July 1952, and in 1953 became planning officer. He was awarded the Navy Commendation Medal for his support of Korean War operations. In June 1954 he reported as director, Procurement Department, Yards and Docks Supply Office, Port Hueneme, under CDR (later VADM) Joe Lyle. In late 1956 Lyle helped him obtain orders from Y&DSO to independent sea duty as supply officer, *USS Hancock* (CV-19), at San Francisco.

In January 1957 Joe Howard heard from his friend and mentor Arleigh Burke, now a four-star admiral and chief of naval operations. Burke needed a speech writer and a special assistant. He wrote Howard that he had another job for him.

Howard showed the letter to Lyle, who thought it was great. When Howard protested that he had a carrier job lined up, Lyle responded, "How can you say no to the CNO?" Howard felt that he did know Burke well enough to say no, however, and informed the CNO that he wanted go ahead with those plans. "You're young yet, you've got plenty of time to get that sea duty." Burke replied. Joe Howard was again persuaded by Burke's rationale and reported to the Office of the Chief of Naval Operations in June 1957 as special assistant.

ADM Burke authorized a staff of three officers to assist Howard in writing speeches, statements, and giving the CNO his views on various subjects, including strategic issues. Once a vice admiral asked Howard, "What the hell is a Supply Corps officer doing in this kind of a job?" It was not the only time that Joe Howard would be asked a similar question while he was on the CNO's staff, but the question had already been answered to the satisfaction of the only person who counted, Arleigh Burke. Joe Howard insists that Arleigh Burke was not hard to work for. "The truth is that every damn time a tough job would come up, Burke would get it." He describes Burke as "an inspiring leader."

In July 1959 the Supply Corps brought CDR Howard home to BuSandA as executive assistant to CAPT Jack G. Dean, director of planning. It was actually a job he requested, because he knew he was not going to get a ship. He was promoted to captain in April 1960 and reported as executive officer of Naval Supply Center San Diego in September 1961. CAPT Howard remained as X.O., NSC San Diego, until July 1964, except for four and a half months in 1962 when he served as commanding officer between the retirement of RADM Joel D. Parks and the arrival of RADM Leland P. (Lee) Kimball. He also spent three months at Cambridge, Massachusetts, in the fall of 1963 to attend the Advanced Management Program at Harvard University.

While at San Diego in 1961, CAPT Howard's book, *Our Modern Navy,* was published. Howard's thesis is that American naval power depends upon the people who *are* the Navy—their attitudes, philosophies, outlooks, and talents. *Navy Times* reviewed CAPT Howard's work in December 1961, commenting, "This book could very well be sub-titled 'The Seapower Primer,' for the author hasn't missed a single bet in telling the Navy's story . . . Capt. Howard has done an excellent job in at least introducing the reader to every non-classified facet of today's Navy."

Joe Howard returned to Washington in August 1964 to work for RADM Bernie Bieri, deputy chief of naval material, first as director of procurement (MAT-02), and later as deputy chief for procurement and production. In June 1966 Howard was holding a meeting of all the contracting officers of the systems commands (which had replaced the bureaus) when he was called to the office of RADM Hersh Goldberg, chief of the Corps. CAPT Howard believed the meeting he was conducting was important and delayed going to Goldberg's office. After repeated calls from the chief, Joe Howard reluctantly went to see Goldberg, who informed Howard and CAPTs Fredric W. Corle and Fowler W. Martin that they had been selected to Flag rank.

RADM Howard testified at a February 1968 hearing of the Government Procurement Committee of the U.S. Senate on the Navy's Small Business Program, representing the assistant SECNAV (installations and logistics). He told the senators that it is, and has been, the continuing policy of the Navy "to encourage increased participation of competent small business concerns as prime contractors and sub-contractors in our procurement program." RADM Howard was awarded the Legion of Merit for his service at NMC. According to the citation, "The strong and capable procurement and production organization within the Navy is largely a result of Rear Admiral Howard's personal effort."

In July 1968 Howard reported to the Defense Supply Agency as deputy director for contract administrative services. He served in the position for two years and during that time decided that the Defense Contract Administrative Services (DCAS) should become an independent agency. At the end of his DCAS tour, RADM Howard was awarded a gold star in lieu of a second Legion of Merit.

Howard thought his next move would be to NSC Norfolk as commanding officer, but received orders as C.O. of NSC Charleston instead. He feels that unspecified political considerations were involved in being given the smaller command. He retired from the Navy in April 1972, with another gold star in lieu of a third Legion of Merit for his outstanding accomplishments while in command of NSC Charleston.

In retirement, Joe Howard wrote a spy novel, *The Diamonite Con-*

spiracy; a history of the Rotary Club of San Diego and a sequel to that; and also *The Life and Times of Madam Schumann-Heink*. He and his wife Rose Ellen live in San Diego, where he has served as president of the San Diego Historical Society since July 1993.

Sources

Burke, Arleigh. *Reminiscences of Admiral Arleigh Burke,* Vol. 4: *Special Services, OP-23*. Annapolis: U.S. Naval Institute, 1983.

Citation. Legion of Merit, May 1968.

Government Procurement, Report No. 15. Office of Legislative Affairs, 6 February 1968.

Howard, CAPT Joseph L. *Our Modern Navy*. New York: D. Van Nostrand, 1961.

Interview of RADM Joseph L. Howard. San Diego, Cal., 5 Oct. 1990.

"Navy Captain Writes a Seapower Primer." *Navy Times,* 21 December 1961.

"The Navy and National Security." *U.S. Naval Institute Proceedings,* July 1951,

Officer Biography Sheet, April 1972.

Official Biography. Defense Supply Agency, July 1968.

"Seabee Supply Was Big Business." *U.S. Naval Institute Proceedings,* January 1947.

"Solving Problems On-the-Spot." *BuSandA Monthly Newsletter,* September 1945.

"Staging Is No Holiday Frolic." *U.S. Naval Institute Proceedings,* April 1949.

The Ney Award for General Messes

In 1958, the secretary of the Navy, in cooperation with the International Food Service Executives Association (IFSEA), established the CAPT Edward Francis Ney Award program to improve and recognize quality in food service by Navy general messes worldwide. Awards, named for the former supply officer of *USS Arizona,* are made annually to winners in various categories of messes afloat and ashore.

Fleet commanders and ashore major claimants nominate candidates, and 63 are selected as semifinalists. They are then evaluated in eight key areas of food service: the food selected and prepared, management, training, facilities and equipment, safety, sanitation, and plastics waste and waste disposal. Semifinalists scoring the highest number of points during the evaluations advance as finalists. Competition is held among 12 afloat, and 6 ashore finalists for recognition as first- or second-place winners.

A Ney Finalist Evaluation Team, with two representatives from the Navy Food Service Systems Office, one from the Bureau of Medicine and Surgery, and one from IFSEA, use the same criteria used during the semifinalist phase. First-place general messes receive trophies from IFSEA.

EAM Requisitioning Procedures

After only a year of existence, the Navy Transportation Control offices at Norfolk and Oakland were disestablished in 1958, and Navy Regional Accounts offices and the Navy Finance Center were transferred from BuSandA to NAVCOMPT. Afloat, a completely mechanized stock and inventory control system was installed in *USS Altair* (AD-11), and electronic accounting machine card requisitioning procedures were implemented in the Fleet.

In August 1958 RADM James W. (Jimmy) Boundy, serving as director of Supply Management and Policy, Office of the Secretary of Defense, was selected to relieve RADM Bear Arnold as chief of BuSandA and paymaster general.

LORE OF THE CORPS

Rear Admiral James William Boundy, SC, USN

Chief, Bureau of Supplies and Accounts, and Paymaster General, 1958–61
Period of Service: 1930–61

RADM Boundy was a member of the first NROTC class at the University of Washington. He started as a line ensign, transferred to the Supply Corps, served on the Asiatic Station, and compiled an outstanding record, including heroic service in World War II, before becoming chief and paymaster general.

James W. Boundy was born in Seattle, Washington, in June 1907. He was fond of saying that growing up in the city on Puget Sound gave him a love of the sea. In September 1930, following graduation from the University of Washington and commissioning in the Naval Reserve in June, he resigned his Reserve commission and accepted a U.S. Navy commission as an assistant paymaster.

He reported for supply training at the Puget Sound Navy Yard and, beginning in 1931, served in *USS Tennessee* (BB-43) and *USS Lexington* (CV-2). He then reported for duty at the Naval Supply Depot San Diego and later at the Naval Air Station San Diego. He also served in China as assistant supply officer, Navy Yard, Cavite, the Philippines, and in the Bureau of Supplies and Accounts before World War II.

LT Boundy went to London as a special naval observer and was on duty there when the Japanese attacked Pearl Harbor. He later joined the staff, Commander Support Force, Atlantic Fleet. He earned the Commendation Ribbon for heroism while serving as supply officer, *USS Pollux* (AKS-2), attached to Task Force 24 in the Atlantic. *Pollux* was wrecked off the coast of Newfoundland in February 1942. The citation for Boundy's heroic action at the time reads, in part, "Lieutenant James W. Boundy, SC, USN, in complete disregard of personal safety, attempted to run a line ashore from the stranded *Pollux* under conditions of heavy sea, icy waters, and below freezing temperature, which combined to make the undertaking extremely hazardous . . . The bravery which LT Boundy displayed in jeopardizing his own life to assist in the rescue of his brother officers and men was in keeping with the highest traditions of U.S. Naval Service."

A year later, while serving on the staff, Air Force, Pacific Fleet, he received the Legion of Merit for "establishing supply depots throughout the forward area, training personnel for these activities, and equipping and maintaining these establishments." In 1945 he was promoted to the temporary rank of commodore at the age of 38, one of the youngest officers to attain Flag rank.

After the war, he reverted to his permanent rank of captain and served as special assistant to the chief, BuSandA, until he was ordered as supply officer in command, Naval Supply Depot Great Lakes, Illinois. He reported in August 1948 for duty under instruction at the National War College, Washington. He remained in Washington as supply officer, Naval Gun Factory in June 1949. During this tour, he was again selected to Flag rank. In July 1950 RADM Boundy became a member of the Joint Logistics Plans Group, Joint Chiefs of Staff.

He reported for duty as assistant chief for accounting and disbursing, BuSandA, and went back to the Pentagon. RADM Boundy returned to BuSandA as chief of the bureau and paymaster general in August 1958, where he helped to bring about major improvements in the Navy supply system. When he completed his tour as chief, Jimmy Boundy singled out what he considered the three most significant improvements made during his administration:

- establishment of the Fleet Readiness Division in BuSandA;
- extensive accomplishments in inventory decisions and improved materials handling equipment for USN ships; and
- added emphasis given to BuSandA's research and development.

In May 1961 he assumed the duties of special assistant to the secretary of the Navy. In this assignment, he played an important role in developing the Navy's policy on unification of supply support for the three armed services. He retired from the Navy in 1961. Boundy and his wife Louise lived in San Raphael, California, but he retained a strong and active interest in the civic affairs of Seattle, which he visited often. He died in October 1969.

Source

Official Biography. Naval Supply Systems Command, n.d.

The Supply Corps and Nuclear Power

Throughout the decade of the 1950s, additional talented Supply Corps officers were assigned to the Rickover organization. One of those was LCDR (later RADM) Kenneth L. Woodfin, who joined in 1958.

LORE OF THE CORPS

Lieutenant Commander Kenneth L. Woodfin, SC, USN

Navy/AEC Contracting Officer, 1958–61
Supply Officer, Director of Naval Reactors, 1961–65
Period of Service: 1942–75

Kenneth Woodfin commanded 2 subchasers as a line officer in World War II before transferring to the Supply Corps, spent 12 years in the Navy Nuclear Propulsion Program, and rose to Flag rank.

Ken Woodfin was born in Dallas, Texas, in July 1923, and was attending Southern Methodist University when the United States entered World War II, He was turned down for military aviation programs for physical reasons and volunteered in 1942 for the Navy V-12 officer training program. In July 1943 he was ordered to active duty and sent to the University of North Carolina, Chapel Hill, where he received an accounting degree. In January 1944 he was sent to the Naval Reserve Midshipman School at Columbia University, New York City, and was commissioned a line ensign in April 1944.

ENS Woodfin served in submarine chasers in both the Atlantic and Pacific. He commanded *No. 660* and *No. 1315,* engaged in active attacks on German U-boats in the Atlantic, but his ships were not credited with any kills. In late 1945 he was on duty with Amphibious Group 15, training in the Philippines for a planned landing at Pusan, Korea, when the war ended abruptly.

Woodfin was promoted to LTJG and decided he wanted to remain in the Navy. He recognized that his interests were in the business aspects of the Navy and obtained a commission in the Supply Corps. He reported to the Navy Supply Corps School Bayonne in a class composed largely of lieutenant and LTJG line officer transferees in December 1946.

His first Supply Corps assignment was in the Accounting Systems Group, Bureau of Supplies and Accounts, from May 1947 to March 1949. His next duty was as accounting officer, Naval Ship Repair Facility, Subic Bay, the Philippines. In July, he was reassigned as comptroller, NAS Sangley Point, the Philippines, and made lieutenant in January 1950. LT Woodfin reported to the University of Kansas in September 1951 as supply instructor in the NROTC program. He also was a part-time accounting instructor for the university. He accompanied a group of NROTC students on the 1952 summer cruise to Europe in *USS Wisconsin* (BB-64).

In June 1955 he was graduated from Stanford University with an M.B.A., first in his class. He had been promoted to lieutenant commander in May and reported as supply officer, *USS League Island* (AKS-30), attached to Commander Service Squadron 3 at Sasebo, Japan, in July 1955. In August 1956 he reported to the Office of the Chief of Naval Operations as comptroller, Office of Naval Intelligence. The director, RADM Lawrence H. Frost, advised him that he would be both the comptroller and the admiral's aide on trips outside the United States. When LCDR Woodfin asked why, the admiral explained, "I want a business advisor to take along with me because I'm deathly tired of trying to answer business problems and you can handle all those for me."

Ken Woodfin recalls that he and Frost visited 48 countries in 2 years, giving him a good insight into how U.S. diplomats operated. In the fall of 1957 he received orders to report to the Bureau of Ships for an interview for the Nuclear Propulsion Program. He passed muster with Rickover and his senior Supply Corps officer, CDR Vince Lascara, and was ordered to report to the Atomic Energy Commission in November.

After a short period at AEC offices in Washington, LCDR Woodfin went to Pittsburgh as Navy/AEC contracting officer at Westinghouse Electric Corporation. Soon, Woodfin was reporting directly to Rickover, who had many ideas of his own about how the Navy should be operated. Ken Woodfin believes that Rickover thought the Navy purchasing system could not deliver what he wanted. So, Rickover encouraged his supply officers to set up sophisticated purchasing operations but did not want them to overwhelm the General Electric and Westinghouse laboratories. He created other organizations that specialized in purchasing operations for the two prime contractors. Rickover was also the catalyst behind the two major contractors setting up a specialized manufacturing operations at each: the Plant Apparatus Department (PAD) at Pittsburgh and Machine Apparatus Operation (MAO) at Schenectady.

Woodfin, who was promoted to commander in May 1960, describes his relationship with Rickover as "highly sparked, if not inflammatory," on a regular basis over a period of three years. They were in frequent dispute over many issues, but he believes that Rickover loved the interaction of the disputes. CDR Woodfin relieved CDR Lascara as principal business assistant to Admiral Rickover in BuShips and the AEC Reactor Development staff in October 1960.

Ken Woodfin had many debates about contractors' costs and cost accounting with Hyman Rickover, who could not comprehend why contractors did not use a standard accounting system so that direct comparisons of costs could be made. Woodfin says that Rickover was a "very quick, but a very stubborn learner." He explained to the admiral that corporations were in control of their own accounting systems, as permitted under generally accepted accounting practices. Rickover would not accept Woodfin's explanations and set about to change to a set of standard accounting rules similar to those of public utility accounting.

The admiral and his accounting expert finally agreed upon a plan to develop cost accounting standards. According to Ken Woodfin, the Rickover team, working with the Government Operations Committee, developed a legislative proposal to certify cost and pricing data and which eventually became the Truth in Negotiations Act.

Woodfin recalls that in the early 1960s, there were more than 30 Supply Corps officers in the Nuclear Propulsion Program. The duties of these officers, called naval reactor representatives (NRs), were stationed in Washington, at the major contractor plants, at shipyards, and other locations. Rickover believed that a five-year tour of duty was the key to a naval officer's success in his program and demanded a commitment from those in his program.

Woodfin says his group insisted that letters were placed in officer jackets indicating the essential nature of their staying in the nuclear program longer than the normal rotation pattern. He says Rickover could never understand why 5 years in his program was not considered more career enhancing than 10 years somewhere else. Eventually, CDR Woodfin convinced Rickover to release him in order for him to move on with his Navy career. He was promoted to captain in July 1965 and was relieved in September by LCDR Mel Greer, who had been his chief assistant at both Pittsburgh and Washington.

CAPT Woodfin reported to the Industrial College of the Armed Forces, from which he was a Distinguished Graduate in July 1966. He reported in August as supply officer, Commander Service Squadron 6 in the Mediterranean and assumed additional duty as staff supply officer, Commander Sixth Fleet in mid-1967.

In July 1968, he reported to a Flag billet, Commander Navy Finance Center Cleveland, Ohio, with instructions to become involved with development of a new military pay system. He was selected for rear admiral and frocked in early 1970.

In July, RADM Woodfin was ordered back to what he calls "the biggest known procurement trouble point in the United States Navy," the Naval Ships Systems Command, as vice commander for procurement. When he took over the new position, he learned that NAVSHIPS was having the same problems with the same shipyards that he had experienced when he had been in the Nuclear Propulsion Program.

Ken Woodfin was again dealing with ADM Rickover. Although he and the feisty Rickover were on the same level of NAVSEA's organization charter as vice commanders, they definitely were not equals. RADM Woodfin's knowledge of, and experience with, Rickover smoothed over a potentially awkward and unpleasant situation. He told Rickover, "I'm here and I'm going to run this contract stuff and you and I are not always going to agree, but we're always going to talk about it." It was an interesting relationship, Ken Woodfin recalls, particularly in view of the friction between Rickover and ADM Ike Kidd, chief of naval material. In July 1973 RADM Woodfin was ordered to duty on Kidd's staff as deputy chief of naval material. Woodfin reports that although he enjoyed his time with Kidd, he had spent more than 13 years on duty in the Navy Department and decided it was time to go on to some other Supply Corps post. However, both the secretary of the Navy and Supply Corps Chief Wally Dowd told him that it would be "a waste to send you anywhere but where you are." So, RADM Woodfin decided to retire in July 1975.

He had several civilian job offers, including one from the National Aeronautics and Space Administration, which was having problems with procurement in the Apollo program. He joined NASA in a senior executive position, with the understanding he would only work there for a year. When he left NASA in 1976, he joined the Burns and Rowe engineering firm in Oradell, New Jersey, engaged in research and development work on the TVA Clinch River breeder reactor for the Department of Energy. Burns employed other officers formerly in the Navy reactor program.

Woodfin testified before a congressional joint subcommittee in June 1976 on the proposed settlement of \$1.8 million in claims against the Navy by four major shipbuilders. He told the subcommittee that he had been involved when the Navy had settled 40 shipbuilding claims for \$1 billion through the normal claim review process. He said that he saw no reason why shipbuilders should be excused from the terms of their contracts, disputed charges that the Navy had awarded inappropriate shipbuilding contracts to the yards, and opposed granting them extra-contractual relief.

In 1985 the Woodfins returned to Dallas, where he continued to perform consulting work for Burns and Rowe. He and his wife Jimmie Ruth live in Dallas and he is still an active consultant, including current assignments with DOE.

Sources

Interview of RADM Kenneth G. Woodfin. Norfolk, Va., January 1992; supplemented by telephone interview, June 1994.

Letters attesting to professional qualification of CDR Woodfin from Chief, Bureau of Naval Personnel, Chief of Bureau of Supplies and Accounts, and VADM Hyman Rickover, December 1962.

Woodfin, RADM Kenneth G. *Economy in Government, Joint Economic Committee, Congress of the United States,* 25 July 1976.

BuSandA and R&D

CAPT Cliff Messenheimer, a serious student of the application of mathematical models to supply planning, was brought into the Bureau in 1959 to take responsibility for the Supply Corps' research and development programs.

LORE OF THE CORPS

Captain Clifford Arthur Messenheimer, SC, USN

Assistant Chief, Research and Development, BuSandA, 1959–60
Period of Service: 1937–60

Cliff Messenheimer was originally a line officer who served in *USS Saratoga* (CV-3), where was impressed by the supply officer, CDR (later VADM) Murrey Royar. Messenheimer transferred to the Supply Corps and became a member of the NF&SS Class of 1939-40 as a LTJG. He later went to Turkey to advise and assist the Turkish navy in setting up a supply school for its personnel.

He was born in January 1914 at Lawrence, Kansas, and was graduated from the Naval Academy in 1937. When he completed NF&SS in the spring of 1940, LTJG Messenheimer was assigned as disbursing officer of *USS Altair* (AD-11), a destroyer tender tied up at Pearl Harbor. He was transferred in March 1941 to the Mare Island Navy Yard, where he was serving when war broke out on 7 December. His next assignment, from April 1943 to August 1944, was as supply officer, *USS Portland* (CA-33), in the North and Central Pacific.

In September 1944,he reported to Norfolk as assistant fleet supply officer, COMSERVLANT, supporting the Atlantic Fleet and shore bases from Iceland, Greenland, and Newfoundland, to Bermuda, Jamaica, and Trinidad, and over to North Africa. He reported to the Bureau of Supplies and Accounts in April 1947 as Atlantic Fleet liaison officer, and in March 1948 became BuSandA's assistant planning officer. In this position CDR Messenheimer was on temporary additional duty with the U.S. Navy Survey Group for Turkey to study supply aspects in the Turkish navy for two months in 1947. He returned to Turkey on Thanksgiving Day 1948 for three weeks as an advisor in setting up a supply school for Turkish naval personnel. RADM T. G. W. Settle, Chief, Naval Group, American Mission for Aid to Turkey, termed the Messenheimer project "of inestimable value to us in carrying on the supply and material ends of our job here."

Cliff Messenheimer entered graduate school at Harvard in September 1949 and earned an M.B.A. When he came back to full-time Navy duty in July 1951, CAPT Messenheimer was given a Supply Corps plum—commanding officer, Naval Supply Depot Guantanamo Bay, Cuba, from 1951 to 1953. While Messenheimer was at "Gitmo," a group of members of Congress came to the base on a junket, including a senator he had met at Harvard. The base commander assigned Messenheimer to escort the senator, who asked to see his quarters, around the base. When the senator, impressed with the quarters, commented that his host "must get quite an entertainment allowance," Messenheimer admitted that he did not. After the junketeers left, the skipper summoned Cliff Messenheimer and said that perhaps he would share *his* entertainment allowance.

CDR Messenheimer had special duty at Washington in January 1953 as personal escort for Kansas Governor Edward F. Arn and his wife during official activities of the inauguration of Dwight D. Eisenhower as the 34th president.

His next duty was as supply officer, Naval Air Station, Memphis, Tennessee, July 1953 to April 1955, where he was promoted to captain. He reported to BuSandA as comptroller in May 1955 and was ordered as assistant Navy inspector general from April 1956 to October 1957. While on the staff of the OPNAV IG, he was on a team that conducted on-site inspections worldwide and became convinced that a systemwide program of stock reduction was in order.

In November 1957 he reported as logistics officer, Commander Sixth Fleet in the Mediterranean. He returned again to BuSandA as assistant chief for research and development in September 1959. CAPT Messenheimer was a strong advocate of closing the gap between research into new ideas and application of sophisticated stock decisions in the field. He also supported programs to analyze supply decisions and improve them through use of new mathematical tools.

CAPT Cliff Messenheimer retired in July 1960 but remained in Villefranche-sur-Mer on the French Riviera, a town that was the home port of the flagship of the Sixth Fleet. There, he accepted a civilian position with an American investment firm. He later was employed in financial management positions in Nassau, Bahamas, in Washington, and in Princeton Junction, New Jersey. He retired from business endeavors in 1981, and he and his wife Margaret live in Bradenton, Florida.

Sources

Additional taped and written notes supplied by CAPT Messenheimer, May 1994.

"Implementation of Advanced Decision Rules Throughout the Navy Supply System." *Navy Supply Corps Newsletter,* July, 1960.

Interview of CAPT Clifford A. Messenheimer. Asheville, N.C., May 1993.

Letters to the Chief, Bureau of Supplies and Accounts from Senior Member, U.S. Naval Survey Group of Turkey, 13 July 1947, and Chief, Naval Group, American Mission for Aid to Turkey, 13 December 1948.

Helicopter Replenishment at Sea

In 1959 the first test of the use of helicopters to replenish ships at seas was carried out in *USS Altair* (AD-11). The tests were successful, and in a short time the practice of helicopter replenishment became routine. When LCDR R. D. Fisher reported as supply officer, *USS Triton* (SSN-586) in 1960, he became the first Supply Corps officer assigned to the permanent crew of a U.S. Navy submarine.

An Unstable Budget Era

The United States had envisioned an era of world peace after the unconditional surrender of the Axis powers at the end of World War II, but during the ensuing 15 years, war of both the hot and cold variety dominated concerns of the U.S. defense establishment. Navy planners were hampered by unstable budgetary levels, which fluctuated from the doldrums of the Louis Johnson era as secretary of defense to the heights of the Korean War.

Despite frequent budget constraints, the Bureau of Supplies and Accounts made major strides in providing enhanced supply support to operating forces and in automating accounting and inventory practices. Peacetime Supply Corps manning levels, drawn down substantially after World War II, rose dramatically during the Korean War but declined once again when hostilities ceased.

The subsequent cold war stalemate with the Soviet Union and her satellite states required higher Navy manning levels than any previous peacetime period. The Supply Corps had achieved recognition throughout the naval establishment as a body of professional business experts and the demand for Supply Corps officers grew commensurately.

Sources

Sources for material used in this chapter and not cited earlier include:

Miller, Nathan. *The U.S. Navy: An Illustrated History*. Annapolis: Naval Institute Press,and New York: American Heritage Press, 1977.

Navy Supply Corps Newsletter, September 1973.

World Almanac and Book of Facts. 1992.

Additional sources for material:

The source of passages on the Navy Air Transport Command role in the Berlin Airlift is LTJG Carl L. Henn, Jr., "The Berlin Airlift, Transport Triumph," *Navy Supply Corps Newsletter,* July 1949.

The source of passages on the U.S. Navy Logistics Support Force 92, operating off Korea, is *The Navy's Role in Korea,* prepared by the Staff, Naval Forces Far East, March 1952. A copy of the presentation is on file at the Navy Supply Corps Museum, Athens, Ga.

CHAPTER ELEVEN

The Age of Naval Technology

1961–72

Shortly after the end of World War II, the Hoover Commission had recommended centralizing management of common military logistical support and introducing uniform financial practices. Initially, the Department of Defense designated eight single managers from among the Navy, Army, and Air Force to manage inventories of common supplies and to provide certain support services for all armed forces. The Navy was selected as single manager for medical supplies, petroleum, and industrial parts.

DOD moved toward further centralization when the Defense Supply Agency (DSA) was authorized 1 October 1961 and became operational on 1 January 1962. The eight single manager agencies became DSA supply centers. Three supply depots were also co-located with the supply centers, and four additional free-standing depots were transferred to DSA in 1963 and 1964. Three DSA supply centers were consolidated into one in 1965. DSA also was given responsibility for the Federal Supply Catalog, the DOD Surplus Disposal Program, the DOD Industrial Plant Equipment Reserve, and the DOD Technical and Scientific Information Program.

Navy Supply Corps officers were assigned to DSA from the start of the new agency's operations. RADM Joseph M. Lyle, Commanding Officer, Aviation Supply Office, was appointed the first deputy director and the second director.

LORE OF THE CORPS

Vice Admiral Joseph Melvin Lyle, SC, USN

Director, Defense Supply Agency, 1964
Period of Service: 1930–64

Joe Lyle served as a Navy enlisted man before entering the Naval Academy. He had the Supply Department duty at Pearl Harbor 7 December 1941. He advanced to the rank of vice admiral and second director of the Defense Supply Agency.

Joseph M. Lyle was born in Augusta, Georgia, in June 1912, and attended the Academy of Richmond County. He enlisted in the Navy in April 1930 and later attended the Naval Academy Preparatory School and was graduated from the Naval Academy in June 1935. He was commissioned a line ensign and reported for duty in *USS Idaho* (BB-42). He was promoted to lieutenant, junior grade, in May 1937, and in June was transferred to the Supply Corps and ordered to the Navy Finance and Supply School at Philadelphia.

LTJG Lyle reported to *USS Beaver* (AS-5) as supply and disbursing officer in July 1938. In October 1939 he was assigned as commissary officer and assistant supply officer at the Pearl Harbor Submarine Base. In October 1940 he moved to the Supply Department, Pearl Harbor Navy Yard. He had been in that assignment for only two months when the Japanese attacked Pearl Harbor. He was Supply Department duty officer and witnessed the actual bombing and torpedoing of ships in Battleship Row. Lyle made the calls that summoned department members to war. LTJG Lyle was promoted to lieutenant in early 1942 and in July 1943 became special assistant to the district supply officer, Fourteenth Naval District, at Pearl Harbor. When he was detached, LT Lyle received a letter of commendation from the Commander-in-Chief U.S. Pacific Fleet for "exceptionally meritorious" service from December 1941 to September 1944.

In October 1944 LCDR Lyle reported as supply and fiscal officer, Naval Air Station, Norfolk, with additional duty as supply officer on the staff, Commander Naval Air Bases, Fifth Naval District. He was promoted to commander and became senior assistant force supply officer, Commander Air Force, U.S. Pacific Fleet, in March 1946.

In August 1948 he reported as executive officer, Aviation Supply Office, Philadelphia, and was promoted to captain. In June 1950 he was ordered as director of naval personnel, Bureau of Supplies and Accounts. CAPT Lyle was commanding officer, Bureau of Yards and Docks Supply Office, at Port Hueneme, California, from January 1953 to July

Supply Office, at Port Hueneme, California, from January 1953 to July 1956. He completed studies at the Naval War College, Newport, in July 1957, when he was promoted to Flag rank, and joined the staff, Commander Naval Air Force Atlantic, as force supply officer. RADM Lyle returned to Philadelphia in June 1959 as commanding officer, Aviation Supply Office.

In December 1961, RADM Lyle was ordered as the first deputy director of the newly established Defense Supply Agency, Cameron Station, Alexandria, Virginia. He became the second director of DSA in July 1964 and was promoted to the rank of vice admiral. When he retired in December 1964, he was awarded the Legion of Merit. The citation read in part: "Exercising marked leadership and professional skill, Vice Admiral Lyle performed essential service in the planning and development of an unprecedented joint logistical organization of the Department of Defense . . . exhibited a remarkable insight into the problems inherent in molding a newly activated joint agency into a cohesive, productive organization."

VADM Lyle retired from the Navy in December 1964 and died in March 1990.

Sources

Memorandum. LTJG J. M. Lyle to CAPT J. J. Gaffney, 19 December 1941
Official Biography. Navy Office of Information, June 1965.

The First Supply Corps Flag Officer with CNO

RADM John W. Crumpacker became the first Supply Corps Flag officer to serve in the Office of Chief of Naval Operations when he was appointed budget officer in July 1959. When he was approached about taking over the Material Division (OP-41), previously a line billet, John Crumpacker suggested that the division be combined with the Budget Division he was then heading. CNO, ADM Arleigh Burke, approved the plan, and it has been a Supply Corps billet ever since.

In early spring 1961, President John F. Kennedy nominated RADM Crumpacker to be chief of the Bureau of Supplies and Accounts and paymaster general, but Senate confirmation was delayed by deliberations not related to the Navy. In May the appointment was finally confirmed, and RADM Crumpacker relieved RADM Boundy as chief.

LORE OF THE CORPS

Rear Admiral John Webber Crumpacker, SC, USN

Chief, Bureau of Supplies and Accounts, and Paymaster General, 1961–65
Period of Service: 1931–61

RADM Crumpacker was another paymaster general, originally a line ensign, who transferred to the Supply Corps and went on to become the first Supply Corps Flag officer to serve on the CNO staff. During his career, he relieved Jimmy Boundy four times, the last as chief of BuSandA.

John Crumpacker was born at LaPorte, Indiana, in July 1908. He developed an interest in the Navy from stories told by his grandmother's cousin, Admiral Royal Ingersoll, who served extensively in the Far East. He entered the Naval Academy in 1927 and graduated in 1931. ENS Crumpacker reported to *USS Saratoga* (CV-3), where his duties included ship's store officer. In May 1933 he was ordered to the first of two one-year tours in the old Reserve destroyers *USS Aaron Ward* and *USS Evans* at San Diego.

Crumpacker recalls that, as torpedo officer, he never missed a shot and won the Battle Force torpedo championship for *Evans*. That earned an opportunity to shoot a live torpedo at an old destroyer, the *Marcus,* which had been stricken from the Navy's register. After two other ships missed, ENS Crumpacker calmly fired his one live torpedo into the old, rock-laden tin can, striking her dead on. Smoke shot 500 feet into the air, and *Marcus* sank stern first into the Pacific.

John Crumpacker's first tour of sea duty in *Saratoga* had generated an interest in naval aviation, so he applied for aviation training but was turned down because of deficient eyesight. He transferred to the Supply Corps and entered the Navy Finance and Supply School Philadelphia in August 1935.

His first Supply Corps assignment after NF&SS was as disbursing officer, *USS Tennessee* (BB-43), in July 1936. LTJG Crumpacker reported in July 1938 as commissary and disbursing officer, Naval Air Station Anacostia, in the District of Columbia. During his tour at Anacostia, the Supply Department was inspected by CDR (later RADM) Brent Young, the assistant to the inspector general of the Supply Corps. Impressed with the young paymaster, Young recommended him for duty in the Purchasing Division, Bureau of Supplies and Accounts. John Crumpacker was promoted to lieutenant in July 1939. In July 1941 he reported to the Naval Station, Tutila, American Samoa, to assume his duties on the staff of the Marine brigade, remaining in the post for about a year. He then became supply officer, with additional duty as treasurer of the Government of Samoa and island purchasing agent. The disbursing officer, LT John Cline, also served as president of the Bank of Samoa. LCDR Crumpacker remained in Samoa until called back to Washington in March 1943 by Paymaster General Brent Young to be his aide and director, Administrative Services Division. He was promoted to commander.

CDR Crumpacker was sent to the Philadelphia Navy Yard in June 1945 as prospective supply officer of *USS Princeton* (CV-37), then on the building ways. Completion of *Princeton* was delayed several months when critical components were redirected to the West Coast for repairs to other Essex-class carriers that had suffered battle damage. By the time *Princeton* made it to sea for trials, the war was virtually over.

John Crumpacker recalls, with some amusement, that he served in four ships that went aground while he was aboard: *Saratoga, Evans, Tennessee,* and *Princeton.* In no instance did he have the con, but when *Princeton* grounded in the flats at Oakland, he rushed ashore to the office of his friend, RADM Murph Royar, C.O. of the nearby Naval Supply Center. Royar mobilized a small fleet of tugs, which pushed and pulled *Princeton* out of the mud. No official report was filed, and, luckily, no press coverage resulted. CDR Crumpacker reported in July 1946 as supply and fiscal officer, Naval Air Station, Quonset Point, Rhode Island, with additional duty on the staff, Commander Naval Bases New England. He was promoted to captain, and in May 1948 became force supply officer, Air Force, Pacific Fleet, then located at NAS Ford Island, Pearl Harbor, where he was instrumental in developing a repair and turnaround system for aircraft materials and parts. CAPT Crumpacker's detailed statistical reports of grounded aircraft, related to funds for fuel and spare parts, were used by the AIRPAC commander in budgetary requests. During this tour, AIRPAC headquarters were moved from Pearl Harbor to NAS North Island, San Diego, as the result of a study that ships could be operated as effectively on a peacetime basis from the West Coast as they could from Pearl Harbor.

CAPT Crumpacker reported in July 1950 to the Naval Gun Factory in Washington, where he relieved CAPT (later RADM) Jimmy Boundy and was heavily involved in providing munitions for the Korean War. In August 1952 he reported to the Industrial College of the Armed Forces at Fort McNair in Washington. He was ordered from ICAF in August 1953 as commanding officer, Naval Supply Depot Puget Sound, Bremerton, Washington, where he was selected to Flag rank. In December 1954 he again relieved Jimmy Boundy as commanding officer, General Stores Supply Office. His tour at GSSO was cut short in July 1956 when he reported as commanding officer, Aviation Supply Office. He recalls that the main challenge was the "enormous turmoil in supply support caused by the gradual shift from propeller-driven aircraft to the jets, and the lack of money to make the shift properly." John Crumpacker discovered that ASO needed nearly a billion dollars to provide an adequate inventory to support Fleet operations. Typical of the major problems facing ASO was that the Navy was facing a 50 percent AOCP (aircraft out of commission, parts) rate for the Super Constellation aircraft then being used in transatlantic and transpacific operations. RADM Crumpacker succeeded in obtaining House of Representatives Naval Affairs Subcommittee approval of a request for an additional $750 million.

RADMs Boundy and Crumpacker had been discussing for some time the desirability of having a Supply Corps Flag officer on the staff of the Chief of Naval Operations and made a presentation in the Pentagon in early 1959. There was no available Flag slot available, so it was agreed that one of the 20 Flag billets in the BuSandA managed claimancy would be used. RADM Crumpacker was relieved at ASO by RADM (later VADM) Joe Lyle, and he reported to the CNO staff in July 1959 as budget officer.

During his tour in the Pentagon, RADM Crumpacker participated in a NATO Navy meeting in Brussels to develop a coordinated program to support the multinational naval operations. In addition to responsibility for developing the operating and procurement budgets for presentation to the secretary of the Navy and to Congress, OP-41 also was responsible for the Navy's nuclear inventory.

While on his Pentagon tour, John Crumpacker tackled a long-standing desire to learn to play the organ. According to the June 1961 issue of *The Navy Supply Corps Newsletter,* "The Admiral is finally teaching himself how to mold the rich, mellow tones of the instrument into recognizable, resonant chords."

When John Crumpacker relieved RADM Jimmy Boundy as chief of BuSandA and paymaster general, it was the fourth time he had followed Boundy into a Navy job. The two friends often needled one another about the unusual circumstances. Boundy would tell Crumpacker that he had cleared the way for him to do a good job, while his friend would say that he once again had been called in to clean up a Boundy mess.

RADM Crumpacker's first major challenge as chief was to face the reality of the newly established Defense Supply Agency. He had opposed the move because he felt that it made no more sense for the three services' regular day-to-day supply requirements to be given to DSA than to GSA (General Services Administration). At the time he assumed command, BuSandA was already under instructions to transfer 220 billets to DSA.

In late 1961, LTGEN Andrew McNamara, the first director of DSA, invited RADM Crumpacker to be his deputy. Crumpacker turned down the offer but wanted to assure that the Navy had a strong say in operations of the new agency, so he recommended RADM Tom Becknell for the job. McNamara chose instead RADM (later VADM) Joe Lyle, who would later become the second director of DSA, succeeding the general in July 1964. Despite his earlier concerns over the role of DSA, John Crumpacker says, "Andy McNamara and Joe Lyle did a wonderful job in getting their office going."

A continuing problem for RADM Crumpacker as chief was a steady stream of significant changes coming out of the Department of Defense under the "other McNamara," Secretary Robert. One was the development of nonsignificant stock numbers to replace the practical Navy system in which alpha-numeric elements gave an immediate clue to the material and its use. "The flood of changes continued during the four years that I was in that job," Crumpacker says, "and some of the programs that we had to take cost me enormous numbers of manhours and manyears." In one instance, he estimated that it would take 84 manyears—or 168 people—to accomplish something SECDEF McNamara wanted in 6 months. "We were confronted with this type of thing constantly."

The study that recommended establishment of the position of chief of naval material envisioned a lean and trim, hard-working group of a few officers. VADM Jim Russell, vice chief of naval operations, asked the chiefs of the bureaus to give him handwritten evaluations of the need for the office, and they all recommended against its establishment. Nevertheless, the proposed small staff was authorized. According to John Crumpacker, it grew into an enormous staff with direct logistics responsibility until it was abolished during the Reagan administration.

RADM John Crumpacker retired in April 1965. When he completed his tour as chief of BuSandA, the London *Daily Express* reported, in an amusing mistaken juxtaposition of stories, that he had been relieved by the Duke of Windsor. Crumpacker wrote to the duke to acquaint him with his "new command" but received no response. Admiral Crumpacker and his wife Vera live at Melbourne, Florida. At 83, he was the most senior Supply Corps officer present for the commissioning of *USS Supply* (AOE-6) at San Diego in February 1994.

Sources

Crumpacker, CDR John. "Supplying the Fleet for 150 Years." *U.S. Naval Institute Proceedings,* June 1945.

Interview of RADM John Crumpacker. Palm Beach, Fla., June 1986.
Navy Supply Crops Newsletter, June 1961, April 1965.

Supply Corps Officers and Special Duties

Navy Supply Corps officers have frequently been called upon to provide unusual requirements for friendly foreign governments. Following is a highly unusual story of one of these officers.

LORE OF THE CORPS

Lieutenant, junior grade, Charles Philip Gibfried, SC, USN

AVP Transfer Team, 1961–62
Period of Service: 1959–86

Chuck Gibfried was called upon to support the conversion of a World War II seaplane tender into a floating palace. He was an expert in computer science and systems and commanded one of the largest supply centers in the Navy.

He was born at Park Ridge, Illinois, in May 1936, and was graduated from the University of Illinois in June 1958 with a B.S. degree. He was employed by International Business Machines (IBM) and joined the Navy to attend Officer Candidate School at Newport, Rhode Island, in January 1959. Upon graduation from OCS, he was commissioned an ensign, Supply Corps, Naval Reserve, and ordered to NSCS Athens.

In December 1959 ENS Gibfried reported to the staff, CRUDESPAC, and placed in a pool for emergency relief of tycom supply officers. He was assigned as supply and disbursing officer, *USS Blair* (DER-147), in February 1960. *Blair* was decommissioned in July of that year, and ENS Gibfried reported as supply officer, *USS Paricutin* (AE-18). He was detached in August 1961 after promotion to LTJG and ordered to Hunter's Point Naval Shipyard as a member of the AVP Transfer Team. This unusual duty involved conversion of the seaplane tender *USS Orca* (AVP-47) into a combination flagship for the tiny Ethiopian fleet and imperial yacht for the Emperor Haile Selassie. The project was the brainchild of the State Department, which sought favor with Ethiopia by lending that nation a replacement for its unseaworthy imperial yacht, originally supplied by Yugoslavia.

LTJG Gibfried was one of 4 U.S. Navy officers and 12 enlisted men who assisted 16 Norwegian navy officers and chief petty officers in the outfitting of the renamed *HMS Ethiopia.* The Ethiopians retained the Norwegians to serve as commanding officer, executive officer, department heads, and leading NCOs. The Americans and Norwegians were assigned to train the Ethiopian crew and sail the ship to its new home port at Massawa, Ethiopia. More than 40 newly commissioned ensigns and 300 young sailors were chosen in their home country for training and assignment to *Ethiopia.*

Amharic was the national language of multiethnic Ethiopia, but fewer than 20 percent of the crew spoke it. With a potpourri of languages native to the crewmen, it was fortunate for the 32 Americans and Norwegians that all ship's instructions, manuals, and formal communications were in English.

When LTJG Gibfried began to supervise food service in *Ethiopia* while still at Hunter's Point, her Ethiopian crew prepared daily rations using standard U.S. Navy recipe cards. However, an entree was not complete until the meat was immersed in blazing hot Sinklai sauce, made with more than 20 varieties of pepper. Contrary to U.S. Navy policy, alcoholic beverages were available at all meals in *Ethiopia* except breakfast. The drinks served in the wardroom were exempt from customs duties and taxes. As a result, beer was just 15 cents and mixed drinks were only a dime. Chuck Gibfried emphasizes that the alcohol consumed aboard was always taken in moderation, but reports that ashore some of the Norwegian officers "lived up to their Viking heritage."

Furnishing the emperor's suite in the after portion of the ship fell to LTJG Gibfried and *Ethiopia*'s supply officer, CDR Rader Yvenes, RNN. Gold wallpaper was supplied by the State Department, but the 24-year-old Gibfried and his Viking associate were to provide everything else. For guidance they only had a bare list of basic items, including a bed, tables, chairs, lamps, draperies, dining china, and silver. The two supply officers were unable to find an emperor-sized bed, but they settled for an elegant king-sized one from Gump's Department Store in San Francisco. Gibfried and Yvenes managed to keep within their budget while supplying all the high-quality yet tasteful furnishings and decor required exclusively for the emperor's use. The project was supposed to be low-key but soon attracted an orgy of unwanted press coverage. Surviving the spotlight's glare, *Ethiopia* (A-01) was commissioned with impressive ceremonies at Hunter's Point in the spring of 1962.

When *Ethiopia* sailed from San Francisco for refresher training at sea, LTJG Gibfried went with her. He was in charge of administration, personnel, and the Combat Information Center. He says his most challenging task was training the Ethiopian sailors in the effective operation of radar and modern communications. The crew's capabilities increased rapidly, and within six weeks they were fully prepared to sail their ship home, with guidance from the permanently assigned Norwegians and the remaining Americans.

LTJG Gibfried left the ship upon arrival at Pearl Harbor in April 1962, and, having completed his obligated tour, returned to inactive duty and to IBM as a marketing representative. He sold and installed computer systems, achieved three 100 Percent Club awards, and was named IBM Man of the Year in Los Angeles and Western Region in 1964. He affiliated with the Naval Reserve in the Los Angeles area and was promoted to lieutenant in July 1963.

In 1966 LT Gibfried applied for recall to active duty. In June he reported to the Command and Control Staff, Commander-in-Chief Pacific, at Pearl Harbor. He served in two software/systems analyst billets, first in the Intelligence Branch until April 1968 and in Logistics/Plans until July 1969. He was promoted to lieutenant commander in November 1968.

LCDR Gibfried reported to NSC San Diego in August 1969, where he was data processing officer. He supervised a staff of 100 and launched a transition from three computer systems into one. He was ordered to the Naval Postgraduate School at Monterey, California, in August 197, and was graduated with distinction, first in his class, and with an M.S. in computer systems. He reported to *USS Enterprise* (CVN-65) as assistant supply officer and was aboard for the first F-14 deployment and the last Vietnam bombing cruise. *Enterprise* received the Blue E award for supply effectiveness, and Gibfried was promoted to commander in February 1975.

Chuck Gibfried returned to the Naval Postgraduate School in March 1975 as assistant professor of computer science and chairman, Computer Sciences Department. He was the first military officer to chair an academic department at NPS. He taught basic, intermediate, and advanced courses in COBOL, management information systems, and data processing management.

It was back to *Enterprise* for CDR Gibfried in June 1977, as supply officer. During this tour, *Enterprise* was the first carrier to reach the CNO readiness standard and won two more Blue E's. CDR Gibfried was ordered to ASO Philadelphia in 1979, where he served as planning officer for two years. He managed the major computer-based information system for supply support/maintenance of naval aviation. He was promoted to captain in November 1980.

In June 1981 he reported as force supply officer, Naval Air Force, U.S. Pacific Fleet. During his three-year tenure, readiness of Navy and

Marine Corps aviation units in the Pacific and Indian oceans increased 19 percent, to the highest level in naval aviation history. CAPT Gibfried was awarded the Legion of Merit for service at AIRPAC for his "significant contributions to supply readiness and to the quality of life of force personnel."

He assumed command of NSC Oakland in August 1984, and oversaw implementation of the state-of-the-art, computer-controlled robotic NISTARS inventory system, already three years behind schedule when he reported aboard. He was highly respected in the Oakland Area and was selected Man of the Year in Oakland in 1985. Chuck Gibfried retired in August 1986 at the end of a two-year tour at Oakland. He received a gold star in lieu of a second Legion of Merit for "markedly improving the efficiency and effectiveness" of NSC Oakland. In retirement, he became executive assistant to the president of Commercial Systems, Science Applications International Corporation (SAIC), San Diego, in November 1986. He spent seven years at SAIC, retired in 1993, but retains the title of vice president and business consultant on a nonexclusive basis. He and his wife Marilyn live at Pebble Beach, California.

Sources

Citation. Gold Star in lieu of 2d Legion of Merit, August 1986.
Citation. Legion of Merit, 3 July 1984.
"An Emperor's 'Yacht'—Aid from U.S." *U.S. News & World Report,* 30 April 1962.
"Man of the Year: CAPT Chuck Gibfried." *The Tribune,* Oakland, Calif., 31 December 1985.
Official Biography. Naval Supply Center, Oakland, n.d.
"A U.S. Navy 'Luxury' Ship for Selassie." *San Francisco Chronicle,* 13 January 1962.

Special Duty in the National Interest

Another Supply Corps officer who performed special duty was Rear Admiral Heinz H. Loeffler, a multilingual naturalized American businessman originally from Germany. Loeffler was a Reservist who carried out highly sensitive assignments, many of them behind the Iron Curtain during the cold war.

LORE OF THE CORPS

Rear Admiral Heinz H. Loeffler, SC, USNR

Special Assignments, Post World War II
Period of Service: 1943–72

Heinz Loeffler left his native Germany in 1928, became an American citizen in 1933, was commissioned a Reserve Supply Corps officer during World War II, and rose to Flag rank in 1967. A recognized world authority in preservation and packing, he was one of the most colorful individuals ever to wear the oak leaf of a Navy Supply Corps officer. His love of country and patriotism were more than the equal of any native-born American's. His sense of humor was legend, and his original limericks enlivened many a gathering of USN and USNR Supply Corps officers.

Born at Nurenberg in July 1910, he was educated in Germany at Nurenberg, and at École Superieure de Commerce, Meuchatel, Switzerland. He came to the United States at the age of 17, with $50 in his pocket, to perfect his English and study American business practices. He lived initially in International House, at the University of Chicago while attending the Institute of Military Studies. Young Loeffler began his business career as a warehouseman in New York City and became president of Kupfer Brothers Paper Company in Chicago in 1936.

Back in Germany, his father, a justice of the German Supreme Court, was ruling against the Nazis, who soon removed him from the bench and arrested him. Heinz Loeffler was eventually able to bring his parents to the United States before World War II after buying his father's freedom. But he was unable to secure release of his sister, who had a Jewish husband, from the concentration camp where she died—a great burden he carried for the rest of his life.

Loeffler first applied for a Navy Supply Corps commission in 1940, but was rejected because of his German birth and his father's connection with the Imperial German government and the German Republic. When the United States declared war on Germany in December 1941, Heinz Loeffler resumed his attempt to secure a Supply Corps commission. His application was rejected 19 additional times, but he finally succeeded in obtaining a direct commission as a lieutenant, junior grade, in 1943. LTJG Loeffler reported to Navy Supply Corps School at Wellesley College, Boston. From NSCS, he went to the Philadelphia Naval Shipyard in the fall of that year, and then to the Navy Purchasing Office, New York, before receiving orders as acting supply officer, Naval Operating Base, Roosevelt Roads, Puerto Rico. He was promoted to lieutenant and served briefly as liaison officer in the French aircraft carrier *Bearne* before being ordered to the European Theater in 1944.

Loeffler's background in the paper industry led to his assignment as packaging officer, U.S. Naval Forces Europe, headquartered in Great Britain. In this role, he was responsible for organizing preservation and packaging units at a number of European and North African naval bases. He also founded a special in-theater school to train naval personnel in proper methods of preservation and packaging. The Commander Amphibious Bases, United Kingdom, extolled LT Loeffler's meritorious service on his staff in supervising and ensuring shipment of supplies and equipment and in training personnel.

Heinz Loeffler quickly developed many strong friendships among the residents of Great Britain during the war. He was so impressed with the indomitable spirit of his British acquaintances that he helped them recover from the privations of more than six years of war, including a severe shortage of clothing. In April 1946 he wrote to a number of Americans, urging them to ship usable surplus clothing to an English business acquaintance who agreed to distribute apparel to needy Britons.

Upon his release from active duty in 1946, LT Loeffler returned to Chicago, resumed his business career, and started a concurrent career in the Naval Reserve. He became the first chairman of the Munitions Board Packaging Advisory Committee at its organizational meeting in 1950 and also served as a member of the Packaging Advisory Committee of the National Security Industrial Association. In the NSIA position, he worked closely with industry to resolve military packaging problems.

Loeffler was promoted to lieutenant commander in 1951, to commander in 1958, to captain in 1963, and to rear admiral in 1967. As a commander, he served as commanding officer of the renowned Volunteer Naval Reserve Supply Company 9-7, Chicago. In 1965 Loeffler was one of six businessmen from throughout the United States asked by the Agency for International Development (AID) to join with two members of Congress to see what could be done to generate small industry in South Vietnam.

His European heritage; his fluency in English, French, German, and Italian; his ability to comprehend a number of Eastern European languages; and his stature in the paper and packaging businesses brought him many opportunities to travel throughout the world, including behind the Iron Curtain. He accepted invitations in June 1969 to address an industry meeting in Czechoslovakia and to give a lecture at Karl Marx University in East Germany. And, as he put it, "to go to Switzerland and England on business to help pay for the trip."

Wherever his travels took him, he met and talked with business and government leaders. He assured them that they would not be named in his writings unless they gave him specific permission to do so. As a result, friends and foes of America alike opened up to him and were candid in their responses. Ever alert to the needs of national security, he always took pains to point out to his readers that his works contained nothing classified.

More than capitalizing on the opportunity to conduct business and to visit parts of the world other Americans could not, Loeffler was a keen observer of geopolitical events and a dedicated listener. He could comprehend the spoken words of others who, unfamiliar with his linguistic expertise, believed he would not understand what they were saying. This ability gave him frequent opportunities to exercise his uncanny knack of picking up bits and pieces of conversation and connecting them into meaningful information. U.S. government officials moved quickly to enlist him in their efforts to compile valuable data. He undertook a number of sensitive and highly classified missions for the Defense Department, State Department, Commerce Department, AID, and other U.S. government entities. To assure safety of his family during his government missions to certain parts of the world, U.S. security officials on several occasions spirited his wife and two daughters off to safe houses until his return.

Customs and immigration officials and police in other parts of the world often were suspicious of this American who sought entry to their countries. Was he a spy or just a businessman intent on capitalistic exploitation of their communist state? They were mystified by the mix of scholarly literature and popular mystery novels that this unusual American who was fluent in their language carried. As a result, he was often subjected to strict scrutiny and intense questioning at national borders.

An avid reader and prolific writer, Heinz Loeffler followed his visits to communist countries and other important areas of the world by writing and publishing—for limited distribution—a series of 10 monographs. These works also are highly informative geopolitical essays. They were written at a time when few Western journalists could gain access to such information in countries under communist rule. Loeffler's writing reveals his deep comprehension of European history and geopolitics. It also provides an interesting description of the challenges of international travel during the early stages of the jet age. A complete set of these books is among the collections of the Navy Supply Corps Museum.

Heinz Loeffler also was frequently in demand to speak before business, civic, and Navy audiences in the United States. In July 1971 he was the guest speaker at the 14th annual observance of Independence Day on the steps of the Harry S. Truman Library at Independence, Missouri. Sharing the platform with RADM Loeffler was William J. Randall, a member of Congress from Missouri. Congressman Randall was so impressed with Loeffler's speech that he had it inserted in the *Congressional Record.* In his remarks on the floor of the House of Representatives introducing the speech, the legislator reported that he had "listened most attentively" and then led the applause when RADM Loeffler told his civilian audience, "Those who would have all the rest of us believe that any defensive action beyond our borders is aggression are themselves misguided souls."

In addition to running his own business—Exeter Paper Company in Chicago—and his dedication to the Navy, Heinz Loeffler was active in many community activities. He directed the training of civil defense volunteers and was active in the Executives Club of Chicago, the Navy League of the United States, the Chicago Council on Foreign Relations, and the Academy of Political Science. He still found time to serve as an officer of many paper and packaging industry associations and committees and as a school board member.

RADM Loeffler retired from the Naval Reserve in 1972, but remained active in Supply Corps and other Navy support organizations. He was a charter member of the Navy Supply Corps Association in addition to being a strong supporter of the Navy Supply Corps Foundation, for which he endowed a scholarship.

Heinz Loeffler sold his business in 1976, but continued to serve as president until his retirement in 1986 at Heinzsite, near Long Grove, Illinois. His final book, *Our Man in Limbo,* written following successful surgery for throat cancer in the spring of 1984, summed up his philosophy: "Concentration on thoughts, words, ideas is wonderful therapy."

In 1986 he relocated to Palm Desert, California, where he died of cancer and Alzheimer's disease in August 1993.

Sources

"In Memoriam—Rear Admiral Heinz H. Loeffler." *Oakleaf,* Fall 1993.

Official papers, correspondence, citations, and news articles provided by RADM Heinz H. Loeffler. Navy Supply Corps Museum, Athens, Ga.

"Reserves of Renown." *BuSandA Monthly Newsletter,* July 1953.

Automatic Materials Handling

In 1961 installation of the first automated materials handling system was completed at the Navy Supply Center Norfolk, and the first Fleet self-service store (Piermart) was established at Newport.

The Bureau of Supplies and Accounts continued to monitor throughout the postwar years how best to meet changing Fleet requirements. In January 1962 the Fleet Material Support Office (FMSO) was established at the Naval Supply Depot Mechanicsburg, Pennsylvania, to apply the latest scientific principles to logistics, whether in material acquisition and distribution or in finding new supply applications for computer technology.

When the Defense Supply Agency was established, FMSO was given responsibility for managing retail stocks bought on a commonality basis by DSA and other interservice buyers such as the General Service Administration. FMSO also had responsibility for writing lists of parts to be carried by Navy ships and shore stations and evaluating effectiveness of supply support for such equipments as missile systems, radars, and sonars.

In 1962 BuSandA advertised for bids to supply a uniform automated data processing system (UADPS) at inventory control points. The first limited UADPS was installed the following year at the Naval Supply Department, Newport, Rhode Island. A Fleet Assistance Group was established on each coast, in 1963, to assist in implementing and maintaining ADP systems.

Women in the Supply Corps

For the first 147 years of Supply Corps history, all officers charged with supplying the Navy were men. That changed in 1943, when the Navy commissioned the first women Supply Corps officers in the Naval Reserve. By 1945 there were 962 women Supply Corps officers on active duty, all Reservists, and they represented 5.7 percent of all Supply Corps officers on active duty.

Congress enacted legislation to permit women to hold regular commissions in the U.S. Navy in 1948. One of the first in the Supply Corps was CDR Betty J. Brown, who became the first woman Supply Corps officer to attain the rank of captain. She also was the first Supply Corps officer, male or female, to become comptroller of a Navy shipyard.

LORE OF THE CORPS

Commander Betty Jane Brown, SC, USN

Comptroller, Norfolk Naval Shipyard, 1963–65
Period of Service: 1943–71

Betty Brown is truly a woman for all seasons. She was the first female

Regular Navy Supply Corps officer to make captain and the first female comptroller of a Navy shipyard. Along the way, she demonstrated her talents as uniform designer, television producer, champion golfer, and champion surf fisher.

Betty J. Brown was born, reared, and educated at Williamsport, Pennsylvania. She earned a bachelor of science degree in education at East Stroudsburg State College (now East Stroudsburg University) and a master of science, also in education, at Pennsylvania State University. She began a teaching career in her hometown just as World War II was breaking out.

With her brother already in the Army, Betty and her mother agreed that she could not stay home when the Armed Services were opening opportunities for women. She first was sworn in as a Marine Corps officer candidate, but when the Marines postponed the first female officer candidate class, Brown did not want to wait. She convinced the Marines to release her and was promptly sworn into the Navy.

In July 1943 she reported to Smith College at Northampton, Massachusetts, and spent three months in the fourth class at the Navy Women's Officer Candidate School. Commissioned as a Naval Reserve line officer, Ensign Brown's first assignment at the Navy Receiving Station, Anacostia, D.C., where she spent three and a half years. She was promoted to lieutenant, junior grade, in 1945 and set up the first Navy liquor mess (package store) in the District of Columbia at Anacostia.

She was promoted to lieutenant in 1946 but decided to return to teaching rather than remain in the Navy as a Reserve officer. When Congress passed the National Security Act of 1948 to permit granting women regular commissions, women Reserve officers were asked to indicate whether they would be interested in regular commissions. Before leaving active duty, Betty Brown signed a statement of interest.

In the summer of 1948, she performed two weeks of active duty. Because she had signed a nonbinding agreement to consider accepting a USN commission in the Supply Corps, the Naval Reserve sent her to the Naval Supply Depot in Bayonne, New Jersey, to learn about supply operations firsthand. Shortly thereafter, the Navy advised her that she had been selected to return to active duty in the Supply Corps as a USN officer. Because she had been on inactive duty for a year, her new commission would be as a LTJG. In December 1948 LTJG Brown returned to active duty at the Navy Supply Corps School, recently moved from Harvard University to Bayonne.

Because the class was not scheduled to start at Bayonne until March 1949, LTJG Brown was assigned temporarily to the Naval Barracks Washington as the assistant officer-in-charge of ship's service. Her first job was to outfit the Navy's WAVE contingent that was to march in the inaugural parade for President Harry Truman in January, and she worked with New York designers to come up with suitable skirts, not too short, but not long.

She returned to Bayonne and NSCS in March with the school's first group of nine women officers. When they reported in, sleeping arrangements had not been completed, but hastily renovated spaces were prepared. Brown's roommate was LT Jane Shopfer, who later left active duty and became the first woman Reserve Supply Corps captain.

More than 80 percent of the NSCS class were ensigns, most only recently graduated from the Naval Academy. The nine women—all LTJGs—outranked the majority of the male students. The women were not put on the station watch bill initially, but eventually that oversight was corrected.

Before completing the nine-month NSCS course, Brown became eligible for promotion and made lieutenant again—this time permanently. LT Brown's first assignment out of NSCS was as assistant supply officer at the Naval Air Station Norfolk, where she was the first woman Supply Corps officer. Although on duty in the Supply Department as assistant accounting officer, she was promptly designated a communications duty watch officer. Responding to her appeals, her boss, Captain Clinton Thro, convinced the commanding officer to assign her to the Supply Department watch list instead. She was responsible for supervising the night crew in filling priority requisitions and involving three or four runs each night to the air terminal to ship priority requisitions to the Fleet.

LT Brown went on her first night duty without benefit of a detailed briefing on what was expected of her. During the evening, word came in that a fight had broken out among civilian workers at the scrapyard. She drove the duty section truck over to the yard to investigate. When she arrived, she found two burly men battling away. Other workers had left their duties and were standing in a group, watching the fight. LT Brown waded in, stopped the fight, and followed up with a stern lecture that succeeded in getting everybody back to work. CAPT Thro rebuked her the next day, "You could have gotten killed. Why did you go out there?" Nobody had warned the newest member of the department of that particular hazard, but never again was there trouble at the scrapyard when Brown had the duty.

She later became NAS Norfolk accounting officer and remained in that job until becoming the control branch officer in 1951. In June 1953 she was transferred to the National Security Agency in Washington as assistant budget and accounting chief, reporting to an Army major.

In February 1954 LT Brown left NSA and went back to the Navy at a familiar spot, the Navy Receiving Station Washington. Her new duty was as assistant supply and fiscal officer and officer-in-charge of the cold storage plant, which supplied all Navy and congressional messes in the Washington area, as well as the White House and Camp David.

In March 1956 she was promoted to lieutenant commander and sent back to Norfolk as assistant officer-in-charge of the commissary store at the naval station. At the time, it was the largest food store in the Navy. Brown's next assignment was across the Elizabeth River as officer-in-charge of the commissary store at the Norfolk Naval Shipyard in Portsmouth.

The commissary store had severe problems, but Brown succeeded in solving them. After three and a half years, she grew tired of "shoppers and groceries." The shipyard supply officer at the time had assured her that she could become one of his assistant supply officers as soon as she had solved the commissary store problems. Betty Brown persevered at the commissary store because the gratifying way of life in the Virginia-North Carolina area outweighed her dislike of Navy-style retail grocery business. She honed her golf skills and discovered the Outer Banks of North Carolina, where she eventually purchased property.

During her time in the area, Brown's golf game flourished, and she began to participate in Navy golf tournaments. In 1961 she won the Norfolk Regional Area Women's Military Golf Tournament and went on to win the Southeast Atlantic Tournament at NAS Jacksonville.

She became shipyard assistant supply officer. Her golfing prowess earned invitations to participate in frequent foursomes, including frequently with the shipyard admiral, the shipyard commanding officer, the supply officer, and the ordnance officer. On one such occasion, the Norfolk Naval Shipyard commander—Rear Admiral William E. Howard—won *her* on the golf course. He had advised his golfing companions that he was ready to implement a new Navy policy of replacing engineering duty only (EDO) officers at Navy shipyards with Supply Corps officers. He added, "I have decided who my first Supply Corps officer will be. It will be Betty." The billet had always been filled by an EDO captain, and many senior Supply Corps captains wanted the prestigious billets as shipyard comptrollers throughout the Navy. Norfolk was one of the most desired of the new Supply Corps shipyard comptroller billets.

When CAPT Major reminded RADM Howard that CDR Brown was in line to become his top assistant, the admiral suggested that he and CDR Brown team up to play 18 holes against Major and CAPT Willy Crenshaw, the shipyard ordnance officer. Howard added, "If we win the match, she becomes the comptroller. If you win, she stays in the Supply Department." Betty Brown played a sterling round that day, and she and her partner took honors.

Howard sent Major to convince RADM John W. Crumpacker, Chief, BuSandA, that a junior female commander should be given the choice assignment over senior male captains who coveted it. In February 1963 CDR Betty Brown became the first Supply Corps officer to be assigned as comptroller of a Navy shipyard.

CAPT Winifred Quick Collins, USN, director of Navy Women, selected her to take on a special project to go to Atlanta to produce, in two days, a television show on women in the service. Brown quickly organized and set up a mock commissary store in the television studio, brought in four enlisted people to describe their jobs, and narrated the show. The telecast was well received.

In August 1965 CDR Brown reported back across the Elizabeth River to the Naval Supply Center Norfolk as director of the Comptroller Division in the Planning Department. When Captain Winston Adair, head of the Planning Department, was promoted to executive officer, Brown succeeded him and was promoted to captain in 1967. When she left NSC Norfolk to transfer to the Naval Supply Systems Command in July 1969, she received the Navy Commendation Medal, primarily for successfully computerizing the center's accounting records.

At NAVSUP, CAPT Brown was assistant deputy commander for financial management, but she was uncomfortable in the job. The death of her brother in a tragic accident hit her hard, and she felt a need to be with her aging mother. Rather than accept a transfer to the Naval Postgraduate School at Monterey, California, she chose retirement after 28½ years of active Navy service and was awarded the Navy Meritorious Service Medal.

CAPT Brown returned to the Norfolk area and to the home she purchased in 1962 by the golf course in her adopted city of Portsmouth, where she has been able to devote considerable time to her love of golf. In 1980 she was the director of the North Carolina Women's State Tournament, and in mid-January 1994 she shot an 86 in Florida—at the age of 77, with an artificial knee, and with three screws in her hip, which she had broken in a fall!

Sources

"CAPT Betty J. Brown Assigned NavSup Duty." *The Supply Chest,* NSC Norfolk, 20 June 1969.

"Eagles for a Wave." *The Virginia-Pilot* [Norfolk, Va.], 11 June 1968.

Interview of CAPT Betty J. Brown. Norfolk, Va., January 1992.

"A Wave Handles the Funds." *The Supply Chest,* NSC Norfolk, 8 May 1969.

The Multistores Fast Combat Ships

In-depth studies by BuSandA and FMSO of how best to provide supply support to operating forces contributed to a decision to construct two classes of larger multipurpose fleet auxiliaries. The first of these fast combat stores ships, *USS Mars* (AFS-1), with 2,625 tons of dry cargo capacity and 1,300 tons of refrigerated capacity, was commissioned in December 1963. CDR C. A. Gardner was commissioning supply officer.

The second lead multistores fast combat support ship, *USS Sacramento* (AOE-1), was commissioned in March of the following year. Her capacity was 177,000 barrels of oil and 2,500 tons of ammunition, as well as 500 tons of dry cargo and 250 tons of refrigerated space. LCDR William H. Riordan was commissioning supply officer. Both of the new classes carried two helicopters for vertical replenishment capability.

Further expansion ashore also took place that year with commissioning of Naval Supply Center Charleston, South Carolina. Continued streamlining of the Navy Supply System in the early 1960s took place in the context of expansion of the Defense Supply Agency. An Integrated Logistics Support Concept was initiated by DOD directive in 1964. The Defense Contract Audit Agency (DCAA) was established in 1964, and Defense Contract Administration Services (DCAS) came into being in 1965 under the DSA.

LORE OF THE CORPS

Rear Admiral Robert Harold Northwood, SC, USN

Commander, Defense Electronic Supply Center, 1963–66
Period of Service: 1937–66

RADM Northwood was duty officer at the Bureau of Supplies and Accounts on 7 December 1941, when the Japanese attacked Pearl Harbor. He went on to become the first Navy Flag officer to head the joint services inventory control point for electronic parts.

Robert H. Northwood was born in Johnstown, Pennsylvania, in May 1914. He developed an interest in the Naval Academy from following its football team and won a Naval Reserve competitive appointment to Annapolis. He was graduated in 1937, but his eyesight deteriorated while he was at the Academy. He was sent to sea in *USS Tennessee* (BB-

43) as a line officer for two years to determine whether his eyesight would improve. It did not, so he transferred to the Supply Corps and attended the Navy Finance and Supply School at Philadelphia with the noted Class of 1939-40. He was graduated in May 1940 and ordered to duty as disbursing officer of Mine Division One, based at Honolulu.

In 1941 he was ordered to duty in BuSandA and assigned to the Officer Personnel Division (OP), with additional duty as aide to the chief, RADM Brent Young. He had the normal weekend duty in the old Main Navy Building on 7 December.

RADM Northwood recalls that OP was a small operation befitting a prewar Corps of only about 600 officers. Officer Personnel was headed by CAPT William J. (Nick) Carter. Sue Dorsey was secretary and Carter's "good right hand." RADM Northwood says that 75 to 100 distinguished senior captains rotated among the best jobs, which were at shipyards and featured luxurious quarters. He also remembers "a couple hundred very professional mustang types who were locked at the lieutenant commander level." The balance of the Corps was composed of junior officers who came in from the Naval Academy in groups of 10 to 20 each year. Sue Dorsey knew them all, Northwood says, and usually handled the detailing of lieutenant commanders and below. LT Northwood remained in the personnel business through the big build-up in Supply Corps officers, which reached nearly 17,000 by the end of 1943. He wanted to get into the action heating up in the Pacific and detailed himself to his old ship, *Tennessee*.

Northwood was sensitive to what he considered a waste of time for junior officers, the assignment of coding duty, a job he felt could better be handled by petty officers. He convinced the commanding officer that Supply Corps officers aboard *Tennessee* should be assigned gun stations or duty in CIC rather than coding duty.

Tennessee had suffered severe damage in the Pearl Harbor attack. When repaired, she was modernized and many 5-inch, 40mm guns were added, requiring an increase in complement from 1,200 to 3,000, but the Navy did not authorize additional scuttlebutts (water fountains).

While on a tour of the Seabee supply storage area when *Tennessee* was in port at Pearl Harbor, Northwood spotted several of the new, flaked ice machines being held for distribution to proposed advance bases. He also noted that all Seabee personnel left for lunch at the same time. He admits that he arranged to have one of the machines and its accompanying ice storage chest liberated over lunch hour the next day and delivered to his ship. By 1300, the badly needed, but unauthorized, ice equipment was aboard *Tennessee*. The skipper asked no questions.

About three weeks later, Secretary of the Navy Forrestal, BuSandA

Chief Nick Carter, and Admiral Ben Morrell, Chief, Bureau of Yards and Docks, came aboard *Tennessee* to observe the landing at Kwajelein Atoll in January 1944. Shortly after arrival, ADM Morrell sent for LCDR Northwood. The Seabee chief had a soft drink with flaked ice, made with a machine not authorized for shipboard use. When he asked where the machine had come from, LCDR Northwood responded, "It came with the ship, sir." Morrell accused Northwood of being a "blankety blank robber," then laughed with the other guests as they all enjoyed cold liquid refreshment in the oven-hot ship.

On the evening before the initial assault on Okinawa, LCDR Northwood was about to turn in when he suddenly realized that the following day was Easter. He had the night galley crew color some 600 dozen hard-boiled eggs with cake icing dye. They put two each in battle station box lunches. During a brief lull in the shore bombardment, runners dashed back to the galley, picked up the boxes, and scurried back to their stations. Firing then resumed. Northwood says, "I often wonder what the Japanese ashore would have thought if they knew that crews in the 14-inch turrets and 5-inch mounts that were pounding them were also engaged in Easter egg hunts."

During the Battle of Surigao Straits leading into the Leyte Gulf, Northwood stood on an outside platform and watched as 14-inch and 16-inch guns of *Tennessee* and five other old battleships fired at long range on a Japanese battleship unseen over the horizon. He returned to auxiliary CIC to observe the enemy's blip disappear from the radar screen upon being hit.

After the Okinawa campaign in 1945, Northwood returned to BuSandA as director of field purchasing and was promoted to commander. He went to the Pentagon in 1947 to serve as aide and special assistant to two successive assistant secretaries of the Navy, Mark E. Andrews and Jack Koehler. He attended graduate school at Harvard in 1949 and was promoted to captain in 1951, when he reported as officer-in-charge of the General Supply Depot, NSC Norfolk. CAPT Northwood was assistant fleet supply officer, U.S. Pacific Fleet, from 1953 to 1956, and commanding officer of the General Stores Supply Office in Philadelphia in 1956. Returning to BuSandA, he was head of OP from 1958 to 1959. He then was commanding officer, Electronics Supply Office at Great Lakes, Illinois, to relieve CAPT Hersh Goldberg, who was selected for rear admiral and returned to BuSandA.

Bob Northwood was the Navy member of a joint committee established by Defense Secretary Robert McNamara to consolidate the various individual services' electronic inventory control points into a new Defense Electronic Supply Center. The services all opposed the consolidation, but McNamara ordered it done anyway. The U.S. Air Force Depot at Dayton, Ohio, was converted to a Defense Supply Agency facility in 1961. Newly promoted Rear Admiral Northwood became deputy commander to an Air Force general in 1961 and was named commander in 1962. During the Vietnam War, Northwood convinced the director of DSA that it was unwise to buy large volumes of slow-moving, solid-state, reliable electronic components only because funds were available.

RADM Northwood retired from the Navy in 1966 and accepted a position as vice president of Mead Corporation. He retired again in 1979 and lives with his wife June at Durham, North Carolina.

Source

Interview of RADM Robert H. Northwood. Asheville, N.C., May 1993.

Commanding the Four Largest BuSandA Field Activities

RADM Hugh C. Haynsworth, Jr., had the distinction of serving as commanding officer of the four largest field activities under the management control of the Bureau of Supplies and Accounts. A native of Sumter, South Carolina, he was graduated from the Naval Academy in 1930 and transferred to the Supply Corps in 1935.

He was on duty with the U.S. Naval Mission to the Republic of Colombia at Cartagena when the attack on Pearl Harbor took place. During World War II, he served successively as head of advance base planning and logistics planning in BusSandA. During this time, he was involved in early development of provisions ordering procedures (POP), underway replenishment systems, automated warehousing, automated order entry, worldwide inventory management, and stock-funded inventories afloat.

He was ordered to duty as C.O. of the BuSandA field branch at Cleveland in 1947, and in 1953 he took command of the Naval Supply Depot Bayonne. In 1959 he became commanding officer of Naval Supply Center Norfolk, followed by a tour as C.O. of NSC Oakland in 1963. He retired in 1964 at Norfolk.

The Vietnam War

The number of American military personnel in South Vietnam gradually increased from a small contingent in 1955 to 15,000 over the next 8 years, and their role changed from advising to fighting. In October 1965 the U.S. Naval Support Activity, Danang, was officially established. It had taken just three months for 900 Navymen to turn a scenic harbor with sandy beaches into a major logistical support base for American Army and Marine forces in the I-Corps Tactical Zone. The Navy turned the quiet city of Danang into a busy seaport and the Navy's largest overseas shore command. CDR Robert S. Leventhal, SC, USN, was the first assistant chief of staff for supply and fiscal for U.S. Navy and Marine forces in Vietnam.

Back in Washington, RADM John Crumpacker completed his four-year tour as Chief, BuSandA, and was relieved by RADM Herschel Goldberg in May 1965. RADM Crumpacker turned over to RADM Goldberg a Bureau of Supplies and Accounts that included 3 inventory control points and 16 supply centers or depots among its field activities. There were 5,601 Supply Corps officers on active duty.

LORE OF THE CORPS

Rear Admiral Herschel Joseph Goldberg, SC, USN

Chief, Bureau of Supplies and Accounts, and Paymaster General, 1965–66;
Commander, Naval Supply Systems Command, and
Chief of Supply Corps, 1966–67
Period of Service: 1935–37

RADM Goldberg was the last chief of the Bureau and the first commander of the Naval Supply Systems Command. On the occasion of the redesignation of the Navy's supply headquarters, Hersh Goldberg reminded his shipmates of the words of Benjamin Disraeli, "Change is inevitable in a progressive society." Goldberg is also the senior of four retired Supply Corps rear admirals to have been reared within a 30-square mile of northwestern Missouri and northeastern Kansas.

Herschel J. Goldberg was born at Highland, Kansas, in May 1913, to parents who immigrated from Lithuania. When he was a child, his family moved to St. Joseph, Missouri, where he attended St. Joseph Academy and was a member of the school's Cadet Corps (ROTC). He received an appointment as an alternate to the Naval Academy and went to Annapolis in the fall of 1931 after the principal candidate failed the physical examination.

Upon graduation in 1935, ENS Herschel Goldberg was ordered to duty in *USS Texas* (BB-35). Two years aboard as a junior watch and division officer convinced him that the line was not for him, so he responded to a call in an ALNAV for volunteers for the Supply Corps. He reported to the

Navy Finance and Supply School in the fall of 1937, completed the course in the spring of 1938, and was promoted to lieutenant, junior grade. He was ordered as disbursing officer of the repair ship *USS Vestal* (AR-4) at San Francisco. When the supply officer suffered a heart attack, Goldberg was given additional duty as his replacement.

The first lieutenant of *USS Houston* (CA-30), moored alongside, came to *Vestal*'s supply office with a problem. He had made local purchases of carpeting, batting, and other materials to refit the Flag quarters for a cruise with President Roosevelt aboard. The supply officer of *Houston,* a lieutenant commander, refused to pay the bill because the first lieutenant had not gone through him. LTJG Goldberg remembered that he had learned at NF&SS that a supply officer "will probably go to jail for violating a law, but never go to jail for violating a regulation." As supply officer, he had the first lieutenant sign the bill, which he then approved. Then, as disbursing officer, Goldberg signed a check and sent it to the vendor. He heard nothing further of the matter.

In July 1940 he reported as supply officer, *USS Brazos* (AO-4), assigned to the Train, Base Force. Six months into the tour, a new C.O. took charge of *Brazos*—the former first lieutenant of *Houston* whose career LTJG Goldberg had saved earlier. *Brazos* was underway almost constantly to convey fuel from the Long Beach-San Pedro area to Alaska, Pearl Harbor, Wake, and Guam.

Goldberg recalls an incident when, in the early days of underway replenishment, the Fleet oiler was using rudimentary gear and engaged in experimental refueling of *USS Saratoga* (CV-3). While refueling was underway, the Flag officer in *Saratoga* decided that the two ships should do some maneuvering. He ran up a zig-zag signal, but it took *Brazos,* not normally a maneuvering vessel, about a half hour to locate the Flag signal book and interpret the message. When the oiler finally signaled that the message was understood, *Saratoga* signaled "execute." One ship zigged and the other zagged on divergent courses. "You never saw such a mess in all your life." Goldberg remembers. "Oil all over both ships." An inquiry later revealed that there were half-hour time zones in that part of the world. One of the ships was on Pearl Harbor time and the other on a different time, so they choose different headings.

LTJG Goldberg was reassigned to the Bremerton (Washington) Navy Yard as the junior officer in the Supply Department shortly before the Japanese attack on Pearl Harbor. The senior assistant was CDR James E. (Eddie) Hunt, whose path Goldberg would cross many times in future years.

LTJG Goldberg was transferred across Puget Sound to the new Navy Supply Depot established at Piers 90 and 91, Seattle, in November 1941.

On 7 December, Goldberg could not believe the first news of the Japanese sneak attack, thinking it to be another dramatic radio show. He changed stations and soon realized the reports were real. He rushed to the office, where "all hell was breaking loose." NSD Seattle started a massive purchase program, with major emphasis on exercising an existing lumber option to obtain every available piece.

Goldberg recalls that they "literally threw the book out" as they anticipated receiving requisitions from stations throughout the Pacific. Puget Sound Supply Department bought "everything from normal hardware-type things to locomotives, and price was never a consideration. Some marvelous Reserves started coming in the Supply Corps at that time." One was ENS Eddie Carlson, who had been manager of the Rainier Club in Seattle. Carlson went on to become chairman and CEO of United Airlines and later was also a member of the Navy Exchange System Advisory Committee.

Hersh Goldberg was promoted to lieutenant in February 1942, and in January 1943 left the Seattle area with orders as supply officer, Naval Station Bora Bora, in the Society Islands. The base had been established only a year before as a fueling stop for ships coming through the Panama Canal en route to Australia. LT Goldberg arrived at Bora Bora two weeks earlier than expected and called on the supply officer he was scheduled to relieve.

He found the supply office a shambles, with pay receipts, small stores chits, and other papers scattered around. He asked his predecessor to see the cash book, but was told that the day's receipts had not yet been posted and he would be shown the book the following morning. LT Goldberg then called on the C.O., who told him, "You know, we asked for this officer to be relieved." Goldberg had not known until that moment.

The supply-disbursing office burned totally that night, and, Goldberg says, suspicions over the cause arose immediately. From the type of smoke and flames, it was obvious that the fire had been set. His predecessor was questioned, but no official inquiry was held. Working from surviving partially burned remnants, LT Goldberg needed about six months to square away pay records, allotments, and other documents.

He was promoted to lieutenant commander in the summer of 1943 and ordered, in October, to Guadalcanal as supply officer. En route to his new duty, he went through Noumea, New Caledonia, where he again encountered his friend CAPT Eddie Hunt, officer-in-charge of the Supply Depot and supply officer of the Submarine Base Noumea. Hunt offered Goldberg the job as his executive officer, but LCDR Goldberg declined and proceeded to Guadalcanal, where his new C.O. did not think any Supply Corps officers were "worth a damn," except CAPT Frank Delahanty, on FADM Halsey's staff. Things went from bad to worse in a hurry, Goldberg says. When Delahanty went to Guadalcanal on an inspection, he and Goldberg discussed matters. Goldberg agreed to return to Noumea as exec in November 1943. In Noumea, there were 2,000 enlisted warehousemen, material handlers, and laborers, nearly half of whom were black. Most of the men were in training for reassignment to advance bases.

Whites were berthed in about 20 barracks on the hill on one side, and blacks berthed on the other hill in another 20 or so barracks. Messing for officers and men was in an old amphitheater. The men ate in the side of the mess hall closest to their barracks. The result was total segregation. The same seating arrangement prevailed when movies were shown in the amphitheater. LCDR Goldberg went to CAPT Hunt to suggest breaking down the de facto segregation, but his superior would have none if it.

After Hunt was transferred as supply officer of the Charleston Navy Yard in the spring of 1944, Goldberg relieved him and promptly proceeded with his plan. He proposed that half of the barracks on each side be populated by each race, while maintaining the practice of messing on the side adjacent to the barracks in which the men resided. The other officers did not like his proposal, but the petty officers, black and white, did, and Goldberg's proposal was implemented. In one stroke he had integrated the work force. There were no problems, and Admiral Goldberg says it was "the most soul-satisfying thing that I've done in my entire career."

During World War II, Supply Corps officers below the rank of captain, detached from duty in the South Pacific, rarely left that area for stateside duty. Officers normally were sent to SERVPAC at Pearl Harbor for reassignment. However, Hersh Goldberg was ordered in November 1944 to report directly to the Charleston Navy Yard as senior assistant to CAPT Eddie Hunt, the supply officer. LCDR Goldberg learned at San Francisco that he had been promoted to commander. He reported to his new duty in December 1944. At Charleston, the new exec encountered, and was impressed by, LT (later CAPT) Gerald L. (Jerry) Griffin, the issue division officer and one of the few Regular Navy Supply Corps officers stationed at the adjacent Navy Yard.

In the fall of 1947, Goldberg went to the Harvard Graduate School of Business for two years. The Bureau of Supplies and Accounts was CDR Goldberg's next duty, where he was originally the fuel division officer under the chief, RADM Dorsey Foster. The services were just beginning to participate in cross-servicing on a voluntary basis. That experience convinced Hersh Goldberg that some sort of merger or combination of supply support among the three services was necessary and inevitable.

In late December 1950, CAPT Joe Lyle, head of Supply Corps personnel offered Goldberg a chance to go to Paris for a two-month fill-in, unaccompanied tour to assist in the setting up of a new NATO command, Supreme Headquarters Allied Powers Europe (SHAPE). Another Supply Corps captain had been hand-picked by GEN Alfred M. Gruenther, GEN Eisenhower's deputy, but was unavailable because of the press of his duties at the Munitions Board. CDR Goldberg left for Paris on New Year's Eve 1950.

The originally assigned captain arrived in 60 days, but in the meantime the senior Navy officer, CAPT (later ADM and CNO) George Anderson, decided he needed more than one Supply Corps officer. As a result, Goldberg's temporary duty became permanent and accompanied, and he stayed in France until June 1953.

CDR Goldberg returned to the United States in the summer of 1953, attended the Industrial College of the Armed Forces at Washington, and in June 1954 was promoted to captain. He reported to the Office of the Chief of Naval Material as assistant chief for supply programs. In January 1957 he became commanding officer, Electronics Supply Office, Great Lakes, Illinois, and was selected for Flag rank in June 1959.

In November of that year, he returned to BuSandA as assistant chief for supply management under RADM Jimmy Boundy and made his number in July 1960. RADM Goldberg had another tour in the Office of Chief of Naval Material, this time as vice chief, from September 1961 to December 1962, when he again went back to BuSandA as deputy chief under RADM John Crumpacker. When Crumpacker retired in April 1965, RADM Goldberg was appointed chief and received the Legion of Merit for "exceptionally meritorious service" as deputy.

Herschel Godlberg's final four jobs in the Navy were in Washington, all of them in offices on the same deck in the old Main Navy building and within several hundred yards of one another. His permanent change-of-duty expenses were the lowest they could possibly be. The four Washington duties were the same ones RADM Bear Arnold had held as a Flag officer.

RADM Goldberg had become a strong believer in joint-service support, but he remembers the subject as "the most serious and far-reaching problem the Corps was facing in those days." He believed the Supply Corps was more attuned to the desirability and necessity of interservice supply than others in the Navy because of the Corps' inventory control point experience.

Comptrollership and procurement were two areas in which assignments were divided between the Supply Corps and the line. RADM Goldberg was concerned over the future of the Supply Corps, and one of his first moves as chief was to establish a committee to examine the question, work with consultants, and report back. CAPTs Jack Scott and Goldberg's old friend Jerry Griffin headed the effort.

Under the old bureau system, replaced by the systems command concept in 1966, the chiefs reported both to the CNO and to his boss, the secretary of the Navy. RADM Goldberg says, "If you did not get what you wanted from your uniformed boss, you would just go around him and try to get it from the civilian boss." Goldberg thought the old system was "nutty" and the new one a "good idea," even though the leader of the Supply Corps was no longer a presidential appointee.

Hersh Goldberg put in his retirement papers in August 1967, but in June ADM David McDonald showed him a recommendation from the chief of Naval Material, ADM I. J. Galantin. It called for transfer of ASO to Air Systems, SPCC to Ships Systems, and ESO to Electronics Systems. Hersh Goldberg thought that he had convinced Galantin, who was also a friend, that the arrangement was "stupid."

ADM Anderson had disapproved Galantin's recommendation and read his negative endorsement to RADM Goldberg, who said, "I couldn't have written it any better. There was nothing but a most superlative praise of the Supply Corps and how wrong this would be." Goldberg told both Anderson and Galantin that if the secretary agreed with Galantin instead of Anderson, he was not going to retire because it would appear as though he were doing so out of pique. The secretary agreed with ADM Anderson's endorsement, the ICPs remained with NAVSUP, and Herschel Goldberg retired in August 1967. He was awarded the Distinguished Service Medal, the citation of which read, in part, "He has held the predominant role in the continued development of a strong, centrally coordinated and fully integrated supply system focused toward an ever-increasing readiness posture for the United States Navy."

In September 1967 Herschel Goldberg accepted a position as special assistant to the president, Levi Strauss Company in San Francisco, and remained with that firm until finally retiring in June 1978. He and his wife Jane live at San Mateo, California.

Sources

Interview of RADM Herschel Goldberg. San Francisco, 29 July 1986.
Official Biography. Navy Office of Information, September 1967.

Reviewing the Role of the Supply Corps

Shortly after he had assumed command of BuSandA in 1965, RADM

Goldberg called in an outside consulting firm, Management and Economics Research, Inc. (MAERI), to review the role of the Bureau and the Supply Corps.

Admiral Goldberg recalls that the MAERI group was headed by Earl Armstrong, a former Supply Corps officer and "a hell of a bright guy," and that the group came up an "excellent study," with a projection through 1980. MAERI concluded that the trend would be toward the consolidation of management functions, that greater emphasis would be placed on integrated and joint logistics, and that a revolution in ADP and information systems would take place. The consultants predicted that the Supply Corps would be in a unique position to meet the critical need in the Navy and DOD for selection, development, and retention of highly competent logistics managers.

From NSC C.O. to College President

CAPT Theodore S. (Ted) Stern reported to NSC Charleston as commanding officer in July 1965. A native of New York, he was graduated from the Johns Hopkins University in 1934. Ted Stern enlisted in the Naval Reserve in October 1940 and was immediately called to active duty. He was commissioned a line ensign in July 1941. He transferred to the Supply Corps in 1947 as a lieutenant commander.

He had several tours in fuel jobs, attended ICAF, and had duty at ESO Great Lakes and BusSandA before being ordered to Charleston. From the beginning of his four-year tour as C.O., NSC Charleston, he was deeply involved in community affairs. He retired from the Navy on a Friday in August 1968 and, on the following Monday, assumed office as the 15th president of the College of Charleston. In that capacity he oversaw an increase in enrollment from 480 students to more than 8,000. He also served as chairman of the Spoleto USA arts festival for nine years and was a Rotary International district governor.

The T. S. Stern Computer Center at NSC Charleston and the Theodore S. Stern Student Center at the College of Charleston were named in his honor in recognition of his contributions to the two local organizations he headed. In 1993 he was named a Navy Supply Corps distinguished alumnus. Ted Stern alternates between his home at Charleston and a farm at Sparta, North Carolina.

Automated Shipboard Supply Systems

In 1966 BuSandA succeeded in installing prototype automated shipboard supply systems designed for tenders. The first was installed in *USS Amphion* (AR-13), a 21-year-old, 7,800-ton repair ship with a complement of 921 and CDR Thomas P. Pettijohn as supply officer. A similar system for carriers was installed in *USS Essex* (CVS-9), a 27,100-ton, World War II ship with a complement of 3,500. CDR Leary B. Kreisslton was supply officer.

Navy Department Reorganization

A major reorganization of the Navy Department took place in 1966, creating a Naval Material Command, eliminating the 124-year old bureau system, and replacing the bureaus with systems commands. As a result, the Bureau of Supplies and Accounts became the Naval Supply Systems Command (NAVSUP). Another provision eliminated the presidential appointment of a paymaster general and designated the Commander Naval Systems Command as chief of Supply Corps.

Afloat forces were recipients of standardized assistance in fitting out new ships when the new Naval Supply Systems Command established Fleet outfitting supply assistance teams (FOSATS). Retail operations were centralized when administration of Navy commissary stores was assigned to the Navy Ship's Store Office.

The Naval Supply Systems Command

Integrated logistics support with the LHA Project for a new class of amphibious assault ships was established in 1967. SPCC and ESO implemented the first phase of a new uniform inventory control point system for inventory control application. ASO and SPCC data processing departments were designated as data processing service centers.

Consolidation of the shore establishment continued in 1967. The Naval Supply Center Bayonne was disestablished, with many functions transferred to Newport, Rhode Island, where the Naval Supply Depot was expanded to a Naval Supply Center, with CAPT Grover V. Clark as commanding officer. The Naval Supply Center Puget Sound was also established in 1967, with CAPT Frank M. Barbero as C.O.

The Diego Garcia Saga

In 1963 CNO ADM George Anderson first proposed the lease from Great Britain of Diego Garcia, in the British Indian Ocean Territory about 1,000 miles south-southwest of the nearest land mass, the Indian subcontinent. The U.S. Navy planned to dredge a 40-foot channel in the lagoon for carrier anchorage, but Defense Secretary Robert McNamara, who opposed additional overseas bases and commitments, forced cancellation of the project.

When President Lyndon Johnson improved ties with Pakistan and approved Navy deterrent patrols in the Indian Ocean, CNO David McDonald revised the Diego Garcia proposal despite Defense Secretary McNamara's continuing opposition. In 1966 McDonald convinced McNamara to agree to negotiation of a 50-year executive agreement for a Fleet radio center on the island. McNamara was adamant in opposition to the Navy's presence in the Indian Ocean, the Arabian Sea, or the Persian Gulf, so the issue of a Fleet base was put on hold.

In 1967 the Navy had not given up its objective of establishing a U.S. base on Diego Garcia. When President Richard Nixon approved sending a carrier task force into the Indian Ocean to counter a number of destabilizing moves by Iraq against Iran and India against Pakistan, the importance of the Indian Ocean base was highlighted. Deprived of use of the major South African naval base at Smithtown by congressional pressure, the U.S. Navy had no base in the area to support the task force.

The strategic situation in Southwest Asia changed dramatically in January 1968, when Prime Minister Harold Wilson announced that the British would withdraw all forces east of the Suez Canal by 1971. Meanwhile, the Soviets had earlier secured bases in Tanzania, India, Aden, and other nations around the Indian Ocean littoral.

Logistics in the Red Sea

USS Joseph P. Kennedy, Jr. (DD-850) was deployed to the Red Sea in March 1967 to protect American interests during rising tensions between Israel and her surrounding neighbors. *Kennedy* transited the Suez Canal southbound in late April and was in the southern Red Sea when the six-day war broke out in early June. *Kennedy* was given the additional assignment of covering the withdrawal of Americans from the area. *Kennedy* was steaming at the head of a northbound convoy to escort it through the canal when directed to escort a southbound convoy. The northbound convoy she had just left was sunk by mines in the canal, stranding shipping, including several American vessels, for months.

Kennedy was assigned to watch for foreign shipping that might bring troops and weapons to the faltering Egyptians. *Kennedy*'s prolonged deployment, without benefit of resupply for more than a month, depleted much of her onboard stores and food. Her supply officer, ENS (later CAPT) Fred L. Meyer, faced a critical endurance problem, requiring bartering for food and stores in local open-air markets at Mombasa, Kenya. North African air space was closed by the Arab-Israeli War, shutting off resupply of technical spares. A joint logistics effort enabled Meyer to obtain critical spares from U.S. communications stations located on mountains in the area.

Fuel became critical as one after another Arab port closed its doors and fueling ports to American ships in support of the Egyptian war effort. In another joint logistics evolution, *Kennedy* was refueled by a British tanker.

NAVILCO Established

The Navy had provided its first supply support to friendly foreign nations in 1947, with shipments of U.S. Navy equipment to Greece and Turkey. As the concept of collective security of the free nations of the Western world led to increased foreign military sales, the U.S. Navy established, in 1967, an International Logistics Control Office (NAVILCO). The new organization, under CAPT Carl L. Henn, Jr., a Supply Corps officer and commissioning commanding officer, was located at Bayonne, New Jersey, in warehouse and pierside facilities freed up by the closing of NSD the previous year. The new organization was charged with providing centralized supply support of U.S. naval equipment being used by dozens of other nations.

NAVILCO provided benefits to all three services by removing the burden of heavy volumes of routine details of supply support from the offices of military, naval, and air attachés in foreign nations. The new organization also shortened the lines of communication between the U.S. supply system and the military services of the customer countries that initiated orders for U.S. equipment.

LORE OF THE CORPS

Captain Carl Leroy Henn, Jr., SC, USN

Commanding Officer, Navy International Logistics Office, 1967–68
Period of Service: 1943–70

As a LTJG, Carl Henn was involved in the Berlin Airlift. He later worked for ADM Hyman Rickover in the Naval Reactors Program, and served on the faculty of the Industrial College of the Armed Forces.

Henn was born in Cleveland, Ohio, in February 1923 and entered Northwestern University in September 1941. He was class and fraternity president and earned academic honors. He was returning to his fraternity house after a stint as a sorority house waiter on Sunday, 7 December 1941, when he learned of the sneak Japanese attack on Pearl Harbor. In July 1943 he enrolled in the Navy V-12 program at Northwestern and transferred to the Midshipman-Officer Program at Harvard University in March 1944. He was graduated in February 1945 and commissioned an ensign, Supply Corps, U.S. Naval Reserve. Northwestern University later gave him credit for his time at Harvard and awarded him a B.S. degree in business administration.

ENS Henn's first duty was at the Naval Air Station Attu in the Aleutian Islands, where he reported in April 1945 as aviation supply officer, In January 1946 he was promoted to lieutenant, junior grade, and moved over to the Naval Operating Base, Kodiak, Alaska, as stores officer. He augmented into the U.S. Navy and returned to Harvard in June 1946 to complete studies at the Graduate School of Business, from which he was graduated with distinction and an M.B.A. in January 1947.

Henn spent February to May 1947 with Trans World Airlines (TWA) in a Navy industrial training program. He then reported to Naval Overseas Air Cargo Terminal (NOACT) at NAS Alameda as air cargo officer. In November Henn became supply officer, Naval Air Transport Squadron VR-8, deployed to Germany to augment U.S. Air Force efforts during the Berlin airlift, code-named Operation Vittles. He transferred from the squadron's terminal at Rhein-Main Air Force Base to the Headquarters Staff, Combined Airlift Task Force (CALTF) at Wiesbaden. During this tour, he conducted special studies for the Bureau of Supplies and Accounts in air-ground coordination and air packaging.

In October 1949 LTJG Henn was ordered to BuSandA for duty as assistant to the director, Air Cargo Section, Transportation Division, where the lessons learned in the Berlin Airlift were important in developing new Navy air cargo procedures. He then served at Westover Air Force Base, Chicopee Falls, Massachusetts, from February to May 1950 as air traffic coordinator in the MATS aerial port of embarkation. He returned to his duties at BuSandA, where he was promoted to lieutenant in January 1951 and served until January 1953. During his three plus years at BuSandA, Henn attended night school at George Washington University and earned an M.A. degree in international economic relations with honors.

LT Henn was ordered to duty as supply officer, *USS Menelaus* (ARL-13), homeported at Naples, Italy, in February 1953. During his two-year tour, *Menelaus* served as aviation stores issue ship with the Sixth Fleet. In April 1955 he reported to Commander Western Sea Frontier at Treasure Island, San Francisco, as project officer for Project PACE, a survey of logistics pipeline management in the Pacific Ocean area. Henn was a prime contributor to the final report, which CINCPACFLT termed "a major contribution in the field of logistics." He was promoted to lieutenant commander in July 1955 and was a member of the team that presented the report to CNO and the Joint Logistics Plans and Joint Military Transportation committees.

LCDR Henn began a five-year tour in October 1957 with the administrative staff, Naval Reactors Division, Atomic Energy Commission. In that position, he had handled preparation and presentation of the budget of all nuclear ship development programs to the Department of Defense and Congress. Henn was also responsible for financial management projects that resulted in significant budget underruns and was promoted to commander in July 1960.

In November 1962 CDR Henn reported as supply officer, Military Advisory Assistance Group, Paris, where he provided supply and logistics assistance in the acquisition and support of American weapons systems by the French Navy. He was awarded the Joint Service Commendation Medal for his performance in the marketing and subsequent support of U.S. fighter aircraft and missile systems purchased by the French.

Henn was promoted to captain in July 1965 and in October was ordered to the Naval Supply Depot Bayonne, where he was head, Material Assistance Department (MAD). MAD was rolled over into a separate entity, the Navy International Logistics Office (NAVILCO), at Bayonne when the supply depot was closed in 1967. CAPT Henn commissioned NAVILCO in February 1967 as a centralized command for the operation and control of the Navy's portion of U.S. defense aid to friendly foreign nations.

In June 1968 CAPT Henn reported to the faculty of the Industrial College of the Armed Forces in Washington as an instructor in management, economics, and international affairs. He retired from the Navy in February 1970 and was awarded the Navy Commendation Medal.

In retirement, Carl Henn worked successively for American Standard, Inc., and Shearson Lehman Hutton before setting up his own financial planning practice in 1989. He also accepted a position with Integrated Energy, Inc./Concord Energy, Inc. He is an author, a speaker, and is involved in a wide variety of community, state, and professional causes. He and his Swiss-born wife Eugenia live in New Brunswick, New Jersey.

Sources

"The Berlin Airlift, Transport Triumph." *Navy Supply Corps Newsletter,* July 1949.
Citation. Joint Service Commendation Medal, July 1965.

"International Supply Operations for Collective Defense." *Senior Foreign Supply Officers Newsletter,* November 1968.
Officer Biography Sheet, 23 August 1960.
"Navy Commissions a World Logistics Control Office." *New York Times,* 1 March 1967.
Telephone interviews of CAPT Carl L. Henn, 4 August and 25 October 1994.
"Window On the World." *Navy Supply Corps Newsletter,* March 1966.

Bieri Relieves Goldberg

RADM Herschel Goldberg was at the helm of the Supply Corps during the Navy's historic evolutionary shift from the bureau system to the systems command mode in 1966. Goldberg retired as Commander Naval Supply Systems Command and chief of Supply Corps in July 1967, and was relieved by RADM Bernard Bieri.

LORE OF THE CORPS

Rear Admiral Bernhard H. Bieri, Jr., SC, USN

Commander, Naval Supply Systems Command, and
Chief of Supply Corps, 1967–70
Period of Service: 1937–70

Bernie Bieri is a Naval Academy graduate, a line transfer, and a member of the transition class at the Navy Finance and Supply School Philadelphia and went on to become the 30th chief of Supply Corps.

Bernhard H. Bieri, Jr., was born at Camden, New Jersey, in October 1915, the son of Vice Admiral Bernhard H. Bieri, USN. Young Bernie lived the typically nomadic life of a Navy "junior" and attended high school in Washington, D.C. He was graduated from the Naval Academy and commissioned a line ensign in June 1937. He served in *USS Maryland* (BB-46) and *USS Phoenix* (CL-46), but his eyesight disqualified him from further line duty. He was faced, in 1939, with becoming a Supply Corps officer or resigning from the Navy.

ENS Bieri reported to the Navy Finance and Supply School Philadelphia, where he was a member of the famous Class of 1939-40. Bernie Bieri and his wife, Peggy, were married during Christmas leave. After his marriage, he reports, his class standing slipped from Number 1 to about Number 15. LTJG Bieri's initial assignment after NF&SS was as disbursing officer, Destroyer Division 10, normally based at San Diego, but which the Pacific Fleet had moved to Pearl Harbor.

In April 1941, after about nine months with DESDIV 10, he was ordered to the Naval Supply Depot San Diego, where CAPT (later RADM) John Hatch, a veteran of World War I overseas duty, was supply officer in charge. LTJG Bieri was assigned as assistant purchasing officer. Things were quiet until Sunday morning, 7 December. He and Peggy were playing doubles tennis at NAS North Island when word of the Japanese sneak attack on Pearl Harbor was passed. He reported immediately to his office for instructions. For another week, everyone in the office dealt with a mass of emergency procurement actions with a "gung ho" spirit, trying to purchase sufficient materials to meet emergency needs at Pearl Harbor.

About 10 days after the United States entered the war, LTJG Bieri was order to NAS North Island for an indoctrination course in aviation supply in preparation for becoming supply officer of one of the "jeep" carriers under construction by the Kaiser Corporation. Before he completed the course, he was promoted to lieutenant and ordered as supply officer, *USS San Francisco* (CA-38), Mare Island Navy Yard, Vallejo, California. *San Francisco* sailed for the South Pacific three weeks later. Although he did not know it at the time, it was on that day when Bernie Bieri became a father for the first time. Two days later, he learned from the Red Cross that his daughter had arrived.

San Francisco escorted six Army transports to New Zealand and then headed north to the Solomon Islands to support the Marines landing on Guadalcanal. After the Battle of Cape Esperance she engaged a superior Japanese force on 13 November 1942 in the Second Battle of Savo Island, where she lost 126 officers and men. Among those killed in the battle, which took place at extremely close quarters, were the task force commander, her skipper, the exec, and first lieutenant.

LT Bieri followed the battle, on radio and radar, from his battle station as head of the coding board, adjacent to the radio shack, and was unhurt in the five minutes his ship was in the fight. He reports that the opposing ships were so close that the larger guns of the more heavily armed Japanese ships could not be depressed enough to damage the hull. *San Francisco* was forced to withdraw after sustaining severe damage above the main deck and escaped to safety through continuing fire and smoke with the navigator, the senior survivor, temporarily in command.

Because the Supply Department spaces located below *San Francisco*'s main deck were spared damage during the ship's terrible ordeal, LT Bieri was able to provide nearly normal supply services afterward. En route back to Espiritu Santo, he and his shipmates watched as *USS Juneau* (CL-52) was torpedoed and sunk about 1,000 yards away. *San*

Francisco limped back to Mare Island for repairs, zig-zagging her way alone.

Upon arrival at Vallejo, Bieri was met by his NF&SS classmate LT (later CAPT) Cliff Messenheimer, assistant supply officer. Messenheimer arranged for the Bieris to move into the vacant servant's apartment above the garage at the quarters of his boss, CDR Hugh Phares, the Mare Island stores officer. The quarters were near the dry dock where the repair work on *San Francisco* would take place. The shipyard began an around-the-clock effort to repair major damage to the ship and completed the nearly impossible task two months later. When the cruiser sailed west in early 1943, she went again briefly to the South Pacific and then was ordered north for the Aleutian campaign. Bieri had to offload his tropical gear and turn it in for cold weather gear before sailing. He recalls the Battle of Kiska as "an absolute fiasco." The Japanese had already evacuated the place 10 days before the landing of several U.S. Army divisions and a Marine detachment.

San Francisco was at anchor at Adak Harbor; nearby was *USS Salt Lake City* (CA-25), Cliff Messenheimer having only recently reported aboard as supply officer. Later, *USS Castor* (AKS-1) came into the harbor, with another Supply Corps friend, LT (later CAPT) Dick Harrison as supply officer. After visiting *Castor,* Bernie Bieri arrived back on board *San Francisco* and checked with his pay clerk to determine whether any messages had come in. "Only routine, except for one strange one which I sent back telling them 'Message not understood.'" The message read: "SUPPLY OFFICER REQUISITION OF JANUARY STOP MALE COUPLING ARRIVED 6 LB 10 OZ STOP RECEIVED INSPECTED AND PASSED THIS DATE."

LT Bieri rushed to the radio shack and was able to cancel the outgoing message. He explained to the baffled pay clerk that he had just become the father of his first son. It was a cause for celebration, and Bieri sent messages to *Salt Lake City* and *Castor* to inform Messenheimer and Harrison that they were to meet him at the Adak Officers Club at 1600. The three met at the club and had quite a celebration.

Bernie Bieri was promoted to lieutenant commander while serving in *San Francisco.* In October 1943 he received orders to Washington for duty in BuSandA, where he relieved his good friend and NF&SS classmate LCDR Bob Northwood in officer personnel. He was involved in a huge increase in the number of Supply Corps officers, Regular and Reserve, on active duty; the number grew from 5,000 in late 1943 to 16,800 by the end of the War. Bieri made commander in August 1945 while on duty in the Bureau.

He left BuSandA in the summer of 1946 for a two-year tour as planning officer and later as officer-in-charge, Ships Supply Depot, Naval Supply Center Pearl Harbor. CDR Bieri reported in the summer of 1948 as executive officer, General Stores Supply Office, Philadelphia, until the summer of 1951, when he was ordered as executive officer, Navy Supply Depot Bayonne, New Jersey. He learned that he had been requested by CAPT Jimmy Boundy, the new C.O., who had been ordered in after the Supply Corps general inspector had described an inspection of the depot as "the worst I've ever had in the history of the Supply Corps." Jimmy Boundy and Bernie Bieri had their work cut out for them. Bieri reports the new programs that CAPT Boundy instituted soon earned the respect of customers and restored the depot's reputation.

In the summer of 1952 CDR Bieri received orders to the Naval War College. When he was graduated in June 1953, he was ordered to Washington duty with the Logistics Planning Group, Joint Chiefs of Staff. He later became supply aide to Raymond H. Fogler, the assistant secretary of the Navy for installations and logistics, from 1954 to 1956.

The chief of naval material, VADM Murrey Royar, and the chief of the Bureau of Supplies and Accounts, Rear Admiral Bear Arnold, were the assistant secretary's principal advisors on matters of supply and logistics. CDR Bieri also became a close, independent advisor on specific supply problems that came to Fogler's attention. One major issue confronting the Navy during Bieri's tour with Secretary Fogler was implementation of Hoover Commission recommendations that the Navy civilianize such operations as the "rope walk" at Boston and coffee plants at Norfolk and Oakland. The Navy followed through by closing the three operations.

Bieri left the Secretariat in April 1956 when he was promoted to captain and reported as supply officer, Long Beach Naval Shipyard, with additional duty as staff supply officer, Commander Naval Base, Los Angeles. The Shipyard Supply Department operated much as a Naval Supply Center, with 83 percent of its work for BuSandA. CAPT Bieri next went to the National War College in Washington in the fall of 1959.

He reported as planning officer, Bureau of Supplies and Accounts in June 1960, but left after a year when the chief, RADM John Crumpacker, sent him to command the Naval Supply Depot Seattle in September 1961. He relieved RADM Emory D. Stanley, Jr., who had just been selected to Flag rank.

As the end of the Korean War brought on the inevitable downsizing, the Naval Station Seattle was disestablished, and certain functions were transferred to NSD Seattle. The Thirteenth Naval District Public Works Department, Class A brig, chapel, VIP quarters in an old BOQ, and the officer, warraant officer, and chief petty officer clubs—all normally the responsibility of line officers—were added to those of CAPT Bieri. In 1962 the Seattle World's Fair drew foreign navy ships from around the globe. NSD Seattle was small compared to other West Coast naval facilities, but CAPT Bieri had "U.S. NAVY" painted in 40-foot high letters on the Pier 90 transit shed, clearly visible from the top of the fair's Space Needle.

Bernie Bieri's selection to Flag rank in the spring of 1962 was celebrated in an unusual fashion by the Royal Canadian Navy. Bieri had developed an acquaintance with LCDR Joe Prosser, the sailing master of the Canadian Naval Academy at Esquimalt on Vancouver Island, British Columbia. The 90-foot Canadian sailing ketch *HMCS Oriole* would make the journey of fewer than 100 miles about once a quarter in company with three or four YP yard craft for a weekend of R&R in Seattle.

On the Canadians' first visit after Bieri's selection, he boarded *Oriole* to greet his visitors. Prosser invited him below for "a touch of Nelson's blood" (rum) and produced a white turtleneck sweater, a yachting cap, and blue trousers. RADM Select Bieri donned his new uniform and was ushered between two rows of midshipmen holding halyards attached to boatswains' chairs. CAPT Bieri and LCDR Prosser were hauled to the top of the mast. There, LCDR Prosser extracted a bottle of champagne and two glasses and pronounced, "We are now toasting the High Admiral."

In December 1962 RADM Bieri returned to Washington as deputy chief of naval material, where he served until March 1965, and he was awarded the Legion of Merit upon detachment. RADM Bieri went back to Pearl Harbor in April 1965 as fleet supply officer, Commander-in-Chief U.S. Pacific Fleet, and force supply officer, Commander Service Force, Pacific Fleet. At SERVPAC, he was responsible for logistics forces that supported both the Fleet and ashore operations in Vietnam. One of his first functions was to visit NSD Guam, NSD Subic Bay, and Vietnam to observe supply operations progress. He received a gold star in lieu of a second Legion of Merit for his contributions during the Vietnam conflict.

In the summer of 1967 RADM Bieri was ordered to relieve RADM Steve Sherwood as vice commander, Naval Supply Systems Command. The timing of the various reliefs was so tight that Bieri could not make a contact relief with Sherwood, so the two arranged to drive to Williamsburg, Virginia, to attend a Supply Corps Commanding Officers Conference. The en route talk comprised the relieving procedure.

When RADM Bieri arrived at NAVSUP on 11 July to take over the job RADM Sherwood had vacated, he was stunned to learn that RADM Goldberg had decided to retire as commander on 30 July to accept an offer in the business community. The question of who would succeed Goldberg as commander of NAVSUP and chief of the Corps was quickly answered: Bernie Bieri would. He immediately called in RADM George E. (Rhythm) Moore to be deputy. Subsequently, Moore was relieved by RADM Ken Wheeler, both of whom later were promoted to vice admiral.

Goldberg had warned Bieri that stock record accuracy throughout the Navy supply system was a problem. NAVSUP had been called to task by Congress and the secretary of defense about the "horrible rate" of inaccuracy in those records. Initially, when NAVSUP officials went to major commercial firms such as Sears Roebuck and the May Company, they learned that Navy stock error rate of only 6 to 7 percent was substantially lower than that of civilian companies. Nonetheless, Bieri is proud of the fact that after a year and a half the Navy's problem was "pretty well under control," with significant improvement over what the business world already considered an acceptable, if not good, rate.

Bernie and Peggy Bieri attended a family wedding at Minot AFB, North Dakota, arriving in civilian clothes and driving a rental car. An Air Force guard closely scrutinized his ID card, saw "RADM," and asked, "What is a raddum?" The admiral sternly replied, "Young man, a 'raddum' is a rear admiral in the Navy." The guard said in a polite and friendly manner, "Gee, admiral, you certainly are a long way from the ocean."

The spirit of Supply Corps officers was exceptionally high during the involvement in Vietnam, Bieri feels. He recalls that "by putting our top-notch people in key slots in the Far East during the Vietnam War, we achieved great recognition from the line and from the commanders in the forward areas. We were continually being asked to provide Supply Corps officers as project managers and for logistics planning, as well as managers of the traditional 'three B's' [beans, bullets, and black oil]."

He points out the many young Supply Corps officers who worked for him and went on to significant positions in military and civilian careers. Among them were future Supply Corps rear admirals Jim Ahern, Wally Dowd, Pat Foley, Fred Haddock, Joe Howard, Doug Lyness, and Jack Scott and civilian corporate executives Jackson Schultz (Wells Fargo Bank), Bob Campbell (Federal Home Bank of Boston), and Carl Wieland (IBM). Another, Pete Malloy, became assistant secretary of defense for procurement and is currently Bernie Bieri's golf partner.

RADM Bieri shared with other chiefs of Supply Corps a keen interest in the future of the Corps. Shortly before he completed his tour as commander of NAVSUP, he wrote a lengthy article in *The Review,* the official journal of the Defense Supply Association. He pointed out that the Supply Corps officer is an integral member of the total Navy team, regardless of where he is located. He concludes, "It is through a well-planned but flexible cycle of experience and formal training that the Navy Supply Corps techno-economist is prepared to shape the future within the U.S. Military Establishment."

RADM Bieri was relieved by RADM Ken Wheeler on 30 June 1970 and was awarded the Distinguished Service Medal. In retirement, he and Peggy returned to the San Diego area and currently live in La Jolla, California, with a summer home in the mountains of Northern California.

Sources

Bieri, RADM B. H., Jr. "Logistics Management in Evolution." *The Review,* May–June, 1970.

Interview of RADM B. H. Bieri, Jr. San Diego, Calif., 4 March 1986.

Official Biography. Naval Supply Systems Command, July 1970.

"RADM B. H. Bieri, Jr. Retires from Navy." *Navy Supply Corps Newsletter,* August 1970.

Vietnam Logistics

As American commitment to the war in Vietnam grew throughout the early 1960s, the complexity of logistics increased. When the battleship *USS New Jersey* (BB-62) was deployed to the war zone, 16-inch shells and powder bags were added to the existing ordnance mix managed by NSA Danang.

In 1967 a huge volume of freight was shipped to Vietnam, and 98 percent went by sea. The combined tonnage transported by Navy and Military Sea Transportation Service (MSTS) ships to Vietnam was roughly equal to all American exports to the rest of the world. Most of this material went directly to U.S. Navy ships through underway replenishment or to the Navy Supply Depot at NSA Danang. The impressive growth of NSA Danang, the first major Navy support base in a combat zone, demonstrated the logistics capability of the Supply Corps. Danang's operations were extended in 1966 to Chu Lai, 45 miles south.

In 1968 Naval Supply Depot Subic Bay became the first ever Naval Supply System Command-managed field activity to receive a Presidential Unit Citation for its support to operating forces deployed to WESTPAC and in Vietnam. CAPT (later RADM) Roland Rieve was the commanding officer.

The *Pueblo* Incident

Cold war tensions heightened on 23 January 1968, when North Korean gunboats attacked *USS Pueblo* (AGER-2), a converted 960-ton Army light cargo ship designated an environmental research ship. In reality it was an intelligence-gathering vessel assigned to the Navy's surface ship surveillance program, originally known as Operation Clickbettle. Her complement was 6 officers, 38 enlisted crew members, 37 enlisted members of a Security Group detachment, and 2 civilian oceanographers. Although the two civilians actually performed oceanographic research, their presence was necessary to substantiate the ship's environmental research cover.

Pueblo's instructions were to operate in international waters, a mandate that the C.O., CDR Lloyd M. Bucher, studiously observed, according to fellow officers. The ship was off Wonsan, North Korea, when three North Korean torpedo boats and a gunboat suddenly surrounded the lightly armed *Pueblo.* CDR Bucher tried to take his ship further out to sea, but the more heavily armed boats scored five direct hits on the flying bridge and wheel house, killing one sailor. Navy air resources were so completely committed to the fighting in Vietnam that no airplanes were available to aid *Pueblo,* which was forced to stop. The North Koreans boarded the vessel, claimed that she was in territorial waters, and seized her. The United States disputed the claim, but *Pueblo* was taken into port by its captors. The surviving 82 Americans, including her supply officer, ENS Tim Harris, were held prisoner for 11 months until the United States issued the demanded apology and repudiated it as soon as the prisoners were released.

LORE OF THE CORPS

Ensign Timothy L. Harris, SC, USN

Supply Officer, *USS Pueblo* (AGER-2), 1967–69
Period of Service: 1965-89

ENS Harris was a line officer when he reported aboard *Pueblo* as its supply officer just five months before the ship was attacked and captured. Following repatriation 11 months later, he transferred to the Supply Corps, completed 24 years of active duty, and retired as a commander.

Timothy Harris was born in Oshkosh, Wisconsin, in August 1945. He entered the Navy through the Aviation Officer Candidate Program in

1965 and was commissioned a line ensign in 1967, when he was graduated from Jacksonville University in Florida with a bachelor's degree in business. He earned a master's of science in education from Michigan State University in 1978.

He was ordered in the summer of 1967 to *Pueblo,* an intelligence-gathering ship operating under cover as an environmental research vessel. With no Supply Corps officer authorized, Harris was advised that he would be assigned collateral duty as supply officer, and so attended Storekeeper First Class School before reporting aboard. *Pueblo*'s Supply Department had five supply rated men and three designated strikers.

ENS Harris was on the bridge on 23 January 1968 when *Pueblo* was confronted by North Korean gunboats in international waters of the Sea of Japan off the coast opposite Wonsan. He hit the deck when the North Koreans fired and blew out the flying wing. Harris was knocked down twice but was able to assist other crew members. CDR Lloyd Bucher, *Pueblo*'s skipper, continued to attempt escape while the ship was being steered by a helmsman lying on the deck as personnel in the pilot house and in the security spaces worked feverishly to destroy classified material.

Tim Harris emphasizes that *Pueblo* was never surrendered and the National Ensign was never struck. The North Korean boats just overtook *Pueblo,* which was plodding along at its maximum 12 knots, and the Koreans jumped aboard the stern at 1445 hours and took over. The North Korean boarding party blindfolded Harris and forced him to stay with several others on the fantail for the trip into Wonsan, which they reached at about 1900 hours.

The *Pueblo* captives were sent to Pyongyang by all-night train, on which the Americans were interrogated by their captors. Thousands of screaming North Koreans greeted the captives' arrival in the capital city. The prisoners were initially kept in wooden frame barracks, with officers housed in separate rooms. Harris was not to see any of the crew for two months. Intensive interrogation continued around the clock.

The North Koreans inflicted physical abuse and psychological harassment throughout the period of captivity. The prisoners learned rapidly that the more bizarre, more insanely absurd and creative they were, the more likely it was the North Koreans would believe them. The Americans learned to think and act like the predictable Koreans in certain situations.

After two months, the entire crew was relocated to military barracks at a remote compound surrounded by rice paddies outside of Pyongyang. The food was mostly turnips, watery soup, and occasional rice. Dysentery was constant and widespread, and medical treatment ranged from nonexistent to rudimentary. The health of crew members deteriorated as they experienced extreme weight loss and lack of protein and vitamins to fight infection.

The prisoners attempted to discredit the North Koreans and to obstruct their propaganda efforts through determination and imagination. Great personal risks were involved. A North Korean general told the prisoners that the election of President Richard Nixon in November 1968 made reparation "most doubtful," and the North Koreans began an unmatched reign of physical and psychological terror. Harassment increased when the Koreans discovered that a popular American magazine had run a propaganda photo carrying a caption that gave the precise definition of an obscene gesture that prisoners were shown making. The Koreans had lost face; they had believed the prisoners' explanation that the gesture was an "Hawaiian good luck sign."

Harris was confined to a dirty, drafty 14 x 20-foot room with only a wooden table and chair and a small bed into which he could just barely squeeze. The window at one end of the room, was covered by a piece of cloth, so the only light was a bare bulb that hung from the ceiling. Bad as the room was, the meals he was forced to eat were even worse. The three-times-a-day fare consisted of stale bread, a small piece of butter, a bowl of turnips, and a pot of tea made with dirty water. A small amount of poor-quality fish was occasionally added.

Pueblo's officers refused to sign the contrived confessions placed before them, but the continued beatings and deprivations took their toll over time. Tim Harris held out as long as he could before finally deciding to sign one of the confessions because the Koreans had the information anyway. He then became remorseful despite his long holdout and frequent acts of defiance. The incarceration dragged on into fall of 1968, when President Lyndon Johnson ordered new negotiations at Panmunjon. These talks eventually resulted in the prisoners' release just before Christmas.

ENS Tim Harris was awarded the Bronze Star for his actions on the day of the attack on Pueblo. The citation reads, in part: "Lieutenant (then Ensign) Harris repeatedly exposed himself to the intense fire while providing the necessary leadership to ensure the destruction of highly classified documents."

He received a gold star in lieu of a second bronze star for his conduct during imprisonment. The citation states, "His courageous stand served to inspire his fellow prisoners and strengthened their will to resist." The Combat Distinguishing Device is authorized for both medals, as well as for the Navy Commendation Medal he received for his participation in "several successful actions to discredit the international propaganda efforts of his captors." Tim Harris also received two Purple Heart medals for combat wounds.

A court of inquiry into circumstances surrounding *Pueblo*'s seizure lasted three months. The result was a recommendation that Bucher and another officer be tried by general court-martial for allowing the capture of the ship when it could still resist and for failure to destroy secret equipment. Secretary of the Navy John H. Chafee overruled the recommendation on the grounds that the two officers had suffered enough.

The application Tim Harris had submitted for transfer to the Supply Corps before capture of *Pueblo* was approved, and he reported to NSCS Athens in May 1969. LTJG Harris served as supply officer, *USS Schenectady* (LST-1185), from November 1969 to June 1971. He next went to Mobile Construction Battalion 14 in May 1972 and to NAS Pensacola in July 1973.

He did two tours with COMFAIRWESTPAC, first at Atsugi, Japan, from July 1975 to July 1977, then with a detachment at Cubi Point, the Philippines, from August 1977 to February 1979. In 1978 he was guest of the U.S. Army at the Bridge of No Return in Panmunjom, over which he had returned from captivity nine years earlier. He then reported to COMNAVAIRPAC, NAS North Island, from July 1983 to June 1985. His final tour was as supply officer, Marine Corps Air Station, El Toro, California, from July 1985 to February 1989. He then retired.

CDR Harris accepted a position with Kay and Company as logistics advisor and arrived at Kuwait in October 1989 to provide logistics and maintenance support for Kuwait Air Force A-4s. When the Iraqis invaded Kuwait on 2 August 1990, Saddam Hussein allowed any westerners in Kuwait to attempt to escape. Harris had no stomach for another imprisonment and made the attempt on 7 August in company with eight other Americans.

The group took off in five vehicles in a daring dash down the expressway to Saudi Arabia through confused Iraqi combat troops who allowed the Americans to move freely. Each time the Americans were stopped, they bribed their way through until, finally, an Iraqi officer told them either to drive through the desert or return to Kuwait City. The group took off across the desert in 125-degree temperature and a sand storm. They lost one of their jeep-style vehicles that became hopelessly bogged down in the sand. During the escape the group counted 250 Iraqi tanks and saw a large amount of destroyed military equipment and 40 to 50 Mercedes and BMW automobiles belonging to fleeing Kuwaiti citizens. It took nearly three hours for the group to reach the Saudi Arabian desert safely. They drove to Dhahran and then to Riyadh for transportation back to the United States.

Tim Harris lives in Yuma, Arizona, and describes himself as a full-time "desert rat," exploring the nearby Sonoran Desert in his 1979 Jeep truck.

Sources

Brandt, Ed. *The Last Voyage of USS Pueblo*. New York: W. W. Norton, 1971.
Documents provided by CDR Timothy L. Harris, May 1994.
Telephone interview of CDR Timothy L. Harris, May 1994.

New Management Tools

NAVSUP implemented two new management tools in 1968. The retail inventory system (RIS) gave stock point commanding officers the authority and responsibility for managing all Navy Stock Fund material at their activities, except for ICP and Fuel Supply Office-managed materials. A resources management system (RMS) was also implemented throughout the Navy supply system.

USS Wichita (AOR-1), lead ship of another new class of multiple-capability fast combat support ships was commissioned in June 1969, with LCDR (later CAPT) Ronald G. Hoopes as her first supply officer. *Wichita* had a light displacement of 13,000 tons and 41,350 tons fully loaded with 160,000 barrels of fuel oil, 600 tons of ammunition, 200 tons of dry, and 100 tons of refrigerated provisions. Her normal complement was 454, and she carried 2 helicopters for vertical replenishment underway.

Logistics Records at NSA Danang

Commitment to the war in Vietnam remained the primary focus for the U.S defense establishment in 1969. CDR Robert S. Leventhal had reported in August 1965 as the first assistant chief of staff, Naval Support Activity Danang. The operation commenced in October. He was relieved in July 1966 by CAPT R. H. (Len) Hazlett, followed by CAPT Wesley J. McClaren in July 1967 and CAPT Norman H. C. Kuhlman in July 1968. CAPT (later RADM) Thomas J. Allshouse reported in July 1969 as the fifth and final ACOS for Supply and Fiscal, NSA Danang.

Although peace talks began in January 1969, American forces continued to pour into Vietnam, reaching 543,400 in April. A few months later, a gradual withdrawal of U.S. personnel began as trained Vietnamese assumed selected functions. At the same time, a large U.S. Navy force remained 100 miles offshore in the South China Sea. The American armada drew supply support from NSA Danang and through refined underway replenishment. Whereas the ammunition ship *USS Lassen* (AE-3) required three days to transfer 342 tons of cargo at sea in 1945, *USS Mount Katmai* (AE-17) took only 56 minutes to transfer the same amount in 1967. Tanker pumping rates in 1945 were 100,000 gallons per hour but were nearly 273,000 gallons by 1967.

A substantial percentage of the supplies going to the war in Southeast Asia originated in the United States and passed through NSC Oakland and NSD Seattle. Before the Vietnam buildup, NSD Seattle shipped 15,000 to 25,000 tons a month into the Pacific. By 1966 the volume of such shipments averaged 65,000 to 75,000 tons a month. The Supply Corps' adoption of automated data processing systems was an important factor in achieving this increased capability. MSTS was responsibile for transporting huge volumes from West Coast ports to the war zone and chartered more than 300 vessels.

In June 1969 there were 132 Navy Supply Corps officers serving under CAPT Allshouse at NSA Danang, up from 92 the year before. Another 30 to 40 Supply Corps officers were serving in NSA detachments spread from Quang Tri, near the border of North Viet Nam, to Chu Lai, about 50 miles south of Danang.

The Largest Logistics Support Operation

NSA Danang was the largest single logistics support organization in U.S. history and supported 210,000 Marine, Army, and Allied troops under combat conditions in the I-Corps area in 1969. Throughput at NSA Danang to forward deployed forces rose to 9.3 million tons in 1968, an average of 773,500 tons a month in 1968, and involved 104,600 line items. Both the volume and number of line items were records.

In the first half of FY69, the logistics operation at Danang accounted for 32 percent of total Supply System sales of general stores material, but only 10.5 percent of the inventory. Stock turnaround in the same period was 3.4 to 1 at Danang compared with 1 to 1 for the Navy Supply System as a whole. The huge inventory of material at Danang was housed in more than 907,000 square feet of covered storage space.

Danang was tasked to fill all bulk fuel and ordnance requirements for the I-Corps operating area and issued more than 50 million gallons of fuel and 80,000 tons of ammunition each month, not including aviation ordnance dropped by B-52s. Danang maintained pay records for 10,000 military personnel and 9,500 Vietnamese employees.

Tom Allshouse compared the level of supply support as measured by the pounds of material required for each person each day. After researching the issue, he found that the individual level of support had increased 400 percent between World War II and Vietnam. Consumption of beer and soft drinks in the I-Corps area averaged 7.2 cans per person daily. Average quarterly stocking at NSA Danang was 45,000 pallets with 2,000 cans per pallet—or 95 million cans. Milk was also a popular beverage at Danang, where Foremost Dairy had a contract to operate the world's largest plant for the manufacture of reconstituted milk, ice cream, cottage cheese, and other dairy products.

LORE OF THE CORPS

Captain Thomas James Allshouse, SC, USN

Assistant Chief of Staff For Supply and Fiscal, Naval Support Activity, Danang, Vietnam, 1969–70
Period of Service: 1947–81

Tom Allshouse decided at the age of 10 that he wanted to go to the Naval Academy and he did. Later, he was the fifth and last ACOS for supply and fiscal, NSA Danang, Vietnam. He achieved Flag rank and was director of OP–41.

Thomas J. Allshouse was born at Duquesne, Pennsylvania, in August 1925. He attended Stevens Institute of Technology, Hoboken, New Jersey, for a year before entering the Naval Academy in June 1944. Upon graduation in July 1947, Allshouse was commissioned an ensign in the Supply Corps and ordered to NSCS Bayonne, New Jersey.

In May 1948 he reported for independent duty as supply and disbursing officer, *USS Hobson* (DMS-26), assigned to the Mine Force, U.S. Atlantic Fleet. The postwar drawdown had left the Navy extremely short of experienced personnel, and *Hobson* had only 8 of an allowance of 25 officers aboard and no storekeepers or disbursing clerks.

New Navy regulations, effective in 1948, allowed officers not eligible for command at sea to perform duties normally performed only by line officers. ENS Allshouse and many of his NSCS classmates were assigned additional duties such as OOD underway, which provided a closer shipboard relationship between line and Supply Corps officers.

His independent tour made him directly responsible for *Hobson*'s operational funds, not as an OPTAR managed by the type commander. *Hobson* had no central storerooms; all spare parts were in parts boxes located in operating spaces throughout the ship. As a result, there was no central control over issues and replacement orders. When the ship went into Charleston Naval Shipyard for overhaul, her allowance list, maintained by the yard, was grossly out of date. ENS Allshouse organized an equipment validation team that found 500 differences between the shipyard master allowance and actual equipment aboard. He had all spares offloaded, inventoried, repackaged, and preserved. He also directed updating of inventory lists and record cards and purged boxes of damaged and useless parts. As a result of this effort, *Hobson* received an unprecedented grade of outstanding for spare parts records and management upon arrival at Guantanamo Bay for postoverhaul underway training.

ENS Allshouse was promoted to LTJG in June 1950, then reported to the Supply and Fiscal Department, Marine Corps Air Station, Cherry Point, North Carolina. Aircraft at Cherry Point and its auxiliary fields used more than 300,000 gallons of three types of fuel each day in 1950, and the base had only a three-day storage capacity, requiring creative planning to maintain the steady flow of fuel. LTJG Allshouse was involved in the buildup of Marine units deploying to Korea, including integration of World War II propeller planes and the newer, more complex, jet planes and helicopters.

In November 1952 Allshouse reported to the Naval Station, Rodman, Canal Zone, for duty in the Supply and Fiscal Department. His major responsibilities were supporting troop ships transiting the canal to and from the Korean Theater and reconfiguring residual supply stocks from World War II support missions to those required by war in Korea. A disposal effort reduced the number of line items stocked by the Rodman S&F Department from 65,000 to 25,000 and improved supply material availability from 64 to 95 percent.

He was ordered to the Bureau of Supplies and Accounts in December 1954 in the Office of the Director of Planning, as head of the Passive Defense Branch, responsible for analysis and development of plans to protect the Navy supply system from atomic, biological, and chemical (ABC) attacks. He was a member of the CNO Special Weapons Test Evaluation Group and participated in atomic device tests. Another issue Allshouse and his associates considered was location of a Navy supply depot in the southeastern United States. Local businessmen, supported by powerful Congressman Carl Vinson, purchased land at Byron, Georgia, for the depot, although studies indicated that the optimum location was Montgomery, Alabama. CAPT (later RADM) Winston H. (Win) Schleef assigned Tom Allshouse the task of resolving the issue. BuSandA and BuDocks agreed to construct a new building at Byron, even though BuSandA deferred establishment of a southeastern supply depot.

Meanwhile, the Navy established a new ICP, the Navy Forms and

Publications Supply Office (NFPSO), which was moved into the new building at Byron in 1956. When Congressman Vinson retired in 1965, the operation was relocated into existing Navy facilities at Scotia, New York. Later, an aircraft carrier and a park at NSCS Athens were named for the Georgia legislator.

LT Allshouse also was a member of the Navy Board of Inspection and Survey Team that accepted the first super carrier, *USS Forrestal* (CVA-59). He was called upon to defend, before Congress, Navy decisions to reduce or close facilities in their districts.

Win Schleef handed Tom Allshouse another hot potato in 1957. RADM Thomas L. Becknell, Deputy and Assistant Chief, BuSandA, decided to close some of the more than a dozen Consolidated Transportation Offices throughout the United States. Schleef told Allshouse to review the situation and recommend which to close. Tom Allshouse researched the issue extensively, found extensive duplication, and decided that half could be eliminated without any loss of service to the Navy. CAPT Schleef secured approval of RADM Bear Arnold, Chief of the Bureau, and RADM Becknell to implement the recommendations.

In November 1957 LT Allshouse went back to sea as assistant supply officer, *USS Orion* (AS-18), which supported 21 submarines assigned to the Submarine Force, Atlantic Fleet. He was promoted to lieutenant commander in July 1958 and left to attend the M.B.A. program at the Graduate School of Business, Harvard University. LCDR Allshouse went to Philadelphia in April 1961 as assistant supply officer, nucleus crew of *USS Kitty Hawk* (CVA-63). He was responsible for directing loading and outfitting of *Kitty Hawk,* assigned to the Pacific Fleet.

Allshouse reported in February 1962 to the Ships Parts Control Center Mechanicsburg, Pennsylvania, where he was assigned as director, Allowance and Load List Division. Shortly after he arrived at SPCC, the Fleet faced a requirement of nearly $300 million to finance shortages in new COSAL requirements emanating from Mechanicsburg. The secretary of the Navy and the chief of naval operations appointed a team of senior Flag officers to work with SPCC to resolve the problem, with Tom Allshouse as the principal briefer. He and his staff worked over the next several months with OPNAV, BuSandA, and BuShips to develop the basic directives and policies reflecting SPCC recommendations for corrective action. New policies and programs were tested on a control ship and, after evaluation, were instituted for all new COSALs except for FBM submarines. Allshouse was promoted to commander in July 1963.

In July 1964 CDR Allshouse was ordered back to duty at BuSandA as assistant chief for supply management. He was to continue the work of planning and implementing the Uniform Inventory Control Point automated data programs with which he had worked at SPCC. He also was involved in activation of ships from the Reserve Fleet and development of urgently needed logistic support for inshore and riverine warfare forces for the war in Vietnam.

Allshouse developed the concept of Fleet outfitting supply assistance teams to expedite outfitting of activated Reserve Fleet ships. The OICs of the two FOSATs—Atlantic and Pacific—reported directly to CDR Allshouse. When ASO projected material requirements appeared to be more than $500 million overstated, he and his staff resolved the differences. They also revised aviation coordinated allowance lists (AVCAL) for carriers and Marine air groups to incorporate many of the improvements developed for COSALs.

Tom Allshouse was promoted to captain in July 1968 and reported in August to the Industrial College of the Armed Forces at Washington, where he became familiar with logistical problems of the other services. In June 1969 CAPT Allshouse and 12 ICAF classmates of all services were ordered to the I-Corps area in the Republic of Vietnam. Allshouse reported to Naval Support Activity Danang as assistant chief of staff, supply and fiscal.

In the spring of 1970, U.S. and ARVN troops, supported by NSA Danang, went into Cambodia to attack Viet Cong bases. CAPT Allshouse was awakened one evening by an emergency call from the Army, which had nearly exhausted its supply of small arms ammunition and requested expedited resupply. Allshouse ordered an emergency stock issue and dispatched it to the dock and an LST for delivery to Cambodia. At about 0400, he assigned his trusted chief boatswains Mate Francis to line up a work party to load the LST by 0600. He specified that loading of the LSTs from 40-ton truckloads be completed as soon as possible. Francis told his boss that he needed help in seeing that Coast Guard inspectors did not impede the loading of the LST to its 500-ton capacity—usually a 72-hour process.

CAPT Allshouse took the two Coast Guard port inspectors out into the harbor in a small skiff, where they spent the morning inspecting several ammunition ships at anchor. He returned to his office and at noon went to the dock, where the LST, with 500 tons of Army ammunition aboard, was backing away from the ramp.

Francis and his gang had accomplished the nearly impossible task of loading the ship in only 6 hours, a fraction of the time usually required, and the Supply Corps had fulfilled the Army's order in fewer than 12 hours from receipt of the request. "You did an outstanding job," Allshouse told Chief Francis, "but I don't want to know how you did it."

Halfway through his tour at NSA, CAPT Allshouse was tasked to develop a plan for the drawdown of U.S. combat forces in the I-Corps area. This involved transporting unit equipment to Danang for loading aboard outbound ships. NSA would concurrently transfer its functions to various Army units and also transfer residual Navy support functions to a new, smaller Naval Support Facility (NSF) Danang for continuing support of the Vietnamese navy.

CAPT Allshouse left Vietnam and reported in July 1970 as supply officer, NAS Quonset Point, Rhode Island, and was ordered to the Aviation Supply Office in April 1971. He took over as ASO operations officer in July 1971. He was assigned responsibility for the ASO requirements determination process and planning and presentation of material budgets at all Navy and DOD levels. Halfway through this tour, CAPT Allshouse became executive officer. He was selected for Flag rank and ordered to the Naval Supply Center Oakland as commanding officer and Twelfth Naval District supply officer.

He reported to Oakland as a frocked rear admiral in July 1973 and made his number in July 1974. At the time he took over, NSC Oakland was still heavily committed to support of operations in Vietnam. In 1973 it was challenged to support the development and construction effort on the new American base at Diego Garcia in the Indian Ocean.

An available Atlantic Fleet construction battalion was sent out from Norfolk to construct a larger communications station. NSC Oakland was tasked to keep the Seabees and other units on Diego Garcia supplied with all material requirements. The stocks on Diego Garcia remained on Oakland's books until issued. Diego Garcia was placed under the administrative command of COMNAVAIRPAC.

RADM Allshouse also initiated a program to immerse his assigned Naval Reserve Supply Corps officers thoroughly into NSC Oakland operations by replacing his Regular Navy command duty officers with Reservists on a continuing basis. He says the performance of Reservists was excellent, the training was valuable, and the program brought the USN and Reserve officers together for the mutual benefit of both.

In July 1975 RADM Allshouse reported to the Office of the Chief of Naval Operations as director, Material Division (OP-41). He was responsible for policy and sponsorship of Navy spares, repair parts and consumables, ammunition, medical supplies and equipment, prepositioned war reserve requirements, transportation management, and energy policies and programs. Allshouse established the Navy's Energy Office and developed the Navy's first energy plan, which became the model for the newly formed Department of Energy.

RADM Allshouse was also responsible for developing a regularly scheduled MAC airlift service between Norfolk and Mediterranean bases.

He provided seed money for Navy field hospital units to support Marine combat operations. He decreed outloading of Army ammunition at NAD Earle, New Jersey, to free King's Bay, Georgia, as an East Coast base for Trident submarines and revised plans to improve missile availability in the Fleet.

In June 1977 RADM Allshouse returned to SPCC as commanding officer. He set up the ICP Academy to train officers and senior civilian employees in the intricacies of inventory control point operations. He also implemented source data automation, mechanized provisioning programs, improved the requirement determination process, and instituted the transfer of depot-level repairables to the Navy Stock Fund.

Tom Allshouse retired from the Navy on 31 August 1981. In retirement, he is chairman, Board of Visitors, Vinson Hall Foundation, and trustee, Navy, Marine, Coast Guard Residence Foundation. He and his wife Elsie live in Woodbridge, Virginia.

Sources

Changes: A History. NSA Danang, 1970.

Copies of documents and reports suppplied by, correspondence from, and telephone interview of RADM Thomas James Allshouse, July, August 1993, July, August 1994.

Naval Support in I-Corps: The Fourth Year. NSA Danang, 1969.

Transcript of Naval Service. Bureau of Naval Personnel, July 1981.

Mortar and Rocket Attack on NSA Danang

Viet Cong guerrillas regularly launched rocket attacks on the Danang complex three or four times a month in 1968 and 1969. CDR (later RADM) Dick Curtis, Director, Navy Supply Depot, routinely worked 14 or 15 hours a day and spent evenings at his office when Navy intelligence reported high probability of a rocket attack. The attacks normally did little damage because of, in Curtis's words, "Our good fortune and the Viet Cong's poor aim." On two occasions, however, the attacks caused extensive damage by setting off explosions in the adjacent South Vietnam Army's ammunition depot.

LORE OF THE CORPS

Commander Richard Earl Curtis, SC, USN

Director, Navy Supply Department, Danang, Vietnam, 1968–69

Period of Service: 1953–82

Dick Curtis frequently surprises friends when he is asked to name his favorite Supply Corps duty. He replies, "Vietnam in 1968–69." He served with distinction at Danang and rose to Flag rank.

Curtis was born in Beckley, West Virginia, in November 1930. He was graduated from the Naval Academy in 1953 and reported to NSCS Bayonne in the final class to go all the way through the course there before the school was moved to Athens, Georgia. ENS Curtis reported to *USS Vulcan* (AR-5) at Norfolk in December 1953 as assistant supply officer. He went to *USS John W. Weeks* (DD-701) in October 1954 as supply officer and was promoted to lieutenant, junior grade, in December. LTJG Curtis came ashore in February 1956 as assistant supply officer, NAS Key West, Florida, where he was promoted to lieutenant in July 1957. The next stop was on the staff of Commander-in-Chief Southern Command at Naples, Italy, from March 1958 to July 1959, when he was detached to attend the Harvard Graduate School of Business. With an M.B.A. degree, LT Curtis reported for duty at SPCC Mechanicsburg from 1961 to 1963 and was promoted to lieutenant commander in April 1963.

In September LCDR Curtis reported to the Office of Chief of Naval Operations for two months of special duty on the Standard Navy Maintenance and Material Management Project. From his Washington duty, he went in November 1963 as supply officer, *USS Chicago* (CG-11). He reported to the staff, Submarine Flotilla Six, at Charleston, where he served from October 1965 to August 1968 and was promoted to commander in July 1967.

CDR Curtis became director, Navy Supply Depot, Naval Support Activities Danang, South Vietnam, in September 1968. NSA Danang, at the time, was one of the Navy's largest supply operations. It was staffed with 31 officers, 537 enlisted personnel, 200 Korean contract workers, and 677 Vietnamese civilian employees. The operation supported Allied troops, primarily U.S. Marines and Army forces, in the I-Corps area, which stretched from the Demilitarized Zone (DMZ) 75 miles to the north to Quang Nai Province, another 75 miles south.

NAVSUP sent its best people to Vietnam. Curtis remembers that he had an outstanding group and singles out for special mention CDRs Jerry Douglas, Gene Goodwin, Charlie Bowne, and Bob Abele, who went on to Flag rank and vice commander, NAVSUP. With little competition for their time, most officers and men in CDR Curtis's command worked 12-hour days, 6 or 7 days a week.

NSD Danang's refrigerated storage was adjacent to a South Vietnamese army ammunition dump, where ordnance was stored in open bunkers and was the frequent target of Viet Cong rocket attacks. When hit by enemy rockets, exploding ammunition would shower the Depot's 750 reefer boxes with flaming debris and molten metal for up to 12 hours before burning out or being extinguished.

At about 0300 hours on 23 February 1969, the Viet Cong struck with a particularly devastating barrage. CDR Curtis immediately checked all perimeter posts and determined that no attempt had been made to breach the fences. He then mustered military and civilian personnel in the duty section and determined two sailors were missing. Dick Curtis did not believe that they had returned to their barracks. Blowing the horn constantly and straining to detect movement through the fire and smoke, he drove his pickup truck down into the area where 250 of the 750 reefer boxes had been badly damaged,

He finally saw the two men huddled under a bridge. He stopped his truck and dashed across an open area through flying shrapnel to reach them. One sailor had sustained a bad head wound. CDR Curtis put his flack vest over the wounded seaman and carried him to the truck. He laid the sailor down in the back and had the other lie beside him. Curtis drove as fast as he could to the Army MASH unit a few miles down the road. A Viet Cong shell exploded ahead of the truck and ruined the front, including the tires. Concerned about the wounded sailor, CDR Curtis drove the remaining two miles to the medical facility on metal rims. The physician's initial report was not good; the young seaman's life hung in the balance. Three days later, however, he was sitting up in his hospital bed and playing his guitar. "Ah, youth!" said an amazed CDR Curtis when he visited the enlisted man. Dick Curtis was awarded the Navy and Marine Corps Medal for his courageous action.

Curtis reports that the Seabees repaired the reefers within a few days and there was little loss of food. However, a large storage area for cement bags was also lost in the attack that left the bags and wooden pallets burning for several days. The Seabees could not use the damaged cement, but it was welcomed by various missionary churches, Buddhist temples, and orphanages in the area. The charred pallets were welcome as firewood. Truckloads were delivered to the local nonprofit organizations. Regular checks verified that the materials were being used for their intended purpose. American forces in Vietnam were being constantly bombarded by adverse publicity over the large quantity of U.S. military supplies constantly on sale in black markets around Saigon. CDR Curtis was determined that material from his command would not end up there, so NSD personnel visited the five market areas around Danang and found only a few Navy Exchange items and some fruit.

Curtis established a team of four storekeepers to track all fruit supplies. Team members coded each box of fruit as it came off ships, assigned another when the box was received and stowed in the reefers, and a third code when it was issued to authorized users. All coded boxes were logged at each stage, and several times a week squads of heavily armed sailors visited the markets and took photographs of fruit boxes, including their codes. The photos were sent to the receiving activity to determine where theft was taking place. Within a month or two, fruit on the black market dwindled to one or two boxes a month.

In early September, 11 days before the end of his tour in Vietnam, CDR Curtis experienced a second rocket attack on the nearby ARVN ammunition dump. The Supply Depot "was inundated with exploding shells and the ground covered with molten metal scattered like confetti." Again, several hundred reefer boxes were rendered inoperable, but this time the depot's two-story office building was leveled, too. The quonset hut containing the depot's antiquated IBM 1401 computer was blown up, and it collapsed on the computer and cards containing the depot's stock records. Within 34 hours, the Seabees constructed an enclosed, air-conditioned computer room in one of the warehouses. IBM technical representatives flew out from the States to put the computer back into operation. Despite considerable damage to his warehouses, only a few of the 12 million combat meals stored outside were lost.

CDR Curtis was relieved by CDR Charlie Bowne in mid-September 1969 and returned to Washington for duty with the Joint Logistics Review Board. In March 1970 he reported to the Naval Supply Systems Command. He went to the Industrial College of the Armed Forces, Washington, in July 1971 and was graduated in June 1972. He reported to the Naval Material Command in the Strategic Systems Project Office (PM-1) and was promoted to captain in October 1972.

In July 1976 CAPT Curtis assumed command of the Naval Supply Center Charleston, South Carolina, where he was selected for Flag rank in the spring of 1978. In June Curtis went back to the Naval Material Command. RADM Curtis returned in June 1979 to the Naval Supply Systems Command as assistant commander for plans and programs. In January 1982 he was appointed vice commander, NAVSUP. He had a heart bypass operation in July and retired on 31 December 1982.

Dick and Pat Curtis settled in the San Diego area, where he worked for four years for U.S. Elevator Company and its parent, Cubic Corporation, then he retired for good. Dick returned to Vietnam in May 1994 with Pat; Truc, his senior Vietnamese employee at Danang; and her husband, a former banker who had served in the ARVN. The foursome visited Saigon (now Ho Chi Minh City), Danang, and Hue. They found the Vietnamese economy in shambles, communism not working in the former South Vietnam, and thousands of small sidewalk businesses operating along every street and road. They say it is still a beautiful country and that the Vietnamese people still admire Americans. Dick and Pat Curtis live in Bonita, California, and enjoy frequent travel.

Sources

Citation. Navy and Marine Corps Medal, Commander-in-Chief, U.S. Pacific Fleet.
Correspondence and reports from RADM Richard E. Curtis, March–July 1994.
Curtis, RADM R. C. *Post Script: Return to Danang, Vietnam*. May 1994.
Naval Support in I-Corps: The Fourth Year. NSA Danang, 1969.

Logistical Larceny

Wartime operational requirements were not always fully appreciated by support activities because they required unusual and sometimes daring action by dedicated Supply Corps officers. One such officer was LT (later CAPT) Dan Solie, supply officer, *USS Frederick* (LST-1184), who has provided the following story.

On her maiden voyage from the States to Danang, Vietnam, in the fall of 1970, *Frederick* suffered a casualty to its surface-search radar. The only spare magnetron aboard was inoperable. LT Solie fired off a requisition for a replacement magnetron to be shipped by air to Kadena AFB on Okinawa, for pickup by the ship en route to Vietnam.

Weather delayed *Frederick*'s arrival at Okinawa until late on a Friday afternoon. Solie and a storekeeper, Gary Sonnenberg, found the Kadena supply receiving area locked. Supply personnel had secured for the weekend, and duty personnel could not be located. *Frederick* was to be underway early on Saturday morning.

LT Solie asked Sonnenberg, a former state lightweight wrestling champion, to scale the fence, locate *Frederick*'s magnetron part in the compound, complete and leave behind the paperwork, and climb back over the fence. The two returned to their ship and delivered the part to operations. *Frederick* was underway to Vietnam with radar operating, thanks to unconventional but effective Supply Department action. CAPT Solie operates a beverage distributorship at Danville, Illinois. He and his wife Beverlee reside at Champaign, Illinois.

Vietnamization

As casualties continued to mount in Vietnam, protests increased against

U.S. involvement. The land war was going badly, despite the U.S. Navy's total command of the sea. With the election of President Richard Nixon in 1968, Vietnamization of the war and the drawdown of U.S. forces accelerated. The U.S. Naval Support Activity Danang, commissioned on 15 October 1965, was formally disestablished by CAPT Tom Allshouse on 30 June 1970, and CDR Charlie Bowne closed down NSD. The following day, a new U.S. facility, the U.S. Naval Support Facility Danang, was established to train Vietnamese sailors to take over from the U.S. Navy upon eventual withdrawal. CDR (later CAPT) Edmund M. (Ed) Waller became supply and fiscal officer. Waller's mission was simply to work NSF and himself out of a job.

Although Vietnam was still the primary ongoing concern of the Navy and the Supply Corps, NAVSUP continued its program of streamlining headquarters and field operations. Ashore in 1969, the Navy Ship's Store Office was assigned responsibility for operating Navy commissaries and was redesignated the Navy Resale System Office. The Military Sea Transportation Service, which was deeply involved in moving the majority of military supplies and equipment to U.S. forces in Vietnam, was renamed the Military Sealift Command (MSC).

As 1971 dawned, the U.S. Navy had turned over primary responsibility for supply support to the Vietnamese. Americans remained purely in an advisory capacity, with little authority or responsibility. But the transition had not taken place as smoothly as had been envisioned. In mid-1971, ADM Chon, the Vietnamese CNO, complained to COMNAVFORV that the U.S. Navy had failed to provide proper logistical support, resulting in ineffective combat forces in the Vietnamese navy. CNO ADM Elmo Zumwalt, a Vietnam veteran, decided that the U.S. Navy should reassume complete control over the Vietnamese navy's supply system, set up proper procedures, train personnel, reinventory material throughout the country, and restock the bases. He also proposed that control revert again to the Vietnamese only when these were completed.

RADM Dowd Goes to Vietnam

In June 1971 Zumwalt ordered RADM Wallace R. Dowd, Jr., Vice Commander, NAVSUP, to Vietnam to trouble-shoot the problem. Wally Dowd already had orders to leave NAVSUP and assume command of NSC Oakland, and his wife, Polly, was due to go into the hospital over the weekend for a heart catheter procedure on Monday. CNO granted RADM Dowd permission for a short delay to see Polly through her medical treatment. Wally and Polly Dowd drove 3,000 miles to Oakland in three days. He relieved RADM Jack Appleby on Saturday, turned over the con to his exec, CAPT Norm Kuhlman, and he and Polly departed on Sunday for Saigon. CDR Harry L. (Lynn) Hazlett, who had served at Danang from 1968 to 1969, was pulled out of the doctoral program at George Washington University and ordered to accompany RADM Dowd to Vietnam.

RADM Dowd and CDR Hazlett traveled around the Saigon-Mekong Delta area for three weeks to evaluate both U.S. and Vietnamese navy logistic support. They found that support was grossly ineffective in light of the high volume of material actually delivered to Vietnam forces in the III-Corps theater. The problems were primarily at the Vietnamese level, but American advisors were also culpable. RADM Dowd was impressed, for the most part, with the Supply Corps officers and enlisted personnel he and CDR Hazlett encountered. He termed them "incredible professionals" and singled out CDRs Don Wilson, Stu Platt, and Phil McGillivary, all of whom later rose to Flag rank; CDR Bill Peek; LCDR (later CAPT) Len Sapera; and LT John Black. RADM Dowd also had high praise for the civilian employees of NSC Oakland, which was the primary CONUS supply support activity for Navy forces in Vietnam. But, the bottom line for the Dowd-Hazlett team was that ADM Chon had been right: supply support was not effective. Their report stressed five conclusions:

- Vietnamese navy supply support had deteriorated to the point that combat units could not get underway.
- Vietnamese navy personnel were not qualified to run a supply system interfacing with the U.S. Navy Supply System.
- No one had any idea what material was on hand and in what condition at the Vietnamese Naval Supply Center Saigon, or at any base throughout the country.
- No transportation system existed to move material to any base in the field.
- Material at the Vietnamese Supply Center and in bases was so deteriorated as to be unusable because of improper or broken packaging.

The seriousness of the situation led GEN Creighton Abrams, the senior in-country commander, to suggest that RADM Dowd be appointed vice CNO, Vietnamese navy. Abrams reportedly sent word to ADM Chon that if he got in the way, Abrams would go to President Thieu, who would either straighten Chon out or see that he was shot. The Navy supply team went to work on the problems. Dowd reports that everything he asked for was provided promptly. He talked each evening with his exec, CAPT Norm Kuhlman, in temporary charge back at Oakland.

The combination of Dowd's commission in the Vietnamese navy, the high-quality officer and enlisted personnel in Vietnam, and solid backing from the United States made it possible to correct the problems in short order.

LORE OF THE CORPS

Rear Admiral Wallace Rutherford Dowd, Jr., SC, USN

Commanding Officer, Naval Supply Center Oakland, 1971–73;
Deputy Commander, Supply, U.S. Naval Forces Vietnam, and
Assistant to Chief of Naval Operations, Vietnamese Navy, 1971
Period of Service: 1942–77

Problems with supply support to the Republic of Vietnam's navy led to RADM Dowd's assuming a unique and unprecedented role as concurrently an admiral in both the U.S. and South Vietnamese navies. The son of an U.S. Navy Flag officer, he went on to become the 32nd chief of Supply Corps.

Wallace (Wally) Dowd was born at Cambridge, Massachusetts, in July 1921, when his father, who later became a line rear admiral, was attending the Massachusetts Institute of Technology. During his teens, Dowd suffered permanent damage to one eye, so when he received an appointment to Annapolis, he was physically disqualified, but was accepted by the NROTC at the University of Washington in the fall of 1938. Dowd was of one of the two graduates of his class in 1942 to receive a regular commission in the Supply Corps and reported the following month to the Navy Supply Corps School at Harvard, in Cambridge, the city where he was born.

The Navy had a desperate need for replacement Supply Corps officers in late 1942 as a result of wartime losses in the Pacific and new ships being rushed to completion. ENS Dowd volunteered to take an accelerated course and in early December was received a set of orders as destroyer division disbursing officer in *USS Alden* (DD-211), a four-stacker launched in 1919.

His orders called for transportation via Seattle, where his girl friend, Polly, met him, and, in his words, "snagged me on the fly." They were married on a Saturday evening and took a train to San Francisco for their honeymoon. He departed for the Pacific on Monday morning and caught up with *Alden* at Pearl Harbor in late December. Polly Dowd found an apartment in San Francisco overlooking the Golden Gate

Bridge and became one of the original employees at the Navy Supply Depot across San Francisco Bay at Oakland.

Dowd's disbursing duty involved, in addition to *Alden,* working three other destroyers, none of which was ever near his ship much of the time. He worked off memorandum pay rolls, which, he reports, "were a mess and constantly out of date." On board *Alden,* he inherited responsibility for the general mess, the storerooms, and for standing OOD watches underway.

Alden transited the Panama Canal in 1943 to go to the South Atlantic to join the hunt for German submarines. His skipper, a full-blooded Cherokee called "Chief" Evans, had orders to take command of a new destroyer, *USS Johnston* (DD-557), under construction at Bremerton. He invited the newly promoted LTJG Dowd to become supply officer of the new ship. Dowd readily accepted, but the Bureau said he was too senior to go to a destroyer, so he was sent to Philadelphia for fitting out of *USS Antietam* (CV-36). The supply officer was LCDR Tom O'Connell. LTJG Dowd was assigned as stores officer, responsible for everything from general to aviation stores, and he assembled his material on the top four floors of a Civil War-era building that had slow, antiquated elevators. According to Dowd, "Everything was a manual operation from start to finish."

Dowd recalls that he over-ordered five boxcar loads of potatoes that he had to peddle to any ship that would take them before morning quarters the next day. He says, "A marvelous pay clerk named Sam Bell did the job and no one was the wiser." LTJG Dowd sailed with *Antietam* in 1944 to the Pacific via the Panama Canal, where it was necessary to remove gun sponsons temporarily in order for the 27,100-ton carrier to squeeze through. *Antietam* made it safely to the Pacific, but *Johnston* was sunk in the Battle of Savo Island in October 1944, with only three survivors. Evans was not among them.

Dowd points out that the Navy did not operate with planned deployments in World War II. Ships were sent where they were needed, and they stayed until the job was done. All resupply—provisions, ordinance, spare parts, food, and other material—was done in port because underway replenishment had not yet been fully developed. *Antietam* supported onboard SB2C Helldivers, TBM Avengers, and F6F Hellcats. Dowd remembers that each ship had an allowance for each type of aircraft and loaded the storerooms to the gills. But once, west of Pearl Harbor, not much was available. Normal resupply was provided from a converted LST, resupply ships in harbors, and through the U.S. mail.

Dowd was promoted to lieutenant and went back to the States in December 1945. He rode one of the Magic Carpet ships, an escort carrier converted temporarily into a transport. He remembers that his crowded, nonair-conditioned ship was "hotter than the hinges of hades, but we were headed home." From San Francisco, he and Polly headed to Washington in one of the first automobiles manufactured after the war, a new Hudson without a horn, back seat, bumpers, or tail lights. The missing automotive parts arrived in Washington months after the Dowds.

LT Dowd reported to NAVSUP and worked in officer personnel for CDR (later RADM) Bernie Bieri and LCDR (later RADM) Jack Appleby. Wally Dowd recalls Sue Dorsey, secretary to the head of OP, as a true lady who knew every Supply Corps officer by his first name. He describes her compatriot, Lorena Boswell, secretary to the chief, as awesome, intimidating, and a powerhouse. At one point, he returned from lunch to find a note advising him that Lorena Boswell wanted to see him. The newly arrived young officer sent back word that if a secretary wanted to see him, she could darned well come to his desk. Dowd describes his reaction as "one of the dumbest things I ever did. I instantly became Number One on Miss Boswell's hit list, and it took me almost a year to get back in her good graces."

When CAPT Jack Appleby fleeted up to head OP, Dowd was given the sea and overseas detail desk. The chief, RADM Dorsey Foster, decided to bring all detailing back to BuSandA from the field, where senior Supply Corps officers in major geographic or functional areas made assignments from pools of junior officers. LCDR Dowd drew the job of making a three-month swing through the Pacific to tell his seniors that they were losing their detailing authority. With him was a letter from Dorsey Foster that underscored his authority and requested all possible assistance. OP resumed authority for assigning all Supply Corps officers with little protest from the field.

Wally Dowd was promoted to lieutenant commander in May 1946 and selected for postgraduate study. LCDR Dowd reported to Stanford University in August 1947 and left with an M.B.A. degree in May 1949 and went on the staff of Commander Fleet Air Wing Four, homeported at Whidbey Island, Washington. Shortly after Dowd reported, the wing was embarked in *USS Salisbury Sound* (AV-13) for a three-month exercise that took the ship to virtually every port in Alaska, out along the Aleutian chain, and then down to the Hawaiian Islands. The wing also consisted of two squadrons of PBM Mariner seaplanes, a squadron of PB4Y Privateers (the Navy version of the Air Force B-24), land-based planes, and an AVP. The objective of the deployment was to exercise the aircraft and ships in the frigid climate. The wing commander was an inveterate fisherman, and he frequently invited Dowd along in his helicopter on trout expeditions. LCDR Dowd recalls several evenings of buzzing streams to chase away bears and bringing gunny sacks of fresh trout back to the ship.

In November 1950 LCDR Dowd was transferred to the staff of Fleet Air Wing One, ostensibly homeported at Guam, but deployed occasionally in *Salisbury Sound* or *USS Pine Island* (AV-12). The wing was assigned to patrol an area from Korea to the Pescadores and the Formosa Straits with the first of the new P2Vs along with PBMs and PB4Ys. During this tour, wing personnel reactivated two old Japanese bases—an air station at Naha and the sparse facilities at Buckner Bay, both on Okinawa.

LCDR Dowd reported in April 1952 as control officer, Supply Department, Puget Sound Naval Shipyard, Bremerton, where he served under CAPT B. D. (Bad Dog) Smith and later CAPT Walt Wright. The senior assistant was CDR (later RADM) Winston Schleef. The return to Bremerton was something of a homecoming for Wally Dowd because he had worked in the yard in the shipfitter and sheet metal shops while finishing high school. In August 1954 he reported to the Command and Staff course at the Naval War College at Newport, Rhode Island. Dowd recalls that 17 members of his NWC class achieved Flag rank, including ADM Bob Long, who served as vice CNO and became CINCPAC. In Dowd's opinion, there is no substitute for a Supply Corps Flag officer serving with and knowing line Flag officers on a first-name basis.

From Newport in the spring of 1955, he was ordered as supply officer of *USS Saint Paul* (CA-73), deployed to WESTPAC 90 percent of the time as flagship, Commander Seventh Fleet. *Saint Paul* visited almost every port in the Western Pacific and went to the Philippines for the funeral of President Ramón Magsaysay. On Christmas Day 1955, Cardinal Terence Cook said mass aboard *Saint Paul* in port at Keelung, Taiwan.

Dowd was ordered to the General Stores Supply Office, Philadelphia, in July 1957. He was assigned as director, Systems Planning, by CAPT (later RADM) Bob Northwood, who was relieved by CAPT (later RADM) John Bottoms. While CDR Dowd was in the job at GSSO, he was promoted to commander. At this point, OSD civil servants made their first attempt to form a fourth service of supply. "I had to fight that bunch for the balance of my naval career," Wally Dowd says. He questions their motives and believes their objective was not to improve the military supply system but to improve their positions and power. At GSSO, CDR Dowd learned that ships did not have adequate allowance lists and that manufacturers of most World War II gears, pumps, valves, and associated equipment had either ceased production of installed equipment or had gone out of business. The major challenge for GSSO was to find companies who could—and would—make the parts so badly needed in the Fleet. That the organization was able to accomplish its new mission was, in Dowd's opinion, a tribute to the dedicated and highly professional group of civilian employees inherited from GSSO. Dowd was also highly impressed with the cooperation between the two ICPs—GSSO and ASO—both located on the same Philadelphia compound. Eventually, GSSO was converted to the first of the Defense Supply Agency activities and redesignated the Military Industrial Supply Agency. Wally Dowd recalls that DSA headquarters was not yet fully functioning, so he and his counterparts from the Army, Air Force, and Marine Corps were left alone to design MISA systems that met the needs of the Navy and the other armed services.

In addition to transfers of civilian personnel between the two, the Navy benefited when CAPT John Bottoms moved from X.O. of ASO to commander of MISA. CDR Dowd left Philadelphia in June 1961 to go to the staff, Commander Service Force, Sixth Fleet, who was also Commander Service Squadron One, homeported at Naples. Dowd's job was force logistics planning officer. His first boss was CAPT Ace Lyles, later relieved by CAPT Grover Clark. Their families lived in Naples, but the staff only spent about 10 percent of its time in port. The balance of time was spent at sea as Sixth Fleet Underway Replenishment Group, with the large fleet oiler *USS Missisinawa* (AO-144) as flagship. The complexities of matching Sixth Fleet operating schedules with the Service Force capabilities kept the supply staff hopping.

Dowd was selected for captain in spring 1962 and relieved CAPT Ray Cope as supply officer, Naval Support Activity, Naples. He soon learned that, because of the money chain, there was friction among personnel at NSA Naples who went to sea. It was not a healthy situation, and the Dowds spent a good part of their time in Naples doing all they could to convince the NSA officers that their reason for being was to serve the Fleet.

In July 1963 Dowd reported to OPNAV as head, Navy Supply Policy Section, and head of the Material Management Branch, Material Division (OP-41). He worked joint staff papers and processed budgets for NAVSUP and its field activities. He was in a sensitive position, working for the line, but serving as the eyes and ears of the commander of NAVSUP. His two superiors were not always in agreement.

He received orders in September 1966 to the staff, Commander Service Force, Pacific, and reported as assistant force supply officer under RADM Bernie Bieri. The buildup of U.S. forces in Vietnam was well underway, and Dowd found himself at the center of supply action. COMSERVPAC was the principal logistical agent for the Commander-in-Chief

Pacific Fleet. The command was responsible for all logistics forces in the Pacific, including the Mobile Logistic Support Force and WESTPAC bases in Japan, the Philippines, and Guam. The logistics support calls were made by CINCPAC at Pearl Harbor.

In spring 1968 Wally Dowd was selected for Flag rank, and in July he assumed command of NSC Charleston, which had worldwide supply support for the Polaris-Poseidon programs. It was RADM Dowd's first real exposure to the complexities of supporting nuclear-powered fleet ballistic missile submarines.

RADM Dowd was relieved by RADM Joe Howard in August 1970 and ordered to Washington as vice commander, NAVSUP, working for RADM Ken Wheeler. Just before completion of that tour, he received orders to report as commanding officer, NSC Oakland, in June 1971. But ADM Zumwalt called him to the war zone. Within two weeks, Polly Dowd had a heart catheter, they had driven across country, and he had assumed command of NSC Oakland, turned over the con to his exec, and departed for special additional duty in Vietnam.

The Vietnamese had not performed well in taking over supply support from the U.S. Navy. Accompanied by CDR Lynn Hazlett, RADM Dowd visited all U.S. and Vietnamese Navy facilities in the III-Corps area and recommended a five-point program to rectify the situation. The program was adopted, but to assure its success and assuage Vietnamese sensitivities, GEN Creighton Abrams decided to have Wally Dowd commissioned a rear admiral in, and appointed vice CNO of, the Republic of Vietnam's navy. This unique appointment is believed to be the only time a U.S. Navy Supply Corps Flag officer has actually served in the Navy of another nation. By October 1971 the program had achieved sufficient results to permit RADM Dowd to resign his commission in the Vietnamese navy and return to the United States to assume on-the-spot command of NSC Oakland.

In January 1973 Wally Dowd became commander, NAVSUP, in relief of Ken Wheeler, who became vice chief of naval material and was promoted to vice admiral. Dowd was concerned about the "nester" philosophy that he perceived was creeping into the Supply Corps. Nesting, sometimes called "homesteading," occurs when officers settle in at a particular location and purchase homes, their wives find good jobs, and the officers are hesitant to relocate when their rotation dates come up.

The new chief arrived in an era of tight money, which required NAVSUP and the Supply Corps to become much smarter in preparing budgets, defending them, and assuring that money was expended wisely. Money for the stock fund and transportation requirements was also a problem, because the "war lords" in the Pentagon wanted more money for sophisticated new weapons systems and did not concern themselves with how the new systems would be supported.

Wally Dowd says, "Moving requisitions is relatively easy. Kicking boxes out the door and getting them to the gents who need them is a major problem." Dowd's solution was to reallocate resources from the ICPs to the stock points. When he became chief of Supply Corps, he found that orders to duty at stock points were perceived as being sent into exile. RADM Dowd was able to reverse that perception, and the "hard-chargers" were subsequently more willing to go to duty at stock points.

When VADM Wheeler retired as vice chief of naval material in September 1974, ADM Ike Kidd, CNM, asked Wally Dowd to take over as his second-in-command on a part-time basis. After handling both jobs for several months, Dowd was offered the VCNM job on a permanent basis. Dowd declined the offer and remained at NAVSUP. Kidd then picked RADM Vince Lascara, who accepted and was promoted to vice admiral.

Wally Dowd retired in March 1977 and received a gold star in lieu of a second Distinguished Service Medal. He and Polly moved to their property on the Hood Canal, west of Puget Sound at Silverdale, Washington. In addition to enjoying the hunting and fishing in the area, Wally Dowd became the CEO of corporations involved with real estate, insurance, development, retail interests, and micrographics.

He has served as chairman of the board of the Seattle Lighthouse for the Blind and as a member of the board of the National Industries for the Blind.

Sources

Interview of RADM W. R. Dowd. Seattle, Wash., 31 May 1986.

Official Biography. Naval Supply Systems Command, August 1973.

"RADM W. R. Dowd Retires from Navy." *Navy Supply Corps Newsletter,* March 1977.

LORE OF THE CORPS

Lieutenant Commander Leonard Joseph Sapera, SC, USN

Supply Officer, Logistics Support Base Cam Rahn Bay, Vietnam, 1971
Period of Service: 1963–91

LCDR Sapera went to war on a commercial airliner. In Vietnam, he dealt decisively with inventory, drug, and morale problems and ended his

Navy career as the only former drilling Reservist ever chosen to become commanding officer of NSCS.

Len Sapera was born in New Orleans, Louisiana, in November 1940, and was graduated in 1962 from Tulane University, where he received a commission as a Reserve Supply Corps ensign through the NROTC Program. He attended NSCS Athens and was ordered as assistant supply officer, *USS Cavalier* (APA-37). Upon completion of that tour in June 1964, he was released from active duty and accepted employment with the Boeing Company at New Orleans. He drilled as a member of Naval Reserve Transportation, Traffic and Terminal Management Division 8-1, New Orleans while on inactive duty.

LTJG Sapera returned to active duty in January 1965 at Naval Air Technical Training Center Glynco, Georgia, as supply officer and comptroller and was promoted to lieutenant in June 1966. LT Sapera served as supply officer, *USS Richard E. Byrd* (DDG-23), from February 1967 to August 1968. He earned an M.B.A. degree in procurement and contracting at George Washington University in September 1969. Sapera was next assigned as chief of contract administration, Defense Contract Administration Services Office, Raytheon Company, Burlington, Massachusetts. He was promoted to lieutenant commander in January 1970.

In January 1971 LCDR Len Sapera reported as senior Navy supply advisor of Military Region II and supply officer of the Navy Logistics Support Base (LSB), Cam Ranh Bay. There were 500 U.S. Navy personnel and hundreds of Vietnamese personnel at the base. The goal of the Navy Advisory Group was to turn the whole base over to the Republic of Vietnam Navy in keeping with President Nixon's Vietnamization Program. LCDR Sapera's assignment was to transfer the supply operation to his Vietnamese counterpart, LT Pham Van Bay.

LCDR Sapera had no knowledge of the Vietnamese language and was struck by the fact that no one smiled or ever seemed afraid. The Vietnamese seemed to just exist in their designated surroundings, which may have accounted for the 39 percent stock record validity Sapera discovered during the relieving process. The major problem of attaining his priority goal, he learned, was a lack of communications between his fellow advisors and their RVN counterparts. He and LT Pham started to work on these and other problems, but it was a slow process.

Sapera's first meeting with his men was blunt and direct. He told them what he expected of them. He then ordered a full-scale inventory of all warehouses. Officers and men alike went to work, counting everything. It took 10 days, but when they finished, reconciled, and stock-checked hundreds of items, they had achieved a 97 percent stock validity. LCDR Sapera now believed that his organization could support the war effort in Military Region II, including the patrol gunboats (PGs) operating from Cam Ranh Bay.

Doors on the supply quonset hut needed repainting. LCDR Sapera had a choice of available colors—black, white, gray, or a gaudy international orange (IO). He chose IO and says, "It turned out to be one of the best management decisions I ever made." The following morning, he heard the Vietnamese sailors laughing and joking with their American counterparts about the color of the doors. The Vietnamese loved orange, and soon Sapera had a big orange sign in Vietnamese and orange wheel rims on his jeep. The orange paint proved to be a big morale booster and led to easing tension between American and Vietnamese personnel.

Each U.S. supply advisor now had a RVN counterpart, and the Vietnamese were learning how to run a supply operation, including the intricacies of warehouse and distribution operations and managing the record-keeping functions. Sapera also held a few social events, where Americans and Vietnamese alike could relax. These informal occasions appeared to contribute to an ever-growing esprit de corps.

The location of LSB Cam Ranh Bay on the southern tip of the peninsula provided an inviting target for Viet Cong rockets, which were fired frequently but randomly, with no apparent target. In April LCDR Sapera decided, "If we give these clowns something to shoot at, they will never hit it!" So, he climbed the roof of the quonset hut and painted a big orange target. The Cong never did hit it. When the Republic of Korea Marine White Horse Battalion relieved the U.S. Army across the peninsula, the rocketing stopped. The Korean Marines meant business, Len Sapera remembers, and were the toughest Allied group he ever served with.

One day, Sapera discovered three large crates, covered by sand, behind the supply quonset hut. They contained crucial engineering parts for the PGs. Sapera believed that they had been left outside and covered over by a sand monsoon. When the crates were taken inside and opened, one of them contained CASREP items for which a PG, *USS Gallup,* tied up at the pier, had outstanding requisitions.

When RADM Wally Dowd arrived in Vietnam in mid-June, he called all Navy Supply Corps advisors in Vietnam to a conference in Saigon. Seventeen attended, and Wally Dowd told them that the reputation and integrity of the Navy Supply Corps were on the line and concluded the meeting by announcing that he would personally visit each base and expected to be shown "everything." After the conference, Wally and Polly Dowd hosted a reception. Polly Dowd could discuss any topic and put the young Supply Corps officers at ease. When she returned home, she wrote to Eileen Sapera and all the other advisors' wives to tell them that she had met their husbands and they were well.

Wally Dowd then began his tour around Vietnam, and rumors of his actions were rampant among the bases. LCDR Sapera knew Dowd did not like what he was finding and had fired the supply advisors of the first two bases he visited. Although things were going well at LSB Cam Ranh Bay, Sapera was concerned about what Dowd's reaction would be to his colorful operation. The Vietnamese sailors were motivated and erected a 12-foot-high Asian sign in front of the supply quonset hut, which was topped by another 10-foot sign that had "#1" on it. Sapera was both astounded and proud.

On 28 June Len Sapera met his visitor, who looked ill. Sapera first took Dowd to see the base doctor, who told the admiral that he had a 104-degree temperature and should go directly to bed. Wally Dowd thanked the doctor and told Len Sapera to show him the warehouses. Dowd delved into every nook and cranny of seven warehouses. At the end, RADM Dowd congratulated everyone on a superb operation, one that he said was, in many ways, better than the one at NSC Oakland. He complimented the RVN storekeepers, especially LT Pham. Then he turned to the large orange sign behind him and said, "LSB Cam Ranh Bay is Number One." Two days later, LCDR Sapera turned over a warehouse with 8,000 repair items to LT Pham and the RVN Navy. The entire Supply Department was turned over in September, but Sapera remained as advisor until December.

When Len Sapera completed his tour at the end of 1971, he returned to NSCS Athens as division officer and instructor and wrote and taught the leadership and management course. He then served two tours at NAVSUP—in OP as head, Shore Detail Branch, from August 1975 to January 1976. He was promoted to commander in June 1977 and selected as executive assistant and aide to the commander, RADM Gene Grinstead, in January 1979.

CDR Sapera traveled more than 114,000 miles with the chief during the 14 months he served as Gene Grinstead's right-hand man. He reports that standard operating procedure was to bring all his paperwork plus assorted chocolate candy to munch on along with an airline Bloody Mary. Sapera claims, "We'd get a lot done on those flights." On one 19-hour Alitalia flight from Bangkok to Rome via Bombay and Dubai, the two had opposite aisle seats with an open seat next to each. At Bombay, Grinstead bet Sapera a drink that a beautiful woman would take the unoccupied seat next to him. An attractive, well-dressed woman came down the aisle, stopped next to the chief, put her makeup kit in the overhead compartment, and sat down next to Sapera. He smiled and said, "Pay up, chief." Sapera remembers that Grinstead grumbled, paid up, then grumbled again when a Catholic priest boarded the plane and took the seat next to him.

The two made a 25,534-mile trip to the Middle East in February 1980, stopping at 19 places in 13 countries on FMS business. Two senior line Flag officers accompanied them. CDR Sapera was impressed with the obvious trust the Saudi navy chief had in RADM Grinstead. In a meeting at Riyadh, the line Flag officers made the presentations but all the questions were asked of Grinstead. The Saudis hosted a lavish buffet at a luxurious downtown hotel. The Americans enjoyed the bountiful meal of roasted goat with all the trimmings. At the end of the meal, the host had the goat's eyes placed on a tray for the honored guests. The line Flag officers politely declined, but Gene Grinstead took one and sent the other to CDR Sapera. The two Supply Corps officers, with nearly 300 Saudis watching, swallowed the eyes and chased them with the nearest available liquid. "The Saudis loved it and the Supply Corps reputation was further enhanced," Sapera reports.

Sapera believes there was a connection between swallowing the goat's eyes and his being asked to step outside the hotel by a Saudi commander, who presented two large boxes. Each contained 24 place settings of 21-carat-gold flatware. CDR Sapera explained that he and the chief were not permitted to accept such gifts, even when offered in generous friendship. He was asked to check with Grinstead and urge him to accept the gift from the Saudi royal family. Sapera went to Grinstead's room, explained the situation, and remembers that the chief said, "It isn't ethical, and we must set the example for others who come over here to do FMS business." They left the place settings behind.

From Washington, CDR Sapera went back to sea in July 1980 as supply officer, *USS San Diego* (AFS-6), deployed with the Sixth Fleet. Len Sapera claims to have had more hang time than any other Supply Corps officer, making 119 vertical transfers from CH-46 helicopters to decks of underway ships. He says *San Diego*'s chief engineer always complained about supply, so CDR Sapera took control of the Engineering Department's OPTAR and managed it himself. Sapera retained the OPTAR even when the chief engineer took over for the executive officer, who went on emergency leave never to return.

Eileen Sapera and their children remained in the Washington area when her husband went to sea. Whenever *San Diego* was in port at Norfolk, he lived aboard during the week and commuted north the approximately 200 miles each weekend. This arrangement resulted in his being, in effect, the command duty officer each weekday night. When CDR Sapera went into the shower each morning, he was doused by extremely cold water. When he repeatedly called the duty engineer, he would be told, "We're working on it." Finally, the supply officer called a local plumber, who informed him that a house call was $35, but he "did not do ships." Sapera told him to park his truck by *San Diego*'s brow, where it could be readily seen by all boarding or leaving the ship. Sapera invited the plumber to his stateroom for coffee, while the engineers demanded to know why a plumber was servicing the ship. The X.O., a former engineering officer, was livid and called Sapera to find out why he had embarrassed his engineers. Sapera, who had given the plumber a personal check and sent him on his way, told the exec that he was tired of taking cold showers. From that point on, the entire ship had hot water at 0600 each day.

In December 1981 Sapera returned to Washington as deputy director, Contracts and Business Review Division, Naval Material Command, where he was promoted to captain in March 1983. CAPT Sapera reported in July 1984 to the Navy Ships Parts Control Center Mechanicsburg, as director, Electronic Systems Department, and later as director, Fleet/Industrial Support Group.

In July 1987 CAPT Sapera assumed command of NSCS Athens, where he placed heightened emphasis on building esprit de corps among officer students and staff. He brought in VIP guests, including successful business people, many of them NSCS alumni, and motivational speakers, to share their experiences with students and staff. He recalls that the most colorful and memorable speaker was Tommy Lasorda, manager of the Los Angeles Dodgers. Sapera had mock-ups of shipboard supply space built in the Russell Hall Academic Building, using salvaged material to bring the real world into the classroom. He was also the driving force behind rebuilding the NSCS chapel and installing new pews and stained glass windows that were purchased with contributions from Supply Corps officers throughout the Navy. NSCS Athens received Training Excellence Awards during his tenure as commanding officer.

One of his most successful undertakings was a gala reunion in July 1989 of old and new Supply Corps officers on the 35th anniversary of the opening of NSCS Athens. More than 625 Supply Corps officers and their guests traveled to Athens for the 4-day event. Len Sapera was highly active and quite visible in the Athens community and hosted many programs involving local citizens during his four-year tour as commanding officer. He obtained a two-ton surplus LST anchor, had it cleaned and painted, and presented it to the city of Athens in 1990 as a highly visible symbol of "NSCS dropping anchor in our permanent home port."

In August 1991 Len Sapera retired from the Navy after 28 years of service, during which he was awarded the Bronze Star, the Legion of Merit, the Meritorious Service Medal (with four gold stars), and the Vietnamese Cross of Gallantry with palm. He and Eileen remained in Athens, where they built a new home after vacating government quarters.

CAPT Sapera is vice president for business development, Athens First Bank and Trust Company, and chairman of the Fund Development Council of the Athens Regional Medical Center. He is a member of the Governor's Military Coordinating Committee and past president of the Rotary Club of Athens.

Sources

"Cam Ranh Bay Warehouse Turnover." *Hai Quan* [base newspaper], 20 June 1971.

Documents supplied by CAPT Leonard J. Sapera, September 1993, July 1994.

Vietnamization Program Memorandum. Supply Dept., LSB, Cam Ranh Bay, 30 August 1971.

NAVSUP Initiatives

A pilot program to establish weapons systems files at inventory control points was successfully implemented in 1970 at the Electronics Supply Office, Great Lakes, Illinois, commanded by CAPT Russell A. (Russ) Jones. In 1971 another important step in speeding the flow of material from stock points to afloat forces occurred when *USS Providence* (CLG-6) transmitted the first requisitions from sea to a supply activity via satellite and Autodin. LCDR (later CAPT) Alan J. Nissalke was the supply officer. NAVSUP also sponsored activation of an improved Mark II UADPS test site at NSC Norfolk in 1971.

Extended Med Deployment

Meanwhile, on the other side of the world the Soviet navy moved in March 1971 to extend its influence in the area by sending a task force on a lengthy visit to Indian ports. These moves threatened Imperial Iran, and the shah questioned the will of the U.S. Navy to fulfill American commitments to insulate Iran from Soviet and Iraqi incursions.

Great Britain agreed in October 1972 to permit the United States to improve the Diego Garcia lagoon anchorage and extend the air strip to 8,000 feet. A new 50-year lease agreement between the two countries was signed in March 1973. The agreement permitted establishment of a U.S. naval station on the strategic Indian Ocean island.

The Sixth Fleet continued to sail the Mediterranean Sea as the major on-site deterrent force of the United States stand-off with the Soviet Union. Supplying ships of such a major deployment, along with the foreign support bases, on a continuing basis, has been an enormous challenge for the Supply Corps.

An AKS was homeported at Barcelona, Spain, and AFs shuttled back and forth from Norfolk, bringing fresh provisions and other supplies to the deployed Sixth Fleet. A destroyer tender, either *USS Yosemite* (AD-19) or *USS Everglades* (AD-24), stayed at Naples most of the time, but the duty AD occasionally ventured out into the Mediterranean to make port calls for short periods. The AFs obtained their prime loads at Norfolk, but fresh fruit and vegetables were picked up at Valencia, Spain. The ADs received industrial support from NSC Norfolk, with the materials brought to the Med by the in-coming AF. The AOs picked up mail and petroleum stocks throughout the Mediterranean. Normally, an AO met the in-coming AF to transfer surface mail, movies, and freight for onward movement. The scheduling was complex and ever changing to meet Fleet movements required whenever world tensions heated up.

Among responsibilities of the Sixth Fleet supply officer was lining up contractors to supply port services for visiting ships and moving Fleet freight arriving by commercial ships and aircraft throughout the Mediterranean. In addition, he was charged with monitoring the flow of Navy resale merchandise originating in Europe and Asia to ship's stores. He also monitored actions of the itinerant merchants who were on hand with unerring regularity when U.S. Navy ships arrived in Mediterranean ports.

The First Woman Supply Corps Officer at Sea

In 1972 the Navy embarked on a pilot program for assigning women to sea duty on noncombatant ships. The first Supply Corps officer assigned under this program was ENS (later CAPT) Rosemary Elaine Nelson (later Dawson), who went to sea as disbursing officer in the hospital ship *USS Sanctuary* (AH-17).

Notes

Sources for material used in this chapter and not cited earlier include:

Miller, Nathan. *The U.S. Navy: An Illustrated History*. Annapolis: Naval Institute Press, and New York: American Heritage Press, 1977.

Navy Supply Corps Newsletter, September 1973.

Supply Corps 2010. Chief of Supply Corps, 1989.

World Almanac and Book of Facts. 1992.

CHAPTER TWELVE

Low-Intensity Conflicts

1973–83

As 1973 dawned, the United States and the Soviet Union were still engaged in an ideological battle and locked in a nuclear arms stalemate. They also were both competing for strategic and tactical advantage in conventional weapons over the entire spectrum of military forces at tremendous cost to their respective economic systems.

Back in Washington in January 1973, RADM Wallace R. Dowd relieved RADM (later VADM) Kenneth R. Wheeler as commander of the Naval Supply Systems Command and chief of Supply Corps.

A four-power Vietnam peace agreement was signed in January 1973, calling for release of American prisoners of war and withdrawal of all U.S. combat troops, but the fighting between North and South Vietnam did not end. By March 1973 Vietnamization was in full swing. Most of the Navy supply advisors had departed South Vietnam, leaving behind a smoothly functioning Vietnamese navy supply system. The linchpin of this operation was the Vietnamese Naval Supply Center at Newport, a suburb of Saigon. The center was responsible for an inventory of 69,000 line items with a value of $19 million.

The drawdown had left only six Navy billets in South Vietnam and two of those were filled by Supply Corps officers, CAPT Henry E. (Hank) Hirschy, Jr., Chief, Vietnamese Navy Supply Support Branch, and LCDR (later RADM) Peter A. (Pete) Bondi, supply advisor to the Vietnamese navy. Hirschy was located at the Defense Attaché Organization (DAO) office adjacent to the Ton Son Nhut Airport. LCDR Bondi's office was at the Newport Shipyard, where he worked closely with the commanding officer of the Vietnamese Naval Supply Center.

The Supply Support Branch had 18 American civilian consultants and 16 Vietnamese employees, but no other military personnel. CAPT Hirschy emphasized fine-tuning the Vietnamese navy supply system, completing a consolidated VNNSC supply complex at Newport, and continuing to train a Vietnamese navy supply command and supply corps. The Hirschy-Bondi team was certain that the ambitious concept was workable, but within three weeks optimism turned to pessimism, then to despair as the communists surged forward.

Withdrawal of Republic of Vietnam (ARVN) troops from the Central Highlands and advance of North Vietnamese troops had a significant impact upon supply operations. As Hue, Danang, Qui Nhon, Cam Ranh, Nha Trang, and other cities fell quickly to communist forces, a tremendous amount of U.S. Navy supplied equipment was lost, and the North Vietnamese stepped up their attacks on Saigon.

The U.S. defense attaché, an Army general, ordered an immediate, significant reduction in the number of American consultants. During the week of 7 April, 15 of the 18 American consultants in the Supply Branch left for home. With only two of the Supply Corps officers and three consultants remaining, the branch continued to run smoothly because of the competence of the Vietnamese supply personnel.

There was a critical need to find additional funds to replace equipment lost by ARVN forces. The Navy agreed to transfer $1.67 million of Vietnamese navy funding to the Army, including $900,000 for planned stock replenishment at VNNSC. Despite the funding degradation and a 63 percent increase in demand, the system provided a net effectiveness of 88 percent in March.

Evacuation Plans

By mid-April, ARVN troops were in general retreat, and it was apparent that remaining Americans would soon have to leave Vietnam. CAPT Hirschy stood watch from 1600 to 2400 hours each day in the Evacuation Control Center. Throughout early April, an important task of the Supply Support Branch had been to develop a plan for the orderly evacuation by Military Sealift Command (MSC) ships of American personnel assigned to the Defense Attaché Office. The ships were to load at Newport under cover of darkness. Loading zones were identified, but the plan was never put into operation. Events moved so quickly that it was replaced by an alternate air evacuation plan.

As enemy forces surged toward Saigon during the week of 20 April, LCDR Bondi was designated the chief scheduler for all personnel being evacuated by air. Loaded planes took off every 30 minutes, 24 hours a day, with some American military dependents and civilians; most of the passengers, however, were the 65,000 loyal Vietnamese considered to be in danger, including those who had worked with the Central Intelligence Agency.

CAPT Hirschy undertook responsibility for holding paydays throughout the Saigon area, including making emergency—sometimes secretive—travel arrangements for both Americans and Vietnamese. These duties were in addition to maintaining an ongoing dialogue with Vietnamese navy officials.

In the final days of April, Americans left in Saigon had abandoned their houses and apartments and were living in one of the two American compounds, venturing out only when necessary. One group was in the U.S. Embassy; the other group was at the Defense Attaché Office opposite the airport. Hirschy and Bondi were living in offices at DAO.

On 28 April, evacuation flights by Military Airlift Command (MAC) C-130 and C-141 aircraft were carried out between attacks. By midnight, only about 1,000 Americans were left in Saigon. Early on 29 April, CAPT Hirschy and LCDR Bondi attempted to take 70 people to the airport by bus for a C-130 flight but were forced to turn back. They then were ordered to lead the Americans for evacuation by Marine helicopters, which were on the way to the U.S. Embassy and DAO.

According to LCDR Bondi, the larger concentration of people seeking safe flights out of Saigon on 29 April was at the DAO complex, not at the U.S. Embassy as highly publicized in the world press and depicted in the play *Miss Saigon*. The people at DAO, in a direct line of fire from the airport, were the ones in dire peril.

The first of the CH-53 helicopters, loaded with heavily armed Marines, arrived shortly after 1500 hours. As the Marines quickly debarked and took up defensive positions around DAO and the embassy, the choppers just as quickly refilled with evacuees and departed for U.S. ships offshore. Some of the helicopters were hit by enemy ground fire, but none was forced down. In a half hour, CAPT Hirschy was safely aboard *USS Mount Vernon* (LSD-34) and LCDR Bondi aboard *USS Duluth* (LPD-6). The ships remained for three more days off the coast of Vietnam before sailing for Subic Bay in the Philippines, which they reached on 4 May.

The Evacuation of South Vietnam

As some Vietnamese were being evacuated by MAC aircraft and Marine helicopters from Saigon at the end of April 1975, thousands of others were using any available transportation to flee the rapidly advancing enemy. At coastal bases, refugees seeking sanctuary crowded into the few former U.S. Navy destroyers, destroyer escorts, and small patrol craft of the Republic of Vietnam Navy that had not already put to sea.

USS Ashtabula (AO-51), a former ESSO tanker launched in 1943, had made two shuttle runs from Subic Bay, the Philippines, to deliver supplies to American ships off the coast of Vietnam. She was in port at Subic Bay, loading for a third run, when she received orders for a special humanitarian mission.

Ashtabula sailed the following morning to meet a motley refugee armada about 40 miles off the coast of Vietnam, near the mouth of the Mekong Delta, and escort the ships to Subic Bay. Her assistant supply officer, LTJG (later CAPT) J. Paul Ochenkowski, was on deck when the sad RVNN fleet came into view, with each ship proudly flying the dying free nation's red and yellow flag. Ochenkowski recorded what he saw: "The decks were jammed, the deck houses packed, even the small platforms located on the masts were each occupied by two or three people, jammed into a small space, willing to stand for over a week for a chance to get to freedom, to escape the North Vietnamese. The crowding was on a truly massive scale."

Ashtabula was designated the escort and supply ship for the Vietnam fleet and was authorized to transfer food without charge. Problems arose immediately. The first challenge was how *Ashtabula* could supply food for so many people for so long. Unsure of the cooking facilities aboard Vietnamese ships, the decision was made to transfer sealed containers of ready-to-eat food that would require no cooking. Heat-treated canned milk, canned processed meat, canned vegetables that could be eaten cold, and large quantities of bread were provided. The food was loaded into *Ashtabula*'s two motor whale boats for humanitarian runs to the crammed ships.

CAPT Ochenkowski reports that crews of the *Ashtabula*'s boats encountered unbelievable crowding and incredible filth, and food supplies were virtually exhausted. The provisions probably made the difference between life and death. The food runs were maintained throughout the slow voyage to the Philippines.

Two days out of Vietnam, a large ocean-going tug flying the South Korean flag came close by *Ashtabula,* reported a low-fuel condition, and requested resupply. Officers of *Ashtabula* hesitated because much of the tug's main weather deck was covered by a large tarpaulin. The specter of the seizure of the American merchant ship *SS Mayaguez* by Cambodians a few days earlier in the Gulf of Siam was foremost in the minds of all aboard *Ashtabula*. At general quarters, *Ashtabula* crewmen waited nervously as the tug's crew complied with an order to pull back the tarp. When American sailors saw another large group of Vietnamese refugees huddled beneath the tarp, the tug was permitted alongside, and *Ashtabula* passed over food and fuel. The replenished tug sped away in the general direction of the Philippines.

As the pathetic little convoy moved slowly on its eight-day journey east, it was overtaken by several merchantmen, also carrying loads of refugees who had pitched tents on their weather decks. Two days out of Subic Bay, *Ashtabula* received word that ships flying the South Vietnamese flag would not be welcomed by the Philippine government, which desired to keep open its options with the communists who had taken control of all Vietnam.

The State and Navy departments decided to help the Vietnamese by providing temporary quarters at a Navy recreation camp on Grande Island in Subic Bay and restricting all movement to the U.S. facilities. However, because the ships would be transiting Philippine territorial waters, it was necessary to find a way for the Marcos government to save face.

A call went out to NSD Subic Bay and all U.S. ships in the area for several dozen U.S. flags for the Vietnamese ships to fly. Enough 48- , 49- , and 50-star flags were rounded up to provide each ship with an American flag. *Ashtabula* distributed the flags, and, on signal, all ships in the convoy hauled down the Republic of Vietnam flags and smartly ran up the Stars and Stripes. Upon arrival at Subic, the Vietnamese ships, now flying U.S. flags, peeled off and anchored at Grande Island while *Ashtabula* tied up at one of the Navy piers.

In 1993 CAPT Ochenkowski, Director, Supply Corps Reserve Personnel at NAVSUP, recorded his onboard observations of *Ashtabula*'s eight-day voyage: "I've thought about these people often. They were the first 'boat people,' and several years later, when the Humanitarian Award was authorized, *USS Ashtabula* received it. . . It was clear from the determination of these people to get away from a communist government, and the incredible hardships that they were willing to put up with, that what the press of the time was saying about our not having the 'hearts and minds' of the people for the war effort in Vietnam was clearly wrong." (Ochenkowski's complete document on the first Vietnamese boat people is on file at the Navy Supply Corps Museum, Athens, Georgia.)

The Supply Corps role in South Vietnam was over. The 1,085 Navy Supply Corps officers who served in Vietnam from 1961 to 1975 could hold their heads high. They had left behind a smooth functioning Republic of Vietnam Navy supply system, run by a well-trained indigenous supply corps.

LORE OF THE CORPS

Lieutenant Commander Peter A. Bondi, SC, USN

Deputy Chief, RVNN Supply Support Branch, U.S. Defense Attaché Office, Saigon, Vietnam, 1974–75
Period of Service: 1963–95

LCDR Bondi may have been the last U.S. Navy Supply Corps officer to leave Vietnam when North Vietnamese and Viet Cong forces overran Saigon in late April 1975. He went on to Flag rank, commanded a DLA depot, oversaw U.S. Navy withdrawal from the Philippines, and is currently serving as fleet supply officer, U.S. Pacific Fleet, at Pearl Harbor.

Peter A. Bondi was born in Philadelphia, Pennsylvania, in February 1941. He attended the University of North Carolina as an NROTC regular, intending to be a line officer. In 1962, his senior year, he changed his mind, was commissioned an ensign in the Supply Corps, and reported to NSCS Athens.

From Athens, his first duty was at the Naval Supply Activity Taipei, Taiwan (Formosa). There were only 12 Supply Corps officers at NSA Taipei, but he was impressed with the group, which included LT (later RADM) Bill Hauenstein, LT (later CAPT) Jim Huffman, and LTJG (later CAPT) Rich Conser. Bondi was promoted to LTJG in December 1963.

In 1964 he went back to his hometown as industrial support superintendent, Philadelphia Naval Shipyard, where he was promoted to lieutenant in December 1965. He was ordered to sea as supply officer, *USS Lawrence* (DDG-4), homeported at Norfolk, in 1966. He returned to Pennsylvania as customer support officer, Ships Parts Control Center Mechanicsburg, from 1968 to 1969. He was promoted to lieutenant commander while at SPCC. He next attended George Washington University in Washington, D.C., from which he was graduated with an M.B.A. degree in contracting in 1971.

LCDR Bondi reported in July 1971 to NSC Oakland, where he served for three years as director of purchase. In 1974, when asked by his wife, Joan, about his chances of going to Vietnam, Pete Bondi replied, "Slim to none," beause only one LCDR billet was left there. Shortly thereafter, he received orders to relieve LCDR Bob Young at Saigon. He reported in December 1974 and stayed until the city fell.

At the time of LCDR Bondi's arrival, all U.S. prisoners of war had been repatriated, American combat troops had been withdrawn from Vietnam, and only 50 U.S. military personnel remained in accordance with the treaty signed at Paris in January 1973. Bondi was one of only two Supply Corps officers left. His job was supply advisor at the Vietnamese Navy Supply Center. Pete Bondi was impressed with the Vietnamese and says, "We could have taken many of those Vietnamese officers and inserted them at Oakland, for example, and they wouldn't have missed a beat."

When the military situation in Vietnam deteriorated, evacuation of the remaining Americans and loyal Vietnamese began. After receiving an urgent telephone call from Lieutenant Dinh V. Manh, a Vietnamese navy officer on duty at NSC Oakland, LCDR Bondi drove a jeep to Dinh's Saigon home and located his wife, four children, and a cousin. Bondi hustled them to the airport, where he put them on one of the last evacuation flights. It was the only time in his final month in Saigon that Pete Bondi had dared venture into the city, but he is pleased that his humanitarian mission worked out well.

On 29 April, their last day in Vietnam, Hank Hirschy and Pete Bondi were responsible for different groups of evacuees. They were evacuated on different helicopters and were taken to different U.S. Navy ships at about the same time. Who was the last Supply Corps officer to leave Saigon remains a question. Pete Bondi has a theory about why the helicopter evacuation was so successful. He believes that the large number of North Vietnamese regulars and guerrillas could have easily taken either the embassy or the DAO compound, but were satisfied to keep the pressure on and force the Americans out of town.

Joan Bondi had a rough 24 hours when the list of evacuees was released and her husband's name was not among them. When his helicopter landed on *USS Duluth* (LPD-6), Pete Bondi was called to the bridge by the skipper, who wanted a complete report on what was transpiring ashore. Bondi spent a couple of hours briefing the captain, and no one recorded his name as being aboard the ship. The error was discovered the following day, and only then did Joan Bondi and their three children learn that LCDR Bondi was safe.

CAPT Hirschy and LCDR Bondi were flown from Subic Bay to Hawaii for two weeks of debriefing. Bondi received message orders to return to Oakland, get his family, and relocate to Hawaii for duty on the staff, Commander-in-Chief Pacific Fleet, where he served from 1975 to 1978. He was involved in Fleet support for about half of his tour, then relieved CAPT (later RADM) Dan McKinnon on the shore desk and was promoted to commander in September 1976.

When time came to return to sea duty in 1978, CDR Bondi was assigned as supply officer in the destroyer tender *USS Bryce Canyon* (AD-36) at Pearl Harbor. In July 1980 he returned to Washington to work in the Contracting Section at Naval Sea Systems Command under RADM Stuart F. (Stu) Platt. NAVSEA was concerned over the length of time ship overhauls were taking, and Bondi was given responsibility for a new unit to develop innovative contracting for overhauls. One result was multiship overhaul contracts. Pete Bondi was promoted to captain in January 1983.

CAPT Bondi finally received duty he had always wanted in the summer of 1983 as head of the Detail Division in OP. The job was rewarding, but probably ulcer-inducing because detailers dealt with people and their plans, desires, and dreams. Bondi was ordered to duty as X.O. at SPCC Mechanicsburg in 1985. He says that duty at Mechanicsburg is a little like overseas duty because it is removed from Washington and engenders a special kind of camaraderie. RADM Robert B. (Bob) Abele was C.O. when he first reported aboard. Bondi considers his SPCC C.O.s—RADMs Abele and J. A. (Jack) Scott—as his role models.

After his SPCC tour, CAPT Bondi reported to San Diego in 1987 as assistant chief of staff for supply, Commander Surface Force, U.S. Pacific Fleet. He was selected for Flag rank in 1988 and reported as commander, Defense General Supply Center Richmond, Virginia, in February 1989. In his first joint service tour, he commanded this major DLA field activity with more than 2,000 employees.

RADM Bondi went back to Pearl Harbor in June 1991 to relieve RADM Ray R. Sareeram as Fleet supply officer on the CINCPACFLT staff, which has overall responsibility for the entire gamut of logistics in the Pacific Ocean area. Before Bondi's arrival, a decision was made to have the three Western Pacific stock points, NSD Guam, NSD Subic Bay, and NSD Yokosuka, report to NAVSUP. The Pacific Fleet remained the stock points' dominant customer despite the fact that the CINCPACFLT staff no longer ran the organizations nor funded them.

NSD Subic Bay was the largest and most important of the supply points in the Western Pacific because of its strategic location. The United States and the Philippine government had negotiated for several years over renewal of base agreements when Mount Pinatubo erupted violently in June 1991. The resultant devastation at Subic Bay Naval Station and nearby Clark AFB significantly reduced the price Uncle Sam was willing to pay for new agreements. Despite substantial damage, the Subic Bay base was functioning fully, but when the negotiations collapsed, CINCPACFLT was assigned the responsibility for withdrawing all American presence. ADM Robert J. Kelly delegated the job to RADM Tom Mercer, Commander U.S. Naval Force, Philippines. Mercer frequently was required to be in Manila for the ongoing political discussions. He was committed to assuring that the Navy could not be charged with abandoning Subic. RADM Bondi was named as Mercer's deputy commander for the withdrawal process.

Pete Bondi was not at Subic on supply business, but as ADM Kelly's representative to plan the entire withdrawal without regard to organization or chain of command. Bondi consulted with the 50 commanding officers of the units based at Subic on the enormous challenge they faced together and set up an organization to accomplish it. Tasks associated with moving people, records, vehicles, and special equipment of a normal base relocation were easily recognizable. However, it was also necessary to determine when the base commissary, dispensary, and schools would close; when material would be turned over or sold; and when and how physical facilities would be turned over to the Philippine government. Photographs were taken of every building to record its condition on turnover.

Bondi's team drew up specific plans for packing up and scheduling transport of the huge amount of retrograde material to be repositioned within the supply system or turned over to Defense Reutilization and Marketing Operation (DRMO) for disposal. A basic principle established from the outset was that nothing would be shipped elsewhere if the transportation cost would exceed the value of the item.

A large volume of material was identified for disposal in the Philippines through procedures prescribed by DRMO. Pete Bondi praises DRMO personnel in the Philippines and in Hawaii, especially CAPT Donald K. Edgerton, and the CINCPACFLT staff at Pearl Harbor. Bondi underscores that everything turned over to agencies of the Philippine government was in strict accordance with U.S. law and in cooperation with the State Department. American officials were convinced that the Philippine military took only what it needed. Everything else was sold locally, transferred to other overseas stock points, or returned to the United States.

Based upon the capability of the base civilian workers in handling cargo, MSC's performance record, and the availability of sufficient gross tonnage afloat in the Pacific, ships were ordered in and out of Subic on a timely basis. They transported more than 98 percent of the material leaving the Philippines and held reverse airlift tonnage to a minimum. Significant volumes of valuable, needed material went to supply points at Yokosuka and Sasebo, Japan, and to Guam, but the preponderance of retrograde cargo went back to the mainland, as determined by NAVSUP and the ICPs. Pete Bondi was promoted to rear admiral, upper half, in October 1992, and the withdrawal was completed in less than a year—in November 1992.

RADM Bondi's bottom line is that the Pacific Fleet was able to align its support posture to compensate fully for the loss of Subic Bay. Other Pacific supply points picked up a share of the logistics mission, including NSD Yokosuka, where the Japanese had built a new, modern, well-equipped warehouse. NSC Guam took over support of deployed AFSs and the advance base at Diego Garcia in the Indian Ocean. Pete Bondi believes that the primary reason for this success is the abundant talent of outstanding Supply Corps officers. He recalls one line Flag officer who told him candidly that he "was absolutely embarrassed that every time he had a job on his staff, he turned to the Supply Corps because they were the ones who could get it done."

As this is written, RADM Bondi and Joan Bondi live in quarters at Pearl Harbor and look forward to retirement in mid-1995.

Sources

Hirschy, CAPT H. D., and LCDR P. A. Bondi. "The Final Hours." *Navy Supply Corps Newsletter,* June–July 1975.

Interview of RADM Peter A. Bondi. Pearl Harbor, Hawaii, 26 January 1993.

Official Biography. CINCPACFLT, n.d.

The Canal Zone Supply Officer and the Circus

Another Supply Corps officer called upon in 1973 to perform unusual duties for which NSCS provided no specific guidance was LCDR (later CDR) Robert D. (Don) Webb, supply officer in tranquil Panama. The Naval Support Activity, Panama Canal Zone, often provided port facilities for ships of Central and South American navies, which owned and operated several former U.S. Navy LSTs. Ecuador had severe budget problems and often chartered its LSTs to civilian firms as cargo carriers.

In March 1973 an Ecuadorian LST, chartered to transport a Mexican circus that had just completed a season of performances during the South American summer, arrived at Balboa, Panama, from Guayaquil. The circus operators had intended to land in Panama and work their way north, performing in Central America en route home in time for the summer season in Mexico.

The government refused to let the circus enter Panama because the animals had not been through quarantine. Before that decision was known, the Ecuadorians had offloaded the circus, animals and all, and the LST left for home. Canal Zone authorities would permit the animals to remain in the Zone only if the Navy allowed the circus to serve quarantine in its extensive real estate for two weeks. The only place the elephants, lions, tigers, apes, and other animals could graze was on the secure, fenced fuel farm guarded by Marines.

Because the Supply Department was responsible for the fuel farm, the NSA commanding officer decided that LCDR Webb was the logical custodian of the circus. It was short on funds, but Webb says he was fortunate to have excellent support personnel who obtained food for the animals, their keepers, and performers. Navy dependents, especially the children, were delighted with the exotic animals and pitched in with food and cash contributions. The appreciative circus personnel put on several informal performances for their hosts.

The keepers lived in tents set up by the Supply Department and adjacent to where their animals were tethered. Two weeks later, when the quarantine requirements had been fulfilled, the circus packed up and headed into northern Panama and Costa Rica. Don Webb believes that he is the only Supply Corps officers ever to be responsible for a circus. He reports that a number of titles were suggested for his temporary duty as circus master, but the most popular was CINCCIR—Commander-in-Chief, Circus.

A Woman Officer in Command

Beginning in the late 1960s, the U.S. Navy instituted several programs to broaden opportunities for minorities, including women, and NAVSUP was among the leaders in implementing such programs. NAVSUP equal employment opportunity (EEO) programs, adopted in the 1960s, were expanded during the early 1970s. In August 1973 CAPT Ruth Tomsuden, became commanding officer, Navy Food Service Systems Office (NAVFSSO). She was the first female to command a major activity in the Naval Material Command claimancy.

LORE OF THE CORPS

Captain Ruth Marie Tomsuden, SC, USN

Commanding Officer, Navy Food Service Systems Office, 1973–75
Period of Service: 1952–75

Captain Tomsuden was commissioned in the Supply Corps Reserve and says that doing so was the best decision she ever made. At the end of her first tour during the Korean War, she was not satisfied with only a two-year obligated tour and augmented into the Regular Navy. She went on to become the first woman to have a major NMC command.

Ruth Marie Tomsuden was born in Brooklyn, New York, in April 1930, and World War II recruiting posters first interested her in the Navy.

She was graduated from Ohio University with a B.S. degree in commerce in 1951 and talked with a Navy recruiter, who encouraged her to apply for a Reserve Supply Corps direct commission in April 1952.

ENS Tomsuden completed the staff corps program at the Navy Officer Candidate School, Newport, Rhode Island, in June 1952 and reported to NSCS Bayonne the following month. In November, she was ordered as disbursing officer for civilian rolls, Mare Island Naval Shipyard, Vallejo, California. Tomsuden was promoted to lieutenant, junior grade, and augmented into the Regular Navy in the spring of 1954.

LTJG Tomsuden reported as disbursing officer in August 1954 on the staff, Commander Service Force, Pacific. She says she had to fine-tune a "can do" attitude among hard-working talented personnel who met the demands of paying all military on staff of CINCPACFLT/COMSERVPAC and settling travel claims on a walk-in basis. Tomsuden was promoted to lieutenant in 1956 and went to NSD Bayonne in December, where she was stock control officer. Two experiences are particularly vivid in her memory. In the first instance, she received an anonymous call at the duty office, alerting her to a theft in progress. She immediately ordered a search of all vehicles leaving the base and went to the main gate to observe the operation. The guards discovered an attempt to remove a truck load of subsistence items and foul weather gear, and the perpetrators were apprehended. She was later a witness in the FBI investigation and subsequent trial.

In the second instance, a guard reported a man calling for help from the mud flats opposite the gate and about 300 yards from shore. The Bayonne Fire Department could not reach him, and he was sinking further into the mud as he struggled to free himself. LT Tomsuden called the Coast Guard, which sent a rescue helicopter to pluck the man, sans trousers, from sure death.

In September 1959 she was ordered to duty in the Office of the Navy Comptroller at Washington as assistant for travel in the Military Pay Division. Here, she encountered her first blatant opposition. A male warrant officer, for whom she was the numerical relief, said that if he were to be replaced by a woman officer, it was time for him to retire. On the positive side, she was involved in Navy travel pay issues ranging from staffing changes in legislation to implementing legislation; in answering questions, which included requests for comptroller general decisions; and was promoted to lieutenant commander.

LCDR Tomsuden was assigned to the Defense Personnel Support Center Philadelphia, in August 1962 as branch chief in the Equipment and Footwear Division, Director of Procurement and Production. In her first procurement assignment, she had to work with commercial firms to gear up for production of tents, boots, and other military equipment.

In 1966 Tomsuden was promoted to commander and reported for duty at the Naval Supply Systems Command, where she was personnel officer and security officer. For the first time, she had an opportunity to work closely with other Supply Corps officers.

CDR Tomsuden reported to new duty in the Systems Analysis Division, Office of Chief of Naval Operations at the Pentagon in August 1968. This duty provided her first opportunity to observe high-level Navy operational procedures. She was also able to acquire experience in procurement processing and budgetary and planning cycles. She was awarded the Navy Commendation Medal for her service on the CNO staff.

When Ruth Tomsuden entered the Navy, women could not aspire to ranks beyond lieutenant commander. She had been contemplating retirement with 20 years of service, but selection to captain changed her mind. In August 1972 CAPT Tomsuden was transferred to the Defense Supply Agency, Cameron Station, in Alexandria, Virginia, where she was assigned to a procurement billet. An incident at Cameron Station reminded Tomsuden that a woman senior officer was still a rarity. When attempting to locate a valued lost silver pen, she posted 3 x 5 cards in strategic locations around DSA headquarters, including one in a woman's room. While she was there, two other women who were unaware of her presence saw CAPT Tomsuden's name on the card. "What do you suppose *he* was doing in here?" one said.

CAPT Tomsuden had been at DSA less than a year when RADM Wally Dowd, Chief of Supply Corps, offered her the opportunity for command. On 31 August 1973, she became commanding officer, Navy Food Service Systems Office, the first woman in command in the Supply Corps and the Naval Material Command. She recalls that she was blessed with "a superlative group of dedicated military and civilian professionals." Her NFSSO post required extensive travel, giving her an opportunity to visit every ship type and every size shore station.

On retirement in August 1975, she was awarded a Gold Star in lieu of a second Navy Commendation Medal. CAPT Tomsuden remained in the Washington area and lives in Falls Church, Virginia. She was an associate real estate broker for 15 years, and retired again in 1991. She still travels and currently is involved in volunteer work with the Area Agency for the Aging and the Animal Welfare League.

Sources

News item. *Club and Food Service Magazine,* June 1975.

Notes and copies of official documents provided by CAPT Ruth M. Tomsuden, August 1994.

Official Biography. Navy Food Service System Office, n.d.

Chronic Underfunding

Austerity was a major NAVSUP thrust during the 1970s, the result of chronic underfunding and successive reduced annual budgets. The situation was brought about by the ravages of continuing inflation and escalating anti-Vietnam pressure on Congress. It required extraordinary efforts by the Supply Corps to continue the high level of support that the Fleet and shore establishment had come to expect.

The situation was compounded in 1973 by the national energy crisis, which had a significant effect on the Navy supply system, one of the nation's largest users of fuel. A substantial increase in prices and new environmental legislation put pressure on operations. In addition, a large portion of the Navy's fuel systems were at, or approaching, the end of their service life. Funding constraints made complete replacement or rebuilding of these facilities impossible. NAVSUP ordered field activities to examine fuel-handling procedures and develop programs to eliminate or severely limit environmental pollution.

Fuel economy programs were mandated throughout the Navy as rising prices ate further into available funds, including major revisions of standard operating procedures for ships and aircraft. The Supply Corps, the Navy's fuel manager, played a major rôle in the fuel conservation effort. NSC Norfolk tested new techniques for the reclamation and recycling of waste oil. The Norfolk Fuel Department worked with commercial firms to test oil-water separation methods for adaption to onboard processing of bilge water. NSC Charleston responded by using sludge-processing systems, overflow alarms, absorbents, and other programs to reduce the threat of environmental damage from petroleum handling.

In 1974 the NAVSUP commander, RADM Wally Dowd, directed all field activities with 500 or more employees to establish EEO offices with full-time staffs. Concurrently, significant reforms were instituted aboard ships to improve relations between officers and enlisted personnel. One outgrowth of the afloat reforms was a decision to abolish the steward rating, long manned primarily by sailors of Asian heritage or by blacks.

Imperial Iran and Foreign Military Sales

Sales of military equipment escalated during the 1970s to the Imperial Iranian Navy (IIN). Shah Mohammed Reza Pahlavi, the Iranian leader, was a staunch ally of the United States. The primary Navy programs involved four of the new construction Spruance-class destroyers especially equipped with costly enhancements specified by the Iranians, 100 F-14 air-superiority fighters, and 8 P-3 patrol planes.

In August 1974 LCDR (later CAPT) Richard E. (Dick) Elliott reported as senior supply advisor, Navy Section, Military Advisory Assistance Group Iran, located at Tehran, in relief of LCDR Steve DeLoach. Dick Elliott had joined the Naval Reserve at the age of 17, was graduated from the University of Oklahoma with a B.B.A. in accounting in 1960, served a year on active duty as an enlisted man, attended OCS, and served another nearly three years as a line officer.

LTJG Elliott decided that he preferred the Supply Corps and applied for a transfer, which was approved and became effective in March 1965, when he reported to NSCS Athens. Upon graduation in October, he was ordered as supply officer, *USS Ashtabula* (AO- 51). During this time, LTJG Elliott received a grade of outstanding on his annual supply inspection. *Ashtabula* won the Ney Award for best general mess afloat among ships of its size and the Arleigh Burke Fleet Trophy for greatest overall improvement in readiness among the more than 500 ships in the Pacific Fleet. LT Elliott left active duty in November 1967, but returned to the Navy through the training and administration of the Naval Reserve (TAR) Program as a lieutenant commander in 1971.

At the time LCDR Elliott went to Iran in 1974, the United States was involved in one of the largest foreign military sales (FMS) programs ever instituted with another nation. The Shah of Imperial Iran was a strong supporter of U.S. objectives in Southwest Asia, ruled with a strong hand, and his police and security forces attempted to hold a growing conservative Islamic movement in check. Dick Elliott's duties involved working with the Imperial Iranian Navy Logistics Office in Tehran and supporting U.S. Navy supply advisors throughout the country. In addition, he handled all FMS financial processing.

Language was a problem in written communications among representatives of the two nations. Letters exchanged between the MAAG and the Iranian navy were sent to an office for translation from English into Farci and vice versa. Elliott wanted to determine the status of a former U.S. Navy LST supplied to Iran. He sent out a letter of inquiry to the IIN and received the following translated response: "Sohrab repair warship which had been allocated IIN under military aids, due to its oldness and putrescence was put out of use as water penetrated into it. Such being the case, in order to prevent its drowning in the navigation lines. Entrance canal or beside the jetty of Bandar-Abbas, it has been drowned at a safe space constrainedly. The matter is reported for information."

It was a response that left the Navy Section perplexed about the ship's fate. It was later discovered that the Iranians had used the ship for target practice and had sunk it in the Persian Gulf. It was not the only time that messages between the navies of the two nations became convoluted.

Dick and Myra Elliott made the most of their unique experience in Iran. Although somewhat restricted in movement by the fact that they lived in a police state, the Elliotts continued to search out and meet citizens of Iran and to absorb the local color. Eight months into LCDR Elliott's tour at Tehran, two USAF colonels were assassinated on their way to work about a mile from the house where the Elliotts lived. This created an atmosphere of tension for the balance of their tour. The Elliotts left Iran in July 1976, 30 months before the shah left in January 1979. The radical Ayatollah Ruhollah Khomeini returned from exile in Paris two weeks after the shah departed. Khomeini supporters routed elite Imperial Guard troops in mid-February, and the Imperial Iranian government was replaced by an Islamic Iranian state.

LCDR Elliott was promoted to commander in July 1977 and became Supply Corps program officer at the headquarters of the chief of Naval Reserve at New Orleans. Later, he returned to New Orleans as deputy chief of staff for logistics, Commander Naval Reserve Force, in August 1983, retired in September 1988 as a captain, and was awarded the Legion of Merit.

In retirement, he joined RCI, a military consulting firm and opened the company's office at New Orleans. In 1994 he was appointed by RCI as site manager, Maintenance Technical Support Center, U.S. Postal Service, Norman, Oklahoma, where he and his wife Myra live.

RADM Grinstead Relieves RADM Dowd as COMNAVSUP

RADM Wallace Dowd made major contributions to the Navy's outstanding support of American forces in Vietnam, and in facilitating Vietnamization, both as C.O. of NSC Oakland and as chief. On 1 March 1977, Rear Admiral Eugene A. (Gene) Grinstead relieved RADM Dowd as commander, NAVSUP, and chief of Supply Corps.

LORE OF THE CORPS

Rear Admiral Eugene Andrew Grinstead, SC, USN

Commander, Naval Supply Systems Command, and
Chief of Supply Corps, 1977–81
Period of Service: 1942–84

Gene Grinstead enlisted in the Naval Reserve during World War II, was commissioned, and served with underwater demolition teams in Korea and China. After the war, he transferred to the Supply Corps, built a reputation in aviation supply, headed both NAVSUP and DLA, and attained the rank of vice admiral.

Eugene Grinstead was born in Durham, North Carolina, in September 1923. He enlisted as a seaman apprentice in the Naval Reserve in December 1942 and reported as a student in the Navy V-12 program at the University of North Carolina in July 1943. He then had instruction at the Naval Reserve Pre-Midshipmen's School, Asbury, New Jersey, and at the Naval Reserve Midshipmen's School at New York City, where he was commissioned an ensign in August 1944.

ENS Grinstead reported to the Naval Officer Training School, Camp Shelton, Norfolk, Virginia, and in September for additional training at the Washington Navy Yard. In April 1945 he went to the Hawaiian island of Maui for further training at the Naval Combat Demolition Training and Experimental Base. He joined Underwater Demolition Team (UDT) Twelve in July 1945 and went into Korea to clear channels and beaches for the U.S. Eighth Army. In January 1946 he became executive officer and communications officer of UDT Team Two, which cleared mines in the mouth of the Yellow River at Tientsin, China. In April 1946 his application for transfer to the Supply Corps was approved. While awaiting orders to NSCS, he had temporary duty from May to August with UDT Team Easy.

His Naval Reserve commission was terminated in August 1946 for augmentation into the Regular Navy Supply Corps as a LTJG. He reported to NSCS Bayonne in October 1946, completed the course of instruction in March 1947, and reported as supply and disbursing officer, *USS Greenwich Bay* (AVP-41), which operated as escort ship for the presidential yacht, *USS Williamsburg*.

In July 1948 he was promoted to lieutenant and ordered as supply officer, Fleet Aviation Support Squadron 108, which supplied maintenance and supply support for land- and sea-based planes at NAS Coco-sola, Panama. LT Grinstead next went to the Naval Air Development Center (NADC), Johnsville, Pennsylvania, in January 1950 as supply officer. At NADC, he was responsible for supply support and contracting for R&D laboratory environments.

In August 1952 Grinstead was ordered as supply officer on the staff, Commander Fleet Air, Eastern Atlantic and Mediterranean. COMFLTAIR-NELM managed all naval air facilities in the European area, operations of antisubmarine patrols, and ashore support for ships deployed into the area. In September 1954 LT Grinstead reported to the Aviation Supply Office at Philadelphia, where he was power plant branch officer, Stock Control Division. He was responsible for support of aircraft engines and related components, which entailed requirements determination, stock positioning, rationing, and commercial overhaul of components. Grinstead was promoted to lieutenant commander in January 1956.

Upon completion of his tour at ASO in January 1958, LCDR Grinstead attended the Armed Forces Staff College. In June 1958 he was ordered to duty as assistant supply officer, *USS Franklin D. Roosevelt* (CVA-42), deployed with the Sixth Fleet in the Mediterranean. He was promoted to commander in July 1960 and ordered to duty at the Bureau of Supplies and Accounts, where he developed and directed a new organization, the Weapons System Section, Inventory Control Point Operations Branch.

Grinstead recalls that RADMs Jimmy Boundy and John Crumpacker, as successive chiefs, decided to test OPNAV to determine if they would give BuSandA an order of priorities in spending appropriated funds. The answer was that the Polaris submarine had priority, and beyond that it was a matter of judgment. That tour was Grinstead's first exposure to the Washington scene and its politics.

From Washington, CDR Grinstead was ordered as supply officer, NAS Oceana, Virginia, in July 1963, when the A-6 was introduced into the Fleet. NAS Oceana was the prototype for field installation of the maintenance material management (3-M) system. Grinstead believes that he was chosen to test the new system because he had served on the 3-M Committee that designed it. The test was a success, and Gene Grinstead was promoted to captain in October 1965.

He moved back to ASO in November, to serve under RADM Howard F. (Howie) Kuehl, and spent nearly four years, successively, as planning director and operations director. Two new aircraft were introduced into the Navy while CAPT Grinstead was at ASO, the P-3 Orion (an antisubmarine patrol version of the civilian Lockheed Electra) and the LTV A-7. Grinstead recalls that these were traumatic experiences because the ICPs could never buy the spares needed to support new aircraft. The budget was always trimmed to whatever funds were available. "We always have to buy our way out as time goes by," he says. Upon detachment from ASO, he was awarded the Legion of Merit. The citation reads, in part, "With exceptional organizational expertise, and a comprehensive knowledge of the aviation supply system, Captain Grinstead effectively directed the planning and preparation of Aviation Consolidate Allowance Lists (AVCAL's) for the Fleet."

In July CAPT Grinstead reported as supply officer, NAS Jacksonville, with additional duty as staff supply officer, Fleet Air Wing, Jacksonville, responsible for far-flung air bases in the Caribbean and the Southeastern United States. The department also supported Fleet ships at the nearby Naval Station, Mayport. This latter responsibility gave Grinstead opportunities to meet frequently with VADM (later ADM) Ike Kidd to discuss support of surface ships. These contacts with Kidd served Gene Grinstead well during the many opportunities the two had to do business later in their careers.

Grinstead stayed at Jacksonville only about a year. In July 1970, VADM Robert L. Townsend, Commander AIRLANT, asked for him to be assigned as his assistant chief of staff for supply. Upon leaving NAS, CAPT Grinstead was awarded the Meritorious Service Medal. AIRLANT was responsible for all the naval air bases in the Atlantic and Mediterranean and for the aircraft carriers operating in the Mediterranean. CAPT Grinstead's duties involved all supply functions in maintaining the command's readiness, effectiveness, and efficiency, budget development, and execution. One of the major challenges he faced involved the immediate elevation of supply inventory accuracy aboard aircraft carriers from an unacceptable rate of 40 percent. Fleet sailors were working night and day, but the ships' high operational rates and constantly changing aircraft deck loads made it virtually impossible to reconstitute inventories accurately at sea. Grinstead obtained funds to hire contractors to inventory the ships to verify the validity of stock locations and inventory. The contract called for payment only when a specified level of inventory accuracy had been achieved. Contractor personnel went aboard inport carriers, took the inventory off, counted it, restored it, removed items no longer applicable to the deckload, and replaced them with items to support replacement aircraft. As a result of this effort, inventory accuracy rose into the 90 percent plus range.

Another supply challenge arose when P-3s were introduced during a crisis in the Mideast. Grinstead says that much of the electronic equipment did not work well. The budget was tight, but the problem received maximum attention and was resolved by replacing the purchase of systems with purchase of subsystems.

In 1972 Gene Grinstead was selected for Flag rank, and in July reported as director, Material Division (OP-41), in the Office of the Deputy Chief of Naval Operations for Logistics. The division was the policy and budget sponsor for munitions, medical, fuel, parts, and freight transportation throughout the Navy. RADM Grinstead remained in the job for more than three years and had three bosses during that period—VADMs Charlie Minter, Walt Gaddis, and (later ADM) Al Whittle.

ADM James Holloway, VCNO when the Israeli crisis broke out in 1973, decided that a Supply Corps officer should run the OPNAV Crisis Center, which was involved largely with logistics issues. Gene Grinstead was the logical candidate for the job, which lasted "somewhere in the neighborhood of 6 to 8 weeks which was about a 24-hour a day job during that period."

RADM Grinstead had a significant role in a major issue that concerned ammunition. The Navy had not funded its ammunition plants, which looked like World War I facilities, for several years. Grinstead proposed that they be turned over to the Army, which had in excess of a billion dollars to modernize its plants. He explains, "If you took the attitude that you needed ammunition for war, you best give the manufacturing responsibility to the guy willing to put his money on it." His proposal was accepted, and the Navy no longer manufactured its own ammunition.

In August 1975, RADM Grinstead returned to NAVSUP as vice commander under RADM Wally Dowd. Gene Grinstead remembers that he worked hard for a tough and demanding boss. When the chief of naval operations proposed that the Supply Corps take a huge share of the plan to bring more women into the Navy, Grinstead told NAVSUP OP, "Take all you can get."

RADM Grinstead relieved RADM Dowd on 1 March 1977. The new chief felt that NAVSUP had been suffering from a lack of funding and inattention to automated data processing (ADP), especially at the inventory control points. Upon assuming command of NAVSUP, Grinstead inaugurated a major project to modernize ADP at the ICPs. The project was launched in 1977, but a contract was not awarded until the mid-1980s.

Another issue Gene Grinstead faced as head of NAVSUP was that of improving the deteriorated support of Navy Grumman F-14 Tomcat fighters, which had been sold to the Imperial government of Iran. The shah complained about the support to CNO, ADM James Holloway, who assigned VADM Forest S. Peterson, commander of NAVAIR, and RADM Grinstead to work on the problem together. They made several trips to Iran and resolved the supply and maintenance problem.

The most challenging issue on his watch, Grinstead recalls, was trying to keep all his people happy in a changing world environment. He faced the same situations his predecessors had in trying to send people to places where not only would the husband be satisfied with his duty, but the wife could also find a job commensurate with her needs. It was a problem that all his successors have had to face and are still facing. Another challenge involved raids by industry on top Supply Corps officers and NAVSUP civilian personnel and on inventory control functions. Detailing the most promising middle-grade Supply Corps officers was compounded by the ongoing demands of ADM Hyman Rickover for the best officers to be made available for his Naval Reactors Program and, once in the program, to stay indefinitely. As chief, Grinstead needed good people in other important places, and he felt an obligation to give his best people sufficient exposure to insure promotional opportunities.

On 18 June 1981, RADM Grinstead was relieved by RADM Andrew A. Giordano and received the Distinguished Service Medal. The citation signed by Secretary of the Navy John Lehman reads, in part, "Rear Admiral Grinstead's enlightened leadership, unequalled knowledge of logistics, and outstanding managerial abilities modernized and transformed the U.S. Navy Supply System."

Gene Grinstead became director, Defense Logistics Agency, with the rank of vice admiral, as relief of LTGEN Gerald J. Post, USAF, in late June 1981. VADM Grinstead was especially pleased with the greatly reduced levels of approval required to get things done at DLA. He could get answers from his bosses in the Pentagon in minutes, often seconds, either over the telephone or in person. He also found that DLA funding remained consistent in contrast with the constant rear-guard action he was forced to wage as commander of NAVSUP in order to protect his funds from diversion to other programs.

DLA awarded literally millions of small contracts and spent a great deal of time answering questions from members of Congress. In early 1983 reports of a wide-ranging press conference quoted Secretary of the Navy Lehman as being critical of DLA. The press coverage prompted a letter of apology from Lehman on 7 March 1983. "The Navy Department appreciates the fine logistic assistance provided by DLA," he wrote. "This support contributes significantly to the improved readiness of Fleet units." VADM Grinstead retired from DLA and the Navy on 1 July 1984 and was awarded the Defense Distinguished Service Medal.

In retirement, Gene Grinstead conducts an international consulting business at McLean, Virginia, where he lives with his wife, Gayle.

Sources

Interview of VADM Eugene A. Grinstead. Arlington, Va., 22 November 1985.
Official Biography. Defense Logistics Agency, n.d.
Official Biography. Naval Supply Systems Command, March 1977.
Transcript of Naval Service. Bureau of Naval Personnel, 1 July 1983.

A New Fiscal Year

In the early 1970s, the congressional budgetary approval process was consistently extending beyond the historic 1 July start of the federal fiscal year. In a move intended ostensibly to assure that approvals would be forthcoming in time for the new fiscal year, the start was pushed back to 1 October. A three-month transitional year was adopted to bridge the gap between FY 77, ending on 30 June 1977, and FY 78, commencing on 1 October 1977.

Just as surely as Murphy wrote his laws, the length of time to approve government budgets expanded to fill the extra three months. The hoped-for elimination of the administrative horrors of relying on continuing resolutions to provide funding when Congress failed to enact appropriation legislation before the start of the ensuing fiscal year did not come to pass.

The Naval Reserve Supply Corps Program

As part of a general reorganization of the Naval Reserve, Supply Corps Reserve programs were completely realigned in 1977. Naval Air Reserve and Reserve construction battalions had traditionally been organized around unit integrity and drilled on two weekend days with assigned Supply Corps officers. They were intended to be mobilized as complete units. Most other Naval Reserve units were primarily organized on the concept of training individuals for augmentation to gaining commands. Most of these units drilled one night a week or two nights a month.

The Naval Reserve reorganization brought major changes. Surface Reserve units were assigned to support designated afloat and ashore commands and trained as integral units, usually to augment existing ships and shore stations to bring them up to wartime manning levels. The Naval Air Reserve and Seabee system of weekend drills was also adopted for surface Reserve units. Supply Corps Reserve drilling units were established to support gaining commands such as ICPs, stock points, advance bases, fuel and transportation commands, and activities of the Defense Logistics Agency. Later, cargo handling and other specialized units were added.

Meanwhile, Supply Corps officers in the Naval Air Reserve units located at more than 30 training sites throughout the country also participated in the Aviation Supply Development and Readiness Project (ASDARP). RADM Raymond (Ray) Hemming was director of the program to coordinate Reserve aviation supply training. Periodic ASDARP meetings were held at one of the drilling sites of the Naval Air Reserve.

Fourth *USS Supply* (AOE-6), 1994, a 48,500-ton, gas-turbine-propelled fast combat support ship commissioned in February 1994, is capable of accompanying deployed battle groups. (National Steel and Shipbuilding Co.)

Officer students attending Navy Supply Corps School, Athens, participate in morning colors at Royar Square. (*Navy Supply Corps Newsletter*)

The Oak Leaf, official insignia of the Navy Supply Corps.

ENS Dan Laurent, disbursing officer, MAAG Laos, boards flight to remote Laotian outposts in 1962. (CDR Daniel Laurent, SC, USN-Ret.)

RADM Dick Curtis, former director, Naval Supply Depot Danang, returned to Vietnam 25 years later, in 1994. He is shown in front of the building that served as Navy headquarters at Danang during the Vietnam War. (RADM Richard E. Curtis, SC, USN-Ret.)

"Tombstone" at Navy Supply Depot Subic Bay spells the end of Navy Supply Corps presence in the Republic of the Philippines. (Naval Supply Depot Subic Bay)

RADMs Jim Miller, Chief of Supply Corps (center), and Lyle Hall (right) arrive at Kuwait International Airport to observe Persian Gulf logistics operations in 1991. (RADM James E. Miller, SC, USN-Ret.)

VADM Ken Wheeler receives Prisoner of War Medal for honorable service as a POW, 1942-45, from RADM Dan McKinnon, Chief of Supply Corps, in July 1989 ceremony at NSCS Athens. (Navy Suppy Corps Museum)

RADM Bob Moore, Chief of Supply Corps, with Roy Anderson, Korean War Supply Corps officer and chairman emeritus, Lockheed Corporation, the 1994 Navy Supply Corps Distinguished Alumnus. (*Navy Supply Corps Newsletter*)

Models demonstrate changes in officer and enlisted uniforms over the 200-year history of the Supply Corps. (*Navy Supply Corps Newsletter*)

Engineering equipment is loaded aboard a MAC Lockheed C-5 at the Navy Air Terminal Norfolk for delivery to the Persian Gulf war zone. (*Navy Supply Corps Newsletter*)

LCDR Bob Engelmann, Chief, Navy Section, Iran, while a hostage in Iran, is shown with visiting Reverend W. J. Howard on Christmas Day, 1979. (*Navy Supply Corps Newsletter*)

RADM Ted Walker, center, visits Air Rework Facility, Marine Corps Air Station, Cherry Point, North Carolina, in 1985. (RADM Ted Walker, SC, USN-Ret.)

RADM Dan McKinnon (standing, 3d from left) and LT Patty Sakowski (standing, far right) with storekeepers and mannequin in MOPP gear at Washington Navy Yard, 1991. (LCDR Patty Sakowski, SC, USNR-R)

Reserve Supply Corps Seminars and Workshops

During the 1960s, senior Naval Reserve Supply Corps officers on both East and West Coasts had begun to examine the idea of holding annual seminars for exchange of professional ideas with other Reservists in other cities. One of the first of these was the Interdistrict Reserve Supply Corps Seminar for officers from the New York City and Philadelphia areas. The seminars were held in the two cities in alternate years. By 1970, Reservists from the Boston and Chicago areas had opted into the programs, with the latter group using Naval Air Reserve airlift to the East Coast.

The first annual West Coast Naval Reserve Supply Corps Seminar was held at Terminal Island, Long Beach, California, on 20 April 1974. Approximately 150 Reserve Supply Corps officers from 6 western states attended. The second West Coast seminar was held at the Naval Air Station, Alameda, California, in 1975.

The seminar concept was so successful that a national Naval Reserve Supply Corps Seminar was scheduled at a central location, the Naval Air Station Glenview, near Chicago, in April 1986. More than 600 Naval Reserve Supply Corps officers went to Glenview, many on Naval Air Reserve, Air Force Reserve, and Air National Guard airplanes and commercial aircraft into nearby O'Hare Field. The seminar was effective despite a Sunday morning early-season surprise snowstorm that delayed the takeoff of return flights.

The ASDARP annual meetings soon were folded into the national seminar program, which was repeated at New Orleans in 1977. However, uncertainty over availability and time required for the lumbering C-119s to make long flights resulted in a decision to return to the annual East and West Coast seminars with similar programs, but on an expanded basis. Attendance at both locations was open to any Reserve Supply Corps officer, and many elected to attend both, usually traveling at the their own expense to at least one. At each seminar, functional workshops were held for the units supporting the various Reserve Supply Corps programs, such as ICPs, stock points, advance bases, fuel, transportation, aviation, Seabee units, and DLA. To update Navy and Supply Corps initiatives, the chief of Supply Corps led impressive lists of guest speakers from DOD, Navy fleet and shore commands, Naval Reserve hierarchy, and industry.

In 1980 the seminars were renamed "readiness workshops" to emphasize the mobilization readiness objective of the professional gatherings. Attendance by supply-rated enlisted personnel was also encouraged. The last year in which two workshops were held was 1985, when administrative and budgetary pressures dictated a return to a single, annual national workshop. A workshop in New Orleans in July 1994 was attended by 460 Reserve Supply Corps officers and 100 enlisted personnel. The next workshop was scheduled for San Francisco in April 1995.

Reserve Direct Commission Program

During the late 1970s, questions arose over junior Supply Corps officer staffing of units in the reorganized Selected Naval Reserve. Manning tables for these units called for nearly 400 more ensigns and LTJGs than were enrolled. The problem worsened because Reserve officers completing active duty and returning to civilian life were either already, or within a few months of becoming, lieutenants. The chief of Naval Reserve made it clear that over-grade waivers would not be issued for assignment of more senior officers to fill vacant junior officer billets.

The seven Reserve Supply Corps Flag officers accepted the challenge of finding a solution to the junior officer shortfall, but no current program offered the answer. In the fall of 1978 the problem was assigned to the "boot admiral," the author of this book, RADM Frank J. Allston, who had recently completed a three-year tour as C.O. of an SPCC unit that drilled in the Chicago area. The outgrowth of this assignment was a proposal to seek authorization to issue direct commissions to qualified, experienced, enlisted personnel who had completed college and also to successful businesspeople without military backgrounds.

The proposed program would grant conditional commissions, to be made permanent only after completion of the basic qualification course (BQC) at NSCS Athens. In recognition of the fact that Reservists were not in position to take off up to six months from civilian jobs to attend the on-site course, the program required that all direct-commissioned officers must:

- have prior military experience, preferably in a Navy supply rating, or outstanding civilian business experience;
- join, and maintain satisfactory performance in, a Selected Reserve unit, preferably one in a NAVSUP-managed program;
- enroll in NSCS Athens-managed correspondence courses;
- perform at least two of the first three two-week active duty training periods at NSCS Athens; and
- complete all requirements within three years.

RADM Andy Giordano, Chief of Supply Corps, was originally lukewarm to the proposal, based upon his belief that officers, in order to wear the oak leaf of the Supply Corps, must complete the resident course at NSCS Athens. When he became convinced that no viable alternative to the proposed program existed, he agreed to it on a trial basis. The first class of seven new direct-commissioned ensigns and two LTJGs reported to NSCS Athens in January 1981.

The program was a success from the start. Enlisted members of drilling Reserve Supply Corps units were among the first to apply. The first fully certified direct-commission officers completed the Reserve BQC and were graduated in February 1981. As of 31 July 1994, 810 Reserve Supply Corps officers had been enrolled in the program, and 574 officers had completed it. Another 50 were under instruction on that date. The demanding requirements took their toll on candidates who were not totally committed, as 186 enrollees failed to complete the course and were disenrolled. RADM Giordano's son, Dean, successfully completed the Reserve BQC program and later augmented into the Regular Navy. In 1994 LT Dean J. Giordano was supply officer, *USS Scott* (DDG-995).

Several evolutionary changes have been made in the program since its inception. The maximum period for completing the BQC program was changed from 5 to 3 years, then to 18 months. The two-week active duty tours at NSCS Athens are required to be performed within the 18 months.

The JUMPS Program

During the decade of the 1970s, Supply Corps officers who specialized in the field of financial management were major participants in the secretary of the Navy's financial improvement plan (FMIP), which included several new programs. In 1977 a successful 10-year effort to automate military pay culminated in adoption of the Joint Uniform Military Pay System (JUMPS) for all naval personnel. JUMPS featured a centralized automated master file of military pay accounts (MPA) for active duty personnel. More than 3,500 local personnel offices and 400 disbursing offices provided optical character recognition information to update MPA files. The first leave and earnings statements were provided to uniformed Navy personnel in 1979.

As more and more women came into the Supply Corps, it was only a matter of time until additional female Supply Corps officers were assigned to afloat duty. A legislative ban on assignment of women to combatant ships came under fire, but Congress made no move to lift the ban. When she reported to *USS Norton Sound* (AVM-1) in 1978, ENS Cindra Brown became the first female Supply Corps officer assigned afloat duty in other than a hospital ship.

Troubles in Iran

By 1978 Iran had become the largest recipient of the U.S. Foreign Military Sales Program. U.S. military personnel assigned to MAAG Iran had numbered almost 1,000 at the height of the FMS contracts with the shah's government. Iran had purchased an essentially American military machine that was totally dependent on military repair parts bought through the FMS program.

As a revolution began in Iran with Muslem riots in 1978, State and Defense officials began to draw up plans for closing out the U.S. involvement in that country. Virtually all members of the American defense contingent were evacuated in January and February 1979, leaving only a handful to close out the FMS program. One of these officers was CDR Ed Brighton, the lone remaining member of the Supply Section. After the successful revolution in February, CDR Brighton moved into the embassy, where he remained until ordered back to the States in early spring.

MAAG and embassy officials pushed NAVSUP for a replacement with a FMS background. LCDR Robert A. (Bob) Engelmann was selected by RADM Gene Grinstead for temporary assignment to Iran. He reported to Tehran for a four-month tour in May 1979, while detailers back in Washington worked to identify an officer to relieve him on PCS orders. Engelmann served as a member of a six-man Navy-Army-Air Force transition team to reestablish relations with the Islamic Iranian military that replaced the Imperial Iranian military. The team included a line commander, who represented the F-14 program, and two each Army and Air Force officers. The remnants of the MAAG were essentially a part of the embassy staff. They had no military identification, carried diplomatic passports, and wore civilian clothes. They were, in effect, State Department employees.

Demonstrators Seize U.S. Embassy

Iranian student demonstrations outside the embassy were commonplace in the fall of 1979. On 4 November, Iranian guards at the American embassy compound opened the gates for the demonstrators. Embassy staff thought the Islamic government would force the demonstrators out as Imperial government predecessors had done during a brief demonstration inside the compound earlier in the year. Bruce Laingen, a former Supply Corps officer and the chargé d'affair in the absence of an ambassador, was in a meeting at the Iranian Foreign Ministry.

However, it soon became apparent that this demonstration had been well orchestrated. LCDR Engelmann was among 52 Americans jeopardized when the demonstrators seized the embassy. The Americans and Iranian employees closed big metal doors that sealed off access to the second deck of the Chancellory Building, but the students had brought torches. The invaders were setting fires on one side of the doors while nearly 80 embassy personnel on the other were trying to put them out.

LCDR Engelmann and other U.S. military personnel retreated into the communications vault, taking as much highly classified material as they could. They planned to destroy sensitive documents and the sophisticated electronic equipment, but first they established radio contact with Washington. The State Department duty officer was unfamiliar with the Iranian situation and failed to comprehend the gravity of the expanding crisis. The beleaguered Americans were also in touch with Bruce Laingen at the Foreign Ministry. Laingen had been told—too late to alert his people back at the embassy—what was going to happen. Meanwhile, the students had marched the embassy security officer to the vault door, which had a small dead-eye observation porthole, put a gun to his head, and threatened to kill him. Laingen advised the Americans inside the vault to surrender, and they did. They would be held prisoner for 443 days.

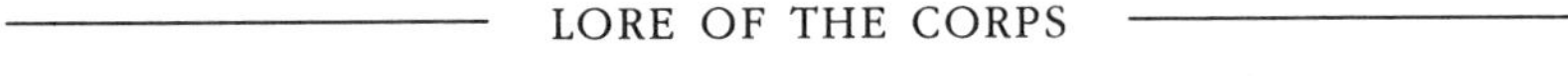

LORE OF THE CORPS

Lieutenant Commander Robert A. Engelmann, SC, USN

Chief, Navy Section, U.S. Embassy, Tehran, Iran, 1979
Period of Service: 1968–92

LCDR Engelmann was serving in a temporary capacity as chief, Navy Section, at the embassy, and he was scheduled to return to the United States the week after the Iranian students had stormed, taken over, and trashed the compound in November 1979. He resumed his Supply Corps career in January 1981, when he was released after nearly 15 months in captivity.

Robert Engelmann was born at Pasadena, California, in September 1946, the son of an Air Force officer. He spent much of the next 15 years in the San Antonio area. Bob Engelmann was graduated from the State University of New York, Stony Brook, with a degree in psychology in 1968. He preferred to be an officer in the Navy to being drafted into the Army and was accepted for Navy Officer Candidate School. After completing a year of graduate school at SUNY Stony Brook, he entered OCS in the fall of 1969.

Engelmann was commissioned a Naval Reserve line ensign in December 1969. He was assigned two consecutive tours of duty in diesel submarines, *USS Dogfish* (SS-350) and *USS Jallao* (SS-368), both of which he helped decommission before sale to foreign navies. He then augmented to the Regular Navy and transferred to the Supply Corps. He reported to NSCS Athens in the fall of 1974 as a lieutenant and was graduated as a line officer because the X.O. of *Jallao* failed to complete some of the paperwork necessary for his transfer from line to staff.

His first orders to duty in *USS Caloosahatchee* (AOJ-98) were amended to instruct the oiler to use him as a supply officer. His transfer to the Supply Corps came through in early 1975. He reported to the Navy International Logistics Control Office (NAVILCO), at Bayonne, New Jersey in April 1977. When NAVILCO moved to Philadelphia in early 1978, he became Iranian project officer.

He next received orders as supply officer and comptroller for the Ship Rework Facility Subic Bay. His household goods had already been shipped to the Philippines when he was sent to Iran on TAD orders to fill in as chief of the Supply Section, MAAG Tehran, in May 1979. LCDR Engelmann was to leave Iran in September, when a permanent relief would report in. The relief had been designated, but Engelmann suggested that he be authorized to delay long enough to spend some time at NAVILCO and take a Defense Department course in basic Farci before coming to Iran. Bob Engelmann had been unable to speak Farci when he arrived in Tehran and says that if an English-speaking embassy driver had not met him, "I'd probably still be trying to figure out how to get out of the airport." His recommendation was the reason that he was still in Tehran on 4 November 1979. LCDR Engelmann had an apartment a little north of the embassy and worked in the Chancellory Building in the embassy compound.

When the demonstrators invaded the embassy, Engelmann and other U.S. military personnel sought refuge in the communications vault, where they planned to destroy all classified materials and sensitive electronic equipment. The revolutionaries threatened to kill the embassy security officer, and Acting Ambassador Bruce Laingen advised the Americans in the vault to surrender. As LCDR Engelmann recalls the event, "Not much got destroyed. All the MAAG's classified material (in the vault) was destroyed, but the Ambassador's safe wasn't even touched. The Defense Attaché's office, which had 13 or 14 big locked file cabinets full of confidential material, was down on the first floor and never brought up. So, we didn't really accomplish all that much in the way of maintaining security or destroying classified material. Now we know."

Being the last to surrender, the group was suspected of being CIA spies, and was roughed up. The revolutionaries feared an American rescue attempt such as the Israelis had pulled off at Entebbe, so Engelmann and nine others were dumped into the trunks of cars and taken to a safe house in northern Tehran.

At this point, a U.S. Army sergeant had identified most of the military personnel to the revolutionaries by rank, but he overlooked Engelmann. The Iranians interrogated U.S. military personnel, but it was late March 1980 before they discovered that Engelmann was military. He was then interrogated for two and a half days, but his questioning was halted on Easter (6 April), when the 52 Americans were taken back to the chancellory to meet with Red Cross representatives and a group of ministers.

On 25 April an American attempt to rescue the hostages failed when aircraft and helicopters crashed in the desert, but the effort unnerved the Iranians. After the failed hostage rescue attempt, they split up the hostages and moved them frequently to widely separated locations around the country, always late at night and locked in the trunks of cars. The hostages assumed the relocations were routine. They were completely isolated from any news and unaware of the rescue attempt until September, when a friend sent crossword puzzles from *The New York Times*. On the reverse side of a puzzle, a television program listing included a special on the failed rescue mission.

The hostages were permitted only limited access to magazines, but they could receive *The Sporting News*. Engelmann says they read everything in the sports paper, including all the classifieds, footnotes, and advertising. They learned of the shah's death in Egypt from a story on a golf match that mentioned television coverage had been interrupted for a program on the deposed Iranian leader's passing. The hostages also managed to extract financial information from *The Sporting News*. An article on the Hickok Sportsman of the Year Belt Award made it possible to calculate that gold had risen to $800 an ounce. From that, they estimated the U.S. inflation rate.

In September, the hostages also were unaware that Iran and Iraq were at war, but knew something was up when they heard planes overhead and bombs exploding at the nearby airport. Able to hear the loudspeakers from a nearby mosque, they decided that a war must have started when President Jimmy Carter lost his place in Iranian prayers as "evil devil" to Saddam Hussein.

On 19 January 1981, one of the peasants assigned to serve meager rations to the hostages and accompany them to the bathroom announced, "This is it. Get your clothes." Each prisoner had only a plastic bag containing a change of underwear. The Iranians first had to come up with 52 pairs of shoes. The hostages were blindfolded, loaded on two buses late at night, and taken to the airport, where three Air Algerian planes waited.

The hostages were forced to walk through a mob of screaming, jeering Iranians. When their plane was loaded, they moved onto the tarmac and sat. Although the hostages did not know it, they were waiting for Ronald Reagan to be sworn in as president of the United States. The planes then took off in different directions to avoid Iraqi pinpointing of the plane with the hostages. Their plane landed at Athens for refueling well away from the terminal and then flew to Algiers. The former hostages passed through a mob of reporters and cameramen to reach U.S. Navy and Air Force MEDEVAC C-9s, which took them to Rhein-Main AFB in Germany. Heavy parkas had been brought from Rhein-Main to insulate the freed Americans from the German winter cold.

At the hospital, the former hostages were given real American food, physical exams, and the opportunity to make telephone calls. Bob Engelmann talked with his parents back in Dallas and his detailer, CDR Al Jones, who was working late at his NAVSUP office. Engelmann learned that his orders to Subic Bay had been canceled when he was detained in Iran. He told Jones that he would take his second choice, NSC Puget Sound, but first had to go back to NAVILCO to check out. Engelmann finally went to bed about 0300.

Later that day, less than 24 hours after they left office, former President Jimmy Carter, former Vice President Walter Mondale, and former DOD Secretary Cyrus Vance visited the released Americans at the U.S. military hospital, Wiesbaden. Three days later, the ex-prisoners flew back to Stewart AFB Base, New York, where they were met by family members, and then flew on to Andrews AFB outside Washington. Receptions hosted by President Reagan and CNO ADM Tom Hayward and parades at both Washington and New York rounded out the activities. LCDR Engelmann met at NAVSUP with RADMs Grinstead and Giordano. He then went home to Dallas, where he learned that LCDR Wayne J. Carter, Jr., who had been designated to relieve him at Tehran, had gone instead to NAS Dallas as supply officer when the embassy was seized. Carter had also been assigned to Engelmann's family as casualty assistance calls officer. Bob Engelmann says, "I lived to meet my CACO. Most people don't."

Two months later, LCDR Engelmann went to Philadelphia, checked out of NAVILCO, and then drove across country via NSCS Athens, where he completed a short refresher course. He reported in early May 1981 to NSC Puget Sound, Bremerton, Washington, and served there for three years, first as physical distribution officer and later as inventory control officer. He was promoted to commander in May 1982. He also met his wife, Elaine, at Puget. They were married in June 1984 and immediately left for Hawaii, where CDR Engelmann was supply officer, Marine Corps Air Station, Kaneohe Bay. In September 1987 he reported to the Defense Construction Supply Center Columbus, Ohio, as assistant technical operations officer. CDR Engelmann's final tour was as supply officer, Naval Surface Warfare Center Dahlgren, Virginia, from September 1990 until his retirement in August 1992.

Bob Engelmann's traumatic adventures in Iran are not his most favored reminiscences, but he has not been able to put them all in the past. Over the years since he has retired, the State Department has required him to sign affidavits for use as depositions in Iran's case for financial restitution before the World Court. Islamic Iran claims that part of the agreement for release of the illegally held hostages was for the United States to refund money in an FMS trust fund into which the Imperial government paid for weapons systems and repair parts. Engelmann signed such an affidavit before a notary public in late July 1994, but emphasizes that recalling specific dates, items, and amounts of 15-year-old individual transactions is exceedingly difficult.

On retirement, he returned to the Pacific Northwest and is currently a personal financial planner in Silverdale, Washington, where he and Elaine live with their daughter and son.

Sources:

"Ex-Iranian Hostage Keeps Eye on Future." *Banner-Herald* [Athens, Ga.], April 1981.

"Supply Corps Hostage Welcomed Home." *Navy Supply Corps Newsletter,* July 1981.

Telephone interview of CDR Robert A. Engelmann, 10 April 1994.

The U.S. Navy Base at Diego Garcia

By 1974, after close encounters of the congressional kind, funds were appropriated to turn Diego Garcia into a major American base. Improvements included deepening the lagoon anchorage to accommodate Nimitz-class carriers and extending and improving the runway to handle Navy P-3 patrol planes, MAC C-5 and C-141 transports, and Air Force B-52 bombers. The U.S. Navy now had an adequate base to provide logistical support to the carrier task force that would be permanently on station in the Indian Ocean. Initially, there were no pier facilities, a fact that required transfer of materials from ship to shore by barge or helicopter. Subsequently, Seabees constructed pier facilities, enabling shuttle of supplies both by Mobile Logistic Force (MLF) ships and by carrier onboard delivery (COD) aircraft over a 1,900-mile logistical pipeline.

Resupply from the United States was provided primarily by ships from the Pacific Fleet, supplemented occasionally by Atlantic Fleet ships that came through the Suez Canal. Air resupply came through an air head at Masirah, Oman. Ship repair was provided by tenders and repair ships anchored in the lagoon at Diego Garcia or offshore in the North Arabian Sea.

Supply Corps officers have been on duty at the Indian Ocean base since the late 1970s; in 1994, 13 served at the four Diego Garcia activities.

High-Tech U.S. Ships and Pennywise Policies

The continued ideological clash between the United States and the Soviet Union further heightened the conventional arms race as each sought development of superior weapons systems. The U.S. Navy was still relying on a core of ships built during World War II, which had ended nearly 35 years earlier, whereas the Soviets were building entire new classes of high-tech ships.

Many of the mainstays of the U.S. Fleet were simply worn out or were rapidly approaching that state. The Johnson administration had made a decision to finance a large portion of the costs of the Vietnam War from the existing Department of Defense budgets. This decision resulted in postponing almost all of the new DOD construction projects. The impact on the Navy was devastating. Funds for the construction of only 88 ships were appropriated between 1966 and 1970. The near halt of construction of new, more modern ships and aircraft came at a critical time in light of declining capability of older ships and airplanes.

Supporting old weapons platforms, including locating spare parts for many systems no longer being manufactured, put a tremendous strain on the Navy supply system. Fortunately, the experts at SPCC and ASO were able to locate the necessary spares needed in the Fleet to keep the older ships and aircraft operational. The danger of these pennywise funding constraints for new construction was brought home in 1973, when war broke out again between the Arab States and Israel over the Suez Canal. The U.S. Navy responded effectively, but at great cost when President Richard Nixon ordered the Sixth Fleet to prevent Soviet intervention in the conflict. Fleet size continued to erode, and by 1977 the

U.S. Navy had the fewest ships—464—of all types in commission since 1939.

The Rapid Deployment Force

In March 1980 President Carter announced establishment of the Rapid Deployment Force and assigned American operations in the Persian Gulf to the new unified command. The nearest American support base was the fledgling facility at Diego Garcia, nearly 2,000 miles away. Obviously, this was a job for the U.S. Navy. The all-nuclear battle group headed by the *USS Nimitz* (CVN-68) was ordered from the Mediterranean into the North Arabian Sea. Another battle group, with the nuclear-powered aircraft carrier *USS Dwight D.Eisenhower* (CVN-69), deployed from Norfolk to the Persian Gulf in early 1980. The deployment lasted an unprecedented eight months, with only a five-day port call at Singapore for relief. In March, the Seventh Fleet amphibious group, with 1,800 embarked Marines, deployed to the Indian Ocean, as did other amphibious groups until the embassy hostages were released by Iran in 1981.

A Defection to a Supply Corps Officer

Captain Marvin W. (Marv) Bledsoe, a Supply Corps officer, was serving as officer-in-charge, Sanno Hotel, Tokyo, in the fall of 1980 when he was approached at a cocktail party at the hotel by a small, somewhat obscure man who tugged on the sleeve of Bledsoe's uniform. "I am MAJ Levchenko of the KGB. I need to contact the naval headquarters at Yokosuka. It's a political matter," the man said. CAPT Bledsoe recalled during a telephone interview in July 1994 that he immediately recognized that he was in an extremely sensitive situation.

He instructed his security people to take the Soviet defector to a room and assure his safety and anonymity. Bledsoe called Naval Investigative Service (NIS) at Yokosuka and advised them of the situation. NIS instructed Bledsoe to make Levchenko comfortable and see that he "stayed put." NIS personnel arrived at the Sanno in two hours and spirited away their prize catch. Several weeks later, the Commander Naval Forces Japan advised Marv Bledsoe that the defector was a very important Soviet agent. He also complimented Bledsoe on the manner in which he handled what could have been an explosive international incident.

When RADM Andy Giordano succeeded RADM Gene Grinstead as Commander NAVSUP in June 1981, the budget situation was beginning to improve. The new Reagan administration, which had taken over in January, had publicly committed to increased defense spending.

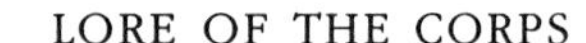

LORE OF THE CORPS

Rear Admiral Andrew Anthony Giordano, SC, USN

Commander, Naval Supply Systems Command, and
Chief of Supply Corps, 1981–84
Period of Service: 1953–58, 1960–84

RADM Giordano was the first commander of NAVSUP and chief of Supply Corps to have been commissioned through the Officer Candidate School, Newport, Rhode Island. He compiled an outstanding record en route to becoming the 34th leader of the Corps.

Andrew Giordano was born at Clifton, New Jersey, in May 1932, and was graduated from high school at Coney Island in Brooklyn. Young Giordano's long-term interest was in the business world, but he also was interested in the military. He was graduated cum laude from the School of Business, College of the City of New York, after having worked one summer in the executive training program at Bloomingdale's in Manhattan. In his senior year, Giordano was drafted into the Marine Corps, with a reporting date a month after graduation in the summer of 1953. He preferred the Navy and was accepted by OCS, voiding the draft notice. Andy Giordano reported to Newport in September 1953, and to NSCS Bayonne in November. He was a member of the last class to enter NSCS Bayonne and the first class to enter NSCS Athens when the move was made over year-end 1953.

ENS Giordano was ordered as disbursing officer and assistant supply officer of *USS Edisto* (AGN-2), an ice-breaker homeported at Boston. *Edisto* spent most of 1954 keeping the sea lanes open for supply ships to get from Greenland to the distant early warning line (DEW) stations in the Arctic. In March 1955 Giordano was promoted to LTJG and ordered in May to independent duty as supply officer, *USS Otterstetter* (DER-214), homeported at Goat Island, Rhode Island, adjacent to Newport. *Otterstetter* stayed on picket stations in the Atlantic Ocean, monitoring aircraft approaching the United States. Giordano took over an unsatisfactory Supply Department and won the Supply E as the best supply department among all DERs in the Fleet.

He was released from active duty at the conclusion of his obligated Reserve tour in October 1956. He was hired by International Telephone and Telegraph Company (now ITT Corp.) as an administrative assistant in the Vacuum Tubes Laboratories at Nutley, New Jersey. Andy Giordano renewed acquaintances with Felice Rochman, a fellow CCNY graduate, and they were married in 1957. He did not join an organized Naval Reserve unit, but was promoted to lieutenant in September 1957. Giordano left ITT in early 1958 and renewed his old association with Bloomingdale's by taking a position as assistant internal auditor.

CDR Nolan Scott, his skipper in *Otterstetter* and then in BuPers, pressed him to return to active duty, so he went back to the Navy in July 1958 and reported to NSCS Athens in August. He became head of the NSCS Disbursing Division. Giordano and two other faculty members, LCDR Hoyle H. (Tip) Daniels II and LCDR (later CDR) Warren P. White, set out to make over the disbursing-oriented curriculum into a more challenging and meaningful experience. They chose the Harvard Business School case method. The three discovered an earlier academic case involving a fictitious ship, *USS Duarte* (DD-901), with the fictitious ENS Wild Bill Ellis as supply officer and an entire Supply Department of imaginary characters developed in 1955. The characters became the curriculum's centerpiece. Lectures were conducted, and exams given, based upon actual real-world supply and disbursing problems in the make-believe *Duarte*.

In April 1959 LT Giordano's appointment in the Naval Reserve was terminated, and he was augmented into the U.S. Navy. Andy Giordano was instrumental in replacing Reserve LTJGs serving their final six months of active duty with career naval officers as NSCS instructors and role models. He reported to the Graduate School of Business, Harvard University, in August 1960 as one of three Supply Corps officers enrolled in the M.B.A. course. At Harvard, he learned of his below-the-zone selection to lieutenant commander.

In July 1962 LCDR Giordano went to the Navy Supply Depot Yokosuka, Japan, where he was a stock control officer in a totally manual operation and later inventory control officer. NSD Yokosuka supported the Navy shore establishment in Japan, the Fleet when in port, the Marine Aviation Force in Japan and Okinawa, and the Naval Aviation Rework Facility (NARF), Japan. Support of Fleet units was controversial because the supply depot C.O. reported to COMSURFPAC, which was also responsible for the resupply and stores ships. LCDR Giordano recalls, "Clearly the staff (SURFPAC) did not want the depot taking business away from the resupply ships, but it made no sense to load the stores ships at the pier, and then have them transfer material to Fleet ships at adjacent piers." He convinced the SURFPAC Supply Department that the depot would provide them the Fleet issue data so they could build up the Fleet load lists. "We finally eliminated the double handling of Fleet support for inport ships," Giordano reports.

The NARF was responsible for more than 300 aircraft and contracted out most of its work to major Japanese companies, which drew needed supplies from NSD Yokosuka. The most automated operation was a transceiver through which data on punched cards was sent via a relay in Japan, through Seattle, to points throughout the United States. LCDR Giordano was demonstrating the operation to a Marine general, who had difficulty understanding how the cards could be sent across the ocean. The female Japanese operator, who barely spoke English, explained it by saying, "General, the cards stay, the holes go."

LCDR Giordano's experience at Yokosuka was his first with stock funding. NSD Yokosuka was the hub of operations in the Orient until much of its mission was later transferred to NSD Subic Bay. Giordano reports that the NSD manual operation was not a problem because of the "extraordinarily industrious Japanese civilian employees."

In July 1965 LCDR Giordano reported to the command and staff course at the Naval War College, where he was selected for promotion to commander. At NWC, he wrote "The Logistical Implications of Weapons Systems Design Decisions," a paper published in the *Naval Engineers Journal* in 1985. He believes that it remains the foundation for integrated logistics support (ILS) planning.

Giordano was detailed to duty at Washington in July 1966, the day that BuSandA became NAVSUP. He was assigned to the Supply Operations Directorate (SUP-04), reporting to RADM (later VADM) George E. (Rhythm) Moore, NAVSUP vice commander. CDR Giordano had been at NAVSUP about a year when he was selected to replace CDR (later RADM) Jim Ahern as executive assistant and aide to RADM Hersh Goldberg, Commander NAVSUP. About a month later, Goldberg confided that he would retire in two months.

Andy Giordano recalls the ongoing tug-of-war between the Naval Material Command and the systems commands over control of logistical issues. In the case of NAVSUP, the primary issue was control of SPCC and ASO. A case study was prepared by Giordano and CDR (later CAPT) John H. (Jack) Garrett for presentation at a NAVSUP commanding officers conference at Williamsburg, Virginia. The case laid out all the logic for NAVSUP retaining the ICPs. Later, Giordano was present at a meeting between Goldberg and Secretary of the Navy Paul Nitze, who ruled that the ICPs would remain with NAVSUP. CDR Giordano continued as EA and aide to the new commander, RADM Bernie Bieri, until June 1968.

The Vietnamese conflict had grown into all-out war, and all ambitious Supply Corps officers knew that a Vietnam tour was a professional necessity for advancement. In September 1968 Giordano reported to *USS Kitty Hawk* (CVA-63) as supply officer. *Kitty Hawk* operated in waters off Vietnam for most of Giordano's tour, as he built a strong reputation in the Supply Corps. In June 1970 he reported to the staff, Commander Naval Air Force Pacific, at NAS North Island. There, CDR Giordano was senior assistant to CAPT Gordon W. (Gordy) Phelps, Jr., force supply officer.

Giordano made frequent WESTPAC trips with VADMs William Bringle and T. J. Walker. He was at AIRPAC when the command began to manage the air stations actively rather than to concentrate solely on the ships. Phelps and Giordano maintained an absolute veto over Supply Corps officers detailed to AIRPAC ships and stations. Although this was a jealously guarded prerogative by CDR Giordano at AIRPAC, it was not as acceptable a limitation to RADM Giordano when he became chief of the Corps.

Andy Giordano was promoted to captain in July 1972 and reported on 1 August to ASO, where he was operations officer. CAPT Giordano believed the assignment was inevitable because of his past criticism of the aviation supply system. A schism between aviation and nonaviation supply officers developed during the early 1970s. In effect, there were two Supply Corps.

ASO was in the early phases of the Closed Loop Aviation Management Program (CLAMP), a system for managing aviation repairable parts and subsystems through a one-for-one exchange between rework and supply facilities. CLAMP totally controlled all the repairable items but was highly controversial. Giordano recalls that "all of us were gaining more visibility than we could stand." He testified at DOD, NAVCOMPT, and NAVSUP in support of CLAMP and attracted the attention of RADM Wally Dowd, Commander of NAVSUP, who was seeking a relief for CAPT Jim Ahern, his comptroller. In June 1974 CAPT Giordano reported to NAVSUP as deputy commander, Financial Management and Comptroller, where he was responsible for all the money—appropriated, nonappropriated, stock fund, and individually funded—in the Naval Supply Systems Command. Andy Giordano became involved, for the first time, with the Navy Stock Fund and had a very simple mission: Get money for the operation of the Naval Supply Systems Command and spare parts.

He points out that the way NAVSUP survived in those extraordinarily austere times was not to do some of the things in the supply commands that should have been done. That negligence would come back to haunt Giordano when he later became NAVSUP commander. For many years, aviation consumable spare parts had been free. "When they had to start paying for those consumables, it was amazing how the Fleet and other consumers treated their resources," Giordano says. CAPT Giordano decided to exploit the flexibility of the stock fund fully for readiness purposes. He consolidated control and updated the NAVSUP Comptroller Office. He was selected for Flag in early 1977, but it would take two years for his actual promotion.

In May 1977 he went to the Pentagon as director, Supply Programs and Policy Division (OP-41) on the CNO staff, where he relieved Rear Admiral Tom Allshouse. Although he was frocked as a rear admiral, he was still officially a captain, a first for OP-41. He became heavily involved in spare parts budgets, spent three years in the Pentagon, and was promoted to rear admiral in June 1979.

He returned to NAVSUP in August 1980 as vice commander under RADM Gene Grinstead. He quickly learned that he could do anything he wanted except detail officers. Gene Grinstead retained that prerogative and made it plain he needed no assistance. When Giordano later became the chief of Supply Corps, he continued that tradition. Andy Giordano says Gene Grinstead was an enormously talented logistician with extraordinary credentials in the aviation community. Grinstead spent about 80 percent of his time on the road—primarily in such Middle Eastern nations as Iran, Saudi Arabia, and Kuwait. While Grinstead was traveling, Giordano stayed in Washington and ran the day-to-day affairs of NAVSUP.

RADM Giordano believed that when the United States sold weapons to allies, the Navy supply system and Supply Corps officers went with the sale. FMS customer requisitions were treated just as those of the U.S. Navy. The French sold weapons at a fairly good price, provided a box of spares, and left their customers to fend for themselves. Giordano was fond of telling Allies that the French were "the best salesmen for the United States Navy Supply Corps."

When RADM Grinstead was promoted to vice admiral and became director of the Defense Logistics Agency in June 1981, RADM Giordano became the new chief. His primary objective was to place all repairables under the stock fund, an idea he had considered at ASO nearly 10 years earlier. Project CLAMP was merely a stop-gap measure, involving pleading, cajoling, and policing, but it did not affect the customer's financial resources. Once repairables were in the stock fund, the system would be automatic. The aviation community strongly opposed the move, but Giordano sold the concept within the Navy, with the Navy Secretariat, with DOD, and on Capitol Hill. Since that time, all consumable repairables in the Navy have been in the stock fund.

RADM Giordano had to deal with congressional inquiries over GAO reports on unreconciled differences between physical and book inventories at Navy stock points. He pointed out to SECNAV John Lehman that the inventory differences resulted from deficiencies in resources, including those to update computers, and not from incompetence at the supply points. Another issue was the highly publicized cases of the $400 hammer, the $100 diode, and the $200 screwdriver. Even though none of these problems occurred in NAVSUP-commanded activities, press and public critics of President Ronald Reagan's defense buildup had a field day at the expense of NAVSUP and RADM Giordano. In response, Giordano initiated the Buy Our Spares Smart (BOSS) Program and Price Fighters. They put the spotlight on resources and attention to detail. As a result, the Supply Corps avoided being permanently tainted by the problems.

Andy Giordano encouraged Supply Corps officers to become more weapons systems oriented. Qualified submarine supply officers wore dolphins, and Giordano advocated wings for qualified aviation supply officers and a device for qualified surface supply officers. He was able to see those programs instituted.

When all physically qualified Naval Academy and NROTC graduates were required to go into the line or Marine Corps, OCS became the primary source of Supply Corps officer input. As Navy officer retention rates rose dramatically at the beginning of the 1980s, the CNO proposed to cease rewarding the top 5 percent of OCS graduates with Regular Navy commissions. Giordano countered with an alternative of giving Reserve commissions to the bottom 5 percent of each Naval Academy class. "Fortunately, we never heard the CNO's idea again," Giordano recalls.

Another of Andy Giordano's interests was NSCS. He encouraged the formalization of graduation procedures, orders, announcements, and a curriculum that gave officer students a broader supply education than the "finger curriculum" then in use. RADM Giordano also built on a program of increased use of assets in the Reserve community, making Supply Corps Reservists a viable part of the Navy supply system. When commanding officers of NAVSUP field activities were slow to integrate their Reserve resources into their commands, Giordano reduced their resources by the amount of Reservists assigned to those activities. Almost overnight, many commanding officers promptly became better acquainted with their Reserve units.

RADM Giordano was relieved by RADM Ted Walker and retired on 1 June 1984. During a distinguished career, he was awarded the Legion of Merit with gold star, the Meritorious Service Medal with gold star, the Navy Commendation Medal with gold star, and the Navy Achievement Medal.

In retirement, Andy Giordano returned to the merchandising field as senior vice president of Donaldson's at Minneapolis. He later was in the merchandising business at Seattle, but returned to the Washington area in 1993. He and his wife Felice live in Arlington, Virginia.

Sources

Interview of RADM Andrew A. Giordano. Minneapolis, Minn., 29 September 1985.
Official Biography. Naval Supply Systems Command, October 1982.
Transcript of Naval Service. Bureau of Naval Personnel, July 1983.

The Maritime Strategy and a 600-Ship Navy

During the early 1980s, the Reagan administration announced a new defense posture, the Maritime Strategy, and set a goal of a 600-ship Navy. The program represented a return of the U.S. Navy to its traditional role of projecting American power throughout the world. Within a few years, the United States had regained undisputed status as the world's leading sea power.

The U.S.-flag Merchant Marine had declined devastatingly during the 1960s. It was briefly revived during the Vietnam War, but resumed the decline when Americans were no longer engaged in combat. American strategic planners had long neglected to include future sealift capability, but the British proved the military value of a merchant fleet in the Falkland Islands conflict with Argentina. By 1983 U.S. Navy logisticians recognized that a continuing substantial decline in the Merchant Marine was a dangerous threat to support of future protracted overseas deployments. Funds were made available in FY 1983 to increase cargo-capable ready reserve ships from 29 to 121 by 1988 through purchase of modern ships from financially distressed commercial operators.

The United States and the Falklands

The British government announcement in 1962 that its forces would be withdrawn from all bases east of Suez sent unintended signals that Great Britain would no longer meet threats to its overseas bases. Among the countries misinterpreting the policy move was Argentina, which disputed the English occupation of the Falkland Islands, 350 miles off the Argentine coastal city of Rio Gallagos. On 4 April 1982 Argentine troops invaded "Islas Melvinas," as they called the 4,700-square mile group of 200 small outcroppings in the South Atlantic Ocean.

The British immediately condemned the move and rushed naval surface and subsurface units to the area while assembling troops and sealift assets for a British Expeditionary Force (BEF) to retake the Falklands, 8,000 miles from England. The British planning and buildup for the expeditionary effort was orchestrated from the Admiralty in London by RADM David Hallifax, RN. Although there was no official acknowledgement, leaks to the press revealed that the United States provided intelligence, control of aircraft movements with AWACS aircraft, and logistical support to the British. RADM Ted Walker, then supply officer, U.S. Atlantic Fleet, confirms that substantial quantities of petroleum products were provided. Fuel was transferred from U.S. Navy assets in Great Britain to Royal Navy bases, and then to British ships.

The Royal Navy had only two small ski-jump deck helicopter-VSTOL carriers capable of launching Harrier jets to repel Argentine attacks and provide air cover for the BEF. Additional Harrier launch and recovery platforms were constructed and mounted atop shipping containers on merchant ships sent to the Falklands. BEF troops landed at East Falkland Island on 21 May and moved swiftly and decisively over the rugged terrain. The outclassed Argentine army surrendered at Port Stanley on 14 June. In a postconflict briefing at SACLANT, a British Ministry of Defence comptroller discussed the costs with RADM Walker. The English official pointed out that the first seven or eight weeks of the Falkland campaign cost the British government more than it would have cost to maintain all U.K. forces east of Suez from the early 1960s to the year 2000.

RADM Hallifax was promoted to vice admiral, and Queen Elizabeth II knighted him for his brilliant planning and support of the Falklands campaign. VADM Sir David Hallifax later served as deputy commander, Supreme Allied Command Atlantic (SACLANT), headquartered at Norfolk. In October 1983 he described the successes, difficulties, and innovations associated with the extended logistics support pipelines of the Falklands expedition at the Naval Reserve Supply Corps Readiness Workshop at Jacksonville, Florida.

The Reagan Doctrine

In 1981, when President Ronald Reagan announced that the United States would confront expansionist moves by the Soviet Union in the Third World, the Reagan Doctrine was born. Reagan made it clear that when any group—the Soviet Union or terrorists—violated the rules of international behavior, they could expect "swift and effective retaliation" by the United States. Libya was providing sanctuary to terrorists, who launched assassinations, skyjackings, and bombings throughout Europe and the Middle East and soon felt the force of this resolve. Previous administrations had chosen not to challenge Libya over obvious flaunting of international law, but in August 1981 a two-carrier (*Nimitz* and *Forrestal*) Navy battle group entered the Gulf of Sidra to conduct exercises and reinforce U.S. rights. When 72 Libyan air force fighter-bombers flew about 140 sorties near the battle group, they were met and escorted out of the area by Navy F-14 Tomcat fighters.

The following day, a Navy E-2 Hawkeye surveillance plane detected 12 Libyan planes headed toward the battle group in a perceived attempt to lure U.S. Navy planes within range of land-based Libyan missiles. Two F-14s were directed to intercept two Libyan planes that threatened to penetrate the U.S. exercise area. When one of the Libyans fired a missile at one of the Tomcats, the two U.S. planes promptly shot down the two aggressors.

The Iowa-class Battleships

In 1982 Secretary Lehman decided to jump-start his goal of a 600-ship Navy by reactivating the four mothballed Iowa-class battleships and equipping them with cruise missiles. One of the battlewagons was the *USS Missouri* (BB-63), which had been declared a national monument in recognition of being the site of the surrender of the Japanese in 1945.

Supply Corps officers were at the heart of reactivating *USS New Jersey* (BB-62). The Navy Regional Contracting Center at Long Beach was given responsibility for all contracting support and procurement of all the materials and services for recommissioning NRCC, and the Long Beach Shipyard did the job for the budgeted $326,000. By 1983 *New Jersey* was in action in the Eastern Mediterranean, with her 16-inch guns blasting hostile forces that had been shelling Marine peacekeepers at Beirut.

Operation Urgent Fury

The 1982 communist takeover of the small, economically deprived Caribbean island of Grenada, the smallest nation in the Western Hemisphere, had opened the way for Cuba to extend its reach in the Caribbean, threatening shipping routes to and from the Panama Canal. In addition, there had been a power struggle on the island among competing communist factions, and 600 American medical students were endangered. On 22 October the Organization of Eastern Caribbean States asked the United States to intervene.

A week later, the Joint Chiefs of Staff initiated planning for rescue of the students in a military evolution code-named Operation Urgent Fury. ADM Wesley L. (Wes) McDonald, CINCLANT, was designated commander of a joint rescue endeavor to dislodge Cuban troops and airport construction workers and unseat the communist government. Operational command was given to VADM Joseph (Joe) Metcalf III, Commander Second Fleet. Development of the Navy logistics plan was the responsibility of RADM Niel P. Ferraro, Atlantic Fleet supply officer.

The *USS Independence* (CV-62) battle group departed Norfolk on 18 October for the Eastern Mediterranean to relieve *USS Eisenhower* (CVN-69) off Beirut, Lebanon. Two days later, the ships were diverted from their easterly transit of the Atlantic and ordered south to the Caribbean. The *Independence* CVBG joined Operation Urgent Fury on 23 October and launched initial air strikes 25 October in support of an amphibious assault by Marine and Army troops.

Logistics Head at Barbados

CAPT (later RADM) Rodney K. (Rod) Squibb, AIRLANT supply officer, dispatched LCDR (later CDR) James M. (Jim) Dykes to Barbados on 26 October to set up a logistics head to push material from Barbados to *Independence* and amphibious ships off Granada. Dykes was designated officer-in-charge, U.S. Atlantic Fleet Logistics Detachment Barbados. An Army transportation unit was already at Grantley Adams Airport to process personnel movements of all services. Security dictated that no advance notice of Dykes's mission be given to the Barbados government, but airport officials cooperated with him. They assigned him two commercial spaces to assemble material arriving by air for delivery to the battle group.

LCDR Dykes then flew out to *Independence,* where CDR (later CAPT) Fred L. Meyer, supply officer, assigned six enlisted men to assist in the airport operation. Dykes involved a retired Supply Corps captain, Verlin C. (Vic) Henson, then a civilian AIRLANT employee at Barbados on a training assignment. Henson rented automobiles, vans, and materials handling equipment, which included the only commercial forklift on the island, with the always useful Form 44.

The first planeload of airlifted material from CONUS arrived at Grantley Adams Airport on 26 October. The Army passenger representatives identified in-coming Navy personnel in supply rates, awaiting further transportation, and they were detailed to supplement Dykes's rapidly expanding supply team. In order to provide sufficient personnel for 12-hour shifts, LCDR Dykes drafted several "supply types" who had been delayed while passing through the airport.

Army Rangers on Grenada were meeting fierce opposition from Marxist forces and armed Cuban workers. Two additional night assaults, involving extremely difficult tactical maneuvers, were made on the island, including a joint operation to rescue 200 of the American students from a hotel at Grand Anse Beach. On 26 October, planes of *Indy*'s air wing made numerous air strikes on key positions.

On the following day, 27 October, the first American casualties arrived aboard *Independence* from the island. Mop-up activities continued over the next few days until the tiny island nation was secured and the American students were safely evacuated. The people of Grenada, who had welcomed arrival of Americans, were jubilant over the successful military operation. Congress waded in with invocation of a war powers resolution, requiring U.S. troops to leave Grenada by 24 December.

Air Force C-5, C-130, and C-141 planes began to arrive at Barbados on the 27th and were unloaded by Air Force personnel, who turned over Navy cargo to LCDR Dykes and his team. Moving the Navy cargo from the Air Force site, a quarter mile from the Navy site, with the single rented forklift proved tedious. Initially, the Air Force would not assist in moving Navy material, so CDR Meyer sent a half-dozen turkeys with all the trimmings from *Independence* so Dykes could have a party for the Air Force. Soon thereafter, Navy cargo began to move by Air Force forklifts. Supply Corps initiative and cooperation had once again surmounted imposing obstacles.

C-1 CODs were originally the primary vehicle for transporting material to *Independence,* but because of their limited capacity, only transportation priority category one (TP1) freight was being moved. TP2 and TP3 cargo began to pile up at the Grantley Adams Airport on Barbados, creating a potential hazard for commercial operations. The supply team covered as much of the palletized material stored outdoors as possible with its limited supply of plastic tarps. LCDR Dykes was instructed to send material for the amphibious group to the Point Salinas Airport on Grenada. The Navy supply team filled a C-130 gun ship with the needed material and sent it to the island.

The Supply Officer and His Unusual Duties

Jim Dykes was the ranking Navy officer at the Grantley Adams Airport, so it became his lot to receive any and all requests for Navy services, most not related to his mission. In one incident, an Army brigadier general ordered him to call in carrier air strikes against opposing forces on coordinates he provided. LCDR Dykes relayed the request to *Indy* over the UHF radio channel used for supply communications. A supply officer's order for an air strike met with skepticism aboard ship, and he was first told to send a message, then to have the general fly out to *Independence,* but the C-1s were all on MEDEVAC runs. The request had been an emergency, so the general quietly thanked Dykes for trying and returned to his office on the opposite side of the terminal.

On another occasion, AIRLANT instructed LCDR Dykes to meet a commercial flight and do whatever the two arriving men wanted. The two individuals showed Jim Dykes their IDs and introduced themselves as CIA agents. They requested entry into Barbados without going through customs. An incredulous Dykes talked with the customs agent, pitching national security and winning the war, but was unsuccessful until he produced a quart of 151-proof rum that he purchased at the airport duty free shop. The two agents passed unchecked into the country without incident, disappeared into a head with their carry-on luggage, emerged fully armed and in camies, and requested a flight to Grenada, which Dykes arranged. "Thankfully, I never saw those guys again."

It soon became clear that Operation Urgent Fury would end much sooner than anticipated, so LCDR Dykes called CAPT Squibb at AIRLANT in Norfolk about returning material, most of it TP2 and TP3, piled up at the airhead. Second-destination funding was short, so the two AIRLANT supply officers decided upon a major vertical replenishment of material to ships deployed off Grenada. CDR Meyer assured Dykes that helicopters would be available, and SURFLANT agreed to provide cargo nets and pennants.

At midnight on the evening of 31 October, LCDR Dykes and his team watched the last commercial flight arrive at Barbados. As soon as the commercial flight left the runway and taxied to the terminal, he and his team swung into action, laying out cargo nets on the runway and taxiways and positioning 175 pallets of cargo for lift to *Independence.* A fleet of nine helicopters from the carrier and *USS Guam* (LPH-9) began arriving at dawn to pick up the cargo. More than 80 lifts completed removal of all remaining Navy cargo in short order.

The *Independence* battle group departed Grenada on 3 November and resumed its Atlantic transit to the Mediterranean. LCDR Dykes closed up shop and returned to Norfolk the same day. His team had handled more than 400 metric tons of Navy freight through the Barbados airport in 9 days. Dykes was awarded the Navy Commendation Medal for his contributions to the success of Operation Urgent Fury.

Independence Relieves *Eisenhower* off Lebanon

Independence passed Gibraltar on 12 November 1983 and arrived off

Lebanon, where she relieved *Eisenhower* on 18 November. Less than a month earlier, Lebanon had been the scene of a suicide bombing of a barracks where 241 Marines and sailors of a U.N. multinational peacekeeping force lost their lives. *Independence* took up position on Beno Station off Lebanon in support of the U.S. peacekeepers.

The men of *Independence* observed her 25th anniversary while off Lebanon on 10 January 1984, and left when relieved by *USS John F. Kennedy* (CV-57) in early March. *Independence* was ordered to participate in Operation Teamwork '84 in the Norwegian Sea. Transition from tropical conditions in early operations off Grenada, through mid-deployment off Lebanon, to end-of-cruise operations in the frigid waters above the Arctic Circle provided a tough test for both the carrier and its supply system. Fred Meyer believes the sequence of events "was proof of the diversity of the aircraft carrier and the robust support provided by the Navy Supply Corps and the DOD logistics system."

LORE OF THE CORPS

Commander Fred Lewis Meyer, SC, USN

Supply Officer, *USS Independence* (CV-62), 1983–85
Period of Service: 1965–92

Fred Meyer was involved in a number of special operations during a 27-year career in the Navy. He was called back to the Industrial College of the Armed Forces, National Defense University in Washington, as a member of the faculty and selected as the first professor of logistics at ICAF, a position he still holds.

He was born in Queens, New York, in September 1943. His father worked on development of Navy combat systems for Sperry Rand during World War II. Young Meyer's interest in the Navy was heightened when his high school guidance counselor, a commander in the Naval Reserve, encouraged him to apply for an NROTC scholarship.

He was awarded a scholarship to attend the University of Rochester and was graduated with an A.B. degree in psychology and a regular commission as a line ensign. He had developed an interest in naval aviation as a midshipman, and his first active duty was on the staff, Commander Naval Air Force, U.S. Atlantic Fleet, in June 1965. ENS Meyer later had duty at NAS Pensacola. He went to sea in December 1965 in *USS Little Rock* (CLG-4), where he was Combat Information Center officer and qualified as OOD. In April 1966 he transferred to the Supply Corps and reported to NSCS Athens.

He was ordered as supply officer, *USS Joseph P. Kennedy, Jr.* (DD-850) in November 1966 and was promoted to LTJG in December. His first cruise was a challenging one when *Kennedy* was deployed to the Mediterranean and the Red Sea in early 1967 as the Arab world and Israel were poised on the brink of war. Meyer exercised creativity in overcoming supply endurance problems when closing of the Suez Canal separated *Kennedy* from the rest of her squadron and resupply facilities in the Mediterranean (chapter 11).

Meyer was promoted to lieutenant in July 1968 and reported to the Naval Air Station, Norfolk, in December as assistant material officer. He remained in Norfolk for a tour on the staff, Commander Naval Air Forces, U.S. Atlantic Fleet, commencing in October 1970 as planning-procedures officer. Fred Meyer reported to the Naval Postgraduate School at Monterey in August 1971 and was graduated with an M.S. degree in operations research and systems analysis. He was ordered to NSC Charleston in October 1973, where he was assistant planning officer and staff operations analyst.

He was promoted to lieutenant commander in January 1974 and went back to sea in September 1975 as assistant supply officer, *USS Saratoga* (CV-60). He was awarded the Navy Commendation Medal and ordered to NAVSUP in October 1977, where he was director, afloat plans, programs, and systems development, serving initially under RADM Shirley D. (Dave) Frost. He spent nearly three years in that billet, but was temporarily assigned to duty in the Office of the Chief of Naval Material from January to September 1978. He was the creator and first director, Fleet Non-Tactical Logistics Information Systems Office. He returned to NAVSUP in September 1978, was promoted to commander in August 1979, and received a gold star in lieu of a second Navy Commendation Medal for his duty at NAVSUP and at CNM.

Fred Meyer went back to school in August 1980 at the Industrial College of the Armed Forces, National Defense University, Fort Lesley J. McNair, Washington. He was graduated from ICAF in June 1981 and reported to ASO Philadelphia, where he was assigned as acting deputy comptroller and as director, systems development and director, international logistics programs.

He was ordered as supply officer, *USS Independence* (CV-62) in June 1983. CDR Meyer had been aboard only four months when *Independence* left Norfolk for deployment to the Eastern Mediterranean as relief of *USS Eisenhower* (CVN-69) on Beno Station off Lebanon. Two days out of Norfolk, the *Independence* battle group was diverted south into the Caribbean to participate in Operation Urgent Fury, the liberation of Grenada. *Indy*'s air wing provided strikes in support of amphibious operations and subsequent ground operations during the 11-day diversion from its primary mission. The carrier battle group then resumed its transatlantic passage and relieved *Eisenhower* in mid-November.

CDR Meyer was awarded the Meritorious Service Medal for his outstanding meritorious service in *Independence*. The citation contains the following: "His clean sweep of outstanding grades for every inspection on his department and a record low 17 percent Not Mission Capable supply requirements attained supporting an average 83 percent Mission Capable and 81 percent Full Mission Capable rates for the Air Wing set new standards."

Meyer reported again to the Naval Supply Systems Command in June 1985 as deputy comptroller for operations research. He was promoted to captain in October 1986 and selected as executive assistant to the deputy assistant and director, Navy International Programs Office. He reported to his new duty in April 1987, and served successively with Navy Undersecretaries James S. Goodrich, H. Lawrence Garrett III, and J. Daniel Howard.

In April 1990 CAPT Meyer became professor of logistics, Industrial College of the Armed Forces, National Defense University, as director of the Defense Industries Study Program. He served as instructor of industry financial analysis advanced studies, acquisition, European Community '92 regional security studies, and aircraft industry studies. He was also professional mentor to all assigned Supply Corps staff members and students and managed 90 percent of ICAF's direct-cost funds.

Fred Meyer thrived in the demanding joint National Defense University environment and took charge of the entire Defense Industries (DIS) Program as director. He selected and motivated a teaching team of 45 senior officers from all services and from academicians and several government agency chairs. Meyer also led a joint National War College-ICAF seminar that developed a national security strategy, a supporting national military strategy and budget through FY 1997, and a plan for deployment of joint forces to solve major national crises projected in FY 1997–2001. Fred Meyer was invited to join the ICAF permanent staff in the Department of Resources Management. He accepted the offer and retired from the Navy in August 1992. In his new status on the academic staff, Meyer became the second-ranking faculty member in the National Military and Resources Strategy and Crisis exercises in 1992.

Fred Meyer and his wife Patricia live in Fairfax, Virginia, and he commutes to ICAF at Fort McNair in the Southwest Section of Washington. The Meyers have three adult children.

Sources

Citation. Meritorious Service Medal, 1986.

Citations. Navy Commendation Medals, 1977, 1980
Copies of official reports supplied by CAPT Fred L. Meyer, August–November, 1994.
Telephone interview of CAPT Fred L. Meyer, 14 September 1994.

The BOSS Program

Despite major efforts to control excessive costs during the early 1980s, a series of problems arose to haunt the Supply Corps. In 1983 the infamous $110 diode, $435 claw hammer, and $900 ashtray received extensive media coverage. Although these incidents were isolated and easily explained, the press had a field day.

RADM Andy Giordano, Commander Naval Supply Systems Command was the point man in a Naval Material Command project to solve the spare parts pricing problem. The result was a NAVSUP program, Buy Our Spares Smart (BOSS). The BOSS program attacked the old practice of buying spare parts items from prime contractors instead of from the subcontractors who actually made them. BOSS challenged the commercial practice of excessive markup on prices of spares and replacement parts and encouraged competition among contractors through the Breakout Program, which separated parts from the procurement cycle for direct and/or competitive purchase.

Competition advocate billets were established at all activities with procurement authority in excess of $25,000. Similar billets were established at customer activities with annual procurement requirements in excess of $1 million. Coordinating this network of 250 competition advocates was a Supply Corps officer, RADM Stuart F. (Stu) Platt, the Navy's first competition advocate general.

A surprise choice to succeed RADM Andy Giordano as Commander Naval Supply Systems Command and chief of Supply Corps in June 1981 was RADM Ted Walker, best known for his service in submarine supply and in the field of comptrollership.

LORE OF THE CORPS

Rear Admiral Edward Keith Walker, Jr., SC, USN

Commander, Naval Supply Systems Command, and
Chief of Supply Corps, 1984–88
Period of Service: 1954–88

RADM Walker lived at various locations throughout the United States as a Navy junior. He was eight when he witnessed the Japanese sneak attack on Pearl Harbor from the roof of his family's quarters. He was graduated from the Naval Academy, was an expert in submarine supply and comptrollership, and became the 35th chief of Supply Corps.

Ted Walker was born at Annapolis, Maryland, in June 1933. At the time, his father was a lieutenant in the Navy and was attending the ordnance program at the Naval Postgraduate School. Young Walker entered the Naval Academy in June 1950, but was disqualified for the line because of his eyes and commissioned an ensign in the Supply Corps in June 1954. He married Carol Ann Turner, his high school sweetheart, in the Naval Academy Chapel eight days after graduation. The Walkers arrived at NSCS Athens only six months after the school had relocated from Bayonne. At NSCS, Ted Walker, whose only radio experience was owning one, was chosen to write, direct, produce, and star in the 15-minute weekly "Navy in Georgia."

Upon graduation from NSCS, he was assigned to the *USS New Jersey* (BB-62) as disbursing officer and later as stores officer. The first lieutenant decided that ENS Walker's Naval Academy background made him the ideal candidate to be *New Jersey*'s boat officer, responsible for scheduling all the battleship's boats, updating all required charts, and providing crew training.

He was promoted to LTJG in early December 1955 and ordered as supply officer, *USS Wren* (DD-568), which he boarded at Beirut, Lebanon, on New Year's Eve. During a later deployment to Northern Europe in the summer of 1956, LTJG Walker had a professional scare when he tried to balance his *Wren* disbursing accounts and came up $420 short. He reconstructed his accounts from original documents, but the shortage persisted. The commanding officer arranged to have the exec witness Walker making the shortage good. The following morning, the exec handed him an envelope containing $405 in cash. The radioman had organized a "blanket muster" to raise the money for the popular supply officer. Walker surmises that he did not spin the dial when he hurriedly closed his safe, and a passing crewman had probably helped himself to enough money for a "really good liberty. That little fiasco cost me $15, a number of sleepless nights, and probably an ulcer before I die," Ted Walker says.

LTJG Walker came ashore from the destroyer in March 1957 and reported to the Navy Ship's Store Office, Brooklyn, for duty under instruction, after which he returned to Norfolk as the assistant Navy Exchange officer, Naval Operating Base. He was promoted to lieutenant in June 1958. In May 1959 he went as Navy Exchange officer, Naval Station, Rodman, Panama Canal Zone. Walker says that this tour provided the usual challenges of trying to run an exchange overseas in the face of irregularly scheduled deliveries, frustrating customer demands, and a foreign national work force. LT Walker was tempted by a possible third Navy Exchange tour—at London—but Carol Ann said that she would not go to another overseas assignment. She wanted to go home, "where she could walk into a store and buy what she wanted without her husband being responsible for being out of stock." LT Walker went instead to NSD Newport, where he was freight terminal division officer and assistant material officer supporting the Destroyer Force, Atlantic Fleet. He also had responsibility for the Navy's first Servmart, called Piermart, at Newport.

He was promoted to lieutenant commander in April 1964 and was ordered as the first Supply Corps officer with primary duty as supply officer of a submarine squadron. In July LCDR Walker reported to Submarine Squadron 16, a newly formed unit of Polaris fleet ballistic missile submarines headquartered in *USS Holland* (AS-32) at Rota, Spain. SUBRON 16 was having logistical and financial problems with the complicated and expensive Polaris submarines as they came into the Fleet. Walker recalls that money was no object to the submarine commanders, but he and CAPT (later VADM) Philip A. Beshany, squadron commodore, agreed they had to get matters under control for the long pull. Beshany and Walker devised a blueprint and operating instructions that formed the basis for the strict submarine logistical discipline that became the hallmark of the Submarine Force over the next three decades.

In July 1966, LCDR Walker was detached from his pioneering duty with SUBRON 16 and reported for duty under instruction at the Armed Forces Staff College at Norfolk. From AFSC, in January 1967, he went to the Strategic Plans and Policy Division (OP-60), Office of the Chief of Naval Operations, as a war planner. He was the only staff corps officer in the division. At the time, the United States was increasingly committed to the Vietnam War, and LCDR Walker was one of the regular daily briefers for CNO.

He remembers that he and line CDR (later RADM) Frederick C. (Fox Charlie) Johnson were on duty on a Sunday morning and speculating over when the Soviets would appear in the Indian Ocean. The discussion resulted in their "inventing" Diego Garcia as a major U.S. base. It became a secret budget line item called Fling Coral. Walker says it was a difficult project, requiring regular correspondence with Britain's Prince Philip and a royal society over preservation of flora and fauna. "We were worried about the blue-footed boobies, pink turtles, and the jackasses."

VADM Thomas F. Connolly, DCNO, Air Warfare, was pushing for a short runway that could accommodate only Navy planes, but Walker envisioned a runway that could accommodate large Air Force cargo aircraft that could airlift significant numbers of troops and huge volumes of cargo into Diego Garcia. Walker's memorandum was approved, and an 8,000-foot runway was authorized.

LCDR Walker was frequently called upon by RADM (later VADM) F. H. (Fritz) Schneider to go to the Naval War College to lecture on war plans. Schneider required Walker to wear civilian clothes and introduced him as "Dr. Walker" because he believed that a Supply Corps lieutenant commander could not command necessary credibility among the predominantly line-officer students. VADM J. T. (Chick) Hayward, President, NWC, participated in one seminar that followed one of Walker's lectures. Ted Walker thinks that Hayward still does not realize that his two-hour dialogue was with a lieutenant commander in the Supply Corps.

Walker, who was promoted to commander in July 1968, was deeply involved in most of the major issues before the Navy during his 30-month tour in the Pentagon. He also developed meaningful relationships with many future Navy leaders. CDR Walker was sent to the George Washington University for postgraduate study in June 1969 and received an M.B.A. in finance in May 1970.

He reported as supply officer, *USS Howard W. Gilmore* (AS-16), located at Charleston and supporting SUBRON 4, which was transitioning from diesel subs to nuclear-powered Sturgeon-class boats. Earlier in the year, *USS Bushnell* (AS-15) had been disabled by a fire. In July, *Gilmore* was ordered to Key West to take over additional support of SUBRON 12 from *Bushnell*. Supporting two squadrons more than 700 miles apart was a real challenge. SUBRON 4 nuclear boats at Charleston had supply officers; the diesel boats of SUBRON 12 did not.

Toward the end of his tour in *Gilmore*, CDR Walker was involved in the turnover of old diesel submarines to allied nations through the Foreign Military Sales program. *Gilmore* was chosen in 1971 to receive the initial fleet shipboard uniform automated data processing system (SUADPS). Ted Walker believes that *Gilmore* was chosen because of the depth of data processing knowledge among the junior officers and enlisted personnel in the Supply Department. The installation was completed in 60 days. In summer 1972 *Gilmore* went to Ingalls Shipbuilding at Pascagoula, Mississippi, for overhaul before reassignment to La Maddalena, Sardinia, Italy. It was Ingalls first major ship overhaul of the size and complexity of *Gilmore*. "It was not fun," Walker recalls.

He left *Gilmore* in mid-August 1972 and reported to the Pentagon as head, Logistics Coordination Section (OP-221D), Office of the Deputy Chief of Naval Operations for Submarine Warfare. CDR Walker soon became the attack submarine programs and budget officer (OP-22M), with responsibility for completing the submarine program objectives memorandum (POM) at a time when the Navy was at the start of a fleet phase-down. At the same time, the Navy was beginning the major Los Angeles-class (SSN-688) nuclear submarine building program.

CDR Walker was in on the planning process for the Navy's cruise missile program, which eventually became the Tomahawk, a highly reliable major surface-ship weapons system. VADM (later ADM and VCNO) Joe Williams, Jr., became commander of the Atlantic Fleet Submarine Force in 1975, and Walker was assigned as his assistant chief of staff for supply. Walker was delayed in leaving the CNO staff until his relief, CDR (later RADM) James A. (Al) Morgart, reported in April 1975. Ted Walker had been selected for captain and was frocked when he left for Norfolk.

CAPT Walker found that the Norfolk submarine base had overextended its budget by more than $800,000, with fewer than two months left in the fiscal year. He recalls that VADM Williams allowed him to do his job, and as far as logistics and finance were concerned, there was never any question that he spoke for the commander of the Submarine Force.

Ted Walker was officially promoted to captain in July 1975. He said he had "super people" on his staff, including his deputy, CDR (later CAPT) Ronald M. (Ron) Bell, assistant supply officer, who was later relieved by CDR (later RADM) Harvey Don Weatherson, and the comptroller, LCDR (later CDR) Martin J. (Marty) Walsh. Walker solved the sub base budget problem by bringing in an MSC T-AK. An SSBN support cargo ship, it was essentially decommissioned, which saved several million dollars in crew and operating expenses. However, the funds saved were the "wrong color," so CAPT Walker arranged a switch of funds with the AIRLANT comptroller.

CAPT Walker reported to SPCC Mechanicsburg as executive officer in June 1980 as relief of CAPT (later RADM) Scott Ebert. It was his first opportunity to meet many Supply Corps officers other than those in the Submarine Force and his first exposure to Reserve Supply Corps units. Later, RADM Tom Allshouse, SPCC C.O., told him that RADM Gene Grinstead, Chief of the Corps, wanted to test him in a non-Submarine Force job. Ted Walker learned the complexity of the range of material support problems and how SPCC operated in provisioning.

His most trying period at SPCC came in March 1979, when there was a major accident at the nearby Three Mile Island nuclear-powered electric generating station. The Mechanicsburg complex was close enough to be vulnerable to serious radiation damage if the containment vessel had ruptured, endangering about 6,000 military and civilian personnel who worked at SPCC, FMSO, and the Defense Depot. Also endangered were about 90,000 reels of sensitive magnetic tape containing the mechanical history records of the U.S. Navy maintained by SPCC and FMSO.

If the governor of Pennsylvania declared an emergency, it fell to RADM Tom Allshouse to determine at what time and under what circumstance the Mechanicsburg complex would be evacuated and what security would be left behind. Individuals up the SPCC military chain of command would not touch the issue. The SPCC nuclear power representative called Washington and was told not to leave under any circumstances; in effect, to die at his post. Relatives of Royal Australian Navy personnel at SPCC called from Australia, concerned that their loved ones were being irradiated. The containment vessel did not erupt, the emergency ended after 96 hours, and everything returned to normal.

Walker was relieved at SPCC by CAPT (later RADM) James B. (Jim) Whittaker in June 1980 and ordered as commanding officer, Naval Supply Center Puget Sound, Bremerton, Washington, where he relieved CAPT William E. (Bill) Lindsay. Puget was deeply involved in support of the Trident submarine base at nearby Bangor, Washington.

CAPT Walker was selected for Flag rank in February 1981. In August, he went back to Norfolk again, this time as assistant chief of staff for supply, U.S. Atlantic Fleet. In December 1981 RADM Walker also became commander, Joint Logistics Over the Shore Task Force. The JLOTS task force tested the use of container ships with new concepts and equipment for projecting U.S. power forward in areas without developed port facilities. In August 1982 his promotion to rear admiral became official.

RADM Walker worked closely with RADM Thomas G. (Tom) Lilly, a Jackson, Mississippi attorney who was director of the Naval Reserve Cargo Handling Program. The two Flag officers put together a new structure to provide sufficient prompt surge capacity in support of deployed U.S. forces. Reserve cargo handling assets were increased from 6 to 12 battalions. The command structure was changed, and a new Cargo Handling Force, similar to the Seabee organization, was established to provide a Reserve force-in-being, fully trained and capable of rapid response.

Walker's staff at CINCLANT included a small fuel unit responsible for petroleum management of the entire Atlantic basin. When the Falklands conflict began in April 1982, the fuel staff managed a significant portion of the petroleum flow to the Royal Navy during its 10-week deployment. VADM Sir David Hallifax, RN, was the architect and planner of the successful logistical evolution for the British recapture of the Falkland Islands. Ted Walker developed a close relationship with the Royal Navy admiral when he came to Norfolk as deputy commander, SACLANT.

RADM Walker returned to Washington in May 1983 as commanding officer, Naval Accounting and Finance Center, and assistant comptroller, Financial Management Systems. He says he and CAPT (later RADM and commander, NAVSUP) Robert M. (Bob) Moore, his deputy at NAFC, developed a "superb working relationship." Walker and his boss, Assistant Secretary of the Navy for Finance and Management Robert H. (Bob) Conn, worked well together but disagreed over the manning of operational comptrollership billets. Conn, a former naval aviator, had superb financial credentials and believed that more line officers should be comptroller. Walker was concerned that the Navy was not getting the proper talent at critical Fleet and major waterfront commands. He was successful in moving more Supply Corps officers into major operational comptroller billets.

Late in the summer of 1983, Conn asked Ted Walker if he were interested in being the next commander of NAVSUP and chief of Supply Corps. When Walker replied affirmatively, Conn advised him shortly after the new year that he would be the next chief, effective in March 1984. Ted Walker invited RADM Bruno Pomponio to remain as vice commander of NAVSUP, but he elected to exchange jobs with COMO (later RADM) Daniel W. (Dan) McKinnon, Jr., deputy commander of DLA.

Ted Walker was pleased that Andy Giordano had scoped out the world situation over the following six to eight months and that his efforts turned out to be right on the mark. "Had Andy not done so," Walker maintains, "the problems we faced with Congress and in the press would have been infinitely more difficult."

RADM Walker was a strong believer in making greater use of Supply Corps Reserve assets. A week after taking command of NAVSUP, he went to San Diego for the weekend Naval Reserve Supply Corps Readiness Workshop and had a firsthand opportunity to become better acquainted with the Supply Corps Reserve.

The new chief faced a number of problems at NAVSUP, including command problems at NSC Oakland, contract irregularities in moving the Navy Exchange Command from Brooklyn to Staten Island, and the Air Force's $700 million disposal problem. At the same time, he had to deal with continuing press hysteria over the $400 hammer and other highly publicized costly military purchases. Fortunately, the command problems were resolved, the Navy had its disposal procedures in order, and Andy Giordano already had the BOSS program in place to address parts pricing issues.

Another problem that arose early in Ted Walker's watch was Navy Resale System military manning. As chief, Walker was always adamant that the Supply Corps should remain in charge of the Navy resale system. He was able to convince DCNO (Logistics), VADM Tom Hughes, to restore half of the previous cuts. Other issues included the material professional designator, jointness, and the demise of the Naval Material Command in 1983. Walker says that 15 to 18 percent of NAVSUP's administrative workload, which he terms "nonproductive overhead labor," went away when CNM went away.

A prototype of the naval integrated storage tracking and retrieval system (NISTARS), a highly sophisticated warehousing system, had serious problems at NSC Oakland although it was about a decade ahead of the civilian world. Walker recognized the need to fix the system, and fix it the Supply Corps did. But, he says, an important lesson was learned: NAVSUP should never prototype a sophisticated, complex system anywhere but on the East Coast.

Walker recalls that Assistant Secretary of the Navy Everett Pyatt came up with the idea of the material professional (MP). Under his plan, specific Flag slots would be reserved for MPs, and Supply Corps officers would have to qualify as MPs to be considered for Flag. Ted Walker credits CAPT (later RADM) William E. (Bill) Powell, then NAVSUP OP, with playing a critical role in moderating the program so that the Supply Corps was not hurt.

The next issue was "jointness," which required that all candidates for Flag rank must have served in certified joint command billets before their records could go before Flag selection boards. Originally, Supply Corps officers were basically promoted on technical or scientific expertise, and it was proposed that Supply Corps officers be excluded from the joint duty requirements. When the Army and Air Force raised serious objections to the exemption, RADM Walker declared that the Supply Corps would "go joint 100 percent."

Walker brought the Reserve Supply Corps Flag officers into full participation in the normal NAVSUP Flag communication channels. He was also concerned that, once retired, Flag officers—Regular and Reserve—were "thrown out to pasture," so he initiated an annual retired Flag officer conference. He was determined that "One Navy" would be the guiding principal for Supply Corps Regular, Reserve, and retired personnel.

When ADM Carl Trost succeeded ADM Jim Watkins as CNO, he asked the chief of Supply Corps how to regain control of uniform decisions from SECNAV John Lehman. Walker recommended reinstatement of the Navy Uniform Board, which Lehman had abolished. Trost immediately reinstated the board upon Lehman's departure.

Ted Walker's three main objectives as chief were to develop a strategic plan for NAVSUP, to change the operating style of management, and to rebuild the image of the Corps. He never lost a chance to remind line officers that the Supply Corps had more people at sea, as a percentage of the total Corps, than the line.

Ted Walker retired on 1 September 1988, and was relieved by RADM Dan McKinnon, vice commander of DLA and Walker's former NAVSUP vice commander. In retirement, Walker accepted a position as vice president for administration and director, corporate strategy for Resource Consultants, Inc. (RCI), in Vienna, Virginia. He has remained active in a wide variety of Navy activities and is president-elect of the Navy Supply Corps Association. He is treasurer of the Naval Memorial Foundation and a trustee of the Naval Academy Foundation. Carol Ann Walker was sponsor of *USS Supply* (AOE-6), the first of a new class of fast combat stores ships, which was launched at San Diego in October 1990 and commissioned in February 1994. The Walkers live at Alexandria, Virginia.

Sources

Interviews of RADM Edward K. Walker. Alexandria, Va., 24 May 1989 and 8 January 1990.

Official Biography. Naval Supply Systems Command, October 1986.

Stillwell, Paul. *Battleship New Jersey: An Illustrated History*. Annapolis: Naval Institute Press, 1986.

Transcript of Naval Service. Bureau of Naval Personnel, July 1987.

The Commodore Rank

In 1982 Congress enacted legislation restoring the venerable Navy rank of commodore to designate Navy officers in the O-7 pay grade. The law also specified that officers of this grade wear only one star in lieu of the two stars they had worn previously. The primary impetus behind restoring the historic rank came from Army and Air Force complaints that the Navy called officers in both the O-7 and O-8 pay grades rear admiral and permitted them to wear two stars.

Representative Ike Skelton (D-Missouri), a University of Missouri classmate of CAPT (later RADM) Dan McKinnon, led the Capitol Hill effort. None of the newly promoted commodores liked the title. It confused officers of other services and friendly nations and also the press. The commodore rank was frequently confused with commander or brigadier general. At one point, the Navy suggested to Congress that the one-star Navy rank be called commodore admiral, an absurdity that died quickly. Eventually, the issue was resolved when the Navy convinced Congress to enact new legislation to formalize rear admiral, lower half, as a one- star rank and rear admiral, upper half, as a two-star rank.

With strong support from the Reagan administration, the Navy was in the most advantageous position since World War II. American forces were on duty in Europe, the Caribbean, and Southeast and Southwest Asia, as well as on the oceans of the world to confront Soviet expansion and retaliate against terrorism, whatever the source.

Sources

Sources for material used in this chapter and not cited earlier include:

Miller, Nathan. *The U.S. Navy: An Illustrated History*. Annapolis: Naval Institute Press, and New York: American Heritage Press, 1977.

Navy Supply Corps Newsletter, September 1973.

Supply Corps 2010. Chief of Supply Corps, 1989.

World Almanac and Book of Facts. 1992.

CHAPTER THIRTEEN

The World's Preeminent Sea Power

1984–92

The U.S. Navy was firmly established as the world's preeminent sea power by 1984, and was the free world's forward-deployed, first-line defense bulwark against threats from the Soviet Union. The Navy operated freely on all seven seas, maintaining deployments in the Western Pacific, Mediterranean, and the North Arabian Sea. The small, long-standing Middle East Force based at Bahrain was beefed up with additional assets.

No other nation could have even considered operating such an extended logistical pipeline to keep its forces on station so long and so far from its home bases. The U.S. supply effort in Southwest Asia functioned smoothly, but the overall command situation was inordinately complicated. RADM E. K. (Ted) Ted Walker, Jr., NAVSUP commander, describes the situation, "We had a command arrangement that looked like something Rube Goldberg had put together." The Army and Air Force also had units there. The theater commander, at that time a Marine four-star general based at Tampa, Florida, had a huge staff, but owned no permanently assigned forces. He was responsible for a part of the world that was roughly 12,000 miles from both American coasts.

Commanders of the respective carrier battle group (CVBG) or surface action group (SAG), deployed to the North Arabian Sea at any time, reported to either CINCLANTFLT or CINCPACFLT, depending upon its origin. The commander of forces in the Persian Gulf reported to the commander-in-chief, Readiness Command, whose naval component commander was a one-star Flag officer at Pearl Harbor, and his logistician was a Supply Corps lieutenant. There was a small naval logistics base, about the size of a parking lot, at Bahrain, with another Supply Corps lieutenant as station supply officer. The staff logistician for the Commander Middle East Force was headed by yet another Supply Corps lieutenant.

The Seaman to Admiral Program

When many officers opted to return to civilian life at the end of obligated service following the Korean War, the Navy experienced a serious leadership problem. The quick fix was to commission senior enlisted personnel with strong leadership potential. The program, adopted in 1957, quickly became known as the Seaman to Admiral Program, although the Navy did not anticipate that many would advance beyond the grade of lieutenant commander.

Chief Storekeeper Rodney K. Squibb, a 12-year Navy veteran, was among the first to take advantage of this new opportunity. He was commissioned an ensign in the Supply Corps, U.S. Navy, in July 1957 and was selected for Flag rank in early 1984. *Navy Times* reported that he was the only U.S. Navy admiral who had risen to chief petty officer before going to Officer Candidate School.

LORE OF THE CORPS

Rear Admiral Rodney Kaye Squibb, SC, USN

Commander, Navy Resale and Services Support Officer, 1987–90
Period of Service: 1945–90

RADM Squibb is believed to be the first Supply Corps officer to serve in every Navy rate and rank from seaman to rear admiral. He enlisted in the Navy at the minimum age of 17½ and left naval service at the mandatory retirement age of 62 after serving 44½ years. He is the only Supply Corps officer to achieve Flag rank through the Seaman to Admiral Program.

Rodney Squibb was born on a farm near Morton, Minnesota, in January 1928. He was intent on joining the Navy upon graduation from high school, but had to wait until October 1945 when he reached the minimum age. During World War II, his older brother served in the Navy, one sister was a WAC in the Army, and another sister was a SPAR in the Coast Guard.

Rod Squibb went through boot camp at NTC San Diego and through Storekeeper A School at NTC Great Lakes before reporting in August 1946 for duty at the Navy Finance Center in Cleveland, where he was advanced to storekeeper, third class. He next reported to *USS Robert L. Wilson* (DD-847) in February 1948, where he served until honorably discharged from the Navy in January 1949; he reenlisted in the Naval Reserve the following day.

He worked as a venetian blind assembler, but was unhappy with civilian life and returned to active Navy duty in May 1949 as a volunteer Reservist because his USN rating was full. Petty Officer Squibb reported to the *USS PC-778,* a Reserve training ship based at Cleveland, where he served for a year and a half. In August 1950 he took the ship through Lake Michigan and down the Illinois and Mississippi rivers to Philadelphia, arriving in November. *PC-778* was decommissioned in April 1951, and Squibb was assigned to the crew to ferry a newly commissioned vessel, *PCE-902,* back to the Great Lakes through the St. Lawrence Seaway to her new home port at Milwaukee, Wisconsin.

He then was reassigned to the crew of *PCE-894,* a Reserve training ship at Chicago, where he served from June 1951 to September 1953, making storekeeper, first class, early in the tour. The Korean War opened up a number of USN rates, including storekeeper, so SK1 Squibb reenlisted in the Navy in July 1953. He was ordered to *USS Fechteler* (DDR-870), a newly recommissioned World War II destroyer, at Long Beach, California, in October 1953. He deployed to Korea in *Fechteler,* which made an around-the-world cruise to change its home port to Newport, Rhode Island.

In June 1955 he was promoted to chief petty officer and reported to *USS Cascade* (AD-16). He served in *Cascade* for about 13 months, during which she made two Mediterranean cruises. SKC Squibb was transferred temporarily to *USS Ticonderoga* (CV-14) for transportation back to the States and duty as an instructor in the NROTC program at the Massachusetts Institute of Technology, Cambridge, starting in August 1956.

Chief Squibb had learned of the Navy's need for officers, and was a successful applicant for the Seaman to Admiral Program. He was commissioned an ensign in the Supply Corps in July 1957 and ordered to the Officer Candidate School, Newport, Rhode Island, in a group of commissioned senior ex-enlisted men. ENS Squibb attended NSCS Athens from November 1957 to February 1958, and then reported to the Navy Ship's Store Office, Brooklyn, for two months of training.

In July 1958 ENS Squibb was given independent duty as officer-in-charge, Ship's Store Ashore, at the Naval Air Station, Oppama, Japan.

He was promoted to lieutenant, junior grade, in December 1958. LTJG Squibb reported to duty as Navy Exchange officer, Naval Air Station, Minneapolis, Minnesota, in June 1960 and was promoted to lieutenant in June 1961. He returned to sea in September 1963 as stores officer and senior assistant supply officer in *Yellowstone* (AD-27) at Mayport, Florida. LT Squibb was ordered to Norfolk in September 1965 as staff supply officer, Service Squadron Eight, which had 37 sea-going tugs, intelligence ships, rescue ships, and other service vessels. He was promoted to lieutenant commander at SERVRON Eight.

Although Squibb was a not a college graduate, he had been attending classes whenever Navy duties permitted, but sea duty prevented completion of requirements for a degree. LCDR Squibb reported to the Naval Postgraduate School, Monterey, California, in November 1967 in a degree program for former naval aviation cadet pilots and former enlisted men. Squibb was graduated with a B.A. degree in international relations in October 1969.

LCDR Squibb's only previous aviation experience was in Navy Exchange duty at two air stations, but he was ordered to *USS Kitty Hawk* (CVA-63), as assistant to CDR (later RADM) Andy Giordano, supply officer. The new duty gave Rod Squibb a good grounding in aviation supply during *Kitty Hawk*'s deployment to Vietnam. He was selected for commander in early 1971, ordered to NAVSUP in August, and became head, Supply Management Branch. RADM Wally Dowd, Commander of NAVSUP, recognized CDR Squibb's aviation background, appointed him assistant inspector general in February 1974, and sent him to inspect air stations around the world. While in the IG shop, Squibb was sent to the University of Pittsburgh for a management executive program in 1974.

CDR Squibb was ordered, in September 1975, as prospective supply officer, *USS Dwight D. Eisenhower* (CVN-69), under construction at Newport News, Virginia. He was the first member of the Supply Department to report to the shipyard. Two years later, at commissioning in October 1977, he had 822 men in his department. Squibb's tour in *Eisenhower* lasted three years, during which his department supported 6,200 men when the air wing was aboard. At sea, he received orders to the Aviation Supply Office at Philadelphia.

He was promoted to captain in September 1978, reported to ASO under RADM Paul Foster, and assigned initially as stock control officer. He later served as planning and data systems officer, and still later as executive officer. He says that he had never been challenged as much as he was by the mathematical and inventory models and the huge Navy parts inventory managed by the aviation inventory control point. He was awarded the first of his four Legions of Merit at the end of his first ASO tour for enhancing the effectiveness of ASO during a period of accelerating technical complexity.

CAPT Squibb's next duty took him back to Norfolk as force supply officer, Naval Air Force, U.S. Atlantic Fleet, responsible for supporting the aircraft carriers and air stations in the AIRLANT claimancy. It was a big job, but Rod Squibb had the right credentials. He traveled extensively with the admirals who headed AIRLANT, including 10 or 12 trips to the Mediterranean. His job was to make certain that the carriers and air stations had the resources to support high readiness levels. CAPT Squibb received a gold star in lieu of a second Legion of Merit.

He was selected for Flag rank in early 1984 and ordered back to ASO in June to relieve RADM John H. Ruehlin as commanding officer. He was frocked as a commodore upon assuming command at a time when the Navy was funding aviation depot level repairables. Shortly after COMO Squibb arrived back in Philadelphia, ASO had its largest budget ever, $5 billion, to buy spares for the aviation community. Squibb and his staff worked overtime to assure they were buying the proper items at the proper price and that the inventory was located at the proper stock points.

ASO led the shift to a posture of more competitive buying of spares and fewer buys from prime contractors. Squibb recalls that they moved from buying 6 percent competitively to 40 percent during his watch. "It was a challenging job, but the rewards were great because we were filling the bins and slowly and surely the material readiness started to increase." Rod Squibb's contributions during his command tour were recognized twice. The first was a gold star in lieu of a third Legion of Merit for the period, June to December 1984, which recognized his increasing competitive procurements from 14.6 percent to 25 percent of total buys.

He made his number as commodore in July 1985 and was redesignated rear admiral, lower half, in 1986. When he left ASO in August 1986, he was awarded the Distinguished Service Medal, which cited his leadership in "fundamental improvement in competition resulting in savings of over $250 million."

RADM Squibb reported to NAVSUP in August 1986 as deputy commander for Fleet support. Rod Squibb was promoted to rear admiral, upper half, in May 1987 and in July relieved RADM Donald E. (Don) Wilson as commander, Navy Resale and Services Support Office, at Fort Wadsworth, Staten Island, New York. At the time, Navy resale system annual sales were $148 million from exchanges, commissaries, ship's stores, and lodges. RADM Squibb says that everything went well for a year and a half until the Department of Defense decided to consolidate all Navy, Marine, Army, and Air Force commissaries. The Defense Commissary Agency was formed in 1989 to operate them.

Rod Squibb believes strongly that it is not enough to rely on attractive prices and the loyalty of sailors and dependents to maintain high usage rates for the Navy's retail operations. He says the exchanges must be more user-friendly in the manner of attractive malls built around such mass merchandisers as Kmart and Wal-Mart, if they are to remain economically viable.

Squibb was recognized both inside and outside the Navy for his stewardship of the ship's store, Navy exchange, and Navy commissary operations around the world when NRSSO sales and profits grew 25 percent and 54 percent, respectively. He was "cover boy" for *Military Market* magazine just three months before he retired. In a wide-ranging interview, "Cheering the NAVRESSO Magic," the publication devoted five pages to words and photographs of Rodney K. Squibb. Summing up his management philosophy, he said, "People like to see the boss, touch the boss. So, I made that one of my primary goals—to get out there. . . . Another thing I found out when you're in senior management is that, if you hang around the office too much, you become the biggest micro manager in the world, and you don't let the potential of your managers be fully executed."

RADM Squibb reached the mandatory retirement age of 62 in January 1990 and retired on 1 February. He had worked for 16 Supply Corps Flag officers and 11 line Flag officers during his 44½-year Navy career. At his retirement, he was awarded a gold star in lieu of a fourth Legion of Merit.

Representative Marvin Leath (D.-Texas) read a tribute to RADM Squibb into the *Congressional Record* just nine days before his retirement at Fort Wadsworth. Rod Squibb says he is enjoying retired life, including traveling and doing some consulting work on a selective basis. He and his wife Lavada have two grown children and live at Newport News, Virginia.

Sources

"An Admiral's Rise Through the Ranks." *Navy Times,* 19 February 1990.

"Cheering the NAVRESSO Magic." *Military Market,* November 1989.

Citation. Distinguished Service Medal, 28 July 1986.

Citation. Legion of Merit, 1981, 1984, 1985, 1990.

Interview of RADM Rodney K. Squibb. Norfolk, Va., 25 January 1992.

Official Biography. Navy Resale and Services Support Office, Staten Island, N.Y., n.d.

Official Transcript. Bureau of Naval Personnel, 1 August 1989.

"A Tribute to Rear Adm. Rodney K. Squibb, SC, USN. *Congressional Record,* 24 January 1990.

New Maritime Strategy and Forward Deployment

In 1985 the Navy was beginning to prove the viability of President Reagan's Maritime Strategy, which called for flanking the Soviet Union from the Norwegian Sea and the North Pacific. The strategy placed emphasis on forward deployment of CVBGs, SAGs, and amphibious assault groups (AAGs) and quick strikes by up to four carrier battle groups in the event of war with the Soviet Union. The real danger of the strategy was that American and Allied forces would outrun their logistics.

One of the early exercises to test this strategy nearly was a disaster when the ships involved almost exhausted their fuel. VADM (later ADM and CNO) Carl Trost, CINCLANTFLT, gave RADM James E. (Jim) Miller, Director, Supply Operations and Readiness, the task of immediately developing a logistics plan to complement the forward deployment element of the strategy. RADM Miller spent a good part of two years in Norway and Great Britain to flesh out details of his proposed Atlantic logistics strategy.

The new logistics strategy required that coastal supply points in the Atlantic Fleet claimancy develop internal procedures to assure maximum support of Fleet operations. To meet this new challenge at Norfolk was an experienced logistician, CAPT William E. (Bill) Powell, a Flag selectee who reported as commanding officer, NSC Norfolk, in May 1985.

LORE OF THE CORPS

Rear Admiral William Egbert Powell, Jr., SC, USN

Commanding Officer, Naval Supply Center Norfolk, 1985–88
Period of Service: 1959–88

Bill Powell was among the first 15 African Americans to enter the Supply Corps and the first to achieve Flag rank. He commanded a supply center and a supply depot and was director of Supply Corps Personnel during his 29 years of active service.

William E. Powell, Jr., was born in Indianapolis, Indiana, in April 1936, was graduated from high school in his hometown, and enlisted in the Navy in 1953. Powell completed recruit training at NTC Bainbridge, Maryland, and was selected to attend the Naval Academy Prep School,

Bainbridge, where he received an appointment to Naval Academy in 1955. Upon graduation in 1959, he attended Navy Supply Corps School at Athens.

ENS Powell was ordered to duty as supply officer, *USS Nicholas* (DDE-449) in January 1960 and was promoted to LTJG in December 1960. His next duty, beginning in December 1961, was at NAS Point Mugu, California, where he was promoted to lieutenant in June 1963. LT Powell reported in April 1964 to the Naval Supply Depot Subic Bay, in the Philippines, and was inventory control officer. In June 1966 he went to the Naval Supply System Command at Washington, where he was involved in ship design. LT Powell was sent in August 1967 to the Fleet Material Support Office Mechanicsburg, Pennsylvania, on a four-month assignment. He returned to NAVSUP in December, and in May 1968 was promoted to lieutenant commander. LCDR Powell attended George Washington University, where he received an M.B.A. in government and business administration in May 1969.

In June 1968 LCDR Powell reported to the Cruiser-Destroyer Force, Atlantic Fleet, as head, Planning and Financial Management Section. Powell was ordered as supply officer, *USS Intrepid* (CVS-11) in August 1971 and was promoted to commander in November. CDR Powell then became head, Industrial Support Branch, Aviation Supply Office, Philadelphia, in March 1974.

Bill Powell went back to school in July 1977 at the Industrial College of the Armed Forces, Fort McNair, Washington. In June 1978 he reported to NSC Oakland, where he served as director, Planning and Management Services Department. CDR Powell was promoted to captain in July 1979 and ordered to duty in the Office of CNO as assistant for aviation supply (OP-51) in June 1980. He formulated aviation logistics policy and planned support for new aircraft and was awarded the Meritorious Service Medal.

Returning to the Philippines in May 1982, CAPT Powell was commanding officer, NSD Subic Bay, where he established a container-handling facility and redesigned the material system. He served as C.O. until June 1984 and received the Legion of Merit. CAPT Powell then returned to NAVSUP in July 1984 as head, Officer Personnel Assignments. In early 1985 Bill Powell was designated a material professional and became the first African American to be selected for Flag rank in the Supply Corps.

As a frocked rear admiral, Powell was designated commanding officer, NSC Norfolk, in May 1985 and formally promoted in October. Under RADM Powell's leadership, an automated procurement process and other innovative programs were developed at NSC Norfolk, frequently recognized as one of the Navy's most productive stock points. Powell participated in a study of joint service capability for senior executives at the Institute of Higher Defense Studies, National Defense University, Ft. McNair, Washington, in 1986. He completed his tour at NSC Norfolk in November 1988 and was awarded a second Legion of Merit.

In retirement, Bill Powell joined E.I. Du Pont de Nemours and Company, where he is vice president—logistics. He and his wife Loretta live in Centerville, Delaware.

Sources

Official Transcript. Naval Military Personnel Command, October 1988.
Summary of Naval Career Assignments, RADM William E. Powell, Jr., n.d.

Navy Mideast Logistics

The U.S. Navy had three Supply Corps lieutenants with logistics responsibility for the enhanced U.S. forces in the Persian Gulf-North Arabian Sea-Indian Ocean area when the Kuwaiti tanker flagging crisis began in the summer of 1987. LT Scott Nibbe was at NAVCENT, LT George Horn was supply officer at Administrative Support Unit (ASU) Bahrain, and LT Tony Mosely was in charge of warehouses at Bahrain. RADM Ted Walker recalls all kinds of problems, ranging from conceptual operating procedures, LANTFLT and PACFLT differences, JCS turf battles, and different perceptions and objectives among the on-scene commanders. Walker says that there was no developed concept or doctrine on how to handle logistical problems.

Meanwhile, the increased number of U.S. ships required huge amounts of material, spare parts, replacement personnel, soft drinks, and mail—official and personal. The only short-term solution was expanded airlift, but the Sheik of Bahrain saw that his sole commercial airport was becoming overloaded with U.S. military cargo aircraft and demanded that they go elsewhere. The solution to that problem was to have the Military Airlift Command contract the mission out to commercial carriers.

The situation heated up in the Persian Gulf in May 1987, when two missiles launched from an Iraqi warplane seriously damaged the *USS Stark* (FFG-31) and killed 37 sailors. That event triggered a threefold increase in U.S. force levels in the theater. The 6- or 7-ship deployment in the North Arabian Sea was quickly boosted to 30 ships. Increased logistical support problems encountered by ASU Bahrain prompted

Commander U.S. Naval Forces, Central Command, to request a visit by a NAVSUP Supply-Logistics Assist Team.

A six-member NAVCHAPGRU detachment arrived at ASU Bahrain in mid-July to assist with cargo operations. The NAVSUP Assist Team was headed by CAPT Michael C. (Mike) Hoyt, a decorated veteran of combat logistics in Vietnam. He was backed up by CDR E. T. Reed from NAVMATO, and R. Dixon from FOSSAC, Norfolk, who arrived a week later. The Assist Team found 965 pallet loads of supplies, which had been shipped to Bahrain by air, but not yet delivered to the Fleet. The material was sitting outside uncovered, and the Naval Facilities Engineering Command (NAVFAC) advised that renting a warehouse would take six or seven months. RADM Walker told RADM Benjamin Montoya, Commander, NAVFAC, "You've got six hours. We're in a war!" NAVFAC quickly located and rented the warehouse.

Navy combatant ships rarely came in to the piers at Bahrain for resupply, so material for the Fleet continued to pile up at the small facility. CAPT Hoyt made local arrangements to lease commercial ships for the movement of material to Navy ships throughout the Gulf and in the North Arabian Sea.

CNO Carl Trost did not want to increase the U.S. Navy presence ashore, and his policy was not to send additional Navy personnel to the Gulf. To untangle the logistics effort, Walker quietly sent Reserve storekeepers, cargo handlers, and transportation experts instead. RADM (later VADM) Anthony (Tony) Less was sent to Southwest Asia to take over and create a single unified command of the ships in the Persian Gulf and in the North Arabian Sea. Less sent Mobile Logistics Force (MLF) ships into the Gulf, and resupply problems rapidly improved. ASU Bahrain requested that Middle East Force ships provide usage data to the Defense Fuel Supply Center (DFSC) and SPCC for planning purposes.

The Supply Assist Team completed its work and recommended that NAVSUP increase ASU manning, finalize the contract for airport services at Bahrain, increase warehouse space, expand limited surface lift to Bahrain, and obtain additional materials handling equipment.

The assist team returned to the United States in August 1987, but RADM Walker sent CAPT Hoyt back again in October for a six-month TAD tour, which was extended for another year in November. Mike Hoyt and other Supply Corps officers managed the normal MLSF replenishment of the combatant ships in the Persian Gulf, and the system eventually became automatic. CAPT Hoyt completed his assignment and returned to the States in December 1988. He made his report to RADM Dan McKinnon, who had relieved Ted Walker as Commander, NAVSUP, in July.

LORE OF THE CORPS

Rear Admiral Daniel W. McKinnon, Jr., SC, USN

Commander, Naval Supply Systems Command, and
Chief of Supply Corps, 1988–91
Period of Service: 1956–91

RADM McKinnon spent four years in Italy, including three in a UN command, ran a Navy R&R facility on Bikini Atoll, was head of NAVSUP OP and C.O. of NSD Subic Bay en route to Flag rank. He capped his career by serving as deputy director of DLA and as commander of NAVSUP and chief of the Supply Corps.

Daniel W. McKinnon, Jr., was born in St. Joseph, Missouri, in April 1934 and attended the same high school as RADM Herschel (Hersh) Goldberg, retired NAVSUP commander, had years earlier. RADMs Charles W. (Woody) Rixey and James B. (Jim) Whittaker, retired Supply Corps Flag officers, also are natives of the same 30 square miles of Northwest Missouri and Northeast Kansas.

Young Dan McKinnon enjoyed dealing with money and was treasurer of every organization in his life from high school through college. Having grown up in an agricultural area and facing the draft, he joined a service that did not "operate in mud." He entered the Navy through the NROTC program at the University of Missouri, from which he was graduated in June 1956 with a B.S. degree in business administration and a commission as an ensign in the Navy Supply Corps.

After graduation from NSCS Athens in early 1957, he reported as assistant supply officer to *USS Boxer* (CVS-21), an aircraft carrier that had seen extensive service in the Korean War. The Marine Corps had wanted to build vertical envelopment, amphibious ships (LPHs) from the ground up. When the LPH program was dropped from the budget, the Navy literally gave the Marine Corps three Essex-class carriers—*Boxer, USS Princeton* (CV-37), and *USS Valley Forge* (CV-45) for use as LPHs. The post-Korean drawdown left the Navy with too few sailors to populate the three ships, and a large portion of their companies were Marines in addition to embarked troops. *Boxer*'s Supply Department had five officers, three of whom were Marines. It took about four years for the Navy to be in a position to re-man the three ships.

McKinnon was promoted to lieutenant, junior grade, in December 1957. Because his three-year obligation was expiring in the spring of 1959, he requested another tour of duty as a Reservist. He received orders to NAS Lakehurst, New Jersey, home of the of the Navy's remaining airships (blimps), and was assigned as stock control officer. NAS

Lakehurst also supported jet and propeller planes and helicopters. LTJG McKinnon ran a profit-making business for NAS Lakehurst, selling the output of the on-base helium plant. He would buy helium from BuAer, sell it to blimps, to the Air Force in bottles, and to other authorized buyers. He was promoted to lieutenant in June 1960.

McKinnon remained a Reservist for only about another year before augmenting as a Regular Navy officer. As a test of the wisdom of his decision, he listed the reasons he stayed in the Navy and referred to his list frequently throughout his career. Years later, he would write an article for the *Supply Corps Newsletter* based on that list as a guide to young Navy officers facing the same decision he faced in 1959.

LT McKinnon reported in August 1961 as purchasing and material officer at Naval Support Activity, Naples. He particularly enjoyed his regular turns as boarding officer, showing ships where to anchor in the harbor. Meanwhile, tensions remained high in the Mideast and Mediterranean following the 1957 Israeli War. A United Nations Emergency Force had been formed, numbering more than 5,000 troops from 13 countries, which operated out of an Italian Air Force base at Pisa, Italy.

The U.S. Sixth Fleet patrolled the Eastern Mediterranean, but did not take sides in the Arab-Israeli conflict. The Navy agreed to be the principal logistics agent to support the United Nations Middle East Force. LT McKinnon relieved LT (later CAPT) Lawrence E. (Larry) Krukin on verbal orders as the supply officer at Pisa in July 1962. Dan McKinnon found that many of the UN troops dispatched to the Mideast were equipped with U.S. Army World War II-vintage equipment. His job was not a typical Navy supply function, because the repair activity primarily involved U.S. Army equipment, which he supplied along with spare parts, C-rations, and radios. He sold the UN troops their jeeps and U.S. Army helmet liners, painted blue with a large, white *UN* on each. He received UN purchase orders, converted them into Department of the Army requisitions, and sent them to the Tumbelo Army Depot, 20 miles away. The English-speaking Canadians ran their own maintenance, supply, and logistics systems and were kept busy fixing everything.

U.S. military personnel were not permitted to go into the Gaza Strip, but LT McKinnon's necessary travel into the area on United Nations business was as a civilian. He had a *lassez-passe* visa in his pocket and an U.S. tourist passport secreted on his person. He kept both CINCUSNAVEUR and the U.S. Embassy in Cairo advised of his movements. Civilians were not allowed to travel into the Sinai Desert, so McKinnon was made an honorary member of the Royal Canadian Hussars in order that he could occasionally visit Canadian desert units in the appropriate uniform.

CAPT (later RADM) Wally Dowd became supply officer at NSA Naples about a year later and assigned LT McKinnon additional duty as naval sea cargo coordinating officer and boarding officer for U.S. Navy ships visiting Italian Riviera ports. The McKinnons enjoyed the necessity of driving over to the Riviera, but LT McKinnon's absences on Navy business did not sit well with the retired Canadian army colonel who ran the UN office at Pisa. He threatened to have McKinnon fired for spending "too much time with the Navy." Nothing ever came of the threat.

Dan McKinnon reported to ASO in October 1964 as head of the Services Division in the Purchase Department, where he worked with three future Supply Corps Flag officers: Howard F. (Howie) Kuehl, D. P. (Phil) McGillivary, and Bruno A. Pomponio. He had been at ASO only 10 months when he and LCDR Jim Whittaker were sent to the University of Michigan for graduate studies. The two Supply Corps officers had a spirited competition for the highest grade-point average. McKinnon claims that they worked from sunrise to sunset, taking off time only for football games. Whittaker finished third in the class; McKinnon was fourth—by one-hundredth of a point.

LCDR McKinnon next reported, in May 1966, as purchasing director at the new Navy Supply Center Charleston, created out of the Supply Department of the Charleston Naval Shipyard, which insisted on keeping its own purchase department. The two purchase organizations were co-located, and Dan McKinnon had orders to both commands. He ran the purchase shop with 66 people; two-thirds of them were supply center employees; the balance were shipyard employees. He says the experience gave him a split personality; he dressed up for supply center meetings and down for shipyard meetings. CAPT Theodore S. (Ted) Stern, NSC Charleston C.O., was active in the community and took on a heavy speaking schedule. He frequently called on Dan McKinnon, who had been active in Toastmasters, to fill in for him.

In April 1968 LCDR McKinnon reported as supply officer, *USS Princeton* (LPH-5), in relief of LCDR (later RADM) Donald E. (Don) Wilson. *Princeton,* along with *Boxer,* and *Valley Forge,* had been assigned full-time duty carrying Marines in their new status as LPHs. Dan McKinnon went to the Vietnamese War in *Princeton* and "spent a lot of time in country and on the helos." He had friends on duty in Vietnam, including CDRs (later RADMs) Woody Rixey and Dick Curtis, with whom he spent time ashore. The Supply Department took over protection of the *Princeton,* which was anchored at Danang. Supply Corps officers would go around the ship in small boats and drop percussion grenades into the water to kill sappers trying to blow up the amphibious carrier by attaching explosives to the hull. When *Princeton* returned to the States in late 1968, the Navy announced that the three carriers that had been converted into LPHs were to be decommissioned in 1969 during a massive downsizing program.

Princeton's retirement was delayed when she was designated as the pickup ship for the Apollo-Saturn 10 moon mission in May. A large press pool came aboard to cover the capsule recovery, and members presented LCDR McKinnon with a large shopping list of items they needed. He agreed to provide their needs in return for costumes for King Neptune and his court, which would be used in ceremonies when the ship crossed the Equator. The press people obtained more than 100 costumes from Hollywood and then taped the ceremonies. A helicopter brought the capsule and astronauts Eugene A. Cernan, Thomas P. Stafford, and John W. Young aboard on 26 May 1969.

Princeton next was involved in atomic tests on Amchitka Island, Alaska. McKinnon was promoted to commander in November 1969, and his ship was finally decommissioned. CDR McKinnon was responsible for disposal of ship's store stocks from *USS New Jersey, USS Valley Forge,* several LSTs, and *Princeton.* The huge sale generated so much money that McKinnon made sure every *Princeton* division had a party, and that everybody on the ship had a dirt-cheap watch, radio, boom box, and other desired items.

CDR McKinnon received orders to NAVSUP to set up the Supply Enlisted Ratings Advisory Group. There was no Class A school for ship's servicemen, but McKinnon was instrumental in establishing one. He later was responsible for detailing officers afloat and ashore overseas, including sending the top 10 percent of Supply Corps officers to Vietnam, as requested by ADM Elmo Zumwalt.

When RADM Wally Dowd relieved RADM Ken Wheeler as commander of NAVSUP and chief of Supply Corps, he wanted Dan McKinnon as his EA and aide. Dowd told him that he would attend all Supply Corps balls and visit all Supply Corps field activities and friendly nations. McKinnon remained in the job for 18 months, traveling with the chief to the Pacific, Asia, South America, Europe, and Iran.

Israel was again at war with the Arabs in October 1973, and it appeared as if they might lose. The United States was quietly airlifting substantial military supplies into Israel. VADM (later ADM and CNM) Ike Kidd, Commander Sixth Fleet, wanted Dowd to come to the Mediterranean to supervise logistics. Dowd and McKinnon flew to the Mediterranean as troops were gathering from all over Europe. They set up a small logistics base at Crete staffed with personnel from CINCUSNAVEUR and NSA Naples and established the Navy Contracting Center Naples, which soon resembled a miniature supply center. The new advance base on Crete needed trucks, fork lifts, buses and other items to become a functioning logistics base. Dowd assigned NCC Naples the task of renting the needed equipment in Athens, Piraieus, or elsewhere in Greece. CDR McKinnon called NCC to check on the status of the needed equipment, and LT Jim Judon asked how he was going to get all the equipment to Crete. McKinnon's answer: "Go rent a ferry." The following day, the rented vehicles, complete with rented drivers, were delivered by ferry and went to work on Crete. The experience reinforced McKinnon's belief in the power of the U.S. Navy purchase order.

CDR McKinnon reported to the Industrial College of the Armed Forces in July 1974. He led an ICAF/International War College study group on a 19-day trip to Africa. The group split its time between Senegal and Ghana, where Ambassador Shirley Temple Black "just became part of the gang."CDR McKinnon was sent to the Logistics Command, CINCPACFLT, at Pearl Harbor, in the summer of 1975. He spent three years in Hawaii on the LOGPAC staff, supporting the ships and shore stations of the Pacific command, and leading inspection trips back to familiar spots, such as Subic Bay, Singapore, Japan, Korea, and Hong Kong. He was promoted to captain in July 1977.

He returned to Washington in June 1978 as assistant to RADM Gerald J. (Jerry) Thompson, as director, Shipbuilding Contract Division at NAVSEA. Dan McKinnon later became director, Contract Administration and Claims Settlement Division at NAVSEA. He wanted to move away from the rigid bid-box routine for ship overhaul contracts, have multiship procurements, using cost-type contracts, and to figure out ways to implement a phased maintenance program.

In May 1980 he reported as commanding officer of NSD Subic Bay, which was the focus and locus of the major events in which the Navy was involved. The war in Afghanistan was brewing, the Iranian hostage crisis came to a conclusion, two carrier battle groups were in the Indian Ocean. Under CAPT McKinnon's leadership, NSD Subic won the Meritorious Unit Commendation, the Environmental Protection Award, and the National Defense Transportation Association Award.

McKinnon recalls: "I was convinced we were wasting massive amounts of money by flying everything by C-5 and C-141 out of Clark AFB and NAS Cubi Point to Missera and Diego Garcia. I was convinced that, if I could shuttle a ship of my own from my piers at NSD Subic, I could save millions of dollars and improve support to Indian Ocean battle groups." McKinnon got his ship.

CAPT (later RADM) James E. (Jim) Miller was assistant chief of staff for supply readiness, CTF-73, when CAPT McKinnon arrived at Subic.

The two worked closely together even though they had separate agenda and agreed that a Seventh Fleet logistics conference would be beneficial. Jim Miller convinced VADM (later ADM and CNO) Carl Trost to call a conference that he and McKinnon conducted. The result: a decision to support deployed battle groups in the Indian Ocean with floating petroleum storage ships rather than to construct storage facilities ashore. Chartered tankers were loaded at Bahrain and at Japanese and Philippine fuel deports and positioned in the Indian Ocean for up to 30 days.

Dan McKinnon developed a close friendship with Dick Gordon, mayor of the town of Olongapo, just outside the main gate of the American base. The two leaders worked together to set up a foundation that provided jobs for unemployed youth. McKinnon describes the people at Subic Bay as loyal, smart, and as capable as any he has seen anywhere, but he admits the country is "a political, ecological, economic tragedy."

CAPT McKinnon reported back to NAVSUP as director of Supply Corps Personnel (OP), and CAPT (later RADM) Ray Sareeram, who relieved CAPT Miller in December 1980, returned to NAVSUP as comptroller in June 1982. Dan McKinnon was selected to Flag rank in 1983 in the second class of the newly reactivated rank of commodore. He became assistant commander of NAVSUP for inventory and systems integrity, responsible for ADP acquisition and modernization programs. RADM Ted Walker took command of NAVSUP in March 1984, and selected COMO McKinnon as his vice commander.

Commodores throughout the Navy were uncomfortable with the title of their new rank despite its rich heritage. The resurrected rank was frequently confused with the rank of commander. The revived rank did not last long, and COMO McKinnon became a rear admiral with a stroke of the president's pen in 1984.

After three years as NAVSUP, RADM McKinnon left in September 1986, to go to the Defense Logistics Agency as deputy director for acquisition management, in charge of an annual $12 billion procurement budget. At DLA he was responsible for the Defense Contract Administration Service (DCAS), later renamed Defense Contract Management Command. He was convinced that a tour at DLA was career-enhancing for Supply Corps officers and maintained that "any activity is as career-enhancing as one wants to make it."

Dan McKinnon says that Ted Walker supported his position and committed to sending outstanding Supply Corps officers to DLA. He was awarded the Defense Distinguished Service Medal for his DLA contributions. RADM McKinnon had held the other two Flag billets in NAVSUP and his credentials made him a strong candidate to succeed Ted

Walker as commander of NAVSUP and chief of Supply Corps. He became the 36th chief in July 1988.

Dan McKinnon challenged the NAVSUP staff to consider radical changes in policy. The solution was to shift workload from Navy and DLA by changing requisition patterns in a manner that would not degrade support to the Fleet.

RADM McKinnon envisioned an enduring agenda aimed at building for the future, including improving relations with other systems commands, particularly NAVSEA. He created a new position of deputy commander for engineering and quality assurance, and brought in an experienced senior civilian to head the function. In March 1989, operating under a charter from the VCNO, he commissioned a group of Supply Corps officers to outline the business areas in which the Corps should be involved. One objective was to stem the loss of Supply Corps billets to other Navy communities. The resulting recommendations produced the *Supply Corps 2010* report, the forward of which includes, "Our mission will continue to include response, stewardship, and accountability in areas of strategic importance to our Navy and nation." RADM McKinnon also fostered the development of a matrix that would define and describe a vision of what a Supply Corps officer would be in the future. The generic matrix, called the "thirteen pillars," was applicable anywhere in the Navy, because it was built around basics people could apply to their work.

Potential problems for the Navy were created by closing of NSD Subic Bay, resulting from the pullout of U.S. forces from the Philippines, and concern over the future of the contracting office at Hong Kong when China takes over the British protectorate in 1997. McKinnon pushed hard to expand a small contracting center at Singapore into a major base. Today, Navy Regional Contracting Center (NRCC) Singapore has a transportation office; a fuel depot; aircraft, ship, and component overhaul; warehouses; hundreds of sets of quarters; and an officers' club. Before he retired, Dan McKinnon was working on a plan to set up a similar operation somewhere along the Persian Gulf littoral.

McKinnon had learned, while at DLA, the importance of working with the staff of the Office of the Secretary of Defense and put some of the best and brightest Supply Corps officers in that organization. The move proved fortuitous when the defense management review (DMR) process began to make major, significant changes in the logistics process.

Dan McKinnon was one of nine senior officers who helped write the mission statement of Navy operating forces. McKinnon believes that relationships between the systems commands and the Navy hierarchy improved when NAVMAT was disestablished. He was asked to draft the acquisition portion of SECNAV's goals.

RADM McKinnon was relieved by his former Western Pacific logistics compatriot, RADM Jim Miller on 14 June 1991. McKinnon received the Distinguished Service Medal for his outstanding performance as head of NAVSUP and chief of Supply Corps. The citation reads: "By employing comprehensive strategic and business planning methods, his command and the supply system performed brilliantly in its Fleet support mission, culminating in the exceptional Navy logistics success achieved during Operation Desert Storm." McKinnon had previously been awarded the Legion of Merit with gold star, the Meritorious Service Medal with two gold stars, and the Navy Achievement Medal with gold star.

In retirement, he continued to serve as chairman of the President's Committee for Purchase from the Blind and Other Severely Handicapped, to which President George Bush appointed him as a member in 1989. In August 1992 he was elected president and chief executive officer of NISH (formerly the National Institute for the Severely Handicapped), headquartered at Vienna, Virginia. He also had more time to engage in his favorite pastime of antiquing. Dan and Rae McKinnon reside at Annandale, Virginia.

Sources

Interview of RADM Daniel W. McKinnon, Jr. Arlington, Va., 15 November 1991.

Official Biography. Naval Supply Systems Command, September 1990.

"Retirements: RADM Daniel W. McKinnon, Jr." *Navy Supply Corps Newsletter*, September-October 1991.

Supply Corps 2010: The Summary Report. Naval Supply Systems Command, December 1989.

Supply Reserve Vision Study: Summary Report. Naval Supply Systems Command, November 1991.

Congress and Military Retail Sales Operations

During the 1980s, Congress had begun to examine military retail sales operations for possible economies. Capital and operating expenses for military commissaries have been historically derived from funds appropriated by Congress, while all other military retail activities were operated with funds generated by profits from sales. The Navy Resale Services and Support Office had responsibility for directing a $3.145 billion system of exchange, commissary, ship's store, and lodge activities throughout the world. The Navy was the only service to operate its co-located exchanges and commissaries with a single retail sales officer.

The first targets for action were the four commissary systems using appropriated funds, resulting in the formation of the Defense Commissary Agency (DECA) in 1989. In 1990 Congress launched yet another study, focusing on consolidating the exchanges operated by the military services. The study found no compelling reason to bring the exchanges under single management, and Congress took no action on consolidation. The Navy undertook a study of consolidation of its exchanges with morale, welfare, and recreation activities in 1989, as the Marine Corps had done earlier, but also took no action.

NSC Oakland and the Bay-Area Earthquake

A strong earthquake, measuring 7.1 on the Richter scale, shook the San Francisco Bay area on 17 October 1989. CDR Barron Bianco, NSC Oakland duty officer, immediately implemented the center's disaster preparedness plan and established a command center to screen and coordinate reports from all departments. His primary concerns were to determine whether there had been injuries, whether dangerous or threatening conditions existed, that all essential services were maintained, and that NAVSUP headquarters was kept apprised of the situation. Because the quake occurred just after 1700 hours and most of the work force had left for the day, he found there were no severe injuries, only cuts or abrasions from fallen glass. Water and gas breaks overwhelmed the NSC Fire Department, so those services into the base complex were shut off. Water seeping into circuit breakers caused small electrical fires, so all electrical power was also cut off.

CAPT Robert Young, NSC commanding officer, was on leave when the earthquake struck. He flew back to Oakland the following day, but suffered a heart attack en route. Despite airline personnel's attempts to revive him through cardiac pulmonary resuscitation, he died at a San Leandro hospital where he was taken directly from the airliner.

New Reserve Supply Roles

Dan McKinnon was another chief who believed in making maximum use of his Reserve assets. He and his Reserve Flag officers developed an efficient and effective method of marrying the Reserve units to their gaining commands. The plan gave him freedom to continue managing his Reserve assets in peace as he had during the Gulf War. McKinnon provided the details of the Supply Corps program to the chief of the Naval Reserve Force to use as a model for other Reserve programs. McKinnon chartered a Reserve version of the 2010 study, the *Supply Reserve Vision Study,* in July 1990. In November 1991 the report identified seven key functional areas, as well as specific operational and managerial elements, in which the Supply Corps Reserve was expected to operate.

McKinnon also was convinced that NAVSUP and the Supply Corps had the background, experience, and expertise to take charge of developing the Navy's business ADP systems. The visionary studies that he initiated in early 1988 paid off when NAVSUP gained greater responsibility for Navy business ADP systems worldwide.

In 1990, the Vice Admiral Robert F. Batchelder Award for exceptional personal contributions to supply readiness was awarded to a woman for the first time: LCDR Laurie Ann McKee, supply officer, *USS Willamette* (AO-180).

LORE OF THE CORPS

Lieutenant Commander Laurie Ann McKee, SC, USN

Supply Officer, *USS Willamette* (AO-180), 1988–90
Period of Service: 1978–

Laurie McKee joined the Navy because she wanted to make a difference. As a Supply Corps officer, she went on to achieve important milestones as the first female to serve in a ship deployed with a carrier battle group and the first female to be chosen to receive the Batchelder Award for excellence in supply readiness. She is a commander on active duty at the Industrial College of the Armed Forces.

Laurie Ann McKee was born at San Diego, California, in December 1952. Two second cousins achieved Flag rank in the Navy: RADMs Logan McKee and Andrew McKee. She entered Indiana University, Bloomington, in 1972, where she was a member of the Singing Hoosiers and the Varsity Singers and also performed with the IU Opera Theater. She used her talents as a singer, dancer, and actress to help finance her college education. She performed at Opreyland and other locations at Nashville, Tennessee, including a stint as one of the Fisherman's Singing Waiters. She also performed in Louisville, Kentucky. In addition to her music, McKee also worked as an undergraduate research assistant in chemistry at the university and as a substitute school teacher. She was graduated from IU with a B.A. degree in biological sciences in spring 1978.

Laurie McKee had a desire to contribute to an organization interested in the greater good and enlisted in the Naval Reserve. She entered Officer Candidate School in October 1978 and was graduated in February 1979 as a line ensign, U.S. Naval Reserve. ENS McKee reported to the Naval Communications Unit at Washington in February 1979 as security director and was assigned collateral duties as nonappropriated funds officer and assistant administrative officer. She was awarded the Navy Commendation Medal and augmented into the Regular Navy in 1980.

She transferred to the Supply Corps in August 1980, and reported to NSCS Athens in September. In May 1981 LTJG McKee went to the Naval Communications Area Master Station at Guam, where she was assistant supply officer with responsibility for food services, customer service, and BOQ-BEQ operations. In July 1982 she returned to NSCS Athens to attend the joint aviation supply material and maintenance (JASMMM) course, and then reported to the Naval Air Station North Island, San Diego, in September. She was director, Control Division, responsible for incoming parts, local cycle repairable assets, and expediting. She was promoted to lieutenant in March 1983.

LT McKee reported for her first sea duty in *USS Simon Lake* (AS-41) at King's Bay, Georgia, in March 1985. She was assigned as stores officer, ADP officer, and repair of other vessels (ROV) officer and was also responsible for overhaul habitability management when *Simon Lake* went into overhaul at Pascagoula, Mississippi. The young supply officer loved to sing in the shower aboard ship and was surprised one day when a romantic chorus reverberated from the other side of the bulkhead. She later discovered that she had been serenaded by the navigator, communications officer, main propulsion and damage control assistants, and two junior officers.

In March 1986 she became the first female and the first Supply Corps officer assigned to a SEAL unit when she reported, as supply officer, SEAL Delivery Team One, at Naval Amphibious Base, Coronado, California. LT McKee created a new department supporting the unique mission for SDV TM-1, which had responsibility for operation of all SEAL delivery vehicles (SDV)—small, free-flooding, battery-powered submersibles assigned to the U.S. Pacific Fleet. She was also exposed to new weapons systems and an unusual working environment. She traveled frequently, including making several trips with SEAL teams in transport planes. McKee also established a supply element of a SDV-TM detachment on Ford Island, Pearl Harbor. She was awarded a gold star in lieu of her second Navy Commendation Medal.

LT McKee reported as supply officer of *USS Willamette* (AO-180) in

June 1988 and became the first female Supply Corps officer of a forward-deployed Combat Logistics Force ship. As the only woman in the entire battle group, she performed her duties in such a manner that she believes few in the battle group were aware of her gender until much later when other women were assigned. "I had no idea how close we supply officers in the battle group would work to ensure our ships and aircraft were properly supported." She was awarded another gold star in lieu of a third Navy Commendation Medal.

McKee was promoted to lieutenant commander in May 1989 and received the Batchelder Award in 1990. The award recognized her exceptional competence in making the most significant personal contributions to the supply readiness of operating forces during 1989. LCDR McKee was ordered for duty at the Naval Postgraduate School at Monterey, California, in October 1990, and received her M.S. degree in management-acquisition in June 1992.

LCDR McKee reported to the Fleet and Industrial Supply Center San Diego, where she was deputy director of business development, planning officer, and director of small purchase, where she served with CAPT (later RADM) John T. Scudi. She says, that because of her proclivity for singing, she was "coerced" into singing in uniform at the 1993 Supply Corps Birthday Ball, held at San Diego on the same weekend as a major conference of active, Reserve, and retired Supply Corps Flag officers. Since that musical performance, she says she has routinely been known as "the girl who sang at the ball."

She reported as a student to the Industrial College of the Armed Forces as a selected commander in June 1994 and made her number in August. She uses her performing talents as an ICAF cheerleader for the ICAF Tigers in the National Defense University intramural athletic program. Laurie McKee lives at Arlington, Virginia.

Sources

Command History, SEAL Delivery Vehicle Team One, n.d.

Personal data on LCDR Laurie Ann McKee supplied by Industrial College of the Armed Forces, September 1994.

Telephone interviews of CDR Laurie Ann McKee, 9 and 23 October 1994.

"Women in the Supply Corps: A Success Story." *Navy Supply Corps Newsletter,* January–February 1991.

War in the Persian Gulf

RADM Dan McKinnon, Commander of NAVSUP, was on a WESTPAC

swing when word came late on 2 August 1990 that Iraq had invaded Kuwait. RADM Jim Miller, vice commander, immediately called VADM (later ADM) Stanley R. (Stan) Arthur, deputy CNO for logistics, for permission to insert two senior Supply Corps officers, experienced in forward operational logistics, into the theater.

CAPT Donald L. (Don) Holland and CDR David E. (Dave) Courter were on an airplane en route to Bahrain within 24 hours. When President George Bush announced the dispatch of U.S. forces to reinforce Saudi Arabia on 7 August, Operation Desert Shield was born. Holland and Courter were already in Bahrain when the first U.S. combat forces—a carrier battle group from the Indian Ocean and the Army's 82nd Airborne Division, to be airlifted from the United States—were ordered into the Persian Gulf.

RADM Miller's foresight paid off, and Holland and Courter immediately took charge of the Navy logistics situation. RADM R. A. K. (Ray) Taylor, Commander, U.S. Naval Forces, Middle East, who was also CENTCOM forward, had little Fleet supply experience and no senior supply officer. Taylor adopted RADM Miller as his de facto fleet supply officer. Thus, NAVSUP was a significant player in developing operational logistics in the Middle East from the beginning of the Persian Gulf War.

The Defense Logistics Agency sent CDR John S. Proctor, a Supply Corps officer on the DLA Procurement Management staff, to the Mideast in August 1990 to be the Commander, DLA (forward). He reported to GEN H. Norman Schwarzkopf's USCENTCOM staff and was attached to the U.S. Army's 22nd Support Command under LTGEN William G. (Gus) Pagonis. In December, General Pagonis selected CDR Proctor from among a group of in-theater logisticians to be the operations officer of the 22nd for Operation Desert Storm's air and ground offensive campaign. CDR Proctor returned to his duties at DLA Headquarters in May 1991.

SEAL Team Two, fresh from its successful work in Operation Just Cause in Panama, rushed 4 of its 8 operating platoons—64 men—to the Gulf. Other SEAL teams also sent platoons. LT David J. (Dave) Dits, Supply Officer, SEAL Team Two, and the rest of his team supply officers outfitted each platoon with full loads of gear. The supply officer remained at Little Creek to process requisitions from the deployed units. Dits says it was an interesting challenge, because SEAL Team Two members were experts in mountain and Arctic warfare. The adjustment to operating in a desert atmosphere required modified procedures for both supply support and training. Dits had to acquire different items from his usual allowance list, particularly clothing. He enjoyed having open purchase authority and calling on makers of top-of-the-line camping gear.

As plans were developed for increasing U.S. forces in the Mideast,

President George Bush launched an intensive and successful effort to convince friendly Western European and Mideastern nations to contribute assets to a coalition force.

Reserve Logistic Unit Priorities

RADM Jim Miller realized that it would be difficult to mobilize Reserve logistics units in a timely fashion, although the need was amply evident. He maintained that the logistics people were required on the ground either before, or at the same time, the operational forces arrived, but the operators had not bought that concept. Miller took the issue to the CNO, ADM Frank Kelso, and the two fleet commanders, who provided the proper priorities for Supply Corps Reserve units going into Desert Shield.

RADM Miller probably understood, better than anyone else in the Navy, what the Supply Corps Reserves brought to the theater, particularly in an expeditionary environment. He pointed out that they not only used their Navy augmenting skills, but they also added business experience through a wide variety of professions. According to Miller, "They didn't ask for things to happen; they made things happen." The can do attitude of Supply Corps Reservists in theater was demonstrated when 30 forklifts arrived at Bahrain to augment existing materials handling equipment. The Public Works Center estimated that it would take three weeks to put them into service. A Reserve storekeeper, second class, who had left a civilian job as service manager of a large automobile agency in Michigan, spoke up, "Give me two or three people and we'll get them going." Within 6 hours, all 30 forklifts were handling the huge influx of cargo. The Reserve team kept the forklifts operating throughout the hostilities.

Supply Corps Reservists voluntarily reported, many in a nonpay status, into CONUS supply centers, ICPs, NAVSUP, and other gaining commands, to augment their active duty counterparts in keeping up with the flow of material to the war zone. RADM Miller estimates that the Supply Corps Reserve provided between 30,000 and 40,000 man days of contributory support to the Gulf War effort.

LT (later LCDR) Patricia E. (Patty) Sakowski, a recalled Supply Corps Reservist from the Washington area, set up a MOPP gear pool at the Washington Navy Yard. She and her Reserve team provided chemical protective gear to all military and civilian technical representatives going into theater, and requests could be filled on short notice. LT Sakowski's team filled the orders and sent the protective gear throughout the country at the end of each day by overnight express. Without the gear, personnel on TDY were not permitted to depart for the Persian Gulf area. The operation was, in effect, a mini-supply center. RADM Miller terms Sakowski "the symbol of excellence" that the Supply Corps Reserves brought to bear in ODS.

When Iraq launched the invasion, the Kuwait air force lost all of its planes except for A-4s that escaped to safety in Saudi Arabia. The Kuwaitis had to leave spare parts behind as there was no time to pack them up when Iraqis poured into lightly defended Kuwait. NAVSUP put together a team with NAVAIR, ASO, and NAS Pensacola representatives that completely outfitted the Kuwaiti planes within 30 days. A support system for the planes was established in Saudi Arabia, from which the free Kuwait aircraft flew missions along with aircraft from America, Britain, France, Italy, Saudi Arabia, and other nations.

Strategists could not have selected a better place to go to war. Coalition forces assembled in Saudi Arabia, a country that had built the world's largest port facilities, more than a dozen modern airfields, and possessed a virtually unlimited supply of petroleum products. The ideal situation will probably never be repeated.

Logisticians held daily crisis action meetings in Saudi Arabia as the Desert Shield buildup continued. They were in regular communication with Bahrain and other locations around the Persian Gulf. By year-end, it was only a matter of time before the strong coalition forces, completing outfiting and training in Saudi Arabia, would be ready to launch the attack to liberate Kuwait.

The Role of Naval Reserve Units in the Gulf

Naval Reserve Supply Corps units activated for the Persian Gulf conflict in 1990 and 1991, notably cargo handling and logistics communications, compiled a record of outstanding performance. Naval Reserve Cargo Handling Battalion Four, headquartered at Charleston, South Carolina, with detachments in Columbia and in Charlotte and Wilmington, North Carolina, was one of the first mobilized. Under the command of CDR (later CAPT) Robert E. (Bob) Davis, NCHB-4 had conducted an arduous and successful prepositioning of Fleet Hospital Six at Sagami, Japan, in May 1989. The following year, in April 1990, the Reserve unit set a record for offload of the Army's 24th Division at Pearl Harbor during Operation Team Spirit.

When it became necessary to supplement the two active duty cargo handling battalions deployed to the Persian Gulf in the summer of 1990, NCHB-4, with 8 officers and 133 enlisted men and women, was the first of six Naval Reserve battalions activated. The call to mobilize for war came on the same day—7 September 1990—that President Bush declared a national emergency, just five months after the NCHB-4's Pearl Harbor evolution. Meanwhile, *USNS Antares* (T-AKR-294), a fast sealift support ship (FSSS) loaded with 5,200 long tons of the Army 24th Division's critically needed combat equipment, suffered a serious midocean engineering plant casualty. Within 80 hours of its callup, NCHB- 4 was at Naval Station, Rota, Spain, where it worked out an unusual, first-of-a-kind emergency ship-to-ship transfer of the 24th Division's 830 vehicles, 70 assault helicopters, and 40 containers from *Antares* to *USNS Altair* (T-AKR-291). Starting on 11 September and working around the clock, NCHB-4 completed unloading and reloading the division's equipment on 14 September. The use of Naval Reserve cargo handlers saved the government $976,000 in stevedoring labor charges. The quick response and safe and successful completion of the mission elicited a personal Bravo Zulu message from VADM Francis R. Donovan, Commander, Military Sealift Command. He noted, "This rapid response and first class performance reflect the total professionalism of your people and their commitments to excellence."

NCHB-4 was soon called upon again to make emergency ship-to-ship transfers of cargo among MSC ships. Between 3 and 7 October, the unit transferred 3,169 long tons of equipment and material of the Army First Air Cavalry Division from the disabled *USNS Cape Mendocino* (T-AKR-5064) to *USNS Cape Douglas* (T-AKR-5062). In this same period, NCHB-4 transferred a complete Army mobile field hospital, totaling 2,012 long tons, from the disabled crane ship *USNS Equality States* (T-ACS-8) to *Cape Douglas*. NCHB-4 completed this demanding three-ship evolution safely and damage-free with only half of its assigned personnel because of other theater commitments and at a savings of $902,000 in stevedoring labor charges. The masters of the three ships praised the unit highly for its extraordinary skill, efficiency, and professionalism.

NCHB-4 undertook another special assignment when it was decided that Fleet Hospital 15, pre-positioned at Bogan Bay, Norway, above the Arctic Circle, was needed in Saudi Arabia. Drawing Arctic gear from CONUS supplies in fewer than 48 hours, NCHB-4 redeployed personnel from multiple sites in the Mediterranean. The Reserve cargo handlers, operating in extreme cold weather and prolonged darkness, completed the loading safely and expeditiously.

During its six-month deployment, NCHB-4 aggressively conducted more than 50 shipboard and 1,1000 aircraft cargo onload-offloadings involving more than 45,000 long tons and operating under the Theater Support Concept of Operations. The tasks performed by the Reserve cargo handlers posed every conceivable challenge, from RO/RO to container handling to traditional break bulk cargo operations. Extensive sheathing and massive amounts of blocking and bracing, both highly intensive and time-consuming operations, were required during ammunition loading, in accordance with maritime regulations. Each operation was completed ahead of schedule and safely without a single incident of serious personal injury or damage to cargo. For its service from 8 September to 31 December 1990, NCHB-4 became the first Naval Reserve unit since World War II to receive the Navy Unit Commendation.

No Reserve Flag officers were recalled to active duty for ODS, but RADM Vance H. Fry, a Chattanooga attorney and businessman and Commander Naval Reserve Cargo Handling Force, had several tours of training duty. CAPT (later RADM) Robert C. (Bobby) Crates, another Chattanooga businessman and the Force chief of staff, was activated and served as the de facto commander. During this period, CAPT William C. (Bill) Ackermann, a recalled publishing executive from Champaign, Illinois, served as Crates's chief of staff. CAPT (FY 96 Flag selectee) Fred J. Schuber III, a New Orleans corporate executive and operations officer, Cargo Handling Staff, and CAPT Peter (Pete) Stiles, a Seattle businessman and planning officer, were also recalled. CAPT C. J. (Hobie) Woods, owner and operator of a LaFayette, California, recreational complex, also was called up and relieved CAPT Ackermann. During one of the periods when RADM Fry was on traing duty at Cheatham Annex, he sent a message to the men and women of NCHB-4. It read, in part, "When the order came to deploy a cargo handling battalion overseas, I did not resitate to call on the officers, men and women, of Navy Cargo Handling Battalion Four. I knew that our Charleston Battalion would perform splendidly. In short, you proved my trust well placed."

CDR Davis and unit members participated in an Naval Station Rota MWR trip to witness a running of the bulls in nearby Arcos de la Frontera, Spain, on Easter Sunday 1991. When a bull broke through a barrier and gored Davis, his wounds required evacuation to Germany where he spent about 20 days in a military hospital before rejoining his unit. Davis, who had qualified as a diving officer in submarines during his first tour out of NSCS Athens, demonstrated traits of flexibility and creativity early in his career as supply officer of *USS Sunfish* (SSN-649) during a Mediterranean deployment in 1974. ENS Davis was challenged when *Sunfish* was in port at La Maddalena, Sardinia, the gasket on her main sea-water pump had hardened, and the pump would not re-seat after repairs. Davis solved the problem by baking the gasket in the ship's oven until the gasket was sufficiently malleable to permit replacement of the pump.

He completed his command tour in June 1991, was awarded the Meritorious Service Medal, and returned to his civilian job with SCANA Corporation, an energy-based holding company at Charleston. Bob Davis joined the South Carolina Department of Education as senior executive assistant in 1992. He was promoted to captain in September 1992,and became director of logistics, Naval Reserve Construction Force Support Command, at Gulfport, Mississippi. He and his wife Sarah (Sally) live in Hopkins, South Carolina.

Logistics Message Traffic Problems

An enormous increase in message traffic at the start of Operation Desert Shield resulted in the imposition of an emergency communications priority system called "Minimize." This effectively eliminated all but the most urgent tactical message traffic originating in the Persian Gulf; only CASREP requisitions could move over military message channels. Navy and Marine Corps supply officers were effectively shut out from the use of electronic message channels to move priority, non-CASREP requisitions.

The burgeoning wave of communications and computer capability in the private sector provided the means to transmit digital information using standard, off-the-shelf hardware and software, but the traditional communications system was severely limited. New voice circuits were provided when VADM Jerry Tuttle, Director of Space and Electronic Warfare, approved the installation of the commercial International Maritime Satellite System (INMARSAT) satellite receivers in Navy ships in late 1990. The impending war in the Gulf provided the catalyst to find an alternative way to transmit vital digital logistics data between the Gulf and CONUS.

Operation Desert Shield became Operation Desert Storm on 17 January 1991, when American soldiers and Marines led their British, French, and other Coalition forces in a brilliant land flanking movement through and around Iraqi positions. The land assault had overwhelming air cover, while the threat posed by a strong U.S. Navy amphibious force offshore froze Iraqi forces in position along the coast. From the beginning, it was obvious that the preparations by the Coalition allies, especially in logistics, had paid off. It was also obvious that despite the ruminations of Iraqi dictator Saddam Hussein, his Revolutionary Guard forces were no match for the Coalition forces. When the first shot was fired, thousands of ill-equipped Iraqi soldiers eagerly surrendered. Land- and carrier-based planes continued to attack strategic targets throughout Iraq, while Coalition supplies continued to flow into Saudi Arabia. Huge mountains of material were stockpiled for the possibility of a long war.

The frustrated Saddam ordered more than 100 Kuwaiti oil wells set afire, but his desperation move did not slow the smoothly functioning Coalition fighting machine. Hostilities had lasted only 100 hours when the Iraqis sued for a cease fire, which was signed 26 February on Iraq territory. Kuwaiti troops reclaimed their country, which had been thoroughly trashed. The Coalition had achieved an unprecedented victory.

At the time, the Navy supply system was still having difficulty supporting the Fleet- and shore-based units because of the communications restrictions. Clearly, this was no way to conduct what was rapidly proving to be a logistics war 10,000 miles and 12 time zones removed from the East Coast of CONUS.

Supply Corps Reservists as Communicators

In mid-January, a concerned RADM Jim Miller, Commander of NAVSUP, tasked RADM James E. (Jim) Eckelberger, C.O., ASO, to develop plans to work around Minimize, especially as it applied to requisitions for aviation spare parts. Eckelberger called upon his Naval Reserve component, which had successfully implemented several information technology projects for ASO, to tackle the problem.

Among the officers and enlisted personnel in ASO New York 202 and a sister Reserve unit, ASO Philadelphia 203, were professionals in the fields of computers, programming, and information transfer. Many Reservists were on the cutting edge of information management for major firms. The Reserve units had established a solid record of presenting the Aviation Supply Office with solutions to internal management information problems. A Reserve team headed by CAPTs J. Herbert (Herb) Dahm and Robert E. (Bob) O'Donnell, C.O. and X.O., respectively, of the New York unit, willingly undertook the challenge to find a way to break the logistics communication logjam. They were ready to get on the job immediately but had to start out under training duty orders because the system could not generate orders promptly to recall them to active duty.

Dahm, a native of Tappan, New York, and a graduate of Clarkson University and Navy OCS, had a strong background in fiber optic communications. When the call came for help from ASO in January 1991, he immediately reported to Philadelphia under 17-day training orders in advance of anticipated orders recalling him and other members of the Reserve unit to active duty. Another 12 aviation storekeepers and data processing personnel of the New York Reserve unit and 8 more from the Philadelphia ASO Reserve unit also reported in advance of recall.

CAPT O'Donnell, a native of New York City and a graduate of Fordham University and OCS, with a strong background in marketing and finance, also was given 17-day training duty orders but not included in the initial recall group. The recall to active duty orders was delayed until the second week of February 1991. Meanwhile, other members of the team began reporting on training duty orders, including LCDR Mark Heilman, a programmer employed by IBM at Poughkeepsie, New York, who was to play a key role in the effort. Heilman began an intensive period of programming, supply requisitioning, and system planning that produced a plan to deploy the team to the Persian Gulf at the end of February.

Bureaucratic Roadblocks

The Naval Reserve recall system dictated that team members travel from Philadelphia back to New York for processing. LCDR Heilman waited in line for a day and a half at the Naval Reserve Center Brooklyn, for issuance of an active duty (green) ID card, which ASO could have issued had the recall system permitted.

CAPT Dahm remained back at ASO to push the procurement process for satellite transceivers, modems, and computers while other team members went to New York for the processing. Dahm encountered frustrations at several points along the way. When he called NAVELEX in California, tasked to procure the special satellite modems needed to put a system in place, he was told it would take 10 days to cut the required paperwork. Dahm reacted strongly, asking whether they had heard of the war, and the modems were at ASO three days later.

The Reserve team planned to collect digital in-theater information, initially MILSTRIP requisitions, on a computer, pass the data through a modem, and use the INMARSAT satellite voice link to carry the data back to ASO in Philadelphia. Because INMARSAT is a commercial system, it was not impeded by Minimize, which applied only to military communications circuits. The data would be processed at ASO and entered into the Navy supply system. The schedule called for the equipment to be shipped to Norfolk for loading aboard a MAC plane that would then pick up team members at Philadelphia at midnight on 28 February and fly CAPT Dahm and six carefully selected team members to Bahrain. CAPT O'Donnell, LCDR Heilman, and other team members continued to work long hours at ASO to complete the software necessary to receive transmissions from the Gulf.

The unusual ASO plan was difficult for many in the Navy to comprehend. CAPT Dahm flew to Norfolk on 27 February and spent a precious day at CINCLANTFLT in cutting through red tape and obtaining the necessary clearance to proceed with the mission. Hours before scheduled departure, part of the plan fell through when Dahm was advised that NAVSUP would approve and fund only a three-person installation team for Marine aviation logistics squadrons (MALS). RADM Eckelberger decided that ASO would fund the full mission. He and Dahm proceeded to obtain permission for the Reservists to enter the war zone. Eckelberger worked the issue with CINCPACFLT at Pearl Harbor, while Dahm advised AIRPAC of the situation.

The team at Philadelphia finally learned late on the 27th that AIRPAC approved the team's mission to make the first installation aboard *USS Midway* (CV-41). CINCPACFLT also gave approval to go to other key locations. The Reservists, Navy and Marine—COL Skip Lane, CDR Keith Flaherty, LT Lou Lesko, DP1 Mark Marziale, SGT Tom Ball, and Gil Young, a civilian in the ASO Data Center—already exhausted from two weeks of virtually nonstop work, boarded a jammed Military Airlift Command flight for the 23-hour journey. Military billeting was unavailable when the flight arrived, but the ASO Reservists were sent to the Bahrain Hilton Hotel. They hailed taxis and rode off to war in style.

While team members were Gulf-bound, CAPT O'Donnell, LCDRs Heilman and John Meacher, DPC Senan Shannon, and other members worked feverishly with CDR David R. (Dave) Bullock and his ASO Data Center staff to complete the system back end on schedule. The first installations on the maintenance aviation support ships *USNS Wright* (T-AVB-3) and *USNS Curtis* (T-AVB-4), located at Jubail, Saudi Arabia, failed because the in-theater Reservists could not raise the satellite. Reservists learned, while en route from the States, the location of the Atlantic East satellite had been changed, and it was no longer in a line-of-sight position relative to the Persian Gulf. It was necessary to switch to the Indian Ocean satellite, which meant that all computers for the project required significant reprogramming. Team members returned to the hotel and assembled on the large balcony of a member's room facing east. The team set up a satellite dish antenna on the balcony, successfully acquired the satellite, and began to reprogram their computers.

CAPT Dahm reports that the technical ingenuity of the team was not restricted to communications equipment and computers. He says that one enlightened member placed a plastic bag in the hotel bidet and then loaded it with ice and enough beer to keep the team going throughout the all-night reprogramming session.

The following day, a test transmission was received at Philadelphia on software that had just been completed by Heilman. "It was primitive, but it worked," Dahm says proudly. The next step was to contact

CDR (later CAPT) James D. (Jim) Reilly, Jr., *Midway* supply officer, via INMARSAT voice phone in the Persian Gulf. Reilly was enthusiastic about the team's plans and arranged for a COD flight to pick the members up at Bahrain the next day and fly them to the ship, which was fewer than 50 miles away.

RADMs Miller and Eckelberger were completely supportive of the project, but not everyone at NAVSUP appreciated the importance of the mission. A message arrived from NAVSUP, advising Dahm that under no circumstances was the team to go aboard any carrier. However, CAPT (later RADM) Edward R. (Bob) Chamberlin, AIRPAC supply officer, forwarded approval for the team to board *Midway*. Dahm advised his bureaucratic adversary that he had all the clearances, from ASO, from AIRPAC, and from CINCPACFLT, but she demanded, "Get me something in writing."

It was 0300 at Bahrain, 1900 at Philadelphia, and 1600 at San Diego. Chamberlin assured Dahm that he would confirm authority for the team to board *Midway,* but NAVSUP was already secured for the weekend with only duty personnel, unfamiliar with the issue, on board. Buoyed by AIRPAC's approval, Dahm determined not to let the opportunity slip away even though the shooting was over in the Gulf and *Midway* was racing for the Straits of Hormuz on her way back to her home port at Yokosuka. By the time the team finished its work, *Midway* was already halfway to Karachi, Pakistan, necessitating a four-hour COD flight back to Bahrain.

Dahm and his team returned to the States with solid evidence of the fundamental capability of the still unnamed system. Marine aviators had been using laptop computers to put requisitions on computer disks and then driving the disks more than 100 miles to Bahrain to use land lines back to the States. They responded enthusiastically to the new system. Now they had a real-time digital pathway to ships and stations around the world, built by the Supply Corps for the supply system and run by the Supply Corps. The Reserve "loggies" had fixed their own problem.

Navy payroll problems, particularly aboard ship, were fast becoming a morale problem. There was obviously a need for real- time transmission of Uniform Microcomputer Disbursing System (UMIDS) data back to the States. It became readily apparent that the new, streamlined communications system offered a solution to the payroll problems, and the ASO Reservists soon had UMIDS data on the air. It also became obvious that the system could carry digits for a word processor as well as digits from a requisition or a payroll system, so a message capability was also added to the system.

New System Becomes SALTS

The new system, finally was named in April 1991 when CDR Bullock constructed an acronym: SALTS (Streamlined Alternative Logistics Transmission System). CAPT Dahm later changed *Alternative* to *Automated* to emphasize that the system had become the standard means of doing business and to position SALTS as a new system, not merely an alternative to traditional Navy communications. SALTS had become quite efficient at collecting, compressing, and transmitting large quantities of data.

The new system achieved even more legitimacy when CAPT Dahm reported to VADM Tuttle that the system was removing millions of lines of message traffic from message boards throughout the Fleet. Herb Dahm says that VADM Tuttle responded with characteristic candor, "Great, the sooner you guys get your crap off my network, the happier I'll be." The communications community considered supply and administrative message traffic junk mail on their system but it could hardly complain when the Supply Corps found a solution to avoiding the communications logjam.

Between the end of the Gulf War to the middle of April 1991, Dahm tried to have recall orders issued to CAPT O'Donnell, who was serving on training duty at ASO without pay. However, the Navy was trying to return all Reservists to inactive status, and OP-41 was pressuring Dahm to tell when the team would be finished. Meanwhile, SALTS was growing from a battlefield patch to a sophisticated information transfer system. It had filled a vacuum, and additional uses seemed to spring from thin air. RADM John T. (Jack) Kavanaugh, then Atlantic Fleet supply officer, dubbed Dahm and O'Donnell "the Frick and Frack of SALTS."

SALTS and Cellular Technology

One of the first technical expansion moves was to incorporate the developing technology of cellular telephones into SALTS. Herb Dahm learned that Bell Atlantic Corporation had developed a portable cellular system, packed into a 30-foot cargo container, to provide disaster communications. The Bell Atlantic System could be airlifted in a C-130 cargo plane or a heavy-lift helicopter. Dahm wanted to provide a less expensive way than using commercial satellites and also to provide a SALTS pathway to communicate with the supply system for ships that did not yet have INMARSAT installed.

With the assistance of Communications Satellite Corporation (COM-

SAT), the U.S. operator of INMARSAT and Bell Atlantic, a SALTS sea van was lifted to the Naval Base at Charleston and loaded on the helicopter deck of *USS R. G. Bradley* (FFG-497). In July 1991 *Bradley* put to sea and successfully transmitted from 40 miles at sea, using SALTS and the cellular package.

Dahm believes the successful *Bradley* test was the first military application of cellular radio by any service or any nation. It led to the routine use of cellular radio by ships close to shore, and the installation of cellular base stations on aircraft carriers for communications while underway in a battle group.

The innovative Supply Corps Reservists next developed the SALTS Expeditionary Logistics Facility (SELF), a small portable cellular-satellite-landline system to provide an ashore logistics team with mobile and satellite data capability upon hitting the beach. SALTS had proved itself so successful in the final hours and days of Desert Storm that it was demanded throughout the Navy, afloat and ashore. The SALTS team proved the cellular concept above the Arctic Circle in Norway, at McMurdo Station in Antarctica, on the equator in Somalia.

CAPT O'Donnell relieved CAPT Dahm as commanding officer of Naval Reserve ASO Philadelphia 202 HQ in October 1991. Over the next two and a half years, SALTS was installed in every ship and shore station in the Navy and in every Marine Corps aviation unit. Even the Army, Air Force, and Coast Guard implemented SALTS in several key areas. SALTS was also implemented in the Kuwait air force to assist in managing procurement of parts for F-18 fighters that the Navy supplied through the Foreign Military Sales Program. Reserve members of the SALTS team circled the globe from the Arctic Circle to Antarctica, from the Persian Gulf to Panama, and from Somalia to Singapore, to bring assured communications to Navy forces.

SALTS was awarded the Department of Defense Gold Nugget Award for innovation in information systems and the Federal Leadership Award for excellence in information technology. CAPTs Dahm and O'Donnell both received the Legion of Merit; LCDR (later CDR) Heilman and LCDR Meacher received the Meritorious Service Medal; and CDR Flaherty the Navy Commendation Medal. Enlisted members of the SALTS team also received personal awards for extraordinary contributions to Navy logistics. RADM Jim Miller hailed them as "logistics heroes."

Gulf War Lessons Learned

In the spring of 1991, after the Gulf War ended, RADM Dan McKinnon called upon the principal logisticians to review the experience of Operation Desert Shield/Desert Storm. Intensive study of ODS logistics evolutions led to publication of a *Logistics Lessons Learned* report by NAVSUP. Principal among them was the absolute requirement for Navy logistics planning. During wartime operations, senior logistics experts must be placed in key positions in-theater, especially on operational, medical, and supply staffs. They can provide the experience to assess emergent requirements and obtain the necessary level of personnel, material, and technical support.

For the most part, the Navy did not experience the logistical difficulties encountered by the other services: significant transportation backlogs, limited sustainability, lack of self-sufficiency on initial deployment, and major wholesale supply system support delays. The Navy avoided these problems because the Fleet operates in war as it does in peace—only the tempo of operations varies. Successful employment of the three echelons of supply support (combat ship allowances, mobile logistics support ships and overseas bases, and the CONUS supply system) directly and dependably supported increased Fleet requirements.

The House Armed Services Committee issued its own report, emphasizing lessons learned from ODS. The report's seven findings, covering four pages, do not include the word *logistics*. One finding deems the Total Force Policy, requiring the integration of Reserve components in a major contingency, a success, but the analyses do not comment upon the major contributions of Naval Reserve supply units.

LTGEN Pagonis, the U.S. Army's chief logistician in ODS, points out that the most difficult phase of the Gulf War for the Army was the final one: redeployment. Almost immediately, the Army commenced a retrograde evolution, Operation Farewell. The huge amounts of ammunition and other material assembled in Saudi Arabia for a long war was no longer needed. Retrograde operations posed no major problems for naval forces.

2,440 Supply Reservists in ODS

NAVSUP (OP-02) records indicate that 2,440 men and women in Naval Reserve supply units were recalled to active duty for Operation Desert Shield/Storm. More than 90 percent of them were in overseas deployable units. The breakdown includes:

- 1,184 in expeditionary logistics and overseas support units—NCHBs, NAVMTOs, FFTUs, tank farms, etc. (37 percent of total onboard);
- 239 in other NAVSUP-sponsored units—NSCs, ICPs, etc. ($1^1/_2$ per-

cent of total onboard); and
- 17 in DLA units (1 percent of total onboard).

The Victory Parade in Washington

On 6 June 1991 victorious American veterans of Operation Desert Shield/Storm marched from the U.S. Capitol down Washington's broad Pennsylvania Avenue in an enormous ODS victory parade past a reviewing stand at the White House. A huge crowd gathered along the route to salute those who had participated in the spectacular victory in the Persian Gulf.

RADM Vance H. Fry, Commander Naval Reserve Cargo Handling Force, who had served more time on active duty training orders during ODS than any other Reserve Flag officer, was asked by the chief of Naval Reserve to lead the Naval Reserve contingent. Members of Naval Reserve supply units mobilized for the Gulf War proudly marched in the parade, which was reviewed by President Bush, JCS Chairman GEN Colin Powell, and GEN H. Norman Schwarzkopf, Commander of Coalition Forces in the Gulf.

Victory and Inevitability

When a latent move toward democracy in Eastern Europe gained momentum during the 1980s, it exploded in November 1989 into the fall of communist governments throughout the region. Raising of the Iron Curtain and elimination of communist governments across Eastern Europe foreshadowed disintegration of the Warsaw Pact, the decades-long foe of NATO. The stunning, quick victory scored by American and Coalition forces in Operation Desert Storm gave Americans a new respect for their Armed Forces. But the ink was barely dry on victory headlines when Congress and the media once again began to clamor to tear down the military. The sudden and unexpected political and military victories led to the antimilitary clique's question, "Who is the enemy?" Throughout the free world, strategists and logisticians had to determine the impact of the suddenly changed world situation and pondered how best to prepare for a wide variety of possible new scenarios, including terrorism. Supporters of "Peace through Strength" urged caution in drawing down the U.S. military establishment, citing uncertainties over objectives of Third World dictators and potential terrorists. In the euphoria that followed victory, the pleas for moderation in downsizing went unheeded.

Within three months of the end of the Gulf War, RADM Dan McKinnon retired and turned over leadership of NAVSUP to his vice commander, RADM Jim Miller. McKinnon was confident that the major initiatives of his tour would remain intact.

LORE OF THE CORPS

Rear Admiral James Edward Miller, SC, USN

Commander, Naval Supply Systems Command, and
Chief of Supply Corps, 1991–93
Period of Service: 1956–93

Rear Admiral Jim Miller became commander of NAVSUP and the 37th chief of Supply Corps with strong credentials from having served in major logistics positions with both the Atlantic and Pacific Fleets, an ICP, and an NSC. He is the second chief to have been commissioned in the Supply Corps from Officer Candidate School.

He was born in San Diego, California, in September 1934, and was graduated from high school in North Hollywood and from the University of Redlands, Redlands, California, in June 1956, with a degree in business administration. He enlisted in the Naval Reserve in August 1956 and was selected for OCS at Newport, Rhode Island.

In December 1956 he was commissioned an ensign in the Supply Corps, U.S. Naval Reserve, and reported to NSCS at the end of the month and in July 1957. ENS Miller went to sea as supply officer of *USS Kidd* (DD-661), which he joined at Pearl Harbor. *Kidd* played a vital role in defending the islands of Quemoy and Matsu a few miles off the coast of China from a possible invasion by the People's Republic of China. When *Kidd* was replenished at sea by *USS Castor* (AKS-1), and requirements were transmitted by flashing lights. ENS Miller ordered "a modest amount" of chicken, but the signalman added an extra zero. For the next month, Miller remembers, the crew had chicken à la king, broiled chicken, fried chicken, chicken on a shingle, chicken "coming out of our ears." Jim Miller was promoted to LTJG in January 1958.

He reported as disbursing officer, Naval Air Station, North Island, San Diego in 1960. The Disbursing Office at North Island handled some 10,000 pay accounts and dealers' bills amounting to hundreds of millions of dollars. CAPT (later RADM) J. P. (Pat) Foley, Jr., supply officer at North Island, played an important part in young Miller's life by introducing him to Anna Brancato from Sicily. Their romance later blossomed into marriage.

In December 1960 Miller was promoted to lieutenant and in January

1961 went back to sea as stock control officer in *USS Delta* (AR-9), a converted former Matson Line pineapple-canning ship. Miller says *Delta* was a good repair ship but had poor watertight integrity and was bent in the middle. Crew members referred to her as the "Swayback Maru." On Christmas Day 1961, LT Miller augmented into the Regular Navy but remained aboard *Delta* for another year and a half. He was next ordered to the Hunter's Point Naval Shipyard at San Francisco, where he worked as industrial material support superintendent for CAPT Walter W. (Walt) Tolson and CDR (later CAPT) Jackson L. (Jack) Schultz.

One tale the Millers are fond of telling about their Hunter's Point duty involves a dinner they attended with the shipyard C.O., the Supply Department bosses, and other department heads. During a lull in the conversation, someone asked Anna Miller what her husband did. When she replied in her pronounced Italian accent, "Oh, my husband runs the whorehouses," there was silence around the table. Jim Miller quickly intervened, "Dear, that's warehouses, the warehouses."

Miller was promoted to lieutenant commander in October 1965 and in July 1966 was ordered to the Naval Postgraduate School at Monterey, California, for duty under instruction. He was graduated with a master of science in management with a specialty in personnel administration.

In July 1967 LCDR Miller reported to the Naval Advisory Group Detachment Korea, at Chinhae, a small town on the southern tip of Korea, which was the major base of the Republic of Korea Navy. Miller was the Fleet and center supply advisor to the commanding officer of the Korean Navy Supply Center. It was an intense period, with North Korean agent infiltration and threats against the U.S. advisors' compound. On one occasion, LCDR Miller could not reconcile fuel levels funded under the Military Assistance Program with steaming hours reported by the Korean navy. Investigation uncovered a large theft ring, so LCDR Miller brought in only enough fuel to satisfy steaming requirements. When the Korean fuel tanks went empty, Korean navy leadership stepped in and solved the theft problem. Miller was awarded the Navy Commendation Medal for his Korean tour.

In October 1969 he became director, Planning and Administrative Division, Navy Subsistence Office at Washington. He was promoted to commander in September 1970 and was ordered as supply officer of *USS Mars* (AFS-1), deployed to WESTPAC off Vietnam. He reported aboard at Hong Kong in June 1972. *Mars*'s Fleet support role involved shuttling between Subic Bay, Kaohsiung, and Yankee Station. The ship did spend some time in the harbor at Danang, where she was a target of some unnerving but inaccurate shelling. Miller recalls that although spare parts were the most important commodity *Mars* delivered to ships at sea, underway replenishment did not go well if she failed to supply fresh lettuce, fresh tomatoes, and ice cream as well.

After a six-month deployment, *Mars* returned to San Francisco for an anticipated long rest, but officers and men learned that their home port was being changed to Sasebo, Japan. CDR Miller had to oversee a complete load adjustment, offload the ship, clean the holds, and reload in only three months. At the same time, the crew had to prepare to transport dependents, pets, household goods, and private vehicles across the Pacific. Ship's company constructed a kennel aft on the main deck. *Mars* then returned to North Vietnamese waters, where she began operating in support of mine clearing and later was involved in early deployments to the Indian Ocean. Upon completion of his *Mars* tour, CDR Miller was awarded the Meritorious Service Medal.

In August 1974 CDR Miller went back to Washington for a tour at NAVSUP as head, Fleet/Interservice Liaison and Procedures Branch at a time when NAVSUP was dissatisfied with both GSA and DLA support. CDR Miller visited all GSA regions and warehouses. A defining moment in the job came when he was explaining the importance of sending out CASREPs by air instead of surface parcel post. A GSA manager asked why taxpayers should pay the higher airmail rates when "all the ships were in San Francisco and New York." Miller was shocked that a senior GSA official did not comprehend Fleet post office operations. GSA personnel were amazed at the explanation of how mail is distributed to ships.

CDR Miller went to the Industrial College of the Armed Forces in August 1976 and headed the ICAF steel industry study team that went to Italy and Spain to visit major industries. He graduated with distinction in June 1977. His next duty in June 1977 was as executive officer to CAPT (later RADM) Richard E. (Dick) Curtis, NSC Charleston. He was promoted to captain in July 1978. CAPT Miller was awarded a second Meritorious Service Medal for the NSC tour.

In May 1979 CAPT Miller reported as assistant chief of staff, Naval Surface Group, WESTPAC, and CTF-73. Familiarity with the area from his earlier service in *Mars* in waters around Korea and Japan facilitated his reacclimation to the Western Pacific, where the U.S. Navy deployed task groups to the Indian Ocean in response to the Iranian hostage crisis. When the Navy decided to expand use of Diego Garcia, Miller made several trips to the isolated midocean atoll to develop air channels. Diego Garcia had no piers, so a reverse underway replenisment was developed, using helicopters to deliver air-lifted material to CLF ships anchored in the harbor.

CAPT Miller was concerned that the CLFs were always running behind the flow of the battle groups, requiring 13 days to replenish the ships in the Indian Ocean. He accompanied RADM (later ADM) Ace Lyons, CTF-73 Commander, on a trip to Guam. During the trip, they determined that AEs and AFSs should be based at Guam. Within a year their proposal was executed.

In January 1981 CAPT Miller was relieved by CAPT (later RADM) Ray Sareeram at CTF-73 and went to Philadelphia as commander, Subsistence Field Activities, Defense Personnel Support Center. DPSC was responsible for buying all the food for the Department of Defense, including meals ready-to-eat (MREs), the replacement for C-rations. He left DPSC in April 1983 with the Legion of Merit.

CAPT Miller reported to SPCC Mechanicsburg as executive officer under CAPT (later RADM) Bob Abele. Miller recalls that he and Abele had a great deal of difficulty in dealing with all the money that SPCC was receiving and being told to spend. Although SPCC did some overbuying at the time, Jim Miller believes the Fleet was well served. Shortly before his record went before a Flag selection board for the first time, he had a severe illness and was not selected. Even though he recovered, he believed that chances for Flag selection were slim the second time around, so he prepared for retirement. He sought assignment to a location in southern New Jersey, where he and Anna built a home.

He was assigned as director, Northeast Region, Naval Audit Service, at Camden, New Jersey, in October 1984 but almost immediately was told to report to Washington for a special SECNAV project. In Washington, he lived in a motel. Several months later, he had just returned from a trip to San Diego and Norfolk when he received a telephone call from RADM Ted Walker, who gave him the good news that he had been selected as a commodore.

While waiting out the approval process for the Flag list, CAPT Miller was assigned as staff director, Assistant Secretary of Defense for Spares Program Management, again living as a geographical bachelor. That was the time of the infamous P-3 toilet seat, which Miller maintains was not really a toilet seat, but rather the cover for an entire toilet assembly. Despite widespread press and congressional criticism of the price the Navy paid for the cover, Jim Miller stresses that commercial airlines have never paid less for the similar item. He says the Department of Defense lost a reported $50 billion in funding authority over the perception of overpriced spares. That was Miller's first real exposure to Washington press and politics.

Upon promotion to commodore, he reported as director, Supply Operations and Readiness and Fleet supply officer, U.S. Atlantic Fleet in September 1985. ADM Frank Kelso, CINCLANTFLT, assigned him to work out the logistics strategy to support the forward deployment of battle groups in the Atlantic Fleet operating area. Miller spent about two years on the project, a good part of that time in Norway and Great Britain.

Midway through Miller's tour, Kelso sponsored the largest logistics-oriented war games ever held at the Naval War College, and Miller was the major game designer. ADM Kelso sat through every minute of the games, which had about 200 participants, including 20 line Flag officers. Miller briefed the players on ammunition inventories and true production rates, which showed the Navy running out of sonobuoys. Rather than to charge the logisticians to produce more, ADM Kelso gave the antisubmarine warfare command two weeks to change their tactics to reflect available inventory. As a result, the Navy pre-positioned sonobuoys and ammunition in Norway to speed response. Jim Miller feels that his greatest contribution at Atlantic Fleet was in developing operational logistics plans for expeditionary scenarios. Many were discussed at Newport and were valuable when Operation Desert Shield was launched in 1990. His LANTFLT and War College experiences led Miller to implement a professional reading program for Supply Corps officers.

Miller was promoted to rear admiral, upper half, in September 1988 and awarded another Legion of Merit for his service at Atlantic Fleet. In August 1989 he relieved RADM Bob Abele as vice commander of NAVSUP. RADM Miller arrived at Washington just as the defense management review process (DMR) was getting underway. Everything that NAVSUP and the Supply Corps were doing came under intense review. NAVSUP Commander RADM Dan McKinnon and his new vice commander were deeply immersed in reviews of consolidating supply centers, supply depots, ICPs, and ADP functions. Miller says, "It was a very arrogant process."

RADM Miller headed the Navy team that reviewed the potential consolidation of the military service ICPs. After six months of intense negotiation and debate, the idea was dropped. NAVSUP did agree to further consumable item transfers, Miller recalls, "because it was the proper thing to do." Based on information then available, he does not think the decision to break apart the supply centers and move the warehouse functions to DLA was valid. He admits that DLA can do the job and has put more money into maintenance than the Navy, but he is concerned that it broke apart an integrated process at the waterfront and probably has not served DOD well. "While we have to accept these consolidations, the manner in which they have been executed is unconscionable. In most cases, they executed the consolidation before they had a viable organization in place to manage them."

Jim Miller believes that the extreme agenda of the comptroller of the Department of Defense was thrust down the throats of the services without regard to the views of functional experts. Occasionally, NAVSUP was permitted to debate the issues, but in general there was no true discussion.

As pressed as NAVSUP was over the DMR process, nothing could match the immediate shock of the Iraqi invasion of Kuwait in August 1990. Early on, RADM Miller went to Saudi Arabia and walked the pipeline there for a firsthand understanding of logistics problems and opportunities. He took RADM J. R. (Ron) Denney, a Reservist from the Philadelphia area, to emphasize the important role of the Supply Corps Reserve to support of ODS.

Several months before Iraq invaded Kuwait, an article by Jim Miller, "Logistics and Maritime Strategy," laid out the basic principles by which NAVSUP was to pursue logistics support for the Gulf War. He began, "Some view the maritime strategy solely in the context of global war; regardless, many of the same principles apply to smaller, less intensive conflicts. This is particularly true when it comes to logistics since the Navy's periodic and fast-paced involvement in containing terrorism and Third World conflicts also calls for flexible and responsive logistics support."

The Gulf War demonstrated to Navy officials that the active duty Navy and mobilized Reservists could work together well and could assure that the supply pipeline was sound and effective. By thoroughly understanding how the supply systems functioned, the Supply Corps team found that both the Army and Air Force were seriously abusing the priority system. The Air Force was rating 96 percent of its requisitions Inventory Priority Group No. 1, the Army 70 percent. As a result of Navy success in leveling the playing field, three to four million pounds of Army and Air Force cargo were diverted to sealift, freeing up air channels for critical cargo for all services, including the Navy. During his tour at NAVSUP, RADM Miller and the other four systems commanders were brought into full partnership with the Navy's leadership team by CNO Frank Kelso. The systems commanders participated in the annual Commander's Conference and the Total Quality Leadership agenda. "It has made a real difference in the ability of NAVSUP to focus fast to changes that are coming in terms of policy," Miller says.

RADM Miller relieved RADM McKinnon as commander of NAVSUP and chief of Supply Corps in May 1991 and quickly returned to the Persian Gulf, this time with RADM Lyle R. Hall, a Reservist from Seattle. They found that all Supply Reservists had been returned to their local Reserve centers. Miller emphasized to Pentagon planners that training Supply Corps Reservists by traditional classroom teaching was not as effective as NAVSUP's plans for training them in a real-world atmosphere. Miller wanted a robust, continuous, on-scene presence by Supply Corps Reservists so they would have firsthand knowledge of the capabilities and shortfalls of the theater. Within 5 months, 170 Reserve Supply billets were identified in-theater, and Reservists were assigned to them for 2 weeks of annual active duty. When the chief went back to the Gulf in 1993, he found the Reservists on annual active duty at every location he visited.

In January 1992 Miller published the *United States Navy Supply System Strategic Plan,* which outlined the mission, vision, guiding principles, and business strategies NAVSUP used to set a course through the period of downsizing and uncertainty. He urged all Supply Corps officers and NAVSUP employees to refer to the plan in carrying out individual roles "in the performance of our mission and the attainment of our vision."

Congress continued to take a sharp knife to the defense budget. The goal of a 600-ship Navy and much of the infrastructure in place to support it were lost. It was obvious to Jim Miller that major reductions in excess capacity and stocks throughout the NAVSUP claimancy were required. A plan to reduce the cost of spare parts and reduce inventories by $5 billion was developed. Under RADM Miller's leadership, NAVSUP developed the fleet and industrial supply center (FISC) concept, which dramatically increased regional supply-procurement responsibilities of the supply centers. This was designed to save of millions of dollars through total asset visibility and other initiatives.

Three naval supply centers were recommended for closure because of plans to close home ports with which they were associated. RADM Miller stepped forward with recommendations of his own. He believed that NAVSUP should not be running two bases for the inventory control points when Mechanicsburg had the physical capacity to accommodate both SPCC and ASO. He did not believe that the Navy should be paying $40 a square foot for leased space in the Crystal City office complex when there was capacity for NAVSUP on government-owned property in south central Pennsylvania. In 1993 the Navy recommended consolidation of SPCC, ASO, and NAVSUP at Mechanicsburg, and the move was scheduled for 1995. The plan to move ASO brought on a chorus of pained indignation from the Pennsylvania congressional delegation, already reeling from an earlier decision to close the Philadelphia Naval Shipyard. In response, the Base Realignment and Closure Commission (BRAC) excluded ASO from the proposed 1995 move.

Following the loss of Navy commissaries to consolidation, Miller supported and executed a proposal by the Commander Navy Exchange Command (NEC), RADM Harvey Don Weatherson, to relocate NEC, formerly the Navy Retail Sales and Service Office (NRSSO), from New York to the Norfolk area. Miller says the move saved $10 million, which effectively was returned to sailors' pockets. He maintained officer flow points during downsizing and led the Corps through turbulent times, including the first three selective early retirement (SER) actions.

RADM Miller also executed a Supply Corps sexual harassment prevention program following the debacle at a Tailhook Association convention, when some attendees were accused of sexual harassment. Every convention registrant was required to prove that he or she was innocent of the broad-sweeping charges. Selection board results were held up, selectees were removed from promotion lists, and reputations were ruined. Supply Corps officers, who had no connection with Tailhook, were tarred with the same broad brush. Although none was found to have been involved in any of the alleged incidents, many suffered from the tarnished Navy reputation. Miller furthered equal opportunities in the Corps when he assigned the first female commanders as supply officers of major noncombatant ships—tenders, supply ships, and repair ships.

RADM Miller was relieved by RADM Robert M. (Bob) Moore on 14 May 1993. He was awarded the Distinguished Service Medal for exceptionally meritorious service as both vice commander and commander of NAVSUP. The citation reads, in part, "Through his dynamic leadership, Rear Admiral Miller caused dramatic, worldwide improvements in logistics and inventory policy. Recognized as one of the Navy's foremost logisticians, he was selected to be the principal architect for the Middle East theater and contributed greatly to unprecedented supply support for *Operations Desert Shield* and *Desert Storm."*

Jim Miller retired in June 1993 and became president and CEO of the Navy Memorial Foundation at Washington. He and Anna live at Annandale, Virginia.

Sources

Interview of RADM James E. Miller. Arlington, Va., 3 May 1993.

"Looking Back, Looking Forward." *Navy Supply Corps Newsletter,* May–June 1993.

Miller, RADM James E. "Logistics and the Maritime Strategy." *United States Naval Institute Proceedings,* June 1990.

Official Biography. Naval Supply Systems Command, June 1991.

Official Transcript of Naval Service. Bureau of naval Personnel, August 1992.

Operation Desert Shield/Desert Storm: Logistics Lessons Learned. Naval Supply Systems Command, April 1992.

United States Navy Supply System Strategic Plan. January 1992.

SALTS in Somalia

The Naval Reserve Supply Corps SALTS team, which had made major contributions in the Persian Gulf and elsewhere, was called upon again in December 1992 to support Operation Restore Hope, the humanitarian relief effort in Somalia. Two weeks before Christmas, CAPTs Herb Dahm and Bob O'Donnell, LCDR Mark Heilman, SK1 Charles Fleming, DP1 Marty Pratt, and DK2 Julio Aponte flew from Mombasa, Kenya, into Mogadishu on a Royal Air Force C-130 Hercules cargo plane. According to CAPT O'Donnell, they arrived in a "dust storm of planes, helicopters, jeeps, armored personnel carriers, U.S. Marines, and Pakistani army security police."

Undeterred by the apparent mayhem around them, the Reservists hitched rides from the airport to the American embassy, where they intended to set up headquarters. Somalis mobbed the gates of the embassy, which had already been pillaged, but the shell had been secured by Marines. The SALTS team staked out office space, set up cots with mosquito netting, and subsisted on C-rations. Despite these primitive conditions, they had established the most complete telecommunications infrastructure in the history of the sad and beleaguered country by sunset the following day. The system O'Donnell's team set up consisted of a PABX telephone switch box, which they screwed onto the wall; a portable INMARSAT satellite transceiver which they stuck out what was once a window; set up an antenna on the roof pointed in the direction of the Indian Ocean satellite, and a three-channel cellular telephone. "We set the system up on a makeshift table consisting of shipping cases and some lumber we acquired along the way," he recalls. "We ran a cable up to the roof where we set up two cellular antenna capable of covering a radius of approximately six miles, which included the Embassy, the airport, the seaport, the Ambassador's residence, and the U.N. compound."

CAPT O'Donnell remembers that word of the presence of the SALTS team in the embassy compound spread quickly. Soon, Marine LTGEN Robert B. Johnston, Commander, Joint Task Force, Somalia; Ambassador Robert Oakley; and senior military staff personnel were equipped with preconfigured cellular telephones. They then had the capability to access the SALTS team's communications hub, through which much of the intra-theater executive communications began to flow, as well as the U.S. Army telephone system.

The Naval Reserve Supply Corps SALTS team stayed in Somalia

through Christmas, subsisting on Spam sandwiches made with shelf-stable bread baked 15 years earlier to supplement their cold C-rations. Travel outside the embassy compound always required flak jackets and helmets and was made under armed guard. CAPT O'Donnell was on a tour of outlying logistics sites with the commander of Canadian forces in theater when the party came under sniper fire. Until the area was secured, they joined a skirmish line of U.S. Marines who were flushing out the snipers, and then they continued on to the next logistics site. The team was relieved just before year-end by a new SALTS team of DP1 Mark Mariale and the first active duty Supply Corps officer on a SALTS team, LCDR John F. De George. The new team remained at Mogadishu for another two weeks until the situation stabilized and they could turn over the system to Marine Corps personnel remaining behind.

The Defense Logistics Agency sent CDR John Proctor, who had served as the agency's representative in the Persian Gulf during ODS, overseas again in December 1992. This time, Proctor went to Somalia to represent the agency to the commander of the United Nations-chartered unified task force of Operation Restore Hope. Proctor returned to DLA headquarters in January 1993.

The First Female C.O. of NAVSUP Field Activity

During the early 1990s, NAVSUP continued to assign Supply Corps officers, regardless of race or gender, to positions of importance. CAPT Rosemary Nelson Dawson, the first female Supply Corps officer assigned to sea duty in 1972, was designated commanding officer, Navy Regional Contracting Center Washington, in July 1992, the first woman to command a NAVSUP field activity.

LORE OF THE CORPS

Captain Rosemary Elaine Nelson Dawson, SC, USN

Commanding Officer, Navy Regional Contracting Center, 1992–94
Period of Service: 1972–94

Rosemary Dawson has the distinction of having been the first female officer to be assigned to three milestone tours for women in the Supply Corps. She was the first woman assigned as a member of ship's company, the first female instructor at NSCS, and the first woman to command a NAVSUP field activity.

Born Rosemary Elaine Nelson in March 1948 at Walla Walla, Washington, she was graduated from Fort Wright College, Spokane, Washington, with a B.S. degree in mathematics and a teaching certificate, but decided she would rather travel than teach. She signed up for Officer Candidate School in June 1971 and was graduated in February 1972 with a commission as ensign, Supply Corps, U.S. Naval Reserve. ENS Nelson reported to NSCS at Athens, Georgia, where she completed the Basic Qualification Course in September 1972, about the time that women (other than nurses) were being assigned to ships' companies for the first time. Nelson received orders as disbursing officer and assistant to the supply officer of the hospital ship *USS Sanctuary* (AH-17), which was undergoing major reconfiguration at Mare Island Naval Shipyard and redesignation as a dependent support ship.

She reported in October, along with several dozen other women, all enlisted personnel. Nelson was the only woman officer in the ship until a line LTJG arrived a few months later and nurses returned aboard about a year later. When *Sanctuary* put to sea on her first coed shakedown cruise after overhaul at Mare Island, Nelson reports that women were in practically every department. She was also assigned additional duty as mess caterer. As the first woman Supply Corps officer of a seagoing Navy vessel, ENS Nelson was aware of the historic significance of the assignment but in true Navy tradition treated it as a normal tour of duty for which she had been trained. To her, it was only "an exciting new job."

Shortly after *Sanctuary* returned from her post-yard shakedown cruise, Rosemary Nelson was interviewed by the *Oak Leaf,* published by the Navy Supply Corps Association. She was, she said, enthusiastic about "getting to use what I learned at Athens." The original plan was to anchor the reconfigured *Sanctuary* off Piraeus, Greece, to support U.S. personnel stationed in that country through onboard medical, administrative, commissary, and exchange facilities. In the event that U.S. forces, with no permanent facilities ashore, would be required to depart Greece suddenly, support activities could just weigh anchor and sail away. The Greek government turned down the idea because it felt the hospital ship's presence could imply planned treatment of casualties from impending hostile U.S. action. An alternate plan was to position *Sanctuary* with a similar mission off La Maddalena, Sardinia, but the Italian government also rejected the idea, so *Sanctuary* cruised in both the Pacific and Atlantic, making good will port calls in South America. With her primary mission having evaporated for political reasons, *Sanctuary* was sent to the Philadelphia Naval Shipyard for decommissioning. LTJG Nelson was aboard for the entire period between *Sanctuary*'s recommissioning in 1972 and her decommissioning in 1975.

Nelson had been promoted to lieutenant, junior grade, in February

1974 and reported back to Athens in April 1975, breaching another all-male tradition as the first female instructor on the NSCS staff. She was promoted to lieutenant in March 1976 and augmented into the Regular Navy while at NSCS. In June 1977, LT Nelson received orders to the Naval Surface Weapons Center (NWSC), White Oak, Maryland, as naval acquisition contracting officer and Navy intern for acquisition and contracting. Two years later, she was ordered to the Naval Postgraduate School, Monterrey, California, and received an M.S. degree in procurement in July 1980.

The next stop for Nelson was the Naval Air Systems Command in September 1980 as contracting officer for the High-Speed Anti-Radiation Missile (HARM) Program. She was promoted to lieutenant commander the month following arrival at her Washington duty. At NAVAIR, LCDR Nelson took the HARM missile through its development and saw it deployed with the Fleet. It was also there that she met her future husband, Paul Dawson, also a NAVAIR contracting officer. They were married in September 1983, just as her NAVAIR tour was coming to an end.

As LCDR Rosemary Dawson, she remained in Washington and moved over to the Naval Material Command for a 21-month tour as contract officer. In June 1985 she was ordered to nearby Fort Belvoir, Virginia, as course director, Program Management Course, Defense Systems Management College. In the DSMC billet she was in charge of quality and content of the joint services' major Weapons Systems Program Management Course, required for all program managers responsible for multi-billion-dollar weapons systems. She coordinated instruction time for the nine functional academic areas. While in the billet, Dawson was promoted to commander in June 1986. CDR Dawson implemented "Just-in-Time" training for an ongoing case study that resulted in greater learning retention. She also instituted instructor training in styles that resulted in developing lessons that would reach all learning styles.

CDR Dawson reported to her fifth consecutive Washington-area duty in August 1989 in a new billet as chief of the Contracting Office, Naval Medical Logistics Command. She was charged with establishing the office, which started with 4 people with only small purchase authority and grew to 25 professionals with unlimited contracting authority. Dawson's command established seven walk-in clinics throughout the United States, with annual sales volume increasing from $25 million to more than $100 million. The command adopted an acquisition strategy for nationwide drug testing kits, which reduced costs of supplies by approximately 40 percent. Contract awards grew during CDR Dawson's three years in command from $3 million to $120 million. She was awarded the Defense Meritorious Service Medal.

She achieved another first in July 1992 when she became the first female commanding officer of a NAVSUP field activity as she took command of the Navy Regional Contracting Center Washington, and was promoted to captain in August. In her new billet, CAPT Dawson established customer-oriented goals and objectives and directed a staff of 130 contract professionals.

Under her command, the Contracting Center increased contract awards by 20 percent—from about $320 to $450 million, including information management services, telecommunications, and engineering technical services. The command expanded its customer base by offering nontraditional contracting services and seeking nontraditional customers. Productivity increased 33 percent during CAPT Dawson's tenure, personnel turnover was reduced by 50 percent, and contracting processes were updated.

CAPT Dawson retired as C.O., NRCC in September 1994. She and her husband Paul, now a contracting consultant, and their two young children live at Middletown, Maryland, near Frederick. In retirement, Rosemary Dawson plans to travel and do some consulting in the field of contracting.

Sources

"History Made at Navy School." *Athens Banner-Herald* [Athens, Ga.], 10 August 1992.

Personal data supplied by CAPT Rosemary Nelson Dawson, October 1994.

"Rosemary Nelson—Ensign at Sea." *Oak Leaf,* Winter 1973; reprinted in the *Navy Supply Corps Newsletter,* April 1973.

An Uncertain Peace

With the end of the cold war, the Soviet Union dissolved, and communism eliminated as the governing philosophy of Eastern Europe, the United States was the sole remaining superpower. However, political realities put severe limitations on how that power could be used. Americans were ready for the peace promised since the end of World War II in 1945. Powerful voices were raised in Congress to make the U.S. defense establishment the centerpiece of a perceived "peace dividend" for the benefit of social programs. A careful and considered downsizing of the military was already underway by the Department of Defense, but the process was accelerated by new congressional action on the defense budget.

By the start of Operation Desert Shield, the Navy had achieved the cherished goal of a 600-ship force—in the Fleet or under contract. As soon as hostilities ceased in the Persian Gulf, ship contracts were either canceled or stretched out. With a smaller Fleet fast becoming a reality, the Navy began downsizing the supporting infrastructure. Which units to deactivate and which bases to close quickly became contentious political issues. Members of Congress would not leave those decision to DOD, but neither would they make the decisions themselves.

Creation of the Base Realignment and Closure Commission (BRAC) in 1990, a supposedly totally independent group, was designed to remove politics from the process by receiving DOD recommendations, reviewing them, and making the final determination. Congress and the president were required by law either to accept the BRAC list as presented, or to reject it in total. Neither the executive nor the legislative branch was empowered to make any changes to the list.

The Navy, and particularly the supply system, was hit hard. Bases at which major stock points were co-located, were scheduled for closing, reflecting the reduced needs of a smaller fleet. The decision to close NSC Pensacola and partially disestablish NSC Charleston took place, but total relocation of the headquarters of the Naval Supply Systems Command to Mechanicsburg was delayed.

Sources

Sources for material used in this chapter and not cited earlier include:

Love, Robert W., Jr. *History of the U.S. Navy,* Vol. 2: *1942–1991.* Harrisburg, Pa.: Stackpole Books, 1992.

Miller, Nathan. *The U.S. Navy: An Illustrated History.* Annapolis: Naval Institute Press, and New York: American Heritage Press, 1977.

Navy Supply Corps Newsletter, February 1970.

Additional sources for material:

Defense for a New Era: Lessons of the Persian Gulf War. Committee on Armed Services, U.S. House of Representatives. Washington, D.C: Government Printing Office, 1992.

Pagonis, LTGEN William G. *Moving Mountains: Lessons in Leadership and Logistics from the Gulf War.* Cambridge: Harvard University Business School Press, 1992.

CHAPTER FOURTEEN

The Challenge of the Future

1993–

Events at the start of the decade of the 1990s had clearly left the United States as the world's only superpower. However, political realities put severe limitations on how that power could be used. As soon as hostilities in the Persian Gulf ceased, ship contracts and long-term acquisition programs were canceled or stretched out. The Department of Defense initiated a careful and considered downsizing of the military, but Congress legislated even deeper cuts in the defense budget to fund social programs. The battle cry in Congress became, "Now that the Soviet threat has disappeared, who is the enemy?"

With a smaller Fleet fast becoming a reality, the Navy began to downsize the supporting infrastructure. Deciding which units to deactivate and which bases to close quickly became contentious political issues. Congress would not leave those decisions to the Defense Department, but neither was it willing to make them itself. In 1990 Congress created the Base Realignment and Closure Commission (BRAC), an independent body, to review recommendations of the services and determine which bases were to be closed or realigned. Congress and the president were required by law either to accept the BRAC list as is, or to reject it completely. Neither the executive nor the legislative branch could make changes.

When the first list of closures and realignments was approved in 1991, President George Bush promptly signed it, and Congress took no action to reject it. Political protests arose from Philadelphia to California. Suits were filed by local, state, and national politicians who felt their respective areas had been wronged but, for the most part, the decisions stuck.

The Navy, particularly the supply system, was hit hard, with bases closing where major stock points were co-located, a reflection of the needs of a smaller Fleet. A decision to close NSC Charleston took effect, but relocating the headquarters of the Naval Supply Systems Command and the Defense Logistics Agency to Mechanicsburg in FY 1995 was delayed. BRAC funds to accomplish the NAVSUP/DLA moves were diverted to recovery efforts associated with three major civil disasters—a hurricane in Florida, an earthquake in California, and floods along the Mississippi River. The moves of NAVSUP and DLA were rescheduled for FY 1996.

Navy Expeditionary Logistics Support Force

The Persian Gulf War proved dramatically that a responsive Navy logistics presence was crucial to the success of major operations. The Navy had successfully deployed USN and Reserve cargo-handling battalions (CHBs), naval overseas air cargo terminal units (NOACTs), and freight terminal units (FTUs) during the Gulf War. Highly efficient, successful Naval Reserve Cargo Handling Force training, organization, and equipage provided the model for the organization and training of other supply and transportation advanced base functional components (AFBCs).

The Supply Corps Reserve Vision Study brought forth a new Navy logistics organization, the Navy Expeditionary Logistics Support Force (ELSF), in response to this need. Designed to meet logistical requirements of future contingencies, ELSF was commissioned in April 1993. It was established as the Navy's primary supply and transportation combat service support ashore, capable of rapid deployment anywhere in the world. ELSF is a key component of the Navy's doctrine of "From the Sea," which is based on a multipolar strategy focused on regional conflicts and littoral warfare.

ELSF was built upon the existing AFBC organization and a foundation of 53 Naval Reserve units of 9 different types. ELSF provides a wide range of ready supply and transportation support critical in any contingency—combat, humanitarian, and peacetime support missions. The support includes offloading of maritime prepositioned ships (MPS), operation of forward air heads, and support to advanced and forward logistics sites. The combination of specialized skills and capabilities provide joint theater commanders with modular choices to move and sustain naval forces. Joint theater commanders have great flexibility in calling on ELSF for the right types and numbers of specialized units needed for each mission.

ELSF units are either designated in specific operating plans (OPLANs) based upon anticipated contingencies, or they can be recalled, as needed, to respond to emergent crises. Units will work at forward logistics sites in-theater for a Navy component commander or the logistics task force commander. Early deployment will be critical to offload and sustain forces at air and sea ports of debarkation. They will establish a transportation and supply network with SALTS capability to provide communication links with existing logistics and transportation networks. In addition to CHBs, NOACTs, and FTUs, the Expeditionary Logistics Support Force includes:

- supply support battalions (SSBs);
- tank farm units (TKFMs);
- mobile mail centers (MMCs);
- fleet mail center augmentation teams (FMCATs); and
- contracting team units (CTUs).

RADM Vance Fry, Commander ELSF, is a Ready Reservist veteran of the ODS logistics support. His staff is comprised of active duty (TAR) and selected Reserve officers and enlisted personnel, headed by TAR CAPT Robert B. (Bob) Miller. The ELSF staff is based at the Cheatham Annex, FISC Norfolk, Williamsburg, Virginia, and is available around-the-clock, sevens day a week.

The 38th Chief of Supply Corps

In May 1993 RADM Robert M. (Bob) Moore relieved RADM Jim Miller to become commander, Naval Supply Systems Command, and the 38th chief of the Supply Corps.

LORE OF THE CORPS

Rear Admiral Robert Marion Moore, SC, USN

Commander, Naval Supply Systems Command, and
Chief of Supply Corps, 1993–
Period of Service: 1961–

Bob Moore put aside a journalism career to enter naval service, left the Navy briefly, and soon returned to go on and command FMSO and NISMC. He was also the logistics expert in the Navy Nuclear Power Program and became the 38th chief of Supply Corps.

Robert M. Moore was born at San Antonio, Texas, in July 1939, the son of a petroleum geologist. He attended the University of Texas, Austin, where he majored in journalism, and worked during the summers for the *Corpus Christi Times*. He enrolled in the contract NROTC program and chose the supply option on the recommendation of a friend. He was graduated and commissioned an ensign, U.S. Naval Reserve, in June 1961.

After four months at NSCS Athens, ENS Moore reported to the staff, Commander, Destroyer Force, U.S. Atlantic Fleet, in October 1961. At DESLANT, he was exposed to such creative supply management concepts as intensive management of the 10 percent of the line items that were "movers." That concept and DESLANT's ideas on OPTAR recordkeeping are routine in the Navy today. Two Supply Corps lieutenants on the DESLANT staff—Stephen (Steve) Lazarus and Allen J. (Al) Lenz, both of whom retired as captains, took Moore along on supply inspections, providing him with a solid grounding in destroyer supply operations. Moore was subsequently assigned as supply officer of a World War II destroyer, *USS Hyman* (DD-732), in December 1961.

Hyman had just received an unsatisfactory annual supply inspection shortly before ENS Moore arrived. In addition to his inspection woes, he had only a month to prepare for an upcoming Mediterranean deployment. At the time, destroyers had only one supply officer to run all four divisions—disbursing, stores, food service, and ship's store. Moore says that he probably never worked harder in his life. During his 18 months in *Hyman,* she also made a deployment to the Caribbean and was underway about 60 percent of the time. He was promoted to LTJG in December 1962 and subsequently received a grade of outstanding on his next supply inspection.

LTJGs Moore and Jerry Shapiro, an NSCS classmate and supply officer of *USS Beatty* (DD-756), both transferred to the DESLANT staff in April 1963. At the time, DESLANT was concerned over the readiness of 13 Reserve training destroyers and destroyer escorts that had been mobilized following erection of the Berlin Wall. DESLANT dispatched the two Supply Corps officers to conduct annual inspections on the Reserve ships, homeported from Maine to New Orleans, to determine their supply readiness. Supplied with a storekeeper, a typewriter, and a station wagon, Moore and Shapiro drove more than 2,200 miles to conduct the inspections all along the eastern seaboard. They even uncovered a kickback scheme in *USS Robert F. Keller* (DE-419) at the Washington Gun Factory.

Bob Moore returned to civilian life to resume a journalistic career in the summer of 1963. His summer work on the *Corpus Christi Times* during college had attracted the attention of the Associated Press bureau chief, who had promised him a job when he completed his Navy obligation. Moore was assigned as the junior reporter in the Louisville, Kentucky, AP bureau, working the midnight shift. The assassination of President John F. Kennedy in November 1963, coupled with good memories of his naval service and dissatisfaction with his budding journalistic career, led him to apply for return to active duty. The Navy was expanding at the time, his request was approved, and LTJG Moore reported to NSCS Athens as a disbursing instructor in January 1964.

Within six months of his arrival at Athens, LTJG Moore was invited to interview with ADM Hyman Rickover for the Naval Nuclear Propulsion Program. He knew little about the program, but was aware of the mercurial personality of the "father of the nuclear Navy." Moore describes his interview with Rickover: "The interview process was just terrible. I ended up having three interviews with Admiral Rickover. He didn't like me the first two times. He finally accepted me for the program, but I didn't know whether I had succeeded or failed at that point because the process was pretty unpleasant."

LTJG Moore later found out that his journalism major was a problem for Rickover, not for technical reasons, but because the admiral felt the public affairs community had not served him well when the nuclear submarine *Thresher* was lost tragically. Rickover had asked him, during a contentious interview session, "just what he knew about anything that entitled him to give out public information."

Moore's stay at Athens was cut short when Rickover selected him for the program, and he reported to Washington in September 1964. For at least six months afterward, LTJG Moore says that he thought he had made the worst decision of his life. He had little authority and worked in spartan offices equipped with surplus furniture. His duty involved contracting for reactor cores for nuclear-powered ships, and he reported to LT (later RADM) Brady M. Cole.

At that time, standard tours in Naval Reactors were five years, and the plan was that Moore, who was promoted to lieutenant in March 1965, would eventually relieve Cole. However, in February 1966 LT Moore was ordered to Schenectady, New York, as contracting officer at General Electric Company, the Navy's prime contractor for reactor plant components. The office was small in terms of personnel, but LT Moore's authority was far-reaching because he was responsible for all the prime contractor's engineering and procurement actions.

Moore remained in the Schenectady job for three years and was in regular contact with Rickover, with whom he met at least monthly. He recalls that he had far more responsibility as a junior lieutenant as the nuclear Navy expanded than he could have imagined in the civilian world. He also credits this tour with providing him a significant education in American business. Naval Reactors duty would also provide the same perspective and insight to 15 of LT Moore's fellow Supply Corps officers who reached Flag rank.

Moore was promoted to lieutenant commander in July 1969 and was selected to attend Harvard University the following month. In the summer of 1970, while attending graduate school, he worked for Ernst and Ernst, a public accounting firm in his hometown of San Antonio. He received an M.B.A. degree from Harvard in May 1971. LCDR Moore's prior extended duty assignments with Naval Reactors had not required him to deal with OP on the subject of detailing, but it now became necessary. CDR (later RADM) Dan McKinnon, head detailer, told him that he needed to come to Washington for a tour at NAVSUP. McKinnon later advised him that he would instead be going to Mechanicsburg to relieve his old boss Brady Cole as director, Nuclear Equipment Support Division at the Ships Parts Control Center. He reported to SPCC in May 1971 to renew his association with Naval Reactors.

At SPCC, LCDR Moore was the junior department head and effectively had his own little inventory control point within the Navy's largest ICP. One of Moore's first projects was to assure that all nuclear-powered ships, both new construction and in overhaul, went to sea with 100 percent of her reactor plant repair parts on board. During his tour at SPCC, he served with seven other officers who achieved Flag rank in the Supply Corps: RADMs Jack Scott, Skip McMorries, Bill Oller, Joe Flores, Jerry Thompson, Woody Rixey, and Phil McGillivary.

Moore had been at SPCC for a year when ADM Rickover called him to Washington for another tour in Naval Reactors, this time as supply officer. He declined, telling Rickover that a year was insufficient time to complete programs he had started. A week later, he received an invitation to interview as aide to the assistant secretary of the Navy for financial management. It was an interview opportunity he could not turn down, but nature intervened when Hurricane Agnes isolated Mechanicsburg for three days. The assistant secretary lost interest. After Moore's second year at SPCC, ADM Rickover contacted him again, and this time would not accept no for an answer. Moore knew that another tour in Naval Reactors would not be considered career enhancing, but he nevertheless rejoined Rickover in June 1973 and was promoted to commander in July 1975.

By 1978 CDR Moore had compiled an outstanding record over a period of 17 years, either in or supporting the Naval Reactors Program. Deciding that early 1979 was time for a mainstream Supply Corps tour, Bob Moore asked RADM Gene Grinstead for duty in *USS Holland* (AS-

32), the submarine tender based at Submarine Refit Site One, Holy Loch, Scotland. *Holland* was reputed to be the toughest submarine-tender job in the Fleet. Grinstead agreed to his request, and CDR Moore reported in May as supply officer of *Holland,* supporting Fleet ballistic missile (Polaris) boats of Commander Submarine Squadron 14.

He made captain in July 1981 and was ordered to the staff of the Chief of Naval Operations for Submarine Warfare (OP-02) as the assistant for programming and budgeting, normally a position filled by up-and-coming O-6 line aviators and surface warfare officers. With his M.B.A. and hands-on experiences in financial, program, and contracting management, CAPT Moore was uniquely qualified for the job.

The OP-02 assignment gave CAPT Moore exposure to senior line officers other than submariners and broadened his perspective. However, Bob Moore had few opportunities to know many of them because he was again short-toured after two years in OP-02. His next assignment kept him in Washington as vice commander, Navy Accounting and Finance Center, working for RADM Ted Walker. Less than a year after CAPT Moore went to work at NAFC, Ted Walker became commander of NAVSUP and chief of the Supply Corps. The new chief assigned Moore to command the Fleet Material Support Office, a highly sought O-6 assignment.

CAPT Moore reported to Mechanicsburg as C.O. of FMSO in July 1985. Again, he had an outstanding tour in a tough job and was selected for Flag in his second year. RADM Stu Platt had resigned as competition advocate general (CAG) in late 1986, and by statute, Platt's successor could only be a Flag officer. Bob Moore was frocked and reported as CAG in May 1987.

After a year in the Secretariat, RADM Moore reported to NAVSUP as assistant commander for inventory and systems integrity in July 1988 in relief of RADM James B. (Jim) Whittaker. Bob Moore's three years (1988-91) in the SUP-OOX job was a period of major change for NAVSUP and the Navy logistics community. In his final year, RADM Moore was the point man in managing the defense management review (DMR) process, including the assumption by DLA of many of NAVSUP's physical distribution functions.

He was promoted to rear admiral, upper half, in June 1990 and in August was assigned the task of creating a new job on the SECNAV staff—commander, Naval Information Systems Management Center. This was an effort to turn a former line Flag billet into a more effective structure for oversight, planning, and policy related to the Navy's multi-billion-dollar information resources budget. After two years at NISMC, RADM Moore was selected as the next commander of NAVSUP, and he relieved Miller in May 1993 to become the 38th chief of Supply Corps.

Within a few weeks of the change-of-command, Bob Moore identified the 10 preeminent issues that he believed the Supply Corps and the supply system must address. Two additional issues were subsequently added. The 12 issues are:

- Fleet and industrial supply centers;
- NAVSUP restructuring;
- hazardous material control and management;
- Supply Corps officer roles;
- afloat automation;
- quality of life;
- Navy field contracting system;
- inventory management/reduction;
- Reserve forces;
- third-tier data processing;
- Navy total asset visibility; and
- DBOF (Defense Business Operations Fund) surcharge.

A year after assuming command of NAVSUP, RADM Moore indicated satisfaction with the progress made but emphasized the Corps' need to continue to focus on these issues. He implemented the fleet and industrial supply center concept. Involving far more that just renaming naval supply centers and supply depots, the FISC concept recognizes that even without physical distribution functions, the Supply Corps should be still deeply involved in other vital Fleet support functions: inventory management, purchasing, hazardous materials, and ship chandlering. The concept has evolved into a partnering arrangement in which FISC manages all support functions at such other Navy installations as air stations, air depots, and shipyards.

In September 1994 NAVSUP and the Naval Ordnance Center concluded an agreement in which the FISCs will manage supply departments at all naval weapons stations. The FISC concept has placed an enormous burden on NAVSUP to prove that it can provide the support services at a lower cost than the other activities could on their own. RADM Moore welcomes the challenge and is confident it will be a success. He points to the successful marriage of supply and maintenance afloat in both the submarine and aviation communities and expects that the Supply Corps will be able to prove its viability ashore as well.

As of 30 September 1994, RADM Moore remained as enthusiastic as the day he took over. He says that he has found the quality of people in the Corps to be exceptional, and they are held in high regard by senior line officers. He further believes that the reputation of Supply Corps officers makes almost anything possible. He notes that some of the turbulence of the years preceding his administration has been muted. "What I believe we've done is to take the realities of some new initiatives and a new order and convert those into some really aggressive programs to make sure that the Navy has the kind of logistics support that it needs for the era beyond the cold war." RADM Moore is a highly decorated officer, with the Legion of Merit (five awards) and the Meritorious Service Medal (two awards). He is also qualified in submarines.

Bob Moore enjoys sailing, and he and his Flag lieutenant, LT John J. Carty, won a sailing competition in the summer of 1994. He also likes to work around his home in Vienna, Virginia.

Sources

"DISA Migration a Central Issue." *Government Computer News,* April 26, 1993.

Interview of RADM Robert M. Moore. Crystal City, Arlington, Va., 15 April 1994.

Official Biography. Naval Supply Systems Command, May 1993.

"RADM Robert M. Moore Becomes 38th Chief of Supply Corps." *Navy Supply Corps Newsletter,* July–August 1993.

Transcript of Naval Service. Bureau of Naval Personnel, August 1994.

"The Year in Review and a Look toward the Future." *Navy Supply Corps Newsletter,* July–August 1994.

The Directorship of DLA

The Defense Logistics Agency, originally the Defense Supply Agency until renamed in 1977, was 30 years old when VADM Edward M. Straw became its 11th director on 6 July 1992. He is the third Supply Corps Flag officer to occupy the billet, following in the footsteps of VADMs Joe Lyle and Gene Grinstead.

LORE OF THE CORPS

Vice Admiral Edward McCown Straw, SC, USN

Director, Defense Logistics Agency, 1992–
Period of Service: 1961–

VADM Ed Straw is the sole three-star Supply Corps officer currently serving on active duty and only the 13th to have served actively as a three-star admiral in the Corps' 200-year history. He is widely experienced in financial management, inventory and acquisition management, material distribution, and joint operational logistics. His career assignments include two aircraft carriers, Naval Material Command, Office of the Chief of Naval Operations, and Naval Supply Systems Command before becoming the 11th director of the Defense Logistics Agency.

Edward M. Straw was born at Harrisburg, Pennsylvania, in March 1939, the son of a former mayor of nearby Marysville. He starred in high school football and basketball. His student athlete credentials attracted the attention of both the Military and Naval academies. He went to Annapolis in July 1957, intending to become a naval aviator. His 20/200 vision precluded that goal, however, as well as a career in the line. He was graduated from the Naval Academy in July 1961, commissioned an ensign in the Supply Corps, and reported to NSCS Athens along with 39 Annapolis classmates.

Following what Straw calls his lackluster record at NSCS, he was assigned to the *USS Forrestal* (CVN-59). From *Forrestal,* he was ordered to duty at Lakehurst, New Jersey, in October 1963, as supply officer, Navy Helicopter Support Squadron Four. The Lakehurst tour was LTJG Straw's first experience with inventory management and maintenance support. He soon reached a decision to make the Navy a career. He was promoted to lieutenant in March 1965 and was ordered to the Naval Supply Depot Subic Bay, the Philippines, where CAPT (later RADM) Roland (Rollo) Rieve was commanding officer. Straw says Rieve gave him his first real understanding of the importance of the supply officer to those who fight wars, an education he credits with making the Supply Corps his long-term career choice. He remembers the exec, CDR (later RADM) Edward E. (Ren) Renfro, as a tough administrator who taught him what it meant to meet deadlines. Straw spent the first year at Subic as material officer, ran the warehouses, and was inventory control officer the second year. NSD Subic Bay won a presidential citation during his tour.

In 1967 LT Straw received orders to NAVSUP as a junior aide, but CAPT Rieve wanted him to go to the Aviation Supply Office to work for CAPT (later VADM) Eugene A. (Gene) Grinstead and "learn something about aviation supply from one of my best students." He reported to ASO in August and was assigned as head, Weapons Section and Stock Control Division. Straw was inventory manager for the F-4 Phantom program and was promoted to lieutenant commander in July 1969. CAPT Grinstead gave him responsibility for fixing a serious support problem for the AWG-10 radar, and Straw, under Grinstead's "hands on" management, turned it around within a year. LCDR Straw's ASO tour was supposed to be two and a half years, but he underwent an operation on a disk in his back and spent an additional year at ASO. During the final year, he managed the A-7 weapons program and worked on introduction of the A-7E.

Ed Straw left ASO in April 1971 to attend George Washington University, from which he was graduated with an M.B.A. in May 1972. He next reported to the Naval Air Station, Corpus Christi, Texas, as comptroller, his first strictly financial experience. Straw's career focus changed from aviation support to hard-core financial management in June 1974, when CAPT (later RADM) Andy Giordano, the first NAVSUP comptroller, called him to Washington to manage the stock fund budget. LCDR Straw was hesitant and told Giordano that he did not know much about the stock fund, but he was assured that "neither does anyone else up here." He reported to the new job in July 1974 and says that Giordano pounded money management into his head. "Andy was way ahead of his time. He understood and brought home to me the value of revolving funds and unit costing when your goal is to receive improved logistics support at lower cost." Straw says that Giordano taught him humility, corporate finance, and the Golden Rule: "He who has the most gold makes the rules."

In 1976 CDR Straw was awarded his second Navy Commendation Medal for obtaining budget approval for the Navy's first authorized retail allowances at operating bases and naval air. The commendation called the Subic Bay super AVCAL program "the turn around of aviation support to WESTPAC carriers."

He reported to the Naval Material Command as assistant to the DCNM for Spare Parts Programs and was promoted to commander in September 1976. In July 1977 CDR Straw headed back to NAVSUP as executive assistant to RADM Gene Grinstead, commander of NAVSUP and chief of Supply Corps. The following year, he globe-trotted with the chief, including three trips to Iran on missions to fix Iran's F-14 readiness crisis when the shah complained to President Carter. "Grinstead had the uncanny ability to smell out the causes of support problems," Straw says. On the first trip, they found 100 of 120 Iranian F-14s not mission capable. In two hours, Grinstead determined that 95 of the fighters were down for brakes because the Iranians had no organic repair capability. The chief found 200 sets of non-RFI brakes piled in a dark warehouse corner. According to Straw, Grinstead made one call to Grumman Corporation on Long Island and had a repair contract in place. Within 24 hours, Grumman started repair on the 200 brake sets airlifted from Iran. In three days, 95 F-14s were back in the air, and Grinstead and his executive assistant were "eating sheep eyes and caviar with the shah."

Straw also recalls another incident when he and Grinstead evaded a terrorist kidnapping plot in the mountains above Tehran but will not divulge details because of the covert nature of the operation.

In July 1978 CDR Straw relieved CDR (later RADM) Rod Squibb as supply officer, *USS Eisenhower* (CVN-69), for her first overseas deployment. Ed Straw points with pride to his "role in earning *Ike*'s three consecutive battle efficiency E's and helping her through the highly acclaimed 300-day deployment to the Indian Ocean during the Iranian hostage crisis."

Following his tour in *Eisenhower,* Ed Straw was selected early for captain, and in June 1980 he relieved CAPT (later RADM) Jim Eckelberger as comptroller, Aviation Supply Office. Later, he was ASO operations officer. CAPT Straw believes that the Eckelberger-Fenick-Hickman-Waldron-Chamberlin team then at ASO was among the best ICP teams ever assembled. Its successes include the celebrated introduction of the F-18 and the stock funding of aviation depot level repairables. "I believe most will agree that the stock funding initiative was most responsible for the dramatic improvements in aviation support in the late 1980s." Ed Straw admits difficulty in reflecting upon his ASO tour since the death of his Academy classmate and friend, CAPT Robert W. (Bob) Fenick, in 1993.

In the summer of 1984, CAPT Straw thought he was headed back to NAVSUP to be RADM Giordano's comptroller, but Giordano retired and RADM Ted Walker took command. Because he and Walker did not know each other, Straw sent Walker a memo, asking if he wanted to bring in his own chief financial officer. He remembers Walker's telephone response, "Straw, get your butt down here." On arrival at Walker's office, CAPT Straw remembers that Walker looked huge in the doorway. The new chief crumpled up Straw's memo and said, "Straw, you may be resigning, but it'll be my call when it happens. Get back to work and keep me out of trouble."

Four years later, Ed Straw was still Walker's comptroller. "He must have liked me. I couldn't escape," Straw recounts. "I believe history will show him to be one of the truly great chiefs of our Corps." Straw believes Walker's aggressive handling of the *Kitty Hawk*-Iranian F-14 spare parts smuggling ring in 1985 may have saved the Supply Corps from being disestablished. According to Straw, "There were some top Navy management decision options that were looking for scapegoats instead of solutions. Ted provided those solutions as we introduced strict inventory accountability requirements that became equal to readiness requirements in our measure of ship supply officers. Because of Ted, the Corps survived to become better for it."

Of all that was accomplished during his four years as NAVSUP's comptroller, Ed Straw is proudest of his introduction of unit costing to the command's management strategy. It resulted in field commanders becoming fully knowledgeable of cost-driven, value-added processes, and overall productivity. In two years, according to Straw, NAVSUP field commanders budgeted and negotiated or mandated goals at lower annual costs. NAVSUP was way ahead of the pack when the strict DBOF unit cost policy was directed by DOD in 1988.

In the fall of 1988, Straw was selected for rear admiral, lower half, and was assigned as director, Supply Programs and Policy (N41) on the OPNAV staff. During his three years in N41, he worked for VADM (later ADM and VCNO) Stanley R. (Stan) Arthur. Says Straw, "Admiral Arthur is the finest leader I have ever worked for. No one can motivate people or back them up as well as he does. The nation has been fortunate to have Stan Arthur in high positions through Desert Storm and Tailhook."

Under VADM Stephen F. (Steve) Loftus, who relieved Arthur, Ed Straw oversaw the flow of logistics support to Desert Storm. He takes great personal pride in N41's role of finding transportation for daily emergent requirements and for the timely allocation of what he calls "our incredibly limited supply" of preferred air-launched weapons. He pursued the weapons shortage as a wartime lesson learned and was credited with improved weapons funding in POM 92.

Straw's pride in the Navy Supply Corps reached new heights during Operation Desert Storm. President George Bush's remarks on the day of the cease-fire are displayed on the wall behind VADM Straw's desk: "In a very real sense, this victory belongs to them, to the privates, to the sergeants and the supply officers, to the men and women in the machines, and to the men and women who made them work." RADM Straw was awarded the Distinguished Service Medal for his performance during Desert Storm and the Defense Management Review.

In July 1991 Straw became NAVSUP's vice commander under RADM Jim Miller. He served in the number two position for a year in what he calls "the role of Mr. Inside to Miller's Mr. Outside." The two highlights of his tour were the elimination of stovepipes through a massive NAVSUP headquarters reorganization and the VCNO logistics infrastructure study. The study uncovered hundreds of millions of dollars in savings driven by reengineering supply, maintenance, and logistics budget processes. Included was Straw's recommendation to build fleet and industrial supply centers to manage regional logistics, which earned him the unofficial title of "Father of the FISC."

In July 1992 RADM Straw was promoted to vice admiral and became the 11th director of the Defense Logistics Agency. He is the first Navy director since VADM Gene Grinstead held the position from 1981 to 1984, when DLA was essentially half the size it now is. The Defense Management Review (DMR) process of the early 1990s brought DLA:

- 25 additional supply depots;
- full distribution responsibility for service-owned inventories of $100 billion;
- inventory management of a million consumable line items previously managed by the individual services; and
- full contract administration responsibility for $800 billion outstanding service, weapons systems contracts.

VADM Straw has followed the philosophy of corporate management reengineering guru Jim Champy: "We blew the place up and started over again." He points out that he did not have time to wait for continuous process improvement and that it takes breakthrough reengineering to bring about the change that will keep DLA's military customers happy. Straw has "reengineered DLA with an overarching objective of providing better quality, better prices, and faster delivery of commodities and spare parts to the warfighter."

In the FY 1996 budget cycle DLA reduced service customer prices for material and material distribution by $5.5 billion. "That's just the beginning of what our streamlined, integrated team approach can do by adopting the best business practices from the private sector," Straw says. His goal of direct vendor delivery, around DLA warehouses, to customers is not only reducing material costs, but also reducing distribution costs. Now, 90 percent of all medical supplies go from private industry directly to military hospitals within 24 hours at one-third lower cost than the previous system. "We're rapidly expanding this concept to all commodities where it makes sense," Straw explains. He predicts that DLA will be 40 percent leaner and 30 percent more efficient by the end of FY 1997. His reengineering accomplishments were recognized by Secretary of Defense William Perry in August 1994, when he named VADM Straw the director of the Defense Performance Review (DPR). Straw's DPR staff is implementing, throughout DLA, Vice President Al Gore's National Performance Review Program to reinvent government.

When asked for his thoughts on the future of the Supply Corps, VADM responded confidently, "It's never been better, as long as we ensure we are using our world class business talent in the right areas. For example, it's sad that we waited so many years to put a fair share of our superstars into DLA. If we had, both Navy and DLA would be better for it today. Our Supply Corps officers are now on the cutting edge of all of DLA's reengineering efforts, saving not only Navy, but all services and the taxpayers billions of dollars. We could have done the same thing years ago."

His response to a question about the future of NAVSUP was unexpected:

> The future of the Supply Corps is not tied to the future of NAVSUP. It's tied to joint logistics, operational logistics and the ships at sea. In fact, I firmly support the merger of NAVSUP and the other systems commands in Crystal City. The Navy can no longer afford the luxury of stovepipes. They need to be integrated like the Army and Air Force logistics commands. We certainly don't need a NAVSEA to buy seven ships a year. I think the outstanding resources of the Supply Corps can be put to better use by bringing standardized integrated logistics support improvements, as the N4 of an integrated systems command.

Straw indicated that as his living legacy to the Corps he wanted to leave Flag officers who are the heirs to the proud traditions and logistics management philosophies of their illustrious predecessors. Flag officers, according to VADM Straw, know how to find the bottom line and understand the value of breakthrough strategies; are masters of inventory management; understand the critical importance of operational and joint logistics to the warfighter; and value hard work and uncompromising performance. "They are the Flag officers who will ensure that our future Flag officers will continue the proud tradition of keeping our Corps virtually indistinguishable from the line" he concluded.

VADM Ed Straw's personal awards include the Distinguished Service Medal, the Legion of Merit with gold star, the Meritorious Service Medal with two gold stars, and the Navy Commendation Medal with two gold stars. He also wears the naval aviation supply officer wings. He serves on several boards, including the Navy Federal Credit Union, the Commission for Savings in America, and the National War College Alumni Association. He is a life member of the National Eagle Scout Association, the Veterans of Foreign Wars, and the Masonic Order and an avid largemouth bass fisherman. Straw has three daughters. He and his wife Christine live with their two young daughters in quarters at the Washington Navy Yard.

Sources

Address by VADM Edward McCown Straw. Graduation Ceremony, Navy Supply Corps School, Athens, Ga., 22 January 1993.

Interview of VADM Edward McCown Straw. Cameron Station, Alexandria, Va., 14 April 1994.

"New Director of Defense Performance Review Named." News release, Office of Assistant Secretary of Defense (Public Affairs), 5 August 1994.
Official Biography. Defense Logistics Agency, n.d.
Transcript of Naval Service. Bureau of Naval Personnel, August 1994.

Logistics Assets in Gulf

In the aftermath of ODS, Combat Logistics Force (CLF) ships and other logistics units in-theater were assigned to the battle group commander or to Commander Logistics Forces Western Pacific, located at Singapore. Supply Corps captains had been assigned on a six-month TAD basis to Commander Middle East Force as assistant chief of staff for logistics. CAPT Daniel P. (Dan) Morrisey, who held the billet in early 1992, met with RADM R. A. K. Taylor, COMIDEASTFOR. The two agreed that, as the command evolved into Commander U.S. Naval Forces Central Command, it would be necessary for the Navy component commander of USCENTCOM to assume control of logistics in-theater.

By late summer of 1992, Taylor and Morrisey had developed a plan to establish an echelon three operational logistics command under COMUSNAVCENT, which would be similar in concept and function to CTF-63 in the Mediterranean and CTF-73 in the Pacific. CTF-153 was established on 1 September 1992, with CAPT John E. Tufts, then ACOS for Logistics, COMIDFEASTFOR, given additional duty as task force commander. CTF-153, manned by six officers and enlisted personnel from the NAVCENT Logistics Department, was given responsibility for all operational logistics in-theater, including deployed Combat Logistics Force (CLF) ships, shore-based logair detachments, and forward logistics sites. CDR Kim F. Kline, NAVCENT staff supply officer, was assigned duties with the new CTF-153. With no operational logistics staff experience and limited manning, the new CTF-153 staff concentrated on developing the command manning document and putting out fires, such as responding to day-to-day logistics requirements of deployed forces.

RADM Jim Miller, Commander of NAVSUP, visited the area in January 1993 and committed to providing a captain with operational logistics staff experience to relieve CAPT Tufts. Commander Service Forces, U.S. Naval Forces, Central Command, (COMSERVFORNAVCENT) was established as the parent command of CTF-153, effective 1 April 1993. The proposed staffing called for a surface line captain to command the new organization with a Supply Corps captain as deputy commander.

CAPT John Tufts was the first Supply Corps officer to be assigned as a task force commander when he was given additional duty during his tour as ACOS for logistics, Commander U.S. Naval Forces, Central Command. Tufts, a native of Los Angeles, California, an NROTC graduate of Oregon State University, and a Vietnam veteran as a midshipman, served in *USS John S. McCain* (DDG-36) on Midway and Diego Garcia islands and in *USS Sacramento* (AOE-1). He also had earlier tours at NSC Puget, NAVSUP, SPCC, and the Navy Exchange Service Center Auburn, Washington, before reporting to the Mideast in May 1992 and being promoted to captain in September. CAPT Tufts served in all three top logistics jobs in the Persian Gulf theater simultaneously during his final three months.

In July 1993 CAPT Tufts was relieved by CAPT Stephen G. (Steve) Crandall and reported as executive officer, FISC Puget Sound, where he was serving at the end of FY 1994. He was recognized for his exceptionally meritorious service in the Mideast with award of the Legion of Merit.

The Supply Corps Role in the Persian Gulf

CAPT Crandall brought experience as replenishment officer, Commander Service Forces, Sixth Fleet and supply officer of *USS John F. Kennedy* (CV-67). While director of logistics, Supreme Allied Commander Atlantic, he also had a significant role in developing CTF-137's operational logistics role to support allied forces in the North Atlantic.

The CTF-153 portion of the ACOS logistics staff still was composed of the same half-dozen officers and enlisted men, pending arrival of the line captain expected to take over by early fall. In the interim, VADM Douglas J. Katz, Commander U.S. Naval Force, Central Command, and Commander Middle East Force, gave CAPT Crandall the broad guidance to take charge of logistics. Steve Crandall lost no time in setting about to make COMSERVFORNAVCENT/CTF-153 the sole operational logistics support for the NAVCENT area. It soon became apparent that VADM Katz was comfortable that CTF-153 was on track and in charge of logistics. Where support was needed, Katz provided it to CTF-153 in taking over the underway replenishment scheduling, material control officer function, and other functions previously performed by battle group commanders of COMLOGWESTPAC.

CAPT Crandall's immediate goal was to capitalize on the unique mission of CTF-153, having operational control of both CLF ships and shore-based logistics aircraft, and to build a logistics support structure integrating sea and air logistic support roles. He adjusted staffing of COMSERVFORNAVCENT for a better fit with the overall logistics mission, including new Supply Corps billets for a commander as logistics plans officer and a lieutenant commander as replenishment officer.

Integrated Logistics Effort for Somalia

Just as the American effort in Somalia was renewed, the new staff proved its merit, supporting Navy and Marine forces operating in and offshore Somalia. CTF-153 integrated Air Force strategic and in-theater airlift with CLF ships offshore to support an amphibious group and a carrier battle group, each with 10,000 personnel.

It soon became necessary to place someone officially and legally in command of SERVFORNAVCENT. CAPT Crandall did not actually command the staff that worked for him. The distinction may have been subtle, and it was not an issue until personnel actually reported for duty with the new staff's unit code. Because the command had been established as a shore staff rather than afloat, Steve Crandall, as a staff corps officer could assume command. CAPT Crandall, was officially designated by COMUSNAVCENT as CTF-153, but no one had been officially designated as COMSERVFORNAVCENT, the new parent of CTF-153. A line officer to take the command had not yet been identified, so VADM Katz secured additional duty orders for CAPT Crandall, officially making him COMSERVFORNAVCENT.

Crandall had a limited number of logistics ships to support combatant forces spread throughout the area from Suez to the Horn of Africa to the Arabian Gulf. CTF-153 needed positive control of all resources to ensure that the right ship was at the right time and place with the right stuff. Maintaining carrier battle group (CVBG) integrity by which commanders controlled logistics ships, forward logistics sites, and material control programs, was a problem for CAPT Crandall and his staff. Control by the battle group commanders just would not work in NAVCENT, where an amphibious group, ships conducting maritime interdiction operations, and other special-purpose units operated simultaneously.

When CAPT Crandall took command, CTF-153 only had three ships: *USNS Walter S. Diehl* (A-AO-193) and two oceanographic survey ships. The *USS Theodore Roosevelt* (CVN-71) CVBG was about to leave the theater, and the CTF-153 AFS had already departed, leaving a gap in coverage for several weeks, but *USS White Plains* (AFS-4) arrived shortly thereafter. She was followed by the *USS Abraham Lincoln* (CVN-72) battle group, whose commodore, RADM Joseph J. (Jack) Dantone, Jr., had known Crandall at AIRLANT and he was skipper of *USS Dwight Eisenhower* (CVN-69).

When VADM Katz and his senior staff flew aboard *Lincoln,* Dantone was surprised to find a Supply Corps officer in command of CTF-153. Dantone had no problem with Crandall taking OPCON of his CLF ships as long as the CVBG had fuel, ammunition, and COD flights when needed. CAPT Crandall later learned that Dantone had decided *Lincoln* should retain its own material control program rather than to turn it over to the MATCONOFFNAVCENT program that was modeled on the program that had served the Sixth Fleet in the Mediterranean so well. Katz backed up Crandall, and by the end of September, all CLF ships were under CTF-153 OPCON and the program was working well.

Thin CTF-153 Resources

The disastrous firefight at Mogadishu, Somalia, in October 1993, resulting in the death of 18 Americans, brought a dramatic change to normal operations of CTF-153. The initial Joint Chiefs of Staff reaction was to divert the arriving amphibious group to Somalia from its Gulf destination. CAPT Crandall and his CTF-153 staff were faced with spreading their already thin logistics support resources across the entire operating area. Crandall quickly set up a forward logistic site (FLS) at Mombasa, Kenya, and positioned *USS Willamette* (AO-180) there to provide petroleum, oil, and lubricant (POL) support and shuttle to Mogadishu as necessary. The supporting structure was so successful and complete that the Army used it for the sea-based withdrawal of its forces from Somalia in the spring of 1994. Using other ship assets as they came into the CTF-153 OPCON area, these arrangements remained in effect until the withdrawal was completed. Even with the American military forces out of Somalia, JCS ordered a continued amphibious group presence off Mogadishu to provide contingency support for noncombatant evacuation operations for the few American citizens still in Somalia. Meanwhile, CAPT Crandall and his CTF-153 staff settled in for the long haul in supporting an amphibious group, whether off Mogadishu or off the Horn of Africa.

By the summer of 1994, staffing of COMSERVFORNAVCENT was nearly complete, and a new Supply Corps deputy commander, CAPT T. A. (Art) Rorex relieved CDR Kline. In September, CTF-153 was once again preparing to support a humanitarian relief operation—this time in Rwanda.

An unrestricted line captain, Kevin P. Cummings, a surface warfare specialist who had just completed a tour as chief of staff, Commander U.S. Naval Forces Marianas, was identified to relieve Steve Crandall in August 1994. At the time CAPT Crandall turned over the reins of COMSERVFORNAVCENT, the staff was composed of 10 line and Supply Corps officers and 17 enlisted personnel. Assigned operational logistics forces included more than 1,500 officers and men in afloat and shore- based units, including seven ships—one each T-AFS, AOR, AE, T- AO, and T-

ATF, and two T-AGOS. Forward logistics sites were located in Egypt, Kenya, and the United Arab Emirates.

LORE OF THE CORPS

Captain Stephen Gary Crandall, SC, USN

Assistant Chief of Staff, Logistics
Commander, U.S. Naval Forces, Central Command, 1994- ;
Commander, Service Forces, U.S. Naval Forces, Central Command, and
Commander, Task Force 153 (CTF-153), 1993–94
Period of Service: 1968–

Steve Crandall had nearly two years of Navy enlisted service before being commissioned in the Supply Corps, was deployed twice to Vietnam, served in three aircraft carriers, and on two Navy and one NATO staff. He eventually became the first Supply Corps officer to be placed officially in command of a Navy task force.

Stephen G. Crandall was born at Carthage, Missouri, in June 1946 and was graduated from Central Methodist College in 1968 with a B.A. degree in political science and a minor in business and economics. The son of a prominent, politically active attorney, Steve Crandall, as many young Americans, could feel the heat of the draft. He says, "Avoiding the draft was acceptable, evading it was incomprehensible." When college deferments were eliminated during his senior year, he searched for options to becoming an Army enlisted man. His father, a decorated and wounded World War II Army artillery officer, advised his son that "three hots and clean sheets in the Navy, even as an enlisted man, beats the hell out of the Army." That wisdom was not lost on the younger Crandall, who hastened to enlist in the Navy and reported to recruit training at NTC San Diego in October 1968.

Crandall's college degree earned him a promotion to airman (E-3) upon graduation from boot camp and orders to the World War II aircraft carrier *USS Ticonderoga* (CV-14) in January 1969, just before she sailed for a Vietnam deployment. Because he was a college graduate and could type, the young sailor was assigned as a yeoman. Crandall lived with 60 other sailors in a non-air conditioned berthing space, but he says it still beat living in a hole in Vietnam.

A subsequent 90 days cleaning the messdeck head and then mess-cooking encouraged Seaman Crandall to take, and pass, the quarterly advancement examination for yeoman, third class. He rode out the rest of *Ticonderoga*'s deployment as a petty officer. Upon return to CONUS, he received orders in January 1970 to the Military Sea Transportation Service Office (MSTSO) at Elmendorf AFB, Anchorage, Alaska. His commanding officer encouraged him to apply for OCS, and Crandall specified the Supply Corps in his application. In June 1970 he reported to Newport in a class of 250, a third of whom were former enlisted, and was promoted to E-5. He was graduated from OCS in October 1970, commissioned an ensign, and ordered to duty at NSCS Athens.

In May 1971 ENS Crandall was ordered as supply and disbursing officer, *USS William C. Lawe* (DD-763), deployed to the Mideast. Crandall rushed to Bahrain to relieve a politically connected officer who had been granted an "early out" rather than to be relieved for cause. Steve Crandall found his new ship on a 124-degree day and set about the difficult relieving process, which took 17 days, because of the poor condition of the records. *Lawe* completed her Persian Gulf-Indian Ocean cruise and returned to Mayport via the Cape of Good Hope. Crandall was promoted to lieutenant, junior grade, in January 1972 and served in *Lawe* during a nine-month deployment to Vietnam in the spring.

LTJG Crandall qualified to stand OOD watches in *Lawe,* whose first combat mission, along with three other destroyers in November 1972, was to attack radar and communication facilities in North Vietnam. The vast majority of ship's company had never fired a shot in anger. A significant percentage of the supposedly flashless powder bags were found to be mislabled, and resultant flashes clearly marked the ship's position, generating prompt return fire from the North Vietnamese. Fortunately, their aim proved to be highly inaccurate.

Lawe returned to the States in the summer of 1973 for transfer to the Naval Reserve Force to relieve *USS Putnam* (DD-767). LTJG Crandall was ordered to COMCRUDESLANT as supply representative at Mayport in August 1973, and in January 1974 reported for duty under instruction at the Navy School Transportation Management, Oakland. Upon graduation in June, he returned to New Orleans, where he and FranCene (Francie) Wing, daughter of *Putnam*'s skipper, were married. He reported in August to NAS Cecil Field, Florida, as material and fuels officer and was promoted to lieutenant in November 1974. LT Crandall went to *USS Saratoga* (CV-60) in July 1976 as stores officer.

His next tour, beginning in November 1978, was at SPCC Mechanicsburg, where he served as head, Load Branch, and head, Provisioning, Outfitting, and Allowance Planning Division. He was promoted to lieutenant commander in December 1979. LCDR Crandall was ordered to the staff, Commander Naval Surface Group, Mediterranean/CTF-63 in March 1982 and assigned as replenishment officer, responsible for scheduling all multiproduct and ammunition ship operations. He also was heavily involved in sea-based logistics support for Lebanese operations and minesweeping in the Red Sea. Crandall was promoted to commander in May 1985.

CDR Crandall reported next to Norfolk as head, Inventory Management and Outfitting Branch, at AIRLANT in June 1985. He drew on his CTF-63 experience while participating in CTF-137 logistics operations in Norway and also served on the 1987 ad hoc Persian Gulf Logistics Strategy Group that developed support plans for tanker convoy-minesweeping operations.

He reported in August 1988 as supply officer, *USS John F. Kennedy* (CV-67) and was promoted to captain in February 1992. CAPT Crandall was detached in June 1990, and became director, Logistics Division, Supreme Allied Command, Atlantic, at Norfolk. By the time he completed his tour at SACLANT, downsizing was well underway and seniority among captains was becoming thin, but CAPT Crandall believed that his chances for a Supply Corps command were good. However, the chief, RADM Jim Miller, had promised VADM Douglas J. Katz that the relief for CAPT John Tufts in the high-profile position would have a broad Fleet and logistics background, including experience with an operational logistics staff.

Jim Miller wanted Crandall to go to Bahrain as ACOS, Logistics, on the staff of Commander U.S. Naval Forces, Central Command. Although the Crandalls preferred stateside duty, he discussed the matter with Miller at length and reluctantly agreed to take the assignment. CAPT Crandall learned that the job probably would carry with it additional duty as Commander Service Forces, Naval Forces, U.S. Central Command and Commander, Task Force 153. Before he was relieved, John Tufts told Crandall, via telephone, that VADM Katz was involved in a serious search for a line officer to take over the additional duties, but had been unsuccessful to date.

Upon completion of his tour at SACLANT, CAPT Crandall was awarded the Defense Superior Service Medal in recognition of his exceptionally superior service. The citation accompanying the award reads, in part, "He was instrumental in the development of the new NATO policy changing logistics from solely a national responsibility to that of a collective responsibility between the nations and NATO commanders. These fundamental changes to NATO logistics represent the most substantive change in over 40 years and are now the standard for the Alliance as it moves into the 21st Century."

Steve Crandall arrived at Bahrain in July 1993, 22 years to the day from the time he reported aboard *USS Lawe* at that sweltering port city as an ensign. CAPT Crandall said that CAPT Tufts had done "a superb job" in a position for which he had no previous operational logistics experience. Crandall found little fault with the manning document and the requisite personnel resourcing for the staff his predecessor had developed after extensive discussions with his counterpart, the commodore at CTF-63 in the Mediterranean.

VADM Katz's guidance to CAPT Crandall was simple: "Take charge, get logistics support under control, and all out-of-theater staffs (particularly COMLOGWESTPAC/CTF-63) out of my business." CAPT Crandall dug into his temporary job as if it were his permanent duty. VADM Katz soon became a strong supporter of Steve Crandall, who promptly established CTF-153 as an efficient, viable organization. Katz kept him in command for nearly 14 months while he sought a line officer with combat logistics experience.

When a strong U.S. presence was established in Somalia under a joint task force, VADM Katz and CAPT Crandall flew to Mogadishu to meet with Army commander MAJGEN Montgomery and other officials. The Navy group spent the night aboard *USS New Orleans* (LPH-11), and VADM Katz reveled in introducing Crandall to an all-officer meeting as the only Supply Corps commodore in the Navy. The most incongruous day of Crandall's tour was the one on which he found himself sitting in the dirt at Mogadishu, wearing a flak jacket, and eating a MRE (meal-ready-to-eat) for lunch and then flying back to Bahrain for dinner with his family at home that evening.

CAPT Steve Crandall's intended 2 or 3 months unofficially in command of a task force had become 14 months with him officially in command. CAPT Kevin P. Cummings, a surface warfare specialist with experience as executive officer of one CLF ship and commanding officer of another, finally relieved CAPT Crandall on 31 August 1994. CAPT Crandall returned to his primary duty as the ACOS Logistics, COMUSNAVCENT.

In addition to the Defense Superior Service Medal, Captain Crandall's personal awards include the Meritorious Service Medal with three gold stars, the Navy Commendation Medal, and the Navy Achievement Medal. He qualified as a surface warfare officer in 1973 and as a naval aviation supply officer in 1990. He and FranCene live in Bahrain with their teenage son. Their daughter attends college in the United States.

Sources

Change of Command Program. Commander, Service Forces, U.S. Naval Forces Central Command, 31 August 1994.

Citation. Defense Superior Service Medal, July 1993.

The NAVCENT History. October 1993.
The NAVCENT Mission. December 1993.
Official Biography. Commander, Service Forces, U.S. Naval Forces Central Command, March 1994.
Personal data supplied by CAPT Stephen G. Crandall, July 1994.
Telephone interview of CAPT Stephen G. Crandall, 30 July 1994.

Supply Corps Flag Officers at DLA

In the fall of 1994, 5 of the 15 active duty Supply Corps Flag officers and a number of captains and selectees were on duty at DLA in headquarters and field positions. RADM Ernest A. (Ernie) Elliott was commander, Defense Construction Supply Center Columbus, Ohio, and RADM Keith W. Lippert was commander, Defense General Supply Center Richmond, Virginia. VADM Edward M. Straw and RADMs Edward R. (Bob) Chamberlin and Leonard (Lenn) Vincent were on duty at DLA headquarters, Cameron Station, Alexandria, Virginia.

LORE OF THE CORPS

Rear Admiral Leonard Vincent, SC, USN

Deputy Director, Acquisition Management, and Commander, Defense Contract Management Command Defense Logistics Agency, 1992–
Period of Service: 1961–

Lenn Vincent says that his career is proof that the American military gives everyone a chance to succeed regardless of how life is started. He overcame enormous obstacles to rise to Flag rank in the Supply Corps and head of a command that administers $800 billion in defense contracts.

Leonard Vincent was born in the hills of Oklahoma near Tulsa in February 1941. His father was part Cherokee and worked in the construction business. One day, when Lenn was 12, his father left for work and never returned. His mother worked long hours in a factory to keep Lenn and his sister together with her in substandard housing without plumbing.

The young Vincent worked at the only odd jobs a youngster could find to provide money to help with family finances. He hung wallpaper, delivered newspapers on horseback, and worked at a service station, bait house, and grocery station. When he was older, he worked in construction, laid hot tar on baked Oklahoma roads, and, after high school, sweated in gritty Texas oil fields.

Vincent was eligible for the draft in 1961, but the Navy held a special fascination for him, and he chose to enlist in the Naval Reserve as a seaman recruit while attending Southeastern State College at Durant, Oklahoma. He and Shirley Morrison were married in 1962, and they had their first child while he was still in college. He had attained the rate of storekeeper, third class, when he was graduated with a B.A. degree in social studies in early 1965. He was accepted for Officer Candidate School and reported for active duty at Newport, Rhode Island, in March 1965. He was originally a candidate for the line, but color blindness forced him to become a candidate for the Supply Corps. Lenn Vincent was graduated from OCS in the top third of his class and commissioned an ensign in the Supply Corps, U.S. Naval Reserve, in July.

ENS Vincent reported to NSCS Athens later in July and completed the basic qualification course in January 1966. His first duty as a qualified supply officer was as disbursing and accounting officer, Naval Ammunition Depot Hawthorne, Nevada. He was promoted to lieutenant, junior grade, in January 1967, but doubts about his Navy career led him to consider teaching. He returned to civilian life at the end of his obligated Navy service in July 1968.

Vincent never did take a teaching job, but went to work in Tulsa for North American Rockwell Corporation and later with Investors Diversified Services. He was promoted to lieutenant in the Naval Reserve in January 1969. After 26 months, Lenn Vincent decided that the civilian world did not offer the same opportunities for him as the Navy did. He responded to the call of the sea in 1970 and found that the fastest route was to enter under the Training and Administration Reserve (TAR) Program. He reported for active duty in September 1970 as supply officer, Naval Special Warfare Group Two at Little Creek, Virginia.

He had been on duty with his new unit less than a month when one of the underwater demolition team members took advantage of the recalled supply officer. He told LT Vincent that he could assist the command and raise the morale of everyone by simply signing a form to requisition a small boat from the salvage yard for the UDT unit's morale, welfare, and recreation program. Vincent trustingly signed the blank form thrust under his nose. He later heard a commotion outside the warehouse and rushed out to see what was going on. He discovered a flatbed truck with a huge gig that looked like a yacht. The cost of fuel for the boat would have bankrupted the MWR fund. Moving quickly to head off the premature end to his naval career, LT Vincent ordered the men to return the gig and fervently hoped that his C.O.

had not witnessed the event. Fortunately, he did not, but Lenn Vincent learned two valuable lessons that day. First, those with authority must have responsibility or they will not be in authority long, and, second, never sign a blank form.

In October 1971 LT Vincent moved to Naval Inshore Warfare Command at Little Creek as staff supply officer. He was awarded the Meritorious Service Medal for efficiently consolidating the individual supply departments of each subordinate component of the multifaceted command, resulting in substantial savings of funds and material inventories.

Vincent became supply officer, *USS Pensacola* (LSD-38), in October 1972. He was promoted to lieutenant commander in early July 1974 and later that month was augmented into the U.S. Navy. A ship's serviceman working in the laundry knocked on LCDR Vincent's stateroom door one evening to request permission to make a personal delivery of one of the captain's laundered white shirts. Lenn Vincent looked at the shirt before responding to the unusual request and saw a dingy, yellow shirt, with a tattered napkin pinned to the collar. On the napkin was written a message to the skipper: "I'm sorry about the color of your shirt, but we ran out of bleach. Once we get back to port, I will rewash it, press it, and guarantee that it will be white."

Lenn Vincent decided to take the heat himself and sheepishly delivered the dingy shirt and napkin note to his skipper, CAPT Ted Fischer, who was fond of exhorting his men to "bite the bullet." Fischer read the sailor's sincere note and laughed heartily. He wrote back to the laundryman, "Thanks for your support, bite the bullet." No matter how many times the captain's shirt was rewashed, it never returned to its original sparkling white color. Vincent says he learned two more valuable lessons: It's always better to take responsibility up front and to bite the bullet; and always have plenty of bleach on hand if you're in charge of the laundry aboard ship.

LCDR Vincent next attended the Armed Forces Staff College from December 1974 to June 1975. He had temporary duty at NSC Norfolk until he reported to George Washington University, where he obtained an M.B.A. in procurement and contracts in August 1976. Vincent then was ordered to duty at NSC Puget Sound as procurement and contracting officer. He was promoted to commander in September 1978. CDR Vincent was awarded the Navy Commendation Medal for this tour when he departed to report as contracts officer, Supervisor of Shipbuilding, Bath, Maine, in June 1979. He was awarded a gold star in lieu of a second Meritorious Service Medal for his exceptional performance that contributed directly to the early Perry-class frigates, "a total of 30 months ahead of contract schedule and $64 million below target cost."

CDR Vincent was then ordered as supply officer, *USS Dixon* (AS-37), in June 1982, where he was awarded another gold star in lieu of a third Meritorious Service Medal. He reported to the Ships Parts Control Center at Mechanicsburg, Pennsylvania, in August 1984 as director of the Combat Systems Department. He was promoted to captain in July 1985, selected into the Material Professional Program in August, and appointed director, SPCC Contract Group. He was awarded another gold star in lieu of a fourth Meritorious Service Medal. The citation described Vincent as "an acknowledged authority in military logistics, supply support, and acquisition."

CAPT Vincent's next duty, in July 1989, was as commander, Defense Contract Management Command, Los Angeles, his first DLA assignment. He was awarded the Defense Meritorious Service Medal for his "unsurpassed leadership and exceptional management of DOD acquisition programs." In August 1990 he reported as commander, Defense Contract Management Command, International, another DLA command, located at Wright-Patterson AFB, Ohio. He served in the billet for a year and was awarded the Defense Superior Service Medal. CAPT Vincent returned to a Navy command in August 1991 as assistant commander for contracts, Naval Air Systems Command. He was promoted to Flag rank in October 1992 and left NAVAIR to return to DLA in November with the Legion of Merit. The citation reads, in part, "Working closely with industry leaders, Rear Admiral Vincent resolved a broad spectrum of contractual issues which resulted in enhanced program affordability during a most difficult time of declining defense budgets."

RADM Vincent's credentials made him an outstanding candidate for the top spots in the acquisition and contracting roles at the Defense Logistics Agency. He was still serving as DLA Deputy Director for Acquisitions and Commander, Defense Contract Management Command at the conclusion of Fiscal Year 1994.

Lenn and Shirley Vincent live in Springfield, Virginia, and have three adult children.

Sources

Citation. Defense Meritorious Service Medal, 23 July 1990.
Citation. Defense Superior Service Medal, 31 July 1991.
Citation. Legion of Merit, 5 February 1993.
Official Biography. Defense Logistics Agency, n.d.
Telephone interview of RADM Leonard Vincent, 14 and 29 September 1994.
Transcript of Naval Service. Bureau of Naval Personnel, August 1994.

Navy Finance Center Becomes DOD Center

The Navy Finance Center, founded in 1942 as the Bureau of Supplies and Accounts Field Branch, handled Navy family allowance, allotments, master accounts, and Government Savings Bond activity. The Field Branch was renamed the Navy Finance Center in 1955 and taken over by DOD in January 1991. To facilitate reduction in the size of the military and its support infrastructure without reducing mission capability of combat forces, Department of Defense finance and accounting functions were consolidated in July 1994 at Cleveland. NFC was again renamed, this time as Defense Finance and Accounting Service—Cleveland Center (DFAS-CL).

The importance to service members and their dependents of uninterrupted and reliable maintenance of pay accounts and allotments cannot be overemphasized. Such service is typical of the "safety net" that the Navy and other armed services provide for their families. Among the wide variety of convenient on-base facilities and services that are available to Navy families are comprehensive medical and dental care, child care, libraries, Navy Exchanges, recreational facilities, and commissary stores.

Another important service available to Navy families, not common in the civilian business world, is the sponsor program, whereby a fellow Navy family is designated to provide guidance and counsel to families ordered to new duty stations on the average of every two to three years. In an organization the size of the Supply Corps, in which so many officers of the same rank know their peers and the families are acquainted, this sponsor support system is particularly effective. Supply Corps spouses have traditionally provided additional support by bonding with one another to provide assistance to those in need when their family members have been deployed for long periods. They have conducted informational programs, sponsored social events, and raised money for such charitable causes as the Navy Supply Corps Foundation, which funds college scholarships for children of Supply Corps officers and enlisted personnel in supply rates. Both official and nonofficial, volunteer services have made major contributions to the ever-improving quality of life for Supply Corps families.

Supply Corps wives have demonstrated the same attributes of dedication, creativity, and initiative on the home front as the men and women of the Corps have shown in the performance of their duties. The enterprising Carol Cole, for example, set about the task of tracking down the roots of a legend involving the command living quarters of NSC San Diego when her husband, CAPT (later RADM) Brady M. Cole was commanding officer. Alleged to be haunted, the quarters have long been the subject of reports of strange happenings. Carol Cole traced the history of the quarters and called upon local parapsychologists to explain the reports of previously unexplained events. She documented both the history of the site as well as the parapsychologists' report. The documents are on file at the Navy Supply Corps Museum.

A Return to Haiti

In September 1994, the U.S. Navy and Marine Corps were called upon again, as they had been in 1915, to restore order in Haiti. However, the Supply Corps officers ordered to Haiti had different duties from those their Navy Pay Corps predecessors had performed earlier in the century, when they were dispatched to restore Haitian financial institutions. Although the Pay Corps' primary role ended in 1916, U.S. Marines continued to occupy the impoverished nation to control political instability for another 19 years. The last Marines left Haiti in 1935, when an acceptable level of stability appeared to have been achieved. Unfortunately, the citizens of Haiti continued to suffer from severe poverty and human rights violations under subsequent dictatorial regimes. Starting in 1991, some 35,000 Haitians used virtually every vessel that would float to escape the totalitarian government of Raul Cedras and reach sanctuary in Florida. The tide of refugees threatened to become a flood, causing the U.S. government to order the Coast Guard to intercept and return the refugees to Haiti.

President Bill Clinton responded to growing political pressure to permit Haitians to enter the United States rather than subject them to retribution upon forced return to Haiti. He issued an executive order on the Friday of Memorial Day weekend in 1994 to activate *USNS Comfort* (T-AH-20), one of the Navy's two 1,000-bed hospital ships and equipped with the world's two largest trauma centers, and send her south. His order did not specify the exact nature of the mission. The ships's officers knew only that they were headed in the general direction of Haiti.

The identical missions of *Comfort* and her sister ship *Mercy* (T-AH-19), in a similar inactive status on the West Coast, required load out on mobilization missions, taking on hospital personnel, and getting underway in 90 days. But in this instance, the 69,300-ton *Comfort,* which had only recently been on routine sea trials, put to sea in just 48 hours without taking on the normal load of food and medical supplies.

Comfort left its Reserve operating status berth at Baltimore, Maryland, on the third day after the president's executive order was issued. The lack of definitive information about *Comfort*'s destination and the specific nature of the mission created an unusual challenge for CDR John Proctor, who had transferred from DLA to the National Naval Medical Center Bethesda, Maryland, in 1993. His collateral duty was as supply officer of *Comfort* whenever the ship was activated. The humanitarian nature of the unspecified mission made it obvious that *Comfort* would be dealing with refugees and not battle casualties. Proctor was knowledgeable of third-world refugee needs from his assignments in ODS and Somalia, and he applied that knowledge to the task of special loading the ship to meet those needs.

While on duty in Somalia 1992, Proctor had observed the severe dehydration of refugees and their basic need for food and shelter. He requisitioned 170,000 personal-size bottles of water and also ordered feminine hygiene products, diapers, and baby formula for the women and children expected aboard. Navy officials were aware of the high incidence of tuberculosis and dysentery frequently suffered by refugees. It was imperative that the ship's company not be exposed to infectious disease that might be brought aboard and distributed throughout *Comfort* by her ventilation system. The decision was made to provide temporary billeting on the weather deck, requiring acquisition of tents and portable toilets.

Requisitions were transmitted electronically to FISC Norfolk, where *Comfort* stopped for loading before leaving for Mayport, Florida. Medical personnel to staff the hospital in *Comfort* were ordered from Navy medical facilities all along the East Coast and reported aboard at Mayport. John Proctor realized that refugees were not accustomed to American food, so he sent commissary personnel ashore to purchase cookbooks with recipes for Caribbean-style and Creole meals. He authorized open market purchases of nonstandard ingredients specified in the cookbooks.

Comfort received orders to deploy as Haitian refugee processing ship off Kingston, on the south shore of Jamaica and out of sight of Haitian boat people, to whom she might have become a beacon. CDR Proctor negotiated contracts with Jamaican vendors to remove trash, including empty water bottles, and to take off, clean, and return the portable toilets each day. In addition to ship's company and a manned hospital, *Comfort* supported personnel from 12 other organizations, including:

- 2nd Battalion, 4th Marines;
- 100 U.S. Immigration and Naturalization Service agents;
- 200 International Organization for Migration translators;
- United Nations High Commission for Refugees (UNHCR) agents;
- State Department personnel; and
- MSC, LANTFLT, and JTF-160 personnel.

Comfort processed 1,500 Haitian refugees brought to her by helicopters and smaller ships, completed her mission, returned to Baltimore in August 1994, and reverted to inactive status. CDR Proctor remained aboard for two weeks to supervise off loading of medical stores and other items before reporting to his primary duty at Bethesda. Less than a month later, the Haitian situation heated up again, and the hospital ship was ordered once more to Haitian waters, this time with only two days' advance notice.

LORE OF THE CORPS

Commander John Stephen Proctor, SC, USN

Director of Supply Management, National Naval Medical Center, and
Supply Officer, *USNS Comfort* (T-AH-20), 1993–
Period of Service: 1966–

The Persian Gulf was Commander Proctor's collegiate specialty, and he is a veteran of several Navy tours of duty in the Mideast. He reported from Supply Corps School directly to Bahrain for more than two years, was involved with FMS in the Mideast and returned during Operation Desert Shield/Desert Storm in 1990, and went to Somalia with Operation Restore Hope in 1992. He had further humanitarian duty in the Haitian Interdiction Program from May to August 1994 and again in September 1994.

John Proctor was born in Washington, D.C., in March 1949, and is a special honors graduate of George Washington University with a B.A. degree in classical archaeology and anthropology and a specialty in studies of the Persian Gulf area. He began his Navy career in 1966 as a hospital corpsman and served two tours in *USS Virgo* (AE-30) in Vietnamese waters. He was commissioned through Navy Officer Candidate School at Newport in June 1975 and was graduated from NSCS Athens in November.

ENS Proctor's first assignment out of Athens was in December 1975 at Bahrain as a quality assurance officer with the Defense Fuel Quality Assurance Office, Middle East, a field operation of the Defense Supply Agency. He also served as supply and fiscal officer and COMIDEASTFOR liaison officer from February 1976 to September 1977. He was promoted to LTJG in July 1977.

LTJG Proctor was next ordered to duty with the Submarine Force and was graduated form the Submarine School at New London, Connecticut, after which he was assigned as supply officer, Gold Crew, *USS Woodrow Wilson* (SSBN-624) in February 1978. Proctor completed four strategic deterrent patrols in *Wilson,* was promoted to lieutenant in July 1979, and was designated submarine-qualified.

He attended the Defense Institute for Security Assistance Management in May 1980 before reporting in June as the program control director for Foreign Military Sales to the Middle East and Africa. He completed his FMS tour in June 1982, when he reported to the Naval Postgraduate School, Monterey, California.

LT Proctor was graduated in April 1984 with an M.S. degree in acquisition and contract management and reported next to NSC Norfolk as director of contracts. He later served as the project officer for the automation of procurement and accounting data entry (APADE) prototype until May 1987. He was promoted to lieutenant commander during his NSC Norfolk tour. LCDR Proctor then served as the assistant supply officer, *USS John F. Kennedy* (CV-67), from July 1987 to July 1989, when he reported to the Armed Forces Staff College, Norfolk. He was then ordered to DLA headquarters on the Procurement Management staff.

CDR Proctor was sent back to the Mideast in August 1990 to serve as the commander, DLA (Forward) and assigned to the USCENTCOM staff. His educational background and in-theater experience made him the ideal candidate to be chosen from among the many on-scene logisticians as operations officer of the Army 22nd Support Command, involving about 50,000 logisticians, when Coalition Forces attacked Iraq in 1991. Army historians have said that CDR Proctor's appointment as operations officer of an Army theater command is a first in U.S. military history. LTGEN William G. (Gus) Pagonis, Commander 22nd Support Command, presented LCDR Proctor the Bronze Star Medal for his meritorious service in support of military operations in ODS. The citation included, "His significant contributions greatly enhanced the effectiveness of the United States and Allied effort against a tenacious enemy. Despite many adversities associated with a combat environment, he served in a resolute manner."

CDR Proctor returned to DLA headquarters in May 1991 and was promoted to commander in June. His invaluable combat experience was called upon again on 16 December 1992 when he was sent to Somalia to head the DLA element of the Joint Logistics Contingency Support Team. He was also designated as the agency's personal representative to the commander of the United Nations-chartered unified task force for Operation Restore Hope. CDR Proctor explains his mission in Somalia:

> Our team was really a new concept the Army and DLA were experimenting with as an aftermath of the Operation Desert Storm experience. . . . Our first major task was to figure out what we would need

> to take with us to sustain us and accomplish our mission. The answer, of course, was that we had to take everything. We knew we were going into a hostile environment in a country where there was no water system or electricity, no sewage system, no food, no infrastructure. There are very few paved roads in the country. We took everything but the kitchen sink; we took buckets instead.

The DLA team Proctor headed was to set up operations in the remnants of the shelled and looted American Embassy. First, it was necessary to clear away rubbish. CDR Proctor says that the place was infested with mosquitoes, scorpions, and snakes. A cobra was living in the walls and rafters of the embassy room where team members set up shop. They saw it once but were never able to capture or kill it and never knew exactly where it was. CDR Proctor reports that lessons learned in Operation Desert Storm really paid off in Operation Restore Hope. Proctor returned again to the more stable atmosphere of DLA headquarters on 26 January 1993. He was awarded the Meritorious Service Medal for his support role in Somalia.

John Proctor reported as director for supply management at the National Naval Medical Center Bethesda, Maryland, in May 1993. In this assignment, he also serves as supply officer of *USNS Comfort* (T-AH-20) when the ship is activated, as she was in May and September 1994. CDR Proctor lives with his two children at Alexandria, Virginia.

Sources

Citation. Bronze Star Medal, 5 April 1991.
Citation. Meritorious Service Medal, June 1993.
"Liaison in Somalia." *Dimensions,* Defense Logistics Agency, March 1993.
Official Biography. National Naval Medical Center, n.d.
Telephone interviews of CDR John S. Proctor, August 1994.

The Fourth *USS Supply*

The fourth Navy ship to carry the proud name *USS Supply* (AOE-6) was commissioned at San Diego on 26 February 1994, 199 years after Tench Francis assumed office as the first U.S. Purveyor of Public Supplies. But this lead ship in a new class is vastly different from her three predecessors bearing the name *Supply*. This latest and fastest Fleet support vessel is classified as a fast combat stores ship and has been assigned to the Service Force, U.S. Atlantic Fleet, homeported at Norfolk. *Supply* displaces 48,500 long tons and is designed to cruise with, and to replenish and rearm, an entire battle force. Her four gas turbine engines provide a speed in excess of 30 knots.

Supply can replenish other ships of a battle group from an inventory of:

- diesel fuel marine (DFM): 1,965,600 gallons;
- JP-5 fuel: 2,620,800 gallons;
- DFM/JP-5 convertible fuel: 1,965,600 gallons;
- lubrication oil: 500 55-gallon drums;
- gas: 800 bottles;
- ordnance: 1,800 long tons;
- chill and freezer stowage: 400 long tons;
- dry stores: 250 long tons; and
- water: 20,000 gallons (for emergency transfer).

For the traditional method of alongside replenishment of other ships underway, *Supply* is also equipped with 6 stream stations (3 on each side), a receive-only sliding padeye, 4 10-ton cargo booms, 3 double-probe stream fueling stations, and 2 single-probe stream fueling stations.

Supply also carries two CH-46 helicopters for vertical replenishment of other ships and can replenish up to four warships simultaneously, using both surface and vertical methods of transfer, while providing its own self-defense. She is equipped with the NATO Sea Sparrow missile system, two close-in weapons systems, two .50-caliber machine guns, an AN/SLQ 32(V)3 electronic warfare system, four decoy launchers, and a Nixie torpedo decoy system.

Plans originally called for a Supply-class of 12 ships—one for each carrier battle group. Downsizing reduced that number to 6. As of the end of FY 1994, construction of three of the five proposed additional ships of the class have been authorized. *Rainier* (AOE-7) was scheduled for commissioning in January 1995, and *Arctic* (AOE-8) in July-August 1995. A contract has been let for *Bridge* (AOE-10), but construction had not yet commenced. For budgetary reasons, there will be no AOE-9. Whether there will be additional ships of the class beyond *Bridge* depends upon future budget actions in DOD and in Congress.

Female Supply Corps Officer in Combatant Ship

When Congress removed restrictions against women serving aboard combatant ships, the Navy moved forward with plans to assign women officers to sea duty in a variety of ships. The Supply Corps quickly nominated one of its bright and experienced young officers, LT Melinda

Matheny, who already had served a successful tour in a tender. She was ordered to duty as supply officer of *USS Briscoe* (DD-977), a modern Spruance-class destroyer, in May 1994.

LORE OF THE CORPS

Lieutenant Melinda Lee Matheny, SC, USN

Supply Officer, *USS Briscoe* (DD-977), 1994–
Period of Service: 1986–

Lieutenant Matheny, the daughter of a retired Supply Corps officer, attended college on a full NROTC scholarship, was commissioned in the Supply Corps, and became the first female Supply Corps officer to be assigned to a combatant ship.

She was born at Norfolk, Virginia, in May 1964, and moved frequently as is typical of a Navy junior. Her father, LT (later LCDR) Arthur (Art) Matheny, had duty as the integrated logistics support officer in the office of the supervisor of shipbuilding, at Ingalls Shipbuilding, Pascagoula, Mississippi. He took his daughter aboard *USS Spruance* (DD-963), under construction at Ingalls, when she was only 11. She became supply officer of a sister ship just 19 years later.

Matheny became interested in the Navy as a way to help defray the cost of a college education and to see the world. She applied to the NROTC program during her senior year in high school and was awarded a four-year scholarship to the University of Michigan. She was graduated with a B.S. degree in mathematics in May 1986 and commissioned an ensign in the Supply Corps. She completed the basic qualification course at NSCS Athens in December 1986.

ENS Matheny was ordered to *USS Jason* (AR-8) at San Diego in January 1987, where she was food service officer for her first five months aboard, then sales and disbursing officer until detached. She was promoted to LTJG in September 1988 and reported in August 1989 to the Navy Regional Finance Center Washington, as director, Commercial Accounts Department. LTJG Matheny was promoted to lieutenant in September 1990.

LT Matheny reported in May 1991 for duty at the Naval Supply Systems Command, as officer program accessions officer in the Office of Supply Corps Personnel. She moved over to Officer Personnel Requirements and Budgets in March 1992 and remained in that billet until she received historic orders as the first woman Supply Corps officer assigned to a combatant ship.

In May 1994, she reported as supply officer, *USS Briscoe* (DD-977). As the first female Supply Department head on a combatant ship, she emphasizes, "I am looking forward to the day when it is not longer news for women to be assigned such positions." The ship was deployed to the Red Sea for maritime interdiction operations in support of United Nations sanctions against Iraq shortly after she reported aboard. LT Matheny credits overwhelming support from the command and crew for making her transition extremely easy. In September 1994 she was still the only female in *Briscoe,* based at Norfolk.

Art Matheny, who retired in 1981 after 27 years of active duty, approves of his daughter following in his Supply Corps footsteps: "I am extremely proud of her. She is an extremely capable lady." He recalls that she was an honor student throughout high school despite the fact that the family moved to the Washington area in the summer between her junior and senior years. She finished 10th in her high school graduating class of 350. She also excelled academically at NSCS Athens.

LT Matheny is married to Paul Martin, a loss control representative for ITT Hartford Insurance Company. They make their home at Norfolk.

Sources

Personal data provided by LCDR Arthur Matheny and LT Melinda Matheny, August 1994.

Records supplied by NAVSUP and NSCS Athens, August 1994.

Telephone interview of LCDR Arthur Matheny, August 1994.

A Bright Future

RADM Bob Moore, Chief of Supply Corps, and VADM Ed Straw, senior Supply Corps officer on active duty, have given their perspectives on the future of the Corps earlier in this chapter. The common thread of their perspectives on the future concerns the professionalism of Supply Corps officers and the fact that there will be no lack of future opportunities to demonstrate that professionalism.

Further elaboration is provided by CAPT John E. Jackson, who holds the Frederick J. Horne Military Chair of Logistics and Sustainability at the Naval War College, Newport. In this position, Jackson, who went to the War college from duty as executive officer of FISC Charleston, serves as the principal conduit for information flowing between NWC and the deputy chief of naval operations (N-4).

CAPT Jackson says that it is becoming increasingly more evident that "the future success of U.S. military forces is inextricably tied to logistics." In the decades ahead, he points out, the ability to apply force or to deter aggression will increasingly rely on the nation's ability to move, support, and sustain forces in remote locations.

The functions normally called *supply* within the Navy, Jackson points out, are only one segment of logistics. Other functions include transportation, maintenance, engineering, health services support, and operating many other services as diverse as mortuary and postal facilities.

One major focus of study at the Naval War College is to ensure that students realize that logistics should be addressed in terms of a multitude of functions and missions. Naval leaders must think in terms of joint logistics, operational logistics, and expeditionary logistics. They must also understand the capabilities and limitations of the other military services and associated defense agencies. Jackson concludes, "The lessons of history clearly demonstrate that it is the height of folly to move troops and equipment into a forward area without the requisite logistics tail being in place and functioning."

All military services and related defense and federal agencies are represented on the faculty and student body of the Naval War College. CAPT Jackson believes that NWC provides the appropriate forum to address the myriad of concerns involved in understanding the important interrelationship of operations and logistics. "A familiarity and understanding between all players is crucial to successful combined operations," he says and is confident about the future for Navy Supply Corps officers.

Ready for Sea

As the Supply Corps moves into its third century of service to the Navy, the men and women of the Corps of the future will face even greater challenges that will require the same attributes as their predecessors demonstrated.

When Fiscal Year 1994 came to an end just five months short of the 200th anniversary of the U.S. Navy Supply Corps, there were 4,025 Supply Corps officers on active duty, including 3,335 USN officers, 382 Reserve officers, 142 Reserve TAR officers, and 166 limited duty officers (LDO). Senior Supply Corps officers expressed confidence that the future of the Corps is in good hands of this talented and well-trained group of men and women. In addition, as of the end of the fiscal year, there were 1,536 Supply Corps officers and 9,268 enlisted men and women drilling in the Ready Reserve.

Supply officers—and their predecessors as naval agents, pursers, paymasters, and Pay Corps officers—have proved extraordinarily capable in a civil war, two world wars, at least six limited wars, three major undeclared wars, and in countless other deployments. More important, they have demonstrated, throughout two centuries, outstanding attributes of courage, determination, dedication, innovation, and flexibility, in addition to their finely honed business acumen.

The United States Navy Supply Corps today—active duty and Ready Reservists—is *Ready for Sea*.

Sources

Sources for material used in this chapter and not cited earlier include:

Commissioning Brochure and Program, *USS Supply (AOE-6)*. Commissioning Committee, February 1994.

The World Almanac and Book of Facts 1994. Mahwah, N.J.: Funk and Wagnalls, 1993.

Index

FRANK J. ALLSTON was the senior drilling Naval Reservist when he retired in June 1985 with more than 34 years of active and Reserve duty.

A native of New Bern, North Carolina, he was graduated from the University of North Carolina, Chapel Hill, with an A.B. in journalism and from the Graduate School of Business, the University of Chicago with an M.B.A. in general management. He was commissioned an ensign in the Naval Reserve Supply Corps in August 1952 through the Reserve Officer Candidate Program. Upon graduation from the Navy Supply Corps School, Bayonne, New Jersey, he served during the Korean War in the Bureau of Supplies and Accounts on the staff of the *BuSandA Monthly Newsletter.*

He returned to civilian life and the Naval Reserve in 1954 and served in management positions with General Electric Company, Bunker Ramo Corporation, and IC Industries before retiring as vice president-corporate affairs, Illinois Central Railroad in 1989. After release from active Navy duty, he embarked on a concurrent career in the Naval Reserve and served as commanding officer of Reserve units in New York City, Greenville, South Carolina, and Chicago. He completed special Naval Reserve senior officer programs at the National War College, Naval War College, U.S. Atlantic Fleet, and Logex '69 at Fort Lee, Virginia. He has been awarded the Legion of Merit and the Navy Meritorious Service Medal.

RADM Allston founded the Recruiting District Assistance Council Program for the Navy Recruiting Command and served as the nation's first RDAC chairman in 1972–73 and was chairman of Armed Forces Week in Chicago in 1978. He was a charter member of the Chief of Naval Operations Sea Power Presentation Team, 1968–80.

He is a past president of both the Navy Supply Corps Association and the Chicago Council, Navy League, of which he is a life member. He is also a member of the Naval Reserve Association, the Naval Institute, the Naval Order of the United States, and the Retired Officers Association.

He and his wife, Barbara, live in Naperville, Illinois.

The **Naval Institute Press** is the book-publishing arm of the U.S. Naval Institute, a private, nonprofit society for sea service professionals and others who share an interest in naval and maritime affairs. Established in 1873 at the U.S. Naval Academy in Annapolis, Maryland, where its offices remain, today the Naval Institute has more than 100,000 members worldwide.

Members of the Naval Institute receive the influential monthly magazine *Proceedings* and discounts on fine nautical prints, ship and aircraft photos, and subscriptions to the bimonthly *Naval History* magazine. They also have access to the transcripts of the Institute's Oral History Program and get discounted admission to any of the Institute-sponsored seminars offered around the country.

The Naval Institute's book-publishing program, begun in 1898 with basic guides to naval practices, has broadened its scope in recent years to include books of more general interest. Now the Naval Institute Press publishes more than seventy titles each year, ranging from how-to books on boating and navigation to battle histories, biographies, ship and aircraft guides, and novels. Institute members receive discounts on the Press's nearly 400 books in print.

Full-time students are eligible for special half-price membership rates. Life memberships are also available.

For a free catalog describing Naval Institute Press books currently available, and for further information about U.S. Naval Institute membership, please write to:

Membership & Communications Department
U.S. Naval Institute
118 Maryland Avenue
Annapolis, Maryland 21402-5035

Or call, toll-free, (800) 233-USNI.